Midwest Studies in Philosophy
Volume XI

Many papers in MIDWEST STUDIES IN PHILOSOPHY are invited and all are previously unpublished. The editors will consider unsolicited manuscripts that are received by January of the year preceding the appearance of a volume. All manuscripts must be pertinent to the topic area of the volume for which they are submitted. Address manuscripts to MIDWEST STUDIES IN PHILOSOPHY, University of Minnesota, Morris, MN 56267, or Department of Philosophy, University of Notre Dame, Notre Dame, IN 46566, or Trinity University, San Antonio, TX 78284.

The articles in MIDWEST STUDIES IN PHILOSOPHY are indexed in THE PHILOSOPHER'S INDEX.

Midwest Studies
in
Philosophy
Volume
XI
Studies
In
Essentialism

Editors
PETER A. FRENCH
Trinity University
THEODORE E. UEHLING, JR.
University of Minnesota, Morris
HOWARD K. WETTSTEIN
University of Notre Dame

University of Minnesota Press • Minneapolis

Copyright ©1986 by the University of Minnesota.

All rights reserved. No part of this publication may be reproduced, stored in a retrieval system, or transmitted, in any form or by any means, electronic, mechanical, photocopying, recording, or otherwise, without the prior written permission of the publisher.

Published by the University of Minnesota Press
2037 University Avenue Southeast, Minneapolis MN 55414.
Published simultaneously in Canada
by Fitzhenry & Whiteside Limited, Markham.
Printed in the United States of America.

Library of Congress Cataloging-in-Publication Data

Studies in essentialism.
  (Midwest studies in philosophy ; v. 11)
    1. Essence (Philosophy) I. French, Peter A.
II. Uehling, Theodore Edward. III. Wettstein, Howard K.
IV. Series.
B105.E65S78 1986   111'.1   86-11240
ISBN 0-8166-1551-9
ISBN 0-8166-1552-7 (pbk.)

Chapter 4, ''Modal Paradox: Parts and Counterparts, Points and Counterpoints,'' copyright ©1986 by Nathan Salmon.

The University of Minnesota
is an equal-opportunity
educator and employer.

This volume is dedicated to
the memory of
Alberto Coffa

Midwest Studies in Philosophy
Volume XI
Studies in Essentialism

Midwest Studies in Philosophy
Volume XI

In Defense of Absolute Essentialism

GRAEME FORBES

She had both brains and beauty. She was a friend of Virginia Woolf and, years later, told her family that Winston Churchill had wanted to marry her. ("Just think," says Francis, "I might have been Randolph.")[1]

1. PRELIMINARIES

A property P is an *essential* property of an object x iff x could not exist and lack P, that is, as they say, iff x has P at every world at which x exists. This paper[2] is about the opposition between two kinds of believer in essential properties. According to an essentialist of the first kind, the *absolute* essentialist, for each P and x there is an unqualifiedly correct yes/no answer to the question: is P essential to x? (and sometimes the answer is "yes"); or, if there is a qualification, it is with respect to the *degree to which* such-and-such is possible or impossible for x. But according to an essentialist of the second kind, the *contextualist*, there is never an unqualified answer to the question. The best that can be said is that *relative to such-and-such a context*, P is essential to x, leaving it open that there are other contexts relative to which P is not essential to x. In almost every public discussion of essentialism in which I have been involved, especially those whose topic was essentialism about origin, I have heard the contextualist position defended; it is implicit, I think, in Mackie (1974) and is explicitly advanced in Johnston (1977). Its best-known proponent is David Lewis, who holds a version of the position that has complex ramifications (1983a). So there is good reason for absolutists to pay more attention to the doctrine than they have hitherto.

The paper is roughly divided into two parts, comprising a defense of absolutism (sections 2–4) and an attack on contextualism (section 5). In the next section, I shall try to clarify some aspects of absolutism as such; this material is slightly technical and could be omitted by a reader with little taste for fine-tuning the purely logical background of our topic. In section 3, I shall briefly review what I think is the strongest case for absolute essentialism about certain properties. I have advanced this case in a number of other places (1980; 1981; 1985, Chapter 6), but I hope here to improve my formulation of exactly what the essentialist theses are. I shall then tackle an unclear aspect of my argument that presents the contextualist with his or her main opportunity to disrupt it. In section 4 I shall apply the argument to a category of thing—fictional entities—that essentialists have not much considered and that may seem especially suited to the contextualist approach, and I shall discuss some difficulties that have been raised for the apparatus I rely on in that case. Finally, in section 5 I shall argue directly for the incoherence of contextualism.

2. DEFINITIONS AND DISTINCTIONS

Essential properties may be trivial or nontrivial. It is characteristic of P's being trivially essential to x that x's possession of P is not grounded in the specific nature of x. The main groups of trivia are (A) the properties of existence, self-identity, or their logical consequences in standard quantified S5;[3] and (B) properties possessed in virtue of some *de dicto* necessary truth. The *de dicto* truth may be a logical truth of nonmodal logic, or it may be logical only more broadly speaking: for example, the property $\lambda x (Bx \rightarrow Mx)$ of being a male if a bachelor would fall under (B). (This is a necessary property, that is, one that is possessed at every world, in addition to being essential; but under reasonable assumptions, $\lambda x ((Bx \text{ v } \sim\text{Exists}(x)) \rightarrow Mx)$ is essential, though not necessary.) There is a special group of essential properties, the "extraneous" essential properties: P is extraneously essential to x iff it is possessed by x at any world w only in virtue of the possession at w of certain properties by other objects (e.g., being such that if snow is white, then it is white). If these properties are nontrivially essential to their possessors, we will count P as nontrivial, otherwise not (the definition is adequate, since I do not think there is an example of an extraneous essential property of x possessed by x at one world because of properties possessed in one kind of way by objects there and possessed by x at another world because of properties possessed in another kind of way by objects there). In later sections, my concern will be only with nontrivially essential properties.

What has been said about properties holds also for relations: e.g., R is essential to x and y (in that order) iff Rxy holds at every world where x and y both exist. A question that then arises concerns how this intuitive trivial/nontrivial distinction relates to the formal characterization of "essentialist theory" initiated in Parsons (1969) and refined and further investigated in Fine (1978b). Consider the schema:

$$(AE) \diamond(\exists x_1) \ldots \diamond(\exists x_n)\diamond[\text{Dif}(x_1 \ldots x_n) \text{ \&}$$
$$\square(E(x_1 \ldots x_n) \rightarrow \phi(x_1 \ldots x_n))] \rightarrow$$
$$\square(\forall x_1) \ldots \square(\forall x_n)\square[\text{Dif}(x_1 \ldots x_n) \rightarrow$$
$$\square(E(x_1 \ldots x_n) \rightarrow \phi(x_1 \ldots x_n))]$$

where ϕ is nonmodal and contains no free variables other than those displayed.[4] An instance of (AE) will say, concerning some condition, that if some n distinct possible objects satisfy it essentially, then *any* n distinct possible objects satisfy it essentially (i.e., whenever they all exist); so the negation of such an instance says of that condition that some n distinct possible objects satisfy it essentially and some n distinct possible objects satisfy it but not essentially. Then an essentialist theory, on Fine's characterization, is one that has a theorem that is a disjunction of negations of instances of (AE); thus in every model of such a theory, there will be some nonmodal condition ϕ that some n distinct possible objects satisfy essentially and that some n distinct possible objects satisfy but not essentially. Given this characterization, we can therefore distinguish two kinds of failure to hold an essentialist theory. An *antiessentialist* theory is one in which every instance of (AE) is a theorem. A *nonessentialist* theory is one with some model that refutes some instance of (AE) but with no theorem that is a disjunction of negations of instances of (AE) (so nonessentialism occupies the middle ground between essentialism and antiessentialism).

Our question is where someone fits into this scheme of things if he or she restricts the properties regarded as essential to the ones we classified as trivially essential. Let us say that an *essentialist sentence* is any sentence with the form of the antecedent of (AE). Suppose that I hold some consistent *de dicto* theory $T,$[5] and that every essentialist sentence I am willing to assert is a consequence of T (this covers group B of trivial essentialist properties, group A being covered by the background logic of T being standard quantified $S5$ with the usual *de re* theory of existence and identity). Then I cannot be an essentialist in Fine's sense, for we can prove that if an essentialist sentence α follows from some *de dicto* theory T, then the *de dicto* generalization of α, which has the form:

$$(DD) \quad \Box(\forall x_1) \ldots (\forall x_n) (\text{Dif}(x_1 \ldots x_n) \rightarrow \phi(x_1 \ldots x_n)),$$

is implied by α in the *de dicto* theory T and is therefore a theorem of T (note that the consequent of (AE) is equivalent in standard $S5$ to (DD)).[6] So if ϕ is a nonmodal condition that is satisfied essentially by some n-tuple of distinct objects in a model of T, then it is satisfied essentially by all such n-tuples in that model; so T could have no theorem of the sort required to be an essentialist theory. But this does not settle whether the holder of T is an antiessentialist or merely a nonessentialist. What we have proved is that if an essentialist sentence is a consequence of T, so is its *de dicto* generalization; therefore T entails every instance of (AE) if it settles all essentialist sentences, i.e., for each sentence with the form of the antecedent of (AE), either it or its negation is a theorem of T. This is hardly an acceptable demand upon a *de dicto* theory, nor would be any other way of arranging for T to be negation complete with respect to essentialist sentences, so the trivial essentialist, as characterized, is most naturally thought of as falling between essentialism and antiessentialism, i.e., into the nonessentialist camp.

One further comment about absolute essentialism should be made (the distinctions involved do not have the same interest in the case of contextualism). We can distinguish between strong and weak versions of absolutism. According to the weak version, although objects have nontrivial essential properties, they do not in general have nontrivial *individual essences*, where a nontrivial individual essence of x is a set S of properties each of whose members is nontrivially essential to x, and furthermore, necessarily no other object could possess all the properties in S. The weak view is sometimes associated with the claim that transworld identity can be primitive ("Haecceitism"), since by denying individual essences, it denies that the conditions that the view admits to be necessary for transworld identity can be assembled into a condition that is also sufficient (the position that objects do have transworld being but their only essential properties are trivial ones, like self-identity, is also Haecceitist). An essentialist can hold the weak view for some categories of entity and not for others. For instance, an essentialist is likely to admit that the weak view is uncontroversially correct for the category (if such there is) of "atomic" objects, or "logical simples," if these have nontrivial essential properties at all (being logically simple would be a plausible candidate). But I think the weak view is less plausible, as an alternative to the strong view, for more common-or-garden categories (1981; 1985, chapter 6).

The weak view should also be distinguished from the claim that there are nontrivially isomorphic possible worlds. A world can be thoughat of as a structure for free logic with the empty domain, the domain of the world being the (perhaps empty) extension of the existence predicate in the structure, and there is a straightforward notion of isomorphism for such constructs. Suppose that distinct worlds correspond to distinct structures ("World Differentiation," in Fine's terms), and that the Falsehood Principle is in force.[7] A nontrivial isomorphism between u and v is then an isomorphism that is not identity on the domain of u. Now the weak view implies the following disjunction: either distinct nontrivially isomorphic worlds exist, or for each world w and each x existing at w, there is some distinct y existing at w such that x and y are "qualitatively indistinguishable" at w, which means that any nonmodal ϕ with one free variable and no individual constants is satisfied by x at w iff it is satisfied by y at w. For suppose there are nonontrivial isomorphisms between distinct worlds and that x exists at w. w itself determines a maximal qualitative possibility for x, x's "unary role" in w.[8] By the supposition, there is no other world in which a distinct y has the same role, so if that role is not to be an essence of x, there must be a distinct y in w itself that has it. However, this implication (that there exist copy worlds or else indistinguishable individuals within a world) does not *characterize* the weak view, for two reasons. First, the other version of Haecceitism (all essential properties are trivial) has the same implication. Second, there are philosophical reasons to hold that plausible examples of nontrivially isomorphic distinct worlds may involve both simple and nonsimple objects and that in these examples the nonsimples have individual essences.[9]

3. YOU ARE WHAT YOU EAT?

Why believe in nontrivial essential properties for some categories of entity? I hold that the plausibility of essentialist views various recent writers have advanced—Putnam's that the fundamental physical properties of a substance are essential to it (1978), Kripke's that the origin of an organism is essential to it (1980), Wiggins's that the biological kind of an organism is essential to it (1980), Fine's that the membership of a set is essential to it (1977), and so on—derives in each case, at least in part, from two conceptual truths about the identity relation:

for any truth of the form:
the object x satisfying condition ϕ at world (or time) u is the same object as
the object y satisfying condition ψ at world (time) v
there must be intrinsic features of x at u and y at v in virtue of which that truth obtains;

and

for any truth of the form
>   the object x satisfying condition ϕ at world (time) u is a different object
>   from the object y satisfying condition ψ at world (time) v

there must be intrinsic features of x at u and y at v in virtue of which that truth obtains.

Here ϕ and ψ are any formulas free of modal (temporal) vocabulary. The point of these principles is to rule out the possibility of ungrounded identities and ungrounded non-identities. For instance, according to Chisholm, there are cases of ungrounded identities involving persons and time; he holds that if Oldman has functionally equivalent brain hemispheres, then if the left one is transplanted into a new body to yield Newman One and the right one to another new body to yield Newman Two, then even though both Newmen are symmetrically related to Oldman in every respect we normally regard as relevant to personal identity, one rather than the other is identical to Oldman (1970). A non-Cartesian may find this extremely peculiar, and my suggestion is that its problematic aspect arises from its violating the principle that identities and nonidentities must be grounded: in this case, because of the symmetry, any one identity is ungrounded, though both nonidentities can be grounded. Another example involves the bare transworld numerical difference between artifacts that those who endorse an accessibility solution to Chisholm's Paradox must swallow (see Forbes [1984]). However, I should say now that those who, to the contrary, cannot see any difficulty in the view that Oldman is one rather than the other of the Newmen will find little below to persuade them otherwise: what follows concentrates on the consequences of finding ungrounded identities and nonidentities objectionable.

To illustrate the relevance of our principles to essentialism, I shall briefly rehearse the role I discern for them in defense of Kripke's well-known essentialism about the origin of organisms (1980, pp. 110–14). But first, I wish to be more cautious than I have been hitherto in deciding what that essentialism amounts to. Kripke doubts whether the Queen could have been born to parents different from her actual ones. It is biological parents that are in question here, since of course sperm-egg transplants are quite conceivable, and presumably there is nothing modally special about human beings in this regard, as opposed to other kinds of organism. So one might extract the following general thesis from Kripke's remarks:

(K) $\Box(\forall x)\Box(\forall y)\Box(x$ originates from $y \rightarrow$
$\Box(\text{Exists}\,(x) \rightarrow x$ originates from $y)).$[10]

But (K) has plausible counterexamples. Suppose z is a human zygote that is formed by fusion of a sperm s with an egg e. Then one can conceive that scientists synthesize a zygote by building it nucleotide by nucleotide, and happen to use exactly the actual matter of z in exactly its actual z-configuration. In such a world, s and e do not exist, or so we can consistently postulate, but it is hard to deny that z exists (one might say that a synthesized "zygote" is not a zygote, hence not the same zygote as z, but this seems strained). So z exists but does not originate from s and e, since they do not exist.[11]

One way of weakening (K) to get around this difficulty is to restrict its application to worlds where z does originate from other cells. One organism is said to be a propagule of another if it fuses or divides to produce the other, so we might try replacing (K) by the claim that if y is a propagule of x at some world, then in any world where x has propagules, y is among them (this implies that x has the same propagules at every world where it has propagules). But our scientists could surely synthesize cells—perhaps half a dozen or so—that fuse to produce the atom-for-atom replica of z as it actually is, which is again a situation in which s and e do not exist. These cases suggest that what is important to the identity of the organism is the identity of the matter from which it originates, together with the configuration of that matter. Let us call the matter of whatever it is from which the organism originates its "original matter."[12] If we think of this matter as a Goodmanian sum, we can introduce a "common quantity" relationship between such sums. Let $C(x,y)$ be the relationship that holds between two sums of matter x and y when a substantial part of the matter of each is a substantial part of the matter of the other (the vagueness here is deliberate, since some tolerance in how much of z's actual original matter the scientists must use in the imagined world if they are to create z seems intuitively justifiable).[13] Then perhaps a better essentialist thesis to extract from Kripke's remarks about the Queen's parents is:

$(K')\ \Box(\forall x)\Box(\forall y)\Box(Myx \rightarrow \Box(\forall z)\Box(Mzx \rightarrow Cyz))$,[14]

which says that if the original matter of x at any two worlds where it has such matter is compared, the two sums will substantially overlap each other. In fact, the thesis (K) that makes the propagule essential seems to be an over-strong amalgam of two distinct doctrines and two implicit assumptions, all of which should be spelled out separately. There is (i) the thesis (K') that most of the original matter is essential, and (ii) another thesis to the effect that a structure or form sufficiently resembling a given one is essential; (i) and (ii) together come close to entailing (K) under the assumptions that a fixed propagule could not have had (iii) very different matter or (iv) very different structure; genuine entailment requires the apparently mistaken extra premise that the original matter could only produce the organism by being the matter of a fixed collection of propagules.

However, I shall not be further concerned with the difference between (K) and (K'), since the difference between them is not very significant in the context of opposition from the antiessentialist or nonessentialist, or from various kinds of deviant essentialist to be introduced below. Whatever precise essentialist claim about origin one chooses to defend, it is clear that the following has to be ruled out: that an organism could develop at one world u from one collection of propagules and at another v from an entirely distinct collection of propagules, where the two collections both exist simultaneously at u, or more weakly, are simultaneously compossible, i.e., all exist together at the same time at some world. This view is inconsistent with both (K) and (K'). How, then, is it to be refuted?

For *reductio* of such a view, let w_1, w_2, w_3, and w_4 be four worlds as follows. w_1 is a world in which there is a certain tree T growing from an acorn α at a place p (it has always been at p), and w_2 is a world inconsistent with essentialism about origin, for in

w_2, T is growing from β, a w_1 -acorn distinct from α. To strengthen the case against (K) and (K'), suppose that w_2 is otherwise as similar to w_1 as is metaphysically possible: T has the same matter, shape, location, and so on as in w_1. w_3 is a world whose existence the nonessentialist has to admit, for in it both α and β grow into trees (if there is no such world, this bestows certain essential properties on α and β). w_3 is to be as similar to w_2 as is otherwise possible, so in particular, the β-tree of w_3 is intrinsically indistinguishable from T as it is in w_2. Suppose we now ask which, if either, tree in w_3 is identical to T. Kripke's opponent cannot say that T is the α-tree of w_3 without violating the principle that there be no ungrounded transworld nonidentities (compare T in w_2 with the β-tree of w_3). But for the same reason, he cannot say that T is the β-tree or neither tree (of w_3), given w_4: in w_4, T is (intrinsically) just as the α-tree is in w_3—it grows in the same place at the same time from the same acorn, has the same matter and shape through time, and so on. So, contradictorily, T must be the α-tree of w_3. Again, the antiessentialist cannot say that there is no such world as w_4, on pain of making some property possessed by T in w_1, such as its location, essential to it.

Modulo a query about the meaning of "intrinsic" both in the statement of the principles about identity and in the above reasoning, this argument shows that uncompromising rejection of origin essentialism as embodied in (K) or (K') is inconsistent with those principles.[15] I shall further maintain that the antiessentialist or nonessentialist (though perhaps not the contextualist) cannot escape the refutation by stretching the meaning of "intrinsic." Suppose such a philosopher responds that he or she can consistently maintain that the α-trees of w_3 and w_4 are different trees because the one in w_3 coexists with a β-tree there, whereas the one in w_4 does not: this is the intrinsic ground of the numerical distinction between the trees. This response seems wrong, for it allows the identity of a given tree at a world to depend on what the other trees that exist there are like. Moreover, if this response is not just *ad hoc* straw-clutching, it commits one to the noncoexistence principle that if a tree T^* possibly has acorn x and possibly has acorn y, it is not possible for T^* to have one of x or y and coexist with some other tree with the other (I am assuming that having an acorn implies existence). For if it is possible, take any world w where it occurs, and generate a world like w_4, where T^* has the acorn that the other tree of w has and is otherwise just like that other tree as it is in w. Here we are back to essential properties again, since, for example, it will be essential to the actual tree T not to originate from any of the acorns $a_1 \ldots a_n$ from which the n other trees of w_1 originate.

But these arguments will not move someone advancing an alternative essentialism to Kripke's, such as location essentialism (place of origin is essential) or composition essentialism (for each moment m of x's existence, counting from the first, x is composed of the same matter at m in all worlds where it has an m' th moment of existence), nor, consequently, will they have any impact on the contextualist. The location (composition) essentialist will deny that T can be as the α-tree of w_3 is, since the position (matter) required for T has been commandeered by the β-tree there; hence both views imply that there is no such world as w_4 (the composition essentialist can admit w_2 provided he or she holds that the acorn's starting to develop is strictly before the tree's beginning to come into existence, analogously to the view about humans in note 12). The contextualist can also accept the principles about identity, maintaining that although some properties are to be held fixed across worlds, the properties in question can vary from context to context: the principles are respected differently in each context, but respected nonetheless. Now it is natural to reply to location essentialists that the location of a tree is not one of its intrinsic features, so that their view does not really accommodate the principles at all. But this reply, in addition to making an explanation of "intrinsic" more urgent, is not obviously applicable to the composition essentialist; for if the original matter of a tree is intrinsic to it, why would its subsequent matter not be so as well? In the case of artifacts, there is also an essentialism about original matter; for instance, it would be said of any particular bronze statue that it could not have been cast from a totally different quantity of bronze. Since the subsequent matter of a fixed statue cannot much differ from its original matter, this results in just essentialism about matter, but that may be held to be a consequence of artifacts not being food-absorbers in the manner of multicellular organisms. If so, the parallel with organisms is preserved and is extended by the thought that the form in which the bronze is cast could not have differed much for the very same statue to have been produced, which seems analogous to structural constraints on the possibilities for the original matter of one and the same organism.[16]

It seems that the justification of a particular essentialist view about things of a given kind may be rooted in the features of the thing that are characteristic of belonging to that kind, but that various features for one kind have parallels in others, which a criterion of the intrinsic/extrinsic distinction should respect.[17] The intuitive idea of "P is extrinsic to x" is something like "P is irrelevant to what makes x the specific F that it is," where F is an ultimate sortal; the problem is to explain this in some way other than "x could be the specific F that it is and lack P," which is an explanation that makes it question-begging to object to an argument that x could not lack P, that P is extrinsic to x. The argument involving the four worlds simply highlights what is plausible in the abstract anyway, that whoever allows at most trivial essentialist properties must violate the requirement that identity-facts be grounded. The case for one specific interesting essentialism about F's over competing essentialist doctrines about F's rests ultimately on what we say about why some properties are germane to grounding the identity of an F and others not.

I shall approach the intrinsic/extrinsic distinction from a starting point that includes a neo-Fregean two-tier semantic theory. The component of the theory that I require is the distinction between the sense of a predicate and its reference; the reference of a predicate is a property or relation, and its sense is a way of thinking of that property or relation; I call the sense of a predicate a "concept."[18] Now one of the data that any theory of essential properties has to explain, or at least one of the features common to the essentialist doctrines of the writers mentioned above for which a theory in sympathy with those doctrines should account, is the fact that things within the same sufficiently broadly circumscribed "category" are homogeneous with respect to essential properties. It is difficult to take seriously the thought that one particular organism has its origin essentially but another does not, or that this set has its members essentially but that set does not. However, from the neo-Fregean perspective, there are two different places one could look for an explanation of the homogeneity: one could look to the senses of the category words "set," "artifact," "organism," and so on—i.e., to the concept of a set, an artifact, an organism—or to the references of those words, the properties those concepts present. What is the *likelier* source of an explanation?

An essentialist thesis like (K) or its analogue for set-membership may seem to have a conceptual "feel" about it. Moreover, if a uniform account of the source of *de re* and *de dicto* necessity is to be sought, then, since it is widely held that the source of *de dicto* necessity is in concepts (see, e.g., Mackie [1974]), it would be the concepts, the ways of thinking of the properties, that we should investigate. But I deny that the source of *de dicto* necessity is in concepts (here and in what follows I depart from Forbes [1985, chapter 9]). Take even the simplest *de dicto* truth, e.g., "the sides of a square forming its corners meet at right angles." On one view, this is necessarily true because "square" is simply defined to mean "four-sided figure whose sides meet at right angles and are of equal length," and the definition specifies a way of thinking, or concept of, squareness. But although this might account for its being *a priori* or uninformative (to most of us) that squares have right angles, it does not explain the necessity. A man might be taught to recognize square-shaped things as square on the basis of encounters with objects that are poised on one of their corners. Perhaps he encounters no squares resting on one of their sides, but if he were to do so, he would judge them to be square only after moving them to see how they look poised on a corner. He may also be taught to recognize right angles by encounters with right-angled triangles resting on their bases. But if one looks at a square poised on a corner, it is not at all obvious that its angles *are* right angles (this is called Mach's illusion). So for this man, by contrast with most of us, even though he has all the concepts (he has ways of thinking of squareness and of being right-angled), it would be informative and *a posteriori* that squares have right angles. But the possibility of such a man does not undermine or tend to relativize the *necessity* of squares being right-angled. The moral of the case, I take it, is that even with simple *de dicto* necessities, the source of the necessity is to be found in the properties to which the predicates of the *de dicto* truth refer. It seems likely, then, that this is also where the explanation of the homogeneity phenomenon that issues in universal *a priori de re* necessities will lie.

The focus on properties helps account for a seeming violation of homogeneity. Propositions (the senses of sentences in the Fregean framework) belong to the category of semantic entities, and a general theory of essential properties should explain why any member of this category has its content essentially. But some propositions have other essential properties that, in apparent exception to homogeneity, are not possessed by all. Some propositions are necessarily, and therefore essentially, true (some may merely be essentially true, given certain assumptions about their existence conditions and the truth property), but other propositions are only contingently true, so if a theory of essential properties is aimed only at explaining such universal *a priori de re* necessities as (K) or (K'), it seems it will not cover all the ground: propositions are not homogeneous with respect to essential truth.[19]

In response to this, I propose to distinguish between derivative and nonderivative essential properties. Sometimes an object has a property essentially derivative from the essential properties of other objects to which it is suitably related. If the approach I propose is to cover all essential properties, I need require only that all non-derivative ones fall under some principle like (K) or (K') manifesting homogeneity, and that all other essential properties of whatever entity of whatever kind are derivative in the sense indicated. And the example bears out that this is the case; e.g., while the proposition that Socrates belongs to singleton-Socrates is necessarily or at least essentially true, the truth-property's being essential to the proposition is derivative from singleton-Socrates having Socrates as a member essentially. But what of *de dicto* necessary propositions? The argument of the previous paragraph suggests that there is no significant difference in this case: the essential truth of the proposition that squares have right angles is derivative from the essential properties—the transworld identity conditions, if you like—of properties, in this case the property of being square.

In the example of squareness, we contrasted someone with a recognitional capacity for the shape square with someone who knows a definition of the predicate. Both subjects have a way of thinking of squareness, but there does seem to be something ''canonical'' about the definitional one: it explicitly specifies what it is to be a square. One way of interpreting this feature is to think of the property of squareness as intrinsically complex and of the definition as articulating its actual nature. If we were to regard such properties as that of being an organism, an artifact, a set, and so on, as having complexity of an analogous kind, perhaps we could explain the idea of intrinsicness that underlies essentialist theses like (K) or (K') in terms of the interaction of our notion of object-identity with the properties mentioned in a ''canonical'' account of what it is to be an organism, an artifact, or a set. We have seen in the four-worlds argument above that an explanation of why origin is essential to an organism and why place of origin is not requires that place be extrinsic to the identity of an organism, so we might hope to explain this contrast in terms of the canonical definition of ''organism'' circumscribing the nature of the beginning of such a thing but not the nature of the place of its beginning.

Artifacts and organisms are continuants, things that persist through time, but the account of what it is to be an artifact is different from the account of what it is to be an organism. Being an artifact is being a functional arrangement of matter, materials with a form imposed on them in accordance with a design and a purpose bestowed externally, the purpose that explains the details of the design.[20] Being an organism is being a thing that typically originates in a reproductive event and typically has the power of self-replication, the product of the originating event fixing a certain nature that in turn determines a pattern of growth and metamorphosis or decay and death (this is just a list of things characteristic of organisms—nothing is being assumed about the boundaries of persistence of a single organism). Most multicellular organisms can postpone death by absorbing sustenance from the environment (food), but the particular food an organism abosrbs, and the particular spatio-temporal path it inhabits, do not figure in what distinguishes one organism from another *if* we restrict the terms of making that distinction to the components of the canonical account of what it is in general to be an organism, as just sketched. In these latter terms, the individuality of the organism resides at least in part in the specific origination it has. On the other hand, restricting ourselves in the same way about artifacts, an artifact's materials of composition are one main source of specificity, design being another; both are needed, since the same design can be multiply instantiated, and the same materials redeployed. The nature of an organism will play a role analogous to an artifacts's design especially if something with a different organic nature could have come from the same originating event.

The view I am advancing, then, is first, that certain features of organisms and artifacts are central to what it is to be a thing of that sort; second, that the particularity of a given organism or artifact derives from its specific manner of instantiating those features (its specific nature or design, and so on); third, that the intrinsic/extrinsic distinction is to be explained by reference to those features; and fourth, that if someone advances a rival essentialist thesis to one that is true, there will be an argument showing that the rival thesis leads to identities and nonidentities that can be "grounded" only by appeal to extrinsic features of the objects in question, i.e., not really grounded at all. Note that there is no context-relativity in the canonical account of the category property that fixes the intrinsic/extrinsic boundary, any more than there is in the canonical account of what it is to be square.

Do my descriptions of what it is to be an organism, or an artifact, beg the question against, say, the location essentialist or composition essentialist about organisms? An organism must have a certain kind of origin and a nature that constrains its life in certain ways, but equally it must originate *somewhere* and at each time be composed of *some* matter. We could say that there is no particular place it must originate and no particular matter that must compose it at the n' th moment of its existence (n suitably larger than 1), but this is precisely what the deviant essentialists deny. However, I think the content I impute to the canonical accounts of the category properties in these two cases is independently defensible. Indeed, it is fair to respond to the deviant essentialists that the canonical account of what it is to be an organism is not something that admits of further explanation, any more than one is obliged to explain why it is four rather than three sides that are mentioned in the account of squareness: four-sided is just what squares are. It is equally as basic that place of origination and composing matter simply do not figure in the story about what being an organism amounts to.

This would introduce a sort of relativity into the defense of (K'): the defense holds water provided we accept a certain account of what an organism is. But that is not the kind of relativity the contextualist seeks to introduce, since deviation from the proposed account of the property "organism" looks very like an attempt to change the subject matter under discussion. It may be true that if we discovered that cats are complex machines placed on this planet by Martians, it would be incorrect to conclude that, after all, there are no cats—we would just have discovered something very surprising about cats. But if we discovered that everything we took to be an organism is instead a complicated electronic device planted by Martians, that would be to discover that, after all, there are no organisms. The organism category, like the cat category, is one we impose on the basis of our experience, to categorize entities according to their observable features and behavior, but in the organism category, unlike the cat category, we do not think there is a single underlying nature, discoverable *a posteriori*, that explains why organisms are thus different from nonorganisms. The general account of what an organism is that *a priori* reflection elicits is constitutive of being an organism. Indeed, it is to the level of categories with *a priori* membership conditions that we must look to explain essentialist principles like (K'), for how else would such principles be known *a priori*?

If my general approach to the justification of (K') is correct, then the advocate of a substantial but quite different alternative to (K') should find that the consequences of his or her view are widely disruptive of our ordinary views about necessity and contingency. This certainly seems so in the case of composition essentialism about organisms. Multicellular organisms are typically potential absorbers of matter and end up being constituted, after some processing, of what, if anything, they absorb. But since the matter such an organism absorbs is what comes within its range as either the organism or the comestibles move through space, it is difficult to see how a necessity of constitution view is consistent with its being contingent what path an organism traces during its life; or else it leads to bizarre transworld identity judgments about matter. So far as location essentialism is concerned, it is less clear that there are absurd wide-ranging consequences once one has swallowed that no organism could have originated slightly to the left of where it actually originated; all one can point to is the lack of rationale for allowing contingency of movement but not of starting point.

4. FICTIONS

The foregoing theory is a justification of absolutism, and it is open to the contextualist to regard as coincidental the harmony it relies on between certain general conceptions and arguments for some essentialist intuitions. The production of a convincing case where such an accord is lacking would lend credence to this response, so I turn now to what looks like a good case for the contextualist to emphasize. It seems to make perfectly good sense to raise modal questions and to make counterfactual assertions about fictional objects (fictions), but essentialist claims about such things appear to have a worrying indeterminacy about them. Could Holmes have been a police detective rather than a private detective, could he have lived in another city, could he have worked without an assistant, could he have really existed and solved real crimes? A contextualist can point to the fact that we seem to have no difficulty in understanding certain counterfactual claims as if their antecedents were genuinely possible, and if they are, the answer to all the previous questions is in the affirmative, for indeed we can argue about whether the nonmeritocratic outlook of the English upper and upper-middle classes would have prevented Holmes from rising to such and such a rank in the police force, about which crimes he would have tackled had he lived in Paris, about whether he would have solved such-and-such an actual crime where real detectives failed, and so on. What is going on here, the contextualist might say, is that in the context of each such discussion, certain agreed properties of Holmes are presupposed to be held fixed across worlds and others allowed to vary, but which properties are fixed can vary from context to context.

To evaluate this position, we first need to settle on some understanding of what a fiction (= fictional object) is. Without arguing for it, I shall adopt what seems to me to be the most plausible view: a fictional object is something that is created by the originator of the first story to involve that object, but although created by a real person, fictions do not really exist: they enjoy only fictional existence. A fiction possesses such properties as it is asserted to possess in the stories in which it figures, and perhaps some others, and its existence is contingent provided the real existence of the stories in which it figures is also contingent.[21] So there would be no such fiction as Holmes had the Holmes stories not been created. With each possible world, then, there is associated not just the domain of real existents, but also the domain of fictional existents, whose content is determined by the activities of real storytellers in that world. Note that in what follows, "merely possible" contrasts with "actual," "real" with "fictional"; *prima facie*, the resulting four possible statuses are all distinct. Note also that in discussing fictions, two distinct notions of existence are involved. There is the notion of being a fiction, that is, of being in the domain of fictions, for which it is necessary and sufficient to be a character created by a storyteller; because they do not really exist, such fictions may be regarded as nonexistent objects, as opposed to real abstract existents. The second notion of existence is that of being implied, in some work of fiction, to exist. If we use the phrase "enjoys fictional existence" for this notion, then a real thing that figures in a story may enjoy fictional existence, though such an entity is not a fiction.[22]

From this point of view on the ontology of fictions, it is plausible to respond in the negative to the questions (a) could Holmes really have existed? and (b) is it possible that a real person could have been the fiction Sherlock Holmes? for if either (a) or (b) is answered in the affirmative, then it is not even essential to Holmes to be fictional, though being fictional is probably the property that an absolutist would first think of as an essential property of fictions ("*P* is essential to x" will now mean "x has P in every world where x exists in either the domain of real things or the domain of fictions"). Note that there is a certain asymmetry between (a) and (b). Someone who answers (a) in the affirmative is proposing that the fictions of a world are among the merely possible real things of that world. The familiar problem here is to say which mere possible Holmes is to be identified with, granted that possibly there is x and possibly there is y such that possibly x really exists and really has the properties that figure in the story and possibly y does also and (necessarily) x is distinct from y. On the other hand, someone who answers (b) in the affirmative is, or at least may be, making a proposal about the nature of mere possibles. Since (b) is doubly modal, an affirmative answer does not imply that some *actual* real person could have been a fiction (this would just raise the same issues as the claim that Holmes could really have existed), but the suggestion might be that the nonactual real things are actual fictions. Pressed for an example of a merely possible real thing, one tends to say something like "Consider the bridge over the Seine which would have resulted had the steel girders in the Eiffel Tower been assembled in such-and-such a way," and saying this much may be enough to introduce a fiction; so in general, the merely possible real things are the actual fictions, which is, so to speak, the converse of the explanatory reduction involved in an affirmative answer to (a).

However, this latter view founders on an insufficiency of actual fictions. To make it work, one might suggest altering the account of membership in the domain of fictions at a world *w* to require only being brought into existence by a storyteller at some world or other, not necessarily *w* itself. The idea would be that the merely possible real stories will provide enough fictions for the domain of fictions at the actual world to correspond one-one with all the real objects that are merely possible at the actual world. But the flaw in this is obvious: one cannot reduce the merely possible real things to the actual fictions if this reduction requires a prior range of unreduced merely possible real things, viz, the stories. It would be pointless to apply the reduction over again to these stories, since their initial unreduced status is required to get the reduction started.

Although these points bear against an affirmative answer to (b), they suggest a way around my earlier objection to the affirmative answer to (a). For all I know, there *actually* is a story about (as one could contentiously put it) the very merely possible bridge specified above, with the "such-and-such" sufficiently expanded: the storyteller simply puts in enough detail so that the strong essentialist can identify precisely which merely possible real bridge is in question. Suppose there is such a story—then the actual fiction is possibly a real bridge. This is a stronger position than the contextualist needs, but he or she might nevertheless be grateful for it. However, the view is intuitively implausible, and it is a merit of the theory of the previous section that it explains why. For we can take a world *w* where both that possible bridge and the actual storytelling exist (in the actual world, we are happy enough to allow that "any similarity between characters in this story and real persons is coincidental," so let the same be true in *w*), and an ungrounded identity results, as with the four worlds in the case of the tree. The best that could be said is that a different fictional bridge exists in *w*, even though the same storytelling occurs, *because* there is a real bridge coincidentally satisfying the specifications of the fictional one. But the identity of the fiction cannot be senesitive to the way real things happen to be, even if whether or not a fiction has been created is sensitive to how storytellers interact with real things, for there is no component of the property of being a fiction that makes similarity to real things relevant to what makes a given fiction the specific fiction that it is.[23]

Against this, contextualists can point to our use of certain counterfactuals whose truth-values we can reasonably disagree about, from case to case. This implies, they say, that we think their antecedents are possible, for if they were impossible, we would only have to decide whether to treat the conditionals as all true or all false. But our problem, they continue, is not one of decision; it is rather whether in fact the antecedents sustain the consequents. However, there is a difficulty for my position here only if the nonstipulative ascription of a truth-value to such a counterfactual as "If Holmes had really existed, he would have solved such-and-such a crime" requires that its antecedent be genuinely ("metaphysically") possible, rather than merely conceivable, or logically possible in some narrower sense, or elliptical for "someone with the salient qualities of Holmes." Admittedly, the last alternative is rather unsatisfactory in the absence of an argument, which does not presuppose the correctness of the essentialist view presently in dispute, that someone who utters that counterfactual "really" means the quantified antecedent.[24] And the first and second alternatives, the ideas that substantive questions of truth-value can arise even if a counterfactual's antecedent is possible only in some narrowly logical sense ("consistent with the meanings of the logical constants") or if "possibly" means "conceivably," could be objected to on the grounds that they are inconsistent with the Lewis-Stalnaker analysis of truth-conditions, which works well enough otherwise. Such objections to this analysis as are based on particular assumptions about the three-place comparison relation on worlds are not to the point here, the problem being with the field of the relation, which is taken to be the class of genuinely possible worlds. But my response to this is that the Lewis-Stalnaker analysis is not sufficiently well confirmed for its success with some cases to suggest that "Sherlock Holmes really exists" is genuinely possible, for there are many other examples of substantive counterfactual claims, which do not raise issues that are presently in dispute, with which that analysis is equally in difficulty. One example is: "If Godel had proved the consistency of real-number theory in Peano Arithmetic, Hilbert's formalism would now be the dominant philosophy of mathematics," which has a narrowly logically possible, but mathematically impossible, antecedent, but which people could reasonably argue about. So I am unimpressed by the contextualist's appeal to counterfactuals.[25]

The usefulness of the case of fictions to the contextualist resided in the indeterminacy there might seem to be over the modal status of certain properties. It may still be wondered if the absolutist approach outlined here settles every substantial question. For example, at each world a fiction is created by a specific storyteller or group of storytellers; but must its creators be the same at every world where it is created? Furthermore, there is no particular type of claim that is characteristically made of fictions in the stories in which they figure, which seems to imply that there are no limits to what could be true, in fiction, of some fictional character. But intuitively, Conan Doyle would not have been writing about Holmes if he had written stories with no content in common with the ones he actually wrote. I take these two points in turn.

Is it really plausible that a fiction has the same creator at every world in which there are stories involving it? The problem case is that of a world where Conan Doyle does not exist but some other author sets down word-for-word replicas of exactly the Sherlock Holmes stories. It might be argued that in the actual world, other authors have extended the corpus of Holmes stories, which is to say that other authors have also written about Holmes. So why would they not have written about Holmes if Conan Doyle had not existed? The obvious reply is that we must give weight to the intentions of these other authors. In the actual world, they intend to write about Conan Doyle's character, and if it is necessary to intend to write about Holmes in order to write about him, then even if they had actually duplicated the exact text of "The Hound of the Baskervilles" but lacked such an intention, they would not thereby have written a Holmes story; so much less would they have written such a story had Conan Doyle not existed.

This reply requires improvement at two points. First, intention to write about Holmes is too strong a necessary condition for writing a Holmes story. For example, someone might unknowingly write about Holmes if he had read Conan Doyle's stories in his youth, forgotten about them, and then wrote detective stories clearly based on the Holmes character, though he believes the conception of the character to be original with himself. It is not easy to formulate a weaker necessary condition to take account of points like this, but perhaps we can say that the new author's creative output involves Holmes only if its content is somehow explained by a cognitive encounter with Holmes stories and if the new author's character sufficiently resembles the Holmes of a Holmes story. But (second) this helps only with intraworld questions about when one story involves the same character as another, and it would be question-begging just to add on that necessarily the first Holmes stories are Conan Doyle's; someone might say that Conan Doyle's nonexistence, or at least lack of any literary activity like his actual work, is exactly the condition needed to open the window of opportunity for someone else to create Sherlock Holmes.

If this view is wrong and our general approach right, we ought to be able to generate a four-world argument like the one used before to show that those who hold the view must explicitly violate the principles about identity or else must appeal to extrinsic factors to justify their identity judgments. And it seems that such an argument is forthcoming, for if we take a purported world w where Conan Doyle does not exist and someone else is the first to write about Holmes, and then move to a world u where that person's literary work (along with its genesis) from w is combined with Conan Doyle's actual work (along with its genesis), then the intraworld criterion implies that they are not writing about the same character, as is guaranteed by transfer of the geneses to the Borges world u. So if one wants to maintain that it *is* Holmes whom the second author creates and also agree that identities and nonidentities must be intrinsically grounded, the question of what other coexisting authors are doing becomes germane to the identity of a fiction created by a given author: at least one author is not writing about Holmes in the Borges world, but only because the other is writing just as he did in a world where he originated Holmes. Hence if our original principles about identity are to be preserved, we have to say that what other authors are doing can be part of the intrinsic grounding of the identity of the character created by *this* author, even if he is working in total isolation from all the others. But no aspect of the property of being a fiction would render such a ground intrinsic.

However, there is a lacuna in this argument for essentiality of creator.[26] The considerations about intraworld identity of fictions produced only a rough *sufficient* condition for identity in terms of cognitive contact. If this condition is necessary as well, then the argument of the previous paragraph goes through for tokens. But why would it be wrong to say that in the Borges world, our two authors create the very same fictional character even though they are cognitively isolated? In the organism case, the distinctness of the trees in w is guaranteed by their spatial separation, but no corresponding *guarantee* of numerical distinctness exists for fictions. We are happy to say that isolated mathematicians may discover the same theorem: the identity of the theorems is established simply by reference to their content. To be sure, fictional characters are not objects of discovery, but what is wrong with the view that identity of text-types is sufficient for identity of fictions introduced by the text tokens?

Since storytelling contrasts with mathematics in this context just in terms of creation as opposed to discovery, at least on nonconventionalist views of mathematics, it is perhaps to the notion of creation that we should look for the nonidentity we need. Now the Borges world has been underdescribed, for the two storytellers can author their stories (a) simultaneously or (b) sequentially. Moreover, it seems that fictions should not be said to exist before the first story involving them is authored, since this is the temporal analogue of the modal doctrine that a fiction does not exist at a world where there is no real story involving it, but that they should be said to exist at all times thereafter.[27] So it would be strange indeed to say, given (a), that the subsequent writer in the Borges world creates the same fiction as the first writer, for it seems to be a trivial truth about the notion of creation that x cannot be created at a time t if x already exists, and continues to exist through t. There is again a contrast with mathematics, where the same theorem can be rediscovered. But by contrast with doing mathematics, storytelling is not supposed to produce something that corresponds to the facts, which is why the notion of discovery is inappropriate. Facts, being objective, can of course be rediscovered, but there is nothing analogous to support the idea of different individuals coincidentally coming across the same thing in storytelling, where the objects are our own subjective creations. Thus, although we can sensibly say that the second author has "re-created" the fictional character of the first, this can mean only that he has produced another token of exactly the same type, not that he has created that very token fiction again. Similar considerations seem to apply to case (b) of simultaneous creation, though the simple principle about creation, that you can't create what already exists, is not applicable. Perhaps what would be wrong with saying that the two authors create the very same fiction is that it would induce a kind of overdetermination of bringing into existence that makes no sense: if the same thing is created by two creators, then if one had done exactly as he did while the other had never existed, that should issue in some difference in the nature of the thing created besides differences logically consequent upon the nonexistence of the alleged second creator. So I conclude that the fictions in the Borges world are distinct tokens of the same type and that the argument for essentiality of creator goes through for tokens.

The other issue to be faced is that there seem to be no restrictions on how differently an author could have written and still have been writing about his actual creation. But surely something of the body of "lore" about Holmes must be preserved in any story about him, or, insofar as those properties are ones a real individual can lose as time passes, it must at least be implicit in a story where Holmes is ascribed none of his standard qualities that such a process of change has occurred. Furthermore, even if the general theory can be shown to imply some restrictions on the amount of disagreement there can be about Holmes's characteristics in the Conan Doyle stories of two different worlds, unless the restrictions are given in the form of an exact list of which qualities can be removed and which introduced, a slippery-slope argument will carry us anyway to a world where there is too much disagreement: the amount of disagreement between adjacent worlds on the slope will be within the bounds of the possible, but the sum of the amounts of disagreement between adjacent worlds will be well beyond those bounds. So on the present approach, if not every alteration is possible, we have to say none are, to stay off the slope. But this is too restrictive; Conan Doyle fixed Holmes's street number in Baker Street as the first number beyond that of the highest-numbered real address at the time he was writing, and it seems uncontroversial that if that latter number had been higher, so would Holmes's street number (this counterfactual has an unproblematic metaphysically possible antecedent). Meanwhile, the contextualist can accommodate the apparently inconsistent intuitions that are making trouble for my own approach here, for he or she can say that we can intelligibly postulate that various fictional features of Holmes, or ranges of features, could have been different, since along with each such postulation, there is an accompanying context in which there is at least the implicit assumption that enough other features are being held fixed to guarantee that it is Holmes we are talking about.

In fact, on the present approach, we can accommodate these intuitions as well as contextualism does. There are two questions: first, are there restrictions on the internal content of a story if Holmes is to be one of its characters? And, second, do we have to go so far as to say that all the fictional properties of Holmes are essential to him, i.e., that Conan Doyle would have created a different fictional object if he had ascribed ever so slightly different a range of characteristics to his central character? A full answer to the first question requires some account of what is involved in creating a fictional character. Literary critics speak of character development in fiction, which contrasts with the initial stages of character introduction. If a Holmes story says that Holmes nodded to a passing policeman on his way to Scotland Yard, it seems excessive to regard "that" policeman as a definite fictional character created by Conan Doyle, just on the basis of this one sentence in the story. Rather, some degree of ascription of character (not necessarily in a psychological sense) is required, though it need not be enough to individuate each fiction from all others: if an author writes a story about two absolutely indiscernible objects, the distinctness of the fictions created may reside just in the intention that they be distinct. So there will be borderline cases where we are unsure whether to say that a fiction has been created (of course, its being vague whether or not a fiction has been created does not entail that a vague fiction has been created). Perhaps we can say that there are certain "marks" of Sherlock Holmes that must hold in any world of the character created by Conan Doyle if, in that world, it is to be Holmes he creates. This allows some of the details to be different, without putting us on a slippery slope.

The contextualist may reply that this is still too strong, since for any candidate mark, it is plausible that Conan Doyle would have created Holmes even if that mark had been absent, provided enough others were present. However, we do not need to dispute this judgment of plausibility, since there is a way of accommodating it without relativizing to context, if we so wish. Suppose we have agreed what the marks of Sherlock Holmes are. Then we can say that lacking such-and-such marks is a possibility for Holmes to such-and-such a degree, and the fewer marks a character Conan Doyle creates in a world w has in common with the marks of his actual creation, the lower is the degree to which the fictional situation of that possible fiction is a possibility for Holmes. The degree to which such-and-such a situation is a possibility for Holmes has as its metalinguistic correlate the degree of truth of a sentence of the form

"$\diamond\phi$(Holmes)," where "ϕ" is an expression spelling out the details of the situation, and once such sentences are ascribed appropriate degrees of truth, the threat of slipping down the slope dissolves (for the same reasons as apply in the solutions to nonmodal Sorites arguments)—see Goguen (1969), Sanford (1975), and Forbes (1983; 1985, chapter 7).[28]

There is still a difference between what the contextualist says about such cases and my own position, a difference that may seem to be to the contextualist's advantage. The contextualist can say that although it is a mark of Holmes that he lived and worked with a medical assistant, Doctor Watson, it is wholly true that he might not have had any such assistant, whereas on my view, it could at best be only *almost* wholly true. To see this, suppose for *reductio* that it is instead wholly true. Then we have a mark of Holmes that can be dropped without any corresponding reduction in degree of possibility for Holmes, and so we have an amount of change, however small, that preserves complete possibility for Holmes. Hence a sequence of worlds as above, with adjacent members differing in relevant respects by less than that amount, will constitute a slippery slope again. Indeed, the fact that ever so slight a change from world to world must reduce degree of possibility has prompted Fine to point to a general difficulty with "degree of possibility" resolutions of modal slippery-slope paradoxes (see note 13). Fine notes that in the nonmodal case, say with the Sorites paradox of smallness (if x is small and y is (to the naked eye) indiscernibly taller than x then y is small, hence everyone is small if anyone is), some height differences do not reduce degree of smallness: take a y who is unqualifiedly small, let x be one millimeter smaller than y, and then in moving along a sequence of men of increasing height, degree of smallness stays the same (maximum) in going from x to y. Similarly, Fine suggests, given sufficiently minimal counterfactual changes in the relevant respects, the result should be completely possible for the chosen object; but then, as indicated above, we are off down the slope.

We can avoid this objection by stipulating that maximum degree of possibility is preserved only by changes within certain bounds from the way things *actually* are, and deny that change within those bounds from u to v, where u and v are *arbitrary* worlds, must preserve degree of possibility. But Fine would justifiably object to this that it embodies an unmotivated bias toward the actual world: what matters is the amount of change, not whether the world with respect to which the change is measured is the actual world, for it is in a good sense contingent which world this is. So either we are left with a brute difference between the modal and the nonmodal cases, or else certain small changes from *any* possible configuration of properties for an object of the appropriate type yield a state that is wholly possible for that object, hence every possible configuration for an object of that type is wholly possible for that object.

However, Fine's problem is resolved when we see that there is a good reason why the modal and the nonmodal cases should differ in the way to which he draws attention: it is not at all a "brute" difference. "Small" is a predicate that we unhesitatingly apply to, say, certain Caucasian male adults in California, and to all Caucasian male adults in California smaller than these: the term is observational, and we have observational encounters with people of different heights, all of whom we un-hesitatingly classify (relative to the standards for the group in question) as small. That is, we are similarly situated, so far as criteria of application of "small" are concerned, with respect to a range of different heights, all of which are unqualifiedly categorized as small. Now consider the predicate "is a possible set of marks for Sherlock Holmes" (similar considerations apply to artifacts and the [matter of the] parts from which they are constructed, and to quantities of original matter in organisms). To be in an analogous situation with respect to this predicate, we would have to be similarly situ-ated, so far as its criteria of application are concerned, with respect to various sets of marks that are unqualifiedly sets of marks for Sherlock Holmes. But there is one set of marks to which we apply that predicate on one kind of ground, the actual set, where the ground of application is that whatever is actual is possible; whereas other sets of marks do not present themselves to us *in the same way* as possible for Holmes; they are only possible in view of the relationship to which they stand to the actual set, which in some sense is an indirect, rather than direct, ground of possibility. Here we have a contrast with the fact that the ground of smallness in a small man does not lie in his being smaller, or just marginally taller, than some other unqualifiedly small man: it is just as intrinsic in each case, having to do with the position of the man's height on the height distribution scale in his group. This scale is roughly calibrated into three bands (small, medium, tall), and two men of different heights can be unqualifiedly small because both have heights well within the bottom band. None of this has any analogue in the modal cases, and there does not seem to be any other source of pressure to admit that some instances of the relationship between a merely possible set of marks of Holmes and the actual set warrant ascribing the same degree of possibility to that set's being a set of marks of Holmes as we must ascribe to the actual set. My conclusion is therefore that there are no difficulties in principle in applying the orthodox essentialist apparatus to resolve what may at first sight appear to be indeterminacies in the modal facts about fictions, and hence that this undeniably rather special case affords the contextualist view no better support than do the cases usually discussed.

5. THE COHERENCE OF CONTEXTUALISM

It is easy enough to describe contextualism in the broadest terms so as to make it sound plausible, but I shall argue that on closer examination, none of its versions are very attractive. A contextualist claims that an essentialist thesis is not made true or false by the modal facts as they stand, but only relative to the specification of some parameter supplied by context. A possible example might be the following: in the context of a discussion of historical facts, it may be speculated how so-and-so would have behaved had he been born in an entirely different epoch; in such a context, character traits are held fixed and origin is allowed to vary (here I am waiving my earlier objection to the assumption that a sensible counterfactual must have a metaphysically possible an-tecedent). But in the context of discussion of biological facts, speculations involving large variations in the grosser features of organisms may be made, the context deter-mining that origin is to be held fixed (see Johnston [1977]). Or perhaps this is too rigid, and something like Lewis's scorekeeping apparatus is involved (1983c): an assumption that is held fixed in a context loses that status as soon as some assertion is made inconsistent with its being fixed, and either less is held fixed, or it is replaced by some different, compensating, essentialist limitation.

In developing this, we should note a broad distinction between two kinds of contextualism. A contextualist of any sort says that a sentence-type of a particular kind does not express a proposition capable of being absolutely true or false, but expresses only a function from contexts to truth-values. Such contextualism may or may not be "debunking." The nondebunking kind is involved when the sentence-types in question contain acknowledged indexical expressions whose references are certain contextually salient items. Indeed, contextualism can be nondebunking even when the contextualist's claim that an expression has an indexical component to its meaning is controversial: according to one kind of modal contextualism, "actual" is an indexical on a par with "local" and "present," and modal operators are indexical in the way tense operators are (see Lewis [1983e]). That this is not thought of as in any way a debunking contextualism presumably has to do with the objectivity of the features of context that determine the reference ("the world of utterance"): there is no sense in which these features are established by convention or involve matters of contingent fact about human psychological states.

When contextualism is nondebunking, the contextualist is happy to say that once the value of the contextual parameter is supplied, an absolute truth-value can be ascribed to the relevant statement. By contrast, although the debunking contextualist *could* say this, he or she will not, since it detracts from the revisionary flavor of his or her position; for instance, ethical relativists would regard it as misleading, even if not technically incorrect, to say that moral statements are absolutely true or false once the relevant societal mores are specified: "absolutely" seems not far removed from "objectively," and it is the relativist's thesis that the nature of that to which ethical statements are relative is not properly described as objective—that is why the contextualism is debunking.

Our first type of modal contextualist is of the same type as the ethical relativist: facts about an object's possibilities are no less problematic than moral facts. To an extent, therefore, the previous sections of this paper transfer the burden of argument, since they have purported to explain how the modal facts in which the absolute essentialist believes can arise; if this explanation or something like it is acceptable, then we can grant the contextualist a context-relative sense of "possibly" (in *de re* occurrences) if one is insisted on, but there will also be the nonrelative sense of broadly logical *de re* possibility just outlined, which we can go on using. However, we can be more aggressive than this, for a plausible contextualism must explain the mechanics of how changes in context lead to changes in the constraints on what is an acceptable possibility judgment, and it is not easy to see what the explanation would be. Take the example of a contextualist view sketched above. What is to prevent the introduction in a biological context of speculation about how an organism would have turned out if it had had a different origin, or speculation in a historical context about what would have happened if so-and-so had had a quite different outlook? There is no plausibility in the bald claim that in such contexts these particular speculations are ruled out. On the other hand, if any such speculation *automatically* pushes back the contextually determined boundary of what is possible for an object of such-and-such a kind, then there will be contexts in which the most obviously impossible things will be within the boundary of the possible. So there must be some mechanism that further constrains *de re* possibility in one respect when it is liberalized in another. But what is this mechanism, and how do thinkers in a context come to agree on its effects? The contextualist has a great deal of explaining to do here.

The motivation for this kind of contextualism, as already remarked, is skepticism about the existence of modal facts that determine the *de re* possibilities. There is thought to be a contrast with the temporal case, where there is less reason for skepticism about facts that determine what the pasts and futures of particular objects are. This kind of skepticism, which could be called *de re* skepticism, or "anti-Haecceitism," regards the transworld identities that arise in standard modal model theory as conventional features of models (see Fine [1978a, p. 126]); so it can be left to context to specify which transworld identifications are to be imposed. From this point of view, however, the theoretical underpinnings of the contextualism advocated in Lewis (1983a, appendix C) seem more natural than those provided by the standard model theory, where it is harder to get a clear picture of what the modal facts are that the contextualist regards as determinate. For Lewis, there is a range of perfectly determinate modal facts, comprising facts about how things are at the various possible worlds with the worldbound individuals existing at those worlds (I ignore niceties about the nonexistents of a world). However, our ordinary modal language is not suited for expressing facts of this kind: it is expressively inadequate with respect to the language of Counterpart Theory, which Lewis holds to be the fundamental language in this context. In modal language, we can express facts about the worldbound individuals of the actual world, but we can speak only of *some* or *all* worlds meeting such-and-such a condition, and we can speak only of the worldbound individuals of other worlds indirectly, picking them out by (implicit) definite or indefinite descriptions that exploit some relation those individuals stand in to the individuals of the actual world. It is the content of this relation about which Lewis is a contextualist: in different contexts, different relations are intended. The relations are all relations of comparative overall similarity, but they differ in various ways:

> (1) as to which respects of similarity and difference are to count at all, (2) as to the relative weights of the respects which do count, (3) as to the minimum standard of similarity which is required, and (4) as to the extent to which we eliminate candidates that are similar enough when they are beaten by competitors with stronger claims . . . the vagueness of the counterpart relation—and hence of essence and *de re* modality generally—may be subject to pragmatic pressures and differently resolved in different contexts. The upshot is that it is hard to say anything false about essences. For any halfway reasonable statement will tend to create a context that (partially) resolves the vagueness of the counterpart relation in such a way as to make that statement true in that context. (1983a, p. 42)

Is there a sense in which Lewis's contextualism is debunking? His position about modality is analogous to a familiar view about time, that identity between objects holds only intratemporally and that the continuants of ordinary thought are in fact sequences of "instantaneous thing-stages," for then a temporal contextualist might argue that which sequences we pick out is not determined by the genuine temporal facts but is rather a matter of our interests or of convention, that is, of something that could be thought to vary with context, sufficiently broadly construed. This temporal contextualism is debunking of our ordinary ontology because it does not ascribe any very favored status to the relation that defines the sequences of thing-stages that constitute the continuants. But note that the stage ontology does not by itself imply contextualism and is not in itself debunking, since a philosopher could accept that ontology yet argue that there is a specially favored relation that defines the continuants, a relation whose status is owed to its intrinsic content, and not to any fact about thinkers; see, for instance, Shoemaker (1979). So whether or not a stage theorist debunks the ordinary ontology depends on what he or she says about the relation that goes proxy, in his or her approach, for transtemporal identity in the ontology of continuants: Shoemaker reconstructs the ordinary ontology, the contextualist does not.

There is no ordinary ontological view that postulates "modal continuants," since the apparatus of possible worlds and transworld identity is the invention of philosophers in a way that the ontology of times and objects that persist through time is not. But as in the temporal case, it is not the choice of ontology that is debunking, but rather Lewis's denial that there is a favored relation that connects worldbound individuals; it is this that eliminates absoluteness in the truth-values of *de re* modal judgments. Evidently, there is room in the modal case for an analogue of Shoemaker's position, a view that accepts Lewis's ontology but rejects his ideology. In criticizing Lewis's contextualism, it would therefore be beside the point to attack his general view about the relative standings of ordinary modal language and the language of Counterpart Theory.

The fate of the contextualist's cause depends on whether he or she can provide a convincing general account of the nature of *de re* possibility on which it seems right to say that there is no favored counterpart relation, or that the identity of individuals is a matter of convention. I will end by mentioning a special temporal case where relativity to context in the truth-value of a tensed sentence might be conceded, to see if the underlying phenomenon is generally applicable to modality. Those who argue for abortion rights often base their position on the doctrine that a human being is not created at conception and that the organism that develops after conception gradually becomes a human being, although it is not definitely a human until, e.g., the fifth month of gestation. To this it is sometimes replied that biologists speak of the human zygote as being a member of the species *homo sapiens*. The natural response to that point is that this is a technical use of "human being" motivated by taxonomical convenience, and that the real question is whether the zygote is a human being in the sense in which these words are used in the moral principles those opposed to abortion often cite. This might be said to translate into a contextual relativity in the question: what is the past of this adult human being? In a biological context, it may be true to say that this human was implanted, but that truth-value does not carry over to a context where questions of public policy are at issue. The relativity arises because the application conditions of the concept of a human being do not determine how it applies to organisms a certain distance removed from the paradigm cases, far enough removed for its application not to be settled by general considerations about the identity of continuants, e.g., the consideration of continuity. Yet practical pressures demand that we make some kind of decision about the penumbral areas. Hence, if we have various purposes of widely different kinds, the decision we make with one in view can be overturned when we consider another. Might it not *always* be like this in the modal case?

My reply is that if the temporal example is to show anything at all, it must involve a contextual relativity in ontology: in the public policy context we are talking about different *entities*. But surely the example establishes nothing of the sort: all that varies with context is the care we have to take over our choice of words. In the temporal case, there is complete agreement on the underlying facts: conception initiates a continuous process of biological development and then decay that constitutes the life cycle of a single organism. The question is whether the sortal "human being" is an ultimate sortal applying to the organism whose life cycle this is at all moments of its existence, or merely a phase-sortal applying only once a certain anatomical and histological structure has been assumed. In the public policy context, given the moral weight of "human being," neither use would be conceded by the other party to the dispute, but in a biological context where such attachments are irrelevant, one may as well use "human being" as an ultimate sortal, given the lack of any other common useful term. But it is the same organism that is in question in all the contexts, as determined by the extent of the temporal continuity. There is little comfort for contextualism in cases such as these.

Notes

1. See "Last of the English Milords," *Sunday Times Magazine* (London), July 15, 1984, p. 28. "Randolph" is Randolph Churchill, son of Sir Winston. "Francis" is Francis Noel-Baker, son of Philip and Irene Noel-Baker (the "she" with brains and beauty).

2. Discussions with Kit Fine have provided much impetus for this paper. I am also grateful to Ronna Burger, Paolo Dau, Dan Lloyd, and Nathan Salmon for comments on earlier versions of this material. I have discussed various aspects of essentialism in my book *The Metaphysics of Modality*, Oxford University Press 1985 (henceforth "Forbes [1985a]"), and although I have tried to concentrate on other aspects here, some overlap was needed for this paper to be self-contained; most of it occurs in the first half of section 3. Part of this typescript was prepared using the *Ophir* and *Dresden* symbol fonts created for the Macintosh computer by B. L. Tapscott of the University of Utah.

3. I follow (more or less) the notation and terminology of Fine (1978a). A *frame* is a pair (W, A) where W is a nonempty set (of worlds) and A is a function from W into sets, at least one of which is nonempty. The domain of all possible objects of the frame is $A = U A_w: w \in W$. A modal structure for L is a triple $A = (W, A, val)$, in which (W, A) is a frame and *val* is a function such that $val(c) \in A$ for c a constant, $val(R) \subset W \times A^n$, for R a predicate of degree n. A *model* M for L is a pair (A, w^*), where A is a modal structure and w^* (the actual world) is a member of W. Models are full (every object has a name), quantifiers are actualist (the range of "∀" at each w is A_w not A), and "□" is strong (the truth of $\ulcorner \Box \phi \urcorner$ at w requires the truth of ϕ at every world, not just at worlds where the referents of ϕ's terms all exist). Suppose L contains no constants. If A is a structure and w a world in W, then A_w, the structure of A at w (or, if A is understood, the structure of w), is (A, val_w), where val_w is the function on L such that $val_w(R)$ is the set of n-tuples $<a_1 \ldots a_n>$ such that $<a_1 \ldots a_n, w> \in val(R)$. $\underline{A_w}$, the *inner* structure of A at w, or the inner structure of w, is $(A_w, \underline{val_w})$

where $\underline{val_w}$ is the function on L given by: $\underline{val_w}(R) = (<a_1 \ldots a_n>: <a_1 \ldots a_n> \in (A_w)^n$ and $<a_1 \ldots a_n, w> \in val(R)]$. Truth of a sentence at a world relative to a model, $(M, u) \models \phi$, is defined inductively, and truth in a model is the special case of truth at its actual world. See Fine (1978a, p. 129) for the case where L has constants.

4. ("AE") is for "antiessentialism"; see Fine (1978b, p. 289, corollary 12) and also Parsons (1969). I have altered the formulation somewhat. "Dif$(x_1 \ldots x_n)$" abbreviates "$\bigwedge(x_i \neq x_j)$, $1 \le i < j \le n$." Similarly, "$E(x_1 \ldots x_n)$" abbreviates "$\bigwedge(E(x_i), 1 \le i \le n$." Fine does not distinguish antiessentialism and nonessentialism.

5. A formula is *de dicto* iff (i) it contains no individual constant or free variable within the scope of a modal operator, and (ii) it contains no variable within the scope of a modal operator unless the variable is bound by a quantifier also within the scope of that operator. Any formula violating (i) or (ii) is *de re*. A *de dicto* theory T is a theory whose axioms are all *de dicto* sentences. If T is a theory, MOD(T) is the class of all its models. The formula/sentence distinction is significant. An open sentence can be said to take the generality interpretation, that is, it is equivalent to the closed sentence obtained by prefixing universal quantifiers to bind the free variables; but these must be *possibilist* (ranging over A at each w) as opposed to actualist universal quantifiers. Since the quantifiers of our language are actualist, a result that holds for *de dicto* sentences may not hold for *de dicto* formulae.

6. The proof is as follows. An essentialist sentence α is a sentence with the form of the antecedent of (AE), and DD(α) is its *de dicto* generalization (which is equivalent to the consequent of (AE)). We want to show that if T is a *de dicto* theory and α an essentialist sentence that is a theorem of T, then $T \vdash (\alpha \to DD(\alpha))$, since this gives us $T \vdash DD(\alpha)$. So assume $T \vdash \alpha$. Suppose $T \nvdash (\alpha \to DD(\alpha))$. Then there is $M \in MOD(T)$ such that $M \models \alpha$ and $M \models \sim DD(\alpha)$. We argue that there must then be $N \in MOD(T)$ such that $N \models \sim\alpha$, contradicting the assumption. To establish the existence of N we use a result of Fine's. Say that two models $M = (A, w^*)$ and $N = (B, v^*)$ are *weakly locally isomorphic* iff $\underline{A}_{w^*} \cong \underline{B}_{v^*}$, for every world $w \in W$ there is $v \in V$ such that $\underline{A}_w \cong \underline{B}_v$ and for every $v \in V$ there is $w \in W$ such that $\underline{A}_w \cong \underline{B}_v$. Thus different isomorphisms may establish $\underline{A}_w \cong \underline{B}_v$ for different $w \in W$. By corollary 14 and the remark on page 137 of Fine (1978a), if T is a *de dicto* theory and M, N are weakly locally isomorphic, then $M \in MOD(T)$ iff $N \in MOD(T)$. Suppose then that $M \in MOD(T)$ refutes ($\alpha \to DD(\alpha)$) as above. Then for some $u \in W$, $(M, u) \models \beta[b_1 \ldots b_n]$, $\beta = \ulcorner$ Dif$(x_1 \ldots x_n)$ & $E(x_1 \ldots x_n)$ & $\sim\phi(x_1 \ldots x_n)\urcorner$, ϕ as in α, $u \in W$, and each b_i assigned to x_i, $1 \le i \le n$. So $DD(\alpha)$ and the consequent of the appropriate instance of (AE) are false in M. We argue that in this case, T does not entail α, by constructing a model N that is weakly locally isomorphic to M, hence also in MOD(T), in which α is false. For each $<a_1 \ldots a_n>$ in A^n such that (i) Dif$(a_1 \ldots a_n)$ and (ii) for some $w \in W$, each a_i exists at W, we introduce a new world w' to obtain a superset V of W, and for each new w' we set $B_{w'} = A_u$ except that if a_i is not in A_u then a_i is in $B_{w'}$ and b_i is not. We fix $B_{w'}$ from A_u by interchanging a_i with b_i throughout, $1 \le i \le n$. That is, if $<c_1 \ldots c_n>$ contains no a_i or b_i then $<c_1 \ldots c_n, w'> \in val'(R)$ iff $<c_1 \ldots c_n, u> \in val(R)$. But if $<c_1 \ldots c_n>$ contains members of $<a_1 \ldots a_n>$, $<c_1 \ldots c_n, w'> \in val'(R)$ iff $<d_1 \ldots d_n, u> \in val(R)$, where $<d_1 \ldots d_n>$ is $<c_1 \ldots c_n>$ with each a_i replaced by the corresponding d_i; *mutatis mutandis* if the c_i's include some b_i's. Evidently, for each w' so introduced, we have $A_u \cong B_{w'}$, hence the two models $M = (A, w^*)$ and $N = (B, v^*)$ are weakly locally isomorphic (set $w^* = v^*$). Thus $N \in MOD(T)$, but $N \models \sim\alpha$, since for any $<a_1 \ldots a_n>$ such that Dif$(a_1 \ldots a_n)$, if there is $w \in W$ where all a_i exist, there is $w' \in V$ where they all exist and satisfy $\sim\phi$.

7. World Differentiation, in the notation of note 3, is: if $A_u = A_v$, then $u = v$. The Falsehood Principle is that an atomic sentence is false at a world if the referent of some individual constant does not exist at that world.

8. For the notion of role, see McMichael (1983).

9. In Adams (1979), there is a plausible example of nontrivially isomorphic distinct worlds. Let w be a world in which there are two indiscernible iron globes, each of which is unqualifiedly a contingent existent, each of which has always existed at and will always exist at w, and each of which has a nature that is contingent in the normal way. u is a world where the first globe ceases to exist at time t, but things are otherwise as in w, and v is a world where the second globe ceases to exist at time t, things otherwise being as in w. Then u and v are nontrivially isomorphic. But the example does not support the weak view over the strong one, except on one interpretation where I have already granted the weak view. One might interpret the case as involving logically simple globes, the identity of which is logically prior to that of the matter that

makes them up, so that the only nontrivial essential properties the globes would have would be, say, being globes and being simple, and the logical consequences of these. But it is more natural to think of the identity of the constituting matter as independent of the identity of the globes, and then we could say that being a globe and being made of that matter is an essence of each globe. If requiring exactly the same matter seems too strict, there will at least be a fuzzy essence available (see Forbes [1985a, chapter 7]). Adams's idea that the case shows that transworld identity is "primitive" in some sense also seems dubious to me: if one thinks of u and v as possible courses of events with an initial segment in common with w (see Forbes [1985a, chapter 6, section 6]), each branching from w at t, then what makes u a world where one globe is immortal and v a *distinct* world where the *other* globe is the immortal one is the totality of facts about transtemporal identity in the two courses of events. On this understanding of the case, there is no sense in which the facts about transworld identity are "brute" facts, and hence they are not primitive, if that is what is meant by "primitive."

10. Earlier I said that R is essential to x and y in that order iff "Rxy" holds at every world where they both exist. But the claim (K) makes is stronger than that origination is essential to x and y: it says that if x originates from y at any world, then x has the essential property of originating from y; this could be written more perspicuously as:

$$(K_\lambda)\ \square(\forall x)\square(\forall y)\square(Rxy \rightarrow [(\lambda z)\square(Ez \rightarrow Rzy)](x)).$$

Note that (K) and (K_λ) are both consistent with origination being strongly rigid, i.e., holding between x and y at every world (whether or not x or y exists) if it holds between them at any world. "Originates" is of course a poor candidate for strong rigidity, but there would be more point to allowing strong rigidity for set-membership: one might want to hold that "Socrates ϵ {Socrates}" is true even with respect to worlds where Socrates, hence {Socrates}, does not exist (the intention is that "ϵ" here be primitive, not defined by "$\Diamond(x\,\epsilon^*\,y)$," where ϵ^* is the relation that is merely essential to Socrates and {Socrates}, in that order).

11. The example, though not the use to which it is put, is from Price (1982, p. 35). Price herself thinks the example shows (K) is false for x a human being, since she identifies the human with the zygote cell from which it develops. She argues that the kind of case Kripke cites (e.g., the case of a world where the Trumans have a daughter who becomes a queen of England, but whom we would say is merely someone who comes to be like the actual Queen, rather than the actual Queen herself) to defend the intuition that origin is essential works because "the essentialist surreptitiously posits that Ms. Truman is someone other than the Queen" (see Price [1982, p. 34]). She thinks we tend to agree that the possible Queen-like daughter of the Trumans is not the actual Queen not because she is the daughter of the Trumans (the moral the defender of (K) draws) but because (i) she arises from a different zygote from the actual Queen's zygote, and (ii) she and that zygote are the same human being, as are the actual Queen and the actual Queen's zygote. Thus transitivity of identity shows the possible daughter is not the actual Queen. But (i) and (ii) explain the essentialist intuition (indeed they constitute essentially the explanation in McGinn [1976]) only if those who have it must be implicitly presupposing that transtemporal identity holds between the zygote cell and what it develops into. Since this presupposition is *prima facie* false by Leibniz's Law (the zygote ceases to exist when it divides), the explanation of the intuition is somewhat uncharitable (see the following note for more on this and the idea of zygotehood as a phase of human life). Kripke's case is supposed to show only that great overall similarity does not suffice for identity; it has force against someone who thinks that the zygote and what it develops into are distinct organisms but that if what develops is sufficiently similar overall to a given object as it is in the actual world, then it is numerically identical to that very object, even if, in the actual world, that object came from a different zygote. However, I should say that Price's example shows that there is a fallacy in the argument of section 5 of Forbes (1980) that no case of the kind hers instantiates threatens (K). Let "x-synthetic" abbreviate "a thing made by scientists which is a molecule-for-molecule replica of x as it actually is." Let S_j be the fusion of s-synthetic and e, and S_k the fusion of s and e-synthetic (where s and e are an actual sperm and an actual egg). Then my confident remark (see Forbes [1980, p. 361]) "it is easy to arrange that S_j is compossible with something non-compossible with S_k," is false.

12. On the view that the zygote cell ceases to exist when it divides, and hence is not identical to the resulting human, one conclusion would be that the human's original matter, the matter of the zygote, is matter that the human was never constituted by. But this is not the only possible view consistent with the ceasing to exist of the zygote cell. "Zygote" is often used ambiguously in these discussions, meaning at one

time "zygote cell" and at another "zygote phase." I have no objection to the position that the human is an organism that once enjoyed a zygote *phase*, and at that time was composed of the very same matter as the zygote *cell* (though I do not assume that the organism was a human being during that phase—see my text *ad fin*). The implication that distinct entities can share matter at a time may seem odd, but can either be lived with or avoided by the stipulation that the organism is constituted at any time by its cell or cells at that time, while the cell or cells are themselves constituted of matter. Now the organism that has a zygote phase continues to exist when the zygote divides, and we might use "the zygote" to refer to the organism in that phase as we use "the child" to refer to it in its childhood phase. Then it will be true that the zygote (in *this* use) and the child are necessarily identical, but it would be a mistake to infer from this that (K) or its refinement (K') below are true (see Forbes [1985a, pp. 134–37] for criticism of this step as it occurs in McGinn [1976]). What (K) requires for its truth is that the organism originate essentially from that very zygote cell, and that cell is not *identical* to the zygote (in the sense "the organism in its zygote phase"), again by Leibniz's Law. The cell merely *constitutes* the zygote (= organism in the zygote phase), and what has to be proved to establish (K) is that the zygote could not have been constituted by some other zygote cell. Similar considerations apply to (K').

13. There is no threat of Sorites paradox from conceding this tolerance. "Mutual substantial overlap" is not transitive, so the apparatus of Forbes (1983, 1985a, chapter 7) can be brought into play.

14. The existence predicate does not figure in (K'), since I am assuming that if "$M\,\alpha\beta$" is true at w then α and β exist at w. If we decided to say that at worlds where β does not exist, it has the empty sum of matter as its original matter, then the existence predicate would be required in both antecedent and consequent of (K').

15. I investigate various compromised ways around (K) in Forbes (1980), and stand by my arguments there, with the exception noted in note 11 above.

16. It might be suggested that a propagule plays a role with respect to the resulting organism more like the role played by the plan with respect to the resulting artifact. But the abstract plan corresponds to the abstract information encoded in the organism's genes, the concrete plan to those sequences of nucleotides themselves. The role of the food an organism ingests seems closer to that of the objects whose function it is to hold the parts of an artifact in the proper spatial relationships.

17. There is an attempted formulation of a category-neutral criterion of extrinsicness in Kim (1982), which is criticized in Lewis (1983b). Kim and Lewis seem more concerned with the relational/nonrelational distinction, which is not quite the same as "extrinsic/intrinsic to the identity of."

18. For a full development of a Fregean semantics with properties as the referents of predicates (and states of affairs as the referents of sentences), see Forbes (1985b). Frege used "concept" as I use "property," i.e., as a word for the referent of a predicate. For my "concept" (= Wiggins's "conception" [1984, p. 128, note 6]), Frege often says "sense of a concept word." As for the legitimacy of using the notion of reference in connection with predicates and sentences, I refer to the justification in Dummett (1984, pp. 203–6).

19. This paragraph and the next respond to an objection of Nathan Salmon's. I note also that it is not easy to arrange for a proposition to be essentially but not necessarily true, for if we let a proposition fail to exist if any of the things it is about fail to exist, then it seems that to accommodate true negative existentials we would have to have a possibilist truth property, which can be possessed at a world by a proposition that does not exist there. But then we could not explain the failure of the proposition that Socrates belongs to {Socrates} to possess truth at a world where Socrates does not exist by reference to Socrates's not existing there, for how then could the proposition that Socrates does not exist be true there? For further discussion of these issues, see the debate between Fine (1985) and Plantinga (1985), and my attempt to adjudicate in Forbes (1985c).

20. We sometimes speak of "nature's artifacts," and if this is to be taken literally, then we should weaken the account of how an artifact acquires a function to allow the production of goal-directedness by chance. But probably the phrase is metaphorical.

21. My ontological position is neutral on various theories about which properties a fiction may be said to possess; see Parsons (1980) and Lewis (1983d) for such theories. Fine (unpublished) has a distinction between two ways of possessing properties, really or fictionally possessing them, which rather neatly resolves a number of problems about what is true of fictions.

22. Fine pointed out to me that the converse is also possible. If an author A writes a story about an author B who writes a story about a character C who turns out, in B's story, to be nonexistent, then C is a fiction created by A who does not enjoy fictional existence.

23. In Fine (1984, p. 127) it is objected to the idea that a fiction x in the fictional domain of w can be identified with a mere possible y at w that a mere possible at w is an existent at some u, and it is easily conceivable that the storytelling activities of w that created x there occur at such a u, so a real existent y at u would be identified with the creation of an author at u. But this objection assumes that the identity of a created fiction at a world is not sensitive to what real existents there are there, and what they are like, which, on my view, is to assume the point most in need of justification.

24. Mark Sainsbury related to me the story of a potter friend of his who dropped a vase she had just made. The vase shattered on impact and she remarked, "I wish I had made it of different clay."

25. Sometimes one tends to say that a could-have-been judgment is a literally false claim of broadly logical possibility in need of expansion into the true claim for which it is elliptical, rather than a true claim involving some other possibility concept. If the potter says "I could have made it of different clay," I tend to hear this as literally true and involving narrowly logical possibility or conceivability, whereas I hear Noel-Baker's "I might have been Randolph" as elliptical for something else. What to say about "Godel could have proved the consistency of $Th(R)$ in PA" depends in part on questions about the relationship between mathematical and logical possibility of the kind explored in Field (1984).

26. This was pointed out to me by Dan Lloyd.

27. Perhaps fictions should be said to exist only so long as stories involving them exist in some concrete form, e.g., on paper or in someone's mind. So suppose that some stories are lost forever. Would it then be possible for a subsequent author to re-create the very same token fiction? This is ruled out by the intrinsicness of identity through time: the identity of the new fiction should not turn on whether or not such-and-such stories still exist in some concrete form.

28. I favor a version of this type of solution of Sorites paradoxes in which *modus ponens* is rejected as a rule that is not universally valid relative to a semantics with infinitely many truth-values, e.g., the real interval $[0,1]$. We define $Val[A \rightarrow B]$ as $1 - (Val[A] \dot{-} Val[B])$, which is justified by the thought that if $Val[A]$ only just exceeds $Val[B]$, then the conditional should be almost wholly true, but if $Val[A]$ exceeds the consequent value by almost the maximum, the conditional should be almost wholly false; in general, the magnitude of the loss of truth in going from antecedent to consequent should be reflected by the degree of truth of the conditional ("$\dot{-}$" is cutoff subtraction). A universally valid rule is one that never delivers a conclusion worse than the premises one starts out with: the value of the conclusion is at worst the value of the least true premise. Then *modus ponens* is not universally valid (let $Val[A] = .9$, $Val[B] = .8$); it is valid only in the restricted sense that when applied to wholly true premises, it always yields a wholly true conclusion.

References

Adams, R. M. 1979. "Primitive Thisness and Primitive Identity." *The Journal of Philosophy* 76: 5–26.

Chisholm, R. 1970. "Identity through Time." In Keifer and Munitz (1970, 163–82).

Dummett, M. 1973. *Frege: Philosophy of Language*. London.

_____ .1983. "An Unsuccessful Dig." In Wright (1984, 194–226).

Field, H. 1984. "Is Mathematical Knowledge Just Logical Knowledge?" *The Philosophical Review* 93:509–52.

Fine, K. 1978a. "Model Theory for Modal Logic Part I: The De Re/De Dicto Distinction." *The Journal of Philosophical Logic* 7:125–56.

_____ . 1978b. "Model Theory for Modal Logic Part II: The Elimination of the De Re." *The Journal of Philosophical Logic* 7:277–306.

_____ . 1984. "Critical Review of Parson's *Non-Existent Objects*." *Philosophical Studies* 45:95–142.

_____ . 1985. "Plantinga on the Reduction of Possibilist Discourse." In Tomberlin and van Inwagen (1985, 145–86).

Forbes, G. 1980. "Origin and Identity." *Philosophical Studies* 37:353–62.
————. 1981. "On The Philosophical Basis of Essentialist Theories." *The Journal of Philosophical Logic* 10:73–99.
————. 1983. "Thisness and Vagueness." *Syntheses* 54:235-59.
————. 1984. "Two Solutions to Chisholm's Paradox." *Philosophical Studies* 46:171-87.
————. 1985a. *The Metaphysics of Modality*. Oxford and New York.
————. 1985b. "States of Affairs, *Bedeutung* and the Contingent A Priori." Forthcoming.
————. 1985c. Review of Tomberlin and van Inwagen (1985). Forthcoming in *Nous*.
French, P. A., T. E. Uehling and H. K. Wettstein, eds. 1979. *Studies in Metaphysics: Midwest Studies in Philosophy*. Vol. 4. Minneapolis.
Guenthner, F. and M. Guenthner-Reutter, eds. 1978. *Meaning and Translation*. London.
Goguen, J. 1969. "The Logic of Inexact Concepts." *Synthese* 19: 325–73.
Johnston, P. 1977. "Origin and Necessity." *Philosophical Studies* 32:413-18.
Kiefer, H. E. and M. Munitz, eds. 1970. *Language, Belief and Metaphysics*. New York.
Kim, J. 1982. "Psychophysical Supervenience." *Philosophical Studies* 41: 51–70.
Kripke, S. 1980. *Naming and Necessity*. Cambridge, Mass.
Lewis, D. 1983. *Philosophical Papers*. Vol. 1. Oxford and New York.
————. 1983a. "Counterpart Theory and Quantified Modal Logic." In Lewis (1983, 26–46).
————. 1983b. "Extrinsic Properties." *Philosophical Studies* 44:199–207.
————. 1983c. "Scorekeeping in a Language Game." In Lewis (1983, 233–49).
————. 1983d. "Truth in Fiction." In Lewis (1983, 261–80).
————. 1983e. "Anselm and Actuality." In Lewis (1983, 10–25).
Mackie, J. L. 1974. "*De* What *Re* Is *De Re* Modality?" *The Journal of Philosophy* 71: 551-61.
McGinn, C. 1976. "On The Necessity of Origin." *The Journal of Philosophy* 73:127–35.
McMichael, A. 1983. "A New Actualist Modal Semantics." *The Journal of Philosophical Logic* 12:73–99.
Parsons, T. 1969. "Essentialism and Quantified Modal Logic." *The Philosophical Review* 78:35–52.
————. 1980. *Nonexistent Ojbects*. New Haven
Plantinga, A. 1985. "Replies." In Tomberlin and van Inwagen (1985, 313–96).
Price, M. S. 1982. "On the Non-Necessity of Origin." *The Canadian Journal of Philosophy* 12:33–45.
Putnam, H. 1978. "Meaning, Reference and Stereotypes." In Guenthner, F. and M. Guenthner-Reutter (1978, 61–81).
Sanford, D. H. 1975. "Borderline Logic." *The American Philosophical Quarterly* 12:29-39.
Shoemaker, S. 1979. "Identity, Properties and Causality." In French *et al.*, eds. (1979, 321–42).
Tomberlin, J. and P. van Inwagen, eds. 1985. *Alvin Plantinga*. Dordrecht and Boston.
Wiggins, D. 1980. *Sameness and Substance*. Oxford.
————. 1984. "The Sense and Reference of Predicates: A Running Repair to Frege's Doctrine and a Plea for the Copula." In Wright (1984, 126–43).
Wright, C. 1984. *Frege: Tradition and Influence*. Oxford and New York.

The Epistemology of Essentialist Claims

ALAN McMICHAEL

E ssentialism is the doctrine that individuals—at least some—have, independently of any particular means of describing them, certain "interesting" necessary properties as well as other merely contingent properties. By a *necessary*, or *essential*, property, I mean one such that necessarily, if the individual exists, then it has that property. By the qualifier (interesting), I mean to exclude properties essential to *all* individuals, such as the property of self-identity. The reason for this exclusion is clear: These are properties that individuals have not in virtue of their own peculiar natures but merely in virtue of general necessary truths. Essentialists plainly want to commit themselves to something more than the existence of general necessary truths and their necessary instances. The same reason justifies a second exclusion. An "interesting" essential property must not be merely the result of "plugging up" a relation, such as identity, that is necessarily totally reflexive. For example, let P be the property of being identical to Carl Sagan. Then it is clearly a necessary truth that:

If Carl Sagan exists, then he has P.

Moreover, P is clearly not essential to everything. Again, however, there is an underlying general necessary truth:

For any X, if X exists, then X has the property *being identical to X*.

Finally, an "interesting" essential property must not be a disjunction one of whose disjuncts is a property of the sort just mentioned.

Essentialism, as I understand it, is not verified by the observation that *numbers* have interesting essential properties. Numbers, if they exist, are properties of classes and so are entities of a higher logical type than individuals. I also wish to confine my remarks to essentialism with regard to finite beings, so that propositions about the essential attributes of God will not constitute a special exception to what I have to say.

There is an alternative way in which to formulate essentialism. For any individual K and property P, we may speak of the *singular proposition* that K has P. This proposition is true of just those worlds in which K exists and has the property P. We may also speak of the *compound* singular proposition that if K exists, then K has P. This proposition is true of all those worlds in which either K does not exist, or K has P. Essentialism is the doctrine that there are necessary singular propositions of this form whose corresponding generalizations (that everything X (that exists) has P, or, if P is a relational property $R(K)$, that everything X (that exists) bears relation R to itself) are not necessary. This second formulation, in terms of singular propositions, will prove useful in what follows.

Essentialism is a problematic doctrine. Among its adherents, serious disputes arise concerning what the essential properties of individuals are, and there exists no consensus on methods for resolving such disputes. There is lacking, in other words, an adequate and generally accepted *epistemology* for essentialist claims.

According to the second formulation of essentialism, the question whether an individual has a certain property essentially reduces to the question whether a certain singular proposition is necessary. This suggests that an adequate essentialist epistemology can be secured as a by-product of an adequate epistemology for necessary truth. However, I shall argue that this suggestion is misleading. The best available epistemology for necessary truth is one that sanctions only, in the primary case, claims of the necessity of certain general propositions and, secondarily, claims of the necessity of their instances. Essentialist claims fall outside these two classes. (This argument requires a single qualification, mentioned below: It does not succeed if necessity is construed, as is not usual, in the weakened sense of temporal modal logic.)

A similar point was made some years ago by W. V Quine.[1] The then popular view was that all necessary truths are analytic. Quine observed that even if this view permits an adequate account of the necessity of general claims, it has no natural and nonarbitrary extension to the singular claims made by essentialists.

Alas, the view that necessary truths must be analytic is no longer dominant. Still, there are philosophers who maintain the traditional view that knowledge of necessary truth, although perhaps not analytic knowledge, is *a priori*. Some of them undoubtably suppose that essentialist claims can be known *a priori*. Recently, however, Saul Kripke called the traditional association between necessity and the *a priori* into question, contending both that some propositions known *a priori* are not necessary and that sometimes we can make wholly *a posteriori* discoveries of the strict necessity of propositions (i.e., of their "logical" or "metaphysical" necessity, not merely the necessity of scientific laws).[2]

If his conclusions are correct, Kripke leaves essentialists in an unclear situation. On the one hand, they cannot maintain that properties that individuals are known to have *a priori* are essential properties, rather than merely contingent properties. On the other hand, Kripke has not ruled out knowledge of essential properties. Indeed, he has opened up the possibility, which he himself believes in, that essential properties can be discovered empirically!

One weakness of Kripke's arguments is that he never actually defines the *a priori*. In what follows, I shall develop a definition of the *a priori*, explore some of its more immediate consequences, then show, using the definition and a companion theory of our grasp of concepts, that although some of Kripke's conclusions are supportable, others must be modified. Indeed, some truths known *a priori* in the sense defined are not necessary. However, the same theory that yields this conclusion also suggests that no propositions, except for a special class that includes logical and mathematical propositions but excludes essentialist propositions, are more strictly necessary than laws of nature. Thus, *contra* Kripke, no essentialist propositions, such as Kripke's "This lectern is composed of wood," can be used as examples of truths we have discovered *a posteriori* to have some stricter variety of necessity than that of natural laws.

Essentialism is tenable, then, only if the modality in terms of which it is defined is no stronger than natural necessity. I suppose that some essentialists may be willing to swallow this conclusion, arguing that natural necessity is necessity enough. The trouble is that because individuals do not seem to enter into natural laws in any (pardon me) essential way, there do not seem to be any necessary singular propositions of the sort that our newly clarified essentialism requires—or at least if there are such propositions, knowledge of their necessity cannot be accounted for by the same mechanism as our knowledge of the necessity of natural laws, and again we are left without an essentialist epistemology.

Finally, the essentialist modality may be weakened still further, so that it is the necessity of temporal modal logic ("it is determined that . . . "). If we do so, then we can indeed claim that individuals have essential properties, but this conception of essential properties is much weaker than what is often desired.

I shall conclude that, at least in the case of the more radical forms of essentialism, we lack any convincing account of how we could come to know essentialist propositions. Of course, it does not *follow* that these forms of essentialism are false. However, I would diagnose their epistemological problems in a way that is relevant to their correctness. The failure to extend epistemologies of necessary truth to essentialist propositions seems to me to show that the relevant concepts of necessity *do not apply* to those propositions. Consequently, none of those propositions are necessary in the relevant senses, and so these forms of essentialism are false after all.

I. ESSENTIALISM AND ANALYTICITY

Some current doubts about essentialism have their roots in the early half of this century, when logical necessity was identified with *analyticity*. Given that identification, essentialism was open to the following attack:

(1) According to the only plausible conception of logical necessity, all necessary truths are analytic.

(2) All analytic truths are either universal generalizations, such as that all bachelors are unmarried, or instances of analytic generalizations, such as that if I am a bachelor, then I am unmarried.

(3) Essentialism entails the existence of necessary singular propositions that are *not* instances of necessary generalizations. Therefore, since there are no such propositions, essentialism is false.

This argument is similar to the one presented in Quine's "Reference and Modality."[3] Although few contemporary philosophers would endorse it, it still merits examination, for present-day essentialism may not be immune from *similar* criticism.

The first premise is the traditional empiricist dogma, and we shall look later at the consequences of denying it. The third premise clearly follows from our second formulation of essentialism. The second premise does all the remaining work. What reason is there for thinking it correct?

According to one popular theory of the analytic, a proposition is analytic just in case there is a way of replacing its constituent concepts with *analyses* that results in a logical truth. Thus the proposition

All bachelors are unmarried

becomes, on substitution in accordance with the analysis,

All and only bachelors are unmarried males,

the logical truth

All unmarried males are unmarried.

Symbolically, the three propositions are represented by:

$(x)(Bx \supset Ux)$
$(x)(Bx \equiv (Ux \, \& \, Mx))$
$(x)((Ux \, \& \, Mx) \supset Ux).$

Notice that the transition to a logical truth is effected *via* the analysis of a *general* concept.

Essentialists want to claim the necessity of singular propositions of the form:

$Ea \supset Pa.$

Such a proposition cannot be transformed into a logical truth merely by analysis of the general concepts E and P—that would merely establish the analyticity of $(x)(Ex \supset Px)$ and so show that P is not an *interesting* essential property. Thus it can only be shown to be analytic, in the sense explained, by analysis of what is signified by the singular term 'a'. It is doubtful, however, that such analysis is possible.

To assess the prospects for analysis, we need to have a better idea of just what we are attempting to analyze. Just what sort of thing is it that corresponds, in a singular proposition, to the individual that is the subject of the proposition? There are four alternatives one might consider:

(1) The individual itself: On this view, a singular proposition has the individual subject itself as a constituent. Given the above account of analysis, there seems to be no sense at all in speaking of an "analysis" of an individual.

(2) An individual essence that is an analyzable compound of general concepts: This view would permit analysis, but there is reason to think that individuals do not have essences of this sort.[4]

(3) An individual essence that is an unanalyzable haecceity: By definition, such concepts are unanalyzable.

(4) A concept that picks out the individual but falls short of an essence: Such a concept would be a merely contingent specification of the relevant individual. A proposition in which it occurred would be only *contingently* about that individual and so would not be the desired singular proposition. (Even if this were denied, the analysis of such a contingent specification could hardly be supposed to yield *essential* properties of the individual.)

In the only tenable cases, (1) and (3), the constituent of a singular proposition corresponding to its subject is unanalyzable. This completes our antiessentialist argument: Essentialists claim the necessity of singular propositions that cannot be transformed, by analysis, into logical truths. Thus they claim the existence of necessary truths that are not analytic. But this is contrary to our empiricist assumptions.

The main problem with the argument is that if an analytic proposition is defined as one that is reducible to a logical truth *via* substitution in accordance with explicit analyses, then the empiricist doctrine that all necessary truths are analytic is *prima facie* implausible. Numerous examples have been presented of putative necessary truths that are not analytic in this sense, for example, the proposition that nothing is both red and green in the same spot on its surface at one time.[5] On the other hand, if the category of the analytic is broadened by dropping the requirement of explicit analysis, as when it is said that the analytic is what is "true in virtue of meaning," then it is not clear that the argument against essentialism holds up. It is also not clear that such a broadened account of analyticity is congenial to empiricism.

All of this may seem beside the point, since almost no one identifies necessity with analyticity anymore. Nevertheless, I do not believe the analyticity conception of necessity can be lightly dismissed. It was intended to provide an account of our *knowledge* of necessary truths within an empiricist framework. *Some* account of our knowledge of necessary truths is needed, whether we choose to be empiricists or not. Let us turn now to an epistemology of necessary truth that is rationalist in character, and let us see whether essentialist claims fare any better under it.

II. A RATIONALIST CONCEPTION OF THE *A PRIORI*

The traditional view, shared by both rationalists and empiricists, is that all knowledge of necessity is ultimately *a priori*. This view is expressed forcefully in Roderick Chisholm's *Theory of Knowledge*.[6] Chisholm quotes Whewell: "Experience can observe and record what has happened; but she cannot find, in any case, or in any accumulation of cases, any reason for what *must* happen." As we shall see, this view has been challenged recently. But for the moment I shall assume that it is correct, so that if there is to be a rationalist account of knowledge of essentialist claims, it is to be found in a rationalist account of *a priori* knowledge.

A priori knowledge is distinguished from *a posteriori* knowledge not because it can arise in the total absence of experience, which is absurd, but rather because experience does not constitute an *evidential* basis for it. What, then, is the role of experience in the acquisition of *a priori* knowledge? There exists a standard account, which can be found, among other places, in the work of Chisholm and also of Philip Kitcher, according to which the experience required for *a priori* knowledge of a proposition is simply that which is needed in order to *grasp* the proposition.[7] Lest the notion of grasping an abstract object such as a proposition seems hopelessly obscure, let me add that one grasps a proposition if one merely *understands* some *sentence* that expresses the proposition.[8] Grasp of propositions, then, is grasp of meanings, and *a priori* knowledge arises from the grasp of meanings.

Clearly there is a strong kinship between this conception of the *a priori* and the analyticity conception. The beliefs and/or abilities required in order to grasp a proposition are an essential part of those required in order to know the meaning of a sentence that expresses that proposition. So *a priori* knowledge is, in a sense, knowledge of meaning, "analytic" knowledge. There are, however, differences of detail between the two conceptions. To see these differences, we need to keep in mind the ways in which the conceptions are customarily elaborated.

First, suppose analyticity is interpreted strictly, so that an analytic proposition is one that can be reduced to a logical truth by means of explicit analyses. Then the rationalist conception we have outlined is at least potentially more liberal. One of its adherents might claim, for example, that we can know *a priori* the proposition

For any act A and person S, if S ought to do A, then S can do A

even though there seems to be no analysis of the notion of obligation that would transform this into a logical truth. This might be claimed on the ground that one who clearly grasps the meaning of 'ought' must realize that it entails ability. Whether or not this claim is correct, at least the rationalist conception supports, and the strict analyticity conception questions, the legitimacy of his move. Similar remarks apply to the proposition, mentioned earlier, that nothing is both red and green.

Second, suppose analyticity is construed more broadly, so that explicit analyses are not required. Would not the rationalist conception then be indistinguishable from the analyticity account? How we may answer depends on how the broad notion of analyticity is explained. Suppose it is said that an analytic proposition is one that is true in virtue of its meaning. Evidently, the word 'proposition' is being used to stand for the *sentence* that *has* the meaning rather than what I am calling a proposition, namely the thing that *is* the meaning. Very well. So the view is that an analytic *sentence* is one that is true in virtue of its meaning. This bogs down in the face of the obvious counter, namely, that every true sentence is, trivially, true in virtue of its meaning—had it meant something else, it might have been false. Suppose we make the usual addition: An analytic sentence is one that is true in virtue of its meaning and not in virtue of any matters of fact. A cursory glance at the literature reveals that matters of fact are none other than *contingent* matters of fact. Thus the new proposal is just a long-winded version of this: An analytic sentence is one that expresses a necessary proposition. This account of analyticity certainly does *not* match the rationalist account of the *a priori*, for it willy-nilly identifies analyticity with necessity and so gives no hint at all why analyticity should be linked with apriority.

Finally, suppose it is said that all these problems are merely due to carelessness of language and that an analytic proposition is really just the sort of proposition that

Chisholm and Kitcher are talking about, namely, one that can be known to be true by anyone who grasps it. The trouble with this is that the notion of the analytic, once meant to be a cornerstone of empiricism, might become the bane of its existence. Empiricists identified the *a priori* with the analytic in order to *trivialize* it. As long as analyticity was identified with something like "true in virtue of explicit definition," the claim of triviality was at least superficially sound.[9] Thus, empiricists could continue to hold onto their fundamental doctrine: All knowledge, except for some trivial exceptions, is *a posteriori*. But once the notion of analyticity is broadened to match the rationalists' notion of the *a priori*, it is of course doubtful that the claim of triviality can be sustained.

III. THE FOUNDATION THEORY OF OUR GRASP OF CONCEPTS

Whether or not the proposed conception of the *a priori* can be squared with traditional empiricism, we are left with a still greater mystery. Just how is it that knowledge can arise from our grasp of propositions? We may plausibly conjecture that the grasp of a proposition entails a grasp of its constituent concepts and an understanding of their manner of combination in the proposition. Clearly, then, we need to know what is involved in our grasp of concepts.

According to one theory, which we may call the *foundation theory,* some concepts, *simple concepts,* are grasped "through temselves," that is, in a way that admits of no further *philosophical* explanation, and other concepts, *complex concepts*, are grasped through acceptance of their *principles of combination* out of simple concepts. At first glance, this seems to mesh neatly with the idea that *a priori* truths are analytic. For example, if I grasp the concept of a bachelor, then I accept that it is the conjunction of the concepts of being unmarried and of being male. My acceptance is justified simply because this is the very principle of combination for bachelorhood. And to explain how knowledge might arise out of this justified belief is perhaps not a difficult philosophical task.

Closer scrutiny explodes these happy relfections. If there are simple concepts, then the concepts that appear in the analysis of bachelorhood, the concept of being married and the concept of being a male, are undoubtably not among them. For our grasp of those concepts is amenable to further philosophical explanation, not perhaps through explicit definitions in terms of other concepts, but in terms of what might be called the *application criteria* for those concepts, the criteria by means of which we judge which things satisfy them.

To find plausible examples of simple concepts, we must look to phenomenal qualities, the "felt qualities" of sensation. These qualities are the objects of what Bertrand Russell calls, in the *Problems of Philosophy*, *acquaintance*, by which he means some sort of direct apprehension.[10]

If we accept such a view, we shall find, contrary to the analyticity conception, that some *a priori* knowledge results not from acceptance of the principles of combination of complex concepts out of simple concepts, but from an intuitive knowledge of relations of inclusion and exclusion among simple concepts. Thus I have intuitive knowledge that the phenomenal visual quality in virtue of which I judge things to be red (in standard observing conditions) excludes that in virtue of which I (standardly) judge things to be green. Furthermore, from my knowledge of this exclusion, I can conclude, by means of criteria of application that I accept, that the *nonphenomenal* concepts of redness and greenness exclude one another.

In summary, the foundation theory divides concepts into the simple and the complex. Some *a priori* knowledge is of relations of inclusion and exclusion among simple concepts. *A priori* knowledge of complex concepts is based in part on knowledge of those relations among simple concepts and in part on acceptance of the principles of combination for the complex concepts, principles that may be either explicit definitions or application criteria.

The foundation theory is refuted by two related objections. First, since concepts are the meanings of words in public use, it must be possible for many different people to grasp one and the same concept, and it *should* be possible to explain how we know that they *in fact* do. The foundation theory seems to preclude any such explanation. Two people grasp the same concept, according to the foundation theory, only if they understand it to be the same combination of the same simple concepts. But simple concepts are *phenomenal* qualities, and there is, at least presently, no available means for determining just what the phenomenal qualities of another person's experience are. Moreover, there is no means for determining just what sort of *combination* of simple qualities another person associates with a word for a complex concept. We nevertheless know that other speakers grasp many of the same concepts we do. Evidently, when we say that a speaker grasps the concept expressed by a certain word, we do not *need* to ascertain what combination of simple concepts that speaker associates with the word. The foundation theory gives a wrong picture of what is really required in order to grasp a given concept.

The second objection is one that Quine leveled against the analaytic-synthetic distinction; it is just as relevant here: There is not, in general, a philosophically significant distinction to be made (1) between *definitions* of concepts and other *lawful connections* among concepts or (2) between *criteria of application* for concepts and other *epistemic connections* among concepts.[11] The foundation theory, in its insistence on specific principles of combination of complex concepts out of simple concepts, presupposes the existence of such distinctions and so, if Quine is right, falls with them. This objection is related to the first. It is because concepts are only *loosely* related to the so-called principles of combination that we can ascertain that someone grasps a concept without knowing any specific way in which that person connects it with ''simple'' concepts.

An example may help to illustrate Quine's point. Consider the concept of momentum in classical physics. The equation $p = mv$ has been regarded as a ''definition'' of momentum, but at least as important to classical physicists' grasp of the concept is the law of momentum conservation. Indeed, we can go so far as to say that classical physicists would be very little interested in the quantity mv were they to lose their belief that it is a conserved quantity. Suppose it should happen that the quantity that is conserved is discovered not to be mv, but some other quantity that typically approximates mv. Almost certainly the physicists would use 'momentum' to denote this new quantity. What, however, should we say about their previous use of the word 'momentum'? We could say that they previously associated a different concept with the word. But it seems slightly more reasonable to say that they meant the very same conserved quantity all along. It seems *least* reasonable to say that they used to mean the quantity mv and not the conserved quantity—despite the "definitional" status of $p = mv$.

Obviously there is some uncertainty here concerning whether a concept change takes place. Of course, that is part of Quine's point, namely, that the question of concept change cannot be settled merely by comparing the new and old "definitions" of the concept. Definitionhood, in the case of concepts like momentum, is a passing status, not a starting point for philosophical theories of meaning.

In some quarters, I suppose, uncertainty over questions of concept change might be taken as an argument *against* loosening the relations between complex concepts and specific definitions or criteria of application. That would be a mistake, however, for such uncertainties are a fact of life. Exactly parallel uncertainties arise concerning the *reference* of *proper names*. For example, suppose it should turn out that the writer of all those fabulous plays is not the man who actually bore the name 'Shakespeare'. What then should we say about our present utterances containing the name 'Shakespeare'? Are they true statements about the writer or false statements about the real bearer of the name? The answer, in any case, is not cut-and-dried.

IV. THE NEXUS THEORY OF OUR GRASP OF CONCEPTS

We found that to determine whether someone grasps a concept, it is not necessary to discover whether that person accepts some particular principle of its combination out of simple concepts. Indeed, it seems sufficient to determine (1) that the person has some "simple representation" for the concept, such as a simple predicate of English, and (2) that the person uses *some* correct criterion of application for the concept—not necessarily the same as that used by others. The person might have a definition of the concept in terms of others that he or she grasps or just a basic ability to make correct attributions using a predicate for the concept.

It might be thought that, on this view, concepts are *extensional*, so that, for all practical purposes, a concept may be identified with the set of things that fall under it. For have I not said, in essence, that to grasp a concept one merely need be able to pick out, in some way or other, the things that fall under it? Not at all. I spoke of the ability correctly to apply the concept. It is at least arguable that this entails not only an ability to pick out the set of things in this world that fall under the concept but also an ability to determine in other, counterfactual situations which things fall under the concept. Or, to put the matter another way, there must not merely be an *actual* correlation between the concept and the criteria by which I apply the concept; the correlation must be *lawful*. For example, suppose I find a book that lists, without explanation, the positions of all Seyfert galaxies in the universe. Suppose I introduce a predicate 'is booked' that is to apply to all and only the galaxies whose positions are listed in the book. I do not thereby grasp the concept of a Seyfert galaxy. If the book were wrong, if there were one Seyfert galaxy left out, then my predicate 'is booked' would not apply to it. Evidently my predicate is not equivalent in its conceptual content to the predicate 'is a Seyfert galaxy'.

On the view I am expounding, the grasp of a concept arises within a *nexus* of beliefs and discriminatory abilities. No one particular belief need constitute a ''definition'' of a given concept; no one set of epistemic rules for the application of the concept need be singled out as its ''main'' criterion of application. Moreover, one can be said to grasp a concept through a discriminatory ability even if that concept happens not to be a ''simple'' phenomenal concept. For example, I may be said to grasp the concept red through my ability to discriminate red things, even though it might also be said that this discriminatory ability can be cashed out in terms of my acceptance of criteria of application that involve recognition of phenomenal qualities and that defy precise articulation.

This view of our grasp of concepts might be called the *nexus theory*. It is not the same as the foundation theory, for it does not assume that concepts must be grasped as specific compounds of specific simples. I would also claim that it is not exactly a *coherence* theory, for it can be argued that there is a ''foundation'' here for our grasp of concepts, namely, ''primitive'' discriminatory abilities, abilities to discriminate phenomenal qualities and relations.

V. DEFINING THE *A PRIORI*

It is convenient to distinguish *basic a priori* knowledge from *a priori* knowledge based on *proof*. The latter is necessary to provide an apriorist account of the unobvious truths of mathematics and logic. Here, we are primarily concerned with the former.

According to the rationalist account we are pursuing, *a priori* knowledge arises from our grasp of concepts. This means, I think, that basic *a priori* propositions are ones that are somehow ''crucial'' to our grasp of their constituent concepts. The sense in which they are crucial can perhaps be captured in a definition of the basic *a priori*:

> p is a basic *a priori* proposition for $S =df S$ believes p and there is no rational contraction of S's system of beliefs that would allow S to withhold belief in p and still grasp p.

The idea is that a basic *a priori* proposition is one that one cannot *doubt*. For example, suppose I grasp a concept A solely through a definition $(x)(Ax \equiv (Bx \ \& \ Cx))$ and not through any other discovered laws or criteria of application. Clearly there is no way for me to abandon my belief in the definition without loosening my hold on the concept A. In saying this, I do not mean to imply that no adjustment of my beliefs whatsoever would allow me to abandon the definition. For example, suppose that I come to accept a true and lawful biconditional $(x)(Ax \equiv (Dx \ \& \ Ex))$ and subsequently come to believe that it conflicts with the original definition. One alternative I have is to give up the definition. If in fact both it and the new biconditional are true, however, I still would grasp the concept A—although I would believe that my concept had changed! But such a possibility is no objection to my claim of apriority. The envisioned adjustment of my beliefs is not a pure contraction, since it involves acceptance of the law $(x)(Ax \equiv (Dx \& Ex))$.

As is clear from my example, the nexus theory does not rule out the possibility of *a priori* knowledge through acceptance of definitions. However, it does have the consequence that once a concept is grasped in more than one way, *via* more than one set of necessary and sufficient conditions or more than one set of application criteria, and so becomes a "cluster concept," then the *a priori* knowledge that stems from one's grasp of the concept is drastically weakened. For example, if I grasp the concept A both through the original definition $(x)(Ax \equiv (Bx \& Cx))$ and through the discovered law $(x)(Ax \equiv (Dx \& Ex))$, then neither of these propositions constitutes *a priori* knowledge for me, although arguably their less interesting disjunctive counterpart, $(x)(Ax \equiv (Bx \& Cx))$ v $(x)(Ax \equiv (Dx \& Ex))$, does.

This observation is the germ of an objection to our whole project, an objection that can be found in Hilary Putnam's writings on the analytic-synthetic distinction.[12] Putnam asserts that all *scientifically interesting* concepts are *cluster concepts*, like the concept A in my example, and so concludes that since the grasp of cluster concepts yields no interesting (that is, nondisjunctive) analytic knowledge (read: *a priori* knowledge), we do not have analytic knowledge that is anywhere near as extensive as philosophers have traditionally supposed. That is, we do indeed have *inconsequential a priori* knowledge involving concepts, such as bachelorhood, that do not enter into any natural laws, except such as are derivative on laws involving the root concepts in terms of which they are defined, but interesting concepts always evolve into cluster concepts and then enter only into merely disjunctive *a priori* propositions.

There is a hole in this reasoning. Some concepts, such as the concept of bachelorhood, fail to enter into natural laws because they are what we would call "unprojectible" concepts.[13] But there is another way in which a concept might fail to enter into any natural laws. A concept might be of such *extraordinary generality* that we cannot expect to find it involved in any laws other than those that follow from its present criteria of application. This might be claimed, plausibly, for the concepts of logic and mathematics.

Consider the connectives of classical propositional logic. The axioms and rules of deduction for any complete system of propositional logic provide an implicit definition of the connectives in the sense that any connectives governed by like rules would be inferentially equivalent to them.[14] Moreover, there is a metatheorem that says that no axiom schema or rule can be consistently added to the system except such as can already be derived within it.[15] Thus, there is a good reason for thinking that these connectives cannot be cluster concepts: No wholly new laws, of generality comparable to those presently derivable in our systems, can be discovered about them.

In order to capture the sense in which logical knowledge is *a priori*, we need a definition that covers not propositional knowledge, but rather intuitive knowledge of the validity of inference rules:

A 1, ..., *An* / *B* is a basic *a priori* valid inference rule for *S* iff *S* accepts the rule *A* 1, ..., *An* / *B*, and there is no rational contraction of *S*'s system of beliefs and methods of inference that would allow *S* to abandon the rule, in the strong sense of divesting himself of any rules from which it might be derived, and still grasp the concepts that the rule contains.

For example, the rule of disjunctive syllogism is a basic *a priori* valid rule of inference for me. I accept the rule, as is evidenced by my immediate acceptance of particular inferences made in accordance with it. Furthermore, I could not abandon it and such rules from which it may be derived (indirect proof, addition, constructive dilemma) without losing my grasp of the concepts of negation and disjunction.

In his writings on quantum logic, Hilary Putnam denies the apriority of classical propositional logic.[16] His denial is consistent with our conception of the *a priori*, for it is based on his belief that the propositional connectives are, contrary to what I have said, cluster concepts. Putnam says that the connectives are grasped not merely through the logical principles we take them to obey, but also through what he calls their ''operational meaning.'' In the case of disjunction, Putnam argues that operational meaning parts company with classical logical rules. He begins by laying down a condition for operational meaningfulness:

> Suppose the proposition '*P* v *Q*' has any operational meaning at all (i.e., that there is any test *T* which is passed by all and only the things which have either property *P* or property *Q*).[17]

We might call this the *independent testability requirement*, for it implies that for any disjunctive proposition '*P* v *Q*', there must exist a single test for the truth-value of the *whole* proposition, and not merely a pair of tests—perhaps not simultaneously applicable—for the truth-values of the parts. When this independent testability requirement is imposed in quantum physics, classical disjunction flunks. That is, we can find a connective that satisfies the rules

> *p* implies *p* v *q*
> *q* implies *p* v *q*
> If *p* implies *r* and *q* implies *r*, then *p* v *q* implies *r*

and that meets the testability requirement, but it is a connective that does not satisfy the classical principle:

> If *p* and *s* together imply *r*, and *q* and *s* together imply *r*, then *p* v *q* and *s* together imply *r*.

The problem with this reasoning is that there seems to be no good ground for supposing that independent testability is part of the meaning of disjunction. Isn't Putnam just resurrecting a particularly virulent form of verificationism?

Let us suppose that Putnam is correct in his claim that classical disjunctions are not generally independently testable. It does not follow that they lack ''operational significance,'' for they may be conceived to receive operational significance from the testability of their parts whether or not they are, as wholes, independently testable.

Putnam is treating disjunction as an operation that transforms a pair of independently testable states into an independently testable state. But there simply is no argument against the alternative of treating it as an operator that transforms testable states into states that *may or may not* be independently testable.

What I have been urging is that there is no reason to suppose that disjunctions *must* be independently testable. Is it, however, something we have *come to believe* about disjunctions, so that we are *now* forced to choose between this belief and the classical logical rules? This is implausible. I think very few of us *ever* believed in the independent testability of all disjunctions. Leaving that aside, it seems to me that independent testability does not compete on a par with the classical rules. If it is a determinant of our concept of disjunction, it is not nearly so crucial a determinant. To be sure, we have seen that there is not always a sharp distinction to be made between beliefs that constitute our grasp of a concept and ancillary beliefs, but in some cases it is clear on which side of the blurry line particular beliefs fall. The testability requirement, involving as it does certain epistemic notions, is of less generality than the classical logical rules. Moreover, it states only a *necessary* condition for a proposition's being a disjunction. Unlike the set of logical rules, it does not give *defining* conditions for disjunction. For these two reasons, a change in the logical rules governing the disjunction sign would reasonably be taken to involve a *change in meaning* of the disjunction sign, whereas a rejection of the testability requirement would not.

I conclude, then, that the transition to quantum logic, with its acceptance of the testability requirement and rejection of certain classical rules, does involve a change in the meanings of the connective signs. The contention that the classical connectives are cluster concepts and so are grasped through alternative criteria of comparable importance has been found wanting.

In summary, we have conjectured that there is *a priori* knowledge of three sorts:

(1) Of the extraordinarily general concepts involved in the axioms and rules of logic and perhaps of mathematics.
(2) Of ordinary empirical concepts that we continue to grasp solely through their orginal definitions or criteria of application.
(3) Of cluster concepts

The third sort consists of weak, disjunctive propositions, and so its importance is open to serious question. The extent and importance of the second sort is also open to question. Some of these concepts are "unprojectible," so do not belong to the sciences. Others are destined to become cluster concepts, in which case the present apriority of propositions in which they occur is only a temporary status. *A priori* knowledge of the first sort, however, cannot be slighted in this way. It remains a thorn in the side of any strict empiricism.

VI. APRIORITY AND NECESSITY

We began our search for an account of our knowledge of necessity by looking at *a priori* knowledge. Our conception of *a priori* knowledge was initially unclear, and we have since developed a more refined view: *A priori* propositions are indubitable propositions, ones that cannot be abandoned without losing a grasp of them. What, however, does indubitability have to do with necessity, the notion we originally sought to understand?

The connection is less clear than one might have supposed. Consider an example of Kripke's:[18] Suppose Leverrier, noting the perturbations in the orbit of Uranus, had said, "Let the body responsible for these perturbations be called 'Neptune'." Then the proposition

Neptune is responsible for the perturbations of Uranus

is, according to our definition, known *a priori* by Leverrier. He cannot abandon this proposition without losing his epistemic grip on the planet Neptune (or, depending on one's theory, on the corresponding concept) and so his grasp of the proposition itself. Yet the proposition is by no means necessary. Neptune might have been torn out of its orbit by a passing black hole, so that perturbations would not now be present in Uranus's orbit.

This phenomenon is not peculiar to *singular a priori* propositions. An analogous phenomenon is exhibited by general propositions. Consider a fictitious history of the development of the concept of mass: Suppose one group of scientists begins with a concept of mass as a quantity that can be measured on a beam balance. Suppose another group of scientists—not in communication with the first—begins with an *inertial* concept of mass, a concept of a quantity that plays a certain role in dynamical experiments. In fact, both groups of scientists grasp the same concept—gravitational mass is the same quantity as inertial mass. For the first group of scientists, however, the proposition

Mass is a quantity that can be measured on a beam balance

is *a priori*, whereas the second group of scientists can discover the truth of this proposition only *a posteriori*. Since it is one and the same proposition, its *modal status* must be the same for both groups. But what then is it? Necessary or contingent?[19]

Our reasoning leads inevitably to one answer, namely, that this proposition has at best the necessity of a law of nature, whatever that may be. This result might have been predicted at the outset. Recall that we asserted that one and the same concept can be grasped by means of distinct application criteria just in case there is a *lawful* equivalence between those criteria. Propositions in which such concepts occur could not be supposed to be "more strictly necessary" than substitutivity of lawful equivalents allows, and lawful equivalence is just equivalence with that necessity characteristic of laws of nature.[20]

Our investigation of the *a priori* has come to a disturbing conclusion. Having set out to explain our knowledge of logical necessity, we were led to develop a theory of *a priori* knowledge. Now we find that the *a priori* includes universal propositions that have no greater necessity than empirical laws and even singular propositions that are wholly contingent. The traditional association between the necessary and the *a priori* has broken down.

One way in which to repair the association is to redefine the *a priori* so as to include only the first of the three classes of *a priori* propositions mentioned above. That is, *a priori* knowledge might be restricted to propositions concerning the extraordinarily general concepts of logic and mathematics, concepts that do not present the clustering difficulty distinctive of empirical concepts, such as mass. All these propositions do seem to be necessary, and necessary in the strictest sense.

The problem with this repair is that it is not at all congenial to essentialism. Typical essentialist claims—such as that Socrates is essentially human—do not depend for their truth solely on the properties of logical or mathematical concepts. So knowledge of them could not be *a priori* in the new, strict sense proposed.

Apparently, if we are to provide an account of knowledge of essentialist claims, we must abandon the traditional line of thought. We must allow that some necessities can be discovered *a posteriori*. This is not so implausible as it might at first sight appear. The traditionalist maintains that when we discover, for example, that water is H_2O, we discover something that can be called ''necessary'' only in some ersatz sense. But this is not obvious. Is it really conceivable that water, being what it is, should not be H_2O? Isn't it just as inconceivable as that $2 + 3$ should be 6?

Such reflections have secured new respectability for the idea of ''*a posteriori*'' necessity. But the idea itself is not really new. From reasoning similar to that used in the mass example above, it can be shown that this ''*a posteriori*'' necessity must be preserved under substitution of lawful equivalents, and this is unaccountable unless ''*a posteriori*'' necessity *is* the sort of necessity that attaches to natural laws. The doctrine that natural laws have a kind of necessity, however, has a long history.

The option remains of defending an essentialism defined in terms of this ''*a posteriori*'' or ''natural'' necessity. We need not *deny* that necessary truths can be known *a priori*. We need admit only that many necessary truths that are known *a priori* are on a par with empirical laws. This point of view has profound consequences for our conception of essential properties, suggesting that knowledge of essential properties arises not merely from the conceptual analyses of metaphysicians, but also from the investigations of natural scientists—a conclusion that others, such as Kripke and Putnam, have already endorsed.

VII. ESSENTIAL PROPERTIES OF NATURAL KINDS

Although we have formulated essentialism as a doctrine about the properties of individuals, it is clearly possible, and indeed fashionable, to speak of the essential properties of ''natural kinds.'' We already have the makings of a theory of such essential properties. For example, consider the natural kind *gold*. Suppose we wish to determine whether a certain property P is essential to that kind. Then all we need to determine is whether it is a natural law that all gold has property P. This, I take it, is a straightforward scientific question.

Aginst this, the objection has been raised that not *all* the natural laws about a certain kind reveal essential properties of that kind, only those that tell us what the kind ''*is*.''[21] Thus (I suppose—examples are lacking), the proposition

All gold has atomic number 79

might be said to reveal an essential property of gold, one pertaining to its *very structure*, whereas the proposition

All gold is soluble in aqua regia,

although lawful, might be said to reveal only an inessential property of gold.

If, however, this distinction is intended to be a distinction in the modal status of these propositions—if, that is, it is alleged that the first is distinguished by being more strictly necessary—then I deny the existence of the distinction.[22] The second proposition, too, indicates a property of gold that is a *necessary consequence of its structure*. And I can conceive of no lawful generalization about gold that would *not* state such a property!

To be sure, the first proposition may be said to state a *manifest* property of gold and the second proposition a *dispositional* property. If that is the distinction intended by those who say that only the first states an essential property, then our disagreement is merely verbal. *I* am using the term 'essential' to indicate only the necessity of a property and not any other characteristic.

VIII. ESSENTIAL PROPERTIES OF INDIVIDUALS

We began our discussion with an objection to essentialism concerning individuals. That objection, premised on the analyticity conception of necessity, concluded that essentialists want to claim the necessity of certain singular propositions and that these singular propositions are of the *wrong form* to be necessary truths. The analyticity conception, however, proved highly questionable, and so we have developed a new conception that apparently identifies necessary truths—except perhaps those of logic and mathematics—with natural laws. But now the old objection returns in a new guise: Essentialists want to claim the necessity of certain singular propositions, propositions that are of the *wrong form* to be natural laws.

One might object that it is a mere prejudice to suppose that singular propositions are never natural laws. But it is not a prejudice at all; rather, it is a claim made plausible by our experience. Never in the course of science has it proved fruitful to suppose that one individual might behave in a certain way in certain circumstances and that yet another individual of the very same kind might behave differently in exactly similar circumstances (*modulo* chance variations). Or, to put the matter another way, all our experience suggests that the laws of nature are preserved under certain general transformations, transformations that ignore mere individuality. Individuals appear to enter into laws only through their general qualities and relations.

This objection is not airtight, because one might argue that although the necessity we have been dealing with is *characteristic* of natural laws, it *also* extends to the singular claims made by essentialists. An *epistemological* difficulty remains, however. Although we arguably do possess methods for determining the natural necessity of various laws, there do not seem to be any *other* methods by which we might come to know the natural necessities postulated by essentialists.

One might try looking again at *a priori* knowledge. Could it be that the essential properties of an individual are those that we know it to have *a priori*? This idea leads to a dead end. The Leverrier example shows that the things we know *a priori* about an individual need not be necessary at all.

Of course, there is a *conditional necessity* that attaches to certain properties of individuals. Suppose it is a law that:

Anything that ever has property P has property P whenever it exists.

This is a law that might be known *a priori*, as a result of the way in which we grasp the property P. For example, it may be said that we know *a priori* that:

Anything that is ever a dog is a dog whenever it exists.

This is a belief we cannot abandon given the way in which we presently individuate dogs. Now suppose, for example, that we know that a certain individual X is a dog. In virtue of the above law, we might claim that the property of being a dog is essential to X *in the sense that X cannot lose that property*.

This is a perfectly good way to use the term 'essential'. However, it is not the sense we defined at the beginning of our inquiry, for there is nothing in the above reasoning to suggest that the proposition that X is a dog if X exists is itself necessary. We have concluded only that X is a dog and necessarily, if X is a dog, then X is a dog whenever X exists.

Not all our trumps are played. There are modal logics in which the following inference is valid:

X is a dog.
Necessarily, if X is a dog, then X is a dog whenever X exists.
Therefore, necessarily, X is a dog whenever X exists.

These are the *temporal modal logics* based on branching time models. In them, 'necessarily' has roughly the same meaning as 'it is determined that'. Thus the conclusion of the inference is merely that this X that is a dog is destined always to be a dog—which is not particularly controversial. So if we construe necessity in the sense provided by temporal modal logic, then we can indeed make essentialist claims—or at least claims that have the *look* of essentialist claims.

Many essentialists want to say more than the interpretation in terms of temporal modal logic allows. Some want to say that given that X is a dog, X is essentially *not* an alligator, and by this they mean not merely what can be expressed in temporal modal logic, namely, that X cannot *become* an alligator, but that X is not "in any possible world" an alligator. Along the same lines, serious disputes arise concerning the essentiality of origins. In temporal modal logic, the answer is trivial: Everything that exists now had the origin it had and that fact cannot be altered. But the same question, raised in terms of "in all possible worlds" talk, resists easy solution. Is there a possible world in which I am conceived a month later than I actually was? Or one in which I have parents different from those I actually have?

Let us call these philosophers, the ones who construe essentialist claims in a strong way that cannot be captured in temporal modal logic, *radical essentialists*. My gripe with radical essentialists is that they make their claims and carry on their disputes without any clear notion of how their statements are to be backed up. Some of them appear to believe that knowledge of essential properties is *a priori*. This will not square with the account of the *a priori* we have developed. Suppose we are acquainted with X. Then perhaps we must think of X under some "individuating concept," such as the concept of a dog. That is, we know *a priori* that X is a dog (in the sense we have defined!). But we have found the connection between the *a priori* and the necessary to be *very* tenuous, especially in the case of singular propositions. So we cannot conclude that the proposition that X is a dog is necessary. Or suppose instead we confine our understanding to the initial, intuitive construal of the *a priori*. There seems to be no reason for thinking that it is required for our *grasp* of the dog concept that we believe that whatever is a dog is so in every possible world. (*I* grasp the dog concept, and I don't believe that the radical essentialist claim is true.)[23]

In the course of our discussion, I have mentioned three varieties of necessity of which we might reasonably be supposed to have some knowledge:

(1) The necessity of temporal modal logic, the necessity of what must come about given the laws of nature and present circumstances.[24]
(2) The necessity of natural laws.
(3) The necessity of laws containing the extraordinarily general concepts of logic and mathematics.[25]

Radical essentialists err in supposing that they have some grip on a fourth variety of necessity. My challenge to them is to reveal the ground of their knowledge of that variety. I see little hope that they will succeed.

The error of radical essentialism seems to me to have two principal sources. First, there is the habit of thinking that we can begin our reasoning on modal matters by assuming the existence of one set of all *complete* possibilities, possible worlds, rather than by investigating the root concepts of necessity and possibility. The thought that such a set is "given" can lead one to suppose that there are definite answers to radical essentialist questions without leading one to any good means for deciding them.[26] Second, there is a tendency to think of essential properties as having some characteristic in addition to their necessity, such as intrinsicality. Indeed, suppose we define an essential property of a thing as one that follows lawfully from its intrinsic properties. Then we can make good sense of such utterances as, "I might have lived in the Andromeda Galaxy rather than the Milky Way"—there is no *intrinsic* property of me that lawfully precludes that. But my very point is that I *cannot* make sense of these claims in terms of "pure" notions of necessity and possibility. Some further elaboration is needed. Radical essentialist claims, when coupled with such elaborations, lose their incendiary quality *and* their independent philosophical interest.[27]

Notes

1. Quine, "Reference and Modality," *From a Logical Point of View* (New York City, 1963), 139–59.

2. Kripke, "Naming and Necessity," in *Semantics of Natural Language,* edited by D. Davidson and G. Harman (Dordrecht, 1972), 253–355.

3. Quine, "Reference and Modality," especially 150.

4. See the symmetrical worlds argument that appears in Robert Adams, "Actualism and Thisness," *Synthese* 49 (1981): 3–42, and also the arguments in my own "A Problem For Actualism About Possible Worlds," *The Philosophical Review* 92 (1983): 49–66. Even if these metaphysical arguments fail, it is still doubtful that essences would be analyzable in the sense required by traditional empiricism—namely, that they can be analyzed, merely by reflection on them, by anyone who understands the relevant singular propositions.

5. For an extended discussion of the putative syntheticity of this proposition, see the Arthur Pap–Hilary Putnam controversy that appears in *Necessary Truth,* edited by Sumner and Woods (New York City, 1969).

6. Chisholm, *Theory of Knowledge,* 2d ed. (Englewood Cliffs, N.J., 1977), 34–37.

7. Chisholm, *Theory of Knowledge,* 40–41. Kitcher, *The Nature of Mathematical Knowledge* (Oxford, 1983), ch. 1, and the earlier *"A Priori* Knowledge," *Philosophical Review* 89 (1980): 3–23.

8. It also seems to me true that one can grasp a proposition *only* by understanding some representation (linguistic or otherwise) of it. Nothing I say seems to hinge on that, however.

9. Only superficially, however. The trick of replacing defined terms by defining terms must stop somewhere, in the case of analytic statements, at logical truths. So things that are true by definition are trivial only if the corresponding logical truths are trivial, which remains to be established.

10. Russell, *The Problems of Philosophy* (1912), ch. 5.

11. Quine, "Two Dogmas of Empiricism," 20–46. Also, "Carnap and Logical Truth," *The Ways of Paradox and Other Essays,* 2d ed. (Cambridge, Mass., 1976), 107–32.

12. In particular, Putnam, "The Analytic and the Synthetic," *Mind, Language, and Reality* (Cambridge, 1975), 33–69.

13. The notion of projectibility was introduced by Goodman's *Fact, Fiction, and Forecast* (Cambridge, Mass., 1954).

14. See Nuel Belnap, "Tonk, Plonk, and Plink," *Contemporary Philosophical Logic*, edited by I. Copi and J. Gould (New York, 1978), 44–48.

15. Theorem 33.1 in Geoffrey Hunter's *Metalogic* (Berkeley, 1971), 116.

16. Putnam, "The Logic of Quantum Mechanics," *Mathematics, Matter, and Method,* 2d ed. (Cambridge, 1979), 174–97.

17. Putnam, "The Logic of Quantum Mechanics," 196.

18. Kripke, "Naming and Necessity," 347–48, n. 33.

19. Some might interpret this situation as a *counterexample* to the nexus theory. They might argue that the scientists do not grasp the same concept on the ground that there are counterfactual situations—although contrary to natural law—in which their attributions systematically differ. But the same may be said for your and my grasp of the concept *green*!

20. The existence of such a notion of necessity is a subject of debate. In my opinion, evidence for the necessity of natural laws can be found in their support of counterfactuals. But we need not settle the question here.

21. Kripke, "Naming and Necessity," 320.

22. Chris Swoyer, in "The Nature of Natural Laws," *Australasian Journal of Philosophy* 60 (1982): 203–23, also denies the distinction, maintaining that all natural laws state essential connections among properties.

23. This sort of argument works only for the basic *a priori*. But isn't it plausible that the claim in question, if *a priori,* would be basic *a priori,* rather than, like some mathematical theorem, a proposition that requires a nontrivial proof?

24. Special relativity would appear to present a problem for a realistic conception of temporal necessity. What counts as "present circumstances" varies from observer to observer, but the realist would presumably not want to say that what is temporally possible at a certain time from the perspective of a given observer might differ from what is temporally possible for another observer!

25. In my opinion, there is a clear distinction between (2) and (3). The necessity of a natural law is contingent on the existence of the natural properties or relations mentioned in the law, and there seem to me to be good reasons for thinking that these natural properties and relations are not entities whose existence is

necessary in the strictest sense. In particular, we can produce mathematical descriptions of worlds in which natural properties and relations exist that are different from those of this world. On the other hand, I do not think we can conceive of worlds in which the logical and mathematical concepts are different. (How would we conceive them?) For more on the contingent existence of natural properties and relations, see my "Why Physics Can't Be Nominalized," *Analysis* 44 (1984): 72–78. Swoyer, in "The Nature of Natural Laws," endorses similar views.

26. I think the wisest course is to adopt *modalism*, the view that necessity and possibility are primitive and that possible worlds are to be explained in terms of them. The modalism-possibilism distinction can be found in Arthur Prior's work. See Kit Fine's postscript to Fine and Prior, *Worlds, Times, and Selves* (London, 1976).

27. I am grateful to Joe Pitt and Eleonore Stump for their comments on an earlier version of this paper. Also helpful was Michael Resnik's NEH Summer Seminar on the philosophy of mathematics, in which I was able to complete much of my research on the problem of *a priori* knowledge.

Mapping Semantic Paths:
Is Essentialism Relevant?

WILLIAM R. CARTER

An individual has an attribute *essentially* if and only if it is true both that this individual has (instantiates) this attribute and is such that it cannot, in some deep sense, exist lacking this attribute. Disputes concerning essentialism may strike nonparticipants as both recondite and pointless. What *difference* does it make whether some individual has some characteristic essentially or not? Unless it can be established that there is—apart from metaphysical controversy—some theoretical 'cash value' attending essentialist claims, the question may elicit a "What does it matter?" response from nonmetaphysicians. One way of meeting such a challenge would be by showing that essentialism matters when it comes to *language*. It is upon one version of this general proposal that attention is focused in this paper. At the outset, I consider a pervasive and radical *skepticism*—said by Kripke to have been "invented" (though not endorsed) by Wittgenstein—concerning language in general and meaning in particular. On one interpretation, radical skeptics would have us reject the idea that ordinary count nouns (sortal terms) such as "cat" and "dog" have a *favored semantic path*. A family of contemporary theories concerning meaning and natural kinds might be thought to provide promising materials for answering the skeptic. Assuming that the 'new' semantic theories concerning natural kinds are such that they (i) provide a way of determining, or "mapping," favored semantic paths for many count nouns, and (ii) rest upon essentialist assumptions, it may appear that essentialism matters very much when it comes to language. This way of looking at things raises interesting neglected questions. Is essentialism somehow required as an antidote to pervasive skepticism concerning ordinary (natural) languages? On Kripke's reading of Wittgenstein, essentialist assumptions apparently play no role at all in Wittgenstein's response to pervasive skepticism concerning linguistic rule-following. The general thrust of Wittgenstein's response seems to be that it is the fact that a general term is employed in a certain way by a community of speakers, and not the fact that objects denoted by this term share some common essence or nature, that is crucial to resolving the skeptic's worries concerning linguistic rules. I argue below that *community defenses* of linguistic rules conflict with the new semantics. If that is so, advocates of the new semantics cannot rely upon the Wittgensteinian proposal for defusing linguistic skepticism. Granting this point, it may appear that new semanticists have no effective reply to the skeptic short of an appeal to some version of essentialism.

For reasons that emerge in the discussion below, I am not convinced that the new semantics presupposes genuine essentialism. What is crucial to the story told by advocates of the new semantics is an assumption of *privileged sameness relations* and not essentialism. Antiessentialist arguments have no force at all when employed against the new semantics. If new semanticists offer an adequate reply to pervasive skepticism concerning language, the case has yet to be made for judging that essentialist assumptions are required in defense of language.

Indeed, there may be reason to judge that the new semantics *supports* a certain nontrivial antiessentialist position. One argument in behalf of this surprising conclusion is developed in the discussion that follows.

I

The main problem is *not*, 'how can we show private language—or some special form of language—to be *impossible*?'; rather it is 'how can we show *any language* at all (public, private, or what-have-you) to be *possible*?'[1]

Arguably it is a corollary of certain semantic and epistemological assumptions concerning sensation terms such as "pain" that each of us speaks a (partly) private language. Many theorists argue that the idea that we speak private languages is incoherent, or in some way absurd. If these theorists are right, any semantics (for any portion of any language) having a private language corollary is thereby discredited. This general line of thought is commonly attributed to Wittgenstein. One of many interesting features of Kripke's recent book is that it portrays a Wittgenstein who takes very seriously skeptical caveats concerning alleged linguistic rules for ordinary terms such as "cat" and "dog." In a sense, the global skeptic (as we might call Wittgenstein's hypothetical skeptic) proposes to extend to language generally arguments that are widely thought to show that private languages are impossible or incoherent. For defenders of so-called private-language arguments—skeptics concerning private languages—global skepticism poses a challenge; perhaps the assumptions that support the conclusion that putative speakers of private languages cannot follow determinate semantic rules also give the "result" that speakers of natural languages cannot (contrary to all appearances) follow determinate semantic rules. Perhaps these assumptions show *too much*, since in fact competent speakers of natural languages appear to follow determinate semantic rules.

Henceforth when I refer to "Wittgenstein" I speak of *Wittgenstein as interpreted by Kripke*.[2] Wittgenstein denies that there generally is any *fact* as to precisely what a speaker *means* by a word. When Kripke discusses this his attention is for the most part fixed upon the mathematical expression "plus." However, it is clear that the thesis that there is no fact as to what you (or I, or anyone) means by an expression is not confined to cases of mathematical expressions. "There can be no fact as to what I mean by 'plus', or any other word at any time" (p. 21). Wittgenstein would argue that there is *no fact* as to what any of us means by the word "table."

> These problems apply throughout language and are not confined to mathematical examples. . . . I think that I have learned the term 'table' in such a way that it will apply to indefinitely many future items. So I can apply the term to a new situation, say when I enter the Eiffel Tower for the first time and see a table at the base. Can I answer a skeptic who supposes that by 'table' in the past I meant *tabair*, where a 'tabair' is anything that is a table not found at the base of the Eiffel Tower, or a chair found there? (p. 19)

Though Wittgenstein does not endorse such skepticism, he does argue that it is a mistake to judge that in fact 'I' (any speaker) employed "table" in the past to mean *table* and not (say) *tabair*. There are indefinitely many hypotheses as to what 'I' meant by this expression in the past. And there is, according to Wittgenstein, no question of determining what in fact is meant. As Kripke puts it in one place, "nothing in my mental history or past behavior—not even what an ominiscient [sic] God would know— could establish" what is meant (p. 21). Thus Wittgenstein "agrees with his own hypothetical skeptic" that there is no fact of the matter—no "condition of the world" that constitutes a speaker meaning one thing by "table" rather than another (p. 69).

It may naturally be thought that Wittgenstein's "no fact" appraisal of what speakers really mean by words poses a threat to the idea that linguistic behavior is *rule-governed*, and so is supportive of a picture of general semantic indeterminacy or anarchy. As Kripke observes, it then is no longer clear how any language is possible. If there are no facts as to what speakers mean by (say) "table," then it seems that there is *no correct* (or incorrect) way of employing this expression. But, as critics of allegedly private languages are fond of asking, how can there be genuine linguistic rules—how can there be a genuine *language*?—in contexts where there is no distinction between "correct" and "incorrect" application of an expression?

II

Privatus reports that he is in pain. A skeptic concerning "other minds" argues that here no one other than Privatus himself can possibly know what Privatus is talking about (referring to) by the term "pain." In the language spoken by Privatus, this term acquires meaning by being associated with a certain inner paradigm—a certain *sensation*—concerning which only Privatus has knowledge. The rest of us can at best conjecture as to what Privatus means by the term "pain." Only Privatus can *know* what is meant.

Critics reject this on the following grounds: if skepticism concerning other minds is correct, then each of us speaks a partly private language. But private languages are impossible, there being no genuine distinction between correct and incorrect applications of allegedly private terms—terms having a meaning that only one person can grasp. So skepticism concerning other minds must be rejected.

At any rate, that is the *general* critical idea. When we look more closely we find that there is some dispute concerning exactly what is wrong with the inner paradigm or "private exemplar" model of the situation. Some critics argue that the mistake lies with the assumption that the semantic paradigm that fixes a meaning for the term "pain" in the language spoken by Privatus is *inaccessible* to other people. Others contest this. As Bruce Goldberg argues:

> [I]t is quite irrelevant whether the object named is a feeling or a physical thing like a table. I think this is true of Wittgenstein's critique also. That is, I believe that the mistake in the conception of language which Wittgenstein criticizes lies not in the supposed inaccessibility of its objects (designata) but in the role they are thought to play.[3]

The central mistake lies, according to Goldberg, not with the idea that the semantic paradigm is accessible to (that is, knowable by) only one person, but rather with the assumption that *any object*, whether "private" or "public," can serve as a semantic paradigm that determines a correct and incorrect way of employing a term. The point holds both for allegedly in-the-mind "entities" such as sensations and for "external objects" such as tables and oak trees. No object, whether private or public, can serve as a semantic paradigm for a general term in the sense of determining or fixing a distinction between correct and incorrect application of this term. Goldberg tells us that if "there is to be such a thing as the correct (or incorrect) use of a word, it must be determined, somehow or other, which of the many possible paths one is supposed to follow in applying it." Speaking of the inner paradigm model of sensation terms, he goes on to say:

> I think there is a mistake involved concerning naming. The assumption that the child invents a word by naming his feeling is a result of not seeing how little can be accomplished in this way. Consider the following. Any object I name will belong to many different classes. Imagine it to be a starting point and the objects in the various classes to which it belongs as occupying positions in paths diverging from it. (p. 88)

The 'object' originally named or baptized is in some sense the speaker's semantic starting point. The various classes having this object among their members represent potential semantic "paths" with which the term involved in the original naming process might be associated. Unless there is a *favored* path—some 'path' made up of all and only states or individuals to which a certain term *correctly* or properly applies—the term in question has no determinate semantics. Goldberg argues convincingly that in alleged cases involving private namings—namings of things or states with which only the speaker can be acquainted—it has not been "determined along which of the paths'' the speaker can correctly proceed. Since there really is no favored semantic path, there is no distinction between correct and incorrect application of terms allegedly employed in ''private namings.'' Such semantic indeterminateness disqualifies a ''private language'' as a genuine *language*. The thesis defended by the global skeptic in Kripke's book is that a similar semantic indeterminateness afflicts natural languages. In the event that indeterminateness is a capital semantic offense, skepticism may appear to be justified with respect to both private languages concerning ''inner'' sensational objects and natural languages concerning things such as tables and oak trees.

III

Kripke argues that Wittgenstein invented a new form of skepticism, one that qualifies as ''the most radical and original skeptical problem that philosophy has seen to date'' (p. 60). The potential problem is that there may appear to be no favored semantic paths for terms such as ''table,'' ''cat,'' and ''dog.'' Nothing in the *head* (mind) of Privatus determines which of many possible semantic paths corresponds to the term ''table.'' Kripke argues at some length against the view that Privatus's *dispositions* fix a unique semantic path for this term. Granting all of this, we might be tempted to judge that the favored path for the term ''table,'' as employed by Privatus, is fixed by some external *paradigm*—some entity that provides something like an *ostensive definition* of tablehood. Goldberg, and I suspect Wittgenstein, as well, would argue that no paradigmatic object can serve to determine the ''favored'' semnatic path for any term.

> for any two objects, there is no (unique) determinate answer to the question concerning whether or not they are the same. In any given case the answer will depend, roughly speaking, on how they are to be compared. (p. 89)

In a sense, many arguments opposing private languages rest upon the assumption that terms lacking favored semantic paths cannot be part of a genuine language. But as advocates of Wittgenstein's radical skepticism will be quick to argue, it can be shown that apparently unproblematic terms such as ''table'' lack favored semantic paths. Neither our dispositions not entities in our head serve to fix such a ''path.'' Not can paradigmatic ''external'' objects do the job. Advocates of radical skepticism conclude that natural languages are no better off than private languages. Many of us are inclined to reject this assessment of the matter; but on precisely what grounds is the skeptic to be answered?

Kripke's account of Wittgenstein's resolution of the challenge presented by radical skepticism is very subtle, and I can here offer only a very rough sketch of the general Wittgensteinian response. Wittgenstein is said to offer not a ''straight solution'' but rather a ''skeptical solution'' to radical linguistic skepticism. We are told that:

> A *skeptical* solution of a skeptical philosophical problem begins . . . by conceding that the skeptic's negative assertions are unanswerable. Nevertheless our ordinary practice or belief is justified because—contrary appearances notwithstanding—it need not require the justification the skeptic has shown to be untenable. (p. 66)

As I interpret this, Wittgenstein would *allow* that favored semantic paths cannot be fixed by (i) what is in the head of any speaker, (ii) the linguistic dispositions of any speaker, or (iii) the intrinsic nature of any paradigmatic object (examplar). At the same time, he would *deny* that it follows from this that there is no favored semantic path for an expression such as "table." The crucial point is apparently that "Wittgenstein stresses the importance of agreement, and of a shared form of life, for his solution to the skeptical problem" (p. 96). Wittgenstein concedes to the radical skeptic that there "is no objective fact" as to exactly what people mean by "table." Or perhaps one should say, revising this slightly, that there is no fact of the matter apart from the fact that speakers of our languages generally employ the word "table" in one way and not in other ways. Using Goldberg's "path" model, we might say that for Wittgenstein the favored semantic path for a term is just the path that most people follow. What makes the class consisting of all and only tables, and not the class consisting of all and only tabairs, the favored path for "table" is the fact that *people agree* in employing the term in this manner (p. 99). It is not that the meaning of a term is something that one grasps in a manner that somehow determines future correct applications of the term in question; it is, rather, the fact that there is general agreement as to future applications of the term that determines meaning.[4] So Wittgenstein argues.

Some people will contest the claim that the author of *Philosophical Investigations* is a 'Wittgensteinian.'[5] For present purposes this does not matter. What does matter is that defenders of the "new semantics" may argue for what Kripke labels a "straight" response to radical linguistic skepticism. Whereas the "skeptical" response defended by Wittgensteinians is generally conciliatory with respect to the claims made by radical skeptics, new semanticists—including, perhaps, Kripke himself—may argue directly the radical skepticism is misconceived. In particular, they may argue that when it comes to so-called *natural kind* terms, paradigmatic objects or paradigmatic samples of stuff serve nicely to determine favored semantic paths. This thesis conflicts both with the position of the Wittgensteinian and that of the radical skeptic.

IV

Semantic *determinateness* can be parsed in terms of a *favored semantic path*— roughly, a "path" representing all and only correct applications of a given word. Radical skeptics deny that there is a favored semantic path for ordinary terms such as "cat" and "dog." Let us say that an *agreement path* for such an expression is a class of objects concerning whose members competent language users agree that the term in question correctly applies. If we follow the Wittgensteinian lead, we then may proceed to judge that the favored semantic path for a term is its agreement path. New semanticists reject this. It is possible, they argue, that by following an agreement path we may be led down the wrong semantic path. It can happen that most or even all speakers of a language do not understand the meaning of commonly employed terms. Thus the meaning of "cat" may be such that many or even all of the objects that lie on the "cat" agreement path are in fact not genuine cats! In such a (possible) situation, the agreement path diverges from the favored semantic path for a general term in a natural language.

Anyone who adopts this anti-Wittgensteinian position owes us an explanation as to how favored semantic paths are properly mapped. In the case of many general terms, the explanation may involve an appeal to *natural kinds*. It is precisely at this point that essentialism may be thought to enter the picture. As one theorist argues, "anything belonging to a natural kind cannot but be of that kind throughout the entirety of its existence."[6] Obviously a natural-kind approach to sortal terms in natural languages such as English has its limits. Terms such as "policemen" and "mathematician" do not represent natural kinds of things, since individual policemen (mathematicians) are not essentially policemen (mathematicians). Things are different when we turn to "cat" and "dog." Since individual cats are essentially cats and individual dogs essentially dogs, these terms represent natural kinds. The favored semantic path for such terms, terms representing natural kinds, is a path made up of all and only individuals of a certain kind. In the event that language users have misconceptions concerning which individuals are things "of the same kind," it can happen that the "agreement" path for a general term diverges sharply from this term's favored path.

On certain traditional conceptions of "meaning" it is very hard to see how agreement paths can diverge from favored paths. Traditionalists may judge, where 'k' represents a *natural kind term*, that there is a set of attributes whose members are somehow "analytically" tied to term k. Occupying a point on the favored k-path is said to be a matter of instantiating all, or most, of these attributes. The meaning of a term is on this view closely aligned with the nominal essence of objects denoted by the expression in question. The favored semantic path for a kind term k is thus made up of all and only individuals satisfying a certain *nominal* essence. Assuming, as is plausible, that the agreement path for k is fixed by the nominal essence of k, it seems that k's agreement path cannot diverge from its favored semantic path.[7]

At least since Locke's time, philosophers have suspected that nominal essence may not correspond at all closely to "real" essence.[8] If natural kinds are classes whose members share some real essence, and natural kinds afford grounds for locating favored semantic paths for certain general terms of natural languages, then it may appear that nominal essence has little, if anything, to do with locating favored semantic paths for such terms.[9] Perhaps nominal essence is a determiner of agreement paths. Since a term's favored semantic path is fixed by real essence, the possibility arises that an agreement path may diverge from a favored path.

This way of looking at the matter has some disquieting features. For one thing, it leaves us with no apparent answer to radical skeptics when it comes to terms that do not represent natural kinds. There is reason to doubt that the class of tables qualifies as a natural kind. Perhaps tables have only a nominal and not a real essence.[10] If so, "table" does not represent a natural kind of thing. In that case there is no question of appealing to natural kinds by way of establishing a favored semantic path for "table."

Why deny that all tables share a common "real" essence? Since Locke, real essence has been viewed in terms of microphysical constitution or "hidden structure."[11] Presumably all tables do not have the same molecular constitution or "deep" physical structure. Thus most tables do not have the same "real" essence. Assuming that members of a genuine natural kind all have the same real essence, tables are not members of a natural kind.

Advocates of the "new semantics"—the so-called *historicoscientific* semantic theory that is defended by Hilary Putnam and Kripke—put great semantic weight on Lockean real essence.[12] Speaking of Quinean pessimism concerning semantic theory generally, Putnam says in one place that "as far as the utility of the traditional notion of 'meaning' is concerned, Quine may well turn out to be right."[13] Putnam and Kripke propose a decidedly nontraditional approach to semantic theory in which natural kinds play a prominent role. The historicoscientific approach to semantics is in important respects decidedly un-Wittgensteinian. Perhaps it is fair to say that the former does while the latter does not offer a "straight" response to the radical skeptic. New semanticists reject the idea that nominal essence is a determiner of favored semantic paths. Assuming, as I think is plausible, the nominal essence fixes agreement paths, new semanticists reject the idea that a term's agreement path must be its favored semantic path.

Water is, a new semanticist might argue, anything that has the same nature as the substance that originally was called "water." Turning from mass nouns to count nouns, cats are entities that stand in "a certain sameness relation"—the *same creature relation,* one might say—to certain paradigmatic objects (the creatures in fact originally called "cats").[14] Wittgensteinians agree with radical skeptics that no such appeal to paradigmatic objects can "determine what is to happen next." If we follow the Wittgensteinian line—which may or may not be the position of the author of the *Philosophical Investigations*—we will judge that the meaning of "cat" is determined not by the real nature of any paradigmatic object or objects but rather by the way speakers employ the term "cat." Defenders of the historicoscientific position deny this. *They* argue that language users generally can be ignorant of the true meaning of a term such as "cat." Accordingly, it may happen that the term is generally (even universally) *misapplied.* Contrary to Wittgensteinians, a term's agreement path may not follow its favored semantic path.[15]

V

Much as scientific investigation is required to determine whether x is the same-L (same liquid) as y, scientific investigation may be required to determine whether x is the same-C (same creature) as y. Being the same creature as certain paradigmatic entities is judged to be a matter of having the same "real nature" as the paradigms. And appeals to real nature generally are taken to be appeals to microstructure. Perhaps Wittgensteinians are correct in judging that there can be no unqualified answers to questions of the form 'Is x the same as y?' Nonetheless, there are unqualified answers to questions such as 'Is x the same-C as y?'

The new semantics is not without its critics. How can something that is *hidden* from the view of nonspecialists play a central role when it comes to the *meaning* of terms such as "water" and "tiger"? Assuming that being a competent speaker of a language involves understanding when to *use* linguistic terms, it is hard to see how something that is "hidden" from the eyes of nonspecialists can be crucial to the semantic story. As one critic, paraphrasing Locke, observes: "since we do not *in fact* know much about real essences these cannot be the basis which we do now use for our classifications of physical things."[16] Those who believe that *use* in somehow a determiner of *meaning* are likely to have reservations concerning the new semantics, since use may well fail to reflect differences in hidden structure.

Whether there is substance to this critical line is not a question I will pursue here.[17] My present concern lies with the alleged essentialist foundations of the historicoscientific position. Critics may make much of this. Note that the Wittgensteinian position has no apparent essentialist corollaries. It may appear that doubts concerning essentialism will carry over to the "new" semantics but will not carry over to the Wittgensteinian position.

For the moment, let's return to Privatus. It is said that Privatus defines what pain is on the basis of certain inner paradigms. Norman Malcolm once objected to this on the following grounds: that alleged sensational paradigms are essentially such that they are experienced only by Privatus. Since the paradigms have this characteristic essentially, it is part of what "pain" means for Privatus that only Privatus can experience pain. Accordingly, it is a contradiction for Privatus to speak of *another's* pain.[18] Since no contradiction is involved in so speaking, it cannot be correct to judge that "pain" is defined in terms of inner paradigms.

Kripke objects to this argument (pp. 115–124). The paradigms from which I form my concept of ducks may be such that certain genetic origins are essential to them. That does not mean that having such origins is "built in" to the meaning of "duck." We can, Kripke argues, *abstract* from (certain) essential properties of paradigmatic objects (p. 124). Such abstraction allows it to happen that many objects to which "duck" correctly applies lack characteristics that are essential to the paradigms.

Here a critic of the historicoscientific view might reply as follows: if we can abstract from essence when it comes to biological origins, then we also can abstract from essence when it comes to microstructure. If individuals lacking origin-essence of paradigms can deserve a place on the favored semantic path for the term "duck," then individuals lacking the microstructure essence of paradigms also may deserve places on this path. But if that is so—if individuals lacking the microstructure of the paradigms qualify as *ducks*—the meaning of "duck" hardly can be such that the term "duck" correctly applies only to individuals having the microstructure of the paradigms. Since the point holds for terms such as "cat" and "water" as well, the straight reply to the radical skeptic proposed by new semanticists is discredited.

This objection is not sound. When Kripke speaks of abstracting from essence he is speaking of abstracting from features that are part of the *individual essence* of certain paradigmatic objects. Such features are essential to certain individual ducks, but not to ducks generally. To say that abstraction is possible with respect to individual essence does not commit one to judging that abstraction is possible with respect to features that are essential to all and only members of a certain natural kind. Defenders of the new semantics will, I take it, deny that this last sort of abstraction is possible. They will deny that any individual that fails to have the same microstructure as certain paradigmatic objects deserves a place on the favored path for "duck." This view of things may turn out to be mistaken; but nothing said in the previous paragraph provides any sound reason to judge that it is mistaken. The objection fails.

Still, anyone who has misgivings concerning essence may have reservations concerning the new semantics. As archenemies of essence, Quineans may well be no less pessimistic about the historicoscientific approach to semantics than about traditional approaches. Perhaps by effectively challenging (genuine) essentialism, Quineans can inflict fatal blows upon the Putnam-Kripke natural-kind approach to the task of mapping favored semantic paths for terms such as "tiger," "cat," and "dog."

I have reservations about this. For reasons that emerge below, I doubt that antiessentialist arguments cut much critical ice with respect to the historicoscientific approach to favored semantic paths. Even if it turns out that respectable antiessence arguments emerge, no critical ice is cut, for advocates of the new semantics for general terms simply are not committed to genuine essentialism (though of course they may endorse essentialism). Perhaps it is true that natural kinds can be employed to fix favored semantic paths for some common nouns; it is nonetheless false that (genuine) *essentialism* lies behind the appeal to natural kinds. Care must be taken not to confuse talk of certain features being essential to some kind, or species, with talk of features being essential to some individual that is a member of the kind in question. Claims of the first sort can be given a *de dicto* reading that involves no commitment to genuine essentialism; not so for claims of the second sort. The historicoscientific approach to favored semantic paths commits us to the first, but not the second, claim.

VI

Perhaps some people are encouraged to believe that the new semantics rests on essentialist underpinnings by the familiar claim that new semanticists hold that "real essences demarcate natural kinds."[19] Thus John Dupre, speaking of Putnam's position, says:

> Having identified the paradigmatic exemplar, the kind is then defined as consisting of all those individuals that bear an appropriate "sameness relation" to this individual. This sameness relation is Putnam's exact equivalent of Locke's real essence. (p. 70)

I have no quarrel with this. But it should be noted that Lockean "real essence" may well not—to put it rather paradoxically—commit us to *essentialism* at all! In the context of work done by Kripke, Putnam, and others, appeals to "real" essence so-called are properly understood in terms of a proposal to replace traditional "nominal (in the mind) essence" accounts of meaning by some "sameness relation" approach to meaning that relies upon microphysical structure of some individual or stuff as the proper determiner of a semantic path. Thus Putnam says in one place that ''if there is a hidden structure, then generally it determines what it is to be member of the natural kind, not only in the actual world, but in all possible worlds.''[20] It is microphysical structure, and not the characteristics that may be listed in a dictionary, that serves to fix meaning. Nothing here commits us to genuine *de re* essentialism. Those feline-appearing creatures on Twin Earth that *look* so much like cats fail to really be cats, since their microphysical structure is (as it turns out) quite different from that of genuine cats. Note that such ersatz ''cats'' may have many or even most of the characteristics traditionalists take to be analytically tied to the meaning, or concept, of ''cat.'' Much as analyticity claims purporting to discover a necessary connection between general concepts do not commit us to judging that any individual has any property essentially (or that any individual necessarily falls under any concept, if it exists at all), the suggestion that microphysical structure determines the proper semantic path for ''cat'' does not commit us to judging that any individual essentially has any particular microphysical structure. Perhaps individual cats are not essentially cats, this because they do not essentially have the microphysical features that are in some way ''definitive'' of cathood. No doubt many theorists will resist this claim. For the moment the point is not that such a claim is true, only that it is consistent with the new semantics proposed by proponents of the Kripke-Putnam program.

Perhaps it will be argued that some ''higher order'' essentialism is in the works. Thus it might be said of the species *tiger* that it essentially includes no individuals that fail to be mammals, or that it is essentially a subkind of *Carnivora*. No doubt some advocates of the historicoscientific approach will endorse such essentialist claims. But there can be no question of *commitment* here, since advocates of the new semantics are free to reject outright the thesis that there are such 'things' as species or biological kinds. Species hardly can have essential properties in the event that there are no species.

It is with first-order essentialism bearing upon concrete individuals that the present paper is concerned. In a work entitled *Reference and Essence,* Nathan Salmon has argued persuasively that ''nontrivial forms of essentialism concerning natural kinds or concrete individuals'' are not entailed by the new semantics.[21] I think Salmon is right about this. Moreover, I believe that an interesting antiessentialist position may be based upon the new semantics. The discussion that follows is largely devoted to this point.

VII

The cell provides the conditions that permit effective performance of the chemistry of life. Essentially, it is a chemical factory. It has a power plant that provides the energy needed for chemical transformation. It has partitions that segregate various pieces of chemical machinery, keeping them from damaging one another.[22]

A *cellular* being is a being that is composed of cells. It is not true, and so is not necessary, that all *organisms* are cellular beings. So even if it were true that every organism is essentially or necessarily an organism, it would not follow that every organism is essentially or necessarily a cellular being. One might grant this and still believe both that every organism is such that it is essentially an organism and that every cellular being is essentially a cellular being. Are these beliefs true? Is it *possible* for any being that is cellular to exist as a noncellular being?

I shall develop an argument supporting an affirmative answer to this question. If the argument is sound, it is not true that any cellular individual is such that it is essentially a cellular being. Assuming that it is a necessary truth that cats (dogs, tigers, and so on) are cellular beings, it then follows that no cat (dog, tiger) is such that it is essentially a cat (dog, tiger). In the event that this conclusion proves to be defensible, something close to Lockean skepticism concerning essence will have been vindicated. The Lockean position is, roughly, that although there are true *de dicto* necessities, *de re* claims ascribing characteristics essentially to individuals are generally and perhaps invariably false.

Some people will reject this at the outset on the grounds that it is not necessarily true that cats (dogs, and so on) are cellular beings.[23] If these people are right, the historicoscientific approach to semantics is based upon fundamental mistakes. On the new semantics, the cellular microstructure of the creatures originally named ''cat'' fixes the meaning of this term. This analysis of meaning in terms of (cellular) hidden structure makes it a necessary truth—if it is true at all—that cats are cellular beings. Of course ''cat'' might have had some meaning other than its present meaning. But given the meaning it has, the favored transworld semantic path for the term ''cat'' is occupied only by cellular beings.[24] New semanticists argue that it is a necessary and not a contingent truth that water is H_2O; for similar reasons, it is a necessary and not a contingent truth that cats are cellular beings. As Salmon notes, it does not follow from this that individual cats are essentially, or necessarily, cellular beings. What is perhaps surprising is that *de dicto* necessity may play a prominent role in a 'Lockean' argument *challenging* the essentialist thesis that individual cats are essentially cellular beings. Felix is a cat. But it is not true that Felix is essentially a cat. There are, contemporary Lockeans may argue, possible worlds in which Felix *exists* as a noncellular individual. In no possible world does a genuine cat exist as a noncellular being. So there are possible worlds in which Felix exists as something other than a cat. Since the argument can be generalized, it is false that any member of $<x: x$ is a cat$>$ is such that it is essentially a member of this class. On some accounts of natural kinds, it follows that ''cat'' does not designate a natural kind of thing.

Such a (broadly) Lockean argument will not get off the ground unless a case can be made for judging that Felix *can* exist as a noncellular being. The basic idea here is that Felix's cellular parts are not essential to Felix. Felix can continue to exist as his parts are replaced by new parts. Indeed, Felix can continue to exist as cellular parts (that is, parts of Felix that are composed of cells) are replaced by noncellular parts. Carrying this replacement process far enough, we might eventually end up with a Felix that fails to qualify as a cellular being.

VIII

Before pursuing cellular beings, we need to say a word concerning artifacts and part-replacement. We start with a certain ship (ship A) and proceed gradually to replace each of its parts with a functionally equivalent 'new' part. Having replaced all of A's original parts, we then reassemble the ship parts that were removed from A in the course of the replacement process. At the end of the story, we are left with two ships, one of which (ship B) has claim to being spatiotemporally continuous with ship A, and the other of which (ship C) is made up of all and only the parts that made up A at the beginning of our story. Question: should we say that $B = A$ or that $C = A$? Orthodox answer: it is true that $B = A$ and false that $C = A$.

There is a strong, if not compelling, argument supporting orthodoxy that is based upon the transitivity of identity. Surely a ship can survive (can continue to exist) as one of its parts is removed and replaced. Assuming this much (assuming that survival over time requires diachronic identity over time), the ship that is present after the first removal-replacement step is identical with ship A (the ship we start with at the beginning of the story). By similar reasoning, the ship that is present after the second removal-replacement step is identical with the ship that was present after the first removal-replacement step; so by the transitivity of identity, the ship that is present after the second step in the removal-replacement process is identical with ship A. Extending the argument, we arrive at the orthodox conclusion that ship B (the ship we are left with following the final removal-replacement step) $=$ ship A. Since it is not true that ship B $=$ ship C, it is not true that $C = A$.

Orthodoxy has it that a ship can continue to exist as all of its parts are gradually replaced by new parts. (It is here assumed that *continuing to exist* is something that requires *strict identity through time*.) I see no conceivable basis for both (a) allowing that a ship existing at one time can be strictly identical with a ship existing at another time even though the 'first' ship and the 'second' have no parts in common, and (b) denying that a cat (dog, and so on) existing at one time can be identical with a cat existing at still another time even though the 'first' cat and the 'second' have no cellular or molecular parts in common. It is true that ships are *artifacts*, while cats, dogs, humans, and trees are not. I fail to see how this fact might sustain the curious claim that whereas ships having (at different times) different parts may be strictly identical, cats having (at different times) different parts are at best "the same" in some *loose and popular* sense that is weaker than identity. The Lockean argument for antiessentialism fails in the event that a case can be made for the conjunction of (a) and (b). However, I doubt that such a case can be made.

Michael Slote has interesting views that bear upon this. Slote tells us:

> When a thing persists through the (total) replacement of its matter, the fact of its persistence as the same thing seems to depend on the fact that the thing itself has organized that replacement. Thus it is clear that our bodies persist through the (total) replacement of their matter (and cells), because it is our bodies themselves that organize this process is a lawful and orderly way. There is, on the other hand, real doubt as to whether a sock that is darned and redarned until none of its original material remains, exists at the end of that process.[25]

Obviously ship *A* does not itself organize the replacement of its parts by new parts. So if Slote is right, it seems that the transitivity argument in behalf of orthodoxy that is sketched above is unsound. It also seems that a similar transitivity argument, applied to a case in which a cat's parts are gradually replaced by new parts, must be unsound. Since the Lockean claim that Felix is not essentially a cat rests upon such a transitivity argument, the case for Lockean skepticism will be rejected by those who share Slote's intuitions concerning part replacement and identity.

When we look closely I believe we find that Slote's proposal encounters transitivity problems. Surely a "natural" object such as a cloud can survive artificial replacement of *some* (say, a very small percentage) of its molecular parts. A series of small replacements may eventually leave us with a cloud that has all new molecular parts. Surely the cloud that exists after the first such replacement is the cloud with which we started; and the cloud that results from the second replacement is the cloud that resulted from the first replacement. Extending the argument, transitivity gives the result that a cloud may survive the artificial replacement of all of its parts. This conflicts with Slote's assessment of the matter.

Perhaps there is a reply to this. Still, it may be worth noting that Slote's intuition conflicts with the standard, or 'orthodox', treatment of Ship of Theseus situations. Anyone who endorses the standard view of Ship of Theseus cases must reject the Slotean view that it is only when part-replacement occurs naturally that one entity endures or persists throughout change of parts.

IX

Advocates of the Lockean position say this: if the orthodox account of Ship of Theseus cases is correct, then it is equally correct to suppose that an individual cat, dog, or tiger can survive as its parts are nonnaturally replaced by new parts. Lockeans judge that orthodoxy is correct in Ship of Theseus situations. Indeed, they argue that we may start with a wooden ship and wind up with a ship that is composed of something other than wood, say, fiberglass. Lockeans further argue that the point can be extended when we turn from artifacts such as ships and bicycles to natural entities such as cats and dogs. We may start with a cellular Felix and wind up with a noncellular Felix.

Felix is a perfectly ordinary cat. It happens in the natural course of things that Felix's cellular parts are replaced by new cellular parts. Perhaps it is possible that natural parts of Felix are replaced by synthetic cat parts designed by bioengineers in laboratories. It is possible that an artificial cat heart could be developed that is functionally 'as good as' a normal cat heart. And it is possible, also, that in time a way could be discovered to replace defective (original) cat hearts with synthetic cat hearts and so prolong the life of a cat that otherwise would perish. Relative to the history of the world to the present, there is a 'possible future' in which this happens to Felix. In such a future, there is a time t_1 (say, one year from now) in which Felix exists with a heart that is made of plastic and transistors and other synthetic materials. And there is a further time t_2 (two years from now) in which other defective natural organs have been replaced by functionally equivalent synthetic 'organs'. The replacement process is, we further may suppose, extended to paw and claw. Indeed, it eventually happens that every original part of Felix has been replaced by a synthetic but functionally equivalent substitute.

Let W^* be a possible world in which things happen this way. The history of W^* corresponds precisely with the history of the actual world through the present. W^* is such that in the period from the present to time t_1 Felix's original heart is replaced by a synthetic heart, other internal organs being replaced in the t_1–t_2 period, and so on, until all of Felix's original cellular parts have been replaced at time t_n. Felix's original heart is not, it may appear, essential to Felix. It is possible for *Felix*, the very cat that presently is napping in a certain armchair, to exist without having *this heart* (that is, the heart that presently is Felix's heart). Indeed, where the value of 'x' is any of Felix's present organic parts, having x as a part is not (let us assume) essential to Felix. Given these assumptions, there seems to be no reason to deny that the survivor of the first replacement step in W^* *is* Felix. Since the survivor of the second replacement step appears to be (numerically) the same entity as the object that existed following the first replacement step, it seems that the survivor of the second replacement step *is* Felix. Relying on the assumption that each replacement step leaves us with numerically the same entity that was present before this step, transitivity of identity gives the 'result' that the final (t_n) survivor is Felix. In world W^*, Felix exists at time t_n. Felix is such that his parts are constituted of synthetic, and nonorganic, material, at time t_n in this world.

Let us now *assume*, for purposes of a *reductio* argument, that Felix is essentially a cat. This implies:

(1) (W) (t) (if Felix exists at time t in world W, then Felix is a cat at t in W).

Since it is (as we assume) true that:

(2) In world W^*, Felix exists at time t_n, it then follows that:

(3) Felix is a cat at time t_n in W^*.

It is a feature of world W^* that the t_n-survivor (Felix, as we suppose) is not an *organic* entity having *cellular* parts.

(4) Felix is not a cellular being at time t_n in W^*.

Conjoining (3) and (4), we get:

(5) (EW) (it happens in world W that a certain being is at a certain time such that it is (i) a cat, and (ii) not a cellular being).

Is this conclusion acceptable? Clearly there is reason to judge that if the Putnam-Kripke position concerning natural kinds is correct, (5) must be false. Since (5) is entailed by the conjunction of (3) and (4), that means that either (3) or (4) must be rejected in the event that the Kripke-Putnam position is correct. Assuming that the t_n-survivor in W^* really is Felix, (4) is beyond question. So if we endorse the Putnam-Kripke position, and also agree that the t_n-survivor in W^* is Felix, it seems we are forced to rejct (3). But if we accept (2), rejecting (3) is something that commits us to denying that Felix, an ordinary cat, is *essentially* a cat.

By relying upon Putnam-like "Twin-Earth" stories one can argue that instantiation of surface features is not what is definitive of *being water* or *being a cat*. The fact that the t_n-survivor in world W^* may look like a cat—may be a mouse-chasing, milk-lapping, feline-appearing, four-legged creature—is not sufficient according to advocates of the Putnam-Kripke position for judging that this creature is a *genuine* cat. I take defenders of this position to hold, first, that it is a necessary truth (an "exotic necessary truth") that cats are *mammals*, and, second, that it is a necessary truth that mammals (genuine mammals, not ersatz mammals, or "fool's mammals") have a *cellular*, and not any *synthetic*, constitution. Since none of *this* implies that any cat is essentially a cat, none of *this* entails that the Lockean assessment of the case of Felix is mistaken. Accordingly, Lockean skeptics about essence are free to endorse the exotic necessities that are revealed by the Putnam-Kripke approach to natural kinds in support of the *reductio* argument above. Arguably we must reject (5), since, as the arguments of Putnam and Kripke establish, it is a necessary truth that cats are cellular beings. What is not true, as Lockeans argue, is that individual cats are essentially cats. This is not true because there are worlds such as W^* in which individuals that in *our* world are cats exist as noncats.

X

Such is the argument for Lockean skepticism concerning the claim that Felix is essentially a cat. One way of challenging the argument is by rejecting the thesis that necessarily genuine cats are cellular beings. As was noted earlier, anyone who responds to the Lockean position in this manner is committed to rejecting an important part of the new semantics.

Conceivably one might have other grounds for rejecting the Lockean argument. Some people with whom I have talked about these matters reject premise (2). Thus we might judge that Felix is such that each of his parts is essential to his continued existence. If such mereological essentialism concerning cats is defensible, (2) is false and the Lockean argument unsound.

But there are problems with this. If we think (as most people do) that a human being can continue to exist throughout a period of time in which a liver or kidney is removed and replaced, then we may be hard-pressed to defend the view that Felix's parts are essential to Felix. The Heraclitean proposal that we cannot encounter the same human being before and after a transplant operation is clearly a piece of thoroughly 'revisionary' metaphysics. If rejecting the Lockean position is something that requires revisionary metaphysics, perhaps there is a good deal to be said for the Lockean position.

Critics of premise (2) needn't endorse mereological essentialism. One might allow that Felix's heart is not essentially a part of Felix, and that Felix's paws and claws are not essentially parts of Felix, while also rejecting (2). It is possible, one might argue, for Felix to survive the replacement of some but not all of his original parts! Since the cat-like entity with which we are left at time t_n in world $W*$ has none of Felix's original parts, this entity isn't Felix. Thus (2) is false.

Orthodoxy has it that artifacts can survive the replacement of all of their parts. Lockeans insist that in this respect cats and dogs are like ships and watches and bicycles. Why judge that Lockeans are mistaken about this? One might judge that some sort of 'threshold' position is defensible when it comes to natural entities such as cats. A cat can lose *just so many* of its 'natural' parts while continuing to exist, one might argue. This may sound like a promising way of steering a course between mereological essentialism concering cats, on the one hand, and endorsement of (2) on the other.

Will such a proposal pan out? One might well suspect that threshold theorists are forced in the end to reject *transworld identity* in favor of some *counterpart theoretical* relation. If—as some philosophers argue[26]—there is good reason to reject counterparts, then there is good reason to reject a 'threshold' approach to living things and their parts.

Let's see what happens when we try to have thresholds without counterparts. Elsewhere I have argued that a threshold approach to a thing's *material origins* is subject to serious problems.[27] For reasons of the sort presented in the paper in question, I believe that similar problems attend "threshold" approaches to existence through replacement of parts. To better see what the difficulties are, let us suppose that W_1 is a world in which only one of Felix's parts is ever replaced (this in the period from the present to t_1), W_2 a world in which two of Felix's original parts are replaced (the first in the present–t_1 period, the second in the t_1–t_2 period), W_3 a world in which three of Felix's parts are replaced, ... and W_n a world in which every present part of Felix is replaced by a new part. Further let F_1 be the t_1 survivor of the replacement process that occurs in W_1, F_2 be the survivor of the second replacement process that transpires in W_2, and ... F_n be the survivor (the t_n-survivor) of the final replacement occurring in W_n. Imagine that a threshold theorist tells us that a cat can survive as 10%, but no more, of its parts are exchanged. The problem is evident. For since (as we may suppose) F_1 and F_2 'share' more than 90% of their parts, $F_2 = F_1$. For similar reasons (F_3 and F_2 sharing more than 90% of their parts), $F_3 = F_2$, $F_4 = F_3$, and ... $F_n = F_{n-1}$. But F_n and Felix fail to have 90% of their parts in common. So our threshold theorist is committed to denying that $F_n =$ Felix. Repeated applications of the transitivity of identity principle ($F_3 = F_2$, $F_2 = F_1$, so $F_3 = F_1$) give the result that $F_n =$ Felix, which in effect secures premise (2) of the Lockean argument. But the threshold theorist is committed to denying that $F_n =$ Felix, since the cat-like F_n has none of Felix's (present) parts. The only hope for thresholdism, I believe, is to reject the idea that the relation that holds between the various 'survivors' of the replacement moves in the worlds under consideration is *transworld identity*. What is true, a threshold theorist may insist, is that F_1 is Felix's counterpart in world W_1, F_2 is F_1's counterpart in world W_2, and so on. Since the counterpart relation is not transitive, nothing here commits the threshold theorist to judging that F_n is (the counterpart of) Felix.

Thus it seems that the present threshold challenge to the Lockean argument will either be inconsistent or will rest upon a counterpart-theoretical modal semantics. Obviously such thresholdism will be unattractive to those who believe that counterparts are metaphysically and semantically *entia non grata*. The question is: upon what grounds can the Lockean argument be challenged, given the proviso that counterpart theory is rejected?

XI

Confirmed essentialists may say this: Felix *is* essentially a cat. Since it is necessary that cats are cellular beings, Felix is essentially a cellular being? But F_n isn't a cellular being. So Felix cannot be F_n. Since the Lockean argument assumes that Felix is F_n, the Lockean argument fails.

This sounds straightforward enough. But perhaps it is not clear how such a position is to be sustained without commitment to some counterpart-theoretical position. Note that F_1, F_2, ..., and F_{n-1} all are *hybrid* individuals having some "biological" (cellular) parts and some synthetic (perhaps electronic) parts. The claim that F_1 *is Felix* surely has great plausibility, this despite the fact that F_1 is only in part a cellular being. How can this be reconciled with the thesis that Felix is essentially a cellular being?

Essentialism is strongly counterintuitive in the event that it commits us to judging that a living being such as Felix can't survive a process in which just one biological part is replaced by a synthetic part. Suppose that an essentialist grants that F_1 is Felix. Then it must be granted that it is not essential to Felix that all of his parts be cellular. Once this is allowed it isn't clear why it should be denied that F_2 is Felix as well. (Reminder: there is great plausibility in the claim that F_1 is F_2.) Essentialists here are confronted by a 'slippery slope' that potentially undercuts the thesis that Felix is essentially a cellular being.

One proposal for defusing the 'slippery slope' is by appealing to the controversial idea that there are *degrees of truth*. The degrees-of-truth gambit with respect to thresholds and material origins is explored by Graeme Forbes in an interesting paper entitled "Thisness and Vagueness."[28] Since F_1 is only partly a cellular being, and since Felix is essentially a cellular being, the claim that Felix is F_1 isn't *perfectly true*. Since F_2 is even less of a cellular being than is F_1, there is even *less* truth in the claim that F_2 is Felix. There is, finally, *no truth* in the claim that F_n is Felix. So judging the matter does not commit an essentialist to denying outright (implausibly) that F_1 is Felix. Assuming that F_1 differs from 'our' Felix only with respect to the fact that where one small part of F_1 is artificial the corresponding part of Felix is natural (cellular), there is a great deal of truth in the claim that F_1 is Felix.

This way of proceeding leads directly to counterparts. Identity, whether within a world or across worlds, is not a matter of degree! Thus if a claim that F_1 is Felix is taken to be a statement of transworld *identity*, this statement cannot be true to some extent only. On the other hand, looking at this from a different vantage point, if there is some but only some truth in the claim that F_1 is Felix, then this claim cannot correctly be parsed as an *identity* claim. But assuming that F_1 is not identical with Felix, it seems that the stage is set (to say the least) for judging that F_1 is merely a *counterpart* of Felix. In short, the appeal to degrees of truth in response to the slippery slope problem leads directly to, and so offers no escape from, counterpart theoretic modal semantics. (Forbes argues along similar lines in "Thisness and Vagueness.") Assuming that there is indeed good reason to reject counterpart theory, there seems to be reason to reject the idea that there is some truth only in the claim that F_1 is Felix. I am inclined to judge that it is *true* that F_1 is Felix, and so am inclined to doubt that Felix is essentially a being all of whose parts are cellular. Since I believe that it is (completely) true that F_2 is F_1, I believe that F_2 is Felix, and so believe that it is possible for Felix to have more than one noncellular part. Readers who perceive the matter this way may well find themselves increasingly distrustful of the proposal that Felix is essentially a cellular being. Such distrust is perfectly consistent with the *de dicto* exotic necessary truths to which Putnam and Kripke call our attention. It is necessary that cats are cellular beings. What is not necessary is that individual cats, if they exist at all, are cellular beings.

If correct, the point carries over from cats to other garden-variety individuals. David Wiggins has argued that "human being" is a *substance* (not a *phase*) sortal that necessarily applies to each of us (that is, to each human being) throughout our entire career.[29] Wiggins judges that the real essence that is in a sense definitive of what it is to be human is essential not just to a certain species (kind) but to individual members of this species:

> Locke lost sight of his objective when confusion or desperation about how the sense of a putative real essence word could be learned in experience led him to supplant the real essence of a natural thing in his semantic account of substance words by the (invariably inaccurate) phenomenal description which he called the nominal essence. With Putnam's proposal to hand, however, which gives the real essence *par excellence*, we may not only solve Locke's problem but also derive substantial consequences from essentialism, e.g., that Julius Caesar had necessarily those genetic properties which flowed from his being a man.[30]

It is not clear that Wiggins is right about this. Perhaps—as the above discussion of Felix's case may suggest—no individual that lies on the favored (transworld) semantic path for "human" fails to have certain genetic characteristics. Perhaps it is necessarily true both that humans have such genetic features and that humans are cellular beings. Lockean antiessentialists may rely upon such assumptions in the process of arguing that those of us who are human are not essentially human. As Dennett and others have suggested, it is possible for any of us to exist as something other than a cellular being and so to exist as something other than a human being.[31] More cautiously, nothing said by either Putnam or Kripke concerning natural kinds and real "essence" implies that Lockean antiessentialists are mistaken. Indeed, as I hope to have indicated, the new semantics may support an interesting version of antiessentialism.

Notes

1. Saul A. Kripke, *Wittgenstein: On Rules and Private Language* (Cambridge, Mass., 1982), 62. Further references to this work appear parenthetically in the text of the paper.

2. Some people deny that Kripke's interpretation of Wittgenstein is correct. See, for example, S. G. Shanker, "Skeptical Confusions About Rule-Following," *Mind* 93 (1984): 423–29.

3. Bruce Goldberg, "The Linguistic Expression of Feeling," *The American Philosophical Quarterly* (January 1971): 88.

4. See Marie McGinn, "Kripke on Wittgenstein's Skeptical Problem," *Ratio* 26 (1984): 21: "the traditional conception of understanding that is allegedly being countered by Wittgenstein's skeptical arguments is linked with a conception of meaning as something that is grasped by a speaker when he understands a word, and which determines all the future correct applications of it."

5. Thus Shanker, "Skeptical Confusions About Rule-Following."

6. Nino Cocchiarella, "Sortals, Natural Kinds and Re-Identification," *Logique et Analyse* 20 (1977): 455. Much the same position is defended by Baruch Bordy, *Abortion and the Sanctity of Human Life: A Philosophical View* (Cambridge, Mass., 1975), 98–99. Brody has much to say concerning natural kinds in a paper entitled "Natural Kinds and Real Essences," *The Journal of Philosophy* 64 (July 1967): 431–46.

7. For a first-rate discussion of these and related matters, see Nathan U. Salmon, *Reference and Essence* (Princeton, N.J., 1981), especially chapter four.

8. See John Dupre, "Natural Kinds and Biological Taxa," *The Philosophical Review* 90 (January 1981). 66–90. Dupre says: "In the case of material things Locke, like his successors, thought that the real essence was some feature of the microscopic structure. . . . [Locke] held that sorts of things were demarcated by nominal essence only" (p. 67). Later in the present paper, it is assumed that Locke is an antiessentialist. For more about this, see Michael R. Ayers, "Locke versus Aristotle on Natural Kinds," *The Journal of Philosophy* 78 (May 1981), 247–72, especially pages 262–63.

9. David Wiggins expresses doubts concerning "nominal essence" approaches to natural kinds in *Sameness and Substance* (Cambridge, Mass., 1980), chapter 3. In one place, Wiggins says that "in the process of teaching and elucidation of the sense of a natural kind predicate everything depends upon the actual extension of the predicate . . . or on what Frege would have called its reference" (p. 83). A more subtle analysis is found in Salmon, where distinctions are drawn between several senses of "sense" and between "sense" and "meaning" (pp. 11–14 and 66–67). Very roughly, Salmon would say that the meaning, but not the sense(s), of natural kind terms are intimately tied to the actual extension of these terms.

10. Wiggins argues for this view in "Essentialism, Continuity, and Identity," *Synthese* 23 (1974): 336.

11. See Ayers, "Locke versus Aristotle on Natural Kinds," especially pages 259 and 263.

12. For a start, see the papers by Putnam and Kripke in *Naming, Necessity, and Natural Kinds*, edited by Stephen P. Schwartz (Ithaca, N.Y., 1977). See also Kripke's "Naming and Necessity," in *Semantics of Natural Language*, edited by Donald Davidson and Gilbert Harman (Dordrecht-Holland, 1972).

13. "Is Semantic Possible?" in Schwartz, ibid., 111.

14. "Meaning and Reference," in Schwartz, ibid., 122–28.

15. Though Wittgenstein is never mentioned, this point emerges when we consider a number of Martian cases constructed by Peter Unger in *Philosophical Relativity* (Minneapolis, 1984), chapter 5. Consider especially the case in which Martians replace each feline animal with a duplicate robot that is indiscernible with respect to its 'surface' features (p. 86). It should be noted that Unger's intuitions seem to be that new semanticists are mistaken in judging that it is necessarily true (if true at all) that cats are animals.

16. Jonathan Bennett, "Substance, Reality, and Primary Qualities," in *Locke and Berkeley*, edited by C. B. Martin and D. M. Armstrong (Garden City, N.Y., 1968), 121.

17. For an argument supporting an affirmative answer, see "Scientific Realism and Ordinary Usage," *Philosophical Investigations* 3 (July 1984): 187–205. For a similar critical line opposing the new semantics, see Eddy M. Zemach, "Putnam's Theory on the Reference of Substance Terms," *The Journal of Philosophy* 73 (March 1976): 116–26.

18. Norman Malcom, "Wittgenstein's *Philosophical Investigations*," in *Knowledge and Certainty* (Englewood Cliffs, N.J., 1963), 105–6.

19. Dupre, "Natural Kinds and Biological Taxa," 68.

20. Salmon, *Reference and Essence*, 97.

21. Salmon's position is extremely subtle, and this does not do it justice. The book is well worth the close attention of anyone interested in these and related matters. I am indebted to Professor Salmon for very insightful critical comments on an ancestor of the present paper.

22. S. E. Luria, *Life: The Unfinished Experiment* (New York City, 1973), 65.

23. Several versions of Unger's Martian story may suggest as much. My intuition is that it is necessary that cats are cellular beings.

24. See Keith S. Donnellan, "Kripke and Putnam on Natural Kind Terms," in *Knowledge and Mind,* edited by Carl Ginet and Sydney Shoemaker (New York City, 1983). Donnellan attributes to Putnam and Kripke the view that it is necessarily true, if true at all, that tigers are mammals (p. 92).

25. Michael A. Slote, "Causality and the Concept of a 'Thing'," in *Midwest Studies in Philosophy* IV, edited by Peter A. French, Theodore E. Uehling, Jr., and Howard K. Wettstein (Minneapolis, 1979), 389.

26. See, for example, Alvin Plantinga's "Transworld Identity or Worldbound Individuals," in Schwartz, *Naming, Necessity, and Natural Kinds.*

27. "Salmon on Artifact Origins and Lost Possibilities," *The Philosophical Review* 92 (April 1983): 223–31. Professor Salmon's reply is in "Impossible Worlds," *Analysis* 44 (1984): 114–17.

28. Graeme Forbes, "Thisness and Vagueness," *Synthese* 54 (1983): 235–59.

29. "Essentialism, Continuity, and Identity," 336.

30. Ibid.

31. Daniel Dennett, "Where am I?" in *The Mind's I,* edited by Daniel Dennett and Douglas R. Hofstadter (New York, 1981).

MIDWEST STUDIES IN PHILOSOPHY, XI (1986)

Modal Paradox:
Parts and Counterparts,
Points and Counterpoints

NATHAN SALMON

I

There is a class of paradoxes that arise from the following (intuitively correct) modal principles concerning the possibility of variation in the original construction of an artifact:[1]

> If a wooden table x is the only table originally formed from a hunk (portion, quantity, bit) of matter y according to a certain plan (form, structure, design, configuration) P, then x is such that it might have been the only table formed according to the same plan P from a distinct but overlapping hunk of matter y' having exactly the same mass, volume, and chemical composition as y.

> If a wooden table x originally formed from a hunk of matter y is such that it might have been originally formed from a hunk of matter y' according to a certain plan P, then for any hunk of matter y'' having exactly the same matter in common with y that y' has, and having exactly the same mass, volume, and chemical composition as y', x is also such that it might have been originally formed from y'' according to the same plan P.

> (0) If a wooden table x is the only table originally formed from a hunk of matter y, then x is such that it could not have been the only table originally formed from entirely different matter, i.e., from a hunk of matter z having no matter in common with y (not even a single molecule, atom, or subatomic particle).

The last of these three modal principles, principle (0), is a nontrivial essentialist principle. It has been argued for by means of the following plausible, and perhaps more fundamental, essentialist principle concerning artifacts and their matter:

> (I) If a wooden table x is such that it might have been the only table originally formed from a hunk of matter z according to a certain plan P, then there could not be a table that is distinct from x and the only table formed from hunk z according to plan P.

The argument proceeds as follows: Let x be any arbitrary wooden table that is the only table formed from its original matter y, and let z be any nonoverlapping hunk of matter. Suppose for a *reductio ad absurdum* that table x is such that it might have been the only table originally formed from hunk z instead of from hunk y. Now necessarily, every table is formed according to some plan or other. Hence there is some plan P such that table x might have been the only table formed from hunk z according to plan P. It follows directly that hunk z is such that it might have been formed into a table (some table or other) according to the very plan P, and hence z might have been so formed only once. Since table x was actually the only table originally formed from hunk y, and since hunk z might have been formed into a table only once according to plan P, it might also have been that both obtained together. That is, it might have been that table x is the only table originally formed from hunk y, just as it actually was, while at the same time some table or other x' is the only table originally formed from hunk z according to plan P. (This is derived from a premise of the argument concerning the compossibility of certain possible states of affairs.) Of course, it is impossible for any one table to be originally formed entirely from one hunk of matter, and also originally formed entirely from some other, nonoverlapping hunk of matter. Thus, it is necessary that if table x is originally formed from hunk y, then any table formed from hunk z is not x. Hence, it is possible for there to be a table x' that is distinct from x and the only table originally formed from hunk z according to plan P. It follows by (I) and *modus tollens* that our original assumption that table x might have been the only table originally formed from hunk z is false.[2]

The first two principles cited above, taken together, imply that a certain *amount* of variation is possible in the original constitution of a table, whereas principle (0) implies that the amount of allowable variation is something short of total. A wooden table might have been originally formed from different wood, but not completely different wood; it might have been originally constructed with some different molecules, but not all. It follows that there is some threshold, some limit point—or if not a definite point, then at least some interval within which it is indeterminate—such that one more change in original constitution must by necessity result in a numerically distinct table.

It seems reasonable to suppose that the threshold consists in an interval of indeterminacy rather than a definite limit point. If a hunk of matter y' differs by only one molecule of wood from the original matter y of a table x, then clearly x is such that it might have been originally formed from y' instead of y. We have just seen an argument that if a hunk of matter z shares not even a single molecule of wood with the original matter of the table x, then x is such that it could not have been originally formed from z. Somewhere between these two extremes is the threshold—the minimum amount of required overlap, the maximum amount of allowable nonoverlap. The idea that this threshold amount should consist in an exact and specific number of shared molecules, or some other sort of sharp cutoff point, seems unrealistic. As with most of our concepts, our concepts of metaphysical possibility and impossibility do not seem to be quite that sharp. It seems more realistic to suppose that the threshold consists in some interval, perhaps some range of numbers of shared molecules. For any hunk of matter y' that shares a greater number of molecules with the actual matter y of the table

x than any number in this range, and that is otherwise just like y, it is determinately true of x that it might have originated from y' instead of from y. For any hunk of matter z sharing fewer molecules with y than any number in the range, it is determinately true of x that it could not have originated from z. For any hunk of matter y'' whose number of shared molecules with y lies within the range, it is indeterminate—vague, neither true nor false, there is no objective fact of the matter—whether x could have originated from y'' instead of from y.

Moreover, even if there is a sharp cutoff point,[3] it seems quite unrealistic to suppose that one could ever establish—say by a philosophical proof—precisely where the cutoff point lies. Thus even if the threshold is some exact and very precise amount of overlap, from an epistemic point of view we can never be in a position to specify with adequate justification just what the threshold is—except by means of some vague locution like 'sufficiently substantial overlap'. We may assert the following:

(II) If a wooden table x is the only table originally formed from a hunk of matter y according to a certain plan P, and y' is any (possibly scattered) hunk of matter that sufficiently substantially overlaps y and has exactly the same mass, volume, and chemical composition as y, then x is such that it might have been the only table originally formed according to the same plan P from y' instead of from y.

(III) If a wooden table x is the only table originally formed from a hunk of matter y, and z is any hunk of matter that does not sufficiently substantially overlap y, then x is such that it could not have been the only table originally formed from z instead of from y.

It is to be understood that being exactly the same matter except for only one or two molecules counts as sufficiently substantial overlap, whereas complete nonoverlap (no shared molecules whatsoever) does not.

Paradox arises when it is noted that none of these modal principles is the sort of proposition that merely happens to be true as a matter of contingent fact. In particular, principle (II) is such that if it is true at all, it is necessarily so. Furthermore, (II) is such that if it is true at all, then it is necessary that it is necessarily true, and it is necessary that it is necessary that it is necessarily true, and so on. In fact, on the conventionally accepted system $S5$ of modal propositional logic, *any* proposition is such that if it is necessarily true, then it is necessary that it is necessarily true, and it is necessary that it is necessary that it is necessarily true, and so on.

One paradox that arises from these observations I call the 'Four Worlds Paradox'. Elsewhere I have developed the paradox using the language and framework of possible-world discourse, i.e., language involving explicit reference to, and quantification over, possible worlds and possible individuals (instead of the ordinary modal locutions 'might have', 'must', or subjunctive mood). The paradox is constructed by considering four distinct but related possible worlds. The Four Worlds Paradox can also be developed within modal-operator discourse, i.e., the language of the modal operators 'necessarily' or 'must', 'possibly' or 'might', and subjunctive mood. The paradox goes as follows: We consider a particular wooden table, a, with its four original legs, L_1, L_2, L_3, and L_4. Let us call the (hunk of) matter from which the table a was originally formed 'h'. The original matter of the four legs is a proper part of hunk h. Suppose for the sake of simplicity (though this is by no means essential to the argument)[4] that the threshold for table a is such that (for example) any table having the same overall plan (form, structure, design, configuration) as a is such that it might have been originally constructed using one leg different from its four actual original legs, as long as whatever other parts there are to the table (the other three original legs, the original table top, original wood screws, original glue, and so on) and the overall plan are the same. Suppose further that no table of this overall plan could have been originally constructed using two or more different legs from the actual original four. Now instead of constructing table a as he did, the artisan who constructed a might have constructed a table according to the same plan using two different table legs L_5 and L_6 in place of L_3 and L_4, keeping everything else the same—where L_5 and L_6 are qualitatively and structurally exactly like L_3 and L_4 actually are, respectively. Let us call this (scattered) hunk of matter 'h''. Hunk h' consists of hunk h with the replacement of the matter in legs L_3 and L_4 (at the time of table a's construction) with the qualitatively identical matter in legs L_5 and L_6. By principle (III), any such (possible) table must be distinct from a itself, but there is no reason why the artisan could not have thus constructed a qualitative duplicate of a instead of a itself. In accordance with S5 modal propositional logic, it follows by the necessitation of principle (II) that the artisan might just as well have constructed a table distinct from a according to the same plan using L_1, L_2, L_3, and L_6 as the four legs instead of L_1, L_2, L_5, and L_6 (keeping everything else the same), since this would involve a change of only one table leg. Let us call this hunk of matter 'h'''. Hunk h'' coincides exactly with hunk h' except for the replacement of the matter in leg L_5 with the matter in leg L_3. Now hunk h'' also coincides exactly with hunk h (table a's actual original matter) except for the replacement of the matter in leg L_4 with the matter in leg L_6. Since the original table a was actually formed according to the same plan from hunk h, it also follows by principle (II) that the artisan might have constructed a itself according to the same plan using the same parts—L_1, L_2, L_3, and L_6, keeping everything else the same. Thus, the artisan might have constructed a by shaping certain matter h'' according to a certain plan, and he also might have constructed a table distinct from a by shaping exactly the same matter h'' according to exactly the same plan. This contradicts (I).

Formally, the Four Worlds Paradox proceeds from the following set of premises, where $\ulcorner M(\alpha, \beta)\urcorner$ means $\ulcorner \alpha$ is the only table originally formed from hunk of matter β according to such-and-such a plan $\urcorner$:

$M(a, h)$	[Given]
$\Diamond(\exists x)M(x, h')$	[Given]
$M(a, h) \supset {\sim}\Diamond M(a, h')$	[from (III)]
$\Box(x)[M(x, h') \supset \Diamond M(x, h'')]$	[from $\Box$(II)]
$M(a, h) \supset \Diamond M(a, h'')$	[from (II)]
$\Diamond M(a, h'') \supset \Box(x)[M(x, h'') \supset x = a]$	[from (I)].

From these (together with the trivial assumption that necessarily, if a table is formed from some matter, then it exists, and the quantified modal logical law of the necessity of identity) the following contradiction is immediately derivable in *S5*, and even the weaker *S4*, modal logic:

$(C_1) \Diamond(\exists x)[x \neq a \,\&\, M(x, h'')] \,\&\, \sim\Diamond(\exists x)[x \neq a \,\&\, M(x, h'')].$

I was once tempted by the view that this paradox is a *reductio ad absurdum* of the last premise cited above, and hence also a *reductio* of the cross-world identity principle (I). But to draw this conclusion is to miss the lesson of the paradox. Even if the last premise cited above is dropped from the list, an equally paradoxical argument can be constructed by invoking a slightly strengthened version of principle (II). To see this, let us first define the notion of a *materially complete* proposition. A proposition is materially complete if it is a complete enumeration of every particle of matter in the cosmos throughout all of a potential history of the world, as well as a complete specification of all the physical interactions and configurations of all the matter in the cosmos in exact chronological sequence throughout that potential history.

Needless to say, no materially complete proposition can be apprehended by the human mind, but of course, that is no reason to suppose that there are no such propositions. There are such propositions, and indeed one of them is true. Presumably, all true materially complete propositions are necessarily equivalent. On the modal logician's conception of propositions as sets of possible worlds (or as functions from possible worlds to truth values), exactly one materially complete "proposition" is true.

Let p be a (the) materially complete proposition that would have been true if the table a had been formed according to the same plan using leg L_6 instead of leg L_4. Notice that the materially complete proposition p surely strictly implies that some table or other is the only table originally formed from hunk h'' according to such-and-such a plan, in the sense that:

$\Box[p \supset (\exists x)M(x, h'')].$

Since p is a materially complete proposition that would have been true if table a had been formed from hunk h'' according to a certain plan, it is trivial that it might have been the case both that p is true and that a is the table formed from h'' according to that plan. By an argument that proceeds exactly as before, except invoking a stronger but still intuitively correct version of (II), it also might have been the case both that p is true and that the table formed from h'' is some table distinct from a. Hence in *S4* we may derive:

$(C_2) \Diamond[p \,\&\, M(a, h'')] \,\&\, \Diamond[p \,\&\, \sim M(a, h'')].$

This means that the question of which (possible) table is formed from hunk h'' (i.e., the question of the *haecceity* of the table formed from h'') is a question whose answer is not decided by a complete accounting of *all* the material facts in the cosmos—including the fact that hunk h'' exists as a physical unit and is table-shaped in such-and-such a particular way. This result is quite unpalatable. A table is in some obvious sense "nothing over and above" its matter and form. Perhaps some facts are underdetermined by the totality of material facts, but surely the question of whether a given actual table *a* is constituted by a certain hunk of matter *h''* must be so determined. The fact that hunk *h''* constitutes table *a*, if it does, is *supervenient* on a complete possible history of all the matter in the cosmos. If for some reason God had preferred to have table *a* originally formed from hunk *h''* instead of from hunk *h*, once He has fixed all of the material facts—all of the facts concerning all of the matter in the cosmos—any further facts concerning which table is formed from which matter will take care of themselves. Hence, at a minimum, the following is true:

$$\Box[p \supset M(a, h'')] \lor \Box[p \supset \sim M(a, h'')].$$

This contradicts (C_2).

II

It is my view that both of the modal principles (II) and (III), and their multiple necessitations, are intuitively and literally true. Paradoxical conclusions are drawn from these principles by invoking defective rules of modal logic, by drawing fallacious modal inferences. Specifically, the conventionally accepted axiom of *S4* modal propositional logic,

$$\Box p \supset \Box\Box p,$$

or equivalently, the presumption that modal accessibility between worlds is transitive, is illegitimate and must be rejected in its unrestricted form. The modal logical system *S4* is fallacious. Its rejection invalidates a modal inference pattern critical to the Four Worlds Paradox:

$$\Box(\phi \supset \Diamond\psi)$$
$$\Diamond\phi$$
$$\overline{\hspace{3cm}}$$
$$\therefore \Diamond\psi.$$

Instead we have only the weaker inference:

$$\Box(\phi \supset \Diamond\psi)$$
$$\Diamond\phi$$
$$\overline{\hspace{3cm}}$$
$$\therefore \Diamond\Diamond\psi.$$

In particular, the hypotheses of the paradox yield the conlcusion that it might have been that it might have been that a table distinct from *a* was originally formed from hunk *h''*, but they do not yield the stronger conclusion that it might have been that a table distinct from *a* was originally formed from *h''*. There is no contradiction with (I).

The primary motivation for rejecting the *S4* axiom, as applied to the origins of artifacts (as well as other sorts of objects), is best given by means of an alternative modal paradox using a sorites-type construction, the main idea of which has been exploited by Roderick Chisholm. We begin with the same actual table *a*. The original matter *h* of table *a* consists of a certain number of molecules. Call this number '*n*'. Now there is a finite sequence of hunks of matter, $h, h_1, h_2, \ldots, h_n$, where each element of the sequence h_i differs from its immediate predecessor h_{i-1} only in the replacement of one molecule by a qualitatively identical but numerically distinct molecule, in such a way that the last element in the sequence, h_n, has no overlap whatsoever with h, the original matter of table a. Now by the necessitation of principle (II), each of the following necessitated conditionals is true, where $\ulcorner M(\alpha, \beta)\urcorner$ again means $\ulcorner \alpha$ is the only table originally formed from hunk of matter β according to such-and-such a plan$\urcorner$:

$$\Box[M(a, h) \supset \Diamond M(a, h_1)]$$
$$\Box[M(a, h_1) \supset \Diamond M(a, h_2)]$$

$$\vdots$$

$$\Box[M(a, h_{n-1}) \supset \Diamond M(a, h_n)].$$

If we head this list with the true sentence '$M(a, h)$', we obtain a finite set of true premises that in *S4* logically entail the conclusion '$\Diamond M(a, h_n)$'. Let us call this argument (premise set plus conclusion) '(CP)', for 'Chisholm's Paradox'. The argument (CP) is *S4*-valid, and each of its premises is true. Yet by principle (III), '$\Box \sim M(a, h_n)$' is also true. Adding this to the list of premises of (CP), we obtain a set of true premises from which a contradiction is derivable in *S4*.

One can see what is amiss with *S4* by considering its import within the framework of possible worlds, to wit, the idea that the relation of modal accessibility between worlds is transitive. Since table a originates from hunk h in the actual world, it follows by (II) that there is a world w_1 possible relative to the actual world, i.e., accessible to the actual world, in which a originates from h_1. Hence by the necessitation of (II), there is a world w_2 possible relative to w_1 in which a originates from h_2. Hence by the *double* necessitation of (II), there is a world w_3 possible relative to w_2 in which a originates from h_3, and so on. Finally, by the $(n-1)$-fold necessitation of (II), there is a world w_n possible relative to w_{n-1} in which a originates from h_n. Thus, there is a world (w_n) bearing the ancestral of the accessibility relation to the actual world and in which a originates from h_n. But by principle (III), there is no *genuinely* possible world, i.e., no world possible relative to the actual world, in which a originates from h_n. Somewhere in the sequence $h_1, h_2, \ldots, h_n$, a hunk of matter $h_m (1 < m < n)$ is the first hunk to exceed the amount of allowable variation from h. Hunk h_m passes the threshold, and so, then, do all of its successors in the sequence. Hence, world w_m is not accessible to the actual world. World w_m is an *impossible world*. That is, w_m is impossible from the standpoint of the actual world, although it is possible relative to its immediate predecessor w_{m-1}, which is itself possible relative to the actual world. World w_m is a possibly possible impossible world.

Similarly, there is a world w_{2m} in which table a originates from hunk h_{2m}. World w_{2m} is possible relative to a world w_{2m-1} in which table a originates from hunk h_{2m-1}, and w_{2m-1} is possible relative to w_m, but w_{2m} is not possible relative to w_m. World w_{2m} is an impossible world that is not even a possibly possible world. It is only a possibly possibly possible world. That is, w_{2m} is a possibly possibly possible impossibly possible world.

This means that the relation of modal accessibility between worlds is not transitive. The premises of the argument (CP) are all true, but its conclusion is false. The argument (CP) is logically invalid.

If there is any defect in this illustration of the intransitivity of modal accessibility, and the consequent illegitimacy of *S4*, it is the assumption that there is some hunk of matter h_m that is the *first* hunk in the sequence to pass the threshold. This is tantamount to the assumption that the threshold consists in some definite number of shared molecules. This assumption, however, is quite inessential to the illustration. Suppose instead that there is a range of hunks, h_k, h_{k+1}, ..., h_{m-1}, such that for any hunk in this range, it is indeterminate—vague, neither true nor false, there is no objective fact of the matter—whether table a could have originated from it. This results in two limit points where before we had only one, and one alone is sufficient for a failure of transitivity. In the sequence of worlds w_1, w_2, ..., w_n, each world is determinately accessible to its immediate predecessor. Furthermore, each of the worlds w_1, w_2, ..., w_{k-1} is determinately accessible to the actual world (since it is determinately true that table a could have originated from hunk h_{k-1} or any of its predecessors), whereas each of the worlds w_m, w_{m+1}, ..., w_n is determinately inaccessible to the actual world (since it is determinately false that table a could have originated from hunk h_m or any of its successors). Each of the remaining worlds w_k, w_{k+1}, ..., w_{m-1} is neither determinately accessible nor determinately inaccessible to the actual world (since it is neither true nor false that a could have originated from h_k, or from h_{m-1}, or from any intervening hunk). This would mean that the accessibility relation is only *partially defined*, in the sense that its characteristic function is not total but partial. There would be a failure of transitivity *via* a region of indeterminacy, but there would still be a failure of transitivity.

Thus the modal paradoxes turn on a fallacy special to *S4* modal logic. In deriving the paradoxes in *S4*, one commits the *fallacy of possibility deletion*, inferring $\ulcorner \Diamond \phi \urcorner$ from $\ulcorner \Diamond \Diamond \phi \urcorner$, or equivalently, the *fallacy of necessity iteration*, inferring $\ulcorner \Box \Box \phi \urcorner$ from $\ulcorner \Box \phi \urcorner$. In particular, though it is necessary that table a does not originate from hunk h_m ($= h'$), it is fallacious to infer that it is necessary that it is necessary that a does not thus originate. In the Four Worlds Paradox, though it might have been that it might have been that some table distinct from a is formed from hunk h'' ($= h_{m-1}$), it is fallacious to infer that it might have been that some table distinct from a is formed from h''.[5]

III

The primary (though not the only) rival to this approach to the modal paradoxes is derived from the modal theory of David Lewis, so-called counterpart theory. Versions of the counterpart-theoretic solution to the paradoxes have been suggested or advocated by a number of philosophers, including Hugh Chandler, Roderick Chisholm, Graeme Forbes, Anil Gupta, Saul Kripke, and Robert Stalnaker.[6] Forbes in particular has recently worked out many of the details of a counterpart-theoretic solution, defending it against criticisms I have made and raising objections to the intransitive-accessibility solution sketched above.[7]

Strictly speaking, one should speak of counterpart theory *with respect to* a certain kind of entity, e.g., artifacts. Counterpart theory with respect to a kind k makes use of a binary cross-world resemblance relation, counterparthood, between possible entities of kind k. The counterpart relation is fixed by considerations of sufficient cross-world similarity in certain relevant respects. Since distinct possible entities of kind k may bear sufficient resemblance to one another across possible worlds, an individual x of kind k will have counterparts at other worlds other than itself. Typically, it is a basic tenet of the theory that each possible individual of kind k exists in one and only one possible world, so that a pair of counterparts existing in distinct worlds are always themselves distinct.

There are certain theoretical constraints on the counterpart relation. For example, any possible individual of kind k is its own counterpart at any (the) world in which it exists. Another minimal constraint is that if a possible individual x of kind k has a counterpart at world w that exists in w, then all of x's counterparts at w exist in w. In the typical case, a counterpart of x at w is something that exists in w and (as it is in w) sufficiently resembles x as it is in its own world. Alternative versions of the theory provide for a possible individual to have a special counterpart at a world even though the counterpart does not itself exist in that world, as does Forbes's, but this happens only when the individual has no existing counterparts at the world in question. Yet another minimal constraint typically imposed is this: if a possible individual y is a counterpart of a possible individual x at a world w, and y itself has counterparts at w that exist in w, then all of y's existing counterparts at w are also counterparts of x at w, i.e., all of a possible individual's existing counterparts at a given world are counterparts at that world of anything that the individual is itself a counterpart of at that world. This constraint can be trivially satisfied by means of the stronger constraint, typically but not always imposed, that any possible individual y that exists in w is its own sole counterpart at w. One condition typically not imposed, however, is transitivity. Since counterparthood is a cross-world similarity relation, and similarity is not transitive, there will be possible individuals x, y, and z, such that y exists in some world w and is a counterpart of x at w, and z exists in some world w' and is a counterpart of y at w', but z does not sufficiently resemble x to be a counterpart of x at w'.

Counterpart theory (with respect to kind k) provides for a possible-world semantic theory that differs in important respects from standard Kripkean possible-world semantics for modal-operator discourse. Let us first briefly review the main ideas that differentiate standard Kripkean possible-world semantics from classical Tarskian semantics. In standard Kripkean possible-world semantics, the extensional semantic attributes—such as singular term reference, predicate application, and sentence truth value—are relativized to possible worlds. In the case of reference and truth value, this relativization to worlds is in addition to the usual Tarskian relativization to assignments of values to individual variables. (Suppressing any reference to a model) if α is an individual variable, *the referent of α with respect to a world w under an assignment s*, or $Ref_{w,s}(\alpha)$, is simply the possible individual assigned to α by s, i.e., $s(\alpha)$. If α is a simple individual constant, it is assigned a referent (or to use Kripke's phrase, its "reference is fixed") independently of any possible world or assignment of values to variables. Thus, simple individual constants and individual variables are *obstinately rigid designators,* [8] expressions that refer to the same thing with respect to every possible world. If π is an n-place predicate, and $\alpha_1, \alpha_2, \ldots, \alpha_n$ are singular terms, then the atomic formula $\ulcorner \pi(\alpha_1, \alpha_2, \ldots, \alpha_n) \urcorner$ is *true with respect to a world w under an assignment s,* or *true $_{w,s}$,* if and only if π *applies with respect to w,* or *applies$_w$,* to the n-tuple consisting of the referents of each of the α_i with respect to w under s, $<Ref_{w,s}(\alpha_1), Ref_{w,s}(\alpha_2), \ldots, Ref_{w,s}(\alpha_n)>$. The connective and quantifier cases similarly follow standard Tarskian semantics. A formula $\ulcorner \Box \phi \urcorner$ is true $_{w,s}$ if and only if ϕ is true$_{w',s}$, for every world w' accessible to w. A formula $\ulcorner \Diamond \phi \urcorner$ is true$_{w,s}$ if and only if ϕ is true$_{w',s}$, for some world w' accessible to w. A sentence is *true (simpliciter)* if and only if it is true $_{the\ actual\ world,\ s}$, for every assignment s.

   Following the lead of Lewis, counterpart theorists typically formulate their theory in terms of translations of sentences (open or closed) involving modal operators into sentences of possible-world discourse, sentences involving explicit attribution of a counterpart relation between individuals in different worlds. This standard sort of formulation of counterpart theory may be regarded as providing a partial semantics for modal-operator discourse, in that it provides truth conditions in terms of possible worlds and counterparts for each sentence (open or closed) of modal-operator discourse. However, the semantics is only partial, since nothing is said explicitly concerning the semantics of subsentential expressions (such as singular terms and predicates) or how the truth conditions of sentences are computed from the semantics of their components. If one wishes to understand the compositional nature of the semantics of modal-operator-discourse sentences in terms of the semantics of their component expressions, one must glean this information, insofar as possible, from the translations into possible-world discourse of the modal-operator-discourse sentences in which the subsentential expressions figure. This feature of the standard formulations of counterpart theory is properly suited to a certain linguistic point of view concerning the synonymy of modal-operator-discourse sentences and the possible-world-discourse sentences giving the truth conditions of the former sentences, and the possibility of exhausting the semantics of modal-operator discourse merely by supplying possible-world-discourse sentential correlates. This point of view is disputable. Moreover, it is quite independent of the issues that separate standard possible-world theorists from counterpart theorists, and it is quite inessential to the main philosophical ideas and intuitions that motivate counterpart theory. If a standard modal theorist adopts this point of view, he or she may easily reformulate the standard modal semantics as a set of instructions for translation of modal-operator-discourse sentences into possible-world-discourse sentences, remaining silent with respect to the compositional nature of the semantics of sentences in terms of the semantics of subsentential expressions. In order to highlight the contrast with standard modal semantics, while clearing away the unimportant differences in what has come to be the usual sort of formulations of each, it is best to reformulate counterpart theory along lines that parallel as closely as possible, within the bounds of the spirit of the philosophical motivation for counterpart theory, the usual formulation of standard possible-world semantics.

I shall do this using the notion of a *counterpart assignment*. A counterpart assignment c_w (with respect to a kind k) for a world w is a function that assigns to any possible individual i (of kind k) a counterpart of i at w, if i has any counterparts at w, and assigns nothing otherwise. If there is no counterpart of i at w existing in w, then depending on the particular counterpart theory in question, the counterpart assignment may be undefined for i, as with Lewis's theory, or it may assign the individual i to itself as its own counterpart at w, as with Forbes's. On Forbes's theory, counterpart assignments are totally defined functions.

Let us call an ordered pair of a world and a counterpart assignment for that world a *world-assignment pair*. In counterpart theory with respect to kind k, reference and truth are relativized not merely to worlds but to world-assignment pairs.[9] Thus one speaks of the referent of a singular term *with respect to* a world-assignment pair $<w, c>$ under an assignment of values to variables s. Equivalently, one may speak of reference with respect to a world w *and* a counterpart assignment c for w, under an assignment of values to variables s. Similarly, one speaks of a sentence (open or closed) as being true, or as not being true, *with respect to* a world-assignment pair under an assignment of values to variables. As in standard possible-world semantics, predicate application is relativized only to worlds. The referents of simple singular terms with respect to world-assignment pairs will depend on whether the term has been assigned something of kind k. If α is an individual variable and s is an assignment of values to variables that assigns to α a possible individual not of kind k, then $Ref_{w,c,s}(\alpha) = s(\alpha)$. If α is an individual variable and s is an assignment that assigns to α a possible individual of kind k, then $Ref_{w,c,s}(\alpha) = c(s(\alpha))$. If α is a simple individual constant that refers to an actual individual x not of kind k, then $Ref_{w,c,s}(\alpha) = x$. If α is a simple individual constant that refers to an actual individual x of kind k, then $Ref_{w,c,s}(\alpha) = c(x)$. An atomic formula $\ulcorner\pi(\alpha_1, \alpha_2, ..., \alpha_n)\urcorner$ is $true_{w,c,s}$ if and only if π applies$_w$ to $<Ref_{w,c,s}(\alpha_1), Ref_{w,c,s}(\alpha_2), ..., Ref_{w,c,s}(\alpha_n)>$. A formula $\ulcorner\Box\phi\urcorner$ is $true_{w,c,s}$ if and only if ϕ is $true_{w',c',s}$ for every world w' and every counterpart assignment c' for w' (i.e., for every world-assignment pair $<w', c'>$). A formula $\ulcorner\Diamond\phi\urcorner$ is $true_{w,c,s}$ if and only if ϕ is $true_{w',c',s}$ for some world w' and some counterpart assignment c' for w' (i.e., for some world-assignment pair $<w', c'>$.)[10] Notice that the clause 'w' is accessible to w' has been deleted; counterpart theory avoids the need for an accessibility relational semantics. A sentence is *true (simpliciter)* if and only if it is $true_{the\ actual\ world,c,s}$ for every counterpart assignment c for the actual world and every assignment of values to variables s.

The major difference between counterpart theory and standard possible-world semantics may be illustrated by means of a simple modal sentence from Chisholm's paradox,

$$\Diamond M(a, h_1).$$

On standard possible-world semantics, this sentence is true exactly on the condition that there is a possible world (determinately) accessible to the actual world in which table a—the very table a itself—is the only table formed according to such-and-such a plan from hunk h_1 (instead of from its actual original matter h). The counterpart theorist does not admit that this condition is fulfilled. Instead, typically the counter-part theorist denies that there is any such possible world. The counterpart theorist is still able to accommodate the truth of the displayed sentence. On counterpart theory with respect to artifacts, the sentence is true exactly on the condition that in some pos-sible world, some counterpart of a —not necessarily the very table a itself—is the only table formed according to such-and-such a plan from hunk h_1. Counterpart theory with respect to artifacts thus assigns a different truth condition to the sentence, one whose fulfillment seems beyond doubt.

In effect, counterpart theory replaces the intransitive accessibility relation with an intransitive counterpart relation. There are glaring technical differences between the two types of solutions to the modal paradoxes, however. (There are glaring moti-vational differences as well. The motivation for counterpart theory, as a solution to the modal paradoxes, is discussed in section V below.) First, certain intuitively correct premises involved in Chisholm's Paradox are counted unequivocally true on the ac-cessibility solution but cannot be thus accommodated on counterpart theory (as I have formulated it). Consider the argument (CP). Suppose again that in the sequence of hunks of matter, $h_1, h_2, \ldots, h_n$, some one hunk h_m is the first in the sequence to pass the threshold. Then on counterpart theory with respect to artifacts, the premise

(P_m) $\Box[M(a, h_{m-1}) \supset \Diamond M(a, h_m)]$

will not be true, since there is a world w_{m-1} in which a counterpart of table a is formed from hunk h_{m-1}, whereas at any world in which a table is formed from hunk h_m, that table, though a counterpart of the counterpart of a at w_{m-1}, is not a counterpart of a itself. (A similar situation obtains if the threshold is vague and there is a range of hunks $h_k, h_{k+1}, \ldots, h_{m-1}$ for which it is indeterminate whether a possible table formed from one of these hunks is a counterpart of a.) Thus whereas the accessibility solution blocks (CP) by counting it logically invalid, counterpart theory with respect to arti-facts (as I have formulated it) blocks (CP) by counting it logically valid but unsound.[11]

Another glaring difference between the two solutions to the modal paradoxes is brought out in their respective treatments of the Four Worlds Paradox. Although coun-terpart theory with respect to artifacts is able to accommodate $S5$ modal propositional logic, in so doing it foregoes certain valid inferences of standard quantified $S5$ modal logic. In particular, it is able to accommodate the truth of the necessitation of the modal principle (II), and of certain sorts of instances of it, like the fourth premise of the Four Worlds Paradox,

$\Box(x)[M(x, h') \supset \Diamond M(x, h'')]$.

In standard quantified modal logic, it follows from this together with the result

$\Diamond(\exists x)[x \neq a \ \& \ M(x, h')]$

and the trivial truism

$\Box(x)\Box[M(x, h'') \supset (\exists y)(y = x)]$

that

$\Diamond\Diamond(\exists x)[x \neq a \ \& \ M(x, h'')]$.

Counterpart theory with respect to artifacts invalidates this inference and thereby blocks the paradox. The accessibility solution, on the other hand, allows the inference, but invalidates further inference by possibility deletion. Thus both solutions to the Four Worlds Paradox count the argument of the paradox invalid, though on distinctly different grounds. Similarly, counterpart theory with respect to artifacts accommodates

$$\Box(x)[M(x, h_{m-1}) \supset \Diamond M(x, h_m)].$$

while blocking the inference from this together with '$\Box[M(a, h_{m-1}) \supset (\exists x)(x = a)]$' to the (CP) premise ($P_m$) displayed above

In the general case, if counterpart-theoretic possible-world semantics is devised in such a way as to preserve S5 modal propositional logic together with the philosophical institutions that motivate the theory, it foregoes the following modal version of universal instantiation, valid in standard quantified modal logic:

(MUI) $\dfrac{\Box(x)\phi_x}{\therefore \Box[(\exists x)(x = \alpha) \supset \phi_\alpha],}$

where α is a simple individual constant or individual variable other than 'x', ϕ_α is just like ϕ_x except for having free occurrences of α wherever ϕ_x has free occurrences of 'x', and ϕ_x may contain occurrences of modal operators. This deviation from standard quantified modal logic prevents the derivation of paradoxical conclusions from the necessitation of (II).[12]

IV

Each of the necessitated conditional premises of the argument (CP) is equivalent in S4 to an unnecessitated material conditional, so that the argument may be recast in S4 into the standard form of a sorites argument in classical propositional logic:

(CP)' $\Diamond M(a, h)$
$\Diamond M(a, h) \supset \Diamond M(a, h_1)$
$\Diamond M(a, h_1) \supset \Diamond M(a, h_2)$

$\vdots$

$\dfrac{\Diamond M(a, h_{n-1}) \supset \Diamond M(a, h_n)}{\therefore \Diamond M(a, h_n).}$

Forbes emphasizes this feature of Chisholm's Paradox and argues that the paradox should be treated in a manner exactly parallel, or as closely as possible, to a contemporary treatment of the standard propositional sorites paradox, such as the paradox of the short person:

Anyone only 5 ft. tall is short.

If anyone 5 ft. tall is short, then so is anyone 5

ft. $\dfrac{1}{1,000,000}$ in. tall.

$\vdots$

If anyone 5 ft. 11 and $\dfrac{999,999}{1,000,000}$ in. tall

is short, then so is anyone 6 ft. tall.

∴   Anyone 6 ft. tall is short.

Standard sorites paradoxes arise from vagueness in some key expression or concept. In the case of the paradox of the short person, the key term is the adjective 'short', which is clearly true of anyone (or at least, any adult human) only 5 feet tall, clearly false of anyone 6 feet tall, but neither clearly true nor clearly false with respect to a range of heights in between. Now one extremely plausible way of diagnosing the problem with this sorites argument is as follows. Assuming that the first premise of the argument is true and that the conclusion is false (its negation true), somewhere down the list of the 12 million conditional premises to the argument—in fact, at least twice, and most plausibly, a large number of times down the list—a conditional premise is neither true nor false. For somewhere down the list there is a conditional with a true antecedent but a consequent neither true nor false, followed by a sequence of conditionals with both antecedent and consequent neither true nor false, followed finally by a conditional with an antecedent neither true nor false and a false consequent. Each of these premises is itself neither true nor false. Thus the classical sorites argument in propositional logic is formally valid but unsound. Not all of its premises are true, even if none are strictly false.[13]

The solution to the modal paradoxes offered in Section II above allows for a treatment of (CP)′ exactly parallel to this. In particular, the critically vague term involved in (CP)′, if any (see note 3), is the accessibility predicate of possible-world discourse, and thereby the possibility operator '$\diamond$' occurring throughout (CP)′. A sentence $\ulcorner \diamond \phi \urcorner$ is true (*simpliciter*) if and only if ϕ is true with respect to some world determinately accessible to the actual world. The same sentence is false (*simpliciter*) if and only if ϕ is false with respect to every world determinately accessible to the actual world and untrue—either false or neither true nor false—with respect to every world neither determinately accessible nor determinately inaccessible to the actual world.[14] The intransitive accessibility account allows that there may be a hunk of matter h_k such that table a originates from it in some world neither determinately accessible nor determinately inaccessible to the actual world, but does not originate from it in any determinately accessible world. If this is so, $\ulcorner \diamond M(a, h_k) \urcorner$ is neither true nor false. Hence at least two of the conditional premises of (CP)′ will be neither true nor false, just as in the paradox of the short person. Insofar as it is desirable for a solution to (CP)′ to parallel as closely as possible a contemporary solution to the classical propositional sorites paradox, the indeterminate accessibility solution does exactly what is desired.

More important than this, the accessibility solution severs the alleged equivalence between (CP) and (CP)', and in fact, the original modal argument (CP) comes out differently in a very important respect from a standard sorites argument. Unlike the premise set of the propositional sorites argument (CP)', all of the premises of the original argument (CP) are determinately true, whereas its conclusion is determinately false. This reflects a crucially important difference between Chisholm's Paradox and the standard sorites paradox. It is important to remember that Chisholm's Paradox, as well as the Four Worlds Paradox and others belonging to the same class, are paradoxes of *modality*. Chisholm's Paradox is not a paradox in classical propositional logic, but a paradox in modal logic. The key feature of Chisholm's Paradox—the feature of it that makes it a peculiarly modal paradox—is its essential use of *nested modalities*. It proceeds from the observation that the truth of the modal principle (II) is no accident but is a necessary truth, thus yielding the nesting of modal operators in the modal premises of (CP). The intransitive-accessibility solution to Chisholm's Paradox properly distinguishes between the original argument (CP) and the propositional recasting (CP)', the latter being a familiarly valid but unsound argument in classical propositional logic and the former an interestingly invalid argument in modal logic. It is a critical defect in the counterpart-theoretic solution (as well as other rivals to the intransitive-accessibility solution) that it is blind to the crucial differences that separate the two cases. The modal paradoxes, as they naturally arise in pondering essentialist doctrines of the sort put forward in principle (III) (and as they did in fact arise in Chisholm's pioneering queries on the subject), are peculiarly modal in that they involve nested modality and depend upon the fallacy of possibility deletion, or equivalently, the presumption that accessibility between worlds is transitive. The counterpart-theoretic solution, in attempting to reduce the modal paradoxes to "the previous case" of standard sorites paradoxes such as the paradox of the short person, recommits the same fallacy and, in so doing, fails to recognize the rightful status, and consequently the proper lesson, of the modal paradoxes.

V

The fundamental defect of the counterpart-theoretic solution to the modal paradoxes is revealed when considering the motivation for invoking counterpart theory in attempting to solve the paradoxes. If Chisholm's Paradox is to be regarded on the model of the paradox of the short person, one must ask what term or expression involved in the former plays the role of the crucially vague term 'short' involved in the latter.

It cannot be expression '*a*' itself. In fact, it is not in the least bit clear what it would mean to say that a proper name—or an individual constant such as '*a*', which functions as a proper name—is "vague," unless it means that '*a*' is ambiguous or nonreferring. We may pretend, for present purposes, that the name '*a*' unambiguously refers to a particular table. The paradoxes still arise. It is even less clear what it would mean to say that the table *a* itself is vague, unless it means that the table has a vague *boundary,* in the sense that with respect to certain molecules at the periphery of the table, it is vague—indeterminate, neither true nor false, there is no objective fact of the matter—whether they are or are not constituents of the table. But vagueness in the table's boundary is not at issue here; the modal paradoxes would arise even if tables came with sharp boundaries.

Nor is there any relevant vagueness in the term 'table', or in the property of being a table. No doubt there are things such that it is vague whether they are to count as tables (as opposed to, say, counters or chests), but we may take it that a itself is a clear and central case of a table. The paradox still arises.

Nor is there any relevant vagueness in the hunks of matter h, h_1, ..., h_n. We may suppose that these are precisely given, with an exact accounting of every molecule included and the exact configuration of their totality. The paradox still arises. Nor is there any relevant vagueness in the relational concept of a table x being originally formed from a hunk of matter y according to such-and-such a plan. Wherein, then, does the vagueness reside?

One might try looking at the matter thus: In the short person paradox, there is a sequence of heights, 5 ft., 5 ft. $\dfrac{1}{1,000,000}$ in., ..., 6 ft., such that, though each height is precise and exact enough in itself, for some of these precisely delineated heights it is vague whether someone of that exact height counts as being *short*. Similarly, in the case of Chisholm's Paradox, we have a sequence of hunks of matter, h_1, h_2, ..., h_n, each precisely given, and a corresponding sequence of worlds, w_1, w_2, ..., w_n, such that in any world w_i there is a table a_i just like a except that it is originally formed from hunk h_i instead of from a's original matter, h. This sequence of possible tables, a_1, a_2, ..., a_n, plays the role analogous to that of the sequence of heights in the short person paradox. Each is precisely given, though for some it is vague whether the table still counts as being a or not. In the actual world, there is also a table just like a originally formed from hunk h. This table is a itself. In world w_n, the table a_n formed from hunk h_n is definitely not a, since by principle (III) there is no genuinely possible world in which a is formed from h_n. With respect to certain worlds w_k intermediate in the sequence between the actual world and w_n, it is vague—indeterminate, neither true nor false, there is no objective fact of the matter—whether the table a_k formed from hunk h_k in that world is or is not the very table a from the actual world. To use the contemporary vernacular, what is indeterminate is whether a_k has a's haecceity—the property of being identical with a—in w_k. Thus the vague concept involved in Chisholm's Paradox would appear to be that of *being identical with a in a possible world,* or more simply, *possibly being a.* More specifically, since the name 'a' is itself nonvague, the relevant vague concept involved would appear to be the relational concept of cross-world identity, or that of possible identity, expressed by '$\Diamond x = y$'. Evidently, this vagueness traces to vagueness in the very concept of identity itself. The ultimate source of the vagueness involved in Chisholm's Paradox thus appears to be the 'is' of identity.

Kripke, apparently having reasoned along lines similar to these, concludes that a counterpart-theoretic approach may be useful in dealing with the vagueness of identity in Chisholm's Paradox. He says that perhaps, . . . given certain counterfactual vicissitudes in the history of the molecule of a table, T, one may ask whether T would exist, in that situation, or whether a certain bunch of molecules, which in that situation would constitute a table, constitute the very same table T. . . . In concrete cases we may be able to answer whether a certain bunch of molecules would still constitute T, though in some cases the answer may be indeterminate. (*Naming and Necessity*, pp. 50–51)

In a footnote to this passage, he writes:

There is some vagueness here. If a chip, or molecule, of a given table had been replaced by another one, we would be content to say that we have the same table. But if too many chips were different, we would seem to have a different one. . . . Where the identity relation is vague, it may seem intransitive; a chain of apparent identities may yield an apparent nonidentity. Some sort of 'counterpart' notion . . . may have some utility here. One could say that strict identity applies only to the particulars (the molecules), and the counterpart relation to the particulars 'composed' of them, the tables. The counterpart relation can then be declared to be vague and intransitive. . . . Logicians have not developed a logic of vagueness. (p. 51, note 18)

There are a number of difficulties with this motivation for the counterpart-theoretic approach. Kripke's idea seems to be that where (the characteristic function of) the concept of identity is undefined, it may facilitate a semantic investigation if the identity concept is represented in the metalanguage by means of a surrogate relation, counterparthood, which is vague and intransitive. Now it may indeed facilitate a semantic investigation into the logic of a vague term or predicate such as 'bald' to consider various regimented or sharpened surrogates or approximations to the vague concept, precisely defined—say, in terms of an exact number of strands of hair on the top portion of the head per square inch of surface area. One might thus verify the validity of the inference $\ulcorner \alpha$ has a full head of hair $\therefore \alpha$ is not bald $\urcorner$. But Kripke is proposing that an allegedly vague concept, identity, be investigated in terms of *another vague concept*, counterparthood. It is difficult to see how there is anything to be gained in representing one vague concept by means of another. If our problem is that we lack a logic of vagueness, we can no more treat the latter than we can the former. If our purpose is to investigate the logic of identity among tables, surely we are better off sticking with genuine identity and doing the best we can, than turning our attention elsewhere only to find the same obstacles arise there.

Perhaps Kripke committed a slip of the pen here and meant to declare the counterpart relation to be *non*vague and intransitive—as opposed to genuine identity among tables, which it represents and which (we are to suppose) is vague but transitive. For example, one might define a relation of counterparthood in such a way that any possible table is a counterpart of itself, i.e., of a determinate self, whereas for any pair of possible tables a_i and a_j for which it is either false or vague (neither true nor false) that they are identical, neither counts as a counterpart of the other. This counterpart relation would thus play the facilitating role of a sharpened or regimented approximation to identity among tables and other artifacts.

Even when Kripke's proposal is modified in this way, it seems confused. It is quite unclear what it means to say that strict identity does not "apply" to tables. Suppose there is a possible table a_k such that a and a_k are neither determinately identical nor determinately distinct. Then on this interpretation of Kripke's proposal, a is a counterpart of a (itself) but not of a_k. It follows directly by Leibniz's Law, or the Indiscernibility of Identicals, that a and a_k are distinct, contradicting the hypothesis. (A similar argument applies if counterparthood is defined so that a and a_k are counterparts.)

The defender of this proposal may protest that within the counterpart-theoretic framework, one is barred from saying anything about the identity or distinctness of a and a_k. One can speak only about the cross-world similarity relations between a and a_k; one must settle for the weak claim that a and a_k are not counterparts. But the Leibniz's Law inference cries out to be drawn; if a is a counterpart of a but not of a_k, then a has a counterpart that a_k does not have. Whether we are allowed to say so or not, it follows that a and a_k *cannot be* one and the very same object and *must be* distinct. Our refraining or being prohibited from saying so does not make it any less true.

When the truth is spoken, incoherence is the result. Consider again the sequence of possible tables $a, a_1, a_2, \ldots, a_n$. Kripke's remarks concerning this sort of situation are highly compressed, and his exact intent is unclear. He says: "Where the identity relation is vague, it may *seem* intransitive; a chain of *apparent* identities may yield an *apparent* nonidentity" (emphasis added). Presumably, if "the identity relation is vague," then things that are *apparently* identical (or *apparently* distinct) need not be *determinately* identical (or *determinately* distinct). A pair of objects x and y may *appear* to be identical (or distinct) when in reality, there is no objective fact of the matter as to their identity (or their distinctness). Perhaps Kripke's view, then, is this: (i) any table in the sequence $a, a_1, a_2, \ldots, a_n$ appears to be identical to its immediate successor in the sequence; (ii) the initial table a and the final table a_n appear to be distinct; but (iii) in reality, for any pair of tables a_i and a_j where $i \neq j$, there is no objective fact of the matter concerning their identity or distinctness.

In that case, Kripke's view would involve rejection of both the modal principles (II) (since a and a_1 only *appear* identical) and (III) (since a and a_n only *appear* distinct). This is not a very satisfactory solution to the modal paradoxes. Both (II) and (III) are intuitively correct, even if it is vague what is to count as "sufficiently substantial overlap." In fact, if Kripke's view is that it is vague—or indeterminate, or neither true nor false, or there is no objective fact of the matter—whether tables a and a_n are distinct, then his view involves rejection of the modal principle (0), a principle that is both weaker than (III) and precisely formulated in a way that (III) is not. It would be difficult, if not impossible, to reconcile this consequence of Kripke's view with his attempt in the very same work to provide "something like proof" for principle (0), or a principle directly like it. (See note 2 above.)

Another possible view might be that in the sequence of possible tables $a, a_1, a_2, \ldots, a_n$, each element is determinately identical with its immediate successor, though there is some range of elements, $a_k, a_{k+1}, \ldots, a_{m-1}$, that are each neither determinately identical with nor determinately distinct from the initial element a, whereas the next element in the sequence, a_m, and all of its successors are determinately distinct from the initial element a. However, this is equally incoherent. If a and a_{k-1} are determinately identical, then they are *one and the very same*, and if a_{k-1} and a_k are determinately identical, then they are also one and the very same. But then there is only one table here. Which table? Well a, aka a_k. Tables a and a_k are one and the very same after all; they are determinately identical. Conversely, if a_m is determinately distinct from a, yet determinately one and the very same table as a_{m-1}, then a_{m-1} must be determinately distinct from a after all. Moreover, if each element in the sequence and its immediate successor are one and the very same, then what we have is simply an n-ary sequence of table a taken n times in a row. It is quite literally impossible for some element in this sequence to be distinct from a. Conversely, if any table in the sequence fails to be determinately identical with the initial table a, then the sequence is not simply the n-ary sequence of a taken n times in a row. Hence it is impossible for each element in the sequence to be one and the very same as its immediate successor.

The idea that the identity relation is vague, in the sense that its characteristic function is undefined for certain pairs of concrete objects like tables, is itself incoherent. In fact, it is provable that the identity concept, or the 'is' of identity, is totally defined for every pair of individuals. The proof, which was foreshadowed in the arguments just given, goes as follows: Suppose, on the contrary, that there is a pair of individuals, x and y, for which the 'is' of identity is undefined—a pair to which neither the predicate 'are one and the very same' nor its negation 'are not one and the very same' correctly applies. Then this pair $<x, y>$ is quite definitely *not* the same pair as the reflexive pair $<x, x>$, since the 'is' of identity—or the predicate 'are one and the very same'—does correctly apply to the latter. That is, the pair $<x, x>$ is an element of the extension of the 'is' of identity (the class of ordered pairs of which the predicate is determinately true), whereas the pair $<x, y>$ is not; hence, they are distinct. It follows by standard ZF set theory that $x \neq y$. But then, contrary to the hypothesis, the 'is' of identity is defined for the pair $<x, y>$. The 'is' of identity is determinately false of the pair; its negation correctly applies. The general form of this argument can be applied to a variety of philosophical issues concerning identity.[15]

In fact, this brief argument also proves that the concepts of identity within a possible world, i.e., intra-world identity, and of cross-world identity (and by analogy, identity at a time and identity over time) are also totally defined. For each is definable in terms of absolute, unrelativized identity as follows:

$$x =_w y =_{def.} x = y.$$
x in w_1 is identical with y in $w_2 =_{def.} x$ exists in
w_1 & y exists in w_2 & $x =_{w_1} (\imath z) [y =_{w_2} z]$.

Perhaps most important, Chisholm's Paradox and the other modal paradoxes do not even involve the concept or relation of identity. The paradoxes *can* be formulated in terms of possible identity or cross-world identity, but they can just as easily be formulated without identity. In fact, the 'is' of identity does not occur in either (CP) or (CP)′—not once, not anywhere. If (CP) and (CP)′ constitute a paradox of vagueness, the vagueness must reside in one or more of the terms actually used in the formulation. Since the identity predicate does not even occur, if there is any vagueness, it must reside elsewhere. It is a mistake to see Chisholm's Paradox as stemming from vagueness in identity.

Forbes's motivation for his counterpart-theoretic approach to Chisholm's Paradox is somewhat different from Kripke's, though he seems to mislocate the vagueness in the same place. He writes:

> [There] is no sharp distinction between those sums [of matter] which could, and those which could not, constitute [the table a]. Given that there is no fuzziness in the boundaries of particular sums of wood or in the constitution relation, it seems that this vagueness must arise from an underlying vagueness in the concept of possibly being identical to [a]; however, in standard [possible-world] semantics, such vagueness could only be represented by vagueness in [a's cross-world] identity conditions, and a solution of the paradox in which we think of identity as vague would be rather unappealing. But [it] does make sense to think of *similarity* as being vague, in the sense of admitting *degrees*. . . . [The] counterpart relation is fixed by similarity considerations—in the present context, similarity of design and constituting matter. ("Two Solutions to Chisholm's Paradox," p. 174)

Forbes's overall argument appears to be this: The orginal argument (CP) is equivalent in *S5* to (CP)$'$, a standard propositional sorites-type argument; hence it is simply a special case of a general and familiar sort of paradox of vagueness. Since the vagueness crucially involved in (CP)$'$ does not reside in the hunks of matter h_1, $h_2 \ldots, h_n$ or in the relation of being a table formed from such-and-such matter, it must reside in the concept of possibly being a. On the standard possible-world semantic analysis of modal-operator discourse, this would mean that there is vagueness in the identity relation itself. But the idea that identity is vague is "rather unappealing" as a solution to Chisholm's Paradox. Counterpart theory provides an alternative possible-world semantic analysis of modal-operator discourse in which the vagueness of possibly being a is derived not from vagueness in identity, but from vagueness in a relation of similarity, the relation of counterparthood. Therefore, a counterpart-theoretic approach should afford a superior solution to Chisholm's Paradox.

This motivation for the counterpart-theoretic solution, though apparently different from Kripke's, is defective in a related way. As I have already noted, neither the argument (CP) nor its alleged equivalent (CP)$'$ involves the concept of identity, and hence neither involves the concept of possibly being identical with a. If (CP)$'$ constitutes a paradox of vagueness, the vagueness must reside elswhere, in some concept essentially involved in the argument.

In fact, despite Forbes's motivational remarks, in his formal treatment the vagueness is indeed located elsewhere. Specifically, by invoking a counterpart theory in which the counterpart relation is vague, Forbes formally locates the vagueness involved in (CP) in a certain second-order modal concept: the concept of a property's being such that a might have had it. Formally, the crucially vague expression involved in (CP)$'$, according to Forbes's formal treatment, is $\ulcorner \Diamond \ldots a \ldots \urcorner$, or $\ulcorner$it might have been that $a \ldots \urcorner$; the crucially vague concept is that designated by '$\lambda F \Diamond F(a)$'.

Forbes's formal treatment may be correct in imputing vagueness to this modal locution, for if there is any vagueness relevantly involved in Chisholm's Paradox, it can be only in such locutions as this. However, it is not at all true that standard possible-world semantics can accommodate the vagueness of this locution only by treating identity as vague. In fact, even if identity is (incoherently) regarded as vague, that would not be sufficient to impute vagueness to the locution in question, since this locution does not involve the identity predicate. It involves only the sentential possibility operator and the proper name (individual constant) 'a'. We have already seen that the name 'a' is not a source of vagueness. Hence, if there is any vagueness relevantly involved in the modal paradoxes, it resides in the modal operators themselves, and the modal operators are precisely where Forbes's formal treatment ultimately locates the vagueness upon which the paradoxes turn.

We have also already seen that nothing so radical as a departure from standard possible-world semantics in favor of a counterpart-theoretic semantics is called for in order to accommodate vagueness in the modal operators. Standard possible-world semantics can accommodate the relevant vagueness in the modal operators in precisely the way I have suggested: one should treat the accessibility relation between worlds as itself vague (its characteristic function partially defined), so that certain pairs of worlds are neither determinately mutually accessible nor determinately mutually inaccessible. When fully worked out, this involves intransitivity in the accessibility relation via a region of indeterminacy, and hence an abandonment of *S4* modal logic in favor of something weaker or independent (such as the modal system *B*). This approach affords a solution to the modal paradoxes that accommodates vagueness precisely where it must arise, if anywhere, and it does so within the framework of standard possible-world semantics without resorting to the entirely unnecessary and unjustified tack of invoking counterparts in place of cross-world identities. This approach also recognizes a crucial difference between the modal paradoxes and the standard paradoxes of vagueness: the former turn on a fallacy special to modal logic—the fallacy of possibility deletion, or equivalently, the fallacy of necessity iteration.

The counterpart-theoretic approach is not merely unnecessary and unjustified. It is positively misleading, and logically distinctly counterintuitive. I shall develop these criticisms each in turn.

VI

Counterpart theory appears to provide an alternative to standard possible-world semantics that is able to accommodate modal principles like (0), (I), (II), and (III), and their multiple necessitations, within an *S5* framework (i.e., maintaining an equivalence accessibility relation) without generating the paradoxes. Yet as it is typically intended, counterpart theory with respect to artifacts accommodates precisely the opposite of (II): if a wooden table x is originally formed from a hunk of matter y, and y' is any hunk of matter distinct from y, then even if y' substantially overlaps y and is otherwise just like y, x is such that it *could not* have been originally formed from y' instead of from y. The reason for this is that, as it is typically intended, counterpart theory with respect to artifacts includes the basic tenet that possible artifacts formed in their respective possible worlds from distinct (even if substantially overlapping) hunks of matter are always themselves distinct (though they may be mutual counterparts). Thus if x is a wooden table originally formed from a hunk of matter y, and y' is a hunk of matter even only one atom or molecule different from y, the counterpart theorist with respect to artifacts would typically deny that there is a genuinely metaphysically possible scenario, a genuinely possible world, in which the one and only very table x—that very table and no other—is formed from y' instead of from y. The counterpart theorist will insist that, strictly speaking, if we are ever to have one and the very same table x—that very table and no other—existing in a counterfactual scenario that might have obtained, x must be originally formed in that scenario from exactly the same matter, atom for atom, quark for quark, right down to the tiniest of subatomic material components. For this reason, counterpart theory with respect to artifacts is, at bottom, a particularly inflexible brand of essentialism. The counterpart theorist with respect to artifacts can mouth the words 'x might have been formed from y' instead of from y', thereby seeming to advocate (II). But in counting this remark true and therefore assertible, the counterpart theorist means to be committed to nothing more than the availability of a possible scenario in which some table or other sufficiently similar to x—not necessarily x itself—is formed from y'. The counterpart theorist thus says one thing and means another.[16]

Forbes has responded to this objection by claiming that

> whether or not [counterpart] theory admits contingency [of the table x's original matter] . . . turns only on whether or not it [counterpart theory] is consistent with the truth of [the sentence 'x is formed from y, and might have existed without being formed from y'], and by this criterion, counterpart theory admits contingency beyond all question. ("Two Solutions to Chisholm's Paradox," p. 179)

This response involves a confusion—or perhaps an equivocation—between two distinct senses in which a theory may be said to "admit" or accommodate a principle or proposition.[17] A theory accommodates a proposition p in the primary sense if the theory embraces p itself, that is, if the proposition p is included as a part of the theory (or at least as a logical consequence of the theory in combination with uncontroversial premises). A theory may be said to accommodate a proposition p in a secondary sense if the theory (or the theory in combination with uncontroversial premises) logically entails the metatheoretic proposition that some particular sentence ϕ is true, where ϕ is in fact a formulation of, or expresses, the proposition p. These two kinds of accommodation should be sharply distinguished. Counterpart theory with respect to artifacts can indeed accommodate modal principles like (0), (I), (II), and (III) in the secondary sense. But this sort of accommodation is deceptive, since as it is typically intended, counterpart theory with respect to artifacts fails to accommodate the critical principle (II) in the primary sense. Consider, by analogy, the following simple theory: (1) A table's exact original matter is always an essential feature of the table; (2) snow is white; and (3) the sentence 'Any particular wooden table might have been formed from metal instead of wood' means in English that snow is white. Call this theory'T'. (To dispel the appearance of inconsistency, imagine the theory T being formulated in Chinese.) The theory T can hardly be said to admit contingency of original matter in any relevant sense, though it does accommodate (II) in the secondary sense. Like counterpart theory with respect to artifacts, the theory T avoids the modal paradoxes by *rejecting* the modal principle (II)—not the *formulation* of (II) given above, but the proposition (II) itself. It may not be entirely futile, but it would be a difficult matter indeed to argue the merits of the doctrine of contingency of original matter with a proponent of T. The advocate of T will apparently join in singing the praises of (II), but the agreement is merely verbal.

Forbes argues that to see counterpart theory on this model, as an inflexible essentialist theory that misrepresents the meanings of modal-operator-discourse formulations of principles such as (II), is

> to think of the extensional sentences of [possible-world discourse] as having some meaning given independently [of modal-operator discourse]. . . . But this conception of [the relation between the two types of discourse] is not very plausible. . . . The threat is that . . . we would have to . . . identify possible worlds with logical constructions of actual entities; and . . . [this identification] has recently been shown [by Alan McMichael] to be problematic. It seems better to think of the meanings of [sentences of possible-world discourse] as being given by those of the modal [-operator-discourse sentences] themselves (so far as this is possible). . . . [In giving the meanings of sentences of possible-world discourse by means of sentences of modal-operator discourse] it would be up to the theorist himself to decide just how to proceed, given his purposes. . . . But from this starting point, one cannot think of the sentences of either [standard or counterpart-theoretic possible world] semantics as yielding perspicuous representations of the 'real' meanings of the modal [-operator-discourse] sentences. . . . Yet Salmon's criticism makes sense only if we think of [possible-world discourse] in these unlikely ways. (ibid., pp. 179–80)

Forbes's conception of the nature and content of possible-world semantics raises large issues concerning the enterprise of semantics generally, issues too broad in scope to be debated adequately in the present forum. It is worth noting, though, that Forbes's conception of the nature of possible-world semantics is distinctly inplausible when extended to temporal semantics for tensed discourse, though Forbes has also suggested that some sort of temporal-counterpart theory may be useful in solving temporal paradoxes analogous to the modal paradoxes.[18] Semantics for tensed discourse usually employs the notion of a time t—perhaps a moment of time or an interval of time—and the relation of earlier-later between times. A semantics for tensed discourse can also be developed using the idea of an *instantaneous total state of the cosmos,* or what I shall call an *i.s.,* and the relation of temporal precedence between successive instantaneous states (assuming no instantaneous state of the cosmos is ever repeated). Using instantaneous states of the cosmos in place of times better emphasizes the analogy between temporal semantics and possible-world semantics. In *i.s.*

semantics for tensed discourse, the semantic attributes of reference, application (of a predicate), and truth value are relativized to *i.s.* 's. On the natural semantic development, a sentence of the form $\ulcorner$ It has been the case that $\phi \urcorner$ is true with respect to an *i.s.* *i* if and only if ϕ is true with respect to some *i.s.*, or some succession of consecutive *i.s.* 's, that precede *i*. Similar clauses may be given for other temporal operators ('it is going to be the case that', 'it has always been the case that', and so on). Now perhaps the meaning of the phrase 'instantaneous total state of the cosmos' is such that it can be explained, or is in fact learned, only by means of tense or other temporal operators; perhaps not. In either case, the phrase has a relatively clear meaning, and contrary to the spirit of Forbes's remarks, this meaning determines the correct correspondence between a sentence of temporal-operator discourse and the expression of its truth condition in *i.s.*-discourse, not vice versa. It is not the prerogative of the semanticist to devise whatever semantic clauses suit his or her philosophical interests and temperament.

Consider, for example, the sentence 'Bill has been baptized'. On the natural semantic development, this sentence is true in English with respect to the present *i.s.* if and only if Bill is baptized in some prior succession of consecutive *i.s.* 's. It is quite incredible to suppose that a philosopher particularly fond of the idea of cross-time resemblance is free to select some other truth condition for this sentence more to his or her liking. A temporal-counterpart theorist might tell us that on his or her theory, the tensed sentence 'Bill has been baptized' is translated into the following sentence of *i.s.*-discourse:

> In some succession of consecutive instantaneous total states of the cosmos that precede the present instantaneous total state, someone bearing such-and-such a resemblance to Bill, as he presently is, is baptized.

The claim that this sentence means simply that Bill has been baptized is bizarre. Even if Bill is now remarkably like his great-grandfather used to be, the fact that his great-grandfather was baptized has no bearing semantically on the truth in English of 'Bill has been baptized'. Of course, one could decide to use the *i.s.*-discourse sentence displayed above in such a way that it is, in effect, a semantically unstructured *idiom,* one that means simply that Bill has been baptized (in the way that the phrase 'kick the bucket' means to die), but such a decision involves a misleading and radical departure from English. The point of introducing such misleading idioms into semantics would be utterly mysterious. Why not use the original straightforward formulations in temporal-operator discourse?

The fact is that sentences of *i.s.*-discourse do not function in *i.s.* semantics as unstructured idioms, whether standard *i.s.* semantics or temporal-counterpart-theoretic *i.s.* semantics. On the contrary, it is the very internal semantic structure of *i.s.*-discourse sentences that makes *i.s.*-discourse suitable for the enterprise of doing a systematic semantics for a tensed language. In fact, the very existence of the theory of instantaneous states and cross-time counterparthood offered by the temporal-counterpart theorist gives the lie to the claim that the meaning of an *i.s.*-discourse sentence (such as the one displayed above) is fixed by its alleged analogue in tensed discourse

('Bill has been baptized'). Rather, the meaning of an *i.s.*-discourse sentence is fixed in the usual way, by the meanings of its components—including the meanings of 'instantaneous total state of the cosmos', 'precede', 'present', and 'resemblance', as they arise in formulating the temporal-counterpart theory. Thus the *i.s.*-discourse sentence displayed above has a meaning that involves the temporal-counterpart theorist's concept of cross-time resemblance. It cannot mean the same thing as the tensed discourse sentence 'Bill has been baptized', for the proposition that Bill has been baptized involves no concept of resemblance, and hence it does not involve the particular resemblance concept given in the temporal-counterpart theory and expressed in the proposed *i.s.*-discourse translation. The same is true if reference to persisting objects is replaced with reference to temporal stages of persisting objects, and if cross-time resemblance is replaced with a notion of spatiotemporal continuity.

Consider now a contemporary follower of Heraclitus who holds that one cannot step into the same river in the same spot twice—i.e., in two different instantaneous states of the cosmos—because new water is continuously flowing through. The contemporary Heraclite (perhaps unlike Heraclitus himself) believes that, in general, the matter that constitutes an object (e.g., the water in a river) is a permanent and unchanging feature of the object. A contemporary Heraclite may devise an elaborate temporal-counterpart theory with respect to material objects to make it possible to "speak with the vulgar"—to utter sentences like 'The Mississippi River once had cleaner water flowing through it than it now has'—but then this clever Heraclite does not mean by this sentence what the rest of us mean, or what the sentence itself means. Any such pronouncement in tensed discourse by this philosopher is merely a verbal camouflage. When the Heraclite says 'The Mississippi is the same river today as yesterday', he or she does not mean the word 'same' in the "strict and philosophic sense," but rather in what he or she believes is a "loose and popular sense," i.e., as a word for temporal counterparthood.[19]

The phrase 'possible world' may not be as clear in meaning as the phrase 'instantaneous total state of the cosmos', but there are a number of conceptions of possible worlds presently in vogue, each of which is clear enough to substantiate my labeling of counterpart theory as a particularly inflexible brand of essentialism. Possible worlds are variously construed as maximal compossible sets of propositions (Robert Adams), total histories the world might have had (Saul Kripke), maximal states of affairs that might have obtained (Alvin Plantinga), total states the cosmos might have been in (Saul Kripke, Robert Stalnaker), total scenarios that might have obtained (myself). For present purposes, these need not be regarded as competing conceptions of possible worlds. If the phrase 'possible world' is unclear in meaning, any of these clearer phrases may be substituted.[20] It is of course true that each of these explications of what a possible world is involves notions from modal-operator discourse: *possibile, compossibile,* or *might have.* The notion of a possible world is defined in terms of concepts like *might have,* rather than vice versa. In this sense, the meanings of sentences of possible-world discourse are not "given independently" of modal-operator discourse. But they do have meaning, and just as in the case of tensed and *i.s.*-discourse, the meanings of sentences in possible-world discourse determine the semantic clauses for modal-operator discourse, and not the other way around. It is not the prerogative of the semanticist to stipulate whatever semantic clauses suit his or her philosophical interests and temperament. The sentence 'Bill might have been a robot' is true if and only if there is a possible scenario—or a possible history, or a possible state of affairs, or a possible state of the cosmos—in which Bill is a robot. The availability of a possible scenario in which not Bill but something rather like Bill in such-and-such respects is a robot is entirely irrelevant.

As in the case of tensed and *i.s.*-discourse, the very existence of the counterpart theorist's theory of possible worlds and counterparthood as a relation of cross-world similarity gives the lie to Forbes's claim about what fixes the meanings of the possible-world-discourse sentences that allegedly give the truth conditions of sentences in modal-operator discourse. The meanings of possible-world-discourse sentences are fixed in the usual way, by the meanings of their grammatical components—including the word 'counterpart', as it arises in the counterpart-theorist's formulation of his or her theory. Another indication of this is the fact that Forbes relies on possible-world discourse, rather than on untutored modal-operator-discourse intuition, as the court of last arbitration to determine the fine detail of which inferences in modal-operator discourse are to count as a valid and which are to count as invalid. The very enterprise of a systematic possible-world semantics for modal logic would be impossible if the sentence giving the truth-in-a-model condition for a particular object language sentence has its meaning fixed by the object language sentence itself.

The fact that counterpart-theoretic semantics misinterprets modal-operator discourse is made evident by the logic the former imposes on the latter. We have already seen that if counterpart theory is devised in such a way as to preserve S5 modal propositional logic, it typically invalidates certain special cases of an intuitively valid modal variant of universal instantiation, (MUI), which permits the inference from ⌜Necessarily, everything is ϕ⌝ to ⌜Necessarily, if α exists, then it is ϕ⌝, where α is a simple singular term. (See note 12.) The misinterpretation of modal-operator discourse is made even more plain if a predicate for the intra-world analogue of counterparthood is added to the latter. For if the counterpart theory includes the usual constraint that all of a possible individual's existing counterparts within a given world are counterparts at that world of anything that the object is itself a counterpart of at that world, then the theory validates the intuitively fallacious inference from

$$\Diamond(\exists x)\,[x \text{ is a counterpart of } a \text{ \& } F(x)]$$

to

$$\Diamond F(a).$$

The validity of this inference in counterpart-theoretic modal logic illustrates the weak interpretation placed on simple possibility sentences such as 'Bill might have been a robot'. Normally, if someone were to utter this sentence, he or she would mean something considerably stronger than, if not entirely independent of, whatever may be entailed by the claim that there might have been a robot counterpart of Bill.[21]

VII

The various explications of possible worlds given in the preceding section support the legitimacy of the idea of an impossible world, as well as the intransitive-accessibility account of the modal paradoxes. Just as there are such things as maximal compossible sets of propositions, there are also such things as maximal consistent but not compossible sets of propositions. If there are such things as total histories the world might have had, maximal states of affairs that might have obtained, and total states the cosmos might have been in, then there are also such things as total histories the world could not have had, maximal states of affairs that could not have obtained, and total states the cosmos could not have been in. Some of these impossible worlds are such that they might have been possible worlds instead of impossible worlds; their modal status as possible or impossible is a contingent feature of them. In fact, among the impossible worlds are those that might have been possible, those that could not have been possible but might have been such that they might have been possible, those that could not have been such that they might have been such that they might have been possible but might have been such that they might have been, and so on, perhaps to infinity. In any case, for some fairly large finite number n, there are worlds that are not possible in the nth degree (not possibly possibly . . . $(n - 1)$ times) . . . possible), but that might have been, i.e., they are possible in the $(n + 1)$th degree. Consider, for example, the possible total scenario (history of the world, and so on) w_1 in which everything is just as it actually is except that the table a is formed from the hunk of matter h_1 instead of from hunk h (and whatever other differences are required by this difference in order to ensure genuine possibility). The total scenario (history, and so on) w_2, that is just like w_1 except that table a is formed from hunk h_2 instead of from h_1, is a possible scenario relative to scenario w_1. That is, in scenario w_1, scenario w_2 is a possible scenario. Eventually, there is a total scenario w_m that is not possible relative to the actual total scenario, i.e., that is not a genuinely possible scenario, but that might have been. That is, w_m is possible in the second degree, but not in the first. Similarly, as we have seen, the total scenario w_{2m}, in which table a is formed from hunk h_{2m}, is possible in the third degree, but not in the second, and hence not in the first. Even the total scenario w_n, in which table a is formed from entirely different matter, is possible in some sufficiently large degree, though presumably it is not possible in only the second or third degree.

Thus far I have ignored the fact that certain sentences may be neither true nor false, perhaps in virtue of a false presupposition, as with the occurrence of a nonreferring definite description (e.g., Russell's 'The present king of France is bald'), or in virtue of the occurrence of a vague predicate (e.g., 'Louis is bald', where Louis has enough hair on his head so that he is not determinately bald but not enough hair so that he is determinately not bald). When we take note of this fact, it emerges that possible worlds are not *maximal* or *total* in the ordinary sense. For example, the proposition that the present king of France is bald is arguably neither true nor false in the actual world, so that the set of true propositions includes neither this proposition nor its negation (the proposition that the present king of France is not bald). If the actual world is just the set of true propositions, then a possible world may be a compossible set of propositions that falls short of being genuinely maximal. Similarly, if the actual world is the true history of the world, or the total state the cosmos is in, and so on, then since the true history of the world, and the total state the cosmos is in, include nothing that determines that the present king of France is bald and also nothing that determines that the present king of France is not bald, a possible world may fall short of being *total* in the sense of deciding 'yes' or 'no' on every possible question of fact. Still, of course, a possible world must approach maximality or totality as closely as possible. A possible world must be *maximal* or *total* in the weaker sense that for any proposition or question of fact p left undecided, there must be enough propositions or questions of fact decided (e.g., that there is no present king of France, or that the number of hairs on the top portion of Louis's head per square inch of surface area is n) to determine that there is no objective fact of the matter concerning p.

This observation supports the feasibility of the indeterminate-accessibility account of the modal paradoxes sketched in section II above. A total (in the weak sense) scenario w' is accessible to a total scenario w if and only if it is a fact in w that w' might have obtained. If the notion of possibility is itself vague, there will be total (in the weak sense) scenarios w_k such that the actual total scenario includes nothing about whether w_k might have obtained or not. World w_k would thus be neither determinately accessible nor determinately inaccessible to the actual world, in the same way that some people are neither determinately bald nor determinately not bald in the actual world.

Forbes objects to these conceptions of what possible worlds are by endorsing a criticism, due to Alan McMichael,[22] that a theory of such entities as maximal compossible sets of propositions or maximal states of affairs that confines itself to things that actually exist—an *actualist* theory of such entities—is problematic. McMichael's criticism, very briefly, is this. The following sentence involving nested modalities is true:

> S: It might have been the case that there exists someone who: (a) does not actually exist; (b) is bald; and (c) might have existed without being bald.

Following the standard approach rather than the counterpart-theoretic approach, S is true if and only if there is a possible world w in which there exists an individual x such that (a) x does not exist in the actual world; (b) x is bald in w; and (c) there is a world w' accessible to w in which x exists but is not bald. McMichael argues that this truth condition apparently cannot be fulfilled within an actualist theory of possible worlds. Suppose for example that possible worlds are identified with maximal compossible sets of states of affairs. Then in order for S's truth condition to be fulfilled, it seems there would have to be one such set w that includes the state of affairs of there existing an individual x who does not actually exist and who is bald, and another such set w' that includes the states of affairs of x's existing and x's not being bald. But since x does not actually exist, there are no such states of affairs as x's existing or x's not being bald, and hence no such set as w'.

The argument here is fallacious, though exposing the fallacy is a delicate matter. No such set as w' is required to exist for the truth of S. Exactly what is required is the existence of a maximal compossible set w of states of affairs that includes the complex state of affairs of there existing an individual x such that: (a) the state of affairs of x's existing does not actually obtain; (b) x is bald, and (c) there is a maximal compossible set of states of affairs w' that includes the states of affairs of x's existing and x's not being bald. This in turn requires the existence, and the possibly obtaining, of the state of affairs of there existing some individual or other who is bald, whose existence does not actually obtain, and whose existence while not being bald might have obtained. But it in no way requires the existence of either the state of affairs of this nonactual individual's existence or of his or her not being bald.

We may put the matter this way: Suppose that possible worlds are maximal compossible sets of propositions. Now it has been observed by a number of philosophers, including McMichael, that within an actualist framework, a set of possibly true propositions may be maximal (in either the strong or weak sense) and yet may include some particular existential generalization without including any singular instance of it. This occurs when the existential generalization is such that no actual entity yields an instance that is possibly true. For example the proposition expressed by '$(\exists x)$ [x does not actually exist]', though false, is such that it might have been true. Since there is no actual entity that can serve as the relevant constituent of a possibly true singular instance of this existential generalization, however, there is no singular instance that is possibly true. Now in order for S to be true, there must be a maximal (in the weak sense) compossible set w of propositions that includes the proposition expressed by the sentence:

$(\exists x)$ [x does not actually exist & x is bald & $(\exists w')$ (w' is possible & the proposition *that x exists and is not bald* $\in w'$)].

As was just indicated, w will include no singular instance of this proposition, since there are none to be included. More importantly, however, the sentence displayed above is equivalent to the following:

$(\exists w')$ [w' is possible & $(\exists x)$ (x does not actually exist & x is bald & the proposition *that x exists and is not bald* $\in w'$)].

This sentence also expresses precisely the sort of existential proposition that is possibly true but has no possibly true singular instance. What the truth of S requires is the existence, and the possible truth, of this existential proposition; it does not require the existence of any singular instance of it.

VIII

My criticisms of counterpart theory are independent of the logic of vagueness that may be supplied to supplement the theory. In fact, the logic of vagueness is all but irrelevant to the main idea behind a counterpart-theoretic approach to the modal paradoxes. Forbes proposes treating the counterpart relation as itself vague and a matter of degree. Essentially the same account results from speaking of *determinate counterparts* in place of counterparts *simpliciter*—where, if it is indeterminate to some degree whether x is a counterpart of y, then it is determinately true that x is not a determinate counterpart of y.

Following J. A. Goguen,[23] Forbes proposes to treat the sort of vagueness found in concepts like that of being short or that of being similar by means of infinitely many *degrees of truth and falsehood* in place of the conventional all-or-nothing dichotomy of truth and falsehood. Accordingly, on Forbes's theory, a sentence containing a vague term may be wholly true, almost wholly true, more true than false, equally as true as false, more false than true, almost wholly false, or wholly false. Degrees of truth and falsehood are represented by means of the real numbers between 0 and 1, inclusive, where 1 represents complete truth, 0 represents complete falsehood, and the sum of the degree of truth of a sentence and its degree of falsehood (the degree of truth of its negation) is 1.

Many find the idea of a sentence being (unambiguously) partly true and partly false grating. Truth and falsehood appear to be mutually exclusive absolutes; nothing ''partly false'' is genuinely and literally true in the ordinary sense. But it would be a mistake to conclude that the concept of degrees of truth and falsehood is utterly without merit in the logic of vagueness. To illustrate: suppose there are two men, Smith and Jones, for whom it is vague—indeterminate, neither true nor false, there is no objective fact of the matter—whether either is bald. Ordinarily, though neither of the two men has little enough hair to qualify as determinately bald, one of the two, say Smith, will be ''balder'' than the other, in the sense that Smith has proportionately less hair on the top portion of his head per square inch of surface area than does Jones. Neither is determinately bald, but Smith is ''closer'' to being determinately bald than Jones is. Although the adjective 'bald' is neither true nor false of both men, it is closer to being true of Smith than it is to being true of Jones. The sentence 'Smith is bald' is closer to being true than is the sentence 'Jones is bald', though neither sentence is true (and neither is false). One may decide to put this another way by saying that both sentences partake of a certain ''degree of truth'' less than the ''maximal degree,'' and that the first is ''more true'' than the second. It does not follow, of course, that the first sentence is true *simpliciter*—any more than Smith's being taller than Jones entails that Smith is tall.

Similarly, though the proportion of hair on Smith's head does not fall squarely into either the category *bald* or the category *not bald,* in all likelihood it is closer to one end of the scale than to the other. Suppose that Smith is such that if he were to lose just a very few more strands of hair, he would become determinately bald rather than indeterminate with respect to baldness, whereas if he grew as many strands of hair, he would remain indeterminate with respect to baldness. Then the sentence 'Smith is bald', though neither true nor false, is closer than its negation to being true; it is closer to being true than it is to being false. One might put this by saying that it is ''more true than false,'' though strictly speaking, of course, it is neither. This interpretation provides significance to the notion of ''degrees of truth'' in the logic of vagueness.

The important point about this construal of a degrees-of-truth approach should not be obscured by the somewhat misleading jargon of a sentence being "more true than false" or "more false than true." A sentence that is true *simpliciter* is now being said to be "wholly" or "completely" true, or true "to the maximum degree," and a sentence that is false *simpliciter* is now being said to be "wholly" or "completely" false, or false "to the maximum degree." A sentence said to be only "partly true," or "less than but almost wholly true," is not true at all, and a sentence said to be "less than but almost wholly false" is not false at all. On the construal I am suggesting of the degrees-of-truth approach, the classical three-way division among *true, false,* and *neither true nor false* is built into that approach—as maximal truth, maximal falsehood, and everything in between. The range of degrees of truth between maximal falsehood and maximal truth, exclusive, are nothing more than gradations of the traditional category of *neither true nor false,* so that classical three-valued logics emerge as subtheories of analogous degrees-of-truth approaches. If a sentence is said to be "more true than false," or "almost but not quite wholly true," it is neither true nor false, though in the sense sketched above it is closer to being true than to being false.

This interpretation of the degrees-of-truth machinery evidently clashes with Forbes's intent. First, Forbes has denounced the traditional three-way division among *true, false,* and *neither* as arbitrary, whereas on the construal suggested this division is embedded in the degrees-of-truth approach.[24] More important, Forbes's definition of *validity* in the logic of vagueness does not accord well with the suggested construal of the nature of the truth value status represented by real numbers between 0 and 1. Forbes calls an argument or inference pattern 'valid' roughly, if in any model, its conclusion is at least as true as the least true of its premises (more accurately, if in any model, the degree of truth of the conclusion is at least as great as the greatest lower bound of the degrees of truth of the premises). This leads him to brand *modus ponens* an invalid inference pattern, since in his logic of vagueness, a conditional that is neither (wholly) true nor (wholly) false may be closer to being true (have a "greater degree of truth") than either its antecedent or its consequent taken individually. Forbes calls the inference pattern of *modus ponens* 'the fallacy of detachment' and blames the standard sorites paradoxes on this alleged fallacy. He sees the choice between the accessibility solution to the modal paradoxes and the counterpart-theoretic approach as a choice between rejecting *S5* modal logic while consequently treating the two arguments (CP) and (CP)′ differently, on the one hand, and rejecting *modus ponens* while treating the two arguments equivalently, on the other. Since *modus ponens* must be rejected in any case, Forbes argues, the counterpart-theoretic approach is superior to the accessibility approach. It retains *S5* modal logic while allegedly reducing (CP) to a familiar paradox of vagueness in classical propositional logic.

Can it be that *modus ponens* is a fallacious inference pattern and that this is the fallacy involved in the traditional sorites paradoxes, such as the paradox of the short person? I can think of no inference pattern whose validity is more obvious than *modus ponens.* Rather than place myself in the hopeless position of Achilles, though, I will say here only that the validity of *modus ponens* is certainly more intuitively obvious and compelling than the alleged validity of the *S4* axiom of modal logic, or equivalently, the inference pattern of necessity iteration (possibility deletion). If the choice were as Forbes sees it, the accessibility approach should be the winner beyond all question!

In fact, though, Forbes has posed a false dichotomy. An inference pattern is properly *valid* if and only if it is truth-preserving. i.e., if and only if for every instance, its conclusion is true in every model in which its premises are true. This is the proper notion of validity even in the logic of vagueness. In a degrees-of-truth logic of vagueness, as I have proposed construing it, an inference pattern is valid (properly so-called) if and only if it preserves "complete truth" or "truth to the maximum degree." By this criterion, *modus ponens* is unquestionably valid even on the degrees-of-truth account. Why place the blame for paradoxes of vagueness on *modus ponens*? In fact, the traditional sorites argument in classical propositional logic is perfectly valid. What goes wrong in a standard sorites paradox, such as the paradox of the short person, is not that the argument is invalid, but that it is unsound. Not all of the conditional premises are (wholly) true. At least two are neither true nor false. In the terminology of the degrees-of-truth approach, at least two conditional premises are "partly true and partly false," or "less than wholly true but true to some degree." The paradox of the short person is dissolved by noting that one should not attempt to establish conclusions by reasoning from premises that are untrue—even if they may be said to be "almost wholly true" in the sense sketched above. Almost is simply not good enough.

The intransitive-accessibility account rejects *S4* and accommodates both of the modal principles (II) and (III) in both the primary and secondary senses, whereas the counterpart-theoretic approach, as I have devised it, retains *S5* but fails to accommodate (II) in the primary sense. This is the real choice. The paraphernalia of degrees-of-truth, the alleged loose and popular sense of 'identity', cross-world counterparts, so-called identity from the point of view of a particular world, and the rest, tend to obscure the point.

IX

On the intransitive-accessibility account that I advocate, there are distinct yet purely qualitatively identical worlds in which the very same matter exists in exactly the same configuration, and in which all matter undergoes exactly the same physical processes, down to the finest detail, throughout all of time. This is not quite the same as the apparent conclusion ($C2$) of the second version of the Four Worlds Paradox, which is surely unacceptable. It is open for the accessibility theorist to argue (as I have elsewhere) that any two distinct such worlds are mutually inaccessible and are not both (determinately) accessible to the actual world. In modal-operator discourse, the accessibility account yields the following conclusion, where p is a (the) materially complete proposition that would have been true if table a had been formed from hunk h'' [$=h_{m-1}$] rather than from hunk h:

($C3$) $\Diamond[p \& M(a, h'')] \& \Diamond\Diamond[p \& \sim M(a, h'')]$.

Some philosophers have objected to this conclusion on the basis of a principle of the identity of materially indiscernible worlds, i.e., worlds in which the same materially complete proposition is true.[25] Conclusion ($C3$) is in fact perfectly compatible with any reasonable version of the Identity of Indiscernibles. Moreover it can be modified to show that the principle of the identity of materially indiscernible worlds in fact contradicts classical Indiscernibility of Identicals. This can be seen through consideration of another conclusion correctly obtainable from the assumptions of the Four Worlds Paradox:

$$\Diamond\Diamond M(a, h').$$

If table a had been formed from hunk h'' instead of from hunk h, then it *would have been* possible for it to have been formed from hunk h' instead of from hunk h''. Let p' be a (the) materially complete proposition that would have been such that it would have been true if table a had been formed from hunk h', if only table a had been formed from hunk h'' instead of from hunk h. Take care here. Since a could not have been formed from h', it is arguable that any proposition, and hence any materially complete proposition, would have been true if a had been formed from h', or alternatively, that no proposition, and hence no materially complete proposition, would have been true if a had been formed from h'. Though it is not *in fact* possible for a to have been formed from h', it *might have been* possible, and indeed it would have been possible if only a had been formed from h''. Proposition p' is a (the) materially complete proposition such that: if a had been formed from h'', then it would have been the case that if a had been formed from h', then p' would have been true. Then we have:

$(C4)$ $\Diamond[p' \And \sim M(a, h')] \And \Diamond\Diamond[p' \And M(a, h')] \And \sim\Diamond[p' \And M(a, h')].$

More intuitively there is a world w accessible to the actual world in which a table distinct from a is formed from hunk h'. There is also a world w' accessible to some world accessible to the actual world (through none accessible to the actual world itself) which is exactly like w in every detail concerning the very matter it contains, with its exact configuration and causal interconnections throughout time, atom for atom, quark for quark, but in which a is the table formed from hunk h'. Worlds w and w' are materially, and hence also purely qualitatively, indistinguishable. Exactly the same material facts obtain in both. Though they are materially indiscernible, they differ in their accessibility relations. World w is accessible to the actual world, whereas world w' is not. Hence, by the Indiscernibility of Identicals, the two worlds are distinct.

An unbridled principle of the identity of materially indiscernible worlds is refuted by the example of the worlds w and w'. Though materially indiscernible, the worlds w and w' are indeed discernible, and not merely by their accessibility relations to the actual world. They also differ as regards which facts obtain in them. World w' includes the fact that a is the table formed from hunk h', whereas world w excludes this. In w, some table distinct from a is the table formed from hunk h'. It follows again by the Indiscernibility of Identicals that the worlds w and w' are distinct.

The temptation to identify the worlds w and w' may stem, in part, from misconceiving possible worlds as material objects, or as entities made solely of matter.[26] Possible worlds are abstract entities whose structure comes from the facts that obtain in them. We saw in section VI that worlds may be conceived as maximal (in the weak sense) consistent sets of propositions, or total (in the weak sense) histories or states of the cosmos, or maximal states of affairs, or total scenarios, and so on. Consider the first conception: worlds as maximal consistent sets of propositions. Then w and w' are maximal consistent sets that both include the materially complete proposition p' as an element. The set w' includes the further proposition that the table formed from hunk h' is a, whereas the set w includes the further proposition that the table formed from hunk h' is some table distinct from a. Both sets are maximal consistent. Thus both are equally legitimate as worlds *per se*. Through they are not disjoint, they are unquestionably distinct sets.

Similar remarks may be made with respect to any of the alternative conceptions of the worlds w and w'. In fact, these various conceptions of worlds strongly suggest an alternative to simple material indiscernibility as a criterion for identity between worlds. They suggest a principle of the identity of *factually* indiscernible worlds, worlds in which the very same facts obtain. One might also endorse an independent principle of the identity of mutually accessible materially indiscernible worlds (a version of the supervenience thesis mentioned at the end of section I above) or a principle of the identity of materially indiscernible worlds accessible to the actual world. On any of the conceptions of worlds mentioned here, an unrestricted principle of the identity of simply materially indiscernible worlds is straightforwardly false.

X

Forbes has raised a second sort of objection to the intransitive-accessibility solution to the modal paradoxes. He argues that if we consider essentialist principles like (III), "we see that there is a conceptual character to such claims," and that metaphysical necessity is "fundamentally an *a priori* matter, to do with the content of our concepts [for example, our concepts of a table and of original matter], even though with the addition of *a posteriori* information, necessary *a posteriori* truths can be inferred."[27] Furthermore, "any *a posteriori* truth p necessary at the actual world is so by being true at the actual world and by some conceptual [*a priori*] truth's entailing that p's truth makes it necessary."[28] Since metaphysical necessity is thus the product of conceptual *a priority*, Forbes argues, every instance of the *S4* axiom schema is indeed true. For if it is conceptually *a priori*, and consequently necessary, that p, then it is also conceptually *a priori* that it is conceptually *a priori* that p. And if it is necessary but *a posteriori* that p, then it is nevertheless conceptually *a priori*, and consequently necessary, that if p then it is necessary that p. From this it follows (in even the weak system T of modal propositional logic) that if it is necessary but *a posteriori* that p, then it is still necessary that it is necessary that p.

It may be true that conceptual *a priority* entails metaphysical necessity, in the sense that (with somewhat rare, and for present purposes irrelevant, exceptions) anything that is conceptually *a priori* is generally *ipso facto* metaphysically necessary. Probably something like this accounts for the fact that (II) is not only necessarily true, but it is also necessary that it is necessarily true, and it is necessary that it is necessary that it is necessarily true, and so on. As Forbes acknowledges in presenting his argument, there are examples—coming primarily from the work of Kripke—of propositions that are metaphysically necessary yet conceptually *a posteriori*. With respect to these examples, the argument that *a priori* necessity iterates—the argument that if it is necessary, because *a priori*, that *p*, then it is also necessary that it is necessary that *p*, and so on—is inapplicable. The argument is inapplicable precisely because the examples in question, though necessary, are not *a priori*, and hence not necessary-by-virtue-of-being-*a-priori*.

The propositions that the intransitive-accessibility account holds to be necessary but not doubly necessary (for example, the proposition that table *a* is not originally formed from hunk h_m) are precisely certain *a posteriori* propositions whose necessity is derived by means of *a priori* modal principles like (III) taken together with certain further information, at least some of which is not *a priori*. That is, the propositions that the intransitive-accessibility account holds to be necessary but not doubly necessary are propositions of precisely the sort that Kripke cites as necessary yet *a posteriori*. The *a priori* principle (III) might be used to establish the necessity of table *a*'s not originating from hunk h_m, but the fact that *a* does not thus originate is itself unquestionably empirical and not *a priori*.

In fact, not even the conditional 'If table *a* is not originally formed from hunk h_m, then it is necessary that *a* is not originally formed from h_m' is *a priori*. For all that is known *a priori*, table *a* may have originated from hunk h_1, in which case *a* would still not have originated from hunk h_m, although it would then be possible for *a* to have thus originated.[29] The necessary *a posteriori* truth that table *a* is not formed from hunk h_m is thus a counterexample to Forbes's claim concerning the source of necessary *a posteriori* truths. Since the conditional proposition that if *a* is not formed from h_m then *a* is necessarily not thus formed is not *a priori*, it cannot be entailed by any conceptual *a priori* truth.

That *a*'s not originating from h_m is in fact necessary yields no reason to suppose that it must also be doubly necessary, triply necessary, and so on. Indeed, the fact *a* does not originate from h_m might not have been necessary at all.

The accessibility account rejects the *S4* axiom in its unrestricted form, but the account allows that there may be interesting special cases of necessity iteration that are logically valid. For example, it may be that, as Forbes's argument suggests, necessity iteration is legitimate whenever the proposition in question is necessary by virtue of being *a priori*. Certainly necessity iteration is legitimate with respect to purely mathematical propositions and (classical) logical truths. Maybe here is a legitimate restricted version of the *S4* axiom schema, or the rule of necessity iteration. Are there others? Necessity iteration is fallacious with respect to certain *a posteriori* propositions, but are there any necessary *a posteriori* propositions with respect to which necessity iteration is a legitimate logical inference? For example, Kripke and Putnam have argued that it is necessary, even though *a posteriori*, that cats are animals, or at least that cats are not robots. Presumably, they would argue that it is even necessary that it is necessary that cats are not robots. Does the latter modal fact follow logically from the former, taken together with certain information concerning the nature of the proposition that cats are not robots? If so, what is it about the proposition that cats are not robots that allows for necessity iteration as a logical inference, whereas necessity iteration with respect to other *a posteriori* propositions is fallacious?

The questions raised here seem to be worthy of further research. These and other challenging philosophical questions arise directly from the modal paradoxes. This alone makes the paradoxes deserving of our attention.

APPENDIX: THE DETERMINACY OF IDENTITY

The proof that identity is nonvague and either determinately true or determinately false for any pair of objects of any kind whatsoever proceeds from the observation that if there is a pair of objects, x and y, of which the 'is' of identity is neither determinately true nor determinately false (i.e., there is no objective, determinate fact of the matter whether x and y are numerically identical), then since the 'is' of identity is absolutely determinately true of the pair $<x, x>$, the two pairs must be different pairs of objects. It follows that the objects x and y are themselves distinct. In that case, the 'is' of identity is, contrary to the hypothesis, defined as determinately false for the pair $<x, y>$. Therefore, there is no pair of objects of any kind for which the question of their identity is metaphysically indeterminate.[30]

Although this proof is very convincing—in fact, to my mind, conclusive—I have found that (like most arguments against firmly entrenched philosophical views) it does not always convince. By far the most common objections I have encountered are based on the contention that the proof relies on principles of classical reasoning, whereas the view it purports to refute demands some special nonclassical logic of vagueness. Hence, it is worth emphasizing that the proof does not illegitimately assume or presuppose classical two-valued logic. To assume that every identity proposition is either true or false would certainly be eristically illegitimate, since the argument is advanced against a view that requires a nonclassical, nonbivalent logic. The critical move in the proof is a simple Leibniz's Law inference from an assumption of the form $\ulcorner \alpha$ has a property F that β does not have$\urcorner$ to its trivial consequence $\ulcorner \alpha \neq \beta \urcorner$. Even on the view being disputed, any inference from something assumed to be true is legitimate if the inference pattern is such as to preserve truth (or such as to preserve "determinate truth," or "complete truth," or "truth to the maximum degree," and so on). Analogously, the term 'bald' (in the sense of 'nearly absolutely bald') is unquestionably vague, in that there are (or at least there could be) individuals who have very little hair on their heads but just enough so that it is neither true nor false (vague, indeterminate, there is no objective fact of the matter) that they are bald. It would be illegitimate to assume that every proposition concerning whether someone is bald is either true or false. A nonclassical, nonbivalent logic is needed in order to reason properly with respect to such propositions. Despite this feature of the term 'bald', if one assumes for the sake of argument (e.g., for a *reductio* argument or for a conditional proof) that Harry has a full head of hair, it is perfectly legitimate to infer that Harry is not bald, for we have assumed as determinately true information that is such that if it is determinately true, then so is the proposition that Harry is not bald. There can be no question but that the Leibniz's Law inference invoked in the proof of the determinacy of identity is likewise such as to preserve determinate truth, and is therefore likewise legitimate. Whatever x and y may be, they are not one thing if they differ in any way, since any one thing has every property it has. Nothing could be more trivial.[31]

The critical premise involved in the proof is the assumption that the 'is' of identity is determinately true of any object and itself, and determinately false of any pair of determinately distinct objects. Lest anyone wish to challenge this assumption, it is important to recall Kripke's powerful '*schmidentity*' method of philosophical argument (which ironically applies virtually unchanged to the present case):[32] We may invent a new sense of 'is'—the 'is' of schmidentity—such that our assumption is true solely by stipulation for this new sense. Then we may prove, by the now familiar argument, that schmidentity is fully defined and determinate for any pair of objects. Yet this allegedly new sense of 'is' is precisely one that gives rise to the very sorts of problems for which the theory of indeterminate identity was introduced in the first place. Who cares about any other alleged sense of 'is' when our concern is with a question of identity? What's so important about x and y being neither determinately ''identical'' nor determinately ''distinct'' in some other sense if they are determinately not one and the very same but two, determinately not schmidentical? Nothing. Where one's concern is with a question of numerical identity, *almost* doesn't count. In fact, it doesn't even make sense.[33]

There is an alternative way of constructing the proof, one which applies the Leibniz's Law inference directly to the objects x and y: Suppose again that it is indeterminate whether x and y are identical. Then x and y differ in that x is determinately identical with x, whereas y is not. That is, y does not have x's property of being such that the 'is' of identity is determinately true of the ordered pair of x together with it. Hence, contrary to the hypothesis, x and y are determinately distinct.

This alternative construction reveals that the general form of the argument is essentially that used in proving the necessity of identity as a theorem of quantified modal logic: for every x and every y, if $x = y$, then it is necessary that $x = y$.[34] More analogously, the argument parallels the proof of the contrapositive of the necessity of identity, a theorem that Alonzo Church has called 'Murphy's Law of Modality': For every x and every y, if it is possible that $x \neq y$, then (since y does not have x's property of being necessarily identical with x) $x \neq y$.

Church has recently used this general form of argument to argue that if quantification into propositional attitude contexts is accepted as meaningful together with the usual laws of classical logic, then it is very likely that for every x and every y, if someone believes that $x \neq y$, then $x \neq y$.[35] The general argument can also be used to establish—or at least to argue compellingly for—a number of other philosophically interesting and highly controversial (in some cases, nearly universally denied) theses, such as the following:

T1: For every x and every y, if $x = y$, then whenever x exists, $x = y$;

T2: For every x and every y, if $x = y$, then if one believes anything at all involving x, one knows that $x = y$;

T3: For every x and every y, the question of whether $x = y$ is not a matter of decision, convention, or convenience, nor of elegance, simplicity, or uniformity of theory;

T4: For every x and every y, if $x = y$, then x is the only possible individual that could possibly have any metaphysically relevant "claim" or "title" to be y;

T5: For every x and every y, the question of whether $x = y$ does not turn on any fact concerning anything other than x and y;

T6: For every x and every y, if $x = y$, then the fact that $x = y$ does not require any "criteria of identity" for things of x's sort or kind;

T7: For every x and every y, if $x = y$, then the fact that $x = y$ is not grounded in, or reducible to, qualitative nonidentity facts about x and y other than x's existence, such as facts concerning material origins, bodily continuity, or memory;

T8: For every x and every y, if $x = y$, then the fact that $x = y$ obtains by virtue of x's existence, and not at all by virtue of any other qualitative nonidentity facts about x and y, such as facts concerning material origins, bodily continuity, or memory;

T9: For every x and every y, if one knows that $x = y$, then one knows this (primarily) solely by logic and by one's acquaintance with x, and not by knowing qualitative nonidentity facts about x and y, such as facts concerning continuity, location, or qualitative persistence or similarity.[36]

Each of these theses is diametrically opposed to the views, theories, or presuppositions of some major segment of the contemporary analytic philosophical community. Much of the literature on cross-time identity (and especially on personal identity), for example, presupposes the opposite of one or more of theses T6, T7, and T8. Many of the most widely held theories in this literature involve denying several (and in some cases all) of the remaining theses. Nearly the same is true of much of the literature on cross-world identity. In particular, that cross-world and cross-time identity facts are grounded in nonidentity facts is a recurrent theme in Forbes's work.[37] Although it is evidently not widely recognized, each of the theses mentioned is in fact, despite its unpopularity, a virtual consequence of Leibniz's Law together with some trivial feature of the reflexive law of identity. The trick (if there is any) is to extract the right property of x from the relevant trivial feature of the law (or proposition or fact) that $x = x$.

Consider thesis T7: Whatever x may be, the trivial fact that $x = x$ is not at all grounded in, or reducible to, any facts about x like those concerning x's material origins, x's bodily continuity through time, or x's memory of past experiences. If the fact that $x = x$ is grounded in any other fact about x, it is only grounded in the mere fact that x exists. Thus x has the complex property of being such that the fact that x is identical with it is not grounded in any qualitative nonidentity facts about x other than x's existence. Hence, by Leibniz's Law, for every y, if x and y are one and the very same, then y also has this complex property. Thus, if $x = y$, then the fact that $x = y$ is not grounded in any qualitative nonidentity facts about x (which are also facts about y) other than x's existence. Indeed, since x and y are one and the very same, the fact that $x = y$ is just the fact that $x = x$. Consequently, the fact that $x = y$ must have the property of the fact that $x = x$ that it is not grounded in any qualitative nonidentity facts about x (which are also facts about y) other than x's existence—*QED*. What a trivial and yet wonderful thing is Leibniz's Law!

The original proof that identity is determinate and fully defined for every pair of objects incidentally yields a persuasive reason for believing that the threshold for the amount of different original matter possible in the construction of an artifact consists in a sharp cutoff point rather than in a range of indeterminacy. A simple thought experiment shows that the threshold for the amount of different matter possible in the *reconstruction* of an artifact at some time after its disassembly does indeed consist in a sharp cutoff point. Recall that the number of molecules in the original matter of table a is n. Suppose that at time t_1, n distinct tables, $a_1, a_2, \ldots, a_n$, each qualitatively identical to a, are constructed from exactly n molecules apiece. At a later time t_2, each table is completely dismantled. At a still later time t_3, n tables, $a_1', a_2', \ldots, a_n'$, are constructed according to the same plan in the following way: a_1' is formed from all of the original molecules of a_1 except for the replacement of one molecule by a qualitative duplicate; a_2' is formed from all of the original molecules of a_2 except for the replacement of two molecules by qualitative duplicates of each; and so on, up to a_n', which is formed from entirely new matter. Clearly $a_1 = a_1'$ whereas $a_n \neq a_n'$. In fact, the construction of the second sequence of tables may be such that, for any i, if $a_i = a_i'$, then $a_{i-1} = a_{i-1}'$, and if $a_i \neq a_i'$, then $a_{i+1} \neq a_{i+1}'$. By the proof of the determinacy of identity, for any i, it is either determinately true that $a_i = a_i'$, or else it is determinately true that $a_i \neq a_i'$. Therefore, there must be some precise amount of different matter that first passes the threshold for the amount of different matter possible in the reconstruction of table a, i.e., there must be some m such that $a_m \neq a_m'$ but $a_{m-1} = a_{m-1}'$. On certain natural assumptions, this yields an excellent reason for supposing that in the sequence of hunks of matter $h_1, h_2, \ldots, h_n$, there is a hunk h_m that is the first to pass the threshold for the amount of different original matter possible in the construction of table a, i.e., that this threshold also consists in a precise cutoff point.

It was noted in section X above that it is *a posteriori*, even though it is necessary, that table a is not originally formed from hunk of matter h_m. Hence, it cannot be *a priori* that a is *necessarily* not originally formed from h_m. Is it then *a posteriori*? It is difficult to imagine establishing, by philosophical argument or otherwise, exactly what number m is, i.e., precisely how many molecules of difference from the actual original matter of table a would first result in a new and different table. It seems likely that it is *unknowable* that table a is necessarily not originally formed from hunk of matter h_m. That is, although it is knowable *a posteriori* that a is not in fact originally formed from h_m, and it is knowable (perhaps even knowable *a priori*) that there is some number m such that a difference of original matter of fewer than m molecules would still result in the same table though a difference of m or greater would result in a different table, it seems unlikely that one could know (*a priori* or *a posteriori*) *of* the relevant number *m,* whatever it is, that it is the threshold number of molecules of difference for the potential construction of table *a.* Whatever number *m* is, the fact that *a* is necessarily not originally formed from precisely that many different molecules from *a'* s actual original matter would appear to be a fact that is neither knowable *a priori* nor knowable *a posteriori,* since it appears not to be knowable at all.[38]

Notes

1. I have discussed some of these paradoxes in "How *Not* to Derive Essentialism from the Theory of Reference," *The Journal of Philosophy* 76 (December 1979): 703–25, at 722–25; "Fregean Theory and the Four Worlds Paradox: A Reply to David Over," *Philosophical Books* 25, no. 1 (January 1984): 7–11, at 9–11; "Impossible Worlds," *Analysis* 44, no. 3 (June 1984): 114–17; and in more detail in *Reference and Essence* (Princeton, N.J., 1981), appendix I, 219–52.

A version of one of the paradoxes was apparently first noted by Saul Kripke in *Naming and Necessity* (Cambridge, Mass., 1980, originally published 1972), at 51, n. 18, where it is briefly discussed. Something directly akin to this paradox was also noted and discussed by Roderick Chisholm in "Parts as Essential to their Wholes," *Review of Metaphysics* 26 (1973): 581–603, at 584–86, and again in *Person and Object* (La Salle, 1976), appendix B, 148–49. This paradox is highly reminiscent of Chisholm's paradoxical queries concerning cross-world identity in his seminal "Identity Through Possible Worlds: Some Questions," *Noûs* 1 (March 1967): 1–8. I follow Graeme Forbes in calling this paradox 'Chisholm's Paradox', though I am uncertain as to the propriety of the epithet. See also Quine, "Worlds Away," *The Journal of Philosophy* 73 (1976): 859–63, at 861; and N. L. Wilson, "Substances Without Substrata," *Review of Metaphysics* 12 (June 1959): 521–39. The general solution to Chisholm's Paradox that I advocate in *Reference and Essence* and defend here was first proposed by Hugh Chandler in "Plantinga and the Contingently Possible," *Analysis* 36 (January 1976): 106–9.

The modal paradoxes have been discussed by other writers, most notably Forbes in "Thisness and Vagueness," *Synthese* 54, no. 2 (February 1983): 235–59; "Two Solutions to Chisholm's Paradox," *Philosophical Studies* 46 (1984): 171–87; and *The Metaphysics of Modality* (Oxford, 1985), 160–90 and *passim;* and Anil Gupta in *The Logic of Common Nouns* (New Haven, 1980), 94–107. See also William R. Carter, "Salmon on Artifact Origins and Lost Possibilities," *The Philosophical Review* 92, no. 2 (April 1983): 223–31; Forbes, "Canonical Counterpart Theory," *Analysis* 42 (1982): 33–37, and "On the Philosophical Basis of Essentialist Theories," *The Journal of Philosophical Logic* 10 (February 1981): 73–99; David Over, "The Consequences of Direct Reference," *Philosophical Books* 25, no. 1 (January 1984): 1–7, at 4–7; and Robert Stalnaker, "Counterparts and Identity," this volume.

2. The argument here is derived from one given by Kripke in *Naming and Necessity,* at 114, n. 56. See also p. 1. The argument is analyzed in *Reference and Essence,* chapter 7, 196–216. For similar arguments, see Forbes, "Origin and Identity," *Philosophical Studies* 37 (1980): 353–62, and "On the Philosophical Basis of Essentialist Theories"; and Colin McGinn, "On the Necessity of Origin," *The Journal of Philosophy* 73 (March 11, 1976): 127–35, at 132. See also Richard Sharvy, "Why a Class Can't Change its Members," *Noûs* 2 (1968): 303–14, and "Individuation, Essence and Plenitude," *Philosophical Studies* 44 (1983): 61–70. (I should mention that I am here merely citing these works for further reference, and not endorsing the arguments or theses put forward in them.)

3. In fact, I believe that the threshold may indeed consist in a sharp cutoff point, though my approach to the modal paradoxes does not depend on this. An argument for a sharp cutoff is presented in the appendix below.

4. See "How *Not* to Derive Essentialism from the Theory of Reference," 723–25, n. 22, and *Reference and Essence,* 251–52, n. 31, for further details concerning the argument of the paradox.

5. If the indeterminate accessibility account sketched here is correct, principle (I) must be regarded as untrue. For suppose that z is a hunk of matter for which it is vague or indeterminate whether a particular actual table a might have been originally formed from it. Then a is not formed from z in any world determinately accessible to the actual world, though it is so formed according to some plan P in some world w_k

neither determinately accessible or determinately inaccessible to the actual world. Now it is determinately possible for a table—some table or other—to be the only table originally formed from hunk z according to plan P. Hence there is a determinately accessible world w in which some table x is formed from hunk z according to plan P. Since w is determinately accessible to the actual world, and a is not formed from z in any determinately accessible world, it follows that tables x and a must be distinct. If (I) were true, it would follow by *modus ponens* from the existence of w that in every world not determinately inaccessible to the actual world (in every world either determinately accessible or neither determinately accessible nor determinately inaccessible), no table distinct from x is the only table formed from hunk z according to plan P. (See note 14 and the appendix, below.) Yet w_k is precisely such a world in which a table distinct from x, viz, a, is the only table formed from hunk z according to plan P. Hence if there is such a world as w_k, then (I) is not true—though (depending on the deails of the three-valued logic) it need not be false, since there need not be any *determinately accessible* world in which a table distinct from x is the only table formed from hunk z according to plan P. (But see note 3 above.)

Even if (I) is untrue for these reasons, it can be maintained that the following weakened version of (I) is necessarily true:

> (I') If a table x is the only table originally formed from a hunk of matter z according to a certain plan P, then there could not be a table that is distinct from x and the only table originally formed from hunk z according to plan P.

The necessitation of (I') is equivalent in *S4* to the necessitation of (I), though in the independent modal propositional logic B, the necessitation of (I') is not sufficient for the derivation of principle (0). Of course, (0) may be true nevertheless.

6. See the works cited in note 1. Differences in terminology and emphasis, as well as certain theoretical differences, tend to obscure the overall fundamental similarity among the theories advocated or suggested by these writers. In place of Lewis's terminology of 'counterparts', Chisholm employs an alleged distinction, due to Joseph Butler, between "identity in the strict and philosophic sense" and "identity in the loose and popular sense," where artifacts made in different possible worlds from different constituent molecules are according to Chisholm never numerically one and the very same ("in the strict and philosophic sense"), though they may be said to be "the same" in the alleged loose and popular sense. The major difference between Chisholm and the other counterpart theorists is that Chisholm does not propose to replace the standard possible-world semantic analysis of formulations in modal-operator discourse of principles like (II) by an interpretation in terms of his counterpart relation, "identity in the loose and popular sense." Thus Chisholm dissents from the formulation of (II), whereas the other counterpart theorists assent to it. Perhaps this difference is enough to disqualify Chisholm as a genuine counterpart theorist, properly so-called, but I maintain that this difference is merely verbal and masks a basic agreement as to the facts (and that in this respect Chisholm is more perspicuous than the others).

Gupta occasionally uses the term 'counterpart' (at 105), but generally prefers to speak, somewhat misleadingly, of 'transworld identity relative to a world'. On Gupta's scheme for handling the modal paradoxes, an artifact x from one world and an artifact y from another world may be said to be "identical relative to" one world w and yet not "identical relative to" another world w'. Since x is "identical" with x (itself) relative to w' (assuming x exists in w'), however, it trivially follows by Leibniz's Law, or the Indiscernibility of Identicals, that x and y are not genuinely identical—they are not one and the very same—but are two distinct artifacts. (The sort of argument just given is discussed in the appendix below.) At most, then, x and y are merely counterparts at w, and it is at best misleading to call them *identical relative to w*. (Gupta's terminology is even more misleading than this, since he gives the title 'absolute identity' to the relation that obtains between a pair of objects when there is a world at which they are counterparts. This prompts him to make the astonishing claim that "absolute identity" is not transitive.)

I received a copy of Robert Stalnaker's "Counterparts and Identity" after the typescript of the present essay was submitted. Although I have not had the opportunity to study Stalnaker's essay carefully, several aspects of his theory seem similar to Gupta's. Stalnaker rejects my argument that his ternary, world-relative notion of "identity" is not genuine identity, but mere counterparthood, basing this rejection on the contention that there is no absolute (non-world-relative), binary notion of identity. This contention coupled with the rest of his theory, however, involves a number of serious difficulties, which I can only outline here.

First, Stalnaker claims (as part of the argument that there is no absolute notion of identity) that absolute truth is truth in the actual world. This gives us a notion of absolute identity: possible individuals are *absolutely identical* if and only if they are identical relative to the actual world. This notion coincides exactly with my intended notion of absolute identity if we assume that every possible individual x is such that, actually, $x = x$. Otherwise, it is better to substitute 'some world' for 'the actual world'. One way or another, absolute identity is definable in terms of world-relative identity, and Stalnaker's theory would thus allow for my notion of absolute identity if only it admitted the notion of intraworld identity. Unfortunately, the notion that Stalnaker calls 'intraworld identity' is not identity at all. This is made clear by Stalnaker's claim (which is essential to the point of his theory) that a single individual a in the actual world (e.g., Theseus's ship) can be two distinct individuals b and c in another possible world w. He defends this claim against the charge of violating the transitivity of identity, in part, by claiming that even though in w, $b \neq c$, in the actual world, $b = c$. But in w, $c = c$. This is inconsistent with (intraworld) Leibniz's Law (which Stalnaker claims to accept), since b does not (actually) have c's (actual) property of *being identical with c in w*. If b and c (actually) differ in this respect, then whatever else they are, they are not (actually) one and the very same object—since one object cannot differ from itself in any repect. In what sense are b and c (actually) ''identical,'' then, except in the highly misleading sense of (actually) being *distinct* counterparts of a? Given that the intraworld relation that Stalnaker calls 'identity' (actually) holds between discernible objects b and c, this relation is not, in fact, genuine intraworld identity but is merely a counterpart relation. Stalnaker purports to explain this relation as genuine identity by saying that it is the binary relation whose extension, in any possible world w, is the set of pairs $<d, d>$ such that d is in the domain of w. The phrase 'the set of pairs $<d, d>$ such that', understood in its standard set-theoretic sense, ultimately involves the notion of identity. Indeed, in fixing the extension (with respect to any possible world) of a genuine identity predicate, the notion of identity is typically invoked in order to exclude pairs of distinct objects from the extension. If Stalnaker's purported explanation thus invokes genuine identity (as it seems to), it is inconsistent (via Leibniz's Law) with his claim that the discernible objects b and c (actually) stand in the relation. If, on the other hand, the purported explanation invokes, instead, Stalnaker's world-relative notion of what he calls 'identity' relative to w, the purported explanation is highly misleading. Moreover, it is circular and does not actually fix the metaphysical intension of the relation in question.

7. See especially ''Thisness and Vagueness''; ''Two Solutions to Chisholm's Paradox''; and *The Metaphysics of Modality*, chapters 3 and 7, the appendix, and *passim*.

8. A term is a *persistent* (or *persistently rigid*) *designator* if and only if it designates the same thing with respect to every possible world in which that thing exists and designates nothing or something else with respect to all other worlds. A term is an *obstinate* (or *obstinately rigid*) *designator* if and only if it designates the same thing with respect to every possible world, whether that thing exists there or not. For more on this distinction between two types of rigid designators, see *Reference and Essence*, 32–41.

9. A notion very similar to that of a counterpart assignment was apparently first introduced by Allen Hazen in his Ph.D. dissertation, ''The Foundations of Modal Logic'' (Pittsburgh, 1977). See his ''Counterpart Theoretic Semantics for Modal Logic,'' *The Journal of Philosophy* 76, no. 6 (June 1979): 319–38, at 333–34, where analogues of counterpart assignments (there called 'representative functions') and world-assignment pairs ('stipulational worlds') are put to a use very similar to (though not exactly the same as) their use here.

10. The truth theoretic analysis that I am formulating here by means of counterpart assignments yields some significant differences in truth value assignments to particular modal-operator-discourse sentences from Lewis's own scheme. Specifically, the following clauses for the modal operators accord better with Lewis's actual scheme:

$\ulcorner \Box \phi \urcorner$ is $true_{w,c,s}$ iff ϕ is $true_{w',c' \circ c,s'}$ for every world w' and every counterpart assignment c' for w';

$\ulcorner \Diamond \phi \urcorner$ is $true_{w,c,s}$ iff ϕ is $true_{w',c' \circ c,s'}$ for some world w' and some counterpart assignment c' for w';

where $c' \circ c$ is the composite of the assignments c' and c, i.e., the function that assigns to any possible individual x, $c'(c(x))$.

Following Forbes, I am devising counterpart-theoretic possible-world semantics in such a way that '$\diamond\diamond F(a)$' is true exactly on the condition that a has an F counterpart at some world, so that '$\diamond\diamond F(a)$' is equivalent to '$\diamond F(a)$', thus preserving $S4$ modal logic. Lewis's original scheme has '$\diamond\diamond F(a)$' true exactly on the condition that a has a counterpart that itself has an F counterpart at some world. Since counterparthood is not transitive, this condition may be fulfilled though a itself has no F counterpart at any world. Lewis's scheme thus fails to preserve $S4$, since '$\diamond\diamond F(a)$' is weaker than '$\diamond F(a)$'. This separates Lewis motivationally from theorists such as Forbes, who invoke counterpart theory precisely to retain $S4$ modal logic in the face of the modal paradoxes. This does not mean, however, that Lewis himself blocks the Four Worlds Paradox in the same way as the accessibility solution. See note 20.

11. On Lewis's original scheme, (P_m) comes out true. See note 10 above.

12. Specifically, counterpart-theoretic possible-world semantics, as I have devised it, invalidates the inference

$$\frac{\Box(x)[G(x) \supset \diamond F(x)]}{\therefore \Box(Exists(a) \supset [G(a) \supset \diamond F(a)]),}$$

since it may be that every possible individual that is G in its own world has an F counterpart at some world, and that a has an existing G counterpart at some world, though a itself (as opposed to its G counterpart) has no F counterpart at any world. The trouble with this instance of (MUI) arises from the nesting of modalities in the conclusion. Lewis's original scheme validates this instance of (MUI), but as noted in note 10 above, it does not preserve $S4$ modal logic. In a sense, then, the counterpart theorist is faced with a choice between $S4$ and such instances of (MUI). Forbes chooses the former, Lewis the latter. Standard quantified $S5$ modal logic validates both $S4$ and (MUI). (Neither version of counterpart theory validates all instances of (MUI).)

Of course, counterpart-theoretic possible-world semantics can be artificially made to capture as much standard quantified $S5$ modal logic as desired by placing further constraints on the counterpart relation. Standard modal logic emerges as the special case of counterpart-theoretic modal logic where counterparthood is identity. It is the philosophical motivation for counterpart theory, and the consequent explication of counterparthood in terms of sufficient cross-world similarity in certain respects, that requires the nontransitive and one-many nature of counterparthood.

13. Here and throughout this essay I am ignoring the possibility that semantic terms like 'true' and 'false' might themselves be vague or have partially defined semantic characteristic functions. If 'true' and 'false' are themelves vague or otherwise partially defined, a simple atomic sentence may suffer from second-order vagueness or second-order failure of truth value, in that the sentence may be, say, determinately untrue though it is indeterminate (vague, neither meta-true nor meta-false, there is no objective fact of the matter) whether the sentence is false or not. Similarly, a sentence that is determinately not false may be neither determinately true nor determinately untrue. The possibility of higher-order vagueness does not directly affect the main points I wish to make concerning the modal paradoxes and sorites paradoxes, and further discussion of this phenomenon in the present essay would introduce unnecessary complications. Notice that it is still reasonable to count a classical propositional sorites argument unsound, even if the sequence of sentences making up the antecedents and consequents of the conditional premises (e.g., sentences of the form ⌐Anyone of height h_i is short⌐) run the full gamut from determinately true to determinately not false but neither determinately true nor determinately untrue, to determinately neither true nor false, to determinately untrue but neither determinately false nor determinately not false, and finally to determinately false. Some of the conditional premises would have to be counted determinately not false while neither detrerminately true nor determinately untrue, but still others should be counted determinately not true. For it would be most reasonable to count a conditional determinately neither true nor false, and hence determinately untrue, whenever its antecedent is determinately not false but its consquent is determinately neither true nor false, and similarly whenever its antecedent is determinately neither true nor false and its consquent is determinately untrue.

14. Here I assume the three-valued modal semantics I put forward in "Impossible Worlds," 114, n. 2, rather than that of *Reference and Essence*, 248, n. 27.

15. The proof just presented that identity is nonvague is discussed further in the appendix.

16. Cf. *Reference and Essence*, 232–38.

118   NATHAN SALMON

17. I am concerned here with theories in the ordinary sense of the word. A theory in this sense is not merely a set of expressions closed under a special syntactic relation, but something more along the lines of a set of fully *interpreted* sentences, or a set of propositions, closed under genuine logical consequence.

18. "Thisness and Vagueness," 252. See also 258, n. 27.

19. Cf. Chisholm's doctrine of *ens successiva* in *Person and Object,* 89–113, 145–58.

20. One might also employ a conception, due to David Lewis, of possible worlds as *way things might have been*. My reason for not including this in the list is that Lewis himself (usually) takes a way-things-might-have-been-but-are-not to be something like an immense concrete object someplace "far, far away," in another dimension of the total cosmos, rather than a way the cosmos might have been, i.e., a possible state of the cosmos. If Lewis insists on this conception of a possible world, strictly speaking his version of counterpart theory is not a brand of essentialism at all, nor is it even relevant to modality in general. It is a fantastic cosmological theory.

21. Cf. *Reference and Essence,* 234–35. Forbes has responded to this objection by claiming, in effect, that the alleged validity of the inference in question does not violate any relevant logical intuition. See "Two Solutions to Chisholm's Paradox," 182; and *The Metaphysics of Modality,* 180. This might be taken as an indication that Forbes does not mean what the rest of us mean by 'Bill might have been a robot'. Most of us understand this sentence in such a way that it is true if and only if there is a scenario that might have obtained—or a history the world might have had, or a state of affairs that might have obtained, or a state the cosmos might have been in—in which Bill himself is a robot. Contrary to Forbes, we have a strong logical intuition that the proposition that Bill himself might have been a robot, whether true or false, is no logical consequence of any proposition to the effect that there might have been a robot counterpart of Bill—unless counterparthood is just identity.

Forbes's reply is based partly on his contention (disputed here) that possible-world-discourse sentences are, in effect, essentially idioms whose meanings are stipulated and fixed by the theorist's proposed translations in modal-operator discourse and not generated from the meanings of their grammatical components.

22. "A Problem for Actualism About Possible Worlds," *The Philosophical Review* 92, no. 1 (January 1983): 49–66.

23. "The Logic of Inexact Concepts," *Synthese* 19, no. 3/4 (April 1969): 325–73.

24. "Two Solutions to Chisholm's Paradox," 177. On the other hand, Forbes is willing to identify his notions of maximal truth and maximal falsehood with the traditional truth values of classical two-valued logic (*The Metaphysics of Modality,* 170).

The possibility of vagueness of infinite order (see footnote 13 above) suggests an alternative interpretation of the degrees-of-truth semantics for vagueness. On my suggested construal of the degrees-of-truth approach, second-order vagueness can be accommodated by allowing that a sentence may be determinately greater than 0 (or determinately less than 1) in truth value status while it is indeterminate whether the sentence takes on the value 1 (or 0) rather than some real between 0 and 1. As with first-order vagueness, the degrees-of-truth approach with indeterminacy allows for finer distinctions than the simple three-valued approach with indeterminacy. Still, on this construal, the latter approach is completely embedded within the former.

25. See for example W. R. Carter, "Salmon on Artifact Origins and Lost Possibilities," 228–29; Forbes, "Two Solutions to Chisholm's Paradox," 182–84, and *The Metaphysics of Modality,* 165n.

Forbes in particular has objected that the acceptance of this conclusion is incompatible with a general metaphysical principle concerning identity facts and the concept of identity—a principle that entails an extreme, cross-world version of the Identity of Indiscernibles (from which the identity of indiscernible worlds is derivable), and that, according to Forbes, provides the ultimate justification for the essentialist principle (III). This is the reductionist or supervenience principle that all facts about the numerical identity or distinctness of a pair of objects, x and y—including facts of cross-time and cross-world identity and distinctness—are metaphysically "grounded in," and "consist in," nonidentity facts about x and y, so that such identity facts do not obtain independently and solely by their own hook but only *in virtue of* nonidentity facts.

Of course, this formulation does not make clear the exact import of the intended principle. Forbes's intent can be gleaned to a certain extent by noting what he takes the principle to entail. An argument purporting to disprove the principle (whatever its precise import) is given in the appendix below.

26. This is not the only likely source of the temptation. Another possible source stems from the natural and plausible reductionist principle that a table is "nothing over and above" its matter, in the sense that a complete accounting of all of the matter in a genuinely possible world, with its exact configuration throughout time, must determine all of the remaining facts about the material objects, like tables, and everything else, present in the world. This immediately yields the supervenience thesis mentioned at the end of section I in connection with the fallaciously obtained false conclusion (*C2*). Within an *S4* framework, the reductionist principle renders the worlds *w* and *w'* exactly alike in all of the facts that obtain in each and in their accessibility relations. Cf. *Reference and Essence*, 237–38.

It should be noted that the conclusion (*C4*), which I claim to be true, is contradictory in *S4* modal logic.

27. "Two Solutions to Chisholm's Paradox," 185.

28. *The Metaphysics of Modality*, 237, n. 26. I have replaced Forbes's letter '*T*' by '*p*' for perspicuity.

29. The epistemological status of such propositions as these is discussed further in the appendix below.

30. The proof is elaborated and defended in *Reference and Essence*, 243–45. The general form of the argument was first given by Gareth Evans in "Can There Be Vague Objects?" *Analysis* 38 (1978): 208, although the argument had occurred to me independently. For further discussion, see John Broome, "Indefiniteness and Identity," *Analysis* 44, no. 1 (January 1984): 6–12; H. W. Noonan, "Vague Objects," *Analysis* 42, no. 1 (January 1982): 3–6; H. W. Noonan, "Indefinite Identity: A Reply to Broome," *Analysis* 44, no. 3 (June 1984): 117–21; David Over, "The Consequences of Direct Reference," 6; Richmond Thomason, "Identity and Vagueness," *Philosophical Studies* 42 (1982): 329–32; and my "Fregean Theory and the Four Worlds Paradox: A Reply to David Over," 10.

31. Cf. *Reference and Essence*, 244n.

32. *Naming and Necessity*, 108.

33. Cf. *Reference and Essence*, 244–45.

34. See Ruth Barcan, "The Identity of Individuals in a Strict Functional Calculus of Second Order," *The Journal of Symbolic Logic* 12 (1947): 12–15.

35. Church concludes from this argument and from the provability of the necessity of identity in quantified modal logic that there are compelling reasons to reject the meaningfulness of quantification into either modal or propositional attitude contexts. See his "A Remark Concerning Quine's Paradox About Modality," in *Propositions and Attitudes*, edited by N. Salmon and S. Soames, forthcoming. For a response, see my "Reflexivity," *The Notre Dame Journal of Formal Logic* 27 (July 1986): 401–29.

36. For a general defense of thesis T9, see my *Frege's Puzzle* (Cambridge, Mass., 1986).

37. See, for example, "Origin and Identity," "Thisness and Vagueness," and *The Metaphysics of Modality*, 126–31 and *passim*.

38. The present essay has benefited from the helpful comments and suggestions of Pascal Engel, Graeme Forbes, David Lewis, and John Pollock.

References

Adams, R. M. 1974. "Theories of Actuality." *Nous* 8: 211–31; also in Loux, 190–209.

Adams, R. M. 1979. "Primitive Thisness and Primitive Identity." *The Journal of Philosophy* 76, no. 1 (January): 5–26.

Adams, R. M. 1981. "Actualism and Thisness." *Synthese* 49: 3–41.

Barcan, R. 1947. "The Identity of Individuals in a Strict Functional Calculus of Second Order." *The Journal of Symbolic Logic* 12: 12–15.

Broome, J. 1984. "Indefiniteness and Identity." *Analysis* 44, no. 1 (January): 6–12.

Burke, M. B. 1983. "Essentialism and the Identity of Indiscernibles." *Philosophy Research Archives* 9: 223–43.

Carter, W. R. 1983. "Salmon on Artifact Origins and Lost Possibilities." *Philosophical Review* 92, No. 2 (April): 223–31.

Chandler, H. 1976. "Plantinga and the Contingently Possible." *Analysis* 36 (January): 106–9.

Chisholm, R. 1967. "Identity Through Possible Worlds: Some Questions." *Noûs* 1 (March): 1–8; also in Loux, 80–87.

Chisholm, R. 1973. "Parts as Essential to their Wholes." *Review of Metaphysics* 26: 581–603.

Chisholm, R. 1975. "Mereological Essentialism: Some Further Considerations." *Review of Metaphysics* 28: 477–84.

Chisholm, R. 1976. *Person and Object.* La Salle.

Church, A. Forthcoming. "A Remark Concerning Quine's Paradox About Modality." In *Propositions and Attitudes,* edited by N. Salmon and S. Soames.

Evans, G. 1978. "Can There Be Vague Objects?" *Analysis* 38: 208.

Forbes, G. 1980. "Origin and Identity." *Philosophical Studies* 37: 353–62.

Forbes, G. 1981. "On the Philosophical Basis of Essentialist Theories." *The Journal of Philosophical Logic* 10 (February): 73–99.

Forbes, G. 1982. "Canonical Counterpart Theory." *Analysis* 42: 33–37.

Forbes, G. 1983. "Thisness and Vagueness." *Synthese* 54, no. 2 (February): 235–59.

Forbes, G. 1984. "Two Solutions to Chisholm's Paradox." *Philosophical Studies* 46, no. 2 (September): 171–87.

Forbes, G. 1985. *The Metaphysics of Modality.* Oxford.

Fumerton, R. A. 1978. "Chandler on the Contingently Possible." *Analysis* 38: 39–40.

Goguen, A. 1969. "The Logic of Inexact Concepts." *Synthese* 19, no. 3/4 (April): 325–73.

Gupta, A. 1980. *The Logic of Common Nouns.* New Haven.

Hazen, A. 1977. "The Foundations of Modal Logic." Ph.D. dissertation. Pittsburgh.

Hazen, A. 1979. "Counterpart Theoretic Semantics for Modal Logic." *The Journal of Philosophy* 76, no. 6 (June): 319–38.

Kaplan, D. 1979. "Transworld Heir Lines." In Loux, 88–109.

Kaplan, D. 1975 "How to Russell a Frege-Church." *The Journal of Philosophy* 72 (November 6): 716–29; also in Loux, 210–24.

Kripke, S. 1971. "Identity and Necessity." In *Identity and Individuation,* edited by M. Munitz, 135–64. New York. Also in *Naming, Necessity, and Natural Kinds,* 1977, edited by S. Schwartz, 66–101. Ithaca, N.Y.

Kripke, S. 1972. *Naming and Necessity.* Cambridge, Mass., and Oxford.

Lewis, D. 1968. "Counterpart Theory and Quantified Modal Logic." *The Journal of Philosophy* 65: 113–26; also in Loux, 110–28; also in Lewis, 1983, with substantive postscripts, 26–46.

Lewis, D. 1973. *Counterfactuals.* Cambridge, Mass.

Lewis, D. 1983. *Philosophical Papers I.* Oxford.

Loux, M., ed. 1979. *The Possible and the Actual.* Ithaca, N.Y.

Marcus, R. B.: See Barcan.

McGinn, C. 1976. "On the Necessity of Origin." *The Journal of Philosophy* 73 (March 11): 127–35.

McMichael, A. 1983. "A Problem for Actualism About Possible Worlds." *The Philosophical Review* 92, no. 1 (January): 49–66.

Noonan, H. W. 1983. "The Necessity of Origin." *Mind* 92, no. 365 (January): 1–20.

Noonan, H. W. 1985. "Indefinite Identity: A Reply to Broome." *Analysis* 44, no. 3 (June): 117–21.

Odegard, D. 1976 "On A Priori Contingency." *Analysis* 36 (June): 201–3.

Over, D. 1984. "The Consequences of Direct Reference." *Philosophical Books* 25, no. 1 (January): 1–7.

Plantinga, A. 1975. "On Mereological Essentialism." *Review of Metaphysics* 28: 468–76.

Plantinga, A. 1974. *The Nature of Necessity.* Oxford.

Quine, W. V. O. 1976. "Worlds Away." *The Journal of Philosophy* 73: 859–63.

Salmon, N. 1979. "How *Not* to Derive Essentialism from the Theory of Reference." *The Journal of Philosophy* 76 (December): 703–25.

Salmon, N. 1981. *Reference and Essence.* Princeton and Oxford.

Salmon, N. 1984. "Fregean Theory and the Four Worlds Paradox: A Reply to David Over." *Philosophical Books* 25, no. 1 (January): 7–11.

Salmon, N. 1984. "Impossible Worlds." *Analysis* 44, no. 3 (June): 114-17.

Salmon, N. 1986. *Frege's Puzzle.* Cambridge, Mass.

Salmon, N. 1986. "Reflexivity." *The Notre Dame Journal of Formal Logic* 27, no. 3 (July): 401–29.

Sharvy, R. 1968. "Why a Class Can't Change its Members." *Noûs* 2 (November): 303–14.

Sharvy, R. 1983. "Individuation, Essence and Plenitude." *Philosophical Studies* 44: 61-70.

Stalnaker, R. 1976 "Possible Worlds." *Noûs* 10: 65–75; also in Loux, 225–34.

Stalnaker, R. 1986. "Counterparts and Identity." In this volume.

Thomason, R. 1982. "Identity and Vagueness." *Philosophical Studies* 42: 329–32.

Wilson, N. L. 1959. "Substances Without Substrata." *Review of Metaphysics* 12 (June): 521–39.

Counterparts and Identity

ROBERT STALNAKER

1. INTRODUCTION

Philosophers who take possible worlds seriously are often divided into two camps. First there are the *possibilists* who hold that possible worlds and other possible objects may exist without *actually* existing. Other possible worlds, according to the possibilist, are concrete universes, spatially and temporally disconnected from our own, but just as real. The claim that such universes are not actual is, in effect, just the claim that we are not located in them. Second, there are the *actualists* who hold that nothing is real except what is actual—that is, except what exists as a part of the actual world. According to the actualist, the things that are (perhaps misleadingly) called "possible worlds" are not really *worlds* but are properties or states of the world, or states of affairs, or propositions or sets of propositions, or perhaps set theoretic constructions of some kind. There are many different versions of actualism; what they have in common is the thesis that possible worlds are things that can be instantiated or realized. A non-actual possible world is not a concrete object that exists in some nonactual place, but an abstract object that actually exists but is uninstantiated.

A second issue that divides the friends of possible worlds concerns the relations between the individuals that exist in the different possible worlds. Just as the possible worlds theorist (possibilist or actualist) explains the claim that something might have been true as the claim that it *is* true in some other possible world, so this theorist explains the claim that some property might have been true *of* a certain individual as the claim that in some other possible world, that property *is* true of some individual suitably related to the actual individual. But what is the suitable relation? The straightforward answer is that the relation is identity. The reason that Daniels might have been a professional pianist is that there is a possible world in which *Daniels,* and not some other individual, is a professional pianist. But according to an alternative line of argument, this cannot be right, since Daniels exists only in our world—he cannot be here and someplace else as well. The pianist in a counterfactual world in virtue of which

Daniels might have been a professional pianist is not Daniels himself, but his *counterpart,* or one of them, in that other world.

These two philosophical issues concerning possible worlds are distinct but related. It happens that David Lewis is the most articulate defender of both the possibilist line about possible worlds and the counterpart line about possible individuals.[1] As a result, the most prominent arguments for counterpart theory, and against strict identity of individuals across possible worlds, are given within a possibilist framework, and some of the motivations and arguments for counterpart theory derive from possibilist assumptions. But counterpart theory has a number of quite different motivations and involves a number of different theses that need to be distinguished. What I want to explore in this paper is a version and a defense of counterpart theory that is quite different from Lewis's version. The version that I will explore is tied to actualism rather than to possibilism. The main thesis that I will, somewhat tentatively, suggest is that the actualist can coherently combine a belief in primitive thisness[2] and genuine identity across possible worlds with a version of counterpart theory that permits one to make sense of contingent identity and distinctness—that is, of the claims that one thing might have been two, and that distinct things might have been identical.

I am not confident that the account of counterparts and identity that I will sketch is a plausible one, but even if it ultimately fails, I think it is important to see that it can be pushed farther than many have supposed. I am confident that if the account I will explore is wrong, it is wrong for reasons quite different from those that are usually given for rejecting counterpart theory and contingent identity. Developing the account and bringing out its problems will, I think, throw some light on the interconnections between some metaphysical and semantical questions concerning possibility, predication, and identity.

I will begin, in section 2, by looking at counterpart theory as it is usually conceived, distinguishing three different motivations for it, and discussing some arguments against it. Then, in section 3, I will look at the thesis of actualism and at the actualist strategy for explaining, or explaining away, merely possible individuals. In section 4, I will consider the thesis, or cluster of theses, that David Kaplan has called *haecceitism*.[3] Here I will argue that haecceitism, properly understood, can be reconciled with a version of counterpart theory, and with the coherence of contingent identity. In section 5, I will look briefly at the temporal analogy, considering some of the similarities and differences between identity through time and identity across possible worlds. Finally, in section 6, I will look quickly at some of the consequences that this account of counterparts and identity has for the abstract semantics of quantified modal logic. The problems come, surprisingly, not with identity, which is perfectly standard, but with variable binding and quantification.

2. COUNTERPART THEORY

Let me begin with an informal sketch of the basic elements of a formal semantic analysis of quantified modal logic in its standard form. The abstract semantics is essentially the same whether it is given a possibilist or an actualist philosophical foundation.

A *frame* or *model structure* for interpreting a quantified modal language consists of a set of possible worlds, each with its domain of individuals—the individuals that exist in that world. The rules for assigning semantic values to the primitive descriptive expressions of the language and for determining the values of complex expressions as a function of the values of their parts are for the most part straightforward generalizations of the rules of extensional semantics; modal semantics does for many possible worlds at once what extensional semantics does for the actual world alone. The semantic values, in extensional semantics, are *extensions* of various kinds: for example, individuals for singular terms, sets of individuals (subsets of the domain) for one-place predicates, truth-values for sentences. The corresponding values in modal semantics are *intensions,* which are identified with functions from possible worlds into extensions of the appropriate kind. So, for example, the intension of a one-place predicate is a function taking a possible world into a set of individuals (a subset of the domain of that world), and the intension of a sentence is a function from possible worlds into truth-values. The semantical rules for the various extensional operators, the quantifier and the identity predicate, are just like the extensional rules, except relativized to possible worlds. For example, the rule for negation says that a sentence $\sim A$ is true *in possible world w* if and only if A is false *in w*. The rule for the one new operator—the necessity operator—captures the familiar slogan, necessity is truth in all possible worlds: $\Box A$ is true in w if and only if A is true in w' for all possible worlds w'.[4]

This simple story can be modified and elaborated in various ways. The counterpart variation of the story requires three changes: it adds a constraint on the domains, adds an element to the structure, and makes some changes in the semantical rules. First, the domains of the different possible worlds are required to be disjoint. Second, a binary counterpart relation is added to the model structure. The third change—the change in the semantical rules—can be carried out in various ways.[5] What the changes must do is to make the modal properties of objects in one possible world depend on the properties, not of the object itself, but of its counterparts in other possible worlds. Consider an open sentence $\Diamond Gx$. The standard semantic rules say that this will be true of an individual a in a world w if and only if Gx is true of a in some possible world w'. In counterpart semantics, the rules must be changed to make $\Diamond Gx$ true of a in w if Gx is true of a counterpart of a in some world w'. Hubert Humphrey, for example, will have the property of being possibly a president of the United States by virtue of the fact that in a different possible world, a different person who is a counterpart of Humphrey was president.

Obviously, the standard theory, allowing the domains of the different possible worlds to overlap and interpreting modal predicates in the straightforward way, is simpler and more natural. What are the motivations for the counterpart move? I will discuss three different motivations. The first is tied to possibilism. The second derives from a metaphysical doctrine about the nature of individuals—a doctrine that is independent of possibilism. The third—again independent of possibilism—derives from intuitions about the contingency of identity and distinctness.

First, the possibilist argument: nothing can be in two places at once. If other possible worlds are really other universes, then clearly, you and I cannot be in them if we are here in this one. People who resemble us in one way or another might be there, but *we* cannot be there. At least we cannot be *wholly* in this world and also in some other possible world. The possibilist will concede that it would be coherent to say that individuals such as you and I are extended across possible worlds, with parts—world-parts analogous to time-slices—in different possible worlds. But it would be intuitively implausible to say that we are (and always will be) only partly actual, the other parts being counterfactual. It would be coherent, but intuitively bizarre, to hold that ordinary individuals are scattered objects with parts existing in many spatially and temporally disconnected locations.[6]

This argument seems to me compelling, given the possibilist framework it presupposes, but it has no force at all for an actualist. For the actualist, the claim that *I* exist in a different possible world is not, as it seems, a claim that I am in some other place as well as here but is, instead, the claim that there is a way the world might have been, different from the way it is, such that had the world been that way, I would still have existed.

A second motivation for counterpart theory derives from the metaphysical doctrine that there is nothing to a particular individual over and above the properties it has, the relations it stands in to other individuals, and the spatial and temporal locations it occupies. There is no *thisness* or individual essence underlying the qualities and relations. It does not strictly follow from this metaphysical doctrine that individuals exist only in one possible world, but it does seem to follow that the relation of identity of individuals across possible worlds must be explained or analyzed in terms of qualitative similarities and differences between individuals within worlds. If things are identified across worlds, these identifications must be supervenient on some kind of counterpart relation between the world-bound parts of individuals.

This metaphysical motivation is independent of the possibilist-actualist contrast. A possibilist, who opted for counterpart theory for the first reason, might believe in irreducible thisness, rejecting the second motivation, and with it the demand that the counterpart relation be explained in qualitative terms. For this kind of counterpart theorist, primitive thisness is represented by a primitive counterpart relation. On the other hand, there is no reason why an actualist who regards other possible worlds as other ways our world might have been could not reject primitive thisness, opting for counterpart theory, not for the first reason, but because it provides a more natural setting for the analysis of identity across possible worlds in qualitative terms.

Finally, a third motivation for the counterpart move derives from intuitive examples and puzzle cases that are difficult to account for on the standard account of modality. I will sketch four examples discussed in the recent philosophical literature that raise problems about identity across possible worlds.

1. Some of the examples that help to motivate counterpart theory are variations on older examples used to raise problems about identity through time. Consider the notorious ship of Theseus. Over the years, the parts are gradually replaced until none of the original parts remain. Then, sometime later, the original parts are gathered up and put back together according to the original plan. We now have two ships. Which is the original? Each seems to have some claim; of each it seems reasonable to say that

it clearly would have been the same as the original ship if it had not been for the other. Suppose we say that continuity is the dominant criterion of identity, and so the original ship is the one that remained afloat throughout, the one that now has all new parts. Now consider this cross-world elaboration of the puzzle, devised by Hugh Chandler:[7] Suppose possible world w_1 is as described in the original ship of Theseus story. In possible world w_2, the story is the same, except that as the old parts are gradually removed, they are not replaced. The ship is gradually dismantled, and then, sometime later, it is reconstructed. The question is, what are the relations between the ships in the two worlds—which ships are identical to which? To avoid begging any questions, I will use different names for each ship that might be thought to be distinct from any other: Let a be the original ship in w_1, b the ship continuous with it with the all new parts, and c the ship constructed, in w_1, from the original parts. Let d be the original ship of w_2, and e the ship constructed, in w_2, from the parts of d. Now which identity statements involving these names are true? First, intraworld identities: We have assumed that $a = b$, and of course it is clear that $b \neq c$. In w_2, it seems clear that $d = e$; the orginal ship was taken apart and put back together. Next, cross-world identities: we can stipulate that $a = d$; the idea is to tell two alternative stories about one original ship. It also seems reasonable to say that $e = c$, since c and e are composed of exactly the same parts, and the history of those parts—their relations to each other at various times—is exactly the same in w_1 as it is in w_2. But we cannot hold all of these identity and distinctness claims at once: they imply a contradiction.

2. Allan Gibbard tells a story about a lump of clay called "Lumpl" and a statue called "Goliath."[8] The statue is made out of the lump, and the lump and the statue came into being, and ceased to exist, at exactly the same moments. It is reasonable to say, Gibbard argues, that in this case, the lump and the statue are identical, but it is clear that they are not necessarily identical. Consider a different possible world in which the statue is destroyed before the lump. In that world, Goliath and Lumpl are distinct. But on the standard theory, one cannot make sense of this. Consider the one thing that is (in the actual world) both Lumpl and Goliath. Is that thing in the domain of the other possible world, and if so, is it the lump or the statue that exists there?

3. It seems reasonable to say that a complex artifact, say a car, a building, or a bicycle, might have been originally made out of slightly different parts from those it was actually made out of. If, in putting together a certain custom-made bicycle, the bicycle-makers had used a different nut, bolt, gear lever, or spoke, they would have made, not a different bicycle, but the same bicycle slightly differently. But if most or all of the parts had been different, then the bicycle constructed would have been a perhaps similar, but distinct, bicycle. If this is right, we are in trouble, for consider a sequence of possible worlds, each containing a bicycle that differs slightly in its composition from the bicycle in the preceding world, but such that the bicycle in the first world in the sequence has no parts in common with the bicycle in the last world.[9] Identity, of course, is transitive. One cannot say that each bicycle is identical to the bicycles in neighboring worlds, but not to the corresponding bicycles in distant worlds.[10] The argument suggests that one must either adopt an extreme form of mereological essentialism, requiring identity of all parts for identity of the whole, or else give up the standard account of identity across possible worlds.[11]

4. Consider the bilingual Pierre who sincerely assents, in French, to the statement ''Londre est jolie'' while dissenting, in English, from ''London is pretty.''[12] It seems that Pierre has a false but coherent conception of the world. In the possible worlds that are the way Pierre thinks the world is, there are two distinct cities, one that is pretty and called (in French) ''Londre,'' and one that is not so pretty and is called (in English) ''London.'' Which of these cities is the city *we* call ''London''? It seems reasonable to say that both of them are. Both of Pierre's beliefs are beliefs about London; when he says either ''Londre est jolie'' or ''London is not pretty,'' he is obviously referring to London, and since he is sincere, he is expressing his beliefs. And it seems that he is successfully describing the world as he believes it to be. But, of course, the standard account will not permit us to say that both of these cities are London while maintaining that they are distinct from each other. Mistakes of identity are familiar: it is not at all uncommon to think one thing is two, or two things one. This kind of mistake creates problems for the semantics of propositional attitudes, since the standard theory does not permit us to describe them in a straightforward way.

These examples remind us what an unyielding relation identity is. The source of the puzzles seems to be that the richness and fluidity of intuitions about possibilities conflict with the inflexible demands of this relation. Loosen up, says the counterpart theorist. A more adequate description of the modal phenomena can be given if we replace the restrictive cross-world identity relation with a more flexible relation that permits intransitivities and asymmetries.

This third motivation for the counterpart move is the one closest to the phenomena and least tied to metaphysical presuppositions. Actualists and believers in primitive thisness may still be troubled by these examples, and so may still have at least one reason to be tempted by counterpart theory. But most philosophers who are troubled by such examples have resisted the temptation to respond with the counterpart move. The following argument, made most explicitly by Alvin Plantinga[13] and Nathan Salmon,[14] spells out one reason for thinking that counterpart theory does not really solve the problems raised by such examples.

One may divide the counterpart doctrine into two parts: the first part is the metaphysical thesis that the domains of the different possible worlds are all disjoint; possible individuals exist in at most one possible world. The second part is the semantical thesis that modal predicates should be interpreted in terms of counterparts (in the way sketched above) rather than straightforwardly in terms of the individuals themselves. If one considers the first thesis by itself, it seems to suggest a rather extreme form of essentialism according to which nothing could have been different in any way from the way it actually is. In fact, according to this form of essentialism, none of us would have existed if anything in the world had been even slightly different. ''If a leaf deep in the mountain fastness of the North Cascades had fallen in October 31, 1876,'' Plantinga writes, ''the day before it actually fell, then (according to Counterpart Theory) I should have been either nonexistent or else a different person from the one I am. And surely this is false.''[15] The metaphysical part of the doctrine, considered alone, does seem quite implausible. How is the addition of the semantical component supposed to help? It cannot, according to the Plantinga-Salmon argument, since it does not retract or qualify the metaphysical thesis in any way. What the second part of the doctrine does, they argue, is to reinterpret the language so as to disguise the metaphysical consequences of the doctrine. One can no longer *say,* in the object language the counterpart theorist sets up, that everything has all of its properties essentially, or that no thing could have been different from the way it was, but these unpalatable essentialist claims remain, in Plantinga's words, "the sober metaphysical truth of the matter,"[16] according to counterpart theory. Nathan Salmon, in his statement of this argument, concludes that counterpart theory "is, at bottom, just a particularly inflexible brand of essentialism. . . . The counterpart theorist can mouth the words 'ship *a* might have been made from slightly different matter,' but any such pronouncement by the counterpart theorist in modal operator discourse is a verbal camouflage that merely postpones the inevitable. What matters is what the counterpart theorist *means* by these words, and more importantly, what is *not meant* by these words."[17]

I am not sure what to think of this argument, mainly because I am not sure how to disentangle the semantical and metaphysical issues. On the one hand, I am inclined to say that the argument just begs the question. The counterpart theorist, in putting forward the semantical part of the doctrine, is not simply proposing that we talk in a different way—that we introduce a "new and looser sense" for certain modal expressions.[18] Rather, the counterpart theorist is proposing an analysis of what we ordinarily say—what we have meant all along—when we talk about the ways things might have been. To say, as Plantinga does, that "the Counterpart Theorist is using that sentence ['Socrates could have been unwise'] to express a proposition different from the one the rest of us express by it"[19] is simply to deny the counterpart theorist's semantical thesis. The argument is not so much an argument against the thesis as it is a rhetorical appeal to its intuitive implausibility. The counterpart theorist replies that although the theory may be surprising, it does account for the phenomena: it can give truth-values to ordinary modal claims that agree with our intuitions about those claims. The semantic thesis, and the contrasting one from the standard theory, should be judged on how well they account for the use of ordinary modal language, and not on alleged intuitions about how the theoretical terms of the theory relate to the modal language they are being used to explain.[20]

On the other hand, I am not entirely persuaded by this reply to the argument because I am inclined to reject the sharp contrast between the theoretical apparatus of semantics and the ordinary discourse it is used to explain. The semantical apparatus, and the theses stated in terms of it, must be understood partly in terms of ordinary modal discourse. For example, possible worlds are explained as ways things might have been, and we are urged to believe in other possible worlds simply on the basis of the intuitive plausibility of the ordinary modal claim that there are many ways things might have been. We get an intuitive grip on what it is for something to be true in a possible world by indentifying it with what would be true simpliciter if that world were actual. This is, of course, to acknowledge some circularity in modal semantics. The apparatus makes clear the abstract structure of modal discourse, but it does not really provide an analysis of that discourse in terms that are understood independently of it. If this is right, then we may be entitled to take seriously our intuitions about theses stated in terms of the apparatus of semantical theory.

In the case of counterpart theory, the worry is that we must use modal locutions in explaining the apparatus in a way that is inconsistent with what the apparatus says that those locutions mean. Consider a statement based on Plantinga's example mentioned above: "If a leaf had fallen a day earlier than it in fact fell, Socrates would still have existed." Intuitively, this should come out true, and it does, according to the counterpart interpretation, since the consequent is true in the relevant possible worlds by virtue of the fact that counterparts of Socrates would have existed there. But to understand what is distinctive about the counterpart move, we must also recognize that it is in some sense not really Socrates who exists in those other possible worlds. If we understand truth in a possible world as what would be true if that world were realized, then the theoretical claim that the individual in the other possible world is not Socrates, but only a counterpart of him, is the claim that if a leaf had fallen a day earlier than it in fact fell, the individual who would have been Socrates would not have been not him but someone else.

This argument is not decisive. The counterpart theorist will not accept these intuitive explanations of possible worlds and of truth in possible worlds. But without them, or some alternative, it is not clear that we know what we are talking about when we talk about possible worlds.

So I am unsure how to evaluate this objection to counterpart theory in its usual form, but I will bypass the issue by defending a version of counterpart theory that is not subject to the Plantinga-Salmon argument. The version that I will suggest is motivated only by the third of the three considerations distinguished above. It will be an actualist theory, and a theory that is compatible with haecceitism, as I will interpret that doctrine. In fact, despite being a version of counterpart theory, it will make the claim that the individual who would be me if things were different really would be identical to me. Before saying how this is possible, I need to make some general remarks, first about actualism, and then about haecceitism.

3. ACTUALISM AND MERELY POSSIBLE INDIVIDUALS

The actualist believes that existing and *actually* existing are the same thing. There exists nothing that is not actual, and this thesis should be understood not as a restrictive metaphysical thesis like materialism and nominalism about what there is in the world, but simply as a trivial consequence of the meaning of the word "actual." How then, according to the actualist, can there be unactualized possibilities? The actualist explains how this is possible by distinguishing two senses of the term "possible world." One the one hand one may mean by "possible world" a way things might be: a property of a certain kind that the world might have, or a state it might be in. On the other hand, one might mean a world that is that way: that has that property, or is in that state. Nonactual possible worlds in the first sense exist, and actually exist, but are unexemplified. Nonactual possible worlds in the second sense do not exist at all, although they could have if things had been different. Modal semantics, in its application (which of course takes place in the actual world), is committed to the existence of possible worlds only in the first sense.[21]

The actualist has a problem about possible individuals, as well as possible worlds, and need to reconcile actualism not only with the intuition that things might have been different from the way they actually are but also with the intuition that there might have been things other than those there actually are. Modal semantics posits nonactual possible worlds; the actualist explains them as uninstantiated ways things might be. Modal semantics may also populate the domains of these possible worlds with nonactual possible individuals. How are these to be explained? The actualist needs a distinction, parallel to the distinction between a world and a state of the world, between an individual and some kind of abstract property or state of an individual that can represent it, something that can exist even when the individual itself does not. Alvin Plantinga, in a discussion of actualism and possible worlds, raises this problem and defends this kind of solution. "How can the actualist understand . . . 'There could have been an object distinct from each object that actually exists'? . . . Easily enough; he must appeal to essences. Socrates is a contingent being; his essence, however, is not. Properties, like propositions and possible worlds, are necessary beings. If Socrates had not existed, his essence would have been unexemplified, but not non-existent.''[22] In the application of modal semantics, Plantinga suggests, we should regard the domains of the various possible worlds, not as sets of individuals themselves, but as sets of essences—the essences that would be exemplified if that world were actual.

Whatever the fate of Plantinga's particular theory of individual essences, the general point is difficult to avoid. Any actualist who accepts the intuitively very plausible thesis that there might have been individuals other than those that actually exist will need to distinguish in some way between *individuals* in the strict sense and their representatives in the domains of the possible worlds. The commitment of an application of possible worlds semantics will be to the representatives that make up the domains. To say that there might have existed an individual with such and such properties is not to say that there *does* exist an individual with those properties in the domain of some possible world, but rather that there exists in the *essential domain* (to use Plantinga's term for the domain of essences) of some possible world a representative of an individual who is represented in that world as having such and such properties.

However the details are spelled out, if we make this kind of distinction, we will need also to distinguish two questions about identity across possible worlds—questions that are easy to conflate if we ignore the distinction required by actualism between individuals and their individual essences or representatives. We may ask, of two "individuals" drawn from the domains of two different possible worlds, whether the essences or representatives are identical, or we may ask whether the individuals represented are identical. The two questions are obviously different and might receive different answers. A particular theory of essences such as Plantinga's may have the consequence that the answers to the two questions will always be the same, but once we have made the general distinction, we can consider alternative theories that answer these two questions differently. An actualist version of counterpart theory, I want to suggest, is one such theory.

Suppose we require that the essential domains of different possible worlds be disjoint. But the essences or representatives that make up these domains will be related by a counterpart relation.[23] The intuitive explanation of the counterpart relation is roughly as follows: the relation holds between representatives *a* and *b* if and only if *a* and *b* represent the same individual. In the application of this version of counterpart theory, it will be true that if a leaf had fallen a day earlier than it did in 1876, Socrates himself would still have existed, even though the essence or whatever it is that the model theory uses to represent him in the domain of the actual world would have been unexemplified. Instead, he would have instantiated a different ''essence.'' Saying this may require a nonstandard theory of essences, but it is no longer a plausible charge against this version of counterpart theory that it is ''at bottom just a particularly inflexible brand of essentialism.''

Still, the critic may respond, what is the point? This theory will surely be just a clumsy notational variation of the standard theory, one that uses an artificial concept of essence to say, in a slightly different way, the same things that could be said with Plantinga's original concept. Here the actualist counterpart theorist may reply in the same way that Lewis replied, in his original exposition of counterpart theory, to a similar suggestion on behalf of the standard theory: ''But beware. Our difference is not just verbal, for I enjoy a generality he cannot match. The counterpart relation will not, in general, be an equivalence relation.''[24] But, the critic is likely to protest at this point, Lewis can say this, since his counterpart relation does not really represent identity, but the actualist counterpart theorist cannot consistently use identity to explain the counterpart relation in the way suggested above and also allow a counterpart relation that is not an equivalence relation. Suppose, the critic continues, the counterpart relation holds between essences *a* and *b,* and also between essences *b* and *c*. It follows that the individual that exemplifies *a* is identical with the individual that exemplifies *b,* and that the individual that exemplifies *b* is identical with the individual that exemplifies *c*. Then, by the transitivity of identity, the individual that exemplifies *a* is identical with the individual that exemplifies *c,* and by the explanation of the counterpart relation, it follows that the counterpart relation holds between *a* and *c*. So, the critic concludes, this relation must be transitive, and a similar argument will show that it must be symmetric.

If this argument were right, then it would show that the actualist counterpart move that I am suggesting would have no point. For our only motivation in making the move is get the added flexibility that will allow us to account for the various puzzle cases, and this requires a nontransitive counterpart relation. But I will argue that the argument does not work—that we can permit the counterpart relation to be nontransitive and nonsymmetric while using it to represent cross-world identity, where ''identity'' really means *identity*. But before giving this argument, I need to make some general remarks about thisness and identity.

4. HAECCEITISM AND ABSOLUTE IDENTITY

David Kaplan has given the name ''haecceitism'' to the doctrine that ''it does make sense to ask—without reference to common attributes and behavior—whether *this* is the same individual in another possible world, that individuals can be extended in logical space (i.e. through possible worlds) in much the way we commonly regard them as extended in physical space and time, and that a common "thisness" may underlie extreme dissimilarity or distinct thisness may underlie great resemblance."[25] The opposite doctrine—antihaecceitism—is the doctrine I cited in section 2 above as the second motivation for counterpart theory, but I have disclaimed this motivation. The version of counterpart theory that I am defending is or may be haecceitist: the counterpart relation may be a primitive relation, irreducible to qualitative similarities and differences. The question is, can a haecceitist version of counterpart theory permit a flexible counterpart relation, one that is nontransitive or nonsymmetric? There is, of course, no reason why a counterpart relation that is primitive and irreducible must be an equivalence relation. The question is whether a counterpart relation that is not an equivalence relation can represent genuine cross-world identity. How does the doctrine of haecceitism rule this out?

Nathan Salmon interprets Kaplan's doctrine to be explicitly about the identity relation. "At least one version of haecceitism," he suggests, "may be described as the view that the logic of possible world discourse includes a binary *absolute* concept of genuine identity between individuals in addition to its ternary *world-relative* concept of identity."[26] Salmon's thesis, as he develops it, is incompatible with my version of haecceitist counterpart theory, but I will argue that the actualist has no reason to accept it. Salmon suggests that we must accept his thesis if we are really to mean *identity* by "identity"—the relation that holds between *x* and *y* "in a world *w* if and only if *x* and *y* are, in an absolute sense, one and the very same thing,"[27] but I will argue that this suggestion is mistaken. The relation that Salmon calls a ternary world-relative relation is as absolute as a relation of genuine identity needs to be.

For an actualist, all statements, including those made by possible worlds theorists when they are talking in their semantical metalanguages, are made in and from the perspective of a possible world. The idea that there is a perspective outside all possible worlds from which we can talk about them is a possibilist myth. Actual semantic theorists, even when they are talking about other possible worlds, speak in the actual world, and their statements are true if and only if they are true at the actual world. Identity statements are not special in this regard: true identity statements are identity statements that are true at the actual world. To say this is not to espouse any kind of relativism. Truth, from the perspective of the actual world, is absolute truth, the only *real* truth there is. Truth in or at other possible worlds is just what would be true if things were different. Of course, *some* things that an actual or possible person might say are necessary truths, and for these statements, it makes no difference whether they are evaluated from the perspective of the actual world or from the perspective of some other possible world. One might mean by an *absolute* property or relation a property or relation that is true in all possible worlds of whatever it is true in any possible world. In this sense, the identity relation is absolute just in case all identities are necessary. But this is not what we usually mean when we talk about properties and relations being absolute. No one would argue against absolute simultaneity, for example, simply on the ground that simultaneity is contingent—that some simultaneous events might not have been simultaneous.

Suppose we reject the assumption that there is an identity relation that is absolute in Salmon's sense. Can we still explain the intraworld or world-relative identity relation as the relation of "being the very same thing," irrespective of ways of conceptualizing the things identified? There is no reason why we cannot: identity is the binary relation whose extension, in any possible world w, is the set of pairs $<d,d>$ such that d is in the domain of w.[28] This is surely identity. But what about cross-world identities? How can we ask and answer questions about whether a member of the domain of one possible world is or is not identical, in the strict sense, with a member of the domain of a different world? The actualist can make sense of such questions, provided it is kept in mind that they, like any other questions, are answered from within a possible world.

There is no reason why we cannot pick out an individual by virtue of the properties it has in one possible world and then talk about the properties or activities of that individual in a different possible world. Consider Nixon, the man who in fact won the 1968 presidential election; suppose he had lost. Here we refer to Nixon, in the actual world, and select a (partial) counterfactual world as a function of him. We might also describe an individual in the counterfactual world, and then locate that individual in the actual world. Consider the person who won the 1968 presidential election in the counterfactual world I have selected. Who is he? He is our very own Hubert Humphrey. That is, the person who (in the counterfactual world) won the 1968 presidential election is (in the actual world) identical to Hubert Humphrey. This is a cross-world identity statement, and it is really identity that we are attributing, an equivalence relation that obeys Leibniz's law, the srongest equivalence relation, the one that holds only between a thing and itself.

We are now in a position to answer the arguments against the coherence of contingent identity. Here is one such argument: suppose it were possible for what is in fact one thing to be two distinct things. Then there will be something a that is one thing in one world, w_1, and two distinct things, call them b and c, in another world, w_2. Then the cross-world identity statements $b = a$ and $a = c$ will both be true, but the intraworld identity statement $b = c$ will be false, and this violates the transitivity of identity.

The problem with this argument becomes clear when we ask which possible world it is given in, or relative to. First, consider the argument from the point of view of w_1: the two cross-world identity statements are both true: $b = a$ and $a = c$. But $b = c$ is also true *in* w_1. That is, it is true in w_1 that the individual that in w_2 is b is identical with the individual that in w_2 is c. So there is no violation of transitivity. Now consider the argument from the point of view of w_2: $b = c$ is clearly false here. What about $b = a$ and $a = c$? What these identity statements do is identify each of b and c with the individual that in w_1 is identical with a. But the description "the individual that in w_1 is identical with a" is, in w_2, an improper description. So the identity statements are, in w_2, either false, truth-valueless, or ambiguous. The fallacy of the w_2 version of the argument, $b = a$, $a = c$, therefore $b = c$, is analogous to the fallacy in the following argument: Russell is the author of *Principia Mathematica*, the author of *Principia Mathematica* is Whitehead, therefore Russell is Whitehead.

A similar answer can be given to the argument sketched in section 3 that the counterpart relation, to represent identity, must be an equivalence relation. Strictly, the intuitive explanation that relates the counterpart relation to identity is as follows: the counterpart relation holds between essence a in the domain of w_1 and essence b in the domain of w_2 if and only if the individual that instantiates a (in w_1) is (in w_1) identical with the individual that instantiates b (in w_2). If the counterpart relation is nontransitive, then there will be identities true in one possible world that conflict with those true in another, but within any world, the identity relation will be perfectly well-behaved.

Our defense of actualist counterpart theory and the coherence of contingent identity requires, first, a distinction between possible individuals themselves and their essences or representatives in the domains of the various possible worlds and, second, the rejection of a world-independent concept of identity. Both, I have argued, are motivated, independently of the defense of contingent identity, by a thoroughgoing actualist conception of possible worlds and possible individuals. Since, according to actualism, there are no merely possible individuals, we need something other than possible individuals to represent the possibility that there be things other than those that actually exist. And since, according to actualism, the actual world is not one place among others but is the only place there really is, real truth is truth at the actual world.

It is not, of course, that actualism *requires* contingent identity or world-bound essences. The examples and intuitions that motivate actualist counterpart theory are themselves controversial and might be rejected or explained away. My aim has been only to argue that one cannot refute the possibility of contingent identity simply on the basis of the semantics and logic of identity. A proper defense of the necessity of all identities must recognize it as the metaphysical thesis that it is.

I will conclude with two sets of brief remarks: first some very impressionistic comments about the analogy between identity across possible worlds and identity through time; second, some informal comments about some problems that arise in constructing a formal semantics for actualist counterpart theory.

5. WORLDS AND TIMES

Can one give an account of identity through time that is analogous to the account that I have sketched of identity across possible worlds—an account that permits *temporary* identity, the branching and merging of individuals through time? It would be nice if we could. There are plenty of puzzle cases that such an account might help to clarify. The literature on personal identity is filled with examples of one person becoming two, cases that are difficult to describe in a plausible way.[29] It is generally assumed in discussions of personal identity that one cannot coherently say, about such cases, that the original person literally *is* each of two later persons, even though the later persons are, at the later time, distinct from each other. But even if the actualist counterpart account of cross-world identity works, there are disanalogies between worlds and times that prevent a straightforward extension of the account to identity through time. This is too large an issue to discuss adequately here; my aim in this section is just to point briefly at some of the relevant analogies and disanalogies.

Start with a spatial analogy: just southwest of Ithaca, Route 13 and Route 96 merge. They go through town together and then divide again; 13 goes east through Cortland while 96 goes north on the west side of the lake. Might we talk of *local* identity, analogous to temporary and contingent identity, in such a case?[30] Southwest of Ithaca, Routes 96 and 13 are distinct, but in town they are identical. We can and do talk this way sometimes, but we are also inclined to say that, strictly, Routes 13 and 96 are nowhere identical; they just share a part. What is identical is that part of Route 13 that is in the city and that part of Route 96 that is in the city. Compare this with the putative cases of contingent identity. There is a possibility that I am tempted to describe as the possibility that I might have been twins. Philosophers may disagree about whether there really is such a possibility, or about how best to describe it, but no one would say that the sober truth of the matter is that there are really two persons where I am who share a common part, the part that *actually* exists—that is located in the actual world. What is the difference between the spatial and the logical-spatial cases? The crucial difference is that while most of us have an actualist conception of possible worlds and possible individuals, we all hold a thesis that is analogous to possibilism about other spatial locations. The regions south and north of Ithaca where 13 and 96 go their separate ways are as real as this place here, within Ithaca. Although there are no individuals that exist only in other possible worlds, there really are things that are located only in other places—for example, that stretch of Route 13 that passes through Cortland. We do not need surrogates that are *here* for things and places that exist only elsewhere; our ontology accommodates the things themselves. Even if there is no world-independent identity relation, there is, it seems plausible to say, a location-independent identity relation. If I say that America's most famous highway is U.S. Route 66, you need not ask where I am when I say this in order to assess its truth.

Are other times more like other places or other possible worlds? Should we admit past and future individuals into our ontology? Is there a temporally neutral perspective—the perspective of eternity—from which objective reality is best described? These are large and elusive questions. I suspect most of us are ambivalent, shifting between a space-like and a world-like conception of time. Some of the puzzles about identity through time may derive from this shift.

If you think of time as space-like, then you will think of continuant individuals—persons and physical objects—as extended through time in the same way that they are extended through space. We are the same as our histories. Only a part of you exists now; other temporal parts are past, or yet to come. On this conception of an object or person, cases of splitting persons should be unproblematic. Suppose *a* undergoes an operation that results in two persons, *b* and *c*, each continuous with *a* in all the psychological and physical ways that would normally make it appropriate to say that it was the same person. The most natural thing to say, from the point of view that sees time as space-like, is that there were two persons all along, but persons with a common temporal part, the part that existed before the operation. Just as two highways pass through Ithaca together, so two persons share the same youth.

If this seems implausible, I think it is because we are inclined to think of a continuant substance—person or physical object—not as something with temporal parts, like an event, but as something that is "all there" in some sense at each moment, even though it is the same thing at different times. We are inclined to say this even if we have trouble explaining what it means. This inclination comes, I think, from a "presentist" conception of time analogous to an actualist conception of worlds—a view according to which we are extended through time in the way we are extended through possible worlds. This conception can, I think, make sense of genuine temporary identity. From this perspective, we can coherently describe the cases of splitting persons as cases of two distinct persons who used to be identical to each other.

6. VARIABLE BINDING

In this concluding section, I will make some informal remarks about the problem of constructing a formal semantics for a modal quantified language that is appropriate to the actualist counterpart theory that I have been exploring. Some serious problems arise when one tries to generalize the usual semantic rules to cover the case that permits contingent identity, although they are problems about variable binding and predication and do not have to do directly with the logic or semantics of identity. The problems can be solved, but only at some cost in complexity and some loss of intuitive naturalness. I will try to say what the problems are, to identify their source, and to point to two alternative solutions.[31]

Variable binding is essentially a device for constructing complex predicates out of sentences. Take any sentence, remove a name, and replace it with a blank, represented by a variable. One then has what is, in effect, a predicate that is true *of* an individual if and only if the sentence would have been true if the name removed had named the individual. Quantification was the original motivation for the device, and in the usual formulation of quantification theory, variable binding is tied to quantification: it is the quantifier that binds the variable. But complex predicates have uses independent of quantification. There is no loss of expressive power, and some gain in conceptual clarity, if we separate the use of variables to construct complex predicates from the application of quantifiers to those predicates. One can formulate ordinary extensional quantification theory so that the only variable binding operator is an abstraction operator taking an open sentence into a one-place predicate. In this formulation, the quantifiers bind no variables but are simply operators that take a predicate, simple or complex, into a sentence.[32]

In extensional semantics, the semantical rule for complex predicates will be something like this: the extension of $\hat{x}A$ (where A is any sentence) will be the set of individuals d in the domain for which A is true when x is assigned the value d. The generalization of this rule to the standard version of modal semantics is relatively straightforward. In general, in standard possible worlds semantics, the semantic values of expressions are *intensions*—functions from possible worlds to extensions. The semantic rules are generalized by relativizing them to possible worlds. They say what the intension of an expression is by saying what its extension is, relative to each possible world. In its standard modal version, the rule for complex predicates will then be somthing like this: For any world w, the extension of $\hat{x}A$ in w will be the set of individuals d from the domain of w for which A is true in w when x is assigned the value d. But this simple generalization will not do for counterpart semantics, at least if the semantics permits individuals to have more than one counterpart in the same possible world. To see why, consider the simplest model of contingent identity: there are two possible worlds, w_1 and w_2. There is one individual in the domain of w_1, a, and two in w_2, b and c. The counterpart relation holds (in both directions) between a and b, and between a and c. Suppose further that the one place predicate G expresses a property that is false of everyithing in w_1, and true just of b in w_2. Now consider whether a is (in w_1) in the extension of the complex predicate $\hat{x}\lozenge Gx$. According to our rule, it is, if $\lozenge Gx$ is true in w_1 when x takes the value a, which in turn will be true if Gx is true in w_2 when x takes the value a. But a has two counterparts in w_2, one of which has the property expressed by G and one of which does not, so how do we decide whether Gx is true there when x takes the value a? The problem is that although the value of G is a well-defined *property* (function taking a possible world to a subset of the domain of that world), the property does not determine a unique *propositional function* (function taking an individual into a proposition, where a proposition is a function from possible worlds to truth-values). As a result, a complex predicate constructed with G may fail to express a determinate property.

One response to the problem—not the one I will recommend—is to stipulate that d should be in the extension of $\hat{x}A$ in w if there is *at least one* way of choosing the counterparts of d in other possible worlds so that A comes out true in w when x takes the value d. This idea can be made precise by assigning to the variables, not individuals themselves, but *individuating functions:* functions that select one counterpart of a given individual for each world in which it has a counterpart.[33] The extension of $\hat{x}A$ in w will then be defined as the set of individuals d in the domain of w such that for at least one of d's individuating functions f, A is true in w when x takes the value f. This is perfectly coherent, but it is complicated and has intuitively and formally unpleasant consequences for the logic of predication and quantification. For example, in our simple model, a will have the property expressed by $\hat{x}\lozenge Gx$ but it will also have the property that seems to be the complement of this one, the one expressed by $\hat{x}\sim\lozenge Gx$. But of course a will not have the contradictory property one gets by conjoining these two, $\hat{x}(\lozenge Gx\,\&\sim\lozenge Gx)$. The abstraction principle that asserts the equivalence of $\hat{x}A\,(y)$ and A^y/x for all y in the domain will be invalid, as will quantifier distribution principles, which implicitly involve abstraction. Even the simple duality relations between the quantifiers will break down. If $\forall\,\hat{x}A$ means that everything has the property $\hat{x}A$, and $\exists\,\hat{x}A$ means that something does, then $\sim\exists\,\hat{x}\sim A$ will not be equivalent, in general, to $\forall\,\hat{x}A$. Our simple abstract model again illustrates this: something, namely a, satisfies $\hat{x}\sim\lozenge Gx$ in w_1, so $\exists\,\hat{x}\sim\lozenge Gx$ is true in w_1. But also everything (since a is the only thing) satisfies $\hat{x}\lozenge Gx$ in w_1, so $\forall\,\hat{x}\lozenge Gx$ will be true in w_1. The problem is that our rule has introduced a hidden existential quantifier into the predicate forming operation—a quantifier over individuating functions—and this has radically distorted the logic of complex predicates and quantifiers.

I prefer a different strategy that seems to me conceptually more natural and that has a less radical effect on the logic. What our model shows, according to the line of thought that motivates the second strategy, is that complex predicates are sometimes ambiguous or indeterminate. $\hat{x} \Diamond Gx$ is true of a on one way of individuating a, false on another. This indeterminacy might be resolved by context—by selecting one set of individuating functions for the purpose of describing things—or we might just leave the predicates with fuzzy boundaries. One can develop this strategy by associating with each possibly indeterminate interpretation a set of determinate extensions of it—all the admissible[34] ways of selecting counterparts so as to resolve all ambiguities. Then the supervaluation move can be used to define truth and falsity in the indeterminate model: A sentence is true if it is true on all determinate extensions, false if false on all determinate extensions, and neither if true on some and false on others.[35]

The logic of abstraction, quantification, and identity will be standard on a theory of this kind, but the counterpart relation may still be nontransitive and nonsymmetric, even in determinate models, and this will give rise to some differences between the logic of the standard combined modal-quantification theory and its counterpart variation. Chandler's case of the bicycle with parts that vary slightly from world to world, for example, can be modeled by a determinate interpretation with a counterpart relation that is nontransitive. I think this theory is worth exploring.

One final comment: what about the sentence of modal quantification theory that says that all identities are necessary?[36]

(NI) $(x)(y)(x = y \rightarrow \Box x = y)$

It has been argued[37] that this can be proved using only Leibniz's law and uncontroversial principles of quantification theory. How does actualist counterpart theory avoid this conclusion? The answer is that it does not, by either of the two ways of doing the semantics that I have described. Both kinds of accounts will validate the statement, although for different reasons. In the first kind of semantics, what the statement says is that for any individuals x and y, if x and y are the same, then there is at least one way of picking counterparts so that in every possible world, the counterpart of x is identical with the counterpart of y. This will of course be true even in our model of contingent identity. Note, though, that a statement that *appears* to be equivalent to the negation of (NI) will also be true in w_1 in this model:

(CI) $(\exists x)(\exists y)(x = y \ \& \ \Diamond x \neq y)$.

On the second way of doing semantics, (NI) is also determinately true, even in our simple model. Obviously, every way of picking counterparts of a will pick the same counterpart for a as the one it picks for a. Because both b and c are, in w_2, self-identical, $x = y$ will be determinately true in w_2 where the values of x and y are both a. There will, however, be more devious ways of expressing the fact that the model represents, in some sense, contingent identity. The inner *necessitation* of (NI), for example, will not be valid:

(NNI) $(x)(y)\Box(x = y \rightarrow \Box x = y)$.

Our model is a countermodel for this principle: in w_2, b and c are examples of individuals such that it is possible that they be identical, but not necessarily identical. That is, where x takes the value b and y the value c, $\Diamond(x = y \ \& \ \Diamond x \neq y)$ will be true in w_2.

If there is such a thing as contingent identity in the sense actualist counterpart theory tries to say that there is, it is not easy to talk about it.[38]

Notes

1. Lewis (1968) introduced counterpart theory. See Lewis (1986) for his most recent and most detailed defense of possibilism.

2. This term is from Adams (1979).

3. Chandler (1975).

4. This is the rule for the simplest semantics for **S5**. In semantic theories for other systems, necessity is relativized to the worlds. A binary accessibility relation between worlds is added to the structure, and the necessity rule says that A is true in w if and only if A is true in w' for all w' that are accessible to w.

5. I discuss two ways of modifying the rules in section 6. See also Lewis (1968) and Hazen (1979). Lewis formulates counterpart theory, not as a semantics for a modal language, but as an extensional theory with quantifiers ranging over possible worlds and possible individuals.

6. Lewis gives an argument like this (1983, 21–22).

7. See Chandler (1975).

8. Gibbard (1975).

9. Chandler (1976) discusses this case. Salmon has a very detailed discussion of the case, which he calls "the four worlds paradox" (1981, 229–52). See also his more recent discussion (1986). Chisholm (1967) had discussed a similar problem much earlier.

10. The form of argument may look superficially like a sorites argument, and it does seem true that the constraints on cross-world identity being appealed to here are vague. But the problem is independent of vagueness. Even if the threshold were perfectly precise, the puzzle would remain.

11. The response that Chandler suggests, and that Salmon adopts in his discussion of the puzzle, is different from either of these: they argue that all the bicycles are identical, but that the more distant possible worlds in the sequence are not accessible to each other. That is, there is a possible world in which the bicycle has totally different parts from those it actually has, but this world is not possible relative to the actual world. Things cannot, of course, lack their essential properties, but according to this solution, it is possibly possible for them to lack their essential properties.

12. This case was invented by Kripke (1979).

13. See Plantinga (1973).

14. Salmon (1981, 232–38).

15. Plantinga (1973), as reprinted in Loux (1979, 164).

16. Ibid., 158.

17. Salmon (1981, 236).

18. Plantinga (1974, 117).

19. Ibid.

20. Hazen (1979) gives an argument like this. Salmon (1981, 235 n) criticizes it.

21. I have defended this actualist account of possible worlds (1976). See (1984, chap. 3) for an expanded version of this paper.

22. Plantinga (1976), as reprinted in Loux (1979, 268).

23. The label "essence" is not really appropriate for the world-bound representatives of individuals, since they are not essential to the individuals that instantiate them, but I will continue to use the term.

24. Lewis (1968), as reprinted in Loux (1979, 112).

25. Kaplan (1975), as reprinted in Loux (1979, 217).

26. Salmon (1981, 127 n).

27. Ibid., 224.

28. There is a general question about how to evaluate predication statements, including identity statements, in possible worlds in which the individuals the predicate is being applied to do not exist. Is, for example, "Socrates is a man" true, false, or neither in possible worlds in which Socrates does not exist at all (and has no counterpart)? I prefer modal semantic theories (whether in their standard or counterpart forms) that require the extension of a predicate in a possible world to be a subset of the domain of that world. On this decision, $x = x$ will be false in a possible world where the value assigned to x does not exist (or has no counterparts). An alternative decision—the one that is usually made in modal semantics—would permit nonexistent things to have properties and stand in relations. On this decision, the extension of the identity relation might include $<d, d>$ in all possible worlds, whether d exists there or not.

29. See, for example, the papers by Derek Parfit, John Perry, Sydney Shoemaker, and Bernard Williams in Perry (1975).

30. Kaplan (1979) mentions the highway analogy in Loux (1979, 103).

31. There are other solutions than the ones I will discuss. See Hazen (1979) for one. Although the strategy I will recommend is different in some ways from the one Hazen has developed, it borrows some ideas from it.

32. See my discussion and defense of this way of formulating quantification theory (1977).

33. Hintikka (1969) formulates a modal semantics in terms of individuating functions rather than a counterpart relation.

34. I say every *admissible* way of choosing counterparts since, as Hazen (1979) has pointed out, there may be links between the counterparts of different individuals. Supose Ronald Reagan and his daughter Maureen (or their "essences") each has two counterparts in a certain possible world. There are four pairs consisting of counterparts of Ronald and Maureen, respectively, but there may be only two pairs that are counterparts of the father-daughter pair in this world.

35. Van Fraassen invented the supervaluation account of semantic indeterminacy. The first application of this strategy was to the problem of nonreferring singular terms (1966). The strategy has since been used to represent many kinds of semantic indeterminacy, including ordinary vagueness of predicates, sortal incorrectness, semantic paradoxes, indeterminate counterfactuals, and future contingent statements.

36. I am ignoring an irrelevant side issue in this discussion: the issue of what to say about predication statements, including identity statements, in possible worlds in which the individuals the statements are about do not exist. (See note 28 above.) If one requires, as I would prefer, that the extensions of all predicates in a given possible world must be subsets of the domain of that world, then $x = x$ will be false of d in w if d does not exist in w. In this case, identities will not be contingent, but for a reason that has nothing to do with the kind of contingent identity at issue in this paper. The real issue is whether identities are essential: whether if $x = y$, it is necessary that if x exists, $x = y$. If one makes the decision about predication that I recommend, the discussion should be, not about (NI), but about the qualified principle:

$$(x)(y)\ (x = y \rightarrow \Box(Ex \rightarrow x = y)).$$

37. See, for example, Wiggins (1980, chap. 1)

38. I would like to thank the National Endowment for the Humanities for fellowship support, and Cornell University for time off during the period when this paper was written.

References

Adams, Robert. 1979. "Primitive Thisness and Primitive Identity." *Journal of Philosophy* 76:5–26.

Chandler, Hugh. 1975. "Rigid Designation." *Journal of Philosophy* 72:362–69.

——————. 1976. "Plantinga and the Contingently Possible." *Analysis* 36:106–9.

Chisholm, Roderick. 1967. "Identity through Possible Worlds: Some Questions." *Nous* 1:1–8. Reprinted in *The Possible and the Actual: Readings in the Metaphysics of Modality,* edited by Michael Loux, 80–87. Ithaca, N.Y.

Gibbard, Allan. 1975. "Contingent Identity." *Journal of Philosophical Logic* 4:187–221.

Hazen, Allen. 1979. "Counterpart-Theoretic Semantics for Modal Logic." *Journal of Philosophy* 76:285–338.

Hintikka, Jaakko. 1969. "Semantics for Propositional Attitudes." In *Philosophical Logic,* edited by J. W. Davis *et. al.,* 21–45. Dordrecht.

Kaplan, David. 1975. "How to Russell a Frege-Church." *Journal of Philosophy* 72: 716–29. Reprinted in *The Possible and the Actual: Readings in the Metaphysics of Modality,* edited by Michael Loux, 210–24. Ithaca, N.Y.

——————. 1979. "Transworld Heir Lines." In *The Possible and the Actual: Readings in the Metaphysics of Modality,* edited by Michael Loux, 88–109. Ithaca, N.Y.

Kripke, Saul. 1979. "A Puzzle About Belief." In *Meaning and Use,* edited by A. Margalit, 239-83. Dordrecht.

Lewis, David. 1968. "Counterpart Theory and Quantified Modal Logic." *Journal of Philosophy* 65:113–26. Reprinted in *The Possible and the Actual: Readings in the Metaphysics of Modality*, edited by Michael Loux, 110–28. Ithaca, N.Y.

————. 1983. "Individuation by Acquaintances and by Stipulation." *Philosophical Review* 9:3–32.

————. 1986. *On the Plurality of Worlds*. Oxford.

Loux, Michael, ed. 1979. *The Possible and the Actual: Readings in the Metaphysics of Modality*. Ithaca, N.Y.

Perry, John, ed. 1975. *Personal Identity*. Berkeley.

Plantinga, Alvin. 1973. "Transworld Identity or Worldbound Individuals?" in *Logic and Ontology*, edited by Milton Munitz. New York City. Reprinted in *The Possible and the Actual: Readings in the Metaphysics of Modality*, edited by Michael Loux, 146–65. Ithaca, N.Y.

————. 1974. *The Nature of Necessity*. Oxford.

————. 1976. "Actualism and Possible Worlds." *Theoria* 42:139–60. Reprinted in *The Possible and the Actual: Readings in the Metaphysics of Modality*, edited by Michael Loux, 253–73. Ithaca, N.Y.

Salmon, Nathan. 1981. *Reference and Essence*. Princeton, N.J.

————. 1986. "Modal Paradox: Parts and Counterparts, Points and Counterpoints." In this volume.

Stalnaker, Robert. 1976. "Possible Worlds." *Nous* 10:65–75. Reprinted in *The Possible and the Actual: Readings in the Metaphysics of Modality*, edited by Michael Loux, 225–34. Ithaca, N.Y.

————. 1977. "Complex Predicates." *The Monist* 60:327–39.

————. 1984. *Inquiry*. Cambridge, Mass.

Van Fraassen, Bas. 1966. "Singular Terms, Truth-Value Gaps, and Free Logic." *Journal of Philosophy* 63:481–95.

Wiggins, David. 1980. *Sameness and Substance*. Cambridge, Mass.

Mereological Essentialism, Mereological Conjunctivism, and Identity Through Time

JAMES VAN CLEVE

Mereological essentialism is the doctrine that no whole can change its parts; mereological conjunctivism is the doctrine that any two objects form a whole. In what follows I shall say something about how the two doctrines are related, defend at least a limited version of each, and draw morals for the problem of identity through time.

I. THREE GRADES OF MEREOLOGICAL ESSENTIALISM

Let us begin by distinguishing three grades of mereological essentialism.

1. A whole cannot survive the *destruction* of a part.
2. A whole cannot survive the *removal* of a part.
3. A whole cannot survive the *rearrangement* of its parts.

Since the rearrangement of a thing's parts is generally a less drastic operation than the removal of one part, and since removal in turn is less drastic than destruction, these doctrines may appear to be progressively stronger. Whether they are really so is a question I shall take up in section III.

As stated, 1–3 are merely temporal versions of essentialism, telling us what changes are compatible with the persistence or identity of a whole through time. A full-blooded essentialist doctrine also has modal force, telling us what ''changes'' are compatible with the ''persistence'' or identity of an object through various possible worlds. The full-strength versions of 1–3 would be as follows:

$1'$. If x is part of y, then x exists in every possible world in which y exists. (Or: If x is part of y, then y is necessarily such that x exists if y does.)

$2'$. If x is part of y, then x is part of y in every possible world in which y exists. (Or: If x is part of y, then y is necessarily such that x is part of it.)[1]

$3'$. If x and y are parts of z related by R, then x and y are parts of z related by R in every possible world in which z exists. (Or: If x and y are parts of z related by R, then z is necessarily such that x and y are parts of it related by R.)

My concern is with the full-strength doctrines, but for the sake of convenience in discussing them, I shall often use the temporal versions. What I have to say should carry over, *mutatis mutandis,* to the modal versions.

Mereological essentialism of the second grade has been espoused by a number of the great philosophers, including Locke, Leibniz, and Hume. In recent times, it has been defended by Chisholm but has found few other adherents.[2]

II. CONJUNCTIVISM, ANTICONJUNCTIVISM, AND EXTREME ANTICONJUNCTIVISM

Before I can explain these doctrines, I must provide several preliminary definitions. An object *z* is *composed of x* and *y* (or, *x* and *y* compose *z*) iff *x* and *y* are parts of *z*, and every part of *z* has a part in common either with *x* or with *y*. An object *z* is *exactly composed* of *x* and *y* iff *z* is composed of *x* and *y,* and *x* and *y* have no parts in common. A *sum* of *x* and *y* is any object composed of them; if there is just one such, let us denote it by '*x* + *y*'.[3] An object with parts is *continuous* iff any two parts of it that exactly compose it are in contact with each other.[4] (The idea is that a continuous object is "all in one piece.") Finally, an object is *scattered* iff it has parts and is not continuous.

The three doctrines listed above may now be described. *Conjunctivism* is the doctrine that for any two concrete objects, there is a third that is composed of them.[5] As a corollary, for any two *nonoverlapping* objects, i.e., objects having no part in common, there is a third that is *exactly* composed of them. It will readily be seen that conjunctivism countenances scattered objects, e.g., objects such as that object exactly composed of the Eiffel Tower and the Statue of Liberty. *Anticonjunctivism* is the direct contradictory of conjunctivism; it denies that any two objects compose a third. Finally, *extreme anticonjunctivism* is the doctrine that two objects *never* compose a third unless they are at least in contact. (Perhaps more than mere contact would be required.) Although anticonjunctivism permits the existence of *some* scattered objects, extreme anticonjunctivism rules out scattered objects altogether.

Among the proponents of conjunctivism have been Brentano, Tarski, and Goodman; among the proponents of anticonjunctivism have been Broad, Wiggins, and Chisholm.[6] I do not know of anyone who has explicitly advocated extreme anticonjunctivism.

III. LOGICAL RELATIONS AMONG THE DOCTRINES

I said earlier that the three grades of essentialism appear to be successively stronger, but whether this is really so depends on what one assumes in regard to the conjunctivism issue.

If we understand 'removal' to cover both the destruction of a part and the detachment of it without destruction, it is clear that grade 2 implies grade 1. (This is clearer yet in the modal versions.) Does 1 imply 2? The answer is that it would be possible for 1 to be true and 2 false *provided* conjunctivism were true, but not if extreme anticonjunctivism were true. To see this, consider the following diagram.

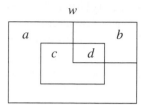

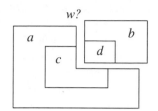

We start with the whole w, composed of a (which has c as a part) and b (which has d as a part). We then remove part b. Does w still exist? Conjunctivists can say yes, for they can hold that no part has been destroyed in the process. The part $c + d$, which was continuous before the removal of b, is now scattered; but it still exists. Extreme anticonjunctivists, on the other hand, *cannot* say that $c + d$ exists any longer. Assuming that it *did* exist before b was removed,[7] they must say that the removal of b has destroyed a part of w. But we are assuming that w cannot survive the destruction of a part; hence, it cannot survive the removal of a part either. QED.

The reader may wonder why I did not use this shorter argument from extreme anticonjunctivism to the nonsurvival of w: w is scattered after the removal of b; hence, it no longer exists. The reason is that my adversaries in this argument—extreme anti-conjunctivists who seek to affirm 1 while denying 2—would not accept the implicit identification of w with the scattered object $a + b$. They would maintain that although w was formerly composed of a and b, it was not then and is not now identical with their sum. That sum may be scattered, but w is not.[8]

This response by grade-2 inessentialists may provoke a further question. If they can evade the shorter argument by refusing to identify a whole with the sum of its parts, why can't they evade my longer argument in the same way? That is, why can't they say that just as the part formerly composed of a and b is not identical with the sum $a + b$, so the part formerly composed of c and d (call it George) is not identical with the sum $c + d$? This would enable them to say that George is still intact after the removal of d, from which one might conclude that no part of w has been destroyed by the removal of b after all.

But this maneuver will not suffice to evade my argument. *George* may have survived the removal of b from w, but that does not alter the fact that $c + d$ did *not* survive. Assuming that $c + d$ was a part of w to begin with (temporarily coinciding with George in material extent), we still have the result that at least one part of w has been destroyed. Grade-1 essentialism then requires us to conclude that w itself has been destroyed.[9]

So extreme anticonjunctivists who affirm grade 1 of mereological essentialism will also have to affirm grade 2. I want to argue next that they will be driven all the way to grade 3.

Typically, rearranging the parts of a thing involves removing some of them and reattaching them elsewhere. If all rearrangement were like this, our result would be immediate: no rearrangement without removal of a part; no removal without destruction of a part; hence, no rerrangement without destruction of a part (and therefore of the whole).[10] But not all rearrangement is like this. A blacksmith might move the head from one end of a nail to the other by bending the nail into a loop, fusing the head to the other end, snipping at the original junction, and then straightening the whole thing out again—a procedure in which no part is ever detached. Moreover, the modal version of grade-3 essentialism rules out *transworld* differences in arrangement, which are not the outcome of any process of rearrangement.

Nonetheless, we can still argue that 2 implies 3 and that 2' implies 3' if extreme anticonjunctivism is true. The strategy is the same as that used above in arguing that 1 implies 2. If a whole w differs in arrangement from a whole w', there will be parts that are adjacent in w but not in w'. For the extreme anticonjunctivist, this means that all those parts that straddled the plane of adjacency in w will no longer exist in w'. Hence, w itself will no longer exist. QED.[11]

So extreme anticonjunctivists cannot affirm grade 1 without affirming the other grades as well. What about conjunctivists? I said above that they can affirm 1 while denying 2. I should say now that although this combination is possible for them so far as logic alone goes, I don't think it is a reasonable one. When we detach a part from a whole, have we "removed" it in the sense of making it no longer a part of that whole? Not if the resulting scattered object is identical with the original whole, for the detached part is certainly a part of the scattered object. It begins to appear that for a conjunctivist, there can be no such thing as mere detachment; the only way to remove a part would be to destroy it.[12] In that case, grade 1 would imply grade 2 after all. The only way to avoid this result would be to refuse to identify the scattered object with the original whole—to reject the principle that anything having all the same parts as w must be w. But anyone who rejects this principle loses any rationale I can see for affirming grade 1 to begin with. So any conjunctivist who affirms 1 ought also to affirm 2.

Matters are otherwise with grade 3, however. The conjunctivist, unlike the extreme anticonjunctivist, can affirm both 1 and 2 while rejecting 3. This seems to me to be the *right* combination. It is also the combination advocated by Locke:

> If two or more atoms be joined together into the same mass . . . the mass, consisting of the same atoms, must be the same mass, or the same body, let the parts be ever so differently jumbled. But if one of these atoms be taken away, or one new one added, it is no longer the same mass or the same body.[13]

He goes on to make exception for living creatures: "in them the variation of great parcels of matter alters not the identity." I shall discuss attempts to limit the scope of mereological essentialism in section VII.

IV. THE CASE FOR CONJUNCTIVISM

To argue for conjunctivism, I shall use the following strategy: first I shall argue that extreme anticonjunctivism is false, i.e., that there are at least *some* scattered wholes;

then I shall argue that once some scattered wholes have been admitted, there is no principled way of excluding the rest.

One argument against extreme anticonjunctivism is already afforded us by the results of the last section. We saw there that grade 1 together with extreme anticonjunctivism implies grade 3. I also asserted there that 1 is true, 3 false. (I assume the reader will agree with me that 3 is false; in section VI, I will say what needs to be said in defense of 1.) It follows, by the principle of antilogism, that extreme anticonjunctivism is false.

Another way to argue against extreme anticonjunctivism is simply to cite examples of scattered objects: the land mass of the state of Michigan, tokens of the letter 'i', and, for that matter, almost any of the familiar objects around us. Physics tells us that even such a paradigm of continuity as my desk is really a scattered swarm of atoms, and that the atoms themselves are scatterings of subatomic particles. Those who would exclude all scattered objects would thus be left with nothing but the basic particles. If what motivates extreme anticonjunctivists is allegiance to common sense, they have joined the wrong camp.

Suppose, then, that we agree to admit at least some scattered objects into our ontology. Does there remain any way to exclude the rest of the objects that the conjunctivist believes in? I doubt that we can find any principle for doing this that is not either vague, arbitrary, or a matter of degree.

Shall we say that scattered objects are permitted only if they are parts of some continuous object? (I mention this proposal because the antilogism above forces upon us only scattered things meeting this restriction.) If we accept what physicists say, this proposal won't get us anything larger than subatomic particles. If we modify the proposal by saying scattered objects are permitted only if they are parts of objects that are not *perceptibly discontinuous,* we will be letting in objects as bizarre as any we keep out. For example, if you and I are standing on the same planet, we will be letting in the sum of my left leg and yours, both limbs being parts of all those not-perceptibly-discontinuous objects that are composed of our two bodies and various connecting tracts of earth.[14]

Shall we say that a collection of objects forms a single object only if the objects can be moved together as a unit? That would admit a house of brick and mortar, but not one of carefully piled stone; and it would admit a pond with its fish in winter (when all are frozen into one block), but not the pond in summer.

Shall we say that a single object must contrast with its environment? That would rule out a ball of cotton if it is packed tightly with others in a bag; it would rule in the contents of the bag if they are scattered about the floor.

One could go on seeking further criteria and trying out various combinations and weightings of them, but I am convinced that the task is bootless. Even if one came up with a formula that jibed with all ordinary judgments about what counts as a unit and what does not, what would that show? Not, I take it, that there exist in nature such objects (and only such) as answer to the formula. The factors that guide our judgments of unity simply do not have that sort of ontological significance.[15]

The position I am contending for can be clarified by comparison with the following passage from Leszek Kolakowski:

> The picture of reality sketched by everyday perception and by scientific thinking is a kind of human creation (not imitation) since both the linguistic and the scientific division of the world into particular objects arise from man's practical needs. In this sense the world's products must be considered artificial. . . . In abstract nothing prevents us from dissecting surrounding material into fragments constructed in a manner completely different from what we are used to. Thus speaking more simply, we could build a world where there would be no such objects as 'horse', 'leaf', 'star', and others allegedly devised by nature. Instead, there might be, for example, such objects as 'half a horse and a piece of river', 'my ear and the moon', and other similar products of a surrealist imagination.[16]

With its mention of such objects as 'my ear and the moon', this passage has an unmistakably conjunctivist ring. But conjunctivists, unlike Kolakowski, do not say that such objects *might* have existed *instead* of the more familiar ones; they say that such objects *do* exist in *addition* to the familiar ones.[17] By suggesting that what objects there are depends on our conceptual practices, Kolakowski intimates a form of idealism or conceptualism that is quite foreign to conjunctivism.

V. ARE MINDS EXCEPTIONS TO CONJUNCTIVISM?

One sometimes encounters the suggestion that the mental and the physical realms are governed by different principles of unity. In the physical realm, so the suggestion goes, things may be compounded and divided as you please, but in the mental realm this is not so. Even if conjunctivism is true of all physical things, it is not true of minds or persons.

This contention might be bolstered by appeal to Kant's principle of *the unity of apperception*. If a subject of consciousness S is to be genuinely *one* subject of consciousness, S must have the following property: if S is aware of p and also aware of q, S must be at least potentially aware of p & q. We could tarry over the exact formulation of this principle, but the application of it is clear. If Smith is aware of seeing lightning and Jones is aware of hearing thunder, it does not follow that anyone is aware (even potentially) of *both* seeing lightning and hearing thunder. (Maybe Smith is deaf and Jones is blind.) Hence, it would be a mistake to fuse Smith and Jones together into one person, as conjunctivism apparently bids us do.[18]

This argument against conjunctivism rests on a confusion. Conjunctivism does indeed imply that two minds or persons must add up to a third *thing*, but it does not imply that two minds must add up to a third *mind*. Conjunctive entities such as Smith + Jones, though composed of minds, are not themselves minds, and for that reason the principle of unity of apperception does not apply to them. (No one would apply that principle to a team or a committee.) There is simply no conflict between unity of apperception and unbridled conjunctivism.

Having seen this, let us go on to consider whether there is anything to the argument for dualism hinted at in the first paragraph of this section. One possible version of the argument would be this:

1. Any two physical things compose a third thing.
2. It is *not* the case that any two *minds* compose a third thing. Therefore,
3. Minds are not physical things.

This argument is valid, provided the conclusion is read as '*Some* minds are not physical things'. But the second premise is not true, or at any rate is not supported by the unity of apperception—that is what we just saw.

Here is another version of the argument:

1. Any two physical things compose a third physical thing.
2. It is not the case that any two minds compose a third *mind*. Therefore,
3. Some minds are not physical things.

This time the second premise is true; in denying it, we *would* run afoul of unity of apperception.[19] But the argument employing it is invalid. Two shoes seldom if ever compose a third *shoe,* but we could not combine that fact with the first premise to conclude that some shoes are not physical things. All that follows from our premises is that it is not the case that for any *x, x* is a mind iff *x* is a physical thing—but that could be true simply because not all physical things are minds.[20]

VI. THE CASE FOR MEREOLOGICAL ESSENTIALISM

There is at least one class of entities to which the application of mereological essentialism (by which hereafter I mean mereological essentialism of the second grade) is not in much dispute—namely, mereological sums, or what Locke calls masses of matter. Mereological essentialism in regard to such entities is highly intuitive. After all, if one particle in a mass of matter is removed, how can it be the very same mass that remains? What is controversial (and usually controverted) is the application of mereological essentialism to entities of other kinds—artifacts, living creatures, and (especially) persons.

My purposes do not require me to affirm mereological essentialism in regard to anything but masses of matter; that is all that is involved in my argument against extreme anticonjunctivism.[21] I should nonetheless like to take the opportunity to argue in the remainder of this section that mereological essentialism should be adopted in regard to artifacts and nonliving things in general.

As an example of an artifact, let us use a plastic letter *T,* such as might be used in a movie marquee. I take it that this is as good an artifact as any, and that our conclusions in regard to it can be extended to coffee cups, sailing ships, and so on.

I am assuming, as noted, that mereological essentialism holds in regard to aggregates of matter. If it does *not* hold in regard to our *T,* this must be because the *T* is something *other* than the aggregate of its matter. It is composed of this matter or constituted out of it, but it is not identical with it. Let us pursue the consequences of denying this identity.

I see only two further possibilities. The first is that the T is not identical with *anything,* because it does not really exist. That is to say, it exists only as a logical construction or in a manner of speaking; to say that a T exists is simply to say that two bars are related in a certain way. The other alternative is that the T exists as a logical subject in its own right, distinct from but coincident with a certain parcel of matter. The 'coincidence' I speak of involves being in exactly the same place and sharing exactly the same matter. Without any pretense of historical fidelity, let me label the first alternative as ''atomist'' and the second as ''Aristotelian.''[22]

One difference between the alternatives may be brought out by asking what happens when two bars cease to be T-related. The Aristotelian would say that something has genuinely ceased to be, namely, a certain T, whereas the atomist would say that the passing away of the T is only nominal, that it is merely a way of describing an alteration in the bars. Another difference is this: although both parties can accept the *de dicto* statement ''necessarily, every T is T-shaped,'' only the Aristotelian can accept the *de re* statement ''every T is necessarily T-shaped.''

Atomism can be developed in a way that accommodates ordinary talk of a thing's gaining and losing parts. For example, the statement that the T on the marquee has lost one of its corners since yesterday could be accepted as meaning that the T that is there now was a proper part of the T that was there yesterday. Such matters are worked out in Chisholm's theory of *entia successiva.* [23]

I have no quarrel with the atomist alternative; I wish simply to point out that it does not give us exceptions to mereological essentialism. At one level, this is because what exists only in a manner of speaking cannot be an exception to any ontological principle. (The average plumber is not an exception to the rule that no one has a fractional number of children.) At another level, it is because the change of parts that is possible on the atomist alternative is only nominal change: it is really a matter of a thing with one set of parts being superseded by a thing with a different set of parts. There is nothing such that *it* first had one set of parts and then another.

For genuine exceptions to mereological essentialism, we must turn to the Aristotelian alternative, which provides us with a real ''it'' or abiding subject that has different parts at different times. What can be said against this view?

Let us imagine that there is language whose alphabet contains the letter *schmee.* A token of *schmee* consists of a vertical bar joined at right angles to the underside of a horizontal bar; it is like our T, except that the upright may be attached at any point along the length of the crossbar. Suppose now that we begin with a T and move the upright gradually to the left. At some point in this operation, the T will cease to be, but the *schmee* will still remain. This shows that the T and the *schmee* must have been two distinct things to start with, since they have different essential properties or persistence conditions. And, of course, each of them must be distinct from the matter of which both are composed.

We have just seen that by the reckoning of the Aristotelian, there are at least three entities sharing the space of our T: the T itself, the *schmee,* and the underlying matter. From here it is but a short step to the recognition that the Aristotelian must admit there there are *infinitely many* distinct objects inhering in any parcel of matter.

In the case at hand, there are the T, the *schmee,* the *squee*—a separate object for each range of displacement (of the upright from the midpoint of the crossbar) that could be used to define a letter.

Perhaps some readers will be tempted to say at this point that there are only *possible* objects corresponding to all these ranges of displacement, and that none of them have actual existence except those actually adopted as letters by some linguistic group. But that would make the number of material beings in the universe a function of human fertility in devising alphabets. Such an attitude is comparable to Kolakowski's and is to be deprecated for the same reason.

Atomists are not implicated in any similar proliferation of entities. In their view, the leftward passage of the upright involves a continuous series of alterations but no infinite number of passings-away.

This, then, is my objection to Aristotelianism: if impartially carried out, it forces us to believe that millions of entities coexist in any parcel of matter. What I find objectionable about this is not the sheer number of entities that are generated; conjunctivism in its own way generates entities aplenty. It is rather that all these entities must occupy exactly the same place and share exactly the same matter, thus violating two plausible philosophical principles: "Two things cannot be in the same place at the same time" and "There cannot be difference of entities without difference of content."[24]

To be sure, these principles probably cannot be accepted without qualification. In stating the first, Locke found it necessary to put it this way: there cannot be two entities of the same *kind* in the same place at the same time.[25] He recognized three kinds of entities: finite souls, bodies, and God; his version thus leaves open the possibility of a soul sharing space with a body or of God sharing space with everything. But even if the list of kinds were much longer than Locke's, a T and a *schmee* would surely belong to the same kind, so even the qualified principle would be violated.

Another proposed qualification of the first principle might be this: two things cannot be in the same place at the same time unless one of them is constituted out of the other. But this principle is still violated by the T and the *schmee,* which are constituted out of the same third thing but not, presumably, out of each other.[26]

To sum up the case for extending mereological essentialism from aggregates to artifacts and nonliving things generally: the only alternative is Aristotelianism, which involves us in an objectionable multiplication of entities.

VII. LIMITING THE SCOPE OF MEREOLOGICAL ESSENTIALISM

Can mereological essentialism be affirmed for aggregates (or for aggregates and artifacts) without being affirmed for living things and persons? I think so, but combining these positions consistently turns out to be trickier than one might expect. I shall illustrate this by considering the views of Locke and Wiggins, both of whom affirm mereological essentialism for aggregates but make exception for living creatures. (Wiggins also makes exception for artifacts.)

Let us begin by noting that unless they are qualified in some way, the two princi-ples I cited above against Aristotelianism can be used to show that mereological essen-tialism holds for entities of any sort whatever, including organisms. Take any entity with parts: it must surely share space and matter with some mereological sum. If things that share space and/or matter are held to be identical, it will follow that everything with parts is a mereological sum; so if mereological essentialism holds for sums, it will hold for all entities with parts. To avoid this result without giving up the case against Aristotelianism, we would have to qualify the two principles somehow. For example, we might say "There can be no difference in *inanimate* things without difference in content" and "There cannot be two *inanimate* things in the same place at the same time."

Let us now see what happens to the attempts of Locke and Wiggins to affirm mereological essentialism for aggregates while denying it for organisms. If this posi-tion is to be tenable, one must be able to say that an organism and the aggregate of its matter are two different things. Locke and Wiggins both say this, but both also fall into inconsistency.

Locke says that an oak tree and the small plant from which it grew are the same oak but not the same mass of matter. Some have seen in this an anticipation of the doctrine of "relative identity" (*x* and *y* can be the same *F* without being the same *G*—even when both are *G*'s), but I think such an interpretation is ruled out because Locke explains further that in this case "identity is not applied to the same thing."[27] I take this to mean: identity is not applied to the same *relata*. So there are two things before us, a certain parcel of matter and a tree composed of it; the tree is identical with a plant that was here twenty years ago, but the matter is not identical with the matter that was here then. Locke's inconsistency arises because he is required to *identify* the tree and its matter by his principle that two things of the same kind exclude each other from the same place. For unless Locke wants to classify a tree as an intelligent spirit, it comes under his category of body and is thus of the same kind as a mass of matter. To avoid this inconsistency, he should either have given up the exclusion principle or added living things to his list of kinds.

Wiggins runs into similar inconsistency. Having argued that mereological es-sentialism holds for sums, he denies that it need also hold for the cat Tibbles, insisting that Tibbles is not identical with Tib + Tail (i.e., the tail of Tibbles plus the rest of Tibbles) or any other sum of its bodily parts.[28] Conformably with this, he also denies that community of all parts is sufficient for identity, since Tibbles has the same parts as any sum of its parts. The inconsistency arises because a crucial part of Wiggins's case for mereological essentialism for sums is Postulate II of Tarski's mereology, which runs as follows:

> For every non-empty class *a* of individuals there exists exactly one individual *x* which is a sum of all elements of *a*.[29]

Well, if there is exactly *one* sum, there cannot be *two* things with all the same parts. Tibbles must be identical with Tib + Tail after all.

Perhaps Wiggins would want to reply to this difficulty as follows: "Postulate II just says there is a unique *sum* having a given set of parts; it does not say there is a unique *thing* having them. There is therefore nothing to prevent two things from having all the same parts so long as one of them is not a sum." This reply would be correct so far as Postulate II by itself is concerned, but it overlooks what happens when the postulate is combined with Tarski's definition of 'sum'. This definition, which is also part of Wiggins's argument for mereological essentialism, runs as follows:

An individual *X* is called a *sum* of all elements of a class *a* of individuals if every element of *a* is a part of *X* and if no part of *X* is disjoint from all elements of *a*. [30]

By this definition, Tibbles is a sum of the set {Tib, Tail}. So, of course, is Tib + Tail. But Postulate II says there is only one such sum; hence, Tibbles = Tib + Tail. More generally, we can point out that this definition counts anything with parts as a sum and thus, in conjunction with Postulate II, implies that there can never be two entities with all the same parts.

If mereological essentialism has the basis Wiggins says it does, it holds for any entities whatever that have parts. If he wants to avoid mereological essentialism for cats while keeping it for sums, he will have to reject as too broad Tarski's definition of sum. But what could he put in its place? Could he say that Tarski's definition, while not giving a sufficient condition by itself, is part of an axiom system (including Postulate II) that implicitly defines the notion of sum? This would raise the following question: what independent characterization of sums is there that will determine whether a given entity with parts is a sum, and therefore subject to the axioms, or a nonsum and exempt from them?

VIII. TEMPORAL CONJUNCTIVISM AND IDENTITY THROUGH TIME

A common approach to the problem of identity through time is to conceive of persisting objects as four-dimensional entities with *temporal* parts as well as spatial ones. [31] The temporal parts, or the ultimate ones anyway, are strictly momentary; they themselves do not persist through time. Things that *do* persist through time do so in this conception by having different temporal parts at different times. Questions about identity through time then get recast as questions about diachronic or cross-temporal unity: how must parts or stages existing at different times be related in order to be parts of one and the same continuing object?

I think this question should be answered as follows: *any* two or more nonsimultaneous temporal parts are *automatically* parts of a continuing whole, no matter *how* they are related. In other words, if objects have temporal parts, *temporal* conjunctivism is just as reasonable in regard to them as spatial conjunctivism is in regard to spatial parts. [32]

Quine, who is one of the leading proponents of temporal parts, makes no bones about accepting the conjunctivist thesis I have enunciated. An object, he says, "comprises simply the content, however heterogeneous, of some portion of space-time, however disconnected and gerrymandered."[33] Among the objects thus countenanced are ''the monetary content of my pocket,'' a temporally scattered object consisting sometimes of nickel and sometimes of copper,[34] and *the President,* a temporally continuous but spatiotemporally discontinuous object that has undergone many changes of political party and may one day undergo nonsurgical change of sex.[35]

My impression is that Quine has few followers in the matter of temporal conjunctivism. I do not see how it can be avoided, however, if one has already taken the first step of admitting temporal parts.[36] Once you allow that things can be chopped up in the temporal dimension, you will have to allow that the pieces can be reassembled as you please.

The doctrine of temporal parts is, in my view, not only sufficient for the existence of entities such as *the President,* but necessary as well. Let me illustrate this point with an example from Eli Hirsch. Hirsch has described an ''identity scheme,'' called Contacti, in which persons ''switch identities'' during any interval when they are in contact. More accurately: if Smith and Jones are what we would normally regard as two persons who come together at $t1$, maintain contact until $t2$, and then go their separate ways, then according to Contacti there is one person corresponding to the shaded portion of the diagram below, and another corresponding to the unshaded portion.[37]

Smith   Jones

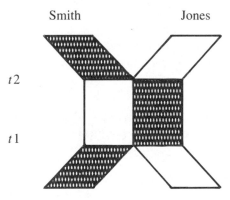

$t2$

$t1$

Now if Smith and Jones have temporal parts, I cannot see any objection to there being a person (or at any rate an object[38]) having some of Smith's parts and some of Jones's. If objects do *not* have temporal parts, however, then it seems to me simply a mistake to suppose that there could be objects such as the Contacti persons—as much a mistake as supposing that there could be an object composed of the left half of A and the right half of B if A and B are metaphysical atoms, i.e., entities without spatial parts.

Of course, one could devise some sort of logical construction answering to the shaded portion of the diagram. One could name it Smones and propose that Smones is F at t iff (i) Smith and Jones are touching at t and Jones is F, or (ii) Smith and Jones are not touching at t and Smith is F. But it would be wrong to think that this construction represents a genuine entity. For example, from the fact that Smones was smiling one moment and frowning the next, it would not follow that anything had changed its facial expression. (Maybe all that happened is that a smiling Smith shook hands with a frowning Jones.)[39]

Let us now return to temporal conjunctivism and its consequences. If any two things belong to indefinitely many temporal sums, then the answer to the question "Is there a continuant to which x and y both belong?" is *automatically yes*, no matter what x and y may be. By the same token, the answer to the question "Do x and y belong to *the* same continuant?" is *automatically no*, no matter what x and y may be. If we want to ask a question to which the answer is not already settled ahead of time, we must indicate what *sort* of continuant we are interested in. We must ask, "Do x and y belong to the same F-*continuant*?" The answer to this may be yes or it may be no, depending on the unity conditions incorporated in the concept of an F. Without such a "covering concept," statements of diachronic unity are vacuous.

We get a further consequence (as Quine has noted[40]) that is reminiscent of the doctrine of relative identity. 'Reminiscent' is the right word, since it is *unity* that is relative, not identity: x and y may be parts of the same F, but not of the same G. For example, if x and y are person-stages, they might be parts of the same lineage (or something more bizarre), but not parts of the same person.

There is also something in all of this akin to the doctrine that identity is conventional. As before, it is not identity that has the feature in question, but unity. Convention enters as follows: out of all the indefinitely many temporal sums that are there, some only are singled out for recognition in our conceptual scheme, and it is with reference to these that questions about diachronic unity get asked and answered. One might say that the role of convention is to specify the covering concepts that are understood when (as is often the case) none are stated.[41]

It should be clear in light of the foregoing that if temporal conjunctivism is true, many questions about identity have no unique answer as typically stated. Or rather, they have an automatic answer if no covering concept is supplied, and as many nonautomatic answers as there are covering concepts. For example, consider the question "Will I still be around in the year 2000—will any object existing then be identical with me?" Before we can answer this, we must restate it as a question about unity, and if we are not to give the automatic answer, we must supply a covering concept. Different covering concepts will yield different answers.

I cannot help thinking to the contrary that the original question has a unique and nonautomatic answer as it stands, and am therefore led to reject the doctrine of temporal parts.[42]

It might be said in reply that the hypothesis of temporal parts does, after all, permit a unique answer to my question, the question being equivalent to this one: "Is my current stage part of any *person*-continuant that will have stages in the year 2000?" But why are person-continuants more pertinent than continuants of any other sort in answering my original question?

In conclusion, then, I should like to put forth the following argument:[43] (1) if objects had temporal parts, temporal conjunctivism would be true; (2) if temporal conjunctivism were true, questions about identity through time would be relative and conventional in the oblique way I have noted; (3) but questions about identity through time are *not* thus relative; therefore, (4) objects do not have temporal parts.[44]

Notes

1. I take this formulation from R. M. Chisholm, *Person and Object* (La Salle, Ill., 1976), 145. Note that 2' implies that a whole cannot survive the *addition* of a part, since it implies that a whole with a new part could not have existed as that very whole previously.

2. For Chisholm's defense, see Chisholm, ibid., 145–58; for references to Leibniz and Hume, see ibid., 221, n. 2. For references to Locke, see below, n. 13.

3. What we really need here is the notion of the sum of an arbitrary number of elements, not just two. Such a notion is defined in section VII.

4. This definition was first suggested to me by Richard Potter; it also occurs in Eli Hirsch, *The Concept of Identity* (Oxford, 1982), 97. Note that for an object to be continuous, it is not enough that *some* two parts of it that exactly compose it be in contact; *any* two such parts must be in contact.

5. And more generally, for *any* number of objects, there is a further object composed of them. I take the term 'conjunctivism' from lectures by Chisholm.

6. Proponents of conjunctivism: Franz Brentano, *The Theory of Categories*, translated by Roderick M. Chisholm and Norbert Guterman (The Hague, 1981), 45–46; Alfred Tarski, "Foundations of the Geometry of Solids," in *Logic, Semantics and Metamathematics* (Oxford, 1956) 24–29; Nelson Goodman, *The Structure of Appearance*, 2d ed. (Indianapolis, 1966), 51. The mereologies of Tarski and Goodman both derive from Lesniewski.

Proponents of anticonjunctivism: C. D. Broad, *Examination of McTaggart's Philosophy* (New York, 1976; reprint of 1933 edition, Cambridge), Vol. 1, 292; David Wiggins, *Sameness and Substance* (Cambridge, Mass., 1980), 138–39; Chisholm, *Person and Object*, 151 (A4)

7. This assumption seems perfectly reasonable to me, but I should acknowledge that some have questioned it. See Peter van Inwagen, "The Doctrine of Arbitrary Undetached Parts," *Pacific Philosophical Quarterly*, 62(1981): 123–37.

8. Instead of saying that $a + b$ is scattered, the extreme anticonjunctivist would say that a is separated from b.

9. Note that anyone who distinguishes George from $c + d$ cannot speak of *the* part composed of c and d, for there are at least two such.

10. Presupposed in this argument is Locke's principle (*An Essay Concerning Human Understanding*, II, xxvii, 4) that nothing can have two beginnings of existence; otherwise the original whole could be said to come back into being upon reassembly.

11. Is it possible to *bend* or *stretch* an object without disturbing any adjacency relations? If so, we must limit the class of rearrangements to which this argument applies.

12. Furthermore, the only way to destroy a part would be to *annihilate* it—or at least to annihilate one of its own parts.

13. Locke, *Essay*, II, xxvii, 4.

14. Perhaps someone will object that your leg, my leg, and the tract of earth between do not make a continuous object because they do not make an *object* at all. But this objection presupposes a criterion of objecthood, which is just what we are seeking.

15. The most detailed discussion of this issue I know of is Hirsch, *The Concept of Identity*, 105–12 and 236–63. Hirsch identifies six "articulation-making" factors (109). But his task is expressly psychological, not ontological; he is asking what induces us to *treat* a portion of matter as a unit, not what *makes* it a unit.

16. Leszek Kolakowski, *Towards a Marxist Humanism* (New York, 1968), 47–48; quoted (with disapproval) in Wiggins, *Sameness and Substance*, 138.

17. Strictly speaking, conjunctivism only says there is such an object as 'my ear and the moon' *if* there are such objects as my ear and the moon separately. To affirm the proviso, we would need something like the doctrine of arbitrary undetached parts. (See n. 7.)

18. When I speak here of two persons being fused into one, I am not referring to the phenomenon (so much discussed in the literature on personal identity) of two persons becoming amalgamated into one; I am referring instead to two persons composing a third. In the first case, we start with two persons and end up with one; in the second, we have three all along.

19. Or at any rate, we would run afoul of unity of apperception if we made this further assumption: a composite of two minds is aware of whatever either component is aware of.

20. Perhaps a similar criticism is applicable to the following argument for dualism in Descartes's Sixth Meditation: any physical thing may be divided in two, but no mind may be divided in two, so no mind is a physical thing. If the second premise says that a mind cannot be divided into two *minds*, the argument is invalid, and if it says that a mind cannot be divided into two entities of *any* kind, it is problematic.

21. In "Why a Set Contains Its Members Essentially," *Nous* 19 (1985), 585-602, I have stated premises from which mereological essentialism may be derived. I do not appeal to this derivation in the present paper because one of its premises is conjunctivism. The only other attempt I know of to provide an axiomatic basis for mereological essentialism (that of Wiggins, cited in n. 28 below) also makes use of conjunctivism.

22. The term 'atomism' is meant to suggest something of Greek atomism and something of logical atomism. As for Aristotelianism, good examples are Baruch Brody, *Identity and Essence* (Princeton, 1980), especially 70–73, and Wiggins, *Sameness and Substance*.

23. See Chisholm, *Person and Object*, 89–113, and Chisholm's replies to criticisms in Ernest Sosa, ed., *Essays on the Philosophy of Roderick M. Chisholm* (Amsterdam, 1979), 384–88.

24. For the latter principle, see Goodman, *The Structure of Appearance*, 36.

25. Locke, *Essay*, II, xxvii, 4.

26. Some of this dialectic occurs in classical Indian philosophy. Members of the Nyaya school maintained that a cloth or a pot is something different from the threads or the clay of which it is composed. Their Buddhist opponents objected that this would permit two things to be in the same place at the same time, thus violating the principle of the impenetrability of matter. The Nyaya reply was that it is all right for two things to be in the same place, provided that there is a one-way relation of ontological dependence or subordination between them. (In their view, the cloth was dependent on the threads, but not vice versa.) For an account of all this, see Bimal K. Matilal, *Epistemology, Logic, and Grammar in Indian Philosophical Analysis* (The Hague, 1971), 55–58, 75.

In connection with the Nyaya point, let me note that although *T*'s could perhaps be said to be subordinate to *schmees* (every *T* implying a *schmee*, but not conversely), one could easily define a character whose permissible range of shapes overlapped the *T* range without containing it; here, there would be cohabitation without subordination.

27. Locke, *Essay*, II, xxvii, 4.

28. David Wiggins, "Mereological Essentialism: Asymmetrical Essential Dependence and the Nature of Continuants," in Sosa, *Essays on the Philosophy of Roderick M. Chisholm*, 297–315, at 309.

29. Ibid, 302

30. Ibid.

31. "A body is thus visualized eternally as a four-dimensional whole, extending up and down, north and south, east and west, hence and ago." W. V. Quine, *Philosophy of Logic* (Englewood Cliffs, N.J., 1970), 30.

32. Chisholm has impressed upon me that the plausibility of temporal conjunctivism may depend on "spatializing time" in a way that goes beyond dividing things into temporal parts: one must also credit past and future parts with some mode of tenseless existence. (Otherwise, they would not come within the range of our quantifiers.) Temporal parts and tenseless existence usually come together in a package deal, but a philosopher who accepted only the first half of the package could perhaps avoid temporal conjunctivism. I do not think, however, that such a one could avoid the *consequences* of temporal conjunctivism I elicit below.

33. W. V. Quine, *Word and Object* (Cambridge, Mass., 1960), 171.

34. W. V. Quine, *Theories and Things* (Cambridge, Mass., 1981), 125.

35. Quine, *Theories and Things*, 13. Another somewhat similar object, Quine adds, "is the Dalai Lama, an example that has been invigorated by a myth of successive reincarnation. But the myth is unnecessary."

36. And tenseless existence; see n. 32.

37. Hirsch, *The Concept of Identity,* 287–93.

38. Perhaps a cross-temporal version of the unity of apperception could be used to show that no such object is a person.

39. On this point, see what Sydney Shoemaker has to say about tables and "klables" on page 339 of "Identity, Properties, and Causality," in *Midwest Studies in Philosophy IV,* edited by Peter A. French, Theodore E. Uehling, Jr., and Howard K. Wettstein (Minneapolis, 1979), 321–42.

I should note that Hirsch himself apparently does not construe the Contacti example in either of the two ways I have suggested—in terms of temporal parts or logical constructions. He says that the issue of whether there are temporal parts is *verbal* (189–92). And he denies that Contacti is necessarily just a code for other statements that better reveal the true logical forms of facts (296).

40. Quine, *Theories and Things,* 125.

41. Compare Shoemaker, "Identity, Properties, and Causality," 322.

42. For criticisms of arguments *for* the doctrine of temporal parts, see Chisholm, *Person and Object,* 138–47.

43. Shoemaker ("Identity, Properties, and Causality") has advanced a view at first sight at odds with what I say here. Despite holding that the problem of identity through time is the problem of specifying the relation that unites momentary thing-stages, and despite holding (or at least not disputing) that arbitrary sums of stages exist, he maintains that not all sums of stages are ontologically on a par: some constitute the histories of continuants, and others do not. It emerges, however, that there is no disagreement between Shoemaker and me. His "thing-stages" are not parts of continuants, but parts of their histories.

The point is worth elaborating. Shoemaker says his thing-stages are *property instantiations* (or, more accurately, sets of property instantiations that are closed under the relation of synchronic unity, but that does not affect my point). He does not tell us what a property instantiation is, but three possibilities come to mind: a property instantiation might be (a) a "particularized property," or (b) an event of a thing's having a property, or (c) an ordered triple $<x, F, t>$, in case this is different from (b). I don't think it matters which alternative we choose—let it be (c). Shoemaker's project is then to seek a relation between $<x,F,t>$ and $<y,G,t'>$ that will guarantee that they belong to the history of the same continuant, i.e., that $x = y$. He is correct in maintaining that two such triples or events do not automatically belong to the history of the same continuant, even if they do belong to many of the same sums or sequences.

In contrast, a proponent of temporal parts who talks of thing-stages is talking of momentary particulars or slices of substances. A sum of *these* automatically determines the history of a continuant, because it *is* a continuant.

I note in passing that Shoemaker finds no relation of diachronic unity that does not conceptually presuppose identity. His favored relation is "immanent causality," which by its very definition holds between $<x,F,t>$ and $<y,G,t'>$ only if $x = y$.

44. I wish to thank Diana Ackerman, Roderick Chisholm, and Ernest Sosa for helpful discussions of the material in this paper.

Possibility without Haecceity

RODERICK M. CHISHOLM

THE PROBLEM OF THE MERELY POSSIBLE

The "problem of the merely possible" is that of describing the merely possible without supposing that there is a realm of *possibilia* falling between being and nonbeing and without violating the principles of contradiction and excluded middle. To solve the problem, one may make use of one or the other of the following two locutions:

(A) x is possibly such that he is an F;
(B) There is a (possible) world in which x is an F.

Some philosophers would attempt to explicate (A) in terms of (B). Suppose I am not a physician but could have been one. Then these philosophers would say that there are possible worlds other than the actual one and that I *am* a physician in those worlds. If this explication is to work, then a possible world must be an entity that is capable of *containing* me. But what is the relevant sense of "in" or "contain?" We may give a meaning to this use of such expressions if we can say that I have an individual essence or haecceity—a set of properties that are "essential to me and repugnant to everything else." We could say, more generally, that an individual thing x exists *in* a possible world w provided that the haecceity of x is exemplified in W.

There is, then, an enormous amount of metaphysics involved in explicating (A) in terms of (B). And, so, let us try to do things the other way around. I will suggest that if (B) is to make any sense, it must be explicated in terms of (A).

How are we to choose between these two approaches to the question? We can ask which one presupposes the simpler ontology. The view that I will set forth does not presuppose that *in addition to* individuals, properties and relations, and states of affairs, there are such things as possible worlds *in* which particular individuals such as you and I may be said to exist. Therefore, we do not need to cope with the problem of "transworld identity," and our view does not require us to presuppose that individual things have individual essences or haecceities.

I will, then, make use of the undefined *de re* locution "*x* is possibly such that it is *F*" and the other modal locutions that may be defined in terms of it. And I will make use of the concepts of properties, relations, and states of affairs.

WORLDS DEFINED

I will begin with a conception of "possible world"—but I will say just "world"—which is essentially that of Leibniz and other philosophers in the Western tradition. It is unlike that presupposed by most contemporary philosophers.

> D1   *W* is a world = *Df W* is a state of affairs; for every state of affairs *p*, either *W* logically implies *p* or *W* logically implies the negation of *p*; and there is no state of affairs *q* such that *W* logically implies both *q* and the negation of *q*.

A world, then, is a self-consistent, maximal state of affairs. That it is maximal is guaranteed by the first clause of our definition; that it is self-consistent is guaranteed by the second.[1] A world is thus a *conjunctive* state of affairs.

I have defined "a *world,*" not "a *possible* world." I have avoided "possible world," since the expression "There are possible worlds" may suggest that there *are* certain things—worlds—that neither exist nor fail to exist and that fall between being and nonbeing. I believe that the concept philosophers have traditionally had in mind when speaking of "possible worlds" can be explicated by reference to those states of affairs that are here called "worlds."[2] If this is so, and if, as I believe, states of affairs are abstract objects existing whether or not they obtain, then *all* so-called "possible worlds" exist. Hence, I use "world," and not "possible world."

"But you can't mean to say that all possible worlds are *actual* worlds. There is—and can be—only *one* actual world!" The word "actual" here is ambiguous. If "*x* is actual" is taken to mean the same as "*x exists,*" then all possible worlds are actual. But when it is said that only *one* world is actual, then "*x* is actual" is taken to mean the same as "*x obtains.*" There is—and can be—only one world that obtains.

It is well to avoid the temptation to speak of "the real world" or "the actual world." Let us, rather, speak of "the *world that obtains,*" or "the *prevailing world.*"

WHAT IS THE ESSENCE OF A THING?

Traditionally, the essence of a thing was said to be a property that is essential to the thing and necessarily repugnant to everything else. The following definition may therefore suggest itself:

> *E* is the essence of *x* = *Df x* is necessarily such that it has *E*; and for all *y*, if *y* is other than *x*, then *y* is necessarily such that it does not have *E*.

But the second clause is not strong enough. Suppose (i) I am necessarily such that I am a person, (ii) all nonpersons are necessarily such that they are nonpersons, and (iii) I am the only person there is. Given the proposed definition, it would follow from these assumptions that the property of being a person is my essence. But it would not follow that being a person is necessarily repugnant to everything else.

How, then, are we to strengthen the second clause in the definition? Shall we say: "It is not possible for there to be a y such that y is other than x and y has E"? This would have to be reducible to our *de re* locution, "x is possibly such that it is F." What we should say is rather this: "x is not possibly such that there is a y such that y is other than x and y has E." Our definition will then be:

> D2 E is the essence of x = Df x is necessarily such that it has E; for every property P, if x is necessarily such it has P, then E implies P; and x is not possibly such that there is a y other than x such that y has E.

Given our definition of essence, we may now say what an *abstract object* is: it is a thing having an essence that is such that *everything* is necessarily such that there is something having that essence. The essence of the property *blue* is the property of being a thing that is necessarily such that it is exemplified in all and only those things that are blue. And if, as I believe, the property blue is an abstract object, then everything is necessarily such that there is something that is necessarily such that it is exemplified in all and only those things that are blue. We will say, then:

> D3 x is an abstract object = Df There is an E that is such that (a) E is the essence of x and (b) everything is necessarily such that there is something that has E.

I will assume that properties, relations, and states of affairs are all abstract objects. I will also assume that individual things—such entities as you and me—are not abstract objects. It will follow (1) that everything is necessarily such that abstract objects exist and (2) that no abstract object is necessarily such that any individual thing exists.

EXISTING IN A WORLD

The conception of a *world* that has just been set forth is to be contrasted with that held by many contemporary philosophers. Worlds, according to them, are things *in* which—in some unanalyzed sense of "in"—individuals such as you and me are to be found. But if a world is a state of affairs, and if states of affairs are abstract or eternal objects, what could it mean to say of an *individual thing* that it exists "in a world"? How could you or I exist "in" an abstract object?

We may *give* a meaning to this use of "in." We could say, for example, that if a world implies the property of being a dog, then at least one dog exists "in" that world. (A state of affairs may be said to imply a given property provided only that the state of affairs is necessarily such that, if it obtains, then something has that property.) Hence, we might say similarly that if a thing x has an essence, and if a given world implies that essence, then x exists "in" that world. And we can also say that everything exists "in" the world that obtains. Let us say, then:

> D4 x exists in W = Df W is a world; and either (a) x has an essence E such that W implies E or (b) W obtains and x exists.

POSSIBILITIES WITHOUT HAECCEITIES

The word "haecceity" has traditionally been used to mean the same as "individual essence," or "essence of an individual thing." Let us use the word in this way:

D5 H is the haecceity of $x = Df$ x is an individual thing; and H is the essence of x.

Is there any reason for supposing that there *are* haecceities—that individual things *have* essences?

Many believe that the doctrine that there are individual essences follows from the assumption that individual things have unrealized possibilities. The reasoning may be illustrated this way: "(1) I am not a physician. Therefore, (2) there is a world W that is other than the world that obtains and that is such that I am a physician *in W*. But (3) if I exist in a world that does not obtain, then I have an essence. (This follows from D4—our definition of what it is to exist *in* a world.) Therefore, (4) I have an essence."

But (2) does not follow from (1). Let us consider how we might describe my unrealized possibilities without assuming that I have an individual essence.

Even if I do not have an individual essence, *some* of my properties are essential to me—i.e., some of my properties are such that I have them necessarily. Suppose that *being a person* is such a property. Now there are some worlds that do not imply the property of being a person ("Some possible worlds don't contain any persons"). If I am necessarily a person, then I am necessarily such that none of those impersonal worlds obtain. We may say that I *exclude* such worlds. (Or we could put it the other way around and say that I am such that I am excluded by certain worlds.) For we may say that a thing x *excludes* a world W, provided only that x is necessarily such that W does not obtain.

It is important to note that from the fact that I am *not* excluded by a certain world W, it does not follow that I *exist in* in that world W. But if I am not excluded by W, then I am *eligible* for W: that is, I am possibly such that W obtains.

If I were to have an essence E such that there is a certain world W that implies E (i.e., a certain world W that is necessarily such that if it obtains then something exemplifies E), then we could say that W is necessarily such that I exist. But if I have no individual essence, then we cannot say of *any* world that it is necessarily such that I exist. And we cannot even say this of "the actual world"—i.e., the world that obtains. The latter point may be put somewhat loosely by saying that this world could have obtained without me. If the world had obtained without me, then someone else would have played the role that I happen to play in this world. Indeed, if neither you nor I have individual essences, then the prevailing world could have obtained with you playing my role and me playing yours. One might say, paradoxically, that you and I would have been very different but the world would have been the same; this gives us a use for the label "existentialism."[3]

We cannot say, therefore, that "x exists in W" means the same as "If W were to obtain, then x would exist." For I exist in this world, but this world could have obtained without me.

AN OBJECTION CONSIDERED

Consider now an objection to what we have been saying: "(1) Your theory implies this: that a world W^1 is identical with a world W^2 if and only if W^1 implies the same states of affairs that W^2 implies. But (2) it is possible (a) that there is a world W^1 implying exactly the same properties as are implied by a world W^2 and yet (b) W^1 may be such that a certain person—say, Jones—is in it, and W^2 may be such that Jones is not in it. Therefore (3) your theory is false."

We are now in a position to see that even if the existentialistic intuition is true, the second premise of the argument is false. The point is not that there are two worlds, W^1 and W^2, such that Jones is "in" one of them and not "in" the other. It is, rather, that there is a world W^1 ($= W^2$) that is such that Jones is eligible for W^1 but does not have an essence that W^1 implies. One might also put this by saying: W^1 is possibly such that it obtains and Jones does not exist. Jones is "in" W^1, but W^1 could have obtained without him.

To say that you and I "could have changed places" in W^1 is to say this: there is a certain set A of properties such that I have the members of A; there is another set B of properties such that you have the members of B; I am possibly such that I have the members of B and W^1 obtains; and you are possibly such that you have the members of A and W^1 obtains.

We should distinguish the following locutions:

(p) It is possible there are no persons;
(q) I am such that possibly there are no persons;
(r) I am possibly such that there are no persons;
(s) I am possibly such that I exist and there are no persons.

There is an ambiguity in (r), for it may be taken to say the same thing as (q), or it may be taken to say the same thing as (s). But although (s) implies (q), it is not the case that (q) implies (s). For if I am essentially a person, then although (p) and (q) will be true, (s) will be false.

Suppose a thing has a certain property necessarily. What does this imply with respect to those characteristics that the prevailing world has necessarily? Next to nothing, I would say. For example, Socrates may be necessarily such that he is a person. It does not follow from this either (a) that Socrates is necessarily such that he is a *person in this world*, or (b) that this world is necessarily such that Socrates exists and is a person.

The fact that I exist only in the prevailing world—if it is a fact—doe not restrict my possibilities. The unrealized possibilities of a given individual are not to be explicated in terms of the different worlds in which that individual might be said to exist. We may speak of such possibilities, using the undefined *de re* modal locution with which we began: "*x* is possibly such that it is *F*." And so we may say of a person who is not a physician that "he could have been a physician." This does not tell us that he is a physician "in some possible world." It tells us no more nor less than that he is possibly such that he is a physician—that none of his essential properties are incompatible with being a physician. "He is possibly such that he is a physician" does *not* tell us that he has a nature that is compatible with being a physician. For what would this "nature" be if the person does not have an individual essence? "He is possibly such that he is a physician" tells us, rather, that he does *not* have an essence that is *incompatible* with his being a physician.

"If he is possibly such that he is a physician, and if he's not a physician in the prevailing world, then isn't it the case that, if he *were* a physician, he would be a physician *in another world?*" This may be correct. But from this fact it does not follow that he *is* a physician in any other world. For unless he has an individual essence, any other world could obtain without him.

AN ARGUMENT FOR THE DOCTRINE OF HAECCEITIES

Alvin Plantinga writes: "Is there any reason to suppose that 'being identical with Socrates' names a property? Well, is there any reason to suuppose that it does not? . . . Surely it is true of Socrates that he is Socrates and that he is identical with Socrates. If these are true of him, then *being Socrates* and *being identical with Socrates* characterize him; they are among his properties or attributes."[4] One could argue similarly, as I did in the book *Person and Object,* that the expression "being me" has the property *being me* as its sense and that the property of *being me* is essential to me and repugnant to everything else. Then one could conlcude that *being me* is my haecceity.

But why assume that terms such as "Socrates" and "I" *have* senses? One can describe their use adequately without such an assumption. The function of proper names in a language may be described without presupposing that they have senses. The same applies to pronouns and demonstratives. We may say that the primary use of the locution "I am F" in English is that of conveying that one has attributed to oneself the property of being F. The primary use of "*That* is F" is that of conveying that the thing one is calling attention to has the property of being F.[5]

Of course, it is true that Socrates is necessarily identical with Socrates and that I am necessarily me. But I see no reason for supposing that these statements commit us to anything other than Socrates, me, and the property of being self-identical.[6] What if one were to say: "That thing is necessarily identical with that thing; therefore, there is the property of *being identical with that thing* that constitutes the sense of 'that thing'"? How do I distinguish this property from the one I may refer to later when, pointing to a different object, I say: "And that thing is necessarily identical with that thing"? Surely I don't contemplate two essences, one for the first occurrence of "that thing" and another for the second.

It has even been suggested that those haecceities that constitute the senses of "Socrates," "that thing," and "me," respectively, are ontologically dependent upon Socrates, that thing, and me. To say that one thing is "ontologically dependent" upon another is, I suppose, to say that the first thing is necessarily such that the second exists. But if what I have suggested is correct, haecceities are abstract objects, and no abstract object is dependent for its being upon any particular thing.

I see no reason, then, to assume that the fact of unrealized possibilities presupposes that individual things have essences or haecceities.

Notes

1. If we wanted to say that there are also "impossible worlds," we should remove the final clause from the definiens. But no useful purpose is served by speaking in this way.

2. Compare Leibniz, *Theodicy* (London, 1952), part III, sec. 414: "These worlds are all here, that is, in ideas [*Ces Mondes sont tous ici, c'est-à-dire en idées*]. I will show you some, wherein shall be found, not absolutely the same Sextus as you have seen (that is not possible, he carries with him always that which he shall be) but several Sextuses resembling him." Compare C. I. Lewis, *An Analysis of Knowledge and Valuation* (La Salle, Ill., 1946), chap. III ("The Modes of Meaning"), especially 56.

3. See Alvin Plantinga, "De Essentia," *Grazer Philosophische Studien* 7/8 (1979): 101–21.

4. "World and Essence," in M. J. Loux, *Universals and Particulars* (Notre Dame, 1976), 369–70. Given (i) that Socrates has a haecceity and (ii) that he exists in a world other than the world that obtains, Plantinga can go on to argue, as he does, that if Socrates is snubnosed in *W*, then he is *necessarily* such that he is snubnosed in *W*. But if what I have said is correct, then it is not the case that individuals have such "world-indexed" properties necessarily. I don't exist in any worlds other than the world that obtains; the world that obtains is not necessarily such that I exist if it obtains; and I am not necessarily such that I exist in it.

5. I have tried to show this in detail in *The First Person* (Minnneapolis and Brighton, 1981), chap. 6, and in "The Primacy of the Intentional," *Synthese* 61 (1984): 89–109.

6. Some philosophers have been unduly impressed by the fact that quantified modal logic happens to have been developed in such a way as to contain the theorem "$(x)N(x = x)$." The philosophical question is whether there is anything for this theorem to express other than the proposition that everything is self-identical.

Individual Essences and Possible Worlds

ROBERT C. COBURN

I

The idea that there exists a vast array of possible worlds and that the totality of facts involving us and all our surroundings, past, present, and future, constitutes but one of these worlds is a very attractive one. We certainly have the notion of situations that could have developed, but did not, of states of affairs that might have obtained, but do not. And the route from this notion to the idea in question is quite direct and, as recent philosophical history indicates, easily taken by those with even modest metaphysical proclivities. Moreover, once this idea of a system of possible worlds scattered through logical space has taken hold, another thought becomes quite irresistible, namely, the thought that we—and lots of other things, too—exist in many of these worlds, that crossworld identities obtain. After all, if we have a grasp of the notion of "counterfactual situations" (of a "possible [but nonactual] state . . . of the world"[1]), surely we also understand what it is for us, and for other things, to be involved in such situations (or states), and this, it seems, is all that crossworld identities require.

The thought that there are nonactual possible worlds in which we exist, however, can readily give rise to perplexity. Consider the question, "If a different possible world had been actual, would I be among its denizens?" It is tempting to hold (1) that there is a correct answer to this question, either yes or no, and (2) that which of these is the correct answer depends upon what properties the individuals in the world in question possess. In particular, it is tempting to thing that the answer to such a question turns on whether the features that individuate me are possessed by any "inhabitant" of the world in question. After all, something about me makes me the individual I am, we want to say. But if we give up the view that it is some feature or features I possess that individuate me, we seem forced to the idea that what makes me the individual I am is just the fact that the possessor of the properties I instantiate is what it is quite independently of any of the features it exhibits— an idea that seems on the face of it unintelligible.

It thus appears that once we embrace possible worlds and crossworld identity, we are quite naturally led to accept the idea that each of us possesses at least one property such that nothing in any possible world that is distinct from us has it and nothing in any possible world that is identical with us lacks it. Put in a slightly different way, we find ourselves led by seemingly faultless steps from ostensibly unimpeachable intuitions to the view that each individual possesses at least one property P such that (a) there is no possible world in which that individual exists and lacks P, and (b) there is no possible world in which P is exemplified by something that is not strictly identical with that individual. Following a now common usage, I shall call such properties "individual essences."[2]

The reason this view gives rise to perplexity is that when we try to get clear about what our individual essences are, we find that none of the candidates that seem at first blush plausible are at all attractive upon further reflection. In sections II-IV, I shall explain why this is so. Then, in sections V and VI, I shall describe two possible ways out of the difficulty this discussion defines and indicate why neither of these is satisfactory either. The upshot will be that here, as elsewhere in philosophy, "nothing works"—at any rate, as well as might be wished.

II

Consider the open sentence 'x = Leibniz'. According to some philosophers, such a sentence expresses a property, and, moreover, a property that is not reducible to (or analyzable into) a collection of "purely qualitative" properties[3] or, indeed, that is not analyzable at all. I shall call such properties "haecceities,"[4] and the doctrine that there are such unanalyzable properties "haecceitism." It is easy to see that if haecceities in this sense exist, they will count as individual essences. For if there is such a property as being identical with Leibniz, it is surely one that Leibniz could not be without; and obviously, there is no possible world in which something has it and is not Leibniz.

However, only a little reflection is required to create the suspicion that haecceities are "creatures of darkness." To begin with, it seems intuitively quite plausible to think that there are logical (or metaphysical) limits on the features things like us might have possessed. I might have been $6'4''$ or red-haired, for example. Virtually no one— at least, before being exposed to certain tracts of philosophical literature—disputes this. But the idea that I might have been a green mothball, or a volcano, or a sneeze, or one of the prime numbers greater than 2^{50}, is hard to credit. On the face of it, judgments like these border on the senseless at best. But if we accept the verdict that it is false or senseless that I might have had properties of these latter kinds, we *ipso facto* embrace "essentialism," i.e., the doctrine that some of our properties are essential to us in the sense that there is no possible world in which we exist and lack these properties. But essentialism, so defined, yields a puzzling consequence when it is combined with haecceitism, the doctrine that all individuals possess haecceities. For these two doctrines together entail that propositions like $[(x)(x \text{ exists and } x = \text{W.V.O. Quine} \supset x \text{ is a rational agent})]$[5]—hereafter Q—are both necessary and synthetic, given that x [x is a rational agent] is one of Quine's essential properties. (If it is not, substitute for the proposition mentioned the proposition [$(x)(x$ exists and x = W.V.O. Quine $\supset x$ is a nonnumber)].) The necessity of Q follows from the thesis that being a rational agent is one of Quine's essential properties. Its syntheticity follows from the fact that given the sort of property a haecceity is, the property of being a rational agent is neither identical with nor a component of Quine's haecceity.

Perhaps synthetic necessary truths are not, as such, all that problematic. Propositions about the "internal structure" of tigers and the chemical constitution of water are plausibly thought to be of this kind.[6] We have at least some understanding of how such propositions can both fail of analyticity and nonetheless hold in all possible worlds, though no doubt our understanding will have to be deepened before we feel completely comfortable with conceiving them in this way. But however this may be, the idea that propositions like Q might be both synthetic and necessary is another matter. There are two reasons for disquietude here. First, there is the difficulty in understanding why Quine's haecceity could not be coinstantiated with properties like x [x is a rock], or even x [x is a number], given the sort of property a haecceity is. After all, one might reason, if the property of being identical with Quine could not be coinstantiated with x [x is a rock], then it is hard to see why it could not also be true (a) that anything having a certain set of purely qualitative properties cannot fail to instantiate this property, and (b) that anything that instantiates this property cannot fail to possess the set of purely qualitative properties in question. But if the property of being identical with Quine is a haecceity, then it is difficult to see how such a purely qualitative individual essence could exist. For if Quine had a purely qualitative individual essence, why couldn't x [x = Quine] be analyzed by reference to it? And, in any case, there are powerful arguments against the existence of purely qualitative individual essences. (I give several of these in section IV.) Second, there is the difficulty in seeing how we could possibly know that there are necessary limits on the properties that given haecceities can be coinstantiated with. The problem here derives from the absence of anything remotely like the sorts of causal connections that underlie and explain our knowledge of the "synthetic" truths we come to know via perception, memory, and various complex inferences from the knowledge perception and memory yield. I am reasonably confident that few will feel content with the suggestion Adams has recently made that perhaps such knowledge results from the fact that God "constructed us in such a way that we would at least commonly recognize necessary truth as necessary."[7] But he may well be right in thinking that the alternatives are even less attractive. These two difficulties are closely connected. To the extent that we find our "knowledge" of these alleged "necessary truths" puzzling, we also feel less than confident that our haecceities could not be coinstantiated with such and such other properties. And independent worrries on the latter issue will tend to throw in doubt the thesis that we know that the propositions in question are indeed necessarily true.

There is another line of thought that also makes for skepticism as regards haecceities. It cannot be a necessary truth, it might be thought, that the only haecceities that exist are exemplified. For if that were so, since I am a contingent being, my haecceity could have failed to exist. But haecceities are properties, and properties, if they exist at all, exist necessarily, i.e., exist in all possible worlds.[8] Also, it seems intuitively obvious that there could have existed an individual who does not in fact exist. After all, the ovum from which I developed might not have been fertilized, and the one that would then have appeared in the following month might have been fertilized instead. Surely the individual that would have developed from that fertilized egg might not have been me or any other human being that exists or ever will exist. (Many would probably insist that he or she certainly would not have been me or any other human being that exists or ever will exist.) But now what can it mean to say that an individual might have existed who does not, never did, and never will, if not that there is a possible world such that had it been actual instead of the world that is, it would have been true that some object exists that never exists in the actual world (hereafter "α"). But that, it seems, is just to say that there is a haecceity that would have been exemplified that is not exemplified as things are. At any rate, once we have embraced haecceitism, this seems a natural way of explicating the truth in question.[9]

The idea that there exist unexemplified haecceities, however, appears, upon reflection, quite unattractive. Suppose that $x[x = $ Plantinga] and $x[x = $ Plantinga*] are two haecceities and that the latter is never exemplified in α. Now picture God prior to the creation. He says in his heart, "Shall I create an instance of $x[x = $ Plantinga] or an instance of $x[x = $ Plantinga*]?" He ponders. Then he decides against $x[x = $ Plantinga*] and forms instead an intention to create an instance of $x[x = $ Plantinga], an instance, furthermore, that exemplifies F, where F is a conjunction of all the time-indexed purely qualitative properties that Plantinga in fact instantiates. This intention, let us suppose, is an element of the larger intention to create just the "world" that in fact exists.[10] Before executing this grand intention, however, he has second thoughts about whether to coinstantiate $x[x = $ Plantinga] with F or $x[x = $ Plantinga*]. Finally, after concluding his reflections, he says in his heart, "Let there be light, an instance of $x[x = $ Plantinga]. . . ." Now if there are unexemplified haecceities, the description of the above process of deliberation and decision, as well as the question whether God's second thoughts involved a change of intention, make sense—or, at any rate, make sense if we assume, perhaps falsely, that the theological story in its general outlines makes sense. Also, the idea would appear to be intelligible, given the assumption indicated, that owing perhaps to some divine unconscious process—a slip of the divine tongue, so to speak—$x[x = $ Planginga*] managed to get coinstantiated with F instead of $x[x = $ Plantinga], God's intentions to the contrary notwithstanding. But none of these consequences are at all plausible. What, one wants to ask, could possibly be the difference between (intending to instantiate) $x[x = $ Plantinga] and (intending to instantiate) $x[x = $ Plantinga*], given that each of these haecceities could be coinstantiated with exactly the same sets of purely qualitative properties? What would the difference consist in if the world contained an instance of $x[x = $ Plantinga*] rather than an instance of $x[x = $ Plantinga], given that Plantinga* would possess all of Plantinga's (time-indexed) purely qualitative properties? The answer that says, "The difference would be that the one world would contain one individual and the other a different individual," will hardly do. For the view that things are individuated by their haecceities is scarcely different at bottom from the view that things are the things they are quite independently of the properties they instantiate, a doctrine that makes individuation an impenetrable mystery.[11]

But if the thought that at least some haecceities are unexemplified is unattractive, the present line of thought continues, the doctrine that they are all exemplified is hardly more satisfactory. To begin with, this doctrine, which is sometimes called "Existentialism,"[12] appears to imply that there are no singular states of affairs involving nonactual individuals. For if there were such states of affairs, then the singular propositions that would be true if these states of affairs had obtained would also exist. And a singular proposition, it would seem, either contains the individual it is "about" or contains a constituent that "refers" to this individual. But this requires either that the individual in question exists or, at least, that unexemplified individual essences exist. The former is impossible: clearly there do not exist any individuals that do not exist. And the latter is ruled out also if Existentialism is true. For either all individual essences are haecceities, or some are not. If all are haecceities and Existentialism is true, none are unexemplified. And if there are some individual essences that are not haecceities, it is hard to see how it could be true that all haecceities are exemplified. For suppose E is such an individual essence. Then surely there will be the property of being identical with the object that would exist if E were instantiated.

But the view that there are no singular states of affairs involving nonactual individuals (and, hence, no singular propositions about nonactual individuals) has some highly counterintuitive consequences. Suppose we agree, for reasons of a kind indicate four paragraphs back, that there might have existed at least one individual who does not (and never has or will) exist in α. Then if there are no states of affairs involving nonactual individuals, something is possible even though there is no state of affairs (or proposition) that might have obtained (or been true) in which this possibility consists. In short, given the plausible assumption that there might have existed something that never exists in α, Existentialism entails that the possible outstrips the possibly-true, and this, on the face of it, is scarcely intelligible.

Also, it is surely true that I am a contingent being. To concede this, however, is to hold that it is possible that I should never have existed. This in turn, it seems, is to hold that there is a possible world in which I never exist. But if there is a possible world in which I never exist, then there is a possible world such that if it had been actual, the proposition [Robert Coburn never exists] would be true. But if there are no singular propositions about nonactual individuals, there would have been no such proposition as [Robert Coburn never exists] had the possible world in question been actual. So it seems that we are compelled by Existentialism to admit, paradoxically, that certain propositions might be true even though if they were, they would not exist.[13]

One might, to be sure, try to avoid this result by giving up the doctrine that nothing has a property in a world unless it exists in that world. But this is a doctrine for which there appears to be a very strong argument. Suppose a has property F in world w. Then surely F is exemplified in w, and furthermore, it is exemplified by something identical with a. But this is tantamount to saying that if w had been actual, a would have existed. Thus, it is very hard to deny that if something has a property in a world, it exists in that world.[14]

Another reason for regarding Existentialism with suspicion is that it requires us to view certain possibilities as spurious that may well seem—and do seem to some—quite unexceptionable. It seems quite possible that I should never have existed, and this possibility may seem quite compatible with the world's being just as it is as regards the purely qualitative features it exhibits. If it is, then I could have failed to exist even though the world that existed instead of α was qualitatively indiscernible from α. But surely what is true of me is true of every individual. So it can appear plausible to think that there is a possible world qualitatively identical with α but containing none of the individuals α contains. But if such a possible world could exist, why couldn't it also be the case that there are two possible worlds, each qualitatively identical with α, but sharing no individuals with either α or each other? It is hard to see why it could not be, if the possible world in question is genuine. An Existentialist, however, is forced to deny that two such possible worlds exist. For given that no singular propositions about nonactual individuals exist, the conceptual resources necessary to distinguish two such worlds are simply not available.[15]

The idea, then, that our individual essences might be (or include) haecceities has severe drawbacks. Unfortunately, for reasons I shall next indicate, the other candidates for our individual essences scarcely fare better.

III

Artifacts, like tables, cars, and computers, are intentionally made, usually according to some more or less determinate plan, from some preexisting hunk of matter or collection of material objects. Biological individuals, like human beings, cats, and snails, come into existence as a result of some unplanned process of development from preexisting biological entities. Probably all persisting things emerge in a way that is analogous to either intentional construction or biological development. If so, then all persisting things have an "origin," were x is the origin of $y =_{df}$ (a) x is a set of one or more objects, severally and jointly distinct from y, from which y developed via some natural biological process or some natural process analogous to a process of biological development, or (b) x is some hunk of stuff that is distinct from y, or a collection of one or more objects that are severally and jointly distinct from y, out of which y was made intentionally and according to some plan, or from which y came to be via some nonintentional process or happenstance. In any case, most of the things in our surroundings with which we have daily commerce have origins in the sense indicated. I shall hereafter refer to an origin of the first kind as an "(a)-origin" and to an origin of the second kind as a "(b)-origin."

Might the property of having such and such as its origin be an individual essence of whatever possesses this property? Or, if not a property like this, perhaps some more complex property that contains such a property as an essential constituent? It is easy to see why such a thought might be, at first glance, attractive. Could you, for example, have come into existence if the ovum from which you in fact developed had never been fertilized? There is, I think, a strong inclination to believe that if the ovum in question had not been fertilized and the next month's egg had been instead, then you would not exist, even if the individual that developed from the fertilization of the later egg were to have been similar to you in all sorts of ways. Moreover, if we imagine a possible world in which the very sperm and egg from which you developed also exist and do get together in the way necessary to give rise via ordinary processes of development to a zygote and eventually a human being, it is equally tempting to think that that is a world in which you exist, and indeed that the human being in question is the one you are— and this even if some other human being in that world is more similar to you as you in fact are and the individual who develops from the sperm and egg in question in that world is quite dissimilar to you as you in fact are. It is perhaps worth mentioning that there is also an argument of considerable force in support of the former intuition concerning the essentiality of (a)-origin, given the correctness of the latter intuition. Suppose that in α, I develop from Jack and Jill and the essentiality of (a)-origin is false. Then there is a possible world w_1 in which I develop from two objects, neither of which is identical with Jack and Jill—Hansel and Gretel, say. But if w_1 exists, surely there is also a possible world—w_2, say—in which I develop from Hansel and Gretel and in which Jack and Jill also exist and give rise to an individual—c, say. But given that nothing diverse from me can have developed from Jack and Jill, it follows that in w_2, I am c. But this is impossible. So the hypothesis that a person's (a)-origin is not essential must be false.[16] (Parallel considerations can be adduced in support of the ideas that a thing's (b)-origin is essential to it and that anything in a nonactual possible world that has the same (b)-origin as an object in α cannot fail to be identical with that object.)

Despite the prima facie attractiveness of the thought that a thing's origin might enter into the construction of an individual essence of the thing, none of the obvious ways of developing this idea yields a problem-free result. In the first place, if E, the property of having such and such as its origin, is an individual essence of an object—a, say—it follows from the definition of an individual essence that $(w)(x)(w$ is a possible world & x exists in w & x has E in $w \supset x = a)$. Now suppose that the property of having developed from sperm s and egg e is an individual essence of me. Then, given any world containing s and e, if a person develops from s and e in that world, that person is identical with me. But then in a possible world w in which the fertilized egg from which I developed undergoes fission in the seventh day after fertilization, with the result that two distinct persons b and c develop from s and e in w, it follows that I am identical with both b and c. But that is absurd: I cannot be identical with both b and c in w, given that b and c are distinct persons.

Moreover, even the weaker doctrine of the essentiality of (a)-origin is suspect. For why couldn't there be a possible world in which s and e fail to exist but in which, nonetheless, a zygote comes into existence at some point that is both qualitatively and materially identical with the zygote from which I in fact developed—at some state of its existence, anyhow. All that is required for this state of affairs to obtain is that such a zygote be created by God *ex nihilo*, or, if this possibility is questionable owing to doubts about the intelligibility of such creation or the idea that such a product could be materially identical with the zygote from which I developed, that such a zygote be created by superscientists who arrange to put together in the right way the very atoms and molecules that constituted the zygote from which I developed. But if such a zygote exists in w and gives rise to a human being there, this human being would seem to have as good a claim to being me as any individual in any world that develops from s and e. [17]

Parallel problems exist for the view that having such and such as its (b)-origin is an individual essence of a thing. Having been made from hunk of matter h is obviously not a sufficient condition of being identical with this table at which I now sit—hereafter t—since a chair might have been made from that very hunk, and no chair in w is identical with t in α. In other words, if the wood of which t was made had been used to make a chair instead, then t would not have existed at all. Nor is a thing's (b)-origin plausibly thought, in all cases, anyhow, to be obviously an essential feature of it. Consider a highly complex artifact like a vacation mansion or a luxury liner. Suppose such a mansion now exists and is called by its owners "Valhalla." Surely Valhalla would still exist even though the stones from which it was constructed had been gotten in Colorado rather than Montana, so long as they were qualitatively the same as the ones that were in fact used. That is, if everything else had been the same—the same kinds of materials had been used, the same architectural plan had been followed in its construction, and so on—Valhalla would have existed, we are inclined to say, despite the fact that it had a different (b)-origin. [18]

The above considerations suggest that if the idea of a thing's origin can be used in constructing properties that have some chance of counting as individual essences of their possessors, it will have to enter into the construction in a more subtle and qualified way. One way of developing an ostensibly more adequate view, at least for artifacts, goes as follows. The property that is the individual essence of the table now before me (t) is not having such and such as its origin—hunk of matter h, say. Rather, it is (a) the property E_1 of having been made from h or a hunk of matter that does not differ very much from h as regards its molecular constituents, in conjunction with (b) the property E_2 of being a table that was made in accordance with plan P or a plan that does not differ very much from P, in conjunction with (c) the property E_3 of being the only P-table that could be made from h or an appropriate h-congener. At any rate, it is easy to see that property E—the complex property whose components are E_1, E_2, and E_3—might plausibly be thought to satisfy the conditions a property must satisfy to be an individual essence. Obviously, E is a property that could be exemplified. And it is at least tempting to hold that it could not fail to be the case that something x has E iff E is essential to x and it is impossible that there be a y distinct from x that also has E. How, after all, could a table in some nonactual possible world be identical with a relatively simple object like t if it were made from some hunk of wood containing mainly different molecules from h? How could something in another world be t if it were not a table of the right sort? If t could lack E_3, it could contain none of the same molecules it contains in the actual world. Also, how could anything t^* in any possible world have E and yet fail to be identical with t? t^*, after all, is a P-table made from h (or an appropriate h-congener), and it is the sole P-table so made. On the face of it, anything meeting these conditions must be t. And so on.

However, attractive as such an individual essence–candidate may at first appear, it is also not without problems. The first of these turns on a line of thought, the central idea of which derives from Chisholm. [19] Assume that E is an individual essence of my table t in the sense just defined. It follows that there is a possible world w_1 in which t originates from a hunk of wood h_1, where h_1 differs by only one molecule from h, the hunk of wood that is t's (b)-origin. But if w_1 exists, there must also be a possible world w_2 in which t originates from a hunk of wood h_2 that differs by only one molecule from h_1. And so on, until we reach a possible world w_n in which t originates from a hunk of wood h_n that shares no molecules at all with h. But if w_n exists, the assumption with which we started must be false: E cannot be an individual essence of t after all. So, if E is an individual essence of t, it is false that E is an individual essence of t. Hence, E cannot be an individual essence of t, appearances to the contrary notwithstanding.

A somewhat different line of thought to the same conclusion goes thus. Suppose that some table t_1 possesses the appropriate analogues of E_1–E_3 and that this complex of properties constitutes an individual essence of t_1. Suppose also that t_1 is exactly constituted of molecules $m_1, \ldots, m_n$, n being, say, 10^8. Then, it would seem, there are distinct possible worlds $w_2, \ldots, w_4$, each of which contains tables whose molecular constituents are as follows:

$$t_2: \{m_1, \ldots, m_{n-3000}\} + \{m_{n+1}, \ldots, m_{n+3000}\}$$
$$t_3: \{m_1, \ldots, m_{n-2000}\} + \{m_{n+1001}, \ldots, m_{n+3000}\}$$
$$t_4: \{m_1, \ldots, m_{n-2000}\} + \{m_{n+1001}, \ldots, m_{n+3000}\}$$

Finally, let us assume that (1) t_1 and t_3 are both constructed in accordance with plan P, t_1 is the sole table made from h_1, t_3 is the sole table made from h_3, and no material is left over in either case; and that (2) t_2 and t_4 are both P-tables, t_2 is the sole table made from h_2, t_4 is the sole table made from h_4, and again no material is left over in either case. It follows that $t_1 = t_3$ and $t_2 = t_4$, given that the threshold principle the analogue of E_1 involves allows a difference of 2000 molecules. Now let us suppose further that h_1 and h_2 are too different as regards molecular structure to satisfy the threshold principle the analogue of E_1 involves. Then $t_1 \neq t_2$. If these possible worlds exist, it follows that $t_3 \neq t_4$. But this is absurd, since t_3 and t_4 contain exactly the same molecules and could exemplify exactly the same purely qualitative properties.[20]

There is a way of stopping these arguments. One could just give up the idea that possibility is nonrelative, thus holding, in the former case, that the fact that w_n is possible relative to w_{n-1}, and that w_{n-1} is possible relative to w_{n-2}, and so on, does not entail that w_n is possible relative to w_1, and, in the latter case, that the fact that w_4 is possible relative to w_2, and that w_3 is possible relative to w_1 does not entail that w_4 is possible relative to w_1.[21] Unfortunately, this way of avoiding the difficulty is also not without its costs. If possibilities are thus relative, then certain states of affairs would be possible if reality had been different in certain ways, even though they are quite impossible as things are. It would also be the case that some propositions are true in all possible worlds—hence, necessary—as things are, but not true in all possible worlds—hence, contingent—had things been different in certain ways: for had things been different in certain ways, different worlds would be possible. But these ideas border on the nonsensical, at least when they concern *metaphysical* possibility. (No one, of course, wants to deny that it would be possible for me to swim the English Channel if years ago I had undertaken a certain training program—perhaps *inter alia*—though as things now stand, such a feat is quite impossible for me. Such possibilities and impossibilities concern not metaphysical but, as we might say, "physiological" possibilities and impossibilities.) The idea of (metaphysically) impossible possible worlds and *a fortiori* the idea of (metaphysically) necessary truths that hold, so to speak, only contingently strike me as ideas to be embraced only with great reluctance.

The arguments indicated are not the only ones that bode ill for the conception of individual essences now under consideration. Another takes the form of a dilemma. Suppose that E is an individual essence in the relevant sense of this table (t). Then either there is an exact cutoff point defining how different a hunk of matter can be from the hunk from which t was in fact made, or there is a region in which there is just no fact of the matter whether a given hunk in a given possible world is sufficiently like h that the sole P-table made from it is t. If the latter is the case, there is a collection of tables scattered around in logical space concerning each of which it will be true that it neither is nor is not identical with t. That is difficult to swallow: what is the identity relation, after all, but a set of pairs of the form $<x,x>$? Now consider the pair $<t,t'>$, where t is our table and t' is a P-table in some nonactual possible world. Either this pair belongs to the set making up the identity relation or it does not. Suppose this is not so. Then $<t,t'>$ is clearly not the same pair as $<t,t>$. for the latter pair is certainly a member of the set defining the identity relation. But then $t \neq t'$, and, hence, there is a fact of the matter as regards the identity of t with t'. Unfortunately, the other horn of the dilemma is equally unattractive. Surely we do not want to be forced into accepting a thesis such as that no P-table that might have existed is identical with t if it was made from a hunk of wood (h') that, though containing the same number of molecules as h, contained exactly 104,396 different molecules, whereas it would be t if only 104,395 of h''s molecules were different from h's.[22]

IV

Once we have given up the idea that there are haecceities, as well as the idea that a thing's origin might be, or play an essential role in, an individual essence of that thing, what candidates for individual essences remain? So far as I can see there are only two. It might be held, first, that a thing's individual essence consists—perhaps *inter alia*—in some subset of its "purely qualitative" properties. However, the possibility that a set of purely qualitative properties that something possesses might constitute its individual essence is not really plausible upon reflection. In the first place, it is hard to rule out the existence of possible worlds that are either radially symmetrical or characterized by Nietzschean "eternal recurrence." If such worlds exist, however, it is possible that there are pairs of distinct individuals that share all their purely qualitative properties. Also, it seems clear that the sperm and egg from which you developed—let us call them "Hansel" and "Gretel," respectively—would have given rise to an individual with very different features had the intrauterine environment surrounding the organism resulting from their union been significantly different. The same is true of Dick and Jane, the sperm and egg from which I developed. If Hansel and Dick had been sufficiently similar and Gretel and Jane sufficiently similar, and if the conditions

surrounding the two zygotes resulting from their respective unions had been sufficiently different from what they in fact were, it is surely plausible to think that any
purely qualitative properties that I possess you could have had, and conversely.

The second of the possibilities to which I have alluded is that a thing's individual
essence consists of a subset of its so-called world-indexed properties, where a world-
indexed property is the property of having some ordinary property in a certain possible
world. In particular, it might be held that whenever a possesses some property P
uniquely in some possible world w, then the property $x[x$ has P in $w]$ is an individual
essence of a.[23]

It is easy to see why such world-indexed properties, if there are any, constitute
individual essences of their possessors. Consider the property—call it Q—of having
authored *The Nature of Necessity* in α. If there are such properties, then clearly something does possess Q. Moreover, it is quite plausibly thought a necessary truth that
whatever has Q has it essentially—how could something be Plantinga in another possible world unless it were true of that thing that it authored *The Nature of Necessity* in
α?—and also that nothing distinct from Plantinga could have it—how could a in w be
distinct from Plantinga and yet have authored *The Nature of Necessity* in α?

Unfortunately, such individuating world-indexed properties seem to be just
haecceities in disguise, or, at any rate, close cousins of haecceities. They are just haecceities in disguise if the logical equivalence of properties P and $P*$ counts (or is taken
as counting) as a sufficient condition of property identity, since it is clear that any individuating world-indexed property is logically equivalent to the corresponding haecceity, that is, the haecceity of whatever possesses the property in question. Thus, it is
obviously a necessary truth that a possesses $x[x = $ Plantinga] iff a possesses Q, since
otherwise there would be a possible world containing an individual identical with
Plantinga of whom it was false that he or she authored *The Nature of Necessity* in α.
These properties are, on the other hand, at least close cousins of haecceities if a more
finc-grained criterion of property identity is accepted or adopted. For like haecceities,
they are, if they exist, individual essences of the things that possess them, and individual essences that are neither reducible to purely qualitative properties, nor such as to
involve the idea of origin. (If they were so reducible, there would be individual
essences that are made up of purely qualitative properties or individual essences that
essentially involve the notion of origin.) In either case, they inherit the problems that
we have seen beset haecceities.

This is obvious, of course, if they just are haecceities. But it appears to be true
even if they are only close cousins of haecceities. For consider: either all such world-
indexed properties are actually exemplified, or some are not. Suppose the former. As
before, there will be no singular propositions about nonexistent individuals, and all
the counterintuitive consequences that fact was shown above to entail will be unavoidable. On the other hand, if some individuating world-indexed properties are unexemplified, we again have to swallow the idea that there are properties just as empty as
haecceities appear to be. In other words, unexemplified individuating world-indexed
properties serve just as well as haecceities in the God-stories described earlier. (Instead of $x[x = $ Plantinga] and $x[x = $ Plantinga*], substitute $x[x$ authors *The Nature of*

Necessity in *w*] and *x* [*x* authors *The Nature of Necessity* in *w'*], understanding the former to be exemplified in α, and the latter not.) So their (ostensible) unintelligibility would seem to count as well against the idea that there are unexemplified individuating world-indexed properties. Indeed, one might wonder how an actually unexemplified property like *x* [*x* and *x* alone has *P* in *w*]—*Z*, say—could exist without its also being true that there is a corresponding haecceity *H*. After all, *Z* is an individual essence of whatever has it. So if *Z* exists, how could there fail to be the haecceity of the individual whose individual essence *Z* would be were *w* to be actual?

V

So far I have set out briefly a line of thought that leads to the conclusion that each of us possesses an individual essence, and I have shown that each of the prima facie possible views about what sorts of properties our alleged individual essences might be carries highly counterintuitive consequences. I turn in this and the following section to consideration of two ways in which it might be thought that we could sidestep the problem that gives rise to these difficulties.

The question that led to the apparent need for individual essences, it will be recalled, was this: "If a different possible world had been actual—*w*, say—would I be among the inhabitants of *w*?" The suggestion was that there must be an answer to this question and that this answer will depend upon whether among the denizens of *w*, there is one that has my individuating feature or features—my individual essence. But, it might be said, there is a different and more appropriate response that does not, or, at least, does not obviously, saddle us with individual essences. It goes thus. Would I exist if *w* were actual? That depends upon *w*'s correct description. If the correct description of *w* includes a sentence containing a rigid designator of me—my name, for example—then I am in *w*. If it does not, there are two possibilities. Either I am not there, or there is no answer to the question whether I am there. The former will be the case if the correct description of *w* is such that every individual in *w* is referred to by a rigid designator that refers as well to an individual in α. In that case, *w* is a world that contains a proper subset of α's individuals (and none besides), and I am among the individuals that α contains and that *w* lacks. It will also be the case if all of the individuals in *w* that are not referred to by rigid designators lack my essential properties—if, as I assume, I have some such properties. The latter will be the case if there are (at least) some individuals in *w* that possess whatever essential properties I possess and are designated in the description of *w* by means of referring devices that are not rigid designators. The reason there will in this case be no answer to the question whether I am in *w* is not that the concept of identity is vague. That is an idea we do well to scotch—for reasons mentioned in section III above. It is rather that in this case, the description of *w* is simply incomplete. In other words, the question whether I am in *w* has no answer—there just is no fact of the matter as to whether I am there or not—because the description is such that a number of distinct worlds all satisfy it, and in some of those worlds I am present, and in others I am not.[24]

Does this sort of response to the question under consideration obviate the need for individual essences? Not if a realistic attitude toward possible worlds is reasonable, that is, not if it is plausible to think of possible worlds as proper objects for the quantifiers in our canonically expressed theory of reality to range over. Then nonactual possible worlds are, in Russell's memorable phrase, "part of the furniture of the world." If this is so, it is intelligible to ask in virtue of what the correct description of one of these worlds—*w*, say—contains the sentence *S* ('Alvin Plantinga authors *The Nature of Necessity*') rather than *S* * ('Robert M. Adams authors *The Nature of Necessity*'). But if such a question makes sense, surely the answer will have to be that the object who authors *The Nature of Necessity* in *w* has (or lacks) the property (or properties) that (singly or together) Plantinga cannot lack and that nothing distinct from Plantinga can possess. After all, if the object in *w* who authors *The Nature of Necessity*—*a*, say—lacks any individuating property of Plantinga, it is not correctly designated by the rigid designator 'Alvin Plantinga', and if *a* has Plantinga's individuating property (or properties), it cannot fail to be Plantinga.

It is worth noting that even if one could see how to avoid commitment to individual essences via the way of thinking about crossworld identity that involves appeal to descriptions of possible worlds that employ rigid designators, one would face some of the same problems that beset proponents of individual essences. Suppose that there are no individual essences in the sense given this expression in section I and that it makes sense to identify individuals across possible worlds only when these worlds are characterized by the use of rigid designators that designate actual individuals. (Without individual essences that can be grasped independently of acquaintance with, or knowledge of, their actual instances, it is hard to see how there could be rigid designators of nonactual individuals.) Then, it would seem, there will be no singular propositions about nonactual individuals. For no such propositions will be within our intellectual grasp—as a matter of metaphysical necessity. And the idea that there might be propositions that we are *of metaphysical necessity* precluded from grasping is hard to accept.[25] If there are no singular propositions about nonactual individuals, once again we find ourselves having to affirm, counterintuitively, that the possible is not exhausted by the possibly-true, since there will be worlds that could have been actual that have the feature that if they had been actual, propositions would be true that do not, as things stand, even exist.

VI

A different way of avoiding the problems developed in sections II–IV involves appeal to the idea of "branching worlds." The central thought here would be that by thinking about possible worlds in a different way, we can both retain a realistic attitude toward them and also allow for crossworld identity while avoiding commitment to any individual essences of a questionable sort. The way of thinking about (nonactual) possible worlds in question involves viewing each as a maximal, possible state of affairs[26]—or, if you wish, a maximal, consistent proposition—that branches off the actual world now or at some time earlier than the present, and thus as being identical with the actual world throughout at least part of its history, namely, the part prior to the point of branching. In other words, each nonactual possible world is, as one might say, a possible but unrealized future outcome of either the present state of affairs or some past state of affairs, together with the entire past of that present or past state of affairs.[27] On this way of conceiving modal matters, an object b in a nonactual possible world w is identical with some object a that exists in the actual world iff b comes into existence in w at some point prior to the point of branching—t, say—and $b = a$ prior to t. Thus, there is a possible world in which I am a lawyer only if there is a possible world that branches off from α after I come into existence and that contains a lawyer who is related in the right way to me as I was before the time of branching.[28] If I am essentially not a rock, i.e., I am a nonrock in all the possible worlds in which I exist, then for each nonactual possible world w, it is true either that I am not among its inhabitants—which will be true if w branches from α before I come into existence—or that (a) none of the rocks that exist in the part of w that α shares is identical with me, and (b) none of the rocks that exist in that part of w that diverges from α is crosstemporally identical with an object that exists prior to the fork and that is identical with me.[29] Accordingly, to the question whether if some nonactual possible world w had been actual I would be there, the answer can be given without recourse to the idea of individual essences. The answer will be yes iff w branches off α at some point after I come into existence in α; the answer will be no otherwise, i.e., provided w branches off α at some point before I come into existence in α.

Unfortunately, the way of thinking about possible worlds and crossworld identity, which I shall call "the branching conception," also abounds in paradox. No one, I take it, thinks it would be correct to say of a bushel of acorns that the bushel contains 279 oak trees. It is similarly incorrect, it seems to me, to include the zygotes when one gives the number of persons (or human beings) currently living in New York City. (This is not to deny that a zygote in a woman's womb is either human or a living organism. But to infer from the fact that such zygotes are living human organisms the proposition that they are human beings [persons] would be legitimate only if it were also legitimate to infer that the sperm produced in human testes are human beings [persons]. After all, they, too, are human and living organisms.) If a zygote is not a human being (or a person), then I am identical with a certain zygote that existed in the past only if I am not essentially a human being or something that has experiences or something that possesses a body with at least a rudimentary nervous system. If it is true that I am distinct from the zygote from which I developed, then on the branching conception, there is no possible world in which I am, say, blind owing to damage to that zygote seven days after fertilization of the ovum from which it developed. For any possible world in which some person develops from such a damaged zygote *ex hypothesi* branches from α prior to my coming into existence and, hence, is a world from which I am absent. But surely we want to hold that I could have been blind owing to some unfortunate occurrence inside my mother prior to my having emerged in the course of fetal development.[30]

Consider the question whether FDR, who in fact died in 1945, could have seen my wife, who was born in 1951. Intuitively, we want to say that this is possible. FDR could have lived a few years longer, i.e., it is at least logically possible that he should have. And if he had, it is at least logically possible that he should have seen my wife shortly after her birth. It is easy to tell a coherent story in which such a thing takes place. But on the branching conception, such a happening is simply impossible because, on that conception, any possible world in which FDR's life ends later than 1945 is a world that branches off α prior to 1951, and any world that branches off α prior to 1951 is a world that lacks my wife. For similar reasons, it is not possible on the branching conception that my wife have ever seen FDR—except in photos, old newsreels, and so on. For any nonactual possible world in which my wife exists is just like α up to 1951 and, hence, is a world in which FDR dies in 1945.

The situation is even worse than the above considerations explicitly bring out. Since on the branching conception, my wife does not exist in any nonactual possible world that is not exactly like α up to the time at which she comes into existence, it follows that if she came into existence in a room with purple wallpaper, she has as an essential property that she came into existence in a room with purple wallpaper. And if her father wore purple socks on his third birthday, it is an essential property of my wife that her father wore purple socks on his third birthday. In short, the branching conception has the unpalatable consequence that any property my wife had when she first came into existence—not excluding relational properties of the sort just mentioned—is a property that she has in any world in which she exists and is therefore, on the standard view, an essential property of hers.[31]

Finally, the branching conception entails that what is possible at one time is different from what is possible at an earlier or later time—in other words, that the possible is temporally relative. This is so because, on this way of developing the metaphysics of modality, after Napoleon, for example, comes into existence, there are nonactual possible worlds containing Napoleon, whereas before he came into existence, there simply were no such worlds. For suppose there were such worlds. Then, it seems, there would be worlds containing Napoleon that branch off α before Napoleon comes into existence, given that possible worlds are maximal, possible states of affairs. There would, after all, be all sorts of states of affairs involving Napoleon, and what could prevent there being assembled with others to make up world-sized states of affairs that involve Napoleon, and what could prevent there being assembled with others to make up world-sized states of affairs that involve Napoleon living in the fifteenth century A.D.? So if we combine the idea that possible worlds are maximal, possible states of affairs with the requirements on crossworld identity that are also built into the branching conception, there is no alternative to holding that what states of affairs (and so possible worlds) exist is temporally relative. But this consequence runs counter to firm intuitions at a number of points.[32]

Suppose one of the nonactual possible worlds that branches off from α before I came into existence had been actual. Then not only would it be the case that I never exist, but it would also be true that α is not, and never will be, among the possible worlds that exist. For if α did (or will) exist, even if one of the nonactual possible worlds that branches off from α earlier than my emergence had been actual, then it is false that I am a member of only those nonactual possible worlds that branch from the actual world after I come into existence. For if α did (or will) exist, in the case imagined, there is (or will be) a nonactual possible world such that (a) if it had been actual I would exist, and such that (b) it does not branch off from the world that is actual at some time later than the time of my emergence onto the scene.[33] But the idea that the actual world would not have been among the possible worlds (that ever exist) had things turned out differently is hard to swallow. If anything is clear in this area of metaphysics, it is the idea that if something does happen, it could happen—that what happens today was at least possible yesterday.[34] Equally difficult to accept is the thought that the proposition [Robert Coburn never exists] might have been true, even though if it had been, there would have been no such proposition.[35]

Also, the idea that possible worlds—worlds, for example, in which Napoleon dies of cancer at age twenty-one—come into existence once, say, Napoleon appears that did not exist *in any sense* prior to a certain date is tantamount to the idea that there is a nonrelative distinction between past, present, and future and that what is commonsensically spoken of as "the passage of time" involves irreducible, objective (i.e., mind-independent) changes, as, for example, Christmas 1994, Easter 1998, and so on draw steadily closer to the present with each passing day. But this view about what temporal passage involves entails the existence of facts—such as that today is August 7, 1985, and that September 1, 1985, is exactly twenty-five days from the day that is now elapsing—that are ineluctably "fugitive," i.e., facts into the expression of which temporal indexicals enter essentially and that thus, of necessity, have the feature that their holding is a temporary matter.[36] For suppose the fact expressed by (certain) utterances of sentences like 'Today is August 7, 1985' were expressible without the use of any temporal indexicals. Then judgments to the effect that event e is past (or present or future) would not be true or false independently of the temporal position of the judger relative to e, and it would be an illusion that the proposition that something is happening now is, if true at all, true absolutely (nonrelatively) and a truth that will inexorably cease to hold quite independently of the existence or thoughts of any thinking subjects.

However, if there are such "fugitive facts," then they surely give the truth-conditions of (tokens of) sentences like 'Today is August 8, 1985' (and the corresponding judgments), i.e., their holding is what makes such token-sentences (and token-judgments) true, when they are true. But in actuality, what makes true my current thought that today is August 7, 1985, is surely just the timeless (and nonfugitive) fact that this judgment takes place on August 7, 1985. The truth-conditions of tokens of such sentences and judgments cannot be both timeless and fugitive, however. So the existence of fugitive facts has to be an illusion; otherwise, it is just false that what makes my current thought that today is August 7, 1985, true is that it occurs on August 7, 1985. Hence, the problem with the view that temporal passage involves irreducible, objective changes of the kind indicated, and *a fortiori* with the branching conception.[37]

It would appear, then, that an appeal to the branching conception of possible worlds and crossworld identity will not help us toward a problem-free escape from the difficulties canvassed earlier either.

VII

What are we to conclude from this recital of apparently intractable problems? If I have not made serious blunders, we should conclude, I suggest, (1) that the best view in this area of metaphysics will fall far short of meeting the desiderata that we might wish it to meet, and (2) that since this is so, we can expect—what seems to be the case—that those fully conversant with the issues will disagree as to the contours of that view. In short, where "nothing works," even the best will be defective, and agreement among the informed and reasonable will be hard to come by.[38]

Notes

1. The phrases are Kripke's. See S. Kripke, *Naming and Necessity* (Cambridge, Mass., 1972), 15 and 19.

2. See, for example, A. Plantinga, "De Essentia," in *Essays on the Philosophy of Roderick M. Chisholm*, edited by E. Sosa (Amsterdam, 1979), 101–2.

3. One way of explicating this notion is given by R. M. Adams thus: *P* is a purely qualitative property just in case "it could be expressed, in a language sufficiently rich, without the aid of such referential devices as proper names, proper adjectives and verbs (such as 'Leibnizean' and 'pegasizes'), indexical expressions, and referential uses of definite descriptions" (Adams, "Primitive Thisness and Primitive Identity," *The Journal of Philosophy* 76 [1979]: 7).

4. Haecceities in my sense are referred to by R. M. Adams as "primitive thisnesses." See his papers "Primitive Thisness and Primitive Identity," *The Journal of Philosophy* 76 (Jan. 1979), 5–26, and "Actualism and Thisness," *Synthese* 49 (1981): 5–26, 3–41. (N. B. Adams uses 'haecceity' and 'thisness' to express the same concept.)

5. Throughout I use Quine's method for forming names of properties, relations, and propositions. See *Word and Object* (New York and London, 1960), 164–65. I am indebted to Graeme Forbes for a proper formulation of *Q*.

6. See Kripke, *Naming and Necessity*, lecture III.

7. R. M. Adams, "Divine Necessity," *The Journal of Philosophy* 80 (1983): 751.

8. This line of thought is suggested by A. Plantinga, "Actualism and Possible Worlds," in *The Possible and the Actual*, edited by M. Loux (Ithaca and London, 1979), 262.

9. Plantinga suggests this way of understanding the truth in question. See ibid., 268–72.

10. I put 'world' in quotes to underscore that the created world ≠ α if God exists, since he is also an inhabitant of α.

11. The basic line of thought in this paragraph is an adaptation of an argument in A. N. Prior, "Identifiable Individuals," in *Papers on Time and Tense* (Oxford, 1968), 718.

12. This use of the word is Plantinga's. See "On Existentialism," *Philosophical Studies* 44 (1983): 1–20.

13. This consequence of existentialism is brought out in R. M. Adams, "Actualism and Thisness," especially sec. 3.

14. The thesis that nothing has a property in a world unless it exists in that world is sometimes called "serious actualism." The argument indicated for this thesis is given by A. Plantinga in his "Reply to Pollock," in *Alvin Plantinga: A Profile*, edited by James Tomberlin and Peter van Inwagen (Dordrecht, forthcoming).

15. This implication of existentialism is also discussed by Adams in "Actualism and Thisness," sec. 4.3.

16. The basic structure of this line of thought derives from Kripke, *Naming and Necessity*, 114–15, n. 56.

17. This counterexample appears in M. Price, "On the Non-Necessity of Origin," *The Canadian Journal of Philosophy* 12 (1982): 33–45.

18. Cf. P. F. Strawson, "May Bes and Might Have Beens," in *Meaning and Use*, edited by A. Margalit (Dordrecht, 1979), 229–38.

19. See R. M. Chisholm, "Identity Across Possible Worlds: Some Questions," in *The Possible and the Actual*, edited by M. Loux, 80–87.

20. The above is an adaptation of the argument N. Salmon gives in *Reference and Essence* (Princeton, 1981), sec. 28.

21. This is Salmon's way of dealing with such arguments. See *ibid*.

22. This last line of thought was suggested to me by remarks in an unpublished paper of Salmon's. The argument against the vagueness of identity is more fully developed in *Reference and Essence*, 243–45.

23. Plantinga has argued that such properties are individual essences. See *The Nature of Necessity* (Oxford, 1974) and "Actualism and Possible Worlds."

24. This line of thought obviously derives from Kripke's *Naming and Necessity*, though he would not accept it as given, I believe.

25. An inability to grasp certain propositions owing to limits on our potentialities for concept formation would not amount to a metaphysical impossibility—unless, of course, it is a metaphysical necessity that we are thus limited, i.e., that our not having a more capacious potential conceptual repertoire is one of our essential properties.

26. This idea is elucidated in Plantinga, "Actualism and Possible Worlds," sec. II.

27. The way of expressing the idea in this sentence derives from A. Prior, "Identifiable Individuals," 69. Here, and hereafter, notions like *the present, the past,* and so on should be understood as relativized to a frame of reference.

28. What the right way is will depend upon the correct view about identity through time for persons.

29. The central idea of the branching conception as conceived here is presented in Prior's "Identifiable Individuals." However, I have built into it the view of crossworld identity that philosophers like Sydney Shoemaker and Allan Gibbard appear to embrace. See Shoemaker, "Comments and Replies," in *Applications of Inductive Logic*, edited by L. J. Cohen and M. Hesse (Oxford, 1980), 321–32; Shoemaker, "Causality and Properties," in *Time and Cause,* edited by P. Van Inwagen (Dordrecht, 1980), 109–35; and Gibbard, "Contingent Identity," *The Journal of Philosophical Logic* 5 (1975): 187–221. Prior, it should be noted, does not appear to have accepted this view of crossworld identity—at least, in the paper cited—since he seems to think that once Napoleon, for example, has appeared, there are possible worlds that include him that branch earlier than the time he came into existence. See "Identifiable Individuals," 77.

30. Cf. Kripke, *Naming and Necessity*, 115, n. 57.

31. My attention was first drawn to this point by Douglas Cannon.

32. It follows that the branching conception as I have developed it differs from the perhaps more familiar view according to which what are temporally relative are only "real (or genuine) possibilities," not possibilities (or possible worlds) *tout court*. I refer to the view according to which the possibility of my remaining a lifelong bachelor does not exist at some times and fail to exist at others, though it is true that it is now no longer a *real* possibility that I remain a lifelong bachelor, as it was prior to 1961 when I in fact relinquished my bachelorhood.

The trouble with this latter view is that it is hard to see exactly how nonactual possible worlds are to be understood if the crossworld identity requirements built into my version are kept. If nonactual possible worlds are not maximal, possible states of affairs, what are they? And if they are maximal, possible states of affairs but not temporally relative, how can these crossworld identity requirements be met?

33. Suppose w is a nonactual possible world that branches from α at t_1 and that I in fact came into existence at t_2. The situation is as depicted below:

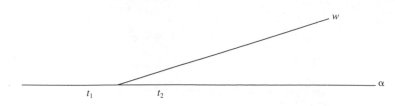

Now suppose that w had been actual and that α was among the nonactual possible worlds that there are. The situation is as follows:

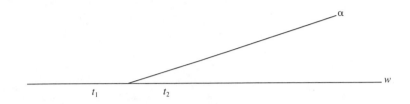

Then it would be the case that a nonactual possible world, namely, α, would exist containing me, even though it branches off from the world that is actual, namely, w, before t_2.

34. Prior recognized that his view carried the untoward consequence noted. See "Identifiable Individuals," 77.

35. This consequence of the branching conception was suggested by Adam's "existentialist" version of actualism in "Actualism and Thisness."

36. Prior also appears to have accepted this consequence. See "Changes in Events and Changes in Things," in *Papers on Times and Tense*, 1-14. The account of "fugitive" facts given in the text appears in M. Dummett, "A Defense of McTaggart's Proof of the Unreality of Time," *The Philosophical Review* 69 (1960): 497-504.

37. The argument against "passage" in this paragraph derives from D. H. Mellor, *Real Time* (Cambridge, 1981), chap. 6.

38. I am grateful to S. Marc Cohen for comments on an early draft that enabled me to improve the paper at a number of points.

Two Concepts of Possible Worlds

PETER VAN INWAGEN

As recently as ten years ago, it was not uncommon to hear philosophers sneer at the newfangled notion of a possible world. Today the sneers have died away, and possible worlds are recognized as a respectable philosophical tool. But what *are* they?

I

Let us approach this question by considering a famous—or notorious—passage from David Lewis's book *Counterfactuals*.

> I believe that there are possible worlds other than the one we happen to inhabit. If an argument is wanted, it is this. It is uncontroversially true that things might have been otherwise than they are. I believe, and so do you, that things could have been different in countless ways. But what does this mean? Ordinary language permits the paraphrase: there are many ways things could have been besides the way they actually are. On the face of it, this sentence is an existential quantification. It says that there exist many entities of a certain description, to wit 'ways things could have been'. I believe that things could have been different in countless ways; I believe permissible paraphrases of what I believe; taking the paraphrase at its face value, I therefore believe in the existence of entities that might be called 'ways things could have been'. I prefer to call them 'possible worlds'.[1]

The notoriety of this passage derives not so much from its content—which I think is pretty unexceptionable—as from its setting. For Lewis did not content himself with saying that there were entities properly called 'ways things could have been'; nor did he content himself with implying that 'possible world' was a heuristically useful stylistic variant on 'way things could have been'. He went on to say that what most of us would call "the universe," the mereological sum of all the furniture of earth and all the choir of heaven, is one among others of these "possible worlds" or "ways things could have been,'' and that the others differ from it ''not in kind but only in what goes on in them'' (p. 85). And to suppose that the existence of a plurality of universes or cosmoi could be established by so casual an application of Quine's criterion of ontological commitment has been regarded by most of Lewis's readers as very exceptionable indeed.

Whether or not the existence of a plurality of universes can be so easily established, the thesis that possible worlds are universes is one of the two ''concepts of possible worlds'' that I mean to discuss. Peter Unger employs a similar concept of possible worlds.[2] The other concept I shall discuss is that employed by various philosophers who would probably regard themselves as constituting the Sensible Party: Saul Kripke, Robert Stalnaker, Robert Adams, R. M. Chisholm, John Pollock, and Alvin Plantinga.[3] These philosophers regard possible worlds as abstract objects of some sort: possible histories of *the* world, for example, or perhaps properties, propositions, or states of affairs.

I shall call these two groups of philosophers Concretists and Abstractionists, respectively.

There are only a few points of agreement between the two parties. Each would accept the words of the passage I have quoted from Lewis: except that it bears the unmistakable stamp of Lewis's prose style, it might have been written by any of the philosophers I have named. And each party would agree that ''worlds'' are objects that are in some sense ''maximal.'' For example, those Abstractionists who hold that worlds are states of affairs would identify worlds with (possible) states of affairs that are maximal with respect to the inclusion (or entailment) of other possible states of affairs: A world is a possible state of affairs W such that the conjunction of W and any state of affairs not entailed by W is *not* a possible state of affairs. And Lewis, who holds that worlds are objects spread out in space and time, identifies worlds with spatiotemporal objects that are maximal with respect to spatiotemporal interrelatedness: A world is a spatiotemporal object W such that the mereological sum of W and any object not a part of W is *not* a spatiotemporal object. Both Abstractionists and Concretists evidently regard the word 'world' as appropriate to the extension they give it. (It could be argued that each party is availing itself of one of the two main historical semantic branches of this word.[4]) This is no doubt at least partly because, whatever else a ''world'' may be, it is certainly something maximal.

Let us introduce the term 'A-world' as a term whose meaning or intension is just that description that Abstractionists give of the objects they say are ''what possible worlds are''; and let us do the same, *mutatis mutandis*, for 'C-world' and the Concretists. (Note that it does not follow that Abstractionists *mean* 'A-world' by 'world', or that Concretists *mean* 'C-world' by 'world'—any more than it follows from the fact that dualists and materialists give different descriptions of the items in the extensions of 'person' or 'sensation' that these two groups of philosophers therefore differ about the *meaning* of 'person' or 'sensation'. We shall return to this point presently.)

It will be useful to define these two terms formally. Let us begin with 'A-world'. We take as undefined 'state of affairs' (e.g., Reagan's having been elected president in 1984), 'obtains' (Mondale's having been elected in 1984 does not obtain; Reagan's having been elected in 1984 does obtain), and 'conjunction' (the conjunction of two states of affairs is the state of affairs that consists in their both obtaining). A state of affairs x is said to *include* a state of affairs y if it is impossible "in the broadly logical sense" for x to obtain without y's also obtaining. Then:

x is an A-world $= df$	x is a possible state of affairs (one that possibly obtains), and the conjunction of x and any state of affairs that x does not include is not a possible state of affairs.

Now 'C-world'. We take as primitive—more for convenience than anything else, since it would be possible to make this notion more precise—the notion of two objects being spatiotemporally related. (Cf. n. 2.) An object will be said to be *spatiotemporal* if, for any x and y, if x and y are parts of that object, then x and y are spatiotemporally related. Then:

x is a C-world $= df$	x is a spatiotemporal object, and the mereological sum of x and any object that is not a part of x is not a spatiotemporal object.

We may note that although "A-world" is obviously a modal concept, "C-world" is a nonmodal concept—at least in the sense that it can be defined using only paradigmatically nonmodal concepts.

I have given the definitions in these forms in order to stress their structural similarity, a similarity that is rooted in the fact that they are both "maximality" definitions. But I might have given (equivalent) definientia that reproduce more closely the forms of Plantinga's and Lewis's official accounts of what a "possible world" is:

> x is a possible state of affairs, and, for any state of affairs, x includes either that state of affairs or its negation (the negation of a state of affairs y being the state of affairs that consists in y's not obtaining)

> Each of x's parts is spatiotemporally related to all of x's parts, and anything spatiotemporally related to any of x's parts is one of x's parts.[5]

This second way of defining 'C-world' makes it clear that there are two ways in which an object that is a sum of spatiotemporal parts could fail to be a C-world: (i) it could be spatiotemporally related to something not one of its parts, as, e.g., the Eiffel Tower is, or (ii) it could have spatiotemporally unrelated parts; this second possibility is realized by the mereological sum of the Eiffel Tower and any spatiotemporal object—assuming that there are such—that is spatiotemporally unrelated to that structure.

Perhaps this is as good a time as any at which to call attention to a puzzling—and to the Abstractionist rather annoying—asymmetry between Abstractionism and Concretism: The difference between Abstractionism and Concretism is thought to be much clearer and more important by Abstractionists than by Concretists. Let the Concretist speak. "You Abstractionists say that a 'world' is a possible state of affairs that is maximal with respect to the inclusion of states of affairs. But *I* say that a 'state of affairs' is a set of worlds and that a state of affairs x 'includes' a state of affairs y if and only if x is a subset of y. Hence, such a 'maximal' state of affairs is just a set whose sole member is an object that is maximal with respect to spatiotemporal interrelatedness. If we ignore the distinction between a set whose sole member is an individual (non-set) and that individual (and Quine has shown us how to dispense with that distinction altogether, if we want to), then A-worlds *are* C-worlds and *vice versa*—even if you Abstractionists don't realize it."

The Abstractionist will find this fantastic. He will protest that he is *called* an Abstractionist because he holds that possible worlds are abstract objects; he will protest that it is incredible to suppose that any state of affairs, even a "maximal" one, is a concrete object. The Concretist will reply (at least he will if he is David Lewis) that *he* did not choose the name 'Concretism' for his position, and that, in fact, he is far from being clear about the (alleged) distinction between abstract and concrete objects. This reply raises large issues.[6] For the moment, let us simply stipulate that it is a part of the Abstractionist's position that states of affairs, whatever they may be, are neither spatiotemporal objects nor mereological sums of spatiotemporal objects nor set-theoretical constructs on mereological sums of spatiotemporal objects.

Those who use the term 'possible world', whether they are Abstractionists or Concretists, use this term in conjunction with certain other closely related terms that, taken together, may be said to constitute "possible-worlds talk." Possible-worlds talk comprises, at a minimum, besides 'possible world' itself, the terms 'actual' and 'in' (or sometimes 'at'). (Various other terms like 'accessible from' and 'closer to' may count as items in possible-worlds talk, but I shall not consider them.)

Abstractionists and Concretists, owing to the fact that they assign very different objects to the extension of 'possible world', see 'actual' and 'in' as marking out very different attributes and relations. Let us do for 'actual' and 'in' what we did for 'world'. We begin with 'actual'. Let us give to the terms 'A-actual' and 'C-actual' senses derived, respectively, from the Abstractionists' and the Concretists' accounts of "actuality."

For the Abstractionist (if he thinks of worlds as states of affairs), actuality is just obtaining: the actual world is the one world—the one among possible states of affairs maximal with respect to the inclusion of other states of affairs—that obtains. (Or if the Abstractionist thinks of worlds as propositions—possible propositions maximal with respect to entailment—he will say that actuality is just truth.) Let us, therefore, define 'A-actual' to mean 'obtaining'. The Concretist, on the other hand, will say that 'actual' is an indexical term. For the Concretist, to call a world actual is to say that one is a part of it. Let us, therefore, define 'x is C-actual' to mean 'I am a part of x' (or, in manifestos and such, 'we are parts of x'). In this connection, some rather delicate ontological points need to be made.

This characterization of 'C-actual' accurately reflects David Lewis's account of actuality. But Lewis is a Quinean as regards existence: he believes that everything exists, that existence is what is expressed by the existential quantifier, that the idea of a non-existent object is self-contradictory.[7] Suppose there were a Concretist who was not a Quinean but a Meinongian (or, better, a Parsonian), that is, someone who believed that there were objects that did not exist. Such a philosopher might well want to say that actuality is just existence; that just as a nonactual horse is a nonexistent horse, a nonactual C-world is just a nonexistent C-world. I do not know of any philosopher who has explicitly endorsed this sort of Concretism in print, but I believe it to be widespread.[8]

Meinongian Concretism is an interesting view. I think that it faces no very grave problems beyond those that it inherits from Meinongianism *simpliciter* (but those are considerable). I will not, however, discuss it in this paper. I mention it only to distinguish it from Lewis's version of Concretism.[9] (I pointed out above that ''C-world,'' which is based on Lewis's account of worlds, is not a modal concept. We should note that a Meinongian account of concrete worlds would have the consequence that ''concrete world'' *was* a modal concept, owing to the fact that Meinongians believe that some objects are impossible, and, therefore, would have to define 'concrete world' in some such way as this: 'object that is maximal with respect to spatiotemporal interrelatedness and is also possibly existent'.[10])

Abstractionists apply the words 'actual' and 'nonactual' only to certain abstract objects. That is, they do *not* apply them to concrete objects. If you asked an Abstractionist to defend this practice, he would reply along these lines: ''It is reasonably clear what it means to say of a state of affairs, which is an abstract object, that it is 'actual': that it obtains. Possible states of affairs are, or represent, ways things could be and are, therefore, the sort of thing that can fail to 'come off'. In a way somewhat analogous to pictures and declarative sentences, they represent things as being arranged in a certain way, and they may represent incorrectly. If they do, we call them 'nonactual'. But what could it mean to say of a concrete object like a horse that it was 'actual'? Horses and other concrete objects do not represent things as being a certain way; they cannot 'fail to come off'—they're just *there*. If we examine the way in which, e.g., 'nonactual horse' has in fact been used, we see that this phrase almost always means, in the mouths of its habitual employers, 'nonexistent horse'. (We must, of course, except David Lewis from this generalization.) And, indeed, it is difficult to see what else it might mean. But we Abstractionists are Quineans (about existence). In this sense of 'actual', we say that there are not, and could not possibly be, nonactual horses. Like 'round square', 'nonactual horse' is a contradiction in terms. Some of us Abstractionists have described themselves as 'actualists', or have said that they were unwilling to countenance nonactual objects. This is what they meant. (Note that even David Lewis is an ''actualist'' in *this* sense. Note also that when Abstractionists call a state of affairs 'nonactual', they don't mean that it does not exist, only that it does not obtain. 'Nonexistent state of affairs' is as much a contradiction in terms as 'nonexistent horse'.)''

Now, as is well-known, the standard formal semantics for quantified modal logic (in conjunction with plausible assumptions about what is possible) strongly suggests a metaphysic of modality according to which there are ''objects that exist only in other possible worlds.'' Sometimes the words 'actual' and 'nonactual' have been introduced this way: an actual object is one that exists in the actual world, and a nonactual object is one that exists only in nonactual worlds.[11] But this way of introducing 'actual' (as an adjective that applies to objects in general, and not only to worlds) depends on the remaining item in the vocabulary of possible-worlds talk, 'in', to which we must turn before we can evaluate this way of introducing 'actual'.

I shall continue with the policy I have followed above and define two terms, one modeled on the Abstractionists' explanation of 'in', and the other modeled on the Concretists' explanation. Since 'A-in' and 'C-in' are awkward, I shall use 'at' for the ''Abstractionist sense'' and 'in' for the ''Concretist sense'' of 'in'.

The Abstractionist uses 'at' or 'in' in two contexts: in ascribing truth or falsity to propositions, and in ascribing existence, or the possession of a property, to objects. Our definitions are:

> p is true [false] at the A-world $w = df$ w is an A-world, and if w were A-actual, p would be true [false];
>
> x exists [has P] at the A-world $w = df$ w is an A-world, and if w were A-actual, x would exist [have P].[12]

No such neat definitions of 'in' are possible. The Concretist, in fact, will probably claim to be using 'in' in more or less its ordinary English sense, the sense exemplified in such adverbial phrases as 'in Australia' or 'in Chicago'. In some sentences, this sense would seem to be closely connected with parthood. If we think of Chicago as a large physical object, the mereological sum of certain people and buildings and so on, we can say that 'In Chicago there is an F' means 'An F is a part of Chicago'. And it might seem that, by analogy, we could write the following definition:

> x exists in the C-world $w = df$ w is a C-world, and x is a part of w.

And, if p is a sentence (rather than a proposition):

> p is true in the C-world $w = df$ w is a C-world and p true if the range of the variables of p is restricted to parts of w.

But this account of truth-in-a-world runs into trouble with certain existential quantifications that would normally be taken to express necessary truths—and, therefore, presumably, to be true in all worlds—such as '$\exists x\, 2 + x = 4$' and '$\exists x\, x$ is a possible world in which all men are blind'. No part of the C-actual C-world (i.e., the universe) is such that when added to 2 it yields 4; nor is any part of the C-actual C-world a C-world having no sighted men as parts. Moreover, there are apparently necessary truths, such as '$2 + 2 = 4$', that contain no variables. These problems can be solved if we assume that although 'in w' *usually* acts so as to restrict our domain of quantification to the parts of w, it sometimes means something we might express by the words 'from the point of view afforded by w'. And these words mean something like, 'people in w who believe that . . . are right'; but, of course, *that* isn't quite right because (at least if C-worlds are as numerous and diverse as the Concretist presumably thinks) some C-worlds are unpopulated.[13] Let us take 'from the point of view afforded by w' as requiring no further explanation. It seems reasonable to read the occurrences of 'in w' in 'in w, $\exists x\, 2 + x = 4$' and 'in w, $\exists x\, x$ is a world in which all men are blind' as meaning 'from the point of view afforded by w'. It could be argued that we are here following the natural semantic bent of the English word 'in'. If I say (perhaps making a point about the economic policies of Mongolia) "Even in Mongolia, $2 + 2 = 4$," presumably I mean that the principles of arithmetic are valid from the point of view afforded by Mongolia, and not just that these principles apply to all the objects in Mongolia: I mean that people doing arithmetic in Mongolia must apply these principles to whatever they reason about arithmetically—even nonspatial objects and spatial objects outside Mongolia. (But one would not say, "In Mongolia, some European countries are democracies,"[14] despite the fact that anyone in Mongolia who believes that some European countries are democracies is right.)

Having defined the Abstractionist 'at' and the Concretist 'in', we may now return to the proposal to introduce 'actual' (as a predicate applying to horses and such) as 'exists in (at) the actual world'. The proposal bifurcates. The Abstractionist will point out that 'x exists at the A-actual A-world' is easily seen to be equivalent to 'x exists', reducing the proposal to one already considered and rejected. The Concretist, however, will find the proposal useful and acceptable: he will point out that 'x exists in the C-actual C-world' is satisfied by many objects that are not worlds. Moreover, he will tell us, there are objects that *fail* to satisfy this open sentence. Or at least he will tell us this if he believes, as he presumably does, that there are any C-worlds besides the one that is C-actual. Furthermore, if he believes, as he presumably does, that there are C-nonacutal C-worlds that have proper parts, he will tell us that there are objects that fail to satisfy this sentence and which are not themselves C-worlds. Suppose we use 'OC-actual' as an actuality-predicate that is applicable to concrete objects in general, and not to C-worlds alone:

x is OC-actual $= df$ x exists in the C-actual C-world.

Inspection of the definitions of 'C-actual' and 'C-world' shows that 'x exists in the C-actual C-world' is equivalent to

Every part of x is spatiotemporally related to me.

We may note that this open sentence is equivalent to the definiens of 'C-actual' in the domain of C-worlds: a C-world is C-actual if and only if it is OC-actual. There is no point, therefore, in our retaining both terms. Let us drop the term 'OC-actual' and redefine 'C-actual':

x is C-actual $= df$ Every part of x is spatiotemporally related to me.

And, of course, a C-nonactual object will be one that has at least some parts that are spatiotemporally unrelated to me. Thus, if the Concretist believes, as presumably he does, that there might have been other horses than those that there are, he will believe that there are C-nonactual horses. Nevertheless, he remains a good Quinean, for he believes that all these C-nonactual horses *exist*. For a Quinean, to say, "Fs exist" is simply to say, "The number of Fs is greater than 0"; and Concretists believe that the number of C-nonactual horses is greater than 0.

But, someone may object, suppose that there are no hairless horses, although there might have been some, and that the Concretist believes that there might have been hairless horses. In possible-worlds talk, his modal belief reads thus: hairless horses exist in some possible world. Or, in explicitly Concretist possible-worlds talk: hairless horses exist in some C-world. And if he accepts this, then, by the argument of the preceding paragraph, he should agree that hairless horses exist—which is false. The Concretist will reply that, *strictly speaking,* hairless horses do exist. But if we say, "Hairless horses exist" in any ordinary context, that context will enforce a tacit domain of quantification on us, the domain of C-actual objects, and what we say will be false. In our present extraordinary context, however—a discussion of the metaphysics of modality—this restricted domain is not forced upon us, and we may say truly that there are hairless horses, or that hairless horses exist. In this context, our quantifiers are, as it were, wide open. Restricted quantification is, of course, common in everyday life, as may be seen by reflecting on everyday utterances like 'There's no beer' or 'Everyone was at the party'.

II

If Abstractionists and Concretists are talking about such very different things when they talk about possible worlds, how can they be talking about the *same* thing? How can an Abstractionist and a Concretist who are discussing a philosophical problem couched in possible-worlds talk be doing anything but equivocating? Well, it would certainly seem that Abstractionists and Concretists *do* have fruitful discussions that are couched in possible-worlds talk. For example, in an autobiographical essay in *Alvin Plantinga*,[15] Plantinga reproduces an elegant simplification of an argument (couched in possible-worlds talk) that he had presented in *The Nature of Necessity*, a simplification communicated to him by David Lewis. But how is such communication possible? What is going on when this happens?

I think that this problem is difficult but not serious. I believe that its solution lies in recognizing that "possible world" is, in some sense, a functional concept: The concept "possible world" is the concept of a thing that plays a certain role. An analogy may give some content to this rather vague thesis. It is widely believed that many of the central concepts studied in philosophical psychology and cognitive science are functional concepts; and this (apparently) means that they are concepts of this form: 'thing that fills the following role . . .'. (For example, some say that the concept of a person is the concept of a thing that mediates in a certain way between sensation and action.) Functional concepts may be distinguished from *ontological* concepts, such as "physical body" or "immaterial substance," which are concepts of the form: 'thing of the following *kind* . . .'. It is, therefore, possible for dualists and materialists to talk to each other without equivocation about persons in the ordinary business of life; it is even possible for the two groups to dispute about what ontological concepts are coextensive with "person" (that is, to dispute about what persons *are*). In philosophical psychology, the "roles" that figure in functional concepts are generally causal roles. But disputes in the more abstract areas of philosophy, disputes about what (say) numbers or propositions or universals are, have the same sort of "feel" as disputes in philosophical psychology about persons. This suggests that "number," "proposition," and "universal" are functional concepts, though, of course, the appropriate roles in these cases cannot be causal roles. Perhaps the concept of a proposition is the concept "bearer of truth-value," for example, and philosophers who argue about "what propositions are" are arguing about what sorts of object (sentence tokens; sentence types; purely abstract objects directly graspable by the mind . . .) fill this role. (This is all very crude, of course. A more sophisticated approach to the idea of a functional concept might be based on the notion that the functional/ontological opposition is context- or level-relative: perhaps "sentence-token" is an ontological concept relative to "proposition"; but perhaps it is a functional concept on another level of analysis, the concept of an object that plays a certain role in linguistic behavior. In the philosophy of mind, "person" may be a functional concept and "physical body" an ontological concept, while in the philosophy of physics, "physical body" may be a functional concept.)

I would suggest that the concept of a possible world is the concept of an object that can fill a certain role in philosophical discourse about modality, essence, counterfactuality, truth-theories for natural languages, and so on, and that a dispute between Plantinga and Lewis about what possible worlds are should be understood on the model of a dispute between Plantinga (a dualist) and Lewis (a materialist) about what persons are. I am not under the illusion that I have said enough to give this idea much content; to do so in any adequate way would be impossible without a fundamental discussion of roles and functional concepts. But perhaps I have said enough to make the question raised at the beginning of this section a bit less worrisome. In terms of the functional/ontological distinction introduced above, we can describe the dispute between the Abstractionists and the Concretists in this way: It is a dispute about which of two ontological concepts ("A-world" or "C-world") is coextensive with the functional concept "possible world," and about what ontological concepts are coextensive with the functional concepts "actual" and "in/at." This explains in what sense the present paper is about "two concepts of possible worlds" and explains the reservations expressed in the previous section about saying that Abstractionists *mean* 'A-world' by 'world' and that Concretists *mean* 'C-world' by 'world'. As to the question, 'How can they be talking about the same thing when they are talking about such different things?', the answer is that they are not talking about different things at all. Unless the Abstractionist and the Concretist are somehow *both* wrong, they are both talking about A-worlds or both talking about C-worlds; one of them, of course, is profoundly mistaken about the nature of the things he is talking about (as is either the dualist or the materialist).

III

What can be said for and against Abstractionism and Concretism? It is not surprising that opinions differ about this. What the Abstractionist says is an awkward or unfortunate feature of Concretism, the Concretist will very likely say is not a feature of Concretism at all—or is a positively desirable one. And of course the same goes for the

defects the Concretist claims to find in Abstractionism. We may outline the principal
claims made on behalf of, and charges brought against, the two theories of possible
worlds in the following table.[16]

Concretism

pro
—Provides a reductive analysis of modality [Lewis].
—Can actually do the work for which it is designed [Lewis].

contra
—Has the consequence that modal statements are equivalent to nonmodal statements,
  ones having (in general) different truth-values from the modal statements they are
  supposedly equivalent to [some Abstractionists].
—Evokes incredulous stares [Lewis].
—Is incredible [all Abstractionists].
—Requires a counterpart-theoretical analysis of modal statements about individuals,
  thus misrepresenting the modal facts [most, if not all, Abstractionists].

Abstractionism

pro
—Is credible; presupposes the existence of nothing beyond what is already needed for
  other philosophical purposes, such as states of affairs or propositions [all Abstrac-
  tionists].

contra
—Cannot provide a reductive analysis of modality [Lewis].
—Cannot do the work for which it is designed [Lewis].

In the remainder of this paper, I shall attempt to evaluate these pros and cons.
With one exception: I shall say nothing about counterpart theory and the analysis of
modal statements *de re*. This is an important issue, but it has been extensively discussed elsewhere, and I have nothing new to say about it. The reader may have been
surprised that I said nothing about counterpart theory in my exposition of Concretism.
This is the explanation: we shall simply ignore the whole topic of *de re* modality, and
an exposition of counterpart theory will, therefore, be unnecessary for our purposes.
(One example—not of my own devising—will involve a particular individual, and the
word 'counterpart' will appear two or three times in connection with this example;
your program contains biographies of the principal players only, and not of the walk-
ons.)

Up to this point, I have tried to preserve a strict neutrality between Abstractionism and Concretism. From now on, however, I shall write as an Abstractionist. My
evaluations of the pros and cons listed above will be frankly partisan and, indeed, are
intended to add up to an argument for Abstractionism and against Concretism.

I begin with an examination of Lewis's claim that Concretism provides a reductive analysis of modality,[17] and of the related charge of the Abstractionists that it is a

consequence of Concretism that modal statements are equivalent to nonmodal statements—ones that they are, in fact, *not* equivalent to.

An example will make clear what is at issue. Consider the modal statement

(1) There is no million-carat diamond, but there could have been one.

In possible-worlds talk, this becomes

(2) No million-carat diamond exists in the actual world, but a million-carat diamond exists in some possible world.

According to Concretism, (2) is equivalent[18] to

(3) No million-carat diamond exists in the C-actual C-world, but a million-carat diamond exists in some C-world.

If we assume, and this seems obviously true, that a diamond could not possibly have spatiotemporally unrelated parts, (3) can be reduced by elementary logical manipulations to

(4) No million-carat diamond is spatiotemporally related to me, and there is a million-carat diamond.

Obviously, (4) contains only paradigmatically nonmodal terms. Since Concretism allows us in a similar way to reduce any modal statement to one containing only paradigmatically nonmodal terms, we can see what David Lewis means when he boasts that Concretism provides a reductive analysis of modality. But let us not be hasty. That Owl can spell 'Tuesday' is no proof of his erudition—not unless he can spell it right; that Owen Glendower can call spirits from the vasty deep is no proof of his sorcerous powers—not unless the spirits do come when he calls for them. And it is no argument for Concretism that it provides a reductive analysis of modality—not unless that analysis is right.

Is it? Specifically, is (4) equivalent to (1)?

One obvious objection to the thesis that (4) and (1) are equivalent is that (4) is a first-person sentence, and (1) is not—or, at any rate, it certainly doesn't seem to be. (That (4) is a first-person sentence is, of course, a consequence of the Concretist's indexical theory of actuality.) This is an interesting point, but I shall not pursue it, since I wish to concentrate on features of (4) unrelated to this one.[19]

A second obvious objection takes as its point of departure the fact that 'There is no million-carat diamond' is a conjunct of (1) and that, moreover, 'There is a million-carat diamond' is a conjunct of (4). This might be thought to be a bad omen for those who hope that (1) and (4) will turn out to be equivalent. I will not develop this objection in detail, since there is a satisfactory reply to it, and this reply does not turn on any matters of detail. The essentials of the reply are found in the closing paragraph of part I. If someone were to utter (1) in any very normal context, that context would restrict his domain of quantification to actual objects. (In general, this will be true of any sentence that employs modal operators—as opposed to quantification over possible but nonactual objects—to convey modal information.) In sentence (4), however, the quantifiers are meant to be unrestricted. In sum, the Concretist's thesis is that the proposition expressed by (4), if the quantifiers in that sentence are unrestricted, is equivalent to the proposition expressed by (1) when its quantifier is restricted to C-actual objects. (Might someone protest that if there are mere *possibilia*, then an unrestricted quantifier is a modal term? Not, I think, unless he was willing to say that an unrestricted quantifier was an astronomical, a geographical, and every other sort of term.)

Keeping the Concretist's point about restricted and unrestricted quantification in mind, let us return to the question whether (4) is equivalent to (1). *I* certainly don't think so. The following two theses seem to me to be true.

—Though there indeed could have been a million-carat diamond, there simply *is* [absolutely unrestricted quantifier] none. (At any rate, there is an n such that there could have been an n-carat diamond and there is none.) At least, this may well be true. I believe it, and I see no reason to feel uneasy about believing it, though I can't prove it.

—Nothing [absolutely unrestricted quantifier] is spatiotemporally unrelated to me (unless, like a number or a proposition, it is not spatiotemporally related to anything). At least, this may well be true. I believe it, and I see no reason to feel uneasy about believing it, though I can't prove it.

The former thesis is, by itself, sufficient for the truth of (1) and the falsity of (4). The latter thesis is sufficient for the falsity of (4).

Abstractionists find these two theses pretty obvious, and that, I think, is the reason, or a part of the reason, for those incredulous stares with which, on Lewis's testimony, he finds himself continually transfixed. Another part of the explanation, of course, is the fact that not only do Concretists believe in million-carat diamonds spatiotemporally unrelated to us, but they believe that fairly mundane modal facts (at least most of us would take them to be facts), expressible in ordinary English by the use of modal operators, are the very same facts as certain facts about objects spatiotemporally unrelated to us. For example, the Concretist must accept the proposition expressed by his utterance of the sentence

> The fact that there is no million-carat diamond but could have been one is the same fact as the fact that although no million-carat diamond is spatiotemporally related to me, some million-carat diamond is spatiotemporally unrelated to me.

This thesis seems to the Abstractionist to be not only incredible in itself, but to entail a further incredible thesis: that if the set of "modal facts" is as rich as even the most conservative estimate makes it, then there is an enormous number and an inconceivable variety of concrete objects. (Well, perhaps the *most* conservative "estimate" is Spinozism, the thesis that if there are no objects of a given kind, it folllows that it is a necessary truth that there are no objects of that kind. Few philosophers these days, I would suppose, are Spinozists. Let us say, "the most conservative estimate after Spinozism.") The reason is simply the inconceivable profusion of sorts of thing that might be but are not. There might have been not only million-carat diamonds but elves and trolls and unicorns (or, at any rate, creatures that looked and acted the way these creatures are supposed to look and act), and French colonies in Australia, and two-hundred-year-old cats, and a falling asteroid that destroyed the Roman Empire. . . . And, if Concretism is true, there are possible worlds that contain all these things. In fact, if Concretism is true, then every possible configuration of matter and radiation in space-time ("physical configuration" for short) must be realized in some C-world. For if a possible physical configuration ϕ were realized in no C-world, then, according to the Concretist, 'It is possible that ϕ occurs' would express a falsehood; but, *ex hypotesi,* this sentence expresses a truth, since ϕ is a *possible* configuration.

It is mildly embarrassing to the Concretist that the requirement that every possible physical configuration be realized in some C-world is, according to *his* view, a trivial requirement, one that is, by definition, automatically satisfied. The triviality of this requirement is a consequence of the fact that, for the Concretist, a possible physical configuration just *is* a C-world (or a part of one). This requirement would be satisfied, in Lewis's words, "if there were only seventeen worlds, or one, or none" (*On the Plurality of Worlds,* p. 86). If it happens that there is no C-world having a million-carat diamond as a part, it is a consequence of this fact and Concretism that (whatever one might have *thought*) the idea of a million-carat diamond is *not* an idea of a possible configuration of matter.

So a problem is posed for the Concretist by the fact that the seemingly substantive requirement that every possible configuration of matter be realized in some C-world is, if Concretism is true, automatically satisfied no matter how small and miscellaneous a collection of C-worlds there is. Lewis calls this problem 'the problem of expressing the plenitude'. He solves it by stipulating, in essence, that the set of possible physical configurations (the set of C-worlds) is not miscellaneous but, in a certain sense, "complete." One way to give content to such a stipulation would be to match "possible physical configurations" one-to-one with some large class of mathematical objects, a class that is in no way arbitrarily restricted. For example, consider the *"Erstaz* worlds" invented by Quine, so named by Lewis, and described in *Counterfactuals.* [20] One might "express the plenitude" of C-worlds by saying that to every Ersatz world, there corresponds at least one C-world. (Call this the plenitude principle). In *On the Plurality of Worlds,* Lewis employs a more sophisticated device for the same purpose,[21] but the device of matching C-worlds to Ersatz worlds at least shows what a solution (even if it is not the best one) to the plenitude problem would look like. And it allows us to put a lower limit on the number of C-worlds: There are at least 2-to-the-c of them. A moment's reflection will show us that if Lewis is right, there must also be at least 2-to-the-c million-carat diamonds.

Lewis apparently thinks that the enormous number of concrete (albeit C-nonactual) objects whose existence is entailed by Concretism is the main source of the incredulous stares he meets when he expounds Concretism. He says:

> [Concretism] *does* disagree, to an extreme extent, with firm common sense opinion about what there is. (Or, in the case of some among the incredulous, it disagrees rather with firmly held agnosticism about what there is.) When [Concretism] tells you—as it does—that there are uncountable infinities of donkeys and protons and puddles and stars, and of planets very like Earth, and of people very like yourself, . . . small wonder if you are reluctant to believe it.[22]

This is not an accurate report of the sources of *my* incredulity. (I don't know about "common sense opinion," by the way. It seems to me that the office of common sense is to keep us from playing cards for high stakes with people we meet on trains, and not to endorse metaphysical opinions.) Most people think that the number of donkeys is finite. If Aristotle is right, the number of donkeys (past, present, and future) is aleph-zero. There are no doubt good reasons to reject the cosmological and biological theories on which this numbering is based, but the number itself doesn't seem to be any reason to reject these theories. And I don't see that the fact that Lewis's theory has the consequence that there are 2-to-the-c or more donkeys is a particularly good reason to reject it.

The good reasons have already been laid out: the theory asks us to believe that there are, e.g., naturally hairless donkeys. And there are none. It asks us to believe that there are donkeys spatiotemporally unrelated to us. And there are none. It's not so much that I object to the thesis that the number of donkeys is uncountably infinite; it's more that I object to the thesis that the number of donkeys spatiotemporally unrelated to us is other than 0—and there are no hairless ones either! (I must, however, concede that if there were uncountable infinities of donkeys, most of them would have to be spatiotemporally unrelated to us; otherwise, there'd be no room for them all. Therefore, I do find an uncountable infinity of donkeys objectionable—but only because of its consequences for the distribution of objects in space and time.)

I find one difficulty in Concretism that could be described as a difficulty about cardinality (one that is not a consequence of the difficulties I have with spatiotemporally unrelated objects). Suppose that there are some C-worlds other than the one we are all parts of. Why should I suppose that there are all the C-worlds that the plenitude principle generates? Now this difficulty is not best described as a difficulty about *cardinality*. The plenitude principle is designed to ensure a *variety* of C-worlds, to make logical space a plenum: it forces a minimum cardinality on the set of worlds only because the variety of worlds it ensures requires that there be at least a certain number of them. Nevertheless, let us consider only the question of cardinality. Suppose I have somehow discovered that the number of C-worlds other than this one is, contrary to my very strong expectations, greater than 0. But suppose that my source of information is absolutely silent about how many of these things there are. How many should I *think* there are? Suppose that I must guess, and you must guess, and lots of people must guess and that the one whose guess is furthest from the truth will suffer an eternity of torment. How shall I guess? No guess, it seems to me, would be much more rational than any other. I note in introspection some slight preference for a finite answer, and, among finite answers, a slight preference for those numbers commonly called "small." I like some infinite numbers a bit better as answers than others. I like aleph-zero best, and 2-to-the-c next best, whatever aleph it may be. Numbers beyond the reach of iterative set-theory are right out, though I am attracted to some small degree by the idea that the C-worlds form a proper class. Lewis doesn't see matters this way. He thinks that 2-to-the-c is a much better guess than six. One does see his point if C-worlds are the same as ways C-worlds could be. I would say that because 2-to-the-c is *not* a better guess than six, C-worlds are *not* the same as ways C-worlds could be.

And, really, how *could* they be? If we think of the universe, we may see some sense in saying that it is (i.e., is identical with) a way a universe could be. Some sense, but not enough. Stalnaker and I have independently contended that this assertion is not even grammatical.[23] What one should say, surely, is that the universe *represents* or *realizes* or *instantiates* a way a universe could be. But the case is worse if we think of unrealized possibilities. How *could* one suppose that the (unrealized) possibility that the universe be thus-and-so is a thing that has a mass of 3.4×10^{37} grams and is rapidly expanding? Or turn the point round: suppose there *is* an object (maximal with respect to spatiotemporal interrelatedness) that has these two features and which is spatiotemporally unrelated to us. What makes it an "unrealized possibility"? What is it besides an enormous physical object that has the feature, cosmologically fascinating but modally irrelevant, of being spatiotemporally unrelated to us? What would such things and their parts have to do with modality? Why should I call a horse that is a part of one of these things a "merely possible horse"? Why is that a good thing to call it? (In José A. Benardete's book *Infinity*,[24] Benardete considers the concept of a "pluriverse" consisting of spatiotemporally unrelated universes in order to show that one can imagine a case in which the higher infinite cardinals would be needed to count physical objects. It never occurred to him that it would be appropriate to describe parts of other universes in the pluriverse as mere *possibilia*, and he still doesn't see it.)

I conclude that Concretism is incredible and, therefore, that the "reductive analysis of modality" that it provides is a *correct* analysis only on the assumption that the incredible is true. The charges against Concretism are thus vindicated, and one of the charges against Abstractionism, that it cannot provide a reductive analysis of modality, is disarmed: better no analysis than an incorrect one. The score in the reductive-analysis game is thus 0 to − 1, in favor of the Abstractionist.

But what of the remaining charge against Abstractionism: that it just doesn't work, that it cannot do the job for which it was designed? If this charge is correct (and if Concretism *can* do the job), the tables are turned. It seems to be the practice of scientists (one we philosophers should adopt) not to reject the only workable theory simply because that theory is (or seems to be) incredible. It is incredible to suppose that something could be both a wave and a particle; it is incredible to suppose that the Galilean Law of the Addition of Velocities should fail; it is incredible to suppose that the geometry of physical space should be non-Euclidean; it is incredible to suppose that there should be a well-defined condition to which no set corresponds. But we have accepted all these incredible things. And if the remaining charge against Abstractionism is correct (and if there is nothing against Concretism other than its being incredible), then we shall have to accept Concretism after all. To that charge, which has been made by David Lewis, I now turn.

IV

What I call Concretism, Lewis calls Genuine Modal Realism. What I call Abstractionism, he calls Ersatz Modal Realism. I shall retain my own terms in my exposition of his argument.[25]

Lewis recognizes three varieties of Abstractionism: Linguistic, Pictorial, and Magical Abstractionism. He believes (i) that each of these varieties of Abstractionism can be refuted, (ii) that any very explicit version of Abstractionism must be of exactly one of these three types, and (iii) that the available writings of Abstractionists (other than those who explicitly espouse Linguistic Abstractionism) are insufficiently informative about the nature of states of affairs (or propositions or whatever A- worlds are supposed to be) to enable one to discover which variety of Abstractionism their authors adhere to. I believe that (ii) and (iii) are correct and that Lewis's refutations of Linguistic and Pictorial Abstractionism are valid. I shall, accordingly, briefly describe these two varieties and outline his objections to them. I shall devote the remainder of this paper to a defense of "Magical" Abstractionism.

Remember that we said earlier (in our explanation in part I of why Abstractionists refuse to apply the word 'actual' to concrete objects) that A-worlds belong to the class of things that can represent concrete objects as being a certain way. (Thus, an A-nonactual A-world is one that *misrepresents* the way concrete things are.) There are three varieties of Abstractionism, in Lewis's view, because there are three kinds of answer to the question 'How does that thing represent?' They are, roughly, 'It represents the way a sentence does'; 'It represents the way a picture does'; 'It just represents, and there's nothing more to be said'.

According to Linguistic Abstractionism, possible worlds represent the way sentences do. Sentences are structures built from a stock of basic elements—characters, we may call them. A sentence represents by convention: By convention, 'The cat is on the mat' represents the cat as being on the mat. Suppose an Abstractionist identified "worlds" with possible distributions of matter and radiation in space-time, and identified possible distributions in their turn with the Quine-Lewis "Ersatz worlds" mentioned in part III in connection with the problem of expressing the plenitude.[26] This philosopher would be a Linguistic Abstractionist, for it is a matter of convention how an Erstaz world represents physical stuff as being distributed—indeed, *whether* it does.

Lewis agrues that Linguistic Abstractionism is defective because it cannot coherently formulate the thesis that the actual world is impoverished in a way in which it probably *is* impoverished. If Linguistic Abstractionism is right, then all *possible* uninstantiated properties are ones that would be instantiated if objects of types that actually exist were sufficiently numerous and properly arranged. (For example, if the Ersatz-world variety of Linguistic Abstractionism is adopted, then any possible property— any property that is instantiated in some possible world—is one that would be instantiated if there were enough filled space-time points and these filled points were arranged in the right way.) We can imagine simple worlds having the following feature: Suppose their inhabitants adopted the view that any possible property would be instantiated if objects of existent types were sufficiently numerous and properly arranged; then their inhabitants would be wrong. Consider, for example, a world in which protons, or the objects that play the role of protons in the physical economy of that world, are not composed of more fundamental particles. Consider some property possessed in our world only by quarks: *having an R-G color-charge of* $-1/2$, say.

This is a possible property, since it is instantiated in some world: the actual one. But it is not instantiated in *any* world that contains only things composed of things of kinds that exist in the simple world we have imagined.

Now if we can imagine a simple world in which Linguistic Abstractionism thus gives the wrong result, is there any reason to suppose that Linguistic Abstractionism gives the right result in the actual world? What warrant have we to suppose that there is in actuality such a rich variety of kinds that every possibility could be realized by some numerical augmentation or diminution and clever arrangement of the things there are? Even if one believed this, surely, one should regard it as a substantive metaphysical thesis (something having to do with God's bounty, perhaps, or with some other causally effective principle that is supposed to make actuality coincide with ontological richness), and not as something that could properly be forced on us by the most general and abstract features of our modal ontology. Is it even evident that there is *any* possible world that is not, in the sense described above, "impoverished"? Or even if there is a nonimpoverished world and it is the actual world, shouldn't we want our modal ontology to "work" in any world? Should we want to say that our modal ontology works only because of the lucky accident that a very rich world happens to be actual? These considerations seem to me to be cogent. Linguistic Abstractionism is defective.

Pictorial Abstractionism, a theory that no one in fact holds, asserts that worlds represent the way pictures or statues or models or maps do: by some sort of (relatively) nonconventional spatiotemporal isomorphism with the things represented and their spatiotemporal arrangement. But this seems impossible. The map is normally simpler than the territory. If something adequately represented (in the pictorial sense) the universe, it would have to be as detailed in its spatiotemporal structure as the universe. The point is tautological: if it left something out it would leave something out. And this point about pictures of the way things are applies to pictures of ways things might be but aren't. They would, of course, be different from, but some at least would have to be as detailed as, a fully accurate picture of the way things are. Suppose there were such detailed pictures of ways things might be. Wouldn't they just be *C*-worlds? Or would they be like *C*-worlds in being spread out in space and time, but, nevertheless, somehow "abstract"? There is no clear sense in this suggestion. Pictorial Abstractionism, like Linguistic Abstractionism, is defective.

The last refuge of the Abstractionist is Magical Abstractionism. (But I will not accept this dyslogistic name for the position I propose to defend. I will call it *Unsound* Abstractionism, which is an acronym for Unscientific Naive Superstitious Obscurantist Unenlightened Neanderthal Dogmatic Abstractionism.)

According to Abstractionists of all three factions, *A*-worlds are proposition-like entities. (The three factions may be said to differ just on the point of what, exactly, a "proposition-like entity" is.) In the previous sections, I have treated *A*-worlds as states of affairs, out of deference to Plantinga, who has done the most to make Abstractionism precise. In the sequel, however, it will simplify matters if we think of *A*-worlds as propositions pure and simple: An *A*-world is a possible proposition that, for any proposition *p*, entails either *p* or the denial of *p*; and actuality is simply truth.

Moreover, these ''propositions'' are not what David Lewis calls 'propositions'; they are not sets of C-worlds. More generally, as I said of states of affairs in part I, a proposition is not, for the Abstractionist, a spatiotemporally extended object, or a sum of extended objects, or a set-theoretical construct on sums of extended objects.[27] (In my view, there are only two of the things Lewis calls propositions—the false one, which is the empty set, and the true one, the set whose only member is the universe.)

A proposition is, of course, either true or false. A contingent proposition—and every A-world is a contingent proposition[28]—is *made true* or *made false* by the way things happen to be arranged. If we allow ourselves the distinction between intrinsic and relational (or extrinsic or ''mere-Cambridge'') properties, we may say that truth and falsity are relational properties of propositions. The proposition that there are cats is true (because there *are* cats); if things had been arranged differently, if cats had never come to be, it would have been false. But its intrinsic properties would have been just as they are. Thus, truth is like accuracy (said of a map). (This simile, however, is dangerous because an inaccurate map can be altered and can thereby become accurate without any change in the territory. But all of a proposition's intrinsic properties are essential to it; it cannot be ''altered.'') We might say that a contingent proposition is indifferent to its own truth-value: remove the cats and you change the truth-values of many propositions, but the propositions remain unchanged—just as a map becomes inaccurate, and yet is unchanged, when the territory changes.

There is, therefore, for the Abstractionist, only one C-world.[29] There is a certain relation borne by this C-world to propositions, which we may call the *makes-true* relation. It bears this relation to the proposition that there are cats because it (the C-world) has feline parts. It fails to bear this relation to the proposition that there are elves because it has no elvish parts. If it, the only C-world, had been at all different in its intrinsic properties, it would have borne the *makes-true* relation to a different set of propositions. Of necessity, it bears the *makes-true* relation to exactly one proposition that is maximal with respect to entailment (to exactly one A-world): if the one C-world bears *makes-true* to both p and q, then p and q are not both A-worlds. The one C-world, in virtue of the way its components are arranged, makes one and only one of the vast array of A-worlds actual. Any Abstractionist will say this much. The Unsound Abstractionist will add that a proposition's ''truth-value dispositions''—dispositions like the one embodied in the conditional 'p would be made true by a C-world having elvish parts'—have nothing to do with human convention (or with divine decree, for that matter). For the Unsound Abstractionist, propositions are necessarily existent objects[30] that have their truth-value dispositions essentially. And, of course, the Unsound Abstractionist will deny that the truth-value dispositions of a proposition are in any way like the ''accuracy dispositions'' of a map: they are not grounded in the spatial or spatiotemporal structure of propositions—a kind of structure wholly alien to their nature.

Lewis's criticism of Unsound Abstractionism is, in a nutshell, that if things were as the Unsound Abstractionist claims, that philosopher could not understand or grasp the *makes-true* relation. Or put the matter this way: the Unsound Abstractionist, in claiming to grasp the *makes-true* relation, is claiming a magical power (hence the epithet 'magical'[31]). Better still: (i) the Unsound Abstractionist has not really said what relation the *makes-true* relation is; (ii) he has made certain negative statements about the relation (it does not hold in virtue of convention or in virtue of spatiotemporal isomorphism between its *relata*), and he has made certain negative statements about the things it is borne to (they are neither spatiotemporal objects nor constructs on spatiotemporal objects), and he has made certain formal statements about it (it is borne by one thing to *some but not all* of the objects to which something might bear it); (iii) although there are doubtless uncountable infinities of relations satisfying the conditions laid down in (ii)—at least there are if there are nonspatiotemporal objects other than pure sets—no one could possibly grasp, or even refer to, any *one* relation satisfying these conditions.

Lewis's argument for this conclusion turns on a distinction between *internal* and *external* relations. Only dyadic relations figure in the argument, and I shall use 'relation' to mean 'dyadic relation'. An internal relation is one grounded in the intrinsic properties of its *relata:* A relation R is internal if, given two objects x and y that stand in R, any two objects having the same intrinsic properties as x and y must stand in R. A relation R is external if there could be a pair of objects that stand in R and could also be a pair of objects that have the same intrinsic properties but do not stand in R. Thus, *being the same shape as* is internal, and *being ten feet from* is external.

Now: *makes-true* is either internal or external.

Suppose it is external. We note that it is not an ordinary external relation, like *being ten feet from,* which a given pair of objects (you and I, say) might or might not stand in. *Makes-true* has modal implications: if the one C-world bears *makes-true* to $p,$ that is no accident. Given the properties of the C-world, it could not have failed to bear *makes-true* to $p.$ But if we suppose that *makes-true* is external, then, since the intrinsic properties of the C-world are obviously relevant to whether it bears *makes-true* to $p,$ we must conclude that the intrinsic properties of p are *irrelevant* to whether it bears *makes-true* to $p.$ In fact, we may as well assume for the sake of convenience that propositions all have the same intrinsic nature: they are individuated by those intrinsic properties of the C-world in virtue of which it bears or fails to bear *makes-true* to them. Thus, the proposition that some donkeys walk and the proposition that some donkeys talk have the same intrinsic properties; the identity of each resides in the fact that (in the former case) the C-world bears *makes-true* to it just in virtue of the fact that the C-world has walking donkeys as parts and (in the latter case) fails to bear *makes-true* to it just in virtue of the fact that the C-world has no talking donkeys as parts. But the modal implications of *makes-true* noted above would appear to be inconsistent with this thesis about the individuation of propositions. I quote Lewis (but where I write 'makes true', he wrote 'selects', and where I write 'proposition', he wrote 'element' or 'abstract simple'; *makes-true* is a special case of what he calls selection, and propositions are a special case of what he calls elements or abstract simples):

> The concrete world makes various propositions true. We are now supposing that this making true has nothing to do with the distinctive natures of the propositions—they haven't any—but it still has to do with what goes on in the concrete

world. Necessarily, if a donkey talks, then the concrete world makes these propositions true; if a cat philosophizes, it makes those true; and so on. I ask: how can these connections be necessary? It seems to be one fact that somewhere within the concrete world, a donkey talks; and an entirely independent fact that the concrete world enters into a certain external relation with this proposition and not with that. What stops it from going the other way? Why can't anything coexist with anything here: any pattern of goings-on within the concrete world, and any pattern of external relations of the concrete world to the propositions?[32]

The implication is that if *makes-true* were really an external relation, and if the intrinsic properties of all propositions were the same, then the following could be the case: though the *C*-world in fact bears *makes-true* to the proposition that there are cats, the *C*-world might have had the very same intrinsic properties and yet have failed to bear *makes-true* to that proposition; it might, in fact, have been just as it is and yet have borne *makes-true* to any set of propositions whatever. But this is clearly absurd, and we must conclude that *makes-true* is an internal relation: whether it holds between the *C*-world and *p* is determined partly by the intrinsic features of the *C*-world and partly by the intrinsic features of *p* and by nothing else. As a consequence, distinct propositions must have distinct intrinsic properties.

Suppose, therefore, that *makes-true* is internal and that propositions have distinct intrinsic natures in which *makes-true* is partly grounded. But how (Lewis asks the Unsound Abstractionist) did you ever manage to single out or grasp that relation? For a configuration of spatiotemporal objects (such as a *C*-world) to bear a graspable internal relation to a proposition must be for the structure of the proposition somehow to match the structure of the configuration of objects. But you say that propositions have neither spatiotemporal nor mereological nor set-theoretical structure. What other sort is there? If you reply that propositions have a *nature* even if they have no structure, I'll ask how you could ever learn the nature of any proposition when you can't observe or examine objects that are nonspatiotemporal and are, therefore, incapable of entering into causal relations. This *a priori* argument for your being unable to learn the intrinsic nature of propositions is underwritten by the observation that you can't individuate them without employing descriptions like 'the proposition that there are cats'. In other words, you can individuate them only by specifying what makes them true: 'the proposition that there are cats' is just a way of saying 'the proposition that is made true just by there being cats'. Note that *I* don't have this limitation. I can refer to the proposition containing all and only those *C*-worlds that have cats as parts. And I can then go on to say what makes it true: I am a part of one of its members. But if you can't discover the intrinsic nature of any proposition, how can you grasp the supposedly internal relation *makes-true*? To grasp an *internal* relation, surely, is to know when *x* bears it to *y*, given the intrinsic properties of *x* and *y*. (To grasp *is the same color as* is to understand what is meant by the color of a thing and to know that this relation is the one that *x* bears to *y* just in virtue of the color of *x* being the color of *y*.)

I will call the problem that Lewis has posed 'the Lewis-Heidegger problem'. Heidegger has pointed out certain difficulties that face the traditional correspondence theory of truth:

We speak of corresponding [*Übereinstimmen*] in various senses. For example, we say when considering two five-mark coins before us on the table: They are in correspondence with each other. The two coins agree [*Übereinkommen*] in appearance. Hence, they have this appearance in common and are in that respect the same. But we also speak of correspondence if we say, for example: The coin is round. Here the statement [*Aussage*] corresponds with the thing. The relation now holds not between thing and thing, but between statement and thing. But in what is the agreement of the thing and the statement supposed to consist, given that they present themselves to us in such manifestly different ways? The coin is made of metal. The statement is not material at all. The coin is round. The statement has no spatial features whatever. One can buy something with the coin. The statement about it is never legal tender. But, for all their dissimilarity, the statement, being true, corresponds with the coin. And this correspondence, according to the common concept of truth, is supposed to be a matching. How can the statement match the coin, to which it is completely dissimilar? It would have to become the coin and so wholly cease to be itself. The statement never succeeds in doing that. The moment it did succeed, it could no longer correspond with the thing in the way a statement does. In the act of matching, the statement must remain   .   .   .   what it is. In what does its essence, so completely different from that of a thing, consist? How does the statement have the power, just precisely by retaining its essence, to match something other than itself, the thing?[33]

Heidegger asks how a proposition could match or correspond structurally with a configuration of matter. Lewis asks this and goes on to ask how, if the supposed internal relation between matter and proposition, the *makes-true* relation, held in virtue of some nonstructural feature of the proposition, we could even *grasp* this relation, owing to the inaccessibility of any nonstructural features that noncausal, and hence imperceptible, objects like propositions might have.

It is evident that the Lewis-Heidegger problem can arise quite independently of any questions about the ontology of possible worlds. It is a problem for anyone who believes that the bearers of truth-value are anything other than constructions out of individuals and the empty set. (If you believe that sentences are the bearers of truth-value, you believe that the bearers of truth-value are such constructions.) It is equally evident that anyone who can solve the Lewis-Heidegger problem can be an Unsound Abstractionist with impunity—or at least he will have nothing to fear from Lewis's argument for the thesis that if *makes-true* is an internal relation, then it cannot be grasped. Let us look carefully at this argument. How does it work? I believe that its most important premise is a principle about language—a principle about terms that purport to name internal relations. Since I wish to have a careful statement of this principle, I will present it in the form of a rather lengthy speech.

Suppose someone makes a claim of the following general form:

There is a certain internal relation I call '*R*'. I cannot define the term '*R*'; it is one of my primitives. I know that each member of a certain set *A* bears *R* to some but not all members of a certain set *B,* that only members of *A* bear R to anything, and that R is borne by things only to members of B. I am absolutely unable to make distinctions within B—except by using the term 'R'. I can sometimes refer to members or nonempty proper subsets of B by calling them things like 'the object that both a_1 and a_2 bear R to' or 'the set of all things a_3 bears R to'; but unless I use 'R', I can single out neither any member nor any nonempty proper subset of B.

This person, in claiming to understand his own relation-name, 'R', is claiming magical powers.

The defense of this principle, I think, is as follows. 'R' is supposed to be a name for an internal relation, a relation that holds between its *relata* wholly in virtue of their intrinsic features. But if R is borne only to members of B, and if I can distinguish among members of B only by considering which objects bear R to them, then I know of no intrinsic features of the members of B that differentiate them one from the other—that fit any of them for the office of having R borne to it by a given object. And to understand or grasp an *internal* relation borne by each of the as to some but not all of the bs is to know how the intrinsic properties of an a must correspond with the intrinsic properties of a b if that relation is to hold between that a and that b.

This is a profoundly tricky argument. Let us try to orientate ourselves within its mazes by considering an example. Suppose I make the following claim.

There are exactly ten cherubim. There is a certain internal relation I call 'typosynthesis'. I cannot define the word 'typosynthesis'; it is one of my primitives. I know that each human being bears typosynthesis to some but not all cherubim, that only human beings bear typosynthesis to anything, and that typosynthesis is borne by things only to cherubim. I am absolutely unable to make distinctions among cherubim—except by using the term 'typosynthesis'. I can sometimes refer to individual cherubim or to nonempty proper subsets of the set of all cherubim by calling them things like 'the one cherub that all Greeks and all Tasmanians bear typosynthesis to' or 'the set of all cherubim that any Cartesian dualist bears typosynthesis to'; but unless I use the term 'typosynthesis', I can single out neither any one of the ten cherubim nor any one of the 1022 one-to-nine-membered sets of cherubim.

Then, according to Lewis, in claiming to understand the term 'typosynthesis', I am claiming a magical power. If typosynthesis is really an internal relation borne by human beings to cherubim, then to understand the word 'typosynthesis' must be to know when to apply this word, given the intrinsic properties of human beings, on the one hand, and the intrinsic properties of cherubim on the other. And, in the example, I know none of the intrinsic properties of cherubim; or, at least, I know of none that are properties of some but not all cherubim. Therefore, Lewis says, in the example I am claiming the magical power of being able to understand a name for an internal relation without knowing any relevant intrinsic features of the things it is borne to.

''And,'' Lewis will tell us Unsound Abstractionists, ''you are claiming magical powers when you claim to understand the relational term '*makes-true*'. You say that the one C-world bears the internal relation *makes-true* to some but not all members of a certain class of things. And yet you cannot differentiate among the things this supposedly internal relation is borne to, except by reference to that relation itself. You tell me that one of those things is the proposition that there are cats, but that's just another way of saying 'the object that a C-world bears *makes-true* to just in virtue of having feline parts'. (And don't tell me that you can differentiate among propositions by means of the English sentences that express them. Expression is an internal relation, and you will have the same problems with this relation that you have with *makes-true*.) It is instructive to compare what you call propositions with what I call propositions. For me, a proposition is a set of possible worlds—of what you call C-worlds. For example, the proposition that Heidegger's coin is round is just the set of all worlds that have round counterparts of that coin as parts. (Note that I picked this proposition out without saying anything about what makes it true.) A proposition is true if and only if it contains the actual world. For example, Heidegger's coin is round; it is a counterpart of itself; it is a worldmate of ours; and, hence, the set of worlds in which it has a round counterpart contains the actual world. Therefore, it is a *true* proposition. According to *my* theory, then, '*makes-true*' can be defined in terms of the relations *is spatiotemporally related to* (which is needed to define 'world'), *is a part of,* and *is a member of,* which we certainly understand.''

This is Lewis's argument against Abstractionism. Let us briefly recapitulate its structure. Abstractionism must be of either the Linguistic, the Pictorial, or the Unsound variety. Linguistic and Pictorial Abstractionism are defective. If Unsound Abstractionism is correct, then the one C-world, in virtue of its intrinsic features, makes one among all the abstract, structureless A-worlds true. This *makes-true* relation is either external or internal. If it is external, then the C-world might have borne *makes-true* to a different set of propositions, even if that world had had exactly the same intrinsic properties; and this is absurd. If it is internal, on the other hand, then it cannot be grasped, and the Unsound Abstractionist does not understand his own theory.

I am convinced that Lewis's argument is defective, if only because, if it weren't, either Concretism or Linguistic Abstractionism or something even worse would have to be right. I will present an argument for the conclusion that there is something wrong with his argument. But I confess I am unable to say what is wrong with it. (I am inclined to think that the defect has something to do with the distinction between intrinsic and relational properties, a distinction that we may not understand as well as we think we do.) What is even more shameful to confess, I am unable to say what is right about it. And there is *something* right about it; the ''cherubim'' case is very convincing, and so is the argument for the thesis that *makes-true* is an internal relation. My argument is a *tu quoque:* by reasoning parallel to Lewis's, we can show that one could grasp set-theoretical membership only by magic; and Lewis's ontology requires at least some set-theoretical constructions.[34]

Suppose we have three individuals, X, Y, and Z. Assume we have no problem in picking out or identifying these individuals. Consider the objects we call '$\{X,Y\}$', '$\{X,Z\}$', and '$\{Y,Z\}$'. Do we understand what it is to bear *is a member of* to one of these objects? We should note that we are unable to individuate these objects except *via* the membership relation: $\{X,Y\}$ is the object to which X and Y bear that relation and to which nothing else bears it, and so on. There is no way to pick out *any* set except by somehow specifying the things that bear membership to it. (Or, at least, this is true in the long run. We can refer to a set as 'Tom's favorite set', but we could not do this unless we—or Tom, or *someone*—could specify the membership of this set.[35]) Does it follow from this fact and from Lewis's principle about terms that purport to name internal relations that in claiming to understand 'is a member of ', we are claiming magical powers? Not unless membership is an internal relation.

And it would seem that it is not. Suppose that X, Y, and Z are three distinct individuals, and that X and Y have the same intrinsic properties. Then, although X is a member of $\{X,Z\}$, Y is not. (I owe this point to David Lewis, who attaches no importance to it.) But there is more to be said. Call the objects to which a (dyadic) relation is borne by something its *range*. (I realize that the distinction between "the objects that bear R to something" and "the objects to which R is borne by something" is, at best, rough and intuitive and, at worst, confuses features of two-place predicates with features of dyadic relations. But this is of no import. As long as our practice is consistent, it will make no difference to our argument whether we take, e.g., the fathers or the children to constitute the "range" of fatherhood.) Call a relation *range-internal* if, necessarily, whatever bears it to x bears it also to anything having the same intrinsic properties as x. Thus, the relation expressed by 'x is ten feet from something the same color as y' is range-internal, but not internal *simpliciter*.

Now if Lewis's principle about names for internal relations is right, it would seem that the corresponding principle about names for range-internal relations is right.

Consider "archetyposynthesis," a relation that human beings bear to seraphim. Its specification is similar to our earlier specification of typosynthesis; but two human beings with the same intrinsic properties may bear it to different seraphim. Nevertheless, if a human being bears it to a given seraph, he bears it to all seraphim having the same intrinsic properties as that seraph: it is range-internal. And let us suppose that we can individuate seraphim only *via* archetyposynthesis. It is clear that if a magical power is required to understand typosynthesis, a magical power would also be required to understand archetyposynthesis—if anything, archetyposynthesis would require even more impressive magical powers.

Well, is membership range-internal? If x bears it to y, must x also bear it to anything having the same intrinsic properties as y? That's hard to say. What, after all, *are* the intrinsic properties of a set? What (to focus our attention) are the intrinsic properties of $\{$the earth, the moon$\}$? It is not at all clear what the intrinsic properties of this object are—other than *being a set,* which is of no use to one who wishes to individuate sets. These would seem to be only two further types of properties that are even superficially plausible candidates for the office "intrinsic properties of a set": containing a given object or objects (type A), and containing various numbers of objects having certain intrinsic properties (type B). For example:

Type A *having the earth as a member*[36]
Type B *having at least one spherical member; having exactly two spherical members; having no nonspherical members.*

We may contrast these properties with such *clearly* extrinsic properties of sets as *having been used as an example by van Inwagen* or *having a member that has passed through the tail of a comet* or *being equinumerous with the set of Martian moons*.

If any property of type *A* is extrinsic, all are; if some property of type *A* is not extrinsic, none are. And the same goes for type *B*. There are, accordingly, four possibilities:

(1) All properties of types A and B that a set has are intrinsic properties of that set, and it has no intrinsic properties other than those entailed by a complete specification of its type-A and type-B properties.

(2) All properties of type A that a set has are intrinsic to it, and it has no intrinsic properties other than those entailed by a complete specification of its type-A properties.

(3) All properties of type B that a set has are intrinsic to it, and it has no intrinsic properties other than those entailed by a complete specification of its type-B properties.

(4) Neither properties of type A nor properties of type B are intrinsic; accordingly a set has no intrinsic properties, other than those it shares with all sets: those entailed by *being a set*.

We may distinguish two cases:

Case One

Either possibility (1) or possibility (2) is realized. In this case, membership is range-internal, since the only object that has all the same intrinsic properties as a given set is that set itself. And if membership is range-internal, then by reasoning parallel to Lewis's, and (apparently) valid if his reasoning is valid, we do not understand membership.

Case Two

Either possibility (3) or possibility (4) is realized. In this case, membership is not range-internal. It is, in fact, *purely external:* it is possible that x belong to y and z not belong to w and, at the same time, possible for either of both of the following conditions to hold: x and z have the same intrinsic properties; y and w have the same intrinsic properties. Suppose, for example, that three individuals, Tom, Tim, and Tam have the same intrinsic properties. Then {Tom, Tim} and {Tom, Tam} have the same intrinsic properties. And Tom is a member of {Tom, Tim}, while Tim is not a member of {Tom, Tam}.

Is it possible that membership is an external relation? Let us adopt the reasoning Lewis used to show that it is absurd to suppose that *makes-true* is external. We recall that in that piece of reasoning, Lewis stipulated that propositions were without distinctive intrinsic properties, justifying this convenient assumption with the observation that such distinctive intrinsic properties as propositions may have play no role in determining whether the *C*-world bears the external relation *makes-true* to them. Let us, with the same justification, assume that sets have no distinctive intrinsic properties: x is a different set from y because and only because different objects bear the external relation of membership to them. Here is an adaptation of Lewis's argument against the externality of *makes-true* to the case of membership:

> Tom and Tim belong to various sets. We are now supposing that this belonging has nothing to do with the distinctive natures of the sets—they haven't any—but does have to do with Tom's and Tim's existence. Necessarily, if Tom and Tim exist, they belong to {Tom, Tim}. I ask: how can these connections be necessary? It seems to be one fact that Tom exists and another that he enters into a certain external relation with this set and not with that. What stops it from going the other way? Why can't anything coexist with anything here: any population of individuals and any pattern of external relations of these individuals to sets?

To take an example, if the intrinsic properties of {Tom, Tim} and {Tom, Tam} really are the same, and if membership really is an external relation, why *couldn't* Tim bear membership to {Tom, Tam} as easily as to {Tom, Tim}? What would prevent it? (Of course, if Tim were a member of {Tom, Tam}, it would presumably be incorrect to *call* that set '{Tom, Tam}'; but why couldn't Tim be a member of *it*?) But this is an absurd result: Tim *could not have* been a member of {Tom, Tam}, and there's an end on't.

Therefore, membership is not a purely external relation, or even a "range-external" relation. And, therefore, we do not understand membership—or we don't if Lewis has made no false step in his argument for the conclusion that the Unsound Abstractionist does not understand *makes-true*.

That we do not understand set-membership entails that we do not understand much of classical mathematics, a hard conclusion to accept. Moreover, as I have remarked, Lewis's own ontology seems to be committed to sets: A proposition is a set of C-worlds, and truth is having the C-actual C-world as a member; a property is a set of objects (C-actual or C-nonactual), and exemplification is membership.[37]

Propositions, perhaps, do not have to be sets of C-worlds. Lewis could as easily have said that a proposition was a mereological sum of C-worlds and that a proposition was true if the C-actual C-world was a part of it. Properties, however, could not survive the demise of set theory so handily. One cannot say that a property is a sum of objects and that an object exemplifies a property if it is a part of that property. If sphericality were the sum of all spheres (including the C-nonactual ones) and if exemplification were parthood, then the sum of two spheres would be spherical, as would a cubical part of a sphere. The problem of representing properties and exemplification in mereological terms has no obvious solution.

I conclude that Lewis's argument against Unsound Abstractionism is as damaging to his own ontology (and to classical mathematics, to boot) as it is to Unsound Abstractionism and that, given the strong *prima facie* case against Concretism, Abstractionism is to be preferred to Concretism.[38]

Notes

1. David Lewis, *Counterfactuals* (Cambridge, Mass., 1973), 84.
2. Lewis's current views can be found in his book *On the Plurality of Worlds* (Oxford, 1986). See also

Peter Unger, "Minimizing Arbitrariness: Toward a Metaphysics of Infinitely Many Isolated Concrete Worlds," *Midwest Studies in Philosophy* IX (1984):29–51.

In the sequel, I am going to treat a "universe" or "cosmos" as a thing spread out in space and time—as a thing all of whose parts are related to one another in space *or* in time *or* in space-time. (Thus, even if a Cartesian ego has no position in *space,* it is still a part of the same universe as the one its body inhabits if the events occurring within it belong to the same temporal series as the events occurring within its body. 'Space-time' is used in its relativistic sense. We may note that even if the products of the Big Bang soon became separated into isolated domains—as one theory holds— the contents of one domain are parts of the same "universe" as the contents of another, since they are connected by a space-time path that skirts the Big Bang.) For short: all the parts of a "universe" are spatiotemporally related. In so treating a "universe," I follow Lewis—but with one simplification. Lewis wants to leave open the question whether there are relations that are not spatiotemporal but which are somehow *analogous* to spatiotemporal relations and which play the role in some possible universes that spatiotemporal relations play in ours (Lewis, *On the Plurality of Worlds,* 75–78). I will ignore this question, which is irrelevant to the problems I wish to discuss.

It might occur to someone to protest that *causally* related objects ought to count as parts of the same universe, even if they are spatiotemporally unrelated. Lewis would reply that spatiotemporally unrelated objects cannot be causally related (78–81). I am doubtful about this, but I will concede it for present purposes.

3. See Saul Kripke, *Naming and Necessity* (Cambridge, Mass., 1980), 15–20, 43–53; Robert C. Stalnaker, "Possible Worlds," *Nous* 10 (1976):65–75; Robert Merrihew Adams, "Theories of Actuality," *Nous* 8 (1974):211–31; Roderick M. Chisholm, *The First Person* (Minneapolis, 1981), appendix; John Pollock, *The Foundations of Philosophical Semantics* (Princeton, 1984), chap. III; Alvin Plantinga, "Actualism and Possible Worlds," *Theoria* 42 (1976):139–60. This concept has its roots in the Carnapian notion of a "state description," but its earliest indisputuable appearance in print was probably in Pollock's "The Logic of Logical Necessity," *Logique et Analyse* 10 (1967):307–23.

4. There is a remarkable passage in the chapter on the word 'world' in C. S. Lewis's book *Studies in Words* (Cambridge, 1960). In the pages immediately preceding the passage I have in mind, Lewis has made a distinction between two senses, or families of senses, associated with the word 'world'; he calls them '*World A*' and '*World B*'. (The similarity between Lewis's term '*World A*' and my '*A*-world' in the text is an accident.) The passage is a description of one of the senses in the *A* family:

> Another way of putting it would be that, just as *World B* is the Region that includes all other regions, so *World A* in the sense we are now considering is the State of Affairs which includes all other states of affairs; the over-all human situation, hence the common lot, the way things go. *Things* or *life* would often translate it. (p. 222)

We may remark in connection with this passage that 'world' in most of its senses is used with varying degrees of inclusiveness. (The metaphysician, naturally enough, uses the word in the most inclusive way possible.) Thus, for *World B* we have the series: the *oikoumene,* the inhabited parts of the surface of the earth, the surface of the earth, the earth, the universe. The metaphysician who calls a possible state of affairs that is maximal with respect to the inclusion of states of affairs a 'world' is simply using 'world' in its *A* sense with a degree of inclusiveness that stands to that of 'the overall human situation' as that of 'the universe' stands to that of 'the inhabited parts of the surface of the earth'.

5. See Plantinga, "Actualism and Possible Worlds," 144, and Lewis, *On the Plurality of Worlds,* 2, 69, 70, 71. See the chapter from Pollock's *The Foundations of Philosophical Semantics* cited in note 3 for an important refinement of Abstractionism involving a distinction between "transient" and "nontransient" states of affairs.

6. Cf. Lewis, *On the Plurality of Worlds,* 81–86.

7. Cf. ibid., 98.

8. Kit Fine once described to me, and endorsed, an ontology of possible worlds that I would describe as Meinongian Concretism. But this endorsement would appear to be contradicted by his published work. (See, for example, his postscript to *Worlds, Times and Selves* [London, 1977], and "Plantinga on the Reduction of Possibilist Discourse," in *Alvin Plantinga* [Dordrecht, 1985], edited by James E. Tomberlin and Peter van Inwagen.) Perhaps the explanation is that Fine believes that, *strictly speaking,* there are no merely

possible worlds (or other "nonactual" objects) and that talk that is apparently about such things should be paraphrasable as talk about proposition-like entities—that is, as talk about the things that Abstractionists say *are* possible worlds. But (if I have Fine right) when we are talking as if there *were* possible worlds—a heuristically useful practice—we should talk about them as the Meinongian Concretist does.

Sometimes Jaakko Hintikka talks rather like a Meinongian Concretist. See, for example, section VIII of "Semantics for Propositional Attitudes," in *Reference and Modality,* edited by Leonard Linsky (Oxford, 1971), 145–67.

9. In "The Trouble with Possible Worlds," in *The Possible and the Actual,* edited by Michael J. Loux (Ithaca, 1979), William G. Lycan mistakenly supposes that Lewis is a Meinongian. See especially note 7, page 277. That such an acute philosopher as Lycan could make this mistake is a tribute to the power of the slippery word 'actual' to confuse people.

10. Lewis's ontology includes things he calls "impossible objects," although none of them is a world. But his notion of an impossible object can be spelled out in nonmodal terms: an object is impossible if it overlaps two or more worlds. Such objects are called impossible because (as will be evident from our discussion of the Concretist's use of 'exists in'), they exist in no world. Cf. Lewis, *On the Plurality of Worlds,* 211.

11. This procedure is the reverse of the procedure adopted by David Lewis in "Counterpart Theory and Quantified Modal Logic" (*The Journal of Philosophy* 65 [1968]:113–26), in which 'actual' as a predicate of objects-in-general is taken as primitive, and an actual *world* is defined as one that contains the actual objects.

12. See the works of Plantinga and Pollock cited in note 3. These definitions need not take a subjunctive form; we might have written, e.g., '*w* includes the state of affairs: *p* 's being true'. 'If *w* were actual, *p* would be true' is equivalent to 'necessarily, if *w* is actual, then *p* is true', since there is only one world, *w* itself, at which the antecedent of the subjunctive conditional holds. The second way of writing the definitions is theoretically preferable, since it allows a noncircular possible-worlds account of subjunctive conditionals. But the definitions in the text are more intuitive. We may also note that the definition of a proposition's having a truth-value at a world is redundant, since this is a special case of an object's having a property at a world.

13. And, of course, unless we call on divine aid, we must assume that in *no* world does anyone believe *all* necessary truths.

14. Or, at least, if one did, one would be describing the Mongolian official "line," or something like that.

15. The book is cited in note 8; 50–52.

16. Here I draw upon Lewis, *On the Plurality of Worlds.* See section 2.8 and chapter 3.

17. Ibid., sec. 1.2; see also ibid., 150–57, 167–70, 176.

18. Not equivalent in meaning, perhaps; but it follows from Concretism that (2) and (3) must have the same truth-value.

19. It is interesting to compare Concretism on this point with Intuitionism in the philosophy of mathematics, according to which seemingly impersonal theorems of mathematics are really of the form 'I have effected a construction, according to which . . . '.

20. Lewis, *Counterfactuals,* 89–91.

21. Lewis, *On the Plurality of Worlds,* 87–92.

22. Ibid., 133 (suspension points in original).

23. Stalnaker, "Possible Worlds," 68; Peter van Inwagen, "Indexicality and Actuality," *The Philosophical Review* 84 (1980): 403–26, especially 406–7.

24. José A. Benardete, *Infinity,* (Oxford, 1964), 143–54.

25. In the sequel, I shall sometimes attribute to Lewis long speeches that are by no means quotations. I believe that these speeches are fairly accurate representations of what Lewis would say in certain circumstances, though I do not, of course, claim that he would have chosen the words I have chosen to express these points. Lewis's own words on these topics can be found in *On the Plurality of Worlds,* chap. 3.

26. In *On the Plurality of Worlds,* Lewis uses "Ersatz world" in a broader sense than in *Counterfactuals.* (In the more recent book, 'Ersatz world' is used in more or less the sense of '*A* -world'.) In the present paragraph, 'Ersatz world' is used in the narrow sense of *Counterfactuals.*

27. This stipulation does not rule out Linguistic Abstractionism, since the Linguistic Abstractionist's "worlds" could be (and may as well be) pure sets—which is what the Ersatz worlds of *Counterfactuals* are. It is hard to see whether it rules out Pictorial Abstractionism, since it is hard to see what kinds of things the "worlds" of that theory are supposed to be.

28. Provided there are any contingent propositions at all: an *A*-world is a contingent proposition unless all truths are necessary truths (in which case, it would be *the A*-world).

29. Or *maybe* there are more. But if there were, they would (according to the Abstractionist) be parts of the one universe. If there are two *C*-worlds, and the other one contains dragons, then (according to the Abstractionist) there *are* dragons, in the same sense as that in which there are donkeys.

30. Or, at any rate, "purely qualitative" propositions are. Some philosophers believe (*a*) that sentences containing proper names express propositions that are not purely qualitative, owing to the fact that these propositions somehow "involve" the individuals to which these names refer, and (*b*) that a proposition of this type would not have existed if one of the individuals it involved had not existed. We shall not consider this thesis.

31. The epithet 'magical' may also partly derive from the fact that the Unsound Abstractionist can give no answer to the question 'How do propositions represent?' beyond 'They just do'.

32. Lewis, *On the Plurality of Worlds*, 180.

33. "Vom Wesen der Wahrheit," *Wegmarken* (Frankfurt am Main, 1967), 78–79.

34. This strategy was suggested to me by Alvin Plantinga, who is, of course, not responsible for the quality of its execution.

35. "Specifying the membership" is a vague enough notion. 'The set that contains just 0 if Jack the Ripper was born in London, and just 1 otherwise' counts; 'the set having just the membership of Tom's favorite set' does not.

36. Let us classify *having no members* as belonging to type *A*: its possession by a set does, after all, determine with respect to each individual whether that individual is a member of that set.

37. See Lewis, *On the Plurality of Worlds*, sec. 1.5.

38. Parts of this paper were read as comments on a paper by David Lewis called "Possibilities: Concrete Worlds or Abstract Simples?" at the 1984 Chapel Hill Philosophy Colloquium. I have benefited from discussion and correspondence with Allen Hazen, David Lewis, Alvin Plantinga, and Peter Unger.

MIDWEST STUDIES IN PHILOSOPHY, XI (1986)

The Necessity of Nature

ALFRED J. FREDDOSO

Y ou struggle out of bed early one dreary winter morning, find your way into the kitchen somehow, and, after a mandatory thirty seconds or so of groping for utensils, faucets, and dials, finally succeed in situating the kettle of water squarely over the blue gas flame. When you return from the other room ten minutes later, the water is beginning to boil. A familiar enough scene, yet one which, like many another such scene, gives rise to philosophical puzzlement.

It is no accident, nearly all of us will grant and, indeed, insist, that *this* water should be boiling at *this* time (call it time '*T*'). But just what sort of nonaccidentalness or necessity is involved here? Obviously, the water's boiling at *T* is not a matter of metaphysical necessity; after all, it is not even metaphysically necessary that the water should so much as exist at *T*, much less be boiling at *T*. The necessity in question seems clearly distinct from the necessity that attaches to the past simply by virtue of its being the past; one can easily conceive of a world that has the same history as our world just after you put the kettle on the flame but in which someone intervenes before *T* to prevent the water from boiling.

What we have lighted on here is the modality commonly dubbed the necessity of nature, or natural necessity. Accordingly, given the scene described above, we might reasonably affirm that the proposition *This water is boiling* is true at *T* by a necessity of nature; or, to pass from the *de dicto* to the *de re*, we might reasonably affirm that it is by a necessity of nature that at *T*, this water has the property of being such that it is boiling. Still, agreement about the name cannot long conceal the deep disagreements about the thing itself.

Since the time of Hume, or, more accurately, since the appearance of occasionalism as championed by the likes of al-Ghazali and Gabriel Biel in the Middle Ages and by Malebranche and Berkeley in a subsequent era, philosophers have been propounding what we might aptly call subjectivistic explications of natural necessity.[1] The occasionalists located the source of this necessity in God's free decision to bring about natural events in accordance with certain arbitrary but (barring only a few exceptions) strictly adhered to rules, rules reflected in the empirical generalizations that scientists strive to discover and systematize. Modern thinkers, as is their wont, shift the focus from the divine mind to the human mind. Hume claimed to have found the source of natural necessity in the psychological habit whereby we come to expect the occurrence of events similar to the effect on the occasion of our experience of events similar to the cause; whereas later, more chastened Humeans have tended to ground natural necessity in one or another epistemic property, e.g., in the explanatory potential or degree of confirmation possessed by lawlike generalizations.[2] Disparate though they be, these theories share in common the conviction that natural necessity, while dependent in a more or less direct way on some knowing or acting subject or subjects, is entirely independent of and extrinsic to the "objective" natural substances that are involved in ordinary causal interactions, or, to use a more neutral locution, ordinary causal sequences. Not surprisingly, subjectivistic accounts of natural necessity typically go hand in hand with what, from a realist point of view, appear to be unduly thin and attenuated metaphysical characterizations of natural substances. By way of corroboration, one need only cite Malebranche, Berkeley, and Hume.

Nearly all the subjectivistic accounts I know of handsomely repay close scrutiny; some are downright ingenious. I have argued at length elsewhere, for instance, that from a theistic standpoint, occasionalism provides a far more impressive and satisfying philosophy of nature than most contemporary theistic intellectuals have cared (or dared) to admit.[3] In this paper, however, I will dutifully set aside such perverse thoughts and accept without argument the now widely held opinion that natural necessity, whatever else might be said about it, is an objective feature of the world. My goal, accordingly, will be to formulate the main contours of an objectivistic account of natural necessity, one that locates the source of this necessity within natural substances themselves.

I will begin in section I by characterizing two other families of modal notions that will be featured prominently in my account of natural necessity, namely, the metaphysical modalities, and what I have elsewhere dubbed the accidental modalities. Then I will proceed in section II to lay out, roughly and informally at first and more precisely later, the core elements of my account of natural necessity. The key claims embodied by this account are (i) that what is true at a given time by a necessity of nature constitutes the culmination at that time of deterministic natural tendencies and inclinations, and (ii) that such tendencies and inclinations are themselves grounded in the essences or natures of natural substances, specifically in the active and passive causal dispositions had essentially by those substances. Finally, in section III I will entertain and respond to some objections.

I

I will commence by explicating the metaphysical modalities and marking them off clearly from much that goes by the name "logical" or "conceptual" or "transcendental" necessity, impossibility, and contingency. The formulas that follow presuppose the necessary existence of such abstract entities as properties, propositions, states of affairs, and possible worlds, though the position I am advancing in this paper in no way hinges on the claim that these formulas cannot be replaced without loss by nominalistic paraphrases.[4] I am taking it for granted that propositions are tensed, so that many of them are capable of being true at one time in a given possible world and false at some other time in that same world. What's more, I am assuming that there is an exact isomorphism between propositions and states of affairs, and hence that states of affairs as well as propositions are tensed. Accordingly, I take a possible world to be a temporally ordered sequence of maximal possible states of affairs.[5]

Let's start with the following equivalences for the *de dicto* metaphysical modalities:

Proposition *p* is *metaphysically necessary* if and only if *p* is true at every moment in every possible world.

Proposition *p* is *metaphysically impossible* if and only if *p* is false at every moment in every possible world.

Proposition *p* is *metaphysically contingent* if and only if *p* is neither metaphysically necessary nor metaphysically impossible.

Notice that *de dicto* metaphysical necessity as characterized here has no obvious connection with the logical form of sentences that express metaphysically necessary propositions, or with the question whether such propositions are knowable *a priori* or *a posteriori* or at all, or with the question whether the truth of some such propositions is presupposed by the very possibility of any human being's or of any rational being's having knowledge. All these topics, engaging though they be, are irrelevant to the matter of just which metaphysical modality a given proposition has. So, for instance, if a proposition is logically necessary only if it is knowable *a priori,* or only if it is expressible by a sentence that is a truth of first-order logic or whose negation is self-contradictory, then not every metaphysically necessary proposition is logically necessary. Since some philosophers seem to use the term "logically necessary" with one or another of these connotations in mind, we must carefully distinguish metaphysical necessity from logical necessity so understood. Again, if a proposition is logically or conceptually necessary only if a sentence expressing it is such that (the meaning of) its subject contains (the meaning of) its predicate or such that whoever understands it thereby sees that (the meaning of) its subject contains (the meaning of) its predicate, then not every metaphysically necessary proposition is logically or conceptually necessary. Since some philosophers seem to use the terms "logically necessary" and "conceptually necessary" with one or another of these connotations in mind, we must carefully distinguish metaphysical necessity from logical or conceptual necessity so understood. Again, if a proposition is transcendentally necessary only if its truth is a basic presupposition of any conceptual framework in terms of which the world can be understood, or only if its truth is required in order for a human being or for a rational being to have knowledge of the world, then not every metaphysically necessary proposition is transcendentally necessary. For there are many metaphysically necessary propositions that are so exotic or arcane as to have nothing at all to do with the possibility that a human being (or a rational being) should have knowledge of the world. Since some philosophers seem to use the term "transcendentally necessary" with one or another of these connotations in mind, we must carefully distinguish metaphysical necessity from transcendental necessity so understood.

Now that these cautionary notes have been issued, we can move on to the *de re* metaphysical modalities. To coordinate this part of the paper with what follows, I will characterize these modalities with respect to a given time in a given possible world:

> It is *metaphysically necessary* for entity x to have property P at moment t in possible world w if and only if
> (a) x exists at t in w, and
> (b) for any moment t^* and any possible world w^* such that x exists at t^* in w^*, x has P at t^* in w^*.

> It is *metaphysically impossible* for entity x to have property P at moment t in possible world w if and only if
> (a) x exists at t in w, and
> (b) for any moment t^* and any possible world w^* such that x exists at t^* in w^*, x lacks P at t^* in w^*.

> It is *metaphysically contingent* for entity x to have property P at moment t in possible world w if and only if
> (a) x exists at t in w, and
> (b) it is neither metaphysically necessary for x to have P at t in w nor metaphysically impossible for x to have P at t in w.

As I understand them, these *de re* modalities exhibit a similar independence of all questions concerning logical form, type of knowability, conceptual frameworks, and relations among concepts. I state this point partly by way of assertion and partly in order to announce an intention. When, dissociating himself from an illustrative example he has just used, D. M. Armstrong comments parenthetically that he does not himself "believe in essential properties, save relative to some conceptual scheme," I construe this remark as implying that he does not believe in essential properties at all.[6] For, as I see it, a property P is essential to a given entity x only if x has P with *metaphysical* necessity and thus has P regardless of how (or even whether) x is conceptualized or described by any human being or by any rational creature whatsoever. In fact, I find it difficult even to imagine how the conceptual framework within which an entity is conceived of or described can have any bearing at all, one way or the other, on which properties are essential to it. If this is too controversial a thesis to be stated baldly and without extended argumentative support, then I will be content here simply to make known my intention to use the term 'essential property' only in the way just adumbrated. Given this usage, which is by no means idiosyncratic, Armstrong's statement can be correctly interpreted as implying, or at least strongly suggesting, that he believes that no entity actually has any property with metaphysical necessity or, hence, essentially. Of course, the above formulas merely *characterize* metaphysical necessity; none of them requires that any entity in fact has any property with metaphysical necessity or that any proposition is in fact metaphysically necessary.

The other family of modalities I will use in fashioning my account of natural necessity are what I call the accidental modalities. Intuitively, a proposition is accidentally necessary at a given time just in case it is a metaphysically contingent proposition that can no longer be false at or after that time. Suppose, for instance, that Michael went swimming yesterday. Then most of us would be inclined to say that the proposition *Michael has gone swimming,* though metaphysically contingent, is now, given the history of our world, no longer possibly such that it is or will be false. If so, this proposition is now accidentally necessary, and its negation, *It is not the case that Michael has ever gone swimming,* is now accidentally impossible. Moreover, all but unrepentant fatalists will cheerfully concede that there are many future-tense propositions that, along with their negations, are now contingent in the corresponding sense.

Clearly, a proposition's accidental modality is relative to a given time. What's more, since the accidental modalities are a function of the world's history at a given moment, and since the history of a possible world w at a moment t may differ from the history of another world w^* at that same moment t, a proposition's accidental modality is relative to a given time in a given possible world. So we have these *de dicto* accidental modalities:

Proposition p is *accidentally necessary* at moment t in possible world w if and only if
    (a) p is not metaphysically necessary, and
    (b) p is true at t and at every moment after t in every possible world w^* such that w^* shares the same history with w at t.

Proposition p is *accidentally impossible* at moment t in possible world w if and only if
    (a) p is not metaphysically impossible, and
    (b) p is false at t and at every moment after t in every possible world w^* such that w^* shares the same history with w at t.

Proposition p is *accidentally contingent* at moment t in possible world w if and only if
    (a) p is metaphysically contingent, and
    (b) p is neither accidentally necessary at t in w nor accidentally impossible at t in w.

What is it for two worlds to have the same history at a given moment? This question can be given substantively diverse answers, each associated with a distinctive response to the challenge of logical determinism. My own, Ockhamistic answer has been set out in detail elsewhere,[7] but it might be worthwhile to outline it here, since I will be presupposing it in the discussion of the natural modalities.

The guiding idea is that what is temporally (as opposed to causally) independent at any given moment is wholly a function of the present-tense (or, as I prefer to say, *immediate*) propositions true at that moment. All nonimmediate, or temporally dependent, propositions true at a time t are true at t only by virtue of the fact that the appropriate immediate propositions were or will be true at moments other than t. So, for instance, the nonimmediate proposition *Michael has gone swimming* is true now by virtue of the fact that the immediate proposition *Michael is swimming* was true at some past time. Moreover, for any moment t in any possible world w there is a set k of immediate propositions that determines all that is true at t in w in a temporally independent way, i.e., true at t but not by virtue of what occurs in w at times other than t. (Keep in mind that the sort of dependence in question here is temporal, and not causal.) I call k the *submoment* of t in w and say that k obtains in w when and only when each of its members is true. Then two worlds share the same history at t if and only if they share all and only the same submoments, obtaining in exactly the same order, prior to t.

Given this overall picture, how are we to distinguish precisely between immediate and nonimmediate propositions? My own explication of this distinction, laid out in the place alluded to above, is too complicated to be presented in passing here. Still, the intuitive idea is relatively clear: what is "purely present" (immediate) at a given moment is distinct from what is strictly past or strictly future (nonimmediate) at that moment. The fact that it is no mean feat to find a general algorithm for separating immediate from nonimmediate propositions does not in any way impugn this guiding intuition.

In addition to the *de dicto* accidental modalities, there are also *de re* accidental modalities. For example, if Michael went swimming yesterday and still exists today, we might reasonably claim that it is now accidentally necessary for him to have the property of having gone swimming, and that it is now accidentally impossible for him to have the property of never having gone swimming.[8] That is, given the present history of the world, it is no longer possible for him ever to lack the former property or ever to have the latter. So, it seems, with the passage of time certain properties that are metaphysically contingent for a given entity to have become accidentally necessary or impossible for it to have, just as, it seems, with the passage of time certain propositions that are metaphysically contingent become accidentally necessary or impossible. By the same token, there are presumably many properties that are now not only metaphysically contingent for Michael to have but also accidentally contingent for him to have. The following formulas seem to capture these *de re* modalities:

It is *accidentally necessary* for entity x to have property P at moment t in possible world w if and only if
  (a) x exists at t in w, and
  (b) it is not metaphysically necessary for x to have P at t in w, and
  (c) for any possible world w^* such that w^* shares the same history with w at t, and for any moment t^* such that t^* is at or after t and x exists at t^* in w^*, x has P at t^* in w^*.

It is *accidentally impossible* for entity x to have property P at moment t in possible world w if and only if
  (a) x exists at t in w, and
  (b) it is not metaphysically impossible for x to have P at t in w, and
  (c) for any possible world w^* such that w^* shares the same history with w at t, and for any moment t^* such that t^* is at or after t and x exists at t^* in w^*, x lacks P at t^* in w^*.

It is *accidentally contingent* for entity x to have property P at moment t in possible world w if and only if

    (a) x exists at t in w, and

    (b) it is not metaphysically contingent for x to have P at t in w, and

    (c) it is neither accidentally necessary for x to have P at t in w nor accidentally impossible for x to have P at t in w.

Remember that the above formulas merely *characterize* the accidental modalities and do not by themselves require that any proposition is, in fact, accidentally necessary or impossible, or that it is now, in fact, accidentally necessary or impossible for any given entity to have any given property. So, as with the discussion of the metaphysical modalities above, many substantive questions are left open. I have simply provided a framework for expressing various theses about the metaphysical and accidental modalities and for asking questions about them and their relation to the natural modalities. For instance, it seems intuitively clear that the necessity of nature is not just a species of the necessity of the past. Pace logical determinism, accidental necessity does not seem to be determinative of the future in the strong way that natural necessity is. But just how do these two types of necessity differ from one another? And just how is natural necessity related to metaphysical necessity? The answers to these questions will, I hope, soon begin to emerge.

II

Nowadays universal causal determinism, though still revered as a regulative ideal in certain influential philosophical circles, has generally speaking lost the well-nigh irresistible charm it had for intellectuals as recently as a century ago. In science, indeterminism with respect to individual entities and events has cropped up in various sectors of physics, chemistry, and biology. In philosophy, strong voices have recently emerged challenging the reigning compatibilist consensus and proclaiming as of old that what I will tendentiously call 'genuinely' free action—be it on the part of God, angels, human beings, or nonhuman animals (with respect to at least some of their movements)—requires the absence of causal necessitation or determinism and the presence in the agent of an ability to choose and to do otherwise in the very same circumstances as those in which the free action is in fact chosen and performed. Since I am hardly in a position to gainsay the scientific case for indeterminism, and since I enthusiastically subscribe to the belief that genuine freedom of action is commonplace, I reject the thesis that every cause brings about its effects deterministically, along with its implication that everything that is caused to be true in the spatiotemporal universe is true by a necessity of nature. However, this rejection is not a part of, nor is it presupposed by, my account of the necessity of nature. The only thing presupposed is the extremely modest methodological claim, able to be conceded in good conscience by even the most fanatical champion of determinism, that in constructing an account of the necessity of nature, we ought to allow for at least the epistemic possibility that genuine indeterminism and genuine freedom are metaphysically possible. Accordingly, I will proceed in my exposition as if there are indeed indeterministic causes, both *natural* (of the sort studied in, say, elementary physics) and *free* (among which are human agents in some of their operations).[9] Still, as will become clear below, the parts of my theory that are meant to accommodate the possible truth of causal indeterminism do not in any way rule out the possible truth of universal causal determinism.

Now if there is genuine indeterminism in the world, then some effects are produced directly by indeterministic causes and, hence, do not occur by a necessity of nature. What's more, even events that do occur by a necessity of nature (assuming that some do) may nonetheless be contingent in the sense that they have indeterministic (whether natural or free) causes somewhere in their causal ancestry. Take, for instance, the scene with which this paper began. When you placed the kettle of water on the flame, you initiated a causal sequence involving the flame, the kettle, and the water. Assume that no indeterministic causes intervened between the time you put the kettle on the flame and the time (T) at which the water began to boil. Then, clearly, it was by a necessity of nature that the water began to boil at T. Yet if you acted (genuinely) freely in putting the kettle on the flame in the first place, it follows that the water's boiling at T, though necessary because of the causes that were operative once you played your role, was not necessitated by any causal sequences that began at times before you acted. That is to say, for any such time $t*$, there are worlds that have the same history as our world at $t*$ but in which even though no indeterministic causes intervene to prevent the water from boiling at T, it is nonetheless not the case that any water is boiling on your stove at T. In short, whenever causal indeterminism is introduced into the world, a certain ultimate sort of contingency diffuses itself outward from that time on, even along causal chains that are thoroughly deterministic. So the fact that an event occurs by a necessity of nature does not entail that there are no indeterministic causes in its causal lineage; it is only a *completely* deterministic world that is such that none of the events occurring in it has any indeterministic causes at all among its causal progenitors.

But why insist that the water's boiling at T is a matter of natural necessity, given that the water would not have boiled at T had you not freely put the kettle on the flame at the appropriate time? Presumably because the water's boiling at T was inevitable or, so to speak, automatic once the relevant causal mechanisms were set into motion and left unimpeded.

This is not to say that those mechanisms were *unable* to be impeded. In fact, there are any number of ways in which they might have been. The gas jet you steadfastly neglected to clean might finally have become clogged; your spouse, deeply concerned about the inordinate amount of coffee you have been consuming lately, might have decided in an imperious moment to put an abrupt halt to your unhealthy ways; the local utility company might have cut off the flow of gas into your home just before T in order to fix a leak two blocks away; it is even conceivable that a vigilant omnipotent agent might for some hidden reason have freely intervened, whether by omission or commission, to keep the water from boiling at T[10]—the possible variations are seemingly endless. Indeed, even though the water did in fact boil at T, it may still be the case that its boiling at T did not result by a necessity of nature from the causal sequence you initiated when you put the kettle on the flame; perhaps some sort of interference took place but was immediately compensated for in a manner dependent upon a further instance of indeterministic causation. Suppose, for example, that when the gas company turned off the natural gas, you noticed it at once and immediately switched over to your emergency supply of propane gas, so that the water began to boil at the very same moment, T, at which it would otherwise have begun to boil. In that case, the water's boiling at T was naturally necessary (let us suppose) because of the causes operative from the time at which you activated the propane tank, but it was not necessitated by the causes operative at the time you put the kettle on the stove.

The upshot is this: what occurs by a necessity of nature at a given time is what is produced by virtue of deterministic natural propensities that are operative before that time and that, since they have been left unimpeded, issue forth automatically in the necessitated event. When, as in the original case, the water begins to boil at T because of causes that act deterministically once you have freely placed the kettle on the flame, we can say that it is naturally necessary that the water boil at T, and we can point to the natural propensities present at the earlier time as evidence for our claim. For in every world which shares the same history with our world just after your action and in which no indeterministic causes intervene before T to prevent the water from boiling, the water begins to boil at T. So what is true by a necessity of nature is what is caused to be true automatically, as it were, once the relevant deterministic causes have been set into motion and left to themselves.

At this juncture, one might be tempted to ask why it is that, left to themselves, these causes automatically produce just this effect. Isn't it conceivable that rather than boiling at T, the water should instead turn into, say, a block of ice or a shrub or even a personal computer? I will return to this question later. For now it is enough to note that a very natural, though apparently controversial, way to respond is simply to claim that it is of the essence or, as the term 'natural necessity' suggests, of the nature of these causes to act in this way and to bring about this effect when unimpeded. Their producing such-and-such an effect in such-and-such circumstances flows from their being the sorts of things and, hence, the sorts of causes they are. They are what they are; they can be no other. And their action follows from what they are. My account of natural necessity will have this sort of essentialism built into it. For according to this account, if a given effect occurs by a necessity of nature, then it occurs in every possible world in which the same unimpeded deterministic causes are operative at the same time and under the same circumstances. There are, to be sure, further subtleties to be spelled out here, and I will attend to some of them below. But the general idea is easy enough to grasp: the deterministic causal propensities that issue forth in natural necessities are themselves grounded in basic causal dispositions, both active and passive, that are had essentially (and so with metaphysical necessity) by natural substances and that, in part, constitute their essences or natures.

How, then, might we build upon the metaphysical and accidental modalities in constructing an account of natural necessity? Let's begin with the *de dicto* natural modalities. First, a proposition that is true by a necessity of nature is *made* or *caused to be* true. Since no metaphysically necessary proposition can, I take it, be *caused* to be true by anyone or anything, and since no metaphysically impossible proposition can be true in any way at all, only metaphysically contingent propositions may be naturally necessary.[11] By the same token, a proposition that is accidentally necessary at a given time is not one that is made true *at that time* by causes then operative. Rather, accidentally necessary propositions constitute the ineradicable present and future vestige of what *was* caused to be true at some previous time. Again, what is accidentally necessary or accidentally impossible at a given time is entirely a function of the history of the world at that time. By contrast, what is naturally necessary or naturally impossible at a given time is in part a function of what is going on causally at that very time. So no proposition that is accidentally necessary at a given time is true by a necessity of nature at that time, and no proposition that is accidentally impossible at a given time is false by a necessity of nature at that time.

I pointed out above that a natural necessity can plausibly be thought of as the culmination of an unimpeded deterministic natural propensity. (In what follows, I will assume that *natural propensities* are divided into *natural tendencies,* which pertain to *de dicto* natural modality, and *natural inclinations,* which pertain to *de re* natural modality. Though natural propensities need not be deterministic, the ones relevant to an account of natural necessity and impossibility are just the deterministic ones.) The distinction between a natural necessity, on the one hand, and a deterministic natural propensity on the other, well-motivated in its own right, has the additional virtue of enabling us to forestall a possible anomaly in the use of terms like 'naturally necessary' and 'naturally impossible'. Given that miracles are at least conceivable, we might be tempted to characterize a miraculous event as one that occurs despite its being naturally impossible that it occur or, alternatively, despite its being naturally necessary that it not occur. To cite a standard medieval example, revived recently by Rom Harre and Edward Madden,[12] when the three young men emerge unharmed from the fiery furnace, we might be tempted to say that they have emerged unharmed despite its being naturally impossible that they do so, or despite its being naturally necessary that they not emerge unharmed. But if we permit such usage, then we must deny that a proposition's being naturally necessary at a given time entails its being true at that time. Worse yet, since a proposition's being naturally necessary should, it seems, be equated with its being true by a necessity of nature, we will be forced to deny that a proposition's being true by a necessity of nature at a given time entails its being true at that time.

However, if we distinguish *de dicto* natural necessities from deterministic natural propensities—more specifically, from deterministic natural tendencies—we can use the term 'naturally necessary' in such a way that it entails truth, and the term 'naturally impossible' in such a way that it entails falsehood. Then we can go on to distinguish various strengths of natural tendencies and to characterize miraculous events as those resulting from causal interference with a natural tendency so strong that only an omnipotent or 'supernatural' agent can have the power to impede or hinder it.[13] An analogous point will hold below for the relationship between *de re* natural necessities and deterministic natural inclinations.

How exactly should we conceive of natural propensities and their relation to the *de dicto* natural modalities? There is bound to be at least a bit of arbitrariness here in the formulation of a semitechnical vocabulary. My own preference is to think of a natural tendency as a relation that a *world* bears to a *proposition* and to think of a deterministic natural tendency as a natural tendency that, if left unimpeded, issues forth in the truth of a given proposition at a given time. As I conceive of them, such tendencies are ultimately a function (i) of the basic causal dispositions had essentially by natural substances and (ii) of the ways in which those dispositions are integrated with one another at the time at which the world is said to have the deterministic natural tendency in question. So, on this picture, a deterministic natural tendency is, as it were, an all-things-considered deterministic natural propensity on the part of the world at a given moment. Accordingly, we can think of the world as having at a moment t a deterministic natural propensity toward a proposition p at a moment t^*, where t^* occurs at or later than t, a propensity such that it automatically issues forth in p's truth at t^* as long as it is unimpeded; and when it does issue forth in p's truth at t^*, we then say that p is true at t^* by a necessity of nature.

Notice, if a natural tendency is deterministic, then it will not be impeded by any *natural* (as opposed to *free*) causes. It will not be impeded by *deterministic* natural causes because, as just noted, deterministic natural tendencies are *ultima facie,* and not merely *prima facie,* deterministic propensities relating the world at one moment to a proposition at a second moment. That is to say, such tendencies are a function not only of the natures of the deterministic causes that will be operative between the two moments in question but also of the history of the world and, hence, the arrangement of causes in the universe at the earlier moment. Nor can any *indeterministic* natural cause impede a deterministic natural tendency, since any propensity that is defeated by an indeterministic *natural* cause is by that very fact not a propensity that might flower into a *natural* necessity.

Consequently, only *free* causes can prevent deterministic natural tendencies from blossoming into full-blown natural necessities. Moreover, as hinted above, natural tendencies in general, and deterministic natural tendencies in particular, can be ordered according to the amount of power it would take to impede or hinder them. In our mundane example of the water's beginning to boil at T, we saw that the obstruction of a natural tendency need not be miraculous; it need not require very much power at all. At the other end of the scale, miracles are conceivable because we are able to conceive of instances of causal interference that exceed the power of any natural or nonomnipotent agent, or that at least exceed the power of any of the natural agents present in the relevant circumstances. So we have:

At moment t, possible world w has a *deterministic natural tendency* toward proposition p at moment t^* (where t^* is at or after t) if and only if

   (a) p is not metaphysically necessary, and
   (b) p is not accidentally necessary at t^* in w, and
   (c) p is true at t^* in every possible world w^* such that (i) w^* shares the same history with w at t and (ii) no freely acting agent brings it about at or after t in w^* that p is false at t^*, and

(d) in at least one possible world w^* such that (i) w^* shares the same history with w at t and (ii) p is true at t^* in w^*, p's being true at t^* is not brought about at or after t in w^* either by a freely acting nonomnipotent agent or by an omnipotent agent acting freely and alone.

Condition (c) captures the idea that a deterministic natural tendency must be impeded in order not to result in the truth of the relevant proposition. Condition (d) has a two-fold purpose. First, it captures the idea that if the world has a deterministic natural tendency toward a proposition, then the truth of that proposition need not result from any free action of the sort described. Second, the stipulation that the truth of the proposition need not be caused by an omnipotent agent acting freely and alone serves to mark off my account clearly from occasionalism, according to which events in nature are brought about by God alone. Also, this stipulation is worded in such a way as not to rule out *a priori* the classical theistic doctrine according to which it is metaphysically necessary that any proposition caused to be true is such that God causally contributes (at least via his permission) to its truth.[14]

We can characterize a *strong* deterministic natural tendency along the same lines by simply adding another condition to the effect that no nonomnipotent agent has the power to bring it about at or after t in w that p is false at t^*. So a strong deterministic natural tendency is one that only a miraculous action can obstruct. Keep in mind, however, that these explications of a deterministic natural tendency and of a strong deterministic natural tendency do not by themselves state that miracles or genuinely free actions are metaphysically possible. Instead, they are meant merely to reflect the fact that *if* miracles and genuinely free actions are, indeed, metaphysically possible, then this is relevant to the question of which deterministic natural tendencies and which strong deterministic natural tendencies a given world has at a given moment.

We can now characterize the contrary of a deterministic natural tendency, what we might call a deterministic natural aversion, as follows:

At time t, possible world w has a *deterministic natural aversion* to proposition p at time t^* if and only if at t, w has a deterministic natural tendency toward not-p at t^*.

We can characterize a *strong* deterministic natural aversion along the same lines by adding the condition that no nonomnipotent agent has the power to bring it about at or after t in w that p is true at t^*. So only a miracle can thwart a strong deterministic natural aversion.

From here it is an easy step to the characterization of *de dicto* natural necessity, since a natural necessity is nothing more than a deterministic natural tendency come of age. So we have:

Proposition p is *naturally necessary* (or: *true by a necessity of nature*) at moment t in possible world w if and only if
(a) p is true at t in w, and
(b) there is a moment t^* such that (i) at every moment from t^* to t, w has a deterministic natural tendency toward p at t, and (ii) p's truth at t is not

brought about at or after $t*$ in w either by a freely acting nonomnipotent agent or by an omnipotent agent acting freely and alone.

To put it succinctly, a natural necessity results from an unimpeded and uninterrputed deterministic natural tendency. Also, we can explicate the idea of a proposition's being *strongly* naturally necessary by simply replacing 'deterministic natural tendency' in clause (b) (i) by 'strong deterministic natural tendency'. So a proposition is strongly naturally necessary at a given moment only if it would have taken a miracle to prevent it from being true at that moment.

Notice, by the way, that clause (b) (ii) is needed in order to exclude a peculiar but, to my mind, perfectly conceivable case. Suppose that just before T, but as close as you wish to T, some free agent (perhaps it would have to be an omnipotent agent) intervenes and impedes the world's deterministic natural tendency toward the proposition *This water is boiling at T*. But suppose further that, for whatever reason, this agent decides after all to bring it about directly that the water should begin boiling at T. In such a case, the proposition *This water is boiling* would obviously be naturally contingent at T, since brought about directly by a free cause. However, without the addition of clause (b) (ii), we would be forced to say that *This water is boiling* is naturally necessary at T. By contrast, once we add clause (b) (ii), our problem is solved. For no matter how close to T it is when our agent impedes the natural tendency in question, the truth at T of *This water is boiling* will have resulted directly from the agent's free action, and not from any deterministic natural tendency.[15]

Notice, too, that on the above account of natural necessity—and an analogous point holds as well for natural impossibility—future-tense propositions may be naturally necessary at given times. This is so, at least, if we grant a thesis that I have argued for at length in another place, namely, that if a cause C brings it about that a proposition p is true (false) at a time t, then C thereby brings it about that it has always been the case that p would be true (false) at t.[16] Let $T*$ be the moment at which you put the kettle on the flame, and assume that at $T*$ the world has a deterministic natural tendency toward the proposition *This water is boiling* at T. It then turns out, on the above account of natural necessity, that if the water in fact boils at T because of the causes put into operation at $T*$, then the future-tense proposition *This water will be boiling at T*, which (as I would argue) was always *true* before T, becomes *naturally necessary* as well at every moment from $T*$ up to, but not including, T.[17] So some future-tense propositions that are accidentally contingent at a given time might nonetheless be naturally necessary at that time. This distinction between the natural and accidental modalities has often been blurred in discussions of logical determinism.

De dicto natural impossibility can be explicated as follows:

Proposition p is *naturally impossible* (or: *false by a necessity of nature*) at moment t in possible world w if and only if
  (a) p is false at t in w, and
  (b) there is a moment $t*$ such that (i) at every moment from $t*$ to t, w has a deterministic natural aversion to p at t and (ii) p's falsity at t is not brought about at or after $t*$ in w either by a freely acting nonomnipotent agent or by an omnipotent agent acting freely and alone.

We can characterize a proposition's being *strongly* naturally impossible, or false by a *strong* necessity of nature, simply by replacing 'deterministic natural aversion' in clause (b) (i) by 'strong deterministic natural aversion'. So a proposition is strongly naturally impossible at a given moment only if it would have taken a miracle to render it true at that moment. And, parallel to what was said above in the case of natural necessity, clause (b) (ii) is meant to exclude the peculiar case in which a free agent first blocks the world's deterministic natural aversion to p at t and then nonetheless directly brings it about that p is false at t.

We can now say that a proposition p is *naturally contingent* at a moment t in a possible world w just in case p is metaphysically contingent, and accidentally contingent at t in w, and neither naturally necessary nor naturally impossible at t in w. So a proposition true at a given moment t is naturally contingent at t only if it is rendered true *directly* (i.e., without the mediation of other causes) by an *indeterministic* cause at t. Note that although logical determinism entails the very strong thesis that no true future-tense propositions are ever *accidentally* contingent, universal causal determinism entails only the much weaker thesis that no true future-tense propositions are ever *naturally* contingent. These two theses are often conflated in discussions of logical determinism.

However, we have seen that there is a further sort of contingency that a theory of natural modality should allow for, namely, the sort of contingency had by a proposition that, even though it might be true by a necessity of nature at a given time t, is nonetheless such that at *some* past time, the world was *not* tending deterministically toward its truth at t. This sort of contingency can be explicated as follows:

> At moment t in possible world w, proposition p is *contingent with respect to the causes operative at moment t^** (where t^* is at or before t) if and only if
> (a) p is metaphysically contingent, and
> (b) p is accidentally contingent at t in w, and
> (c) p is true at t in w, and
> (d) it is not the case that at t^*, w has a deterministic natural tendency toward p at t.

So, in keeping with what was said above, even though the proposition *This water is boiling* is true at T by a necessity of nature, it is nonetheless contingent with respect to any deterministic causal sequence set in motion before you freely put the kettle on the flame.

Now for the *de re* natural modalities. On the picture I have been developing here, the natural tendencies in terms of which we explicate *de dicto* natural necessity reflect natural inclinations had by the various natural substances. Natural inclinations in general are propensities on the part of a substance toward the possession of a given property at a given time, and deterministic natural inclinations in particular are all-things-considered deterministic propensities of this sort. Parallel to the relationship between a world and a deterministic natural tendency, a substance has a deterministic natural inclination toward a property P at a time t only if it can be prevented from having P at t by the action of some free agent, perhaps a very powerful one. Consequently, no entity can have a deterministic natural propensity toward any property that it has essentially, and so with metaphysical necessity; nor can an entity have a deterministic natural propensity toward any property that it has by accidental necessity. What's more, deterministic natural inclinations are *ultima facie*, and not merely *prima facie*, deterministic propensities relating a substance at one moment to a property at a second moment. That is to say, such inclinations are a function not only of the natures of the deterministic causes that will be operative between the two moments in question, but also of the history of the world and, hence, the arrangement of causes in the universe at the earlier moment. More formally, we have:[18]

> At moment t in possible world w, entity x has a *deterministic natural inclination* toward property P at moment t^* (where t^* is at or after t) if and only if
> (a) x exists at t in w, and
> (b) it is not metaphysically necessary for x to have P at t^* in w, and
> (c) it is not accidentally necessary for x to have P at t^* in w, and
> (d) x has P at t^* in every possible world w^* such that (i) w^* shares the same history with w at t, and (ii) no freely acting agent brings it about at or after t in w^* that x does not have P at t^*, and
> (e) in at least one possible world w^* such that (i) w^* shares the same history with w at t and (ii) x has P at t^* in w^*, x's having P at t^* is not brought about at or after t in w^* either by a freely acting nonomnipotent agent or by an omnipotent agent acting freely and alone.

Conditions (d) and (e) parallel conditions (c) and (d) in the formula for a deterministic natural tendency. To explicate what it is for an entity to have a *strong* deterministic inclination toward a given property, we need add only that no nonomnipotent agent has the power to bring it about at or after t in w that x does not have P at t^*. So if a substance has a strong deterministic natural inclination toward a property at a given time, then only a miracle can prevent it from having that property at that time.

The contrary of a deterministic natural inclination, what I will call a deterministic natural repugnance, can be characterized in this way:

> At moment t in possible world w, entity x has a *deterministic natural repugnance* to property P at moment t^* (where t^* is at or after t) if and only if at t in w, x has a deterministic natural inclination toward the complement of P at t^*.

Again, by adding the condition that no nonomnipotent agent has the power to bring it about at or after t in w that x has P at t^*, we arrive at an explication of what it is for a substance to have a *strong* deterministic natural repugnance to a property. So if a substance has a strong deterministic natural repugnance to a property at a given time, then it takes a miracle for the substance to have the property at that time.

From here we simply follow a route analogous to the one already traveled with the *de dicto* modalities in order to characterize *de re* natural necessity and impossibility. To wit:

> It is *naturally necessary* for entity x to have property P at moment t in possible world w (or: x has P by a *necessity of nature* at t in w) if and only if

(a) x has P at T in w, and

(b) there is a moment t^* such that (i) at every moment from t^* to t in w, x has a deterministic natural inclination toward P at t and (ii) x's having P at t is not brought about at or after t^* in w either by a freely acting nonomnipotent agent or by an omnipotent agent acting freely and alone.

It is *naturally impossible* for entity x to have property P at moment t in possible world w (or: x lacks P by a *necessity of nature* at t in w) if and only if

(a) x lacks P at t in w, and

(b) there is a moment t^* such that (i) at every moment from t^* to t in w, x has a deterministic natural repugnance to P at t and (ii) x's lacking P at t is not brought about at or after t^* in w either by a freely acting nonomnipotent agent or by an omnipotent agent acting freely and alone.

Again, parallel to the explication of the *de dicto* modalities, we can give an account of what it is for a substance to have a property by a *strong* necessity of nature, or what it is for it to lack a property by a *strong* necessity of nature. We need merely preface the occurrences of 'deterministic natural inclination' and 'deterministic natural repugnance' in the above formulas with the word 'strong'. So if a substance has a given property by a strong necessity of nature at a given time, it could have lacked that property at that time only by virtue of a miraculous action; and if it lacks a given property by a strong necessity of nature at a given time, then it could have had that property at that time only by virtue of a miraculous action.

In addition, natural substances are said to *act* or to *be acted upon by a necessity of nature* just when it is naturally necessary for them to have the property of acting in such-and-such a way or the property of being acted upon in such-and-such a way. So, in our example, the flaming gas acts by a necessity of nature during the time when it is heating the water, and the water is acted upon by a necessity of nature during the time when it is being heated by the flame.[19]

We can now go on to say that it is *naturally contingent* for entity x to have property P at moment t in possible world w if and only if it is metaphysically contingent for x to have P at t in w, and accidentally contingent for x to have P at t in w, and neither naturally necessary for x to have P at t in w nor naturally impossible for x to have P at t in w. So if a substance x, in fact, has a given property P at a time t, it is naturally contingent for x to have P at t only if x has P at t by the direct action of some indeterministic cause, be it natural or free. And, as with the *de dicto* modalities, we must distinguish sharply between *natural* contingency and *accidental* contingency.

Finally, we can formulate the *de re* counterpart of the *de dicto* notion of a proposition's being contingent relative to the causes operative at a certain time:

At moment t in possible world w, it is *contingent* for entity x to have property P *relative to the causes operative at moment t^** (where t^* is at or before t) if and only if

(a) it is metaphysically contingent for x to have P at t in w, and

(b) it is accidentally contingent for x to have P at t in w, and

(c) x has P at t in w, and

(d) it is not the case that at t^* in w, x has a deterministic natural inclination toward P at t.

Thus, in our example, it is contingent for the water to have the property of boiling at T relative to the causes operative at times before you freely put the kettle on the flame, and it is contingent for the gas now being consumed in the flame to be so consumed relative to the causes that were operative before you ignited it by turning the appropriate dial.

There are other satellite notions we could go on to explicate, but these should be sufficient to convey clearly the main contours of my account of the natural modalities.[20] To recapitulate, the key concept is that of a deterministic natural propensity, with such propensities being subdivided into deterministic natural tendencies (which are had by whole worlds) and deterministic natural inclinations (which are had by individual natural substances). I have previously claimed that deterministic natural tendencies merely reflect deterministic natural inclinations. Now I wish to emphasize the further point, adumbrated above, that such natural inclinations are in turn grounded in those basic causal *dispositions* that natural substances have essentially, and thus with metaphysical necessity.

The idea is this: by virtue of being the kind of thing it is, a natural substance is disposed toward making characteristic causal contributions, both active and passive, to the actualization of various states of affairs. These dispositions are triggered in some circumstances, frustrated in others, and, in still others, integrated with the dispositions of other substances to produce some intermediate effect. The all-things-considered natural tendencies and inclinations we have been speaking about, indeterministic as well as deterministic, are in effect the result of the integration of the causal dispositions of existing natural substances with the arrangement, both spatial and temporal, of these substances in the universe. So the fact that, say, this sample of phosphorus or this flower or this insect or this lepton has just these causal dispositions, i.e., active and passive causal powers, is a necessary fact about it, one that is true of it at any moment it exists in any possible world. Consequently, this sample of phosphorus could not have been a flower or an animal or a sample of hydrogen instead. It is of its essence or nature to be phosphorus and to have the causal dispositions, both active and passive, that are characteristic of phosphorus. And this is why natural necessity can be characterized in terms of what occurs in every possible world with a given history.[21]

Of course, none of the above requires that any proposition is, in fact, naturally necessary, or that any substance has, in fact, any property with natural necessity. Nor does the above account require the truth of essentialism. So it does not by itself generate the controversial theses hovering in the neighborhood. Still, it does require that *if* any proposition is ever naturally necessary, or *if* it is ever naturally necessary for any substance to have a given property, then it has to be the case that natural substances have natures and, thus, that they have essentially a full array of causal dispositions.

III

I will now briefly consider some objections:

(a) "It's astonishing that you should have come this far in a paper on the necessity of nature without so much as alluding to natural laws. After all, contemporary discussions of natural necessity often focus from the beginning on such laws and treat little else. It is just the necessity of laws of nature, some would argue, that serves as the foundation for natural modalities of the sort you have explicated, since these modalities are best thought of as functions of (i) the history of the world at a given time and (ii) the laws of nature obtaining at that time. Yet your theory makes no mention of laws of nature.''

The account of natural necessity proposed above can easily accommodate laws of nature as long as these laws are conceived of in the way I will now specify.[22] First, notice that the foundational role ascribed in the objection to these laws corresponds exactly to the foundational role played in my account by the various active and passive causal dispositions that natural substances have as essential properties. Next, grant that a law of nature is of the form

It is a law of nature that F's are G,

and assume with such philosophers as D. M. Armstrong, Fred Dretske, and Michael Tooley that a statement of this form, far from being equivalent to the corresponding universal generalization, is instead correctly taken to express a modal relation between universal properties, a relation most perspicuously represented by the formula

Being an F necessitates *being a G*.[23]

Assume further that the first property named in such a formula is in the paradigmatic instance a natural kind, that the second property named is an active or passive causal disposition, and that the sort of necessity linking them together is metaphysical necessity. Finally, suppose it to be a metaphysically necessary truth that any substance that instantiates a natural kind essentially instantiates that kind. From all this, it follows that, on my account, natural modalities are indeed functions of (i) the history of the world at a given time and (ii) the laws of nature obtaining at that time. For laws of nature so understood simply specify those metaphysically necessary connections between natural kinds and causal dispositions that, as I claimed at the end of section II, serve as the foundation of all deterministic natural tendencies, aversions, inclinations, and repugnances.

(b) ''But few will agree that natural laws are metaphysically necessary propositions linking causal dispositions to natural kinds. Indeed, even those who argue that natural laws are relations among universals shy away from the thesis that such laws are metaphysically necessary. The most straightforward reason for their reluctance is that many laws of nature are manifestly *not* metaphysically necessary. How can you ignore this fact?''

Whoever sets out to analyze the notion of a law of nature has to contend right from the start with the evident fact that the term 'law of nature' is used in a variety of substantively distinct ways. So no resultant analysis will be wholly untainted by arbitrariness, though this is not to say that some terminological decisions might not be more illuminating than others. I myself am inclined to draw a sharp distinction between *laws of nature,* strictly speaking, which are metaphysically necessary propositions, and corresponding *statements of regularity,* which are metaphysically contingent propositions depicting what happens "always or for the most part," to use Aristotle's phrase. For instance, the proposition *Salt has a disposition to dissolve in water* is a paradigmatic law of nature stating a metaphysically necessary connection between the natural kind *salt* and the causal property *being disposed to dissolve in water*. By contrast, the proposition *Salt dissolves in water* describes only a metaphysically contingent regularity, since *in our world* salt's disposition to dissolve in water will not *normally* be thwarted—as it is, say, when the water in question has already exhausted its capacity for dissolving salt. Further, the more stable and significant the relevant normal conditions, the more 'lawlike' the regularity, with the result that some regularities attain the status of what are sometimes called 'derived laws'. An example would be the laws of planetary motion operative in our solar system. Still, on the view I am defending, all such regularities are firmly grounded in natural laws, strictly speaking, since they merely reflect the continuous integration of these metaphysically necessary laws with metaphysically contingent antecedent conditions.

(c) "But isn't it obviously conceivable that the laws of nature should be suspended or violated, or at least that there should have been different such laws? This is the basis for the Humean (or, to be fair, Ghazalian) dictum that there are no logically necessary connections between causes and effects, i.e., that there are no *conceptual* limitations on what sorts of *causal* transformations are possible. Yet, on your view, it is metaphysically necessary for, say, water to have a causal disposition to be heated when brought into suitable proximity to fire, and metaphysically impossible for it to have a causal disposition to be transformed into a personal computer under the same circumstances. So you are committed to claiming, pace Hume and al-Ghazali, that it is *logically* (and not just naturally) necessary that in those circumstances, the water should be heated, and that it is *logically* (and not just naturally) impossible that in those circumstances, the water should turn into a computer. Isn't this clearly wrongheaded?"

This objection provides me with a welcome opportunity to show how I am able to accommodate the truth contained in the Ghazali-Humean dictum without at the same time falling into the causal anarchism characteristic of occasionalism and positivism. Recall that on my position, metaphysical necessity enters into natural modality in two distinct ways. First, the relation between the universals involved in a natural law is metaphysically necessary, with the result that laws like the one cited above have *de dicto* metaphysical necessity. (This does not mean, however, that the natural kinds they involve are necessarily instantiated.) Second, every possible natural substance essentially instantiates the natural kind that it instantiates, and so in every possible world in which it exists, each such substance has essentially, and hence with *de re* metaphysical necessity, the causal dispositions endemic to its natural kind.

So it is, indeed, impossible that there should have been different laws of nature if by this we mean either (i) that the substances that, in fact, exist could have had different natures, i.e., could have instantiated different natural kinds, or (ii) that the natural kinds instantiated by these substances could have been necessarily tied to basic causal dispositions different from those they are, in fact, necessarily tied to. Nonetheless, there could have been different laws of nature in the sense that it is metaphysically possible (i) that there should exist natural substances of kinds that have, in fact, never been instantiated and/or (ii) that the natural kinds that are, in fact, instantiated should not have been.[24] So, for instance, my position does not rule out the possibility that there should have been elementary physical particles of types that are different from those that are, in fact, instantiated and that are such that if they had been instantiated instead, then the strengths of the fundamental forces in nature would be slightly different or even greatly different from what they are in our universe. Under those circumstances, the scientific theories that hold for our universe would not have held. Nor does my position rule out the possibility that natural kinds themselves are necessarily interrelated in such a way that certain of them can be instantiated only if certain others are; perhaps no natural kind instantiated in our universe is instantiated in worlds in which the elementary physical particles differ in kind from those that exist in our world. Further, my position does not rule out the possibility that a universe should be instantaneously transformed from one in which a certain set of natural kinds is instantiated into one in which some disjoint set of natural kinds is instantiated. A fortiori, my position does not rule out the more modest Ghazali-Humean possibility that the water on your stove should ''turn into,'' or at least be replaced by, a personal computer when brought into proximity to fire. Whether this causal transformation is metaphysically possible depends only on whether it is metaphysically possible for there to be a causal agent powerful enough to effect it. Nothing I have said rules this out. Given that our current understanding of the natures of water, fire, and personal computers is substantially correct, all I am forced to deny is that the water's transformation into a personal computer on the occasion of its being brought into proximity to fire is a transformation that might result from the natural tendencies (whether deterministic or indeterministic) operative at the time in question. If this denial is sufficient to entail that transformations of this sort are 'logically' or 'conceptually' impossible in one or another of the senses alluded to in section I, then so be it. As I see it, the truth contained in the Ghazali-Humean dictum is adequately safeguarded as long as we do not antecedently rule out such transformations as *metaphysically* impossible.

So, correctly understood, the conception of natural laws most congenial to my account of natural necessity allows for ample flexibility regarding which natural laws hold at any given time or in any given possible world, and also regarding which causal transformations are metaphysically possible.

(d) ''Despite what you say, this response does not preserve the whole truth contained in the Ghazali-Humean dictum. To see this clearly, call to mind the miracle of the fiery furnace. As told in chapter three of Daniel, the story seems to entail that real human flesh was exposed without protection to real fire and yet was not incinerated. This is clearly conceivable. Yet Harre and Madden, whose views you have been closely adhering to throughout this discussion of natural laws, rule it out as impossible.[25] They do not, to be sure, rule out *every* kind of miraculous intervention in this situation. They allow, for instance, that God might conceivably have replaced the human flesh of the young men with stone for the duration of the fire. (This is analogous to the water's being replaced by a personal computer in your example.) But clearly this is not enough. The miracle *as told* is conceivable, and your position cannot accommodate this fact.''

Anyone familiar with their pioneering work *Causal Powers* (now, inexplicably, out of print in America) will recognize how deeply indebted I am to Harre and Madden for my understanding of natural necessity and natural laws. As I see it, however, their discussion of the miracle of the fiery furnace is flawed in a way that misrepresents the real difference between their (and my) general understanding of natural modality, on the one hand, and the occasionalist/positivist position on the other hand.

As noted in the objection, Harre and Madden are perfectly willing to concede that human flesh exposed to fire might be instantaneously transformed into stone; yet they adamantly refuse to concede that unprotected human flesh might not be incinerated when exposed to fire. But why the asymmetry here? Neither of these events could be explained by an appeal to the natures of fire, human flesh, and stone—or, hence, by an appeal to any natural tendencies operative at the time in question—at least not if we suppose that our current scientific understanding of these natures is substantially correct. Both events would seem to involve the thwarting of the same deterministic natural tendency, namely, the world's tendency toward the proposition *This human flesh is incinerated* at the time in question. So why should just one of them be counted as metaphysically possible?

The only plausible response open to Harre and Madden is this: In the miracle story as told in Daniel, chapter three, all the conditions obtain that are necessary for the exercise of the relevant causal dispositions on the part of the fire and the flesh, and it is metaphysically impossible that all those conditions should obtain and yet that the flesh not be incinerated; but in the alternative story involving the transformation of the flesh into stone, one of those conditions fails to obtain, since an omnipotent being steps in at the last moment to interfere with the operative natural tendency by turning the flesh into stone.

This response, however, is far from adequate. I willingly grant that one of the conditions necessary for the fire's incinerating the flesh is that no agent, omnipotent or otherwise, should interfere with the natural tendency in question. Such a condition is explicitly built into the account of natural modality propounded in section II. But just which ways of interfering with this tendency are metaphysically possible? What are the metaphysically possible ways in which an agent might bring it about that the fire does not incinerate the flesh? Suppose for a moment that no natural substance can exercise an active causal disposition unless God acts along with it to bring about its natural effect—an idea that lay at the heart of late medieval and early modern theories of God's 'general concourse' or 'general concurrence'.[26] In that case, God can bring it about that the (real) fire does not incinerate the (real) human flesh merely by withholding his causal concurrence, even if all the other conditions obtain that are necessary for the exercise of the fire's active disposition to incinerate human flesh brought into proximity to it. On what grounds do Harre and Madden rule out such a possibility? What reasons do they have for thinking that the doctrine of divine general concurrence is metaphysically impossible? After all, to the naked philosophical eye, this doctrine does not seem incoherent; and it is certainly no more wondrous, shall we say, than the thesis, wholeheartedly endorsed by Harre and Madden, that God might conceivably transform human flesh into stone.

Now it is not my purpose in this paper to defend or even to articulate the doctrine of divine general concurrence. The point I wish to make is simply that Harre and Madden have not provided a satisfactory argument—or, for that matter, any argument at all—against its possibility; hence, they have not furnished us with any reason for thinking that the ostensibly coherent mode of causal interference associated with this doctrine is metaphysically impossible. Perhaps it is, indeed, impossible; perhaps it is not. But the issue should certainly not be decided by fiat.

What's worse, by putting such undue emphasis on the miracle of the fiery furnace, Harre and Madden give the impression that the distinctiveness of their (and my) general account of natural modality and natural laws depends crucially on the claim that the miracle as described in the book of Daniel is metaphysically impossible. Nothing could be more misleading. In order to distinguish our general account of natural modality and natural law from that of the occasionalists and positivists, we need only point out that even if this miracle is metaphysically possible (whether conceived of as the transformation of human flesh into stone or as the simpe nonincineration of real human flesh), it cannot be accounted for in terms of the natural tendencies and inclinations operative at the time in question. That is why, pace al-Ghazali and Hume, this event and others like it must be treated as having a *special* causal ancestry and as not being of a piece with events that do constitute the culmination of natural tendencies and inclinations.

(e) "Despite what you have suggested, your position is not the only alternative to occasionalism and positivism. After all, those philosophers who reject the positivist conception of natural necessity and hold that natural laws are relations among universals reject as well the sort of view you are proposing. Their arguments are surely more persuasive than those you have cited so far."

Where, exactly, are these persuasive arguments? A few years ago, someone might have charged that if the laws of nature are metaphysically necessary, then they must be analytic or, at least, knowable *a priori,* and not empirically. Perhaps, on one of the meanings of 'logically necessary' mentioned in section I, it is true that every logically necessary proposition is analytic or knowable *a priori.* But my account entails only that the laws of nature are *metaphysically* necessary, not that they are *logically* necessary. And nowadays few philosophers will be inclined to insist that no metaphysically necessary proposition can be known empirically or *a posteriori.*

The fact is, I think, that there are no compelling arguments against the view of laws I am taking here. This judgment is borne out by a brief survey of some of the best contemporary work on laws of nature. Dretske and Tooley, for example, simply assume without argument that laws of nature, despite being relations among universals, are not metaphysically necessary but, instead, have a special modal status falling somewhere between metaphysical necessity, on the one hand, and unqualified metaphysical contingency on the other.[27]

Armstrong, to be sure, does treat the issue at some length, but as he is honest enough to admit, his arguments against the metaphysical necessity of natural laws all rest on the highly controvertible assumptions that form the basis of his distinctive

metaphysical system. For instance, his main objection to the doctrine of strong necessity, i.e., the doctrine that laws of nature are metaphysically necessary, is that it requires that universals are necessary rather than contingent beings and, thus, violates
the principle that there cannot be any uninstantiated universals. Elsewhere he ties his
acceptance of this principle to his antecedent commitment to naturalism, the view that
"nothing else exists except the single, spatio-temporal world, the world studied by
physics, chemistry, cosmology and so on."[28] The objection will thus not have much
power to sway those of us who do not fancy naturalism, or even those naturalists who
feel that uninstantiated or necessarily existent universals pose no more threat to naturalism than instantiated and contingently existing ones do.

In rejecting the fallback to the doctrine of weak necessity, according to which
two universals connected nomologically in any possible world are so connected in every possible world in which they both exist, Armstrong explains that this doctrine has
a difficulty with certain kinds of complex laws. That difficulty need not detain us here,
since it is a genuine difficulty only on the assumption that universals are contingent
beings, an assumption I for one am not inclined to accept. However, it turns out that
one way to avoid the difficulty is to adopt a view of laws that, leaving aside questions
about whether universals are necessary or contingent beings, is much like the one I
have proffered here. Armstrong retorts:

> The old tradition which links powers with necessity is here upheld. The Weak
> Necessity view requires irreducible powers. But if we wish to uphold a purely
> Actualist metaphysics, then it seems that we should reject the Weak Necessity
> view of laws of nature and declare them to be contingent.[29]

An actualist metaphysics, in turn, is one that

> debars us from postulating such properties as dispositions and powers where
> these are conceived of as properties over and above the categorical properties of
> objects. It is not denied that statements attributing dispositions and/or powers to
> objects, or sorts of objects, are often true. But the truth-makers or ontological
> ground for such true statements must always be found in the actual, or categori-
> cal, properties of the objects involved.[30]

Actualism, Armstrong tells us, is the "most difficult and uncertain" of the basic
assumptions he makes in his treatment of laws of nature.[31] Indeed it is. Why, after all,
should we believe that every dispositional property must have a 'categorical basis'?
What is a categorical basis, anyway? How exactly is it supposed to 'ground' a property, especially if, as Armstrong must apparently hold, it is only contingently related
to the properties it grounds? How, for example, is salt's disposition to dissolve in water grounded in its chemical structure? What exactly is wrong with the claim that when
scientists explain a thing's causal dispositions and powers by appeal to its microstructure, they are explaining those dispositions and powers by appeal to the dispositions
and powers of the relevant microentities? In some instances, the first set of dispositions and powers might be strictly reducible to the second; in others, the first set might
necessarily emerge from the second. In any case, the fact that structural explanation

has turned out to be a significant scientific tool does not, it would seem, militate against the philosophical understanding of natural modality and natural law proposed here.

Then, too, look at the consequences that follow from Armstrong's thesis that the laws of nature are metaphysically contingent and that none of the ties connecting individual natural substances with their causal dispositions are metaphysically necessary. First, on this thesis, it is a primitive, unexplained, and rather mysterious fact that the laws of nature that hold in our world are true. Second, even though, as in the passage cited above, Armstrong often insists on the importance of 'ontological grounds', there are on his own view no such grounds for the alleged possibility that propositions that are in fact false might have been laws of nature. At this point, the occasionalists could at least appeal to God's power to promulgate laws of nature different from those he has in fact promulgated. (Does Dretske have this precedent in mind when he likens the modal status of natural laws to that of the duly promulgated, though contingent, constitutional delineation of the powers of the president of the United States?)[32] But what will a self-avowed naturalist appeal to? Third, is it plausible, or even coherent, to suppose, as Armstrong must, that the kind *salt* could have been linked to the causal dispositions and powers associated in our world with, say, the kind *pin oak*? Finally, what of his rejection of the thesis that natural substances have various causal dispositions essentially or with metaphysical necessity? Is it at all reasonable to suppose that this grain of salt before me could have had all and only the causal dispositions characteristic of, say, a piece of phosphorus or a rhododendron or an armadillo, or that it could have belonged to some uninstantiated and, perhaps, unimaginable natural kind?

I do not mean to suggest by the tendentious tone of these questions that Armstrong and the others have no resources to draw upon here. I intend to explore the matter in more detail elsewhere. Nor do I mean to suggest that the view I have been defending is anything but 'old' or even old-fashioned. The account of natural modality proposed in this paper is, in fact, little more than a dusted-off and updated version of what was standard fare among the Aristotelian scholastics from Aquinas to Suarez. What I do mean to suggest, however, is that, at least on the surface, this old-fashioned account has virtues that we can now begin to appreciate anew in the current postpositivistic philosophical milieu.[33]

Notes

1. Berkeley himself frowns upon at least certain uses of the term 'occasion' because they presuppose a belief in matter. See *Three Dialogues between Hylas and Philonous,* edited by Robert M. Adams (Indianapolis, Ind. 1979), 54–55, and *A Treatise concerning the Principles of Human Knowledge,* edited by Kenneth Winkler (Indianapolis, Ind., 1982), 52–57. I myself prefer the name 'no-nature view' to the traditional 'occasionalism' and see Berkeley's account of God's causal activity in nature as, metaphysically speaking, the purest instance of such a doctrine. This subject is treated at length in my "Medieval Aristotelianism and the Case against Secondary Causation in Nature," as yet unpublished. Pertinent references to the work of the other philosophers mentioned here include problem XVII, "Refutation of Their Belief in the Impossibility of a Departure from the Natural Course of Events," 185–96 in *al-Ghazali's Tahafut al-falasifah: The Incoherence of the Philosophers,* translated by Sabih Ahmad Kamali (Lahore, 1963); Gabriel Biel, *Collectorium circa quattor libros Sententiarum* IV, pt. 1, edited by Wilfridus Urbeck and Udo Hoffman

(Tuebingen, 1975), question 1, "Utrum sacramenta legis novae sint causae effectivae gratiae," 1–36, especially 14–18 and 27–36 (I have made a translation of the relevant sections for anyone who might be interested); and *Nicolas Malebranche: The Search After Truth and Elucidations of the Search After Truth,* translated by Thomas M. Lennon and Paul J. Olscamp (Columbus, Ohio, 1980), bk. 6, pt. two, chaps. 2 and 3, 440–52, and elucidation 15, 657–83.

2. For a list of some of these epistemic properties, see pages 251–52 in Fred I. Dretske, "Laws of Nature," *Philosophy of Science* 44 (1977):248–68.

3. See my "Medieval Aristotelianism and the Case against Secondary Causation in Nature," to appear in *Divine and Human Action: Essays in the Metaphysics of Theism,* edited by Thomas V. Morris (Ithaca, N.Y., forthcoming).

4. In fact, I find myself in deep sympathy with at least the main contours, if not all the details, of the theistic conceptualism proposed in Michael Loux's contribution to this volume.

5. Following Alvin Plantinga, I take a state of affairs *S* to be *maximal* just in case for any state of affairs *S**, *S* either includes *S** or precludes *S**.

6. D. M. Armstrong, *What Is a Law of Nature?* (Cambridge, 1983), 166.

7. See my "Accidental Necessity and Logical Determinism," *The Journal of Philosophy* 80 (1983):257–78.

8. If there are no tensed properties, but only tensed exemplifications instead, we can say that it is now accidentally necessary for Michael to have exemplified the property of swimming. The formulas below can all be restated accordingly. Incidentally, besides the *de re* temporal modalities spelled out here, there are several others that are philosophically significant. See Thomas V. Morris, "Properties, Modalities, and God," *The Philosophical Review* 93 (1984):35–55.

9. I here endorse Elizabeth Anscombe's sundering of causation from determinism and deterministic explanation, since there seems to be nothing incoherent in the notion of an indeterministic cause. See her now classic paper "Causality and Determinism," reprinted in *Causation and Conditionals,* edited by Ernest Sosa (Oxford, 1975), 63–81. The root notion involved in causation is that of *producing* or *bringing about* or *effecting* some state of affairs, a notion that seems obviously independent of and prior to questions regarding determinism and indeterminism. The distinction between free and natural causes is a hallowed one, and although I have no precise definitions to offer, I assume that free causes are beings equipped with rather substantial cognitive and volitional capacities, whereas natural causes lack such capacities. Also, as should be obvious, I am assuming that causes are paradigmatically substances rather than events. However, events may still be causes in a derived sense as long as they involve causal contributions on the part of substances. Here I follow Rom Harre and Edward Madden, *Causal Powers* (Totowa, N.J., 1975), 5. This is an ontological issue that requires more extended discussion than I am able to provide here, so I must beg the indulgence of those who take so-called event causation to be basic. However, anyone unwilling to countenance even provisionally the idea that agent causation (on the part of natural as well as free agents) is primitive should be able to recast the following discussion of natural necessity into a more congenial idiom.

10. I allow for the possibility of interference by omission because this sort of interference figured prominently in late medieval and early modern theories of God's general concurrence in the ordinary course of nature. See the response to objection (d) in section III below.

11. I do not mean to rule out antecedently *every* sort of quasi-causal dependence on the part of necessary truths. For instance, even though propositions are not, strictly speaking, caused to exist, it still seems conceivable that they should depend for their existence on the divine intellect in a way analogous to that in which thoughts depend for their existence on those who think them. If this thesis is true, then the necessary truth *There are propositions* would depend upon God for its truth. Again, in the traditional explication of the Christian doctrine of the Trinity, even though the divine persons are uncaused and necessary beings, the Son is said to be begotten by the Father, so that the existence of the Son depends on that of the Father, but not vice versa. If this thesis is true, then the necessary truth *The Son exists* depends for its truth on the activity of the Father. The conceivability and coherence of such theses is closely tied to the claim that at least some subjunctive conditionals with metaphysically impossible antecedents are false.

12. Harre and Madden, *Causal Powers,* 46–47. The biblical story in question is found in the third chapter of the book of Daniel.

13. Here and below I am building upon previous work by presupposing the correctness of the account of omnipotence found in Thomas P. Flint and Alfred J. Freddoso, "Maximal Power," in *The Existence and Nature of God*, edited by Alfred J. Freddoso (Notre Dame, Ind., 1983), 81–113.

14. Condition (d) has the desirable side effect of excluding the world's having a deterministic natural tendency toward propositions, e.g., *Adam freely chooses to eat the apple,* that cannot be brought about without the free action of a nonomnipotent agent. Also, condition (d) guarantees that if a proposition *p* is true at *t* in *w* but could not, given the history of the world, have come to be true at *t* in *w* had it not been brought about by the free action of some nonomnipotent agent or of some omnipotent agent acting alone, then *w* did not have before *t* a deterministic natural tendency toward it. So, for instance, if *Adam eats the apple* was freely brought about by some nonomnipotent agent at *t* in our world, then condition (d) ensures that the world was not deterministically tending toward its truth at any previous time. For in the choice-situation obtaining at the time Adam freely chose to eat the apple, this proposition could be rendered true only by a free action of one of the sorts just specified.

15. I leave open the question of whether an agent can *simultaneously* obstruct the natural tendency in question and bring about the relevant state of affairs. Such an agent, it seems, would be preventing and bringing about the same state of affairs at the same time.

16. See my "Accidental Necessity and Power over the Past," *Pacific Philosophical Quarterly* 63 (1982):54–68. So anyone who brings it about that the water does not boil at *T* thereby brings it about that the proposition *This water will boil at T* has always been false and, more to the point, that it has been false from the time you acted up until *T*.

17. To be sure, characteristic indicators of the future tense in English, both 'will' and 'shall', on the one hand, and 'going to' on the other, are sometimes used to express natural tendencies (both deterministic and indeterministic) rather than unadorned future truth. In "Omniscience and the Future," which constitutes chapter three of *Providence and Evil* (Cambridge, 1977), Peter Geach emphasizes the former use of these locutions to the complete exclusion of the latter use. This seems to me to be a mistake, though it is true that the use of future-tense locutions to express natural tendencies (as well as intentions) is often overlooked.

18. The consequent in condition (d), namely, '*x* does not have *P* at *t** in *w**', is being read in such a way as to be true if either (i) *x* does not exist at *t** in *w**, or (ii) *x* exists but lacks *P* at *t** in *w**.

19. The suggestion here and elsewhere that there are inanimate causal agents is likely to be offensive to pious philosophical ears nowadays. However, I not only do not apologize for this suggestion, but I even make bold to claim that many of the puzzles surrounding human agency can be dealt with adequately only if we begin by looking at agency in nature.

20. One such notion, obediential potency, occupies a prominent place in medieval discussions of the Christian doctrine of the Incarnation. It can be characterized as follows:

> At moment *t* in possible world *w,* entity *x* is in *obediential potency* toward property *P* at moment *t**
> (where *t** is at or after *t*) if and only if
> (a) at *t* in *w*, *x* has a strong natural repugnance to *P* at *t**, and
> (b) God has the power to bring it about at or after *t* in *w* that *x* has *P* at *t**.

See my "Human Nature, Potency and the Incarnation," *Faith and Philosophy* 3 (1986):27–53, for a discussion of this and other natural modalities involved in the explication of the Incarnation. The present treatment of these modalities supersedes and, in some instances, corrects that found in the paper just alluded to.

21. Of course, things are somewhat more complicated than indicated so far, since essential dispositions must be carefully distinguished from various nonessential dispositions, capacities, and abilities that natural substances might come to have at various stages of their development (as in the case of living organisms) or in combinations with other substances (as in the case of chemical compounds). Still, all of these developmental and combinatorial properties, which are, strictly speaking, nonessential because their exemplification depends in part on contingent antecedent conditions, must on my account be firmly rooted in higher order dispositions that are essential to the things in question. See Harre and Madden, *Causal Powers*, especially chapters five and six, for a treatment of some of the complexities involved here.

22. I do not wish to give the impression that I have invented the account that follows. As I indicate below, much of what I have to say was at least implicit in late medieval and early modern philosophy. In

addition, my views on natural laws have been deeply influenced by a close reading of the work of several contemporary philosophers, even if I do not find myself in complete agreement with them on all the relevant issues. The list includes Peter Geach, pt. II, "Aquinas," in *Three Philosophers* (Ithaca, 1961), especially 101–9; Milton Fisk, "Are There Necessary Connections in Nature?," *Philosophy of Science* 37 (1970):385–404; Harre and Madden, *Causal Powers,* and also "Natural Powers and Powerful Natures," *Philosophy* 48 (1973):209–30; Sydney Shoemaker, "Causality and Properties," in *Time and Cause,* edited by Peter van Inwagen (Dordrecht, 1980), 109–35; and Baruch Brody, *Identity and Essence* (Princeton, N.J., 1980), especially chapter six.

23. See Armstrong, *What Is a Law of Nature?,* chap. 6; Dretske, "Laws of Nature"; and Tooley, "The Nature of Laws," *Canadian Journal of Philosophy* 7 (1977):667–98. To be accurate, Dretske denies that there is, strictly speaking, a modal relation between the universals, call them '*F*' and '*G*', and affirms instead that such a relation holds only between an individual substance's being *F* and its being *G*. However, this point is not relevant to the discussion that follows.

24. Here we are faced with a choice. On the one hand, we might claim that all true propositions of the form 'It is metaphysically necessary that *F*'s are *G*' (where '*F*' stands for a natural kind and '*G*' for an active or passive causal disposition) are laws of nature but that only those laws that involve instantiated natural kinds are *operative* laws of nature. On the other hand, we might claim instead that true propositions of the sort in question are laws of nature only if they involve instantiated natural kinds, whereas they are merely *potential* laws of nature if they involve uninstantiated natural kinds. I have no strong preference one way or the other, though I suspect that the second alternative is more in keeping with the manner in which we normally speak of laws of nature.

25. See Harre and Madden, *Causal Powers,* 46–47. Al-Ghazali appeals to a parallel story from the Quran (21:69–70 and 37:98) in which Abraham is thrown into a fire and emerges unharmed. The present objection, by the way, is very much in the spirit of J. L. Mackie's argument against irreducibly (or what Mackie calls 'distinctively') dispositional properties in *Truth, Probability and Paradox* (Oxford, 1973), 137–43.

26. The relevant medieval literature includes Aquinas, *Summa Contra Gentiles* III, chaps. 66–70, and *De Potentia,* question 3, art. 7; Luis de Molina, *Liberi Arbitrii cum Gratiae Donis, Divina Praescientia, Providentia, Praedestinatione et Reprobatione Concordia,* pt. II, "De concursu Dei generali"; and Francisco Suarez, *Disputationes Metaphysicae,* disputation 22, "De Prima Causa et alia eius actione, quae est cooperatio, seu concursus, cum causis secundis." (The selections from Molina and Suarez are not yet available in English translation, though I have made a translation of some of the relevant sections from Molina for anyone who might be interested.)

27. In "Laws of Nature," 263–64, Dretske has this to say:

> Although true statements having the form [of laws of nature] are not themselves *necessary* truths, nor do they describe a modal relationship between the respective qualities, the contingent relationship between properties that is described imposes a modal quality on the particular events falling within its scope. This F *must* be G. Why? Because F-ness is linked to G-ness; the one property yields or generates the other in much the way a change in the thermal conductivity of a metal yields a change in its electrical conductivity.

In "The Nature of Laws," 672–73, Tooley remarks:

> The idea of a statement about particulars being entailed by a statement about a relation among universals is familiar enough in another context, since some philosophers have maintained that analytical statements are true in virtue of relations among universals. In this latter case, the relations must be necessary ones, in order for the statement about particulars which is entailed to be itself logically necessary. Nomological statements, on the other hand, are not logically necessary, and because of this the relations among universals involved here must be *contingent* ones.

It may be that Dretske and Tooley take the contingency of natural laws for granted because they are thinking of these laws as linking natural kinds to the *manifestation* by instances of those kinds of the relevant dispositional properties. What I have said also entails that such links are contingent. On my view, however, natural laws link the kinds in question directly with the dispositions, and not with the manifestations of those dispositions. So perhaps Dretske and Tooley are calling 'laws' what I would call 'statements of regularity' instead.

28. Armstrong, *What Is a Law of Nature?*, 82.
29. Ibid., 168.
30. Ibid., 9.
31. Ibid.
32. Dretske, "Laws of Nature," 264–66.
33. I wish to thank Thomas Flint and Philip Quinn for their helpful comments.

Metaphysical Necessity and Conceptual Truth

ELI HIRSCH

Kripke's discussion of the relationship between necessity and *a priori* knowledge suggests several related distinctions that he does not explicitly formulate.[1] One of these is the following:

(1) A sentence, when uttered in a certain context, may express a proposition that is necessarily true.

(2) A sentence's meaning may be such that it is necessarily the case that any sentence with that meaning, when uttered in any context, expresses a true proposition.

The notion of "meaning" that is relevant to (2) is that of a semantical rule that one grasps when one understands an expression, a rule that determines how the expression is to be used. Meaning in this sense is that Kaplan calls "character."[2] Evidently, meaning as character is closely related to the cognitive states that people are (supposed to be) in when uttering an expression.[3] It may be that this notion of meaning is problematical in certain cases, most especially with respect to proper names. But the notion seems straightforwardly applicable in many cases, and at least with respect to these cases, (2) is sufficiently clear.

It is obvious (since Kripke and Kaplan) that (1) and (2) need not coincide. In (1), we have a sentence that in a given context expresses a necessary proposition, a proposition that holds true in every possible world, but the meaning of the sentence might allow that in some other context it would express a proposition that is not even true, let alone necessarily true. In (2), on the other hand, we have a sentence whose meaning guarantees that in any context it must express a truth, but this need not be a necessary truth.

It may be immediately evident that (2) is closely connected to *a priori* knowledge, but this connection is not completely straightforward—on the face of it, (2) contains no epistemological notions. The connection will be examined later. In the meantime, to fix our terminology, let us say that a sentence satisfying (2) is a "conceptual truth."[4] Such a sentence might also be called "true in virtue of meaning." (2), then, defines the distinction between conceptual and nonconceptual truth. On the other hand, a sentence in a context (or, more strictly, a proposition expressed by a sentence in a context) is necessary or contingent depending on whether it satisfies (1).

A trivial example of a nonconceptual necessity, satisfying (1) but not (2), is "There are dogs in this (the actual) world." This sentence as uttered in the actual world is necessary because no matter what would have been the case, there would have been dogs in *this* world. But the sentence is not a conceptual truth because when uttered with its ordinary meaning in a world that has no dogs, it would express a falsehood. A trivial example of a conceptual truth that is contingent—satisfying (2) but not (1)—is "If there are dogs in this world then there are dogs." Clearly the meaning of this sentence ensures that for any possible context in which it is uttered, it must express a truth, but as uttered in the actual world (where the antecedent is true), it expresses a contingent proposition that fails to hold true with respect to any world not containing dogs.

To consider a less trivial example, let us assume that the term "heat" functions in the way described by Kripke.[5] That is, there is a certain sensation that we rigidly call "the sensation of heat," and we then use the term "heat" to refer rigidly to whatever phenomenon normally produces that sensation. In the actual world, this phenomenon turns out to be molecular motion. On this understanding of the meaning (character) of "heat," it can readily be seen that "Heat is molecular motion" as uttered in the actual world is a nonconceptual necessity. And "Heat normally produces the sensation of heat if anything does" is a contingent conceptual truth.

Other examples involve personal pronouns. Assuming that the meaning (character) of "I" and "you," respectively, is defined by the rules that "I" refers rigidly to the speaker and "you" refers rigidly to someone being spoken to, then "I exist (and think)" is conceptually true but contingent, as is, perhaps, "You are someone I'm talking to if I'm talking to anyone." And if certain facts about how I originated are essential to me, as Kripke maintains, then a sentence like "I originated from a sperm cell and an egg cell," when uttered by me, may express a necessary truth. But the sentence is not conceptually true, since a sentient being who originated differently might possibly have uttered the sentence with its ordinary meaning and thereby have expressed a falsehood.

In the examples cited above, it seems that the conceptual truths can be known *a priori*, but the nonconceptual truths cannot. This may suggest the general principle that all and only conceptual truths are knowable *a priori*. Such a principle has some initial plausibility, for one might suppose that if and only if a sentence's meaning guarantees that its utterance must express a truth can one determine *a priori* that in uttering the sentence, one has expressed a truth.

I think, in fact, that this is roughly correct. However, there are certain complications that have to be acknowledged.

Let me first brush aside one point that I think is not seriously relevant. In a footnote in *Naming and Necessity,* Kripke remarks, perhaps only half seriously, that even the most mundane fact (e.g., that a lecture would take place at a certain time) might be known *a priori* by someone who was born with (reliable) innate beliefs about that (kind of) fact.[6] But I think it is clear that most (at least recent) philosophers who have talked about *a priori* knowledge have meant knowledge that derives in some sense entirely from our rational faculty, that is, knowledge that depends upon nothing beyond our capacity to understand and to reason. Although I have no analysis to offer of what "understanding" and "reasoning" consist in, it seems plain enough that inborn (innate) beliefs about mundane facts do not qualify as knowledge deriving entirely from our understanding and reasoning. Let us assume, then, that such beliefs do not qualify as *a priori* knowledge in the sense that concerns us.

Given this assumption, it may well be that all truths knowable *a priori* are conceptual truths. However, the converse principle, that all conceptual truths are knowable *a priori*, seems to be threatened by certain mathematical examples, such as Goldbach's conjecture. Kripke points out that if Goldbach's conjecture is true, it is necessarily true, though, for all we know, it may be impossible (for any finite mind) to prove *a priori* that the conjecture is true.[7] What I want to add is that Goldbach's conjecture, if true, is not only necessary but conceptually true (the meaning of Goldbach's sentence guarantees that in any possible context, it expresses a truth). So we may have here the possibility of a conceptual truth not being knowable *a priori*.

I think it is important, however, not to exaggerate the general relevance of this kind of mathematical example. The reason why Goldbach's conjecture may be conceptually true without being knowable *a priori* is because the conjecture is in some (perhaps not very clear) sense infinitely complex. This kind of mathematical example ought not to license the general possibility that *any* example of a conceptual truth might be not knowable *a priori*. In general, if the meaning of what you say necessitates that you have said the truth, then it should be possible to reason *a priori* that what you have said is true.

We can distinguish between two senses of *a priori* knowability. A truth is knowable *a priori* in the narrow sense if it is metaphysically possible that we (human beings) should know this truth *a priori*, i.e., that we should know it purely on the basis of our understanding and reasoning. A truth is knowable *a priori* in the wide sense if it is metaphysically possible that some being, human or not, should know it *a priori*.

Now, as Kripke notes, an "infinite mind" could find out whether Goldbach's conjecture is true by searching through all the numbers.[8] Assuming the possibility of such a mind, if Goldbach's conjecture is true, this truth is knowable *a priori* in at least the wide sense. It may also be knowable *a priori* in the narrow sense. We do not know that it is not. Could we know that it is not? It seems plausible to answer that at least we could not possibly know this *a priori*. In other words, if the assumed truth of Goldbach's conjecture is not knowable *a priori* in the narrow sense, then this fact itself is not knowable *a priori* in the narrow sense.

In the discussion below, I will assume the simplified principle that a sentence is conceptually true if and only if it is knowable *a priori*. Even given the narrow sense of "*a priori* knowability," this principle seems to hold in almost all cases and may, indeed, hold without exception. A more cautious principle would be the following: If the truth of a sentence is knowable *a priori*, then the sentence is conceptually true, and if a sentence is conceptually true, then either its truth is knowable *a priori* or the fact that its truth is not knowable *a priori* is not itself knowable *a priori*. When I argue later from the simplified principle, one could, at the expense of some complications, substitute the more cautious principle.[9]

Having expressed a connection between conceptual truth and *a priori* knowledge, let me now express a connection between conceputal truth and metaphysical necessity. The connection is the following *Principle A:* If the meaning of a sentence is context-free, then if the sentence expresses a necessary truth, it is conceptually true.[10] (The converse principle does not hold, as will be shown shortly.)

Let me try to indicate what I mean by "context-free meaning." The meaning of an expression (in the sense of "meaning" being employed here) determines, for any context in which the expression is uttered, its intension, that is, its application with respect to (when talking about) each possible world (or perhaps each time and place in each possible world—I will ignore this complication). The intension of a sentence consists of a truth-value for each possible world; the intension of a term consists of a set of individuals or n-tuplets for each possible world. Now an expression has *context-free meaning* if its intension does not vary with its context of utterance; it has one and the same intension for all (actual and possible) contexts of utterance.

An obvious example of a term that is not context-free is a personal pronoun like "I." The intension of "I" varies with the agent who utters "I." It may be noted, further, that although the intension of "I" varies from context to context, given a particular context (agent) of utterance, "I" refers to the same individual with respect to every possible world. Hence, "I" is rigid in Kripke's sense, though it is not context-free. Let us note that we can readily extend Kripke's notion of rigidity to general terms and sentences—these might be said to be rigid if, when uttered in a given context, their intensions assign constant values to all worlds.

Another example of a term that is rigid but not context-free is "heat," assuming still the Kripkean account of "heat" described above.[11] In this respect, it may be worth comparing the abstract singular term "heat" to the concrete general term "hot." The latter term, like the former, is not context-free, but unlike the former, the latter also is not rigid. First, "hot" is not context-free because when uttered in any world W, it denotes with respect to each possible world W' those things that have an internal structure that would normally produce the sensation of heat in W (rather than in W'). If "hot" is uttered in a world in which some magnetic phenomenon normally produces the sensation, it will denote, with respect to each world, not (what we call) hot things, but magnetic things. Hence, the intension of "hot" varies with the context of utterance, and "hot" is not context-free. Furthermore, given any context of utterance, the things that are called "hot" with respect to one world will differ from the things that are called "hot" with respect to a different world (different things will have the relevant internal structure in different possible worlds). So "hot" also is not rigid.

Perhaps we should also briefly compare the term "heat" to the nonrigid description "the phenomenon that normally produces the sensation of heat." The latter term, precisely because it is not rigid, does appear to be context-free, for when uttered in any possible context, it refers, with respect to any possible situation, to whatever produces the sensation in that situation.

The term "the phenomenon that normally produces the sensation of heat" appears to be context-free on the assumption that the constituent expression "the sensation of heat" is context-free. This assumption may be controversial. Indeed, apart perhaps from certain mathematical expressions, it may not be possible to cite any uncontroversial example of context-free meaning. To me, however, it seems that rather clear examples are found among basic mentalistic terms: general terms such as "angry," "afraid," "in pain," and correlative abstract singular terms such as "anger," "fear," "pain." Take "angry," for example. To treat this term as not being context-free is to suppose that we can imagine a possible context in which someone utters the word "angry" with the meaning it actually has but without denoting (with respect to any world) the angry things (in that world). On this supposition, one might have uttered "I am angry," meaning by these words just what we do, but without asserting that one is angry. A speaker's utterance "I am angry" might express a proposition that is true even though the speaker is not angry, or false even though the speaker is angry—all of this with the speaker's meaning by "I am angry" what we mean. This seems to me absurd. So I would say that "angry" is context-free.

There is, as I am conceiving of this, an easily statable (though not always easily decidable) test for whether an expression is context-free. Considering an expression, I ask myself whether I might have, in some possible world, a phenomenological twin, someone whose inner mental life is indistinguishable from the one I actually have, who uses the expression in question with a different intension from the one that I attach to the expression.[12] If the answer is no, the expression has context-free meaning. If the answer is yes, the expression does not have context-free meaning (in some examples of a yes answer, notably proper names, there may be resistance to regarding the term as having any meaning at all—but then the term still does not have context-free meaning).[13]

The above test is useful insofar as it can be applied to an expression without first determining with any precision what its meaning is. We know that our phenomenological twins will share this meaning, whatever precisely it is. The test will fail, however, for certain special expressions such as "person whose inner mental life is indistinguishable from the one I actually have," which evidently is not context-free, though, trivially, its intension cannot vary between me and my phenomenological twins. Such exceptions aside, the test may be useful. (In any case, an affirmative answer to the test question does seem to quarantee that the expression is not context-free.)

Let us now return to the *Principle A* stated earlier, that for sentences with context-free meaning, necessity entails conceptual truth. The justification of this principle is not difficult to see. Suppose that the sentence S has context-free meaning and that, as uttered in a given context, S expresses a necessary truth. Since S is context-free, its intension must not vary from context to context. So S must express a necessary truth when uttered in any context. Obviously, then, S expresses a truth when uttered in any context. This makes S conceptually true. (However, the converse principle, that conceptual truth entails necessity in cases of context-free meaning, does not hold as is illustrated by "Someone thinks," which, although apparently context-free, is conceptually true and contingent.)

Given the connection suggested earlier between conceptual truth and *a priori* knowledge, we can state the following further *Principle B:* If a sentence with context-free meaning expresses a necessary truth, it is knowable *a priori*. (The more cautious version of *Principle B* would be: If a sentence with context-free meaning expresses a necessary truth, either it is knowable *a priori* or the fact that it is not knowable *a priori* is not itself knowable *a priori*.)

The above principles seriously restrict the categories of *a posteriori* necessity and nonconceptual necessity. And they draw attention to the outstanding importance of trying to determine which expressions are context-free.

I think that the principles have a critical bearing on a number of philosophical issues. I will mention several examples, but I want to discuss only one of these. One obvious example is the question of which laws of nature might be regarded as *a posteriori* necessary. Some people nowadays seem to think that maybe all laws are *a posteriori* necessary, but this would seem to require (most problematically, I would think) that no laws have context-free meanings. Many other examples relate to scientific statements that, though they are presumably not knowable *a priori,* seem to be necessary if true. Various theoretical identifications, such as "Water is H₂O," belong to this class. It must be possible, given the above principles, to regard such identifications as not context-free. A problematical kind of example of this class is the statement "Temporal relations are relativized to a framework." I think that this statement must be necessary if it is true. (Could simultaneity be dyadic in one world and not in another?) Assuming that it is not knowable *a priori,* it apparently must not be context-free. But how could it *not* be context-free? I think this may be a serious problem, but I cannot pursue it here.

The example that I want to discuss at some length concerns a certain version of the identity thesis, what Kripke calls the "type-type" version, that is, the view that identifies physical types or properties with mental types or properties.[14] Kripke's example is "Pain is C-fiber stimulation." The argument that follows is an adaptation of Kripke's up to a point, but I want to develop the argument in a certain direction that Kripke ignores.

Suppose that the claim is made that pain is C-fiber stimulation. It seems evident (here I will rely on Kripke's discussion) that if this claim is true, it is necessary.[15] On the other hand, it is obviously not knowable *a priori* that pain is C-fiber stimulation, and therefore, by *Principle B,* the sentence "Pain is C-fiber stimulation" must not be context-free. (One might argue to this conclusion from the clearer *Principle A* if it is immediately conceded that "Pain is C-fiber stimulation" is not a conceptual truth.)

Now it seems evident that if a sentence is not context-free, this must be because some of its parts are not context-free. In the present instance, the only reasonable candidates for such parts are "pain" and "C-fiber stimulation." So we are led to the conclusion that if pain is C-fiber stimulation, then either "pain" or "C-fiber stimulation" is not context-free.

I think we should immediately dismiss the first alternative. As I have already said, basic mentalistic terms like "pain" surely seem to be context-free. We cannot imagine that in some other context, someone might have used "pain" with its ordinary meaning but have referred to something other than pain; nor can we imagine that our phenomenological twins might have used "pain" to refer to something else.

The second alternative seems more interesting (though this alternative is in effect ignored by Kripke). It seems in fact quite plausible to regard a relatively theoretical term like "C-fiber stimulation" as not being context-free. What fixes the reference of such a term? Perhaps the answer, at least in rough outline, is as follows. We have a general physiological theory that posits C-fiber stimulation as a process that is related in certain ways to various other processes. Within the context of this theory, the term "C-fiber stimulation" may in effect be used to refer rigidly to whatever in reality turns out to answer (best) to the requirements of the theory. For example, the theory may require C-fiber stimulation to produce certain changes in certain instruments that are attached to a subject's brain. It seems that it could turn out that pain—the subject's very experience of pain—is what produces these changes. Then pain has turned out *a posteriori* to be (necessarily) C-fiber stimulation. This identity is not knowable *a priori* because "C-fiber stimulation" is not context-free and could have referred to something else.

It may be instructive to compare the treatment of "Pain is C-fiber stimulation," just suggested, with Kripke's treatment of "Heat is molecular motion." Kripke explains that the latter can be *a posteriori* necessary because the reference of "heat" is rigidly fixed by a contingent property of its referent, i.e., the property of producing a certain kind of sensation. This is why it can turn out *a posteriori* that the thing that has this contingent property is molecular motion. Analogously, on the above proposal, the reference of C-fiber stimulation is rigidly fixed by a contingent property of its referent, the property of being related to various things in the way required by the physiological theory. So here, too, it can turn out *a posteriori* that the thing that has the contingent property is the experience of pain.

Let me reformulate this point by introducing another idea. I will say that a singular term *refers essentially* if the term is both rigid and context-free.[16] Clearly, when a term refers essentially to something, there is an especially intimate connection between the term's meaning and its referent, for the meaning necessitates that the referent be none other than that thing. I will not discuss here the interesting question whether particulars (such as bodies and persons) can be referred to essentially. This probably depends at least in part on whether there are "purely qualitative" criteria of transworld identity for particulars. I think it is quite evident, however, that many properties (most obviously, mental properties) can be referred to essentially. Of course, it is also possible to refer nonessentially to a property.

It follows from the principles discussed earlier that if "*a*" and "*b*" both refer essentially, then if the identity statement "*a* is *b*" is true, it is both necessary and conceptually true (necessary because the terms are rigid, and conceptually true because the terms are context-free). Furthermore, such a statement should also be knowable *a priori*.

Kripke's account of "Heat is molecular motion" amounts to this: the statement can be *a posteriori* necessary because "heat" does not refer essentially. Analogously, on the proposal presently under consideration, "Pain is C-fiber stimulation" can be *a posteriori* necessary because "C-fiber stimulation" does not refer essentially. It can turn out *a posteriori* that "C-fiber stimulation" refers nonessentially to the same thing that "pain" refers to essentially.

But the argument cannot end here. It must be noted that someone who holds that pain is C-fiber stimulation is committed to various mental-physical identifications of a far less technical nature. I assume that C-fiber stimulation is something on the order of a certain kind of motion of certain kinds of parts of the nervous system. To fix our ideas, let us assume that this motion is a vibration of some sort so that there will be a truth of the form "C-fiber stimulation is such and such a vibratory motion of things of such and such a kind." The details of this assumption are not important. My point is that the person who holds that pain is C-fiber stimulation must also believe that there is some true statement on the general order of "Pain is a certain kind of vibratory motion of things of a certain kind." (Another formulation much to the same effect is "There is a certain kind of thing and a certain way of vibrating such that the property of being in pain is the property of containing parts of that kind that vibrate in that way.")

But now our argument gets repeated with respect to the latter statements. Perhaps it will be worthwhile this time to spell out the argument in a stepwise fashion. Let *S* abbreviate "Pain is a certain kind of vibratory motion of things of a certain kind."

1. If *S* is true, it is necessarily true. (This seems fairly evident. It follows on the assumption that if *S* is true, there is a necessary identity of rigid terms of the form "Pain is such and such a vibratory motion of things of such and such a kind.")
2. It is not knowable *a priori* that *S* is true. (Presumably everyone agrees on this.)
3. If *S* is true and *S* is context-free, then it is knowable *a priori* that *S* is true. (From 1 and *Principle B*.)[17]
4. Therefore, if *S* is true, *S* is not context-free. (From 2 and 3.)
5. Therefore, if *S* is true, either "pain" or "vibratory motion" is not context-free. (From 4 and the fact that the only parts of *S* that could make it not context-free are "pain" and "vibratory motion.")
6. "Pain" is context-free. (As argued earlier.)
7. Therefore, if *S* is true, "vibratory motion" is not context-free (and hence does not refer essentially). (From 5 and 6 and the definition of "essential reference.")

So just as the identity theorists were forced earlier to hold that "C-fiber stimulation" is not context-free and does not refer essentially, they are now forced to hold that "vibratory motion" is not context-free and does not refer essentially. Here again, the argument might proceed from the clearer *Principle A* if it is immediately conceded that *S* is not a conceptual truth.

The term "vibratory motion," or even more simply "back and forth motion," belongs to, or is at least definable in terms of, the most basic vocabulary of physical science. If the identity theorists treat this term as not referring essentially, then I think the position they are probably going to be led to is that even our most basic physical terms—terms for sizes, shapes, spatial relations, motions—do not refer essentially. The idea would have to be that all of these terms have their references fixed by how they relate to one another and, ultimately, to our experience.

The simplest way to try to develop this idea would be to suppose that many of these terms have their references fixed in the manner suggested by Kripke for "heat." Thus, the term "being spherical" might be said to have its reference fixed by some such description as "the property that (when instantiated) normally produces the experience of a spherical shape." Consider the sentence "There exists a spherical object in contact with a cubical object." According to the proposal under consideration, this sentence would assert something along the following lines: There is a property P that normally produces the experience of a spherical shape, and a property P' that normally produces the experience of a cubical shape, and a relationship R that normally produces the experience of two things being in contact, and there exists an object x that has P and an object y that has P', and x and y stand to each other in the relationship R.

The details of this view are problematical and might be worked out in several different ways. The crucial point for our present purposes is the idea that physical terms do not refer essentially, and therefore, the properties and relations corresponding to these terms might turn out to be anything. A term of the form "such and such a vibratory motion of things of such and such a kind" can therefore turn out to refer nonessentially to the property that "pain" refers to essentially.

Russell advanced an idea like this. Frequently, Russell insisted that physical science tells us nothing about the "intrinsic nature" of the world, but only about the world's "abstract structure." Consequently, there is nothing to block the identification of mind and matter: "The physical world is only known as regards certain abstract features of its space-time structure—features which, because of their abstractness, do not suffice to show whether the physical world is or is not different in intrinsic character from the world of mind."[18] Russell goes on to conclude that it is probable that certain kinds of physical movements within living organisms are mental events (and that no other physical movements are mental events).

In a paper discussing Russell's position, Grover Maxwell aptly dubs the position "structural realism."[19] In terms of the categories of the present discussion, structural realism can be defined as the view that all of the basic terms for describing physical reality refer nonessentially, whereas many psychological terms refer essentially. This position must not be confused with phenomenalism or any doctrine that attempts to reduce the physical to the mental. It is, or at least purports to be, a form of realism as regards extramental reality, which includes all of physical reality outside living organisms. The point is that we cannot grasp the "intrinsic (or essential) nature" of extramental reality in that we cannot refer essentially to any extramental properties or relations. Russell's position should also be distinguished from the far more common "materialist" line that seems to imply that physical terms refer essentially and psychological terms have their references fixed by descriptions containing physical terms. In Russell's account, the relationship between our physical and psychological vocabulary is exactly the opposite.

I think that Russell's version of the identity thesis, rooted in structural realism, is the most important alternative to dualism that has been formulated. The position seems, however, to be open to a number of serious objections. I will here address only a few of these that are most closely related to the sorts of issues I have been discussing.

One question that we might raise is whether, even given the premise of structural realism, the identity thesis is viable. We are invited to believe, to resume our previous example, that pain is a certain kind of vibratory motion of things of a certain kind. Given the premise of structural realism we have no grasp of the "essential nature" of that phenomenon we call "vibratory motion": this is something-we-know-not-what that is related in certain ways to our experience. Still, if pain is a certain kind of vibratory motion of things of a certain kind, then it seems at least to follow that pain is a highly complex phenomenon, involving various things with various properties and relations. This surely seems problematical, for don't we want to say that the property of being in pain is *logically simple*?

One's reaction to this objection will depend in part on one's general attitude toward the notion of logical simplicity. Some people, of course, reject the notion of simplicity, or regard simplicity as being merely language-relative, and they would, perhaps, not need to worry about this objection at all. But if one takes the notion of simplicity quite straightforwardly and assumes that properties can be objectively ordered as more or less simple, the difficulty seems rather acute. The difficulty is not just that we are not inclined to regard pain as complex. The more serious problem is that since we surely do not seem able to know *a priori* that pain is complex (if anything, we seem to know the opposite *a priori*), our same old argument applies to the sentence "Pain is complex." It seems obvious that if this sentence is true, it is necessary. Since we cannot know it *a priori*, it must be *a posteriori* necessary and, hence, presumably not context-free. But how could "Pain is complex" not be context-free? Is the Russellian going to try to say that "complex" is not context-free? That, I think, is scarcely intelligible.

I can think of one possible answer to this objection, but I am not sure how convincing it is. It might be said that if we have a set of properties that we can refer to essentially, so that we grasp the essential nature of these properties, then we can say *a priori* that one of these propertiers is not compounded out of the others. But Russell's identity thesis implies that pain is compounded out of properties whose essential nature we do not grasp. This is why we cannot know *a priori* that pain is complex even though it is both necessary and conceptually true that pain is complex.[20]

Let me pass on to another objection. Even if Russell's identity thesis is viable given the premise of structural realism, we have to ask whether structural realism itself is a viable position. One point I want to make is that structural realism seems to be extremely counterintuitive. According to this position, all of the following physical terms refer nonessentially: "spherical shape," "cubical shape," "straightness," "contact," "congruence," "betweenness," "being inside of." I omit mentioning temporal and causal notions, since the structural realist could say, perhaps, that these notions refer essentially insofar as they apply within the mental, as well as the physical, domain. It seems sufficiently incredible to suppose that the purely physical terms mentioned refer nonessentially.

I take it for granted that these terms are at least rigid. The question, then, is whether they are context-free. Take the term "contact." Can we really suppose that someone might have used the term "contact" with its actual meaning and have referred to something other than the relationship of contact? Might we have had phenomenological twins who say "Two things are in contact" without thereby asserting something that is true if and only if two things are in contact? This seems intuitively incredible.

It might be answered that if it sounds counterintuitive to suppose that someone who means by "contact" what we do uses this term to refer to something other than contact, it also sounds counterintuitive to suppose that someone who means by "heat" what we do uses this term to refer to something other than heat. But if we are prepared to accept this point about "heat," which follows from the Kripkean account of "heat," why should we balk at accepting the corresponding point about "contact"?

I would concede a certain degree of force to this rejoinder. Although I have several times appealed to the Kripkean account of "heat" for illustrative purposes, I am not convinced that the account is intuitively acceptable. Whether any other account does better is another question. A familiar alternative would be to hold, in effect, that "heat" refers essentially to a dispositional property, that is, to an object's disposition to produce in us the sensation of heat. On this account, in a world in which some magnetic phenomenon produced the sensation, magnetic things would have been hot (whereas on Kripke's account, they would not have been hot). But does it sound right to say that whether things are hot depends upon the workings of our nervous system? Another possibility found in the literature is to say that "heat" refers essentially to a nondispositional property but that science teaches us that this property is not instantiated. In other words, there is no heat; nothing is hot. Of course that sounds funny. Kripke's account has the virtue of at least making literal sense of the statement that heat is (identical with) molecular motion. But I really do not know of anything to say here that sounds quite right. And I would make the same judgment for the case of color: There is no philosophical account that satisfies all of our main intuitions about color. Four apparently irreconcilable intuitive assumptions are: (a) Some physical things are colored, (b) colors are not dispositional properties, (c) contemporary science can describe and explain how things are colored, and (d) color terms refer essentially. Kripke's account sustains the first three of these assumptions, but not the fourth.[21] Other accounts may sustain a different two or three of the four assumptions, but no account seems able to sustain all of them.

I would agree, then, that our intuitions may have to bend in these areas. Still, it seems to me that there is something especially baffling in Russell's structural realism. When the Kripkean says that "heat" does not refer essentially to heat or that "yellowness" does not refer essentially to yellowness, the implication is that we can discover (or introduce) other terms that do refer essentially to these properties, terms that (as we might say) reveal the essential nature of these properties. But when the Russellian says that such terms as "motion" or "contact" do not refer essentially, the implication seems to be the opposite, that we cannot possibly refer essentially to motion or contact. So there is a big difference, indeed, between the Kripkean claim that "secondary quality" terms do not refer essentially and the Russellian claim that even "primary quality" terms do not refer essentially.

Consider an analogy that Russell offers.[22] He suggests that we stand to extramental properties in the way that people blind from birth stand to visual experience. Russell's suggestion is that just as born-blind people cannot grasp the essential nature of different kinds of visual experience even though they can refer nonessentially to such experiences (e.g., as "the kind of experience sighted people call 'the sensation of yellow'"), in the same way, we cannot grasp the essential nature of such a relationship as contact even though we can use the term "contact" to refer nonessentially to this relationship. But Russell's comparison is misleading in at least one way. Born-blind people cannot refer essentially to the sensation of yellow, but sighted people can. In contrast, according to Russell, no one can possibly refer essentially to the relationship of contact.

Or might it be that I am misinterpreting Russell? Might he say, instead, that it is possible, at least metaphysically possible, for someone to refer essentially to the relationship of contact even though we cannot? But such an idea strikes me as incomprehensible. What could this person who is able to refer essentially to contact have that we lack? How can anyone get *closer* to that relationship than we are? One wants to insist, I think, that if the term "contact" does not refer essentially to contact, then surely no term possibly could. And I think that this is really what Russell himself would say, that the extramental properties and relationships cannot possibly be referred to esentially. But that, too, seems mystifying. I doubt that we can make good sense out of a view that characterizes physical reality in terms of properties and relationships that are in principle "beyond understanding," at least in a most important sense.

What is an alternative to structural realism? If we remain within a realist framework, the alternative must be to regard at least some of our basic physical terms as referring essentially to extramental (and nondispositional) properties and relationships. Such a view might be called "intuitive realism," for it captures our natural intuition that the physical properties and relationships we ordinarily talk about do not have the status of some unknowable Ps and Rs that produce our experience, but that we do grasp the essential nature of these properties and relationships. However, as the arguments above show, intuitive realism appears to hold out no hope for any view that attempts to identify types of mental states with types of movements in the nervous system. I think that similar arguments might show that various other alternatives to (type-type) dualism are untenable, given the premise of intuitive realism.[23] The general point is that if we have a mental term and a physical term that both refer essentially, and we combine these terms in an identity sentence, then as soon as it is at least granted that (we know *a priori* that) the truth of this sentence is not knowable *a priori* and, hence, that the sentence is not conceptually true, it is already settled that the sentence is not true at all.[24]

Notes

1. Saul A. Kripke, *Naming and Necessity* (Cambridge, Mass., 1980), and "Identity and Necessity," in *Identity and Individuation,* edited by M. K. Munitz (New York, 1971), 135–64. In the present discussion, "necessity" is always to be understood in the sense of metaphysical necessity.

2. David Kaplan, *Demonstratives* (Unpublished manuscript, UCLA Department of Philosophy, 1977), 24–27.

3. See ibid., 59–70.

4. What I am calling "conceptual truth" is closely related to what Kaplan calls "logical truth" (*Demonstratives,* 48), but the former notion applies even to sentences whose truth depends upon the meanings of nonlogical expressions, whereas Kaplan's notion may not.

5. Kripke, *Naming and Necessity,* 131, 132, 136. See especially Kripke's remark that the statement "Heat = that which is sensed by sensation S [the sensation of heat]" is *a priori* (136).

6. Kripke, ibid., 39 n.

7. Ibid., 37.

8. Ibid.

9. Even the more cautious principle may be questioned; for a possible counterexample, see note 20 below. I believe, however, that there is a strong presumption in favor of this principle's applying to any given case. (The principle in question is, of course, not intended to deny Gödelian results about the limitations of formal proof procedures.)

10. Compare with Kaplan's principle (i) in *Demonstratives* (81). What I am calling "context-free meaning" is, I think, what Kaplan calls "stable character" (80). I assume in what follows, as does Kaplan (see especially *Demonstratives,* page 98), that even ambiguous expressions may have context-free meaning (stable character).

11. Kaplan (ibid., 82) asserts that all of the rigid terms discussed by Kripke have stable character. This is surely incorrect if I have not misrepresented Kripke's account of "heat" (and if Kaplan's "stable character" is, indeed, the same as my "context-free meaning"). One must not be misled by the fact that the intension of "heat" cannot, perhaps, vary from context to context *in a given world.* The term still lacks stable character—is not context-free—insofar as its intension varies from context to context in different worlds.

12. This formulation of the test for context-free meaning may be "individualistic" in the sense opposed by Tyler Burge, "Individualism and the Mental," in *Midwest Studies in Philosophy IV: Studies in Metaphysics,* edited by P. A. French, T. E. Uehling, H. K. Wettstein (Minneapolis, 1979), 73–121. For one who agrees with Burge's position, the test question could perhaps be reformulated along the following lines: Might there be a linguistic community in some possible world containing phenomenological twins of all of the actual members (including the "experts") of our linguistic community such that these twins use the expression in question with an intension different from the one we attach to the expression?

13. Kaplan sometimes seems to suggest that proper names have no character (meaning) (*Demonstratives,* 107, n. 13) and, at other times, that they have stable character (context-free meaning) (*Demonstratives,* 83, 98). I am unable to understand the second alternative. (Clearly, our phenomenological twins might use our proper names with different referents.)

14. Kripke, *Naming and Necessity,* 148–55, and "Identity and Necessity," 161–64.

15. Kripke's assumption, which I share, is that "pain" is evidently rigid. However, this is denied in David Lewis, "An Argument for the Identity Theory," in *Matrialism and the Mind-Body Problem,* edited by David M. Rosenthal (Englewood Cliffs, N.J., 1971), addendum to page 164, and "Mad Pain and Martian Pain," in *Readings in Philosophy of Psychology* vol. 1, edited by Ned Block (Cambridge, Mass., 1980), 218.

16. Compare with Kripke's notion of "picking something out essentially" in "Identity and Necessity," 162 (the same notion, in slightly different words, is found in *Naming and Necessity,* 152.)

17. If we want to appeal to the more cautious version of *Principle B,* we need merely change premise 2 to "We know *a priori* that it is not knowable *a priori* that S is true" and premise 3 to "If S is true and S is context-free, then it is not knowable *a priori* that it is not knowable *a priori* that S is true."

18. Bertrand Russell, *Human Knowledge: Its Scope and Limits* (New York, 1948), 224. A view similar to Russell's is found in J. Kim and R. Brandt, "The Logic of the Identity Theory," *Journal of Philosophy*

64, no 17 (1976):515–37. Insofar as Russell believed in sense-data, he apparently held that many typical expressions have two meanings, since they refer essentially to sense-data properties while referring nonessentially to quite distinct physical properties. In what follows, the expressions I mention are always to be understood in their physical applications. (I ignore Russell's perplexing suggestion on page 329 that ''compresence'' applies univocally to sense-data and physical events. In general, my references to Russell may not be exegetically strict; rather, my aim is to address what I take to be the most straightforward version of Russell's position.)

19. Grover Maxwell, ''Structural Realism and the Meaning of Theoretical Terms,'' in *Minnesota Studies in the Philosophy of Science IV,* edited by M. Radner and S. Winoker (Minneapolis, 1970), 181–92.

20. Hence, ''Pain is complex'' might be accepted as an exception to the general principle that conceptual truths are knowable *a priori* (or to the more cautious principle that one cannot possibly know *a priori* of a conceptual truth that it is not knowable *a priori*). Alternatively, the suggestion might be that ''Pain is complex'' *is* knowable *a priori* by a possible being who can refer essentially to the properties from which pain is compounded. (But I will question in a moment whether Russell held that any being could possibly refer essentially to these properties.) It should be observed that on our present argument, Russell's identity thesis appears to be *incompatible* with panpsychism, where the latter implies that each physical property is identical with some combination of ordinary mental properties. A panpsychist identity thesis would apparently entail that pain is compounded out of properties whose essential nature we do grasp, in which case we ought to be able to know this *a priori*.

21. See *Naming and Necessity* (140n), where Kripke treats color in the same way that he treats heat. The same footnote may suggest that Kripke would not extend this treatment to ''primary qualities'' like spherical shape.

22. Bertrand Russell, *The Problems of Philosophy* (Oxford: 1959), 32.

23. The arguments apply most obviously to traditional central state materialism but may also apply to some versions of functionalism. Ned Block distinguishes between ''*a priori* functionalism'' and ''empirical functionalism'' depending on whether statements of the form ''Such and such mental state is identical with such and such functional state'' are claimed to be *a priori* or *a posteriori*. The present argument would threaten at least the *a posteriori* position. See Ned Block, ''Troubles with Functionalism,'' in *Readings in Philosophy of Psychology* vol. 1, edited by Ned Block, 271–72.

24. My thanks to Jerry Samet for helpful comments on this paper.

Available Properties

FABRIZIO MONDADORI

The threat is stronger than the execution.
—*A. Nimzowitsch*

1. A KIND OF INDIVIDUAL NATURE

Given a sufficiently rich, detailed, and intelligible way of qualifying—or categorizing—possibilities,[1] the character, content, and quality of the actual course of a life can be described, to a fairly large extent, in terms of the possibilities that inhere (and inhered) to it: its insignificant parts, in terms of impersonal/generic possibilities; its significant parts, in terms of partly distinct, nearly distinct, and distinct ('real') possibilities; its fortuitous parts, in terms of possibilities that are (or were at one point) fortuitous; its unexpected and surprising parts, in terms of possibilities that are (or were at one point) both unexpected—or unusual, or exceptional—and surprising; its unitelligible parts, in terms of atypical or uncharacteristic possibilities; its remote parts, ... ; ... ; and so on; and so forth, along similar lines. The following three points are worthy of notice here.

First, not all those possibilities need be possibilities that managed to get realized: the insignificant parts of the course of a life, for example, may either be the result of the (impersonal, and sometimes also fortuitous) realization of impersonal/generic possibilities, or else consist of unrealized (and never to be realized) impersonal/generic possibilities—or, of course, both. In fact, more precisely, an unrealized (and never to be realized) distinct possibility stands to bring out more, and to say more, about the 'real' character (content, quality) of the course of a life, as distinguished from other actual courses of life, than a fortuitous, or an impersonal/generic, possibility that managed to get realized: the former is certainly more representative of the individuality of that course of life than the latter. Important as it may be, then, that a given possibility managed to get realized, it is equally (and probably more) important that it was once realizable, that it once inhered to a given course of life, that it had such-and-such a *quality*: the quality of the possibility is what makes the essential difference, intuitively, to the content, character, and quality of a given course of life.

257

Second, possibilities may well change in quality as time goes by. Possibilities that 'originated' as impersonal/generic, and thereby as remote, possibilities may well become, in the course of time, partly distinct, or nearly distinct, or distinct, possibilities: or they may either remain as impersonal/generic as they 'originally' were, or become more and more remote from actuality, until the point is reached at which we should not think of them as possibilities any more—or think of them as possibilities purely in a *façon de parler*. Third, talk of an actual course of life is, plainly, really talk of the actual course of life *of* an actual individual *i*: the content, character, and quality (in a word: the individuality) of a given course of life reflect(s)— or simply *are* (*is*)— the individuality of the individual *i* whose course of life it is. What is true of the former is true, obviously, of the latter as well.

Now this holds, most importantly, for the first of the three points just made: so, for example, possession, by *i,* of such-and-such (unrealized) distinct possibilities says, intuitively, a lot more about *i* than possession, by *i,* of such-and-such impersonal/generic, and fortuitous, possibilities, quite independently of whether the latter managed to get realized or not. We tend, naturally and understandably, to focus on possibilities that were once, and on possibilities that are now, partly distinct, or nearly distinct, or distinct, possibilities for *i* (distinct possibilities having the clear edge on both partly distinct and nearly distinct possibilities), and to regard, for example, those that were once, and those that are now, impersonal/generic, and fortuitous, possibilities for *i* as having little or no connection with the way *i* 'really', 'characteristically' is—or, if you will, with *i*'s 'individuality'. So, also, the fact that *i* fortuitously managed to realize a possibility that was once a distinct possibility (for *i*) counts, intuitively, as far less significant, or as far less relevant, to *i*'s 'individuality' than the seemingly less significant fact that such a possibility once pertained to *i*: never mind *whether* it was realized or not; never mind, either, *that* (and *how*) it was realized. The only important consideration, modally and metaphysically speaking, is that such a possibility was once a *distinct* possibility for *i*.

Comparisons are drawn, accordingly, not only among the qualities of the possibilities that belonged once, and belong now, to *i,* but also between the possibilities (of a given quality) that *i* did not succeed in realizing and the possibilities (of the same, or of a different, quality) that *i* did, in fact, manage to realize: what such comparisons bring out is something that might not implausibly be called *i*'s individual nature, at least on a fairly ordinary and intuitive notion of an individual nature.[2] (What such comparisons bring out is something that surely counts as *at least* uniquely distinctive of *i,* given, at any rate, the conception of possibility I shall put forth later.)

We hold, not implausibly (to pick out the extreme case): the fact (1) that *i*'s possibilities consistently failed, and fail, to reach the threshold even of partial distinctness, and (2) that most of *i*'s properties were once the 'object' of fortuitously, or else impersonally, realized impersonal/generic possibilities[3] suggests the presence of a nature that is the (almost) perfect instance of a generic/impersonal/characterless nature—there is nothing really *individual* about it. Add to the lot, however, just one, exceptional—unrealized—possibility that would (or, even, might) have been a distinct possibility for *i* (had things been otherwise), and you have cast an entirely different light, and bestowed an entirely different quality (an individuality of sorts), on what would otherwise be, or have been, a hopelessly nondescript nature.

The kind of individual nature I have just been talking about (call it a *modal* nature) belongs in a spectrum of (kinds of) individual natures whose distinctive—and somewhat disturbing—trait is that, unlike the more standard and well-known kind of individual nature commonly referred to as an individual *essence,* each of them can intelligibly be said to be *contingent*—either in the sense that it could have been different (in such-and-such respects), or in the sense that it could, as it were, be (or have been) violated. An example of the former type of contingency is provided by individual natures of the sort I have described in the previous paragraph: I shall return to it later.

An example of the latter type of contingency, on the other hand, is provided by the kind of individual nature (talk of character, or of personality, may be more appropriate here)[4] that is implicitly appealed to in such not-so-uncommon remarks as, "If Kleist had not committed suicide, Kleist would not have been Kleist." We do not mean to say, of course: The property of *committing suicide* was an essential property of Kleist (i.e., a property Kleist could not have lacked while still existing/while still being Kleist); Kleist could not but have committed suicide; ... ; and the like. (A different antecedent, however, and we might have been dealing with individual essences instead: cf., "If Kleist had originated from different parents, Kleist would not have been Kleist.")[5] We mean to say, rather (and rather more plausibly): Had Kleist not committed suicide, Kleist would not have been *true to* his (individual) nature. And we in no way rule out the possibility that Kleist should, in fact, not have committed suicide at all: on the contrary, the (implicit) suggestion here is that Kleist—or any other actual individual for that matter—could have failed to be true to his own (individual) nature, could have violated it, could have acted in a way that was not really consistent with it—and this in spite of the fact that the explanation of Kleist's having committed suicide is to be found, precisely, in the (kind of) individual nature he had.

It is not the only kind of individual nature we should ascribe to an actual individual: there is the kind of individual nature that is intimately bound up with a given individual's (distinct) possibilities (we have seen above), and there is the often unreliable and slippery kind of individual nature (again, talk of character, or of personality, may be more appropriate here) which gets to be reflected in, or displayed by, a given individual *i*'s reaction(s) to a possibility that has opened up for him or her (*i* may shun it—the possibility—or may decide to enforce it, or may regard it as a possibility not to be seriously entertained, or ...). There is the kind of individual nature ... : but enough of this. It should be clear from our considerations so far that—unlike individual essences—none of the kinds of individual natures I have been talking about is really anything to do with properties a given individual could not have failed to possess, and that none of them yields anything like a distinction (the 'classical' distinction, I mean) between essential and accidental properties of individuals. We could say, of course, by appealing for example to the modal conception of individual natures, that the 'essential' side of e.g. Kleist is captured by the set of Kleist's distinct possibilities, or by the set of properties (Kleist's) that 'underlie' those possibilities—but that would only be a wanton and pointless appropriation of an inappropriate vocabulary. There simply is no such thing as the 'essential' (in the now current sense of ''essential'') side of Kleist, on the modal conception of individual natures—or, at least, no such side can be characterized in terms of it.

According to that conception, it will be recalled, the individual nature of an individual i (or better: *a* kind of individual nature) is brought out by the set of possibilities that counted once, and of those that count now, as distinct possibilities for i. It is a fairly select and distinguished set, each possibility in the set being as distinctive of i as a possibility (for i) could ever get (or hope) to be. All the more so, in fact, if one holds, as I do, that actuality is the root of all possibility; that i's own possibilities are grounded, on the whole, in (nonmodal) actual traits and properties of i; and that, in particular, it is to a large extent i's own (nonmodal) traits and properties that render determinate, and then distinct, i's originally impersonal/generic (and now determinate, and then distinct) possibilities. Given, accordingly, that i's distinct possibilities (plus, of course, the comparisons alluded to a few paragraphs back) display i's (individual: modal) nature, and given that only so many of i's possibilities are allowed to qualify as distinct possibilities for i, regarding that particular group of possibilities the obvious question arises: what determines such a group?

In view of the considerations of the previous paragraph, the answer naturally suggests itself: i's modal nature itself. We may think of the latter, then, either as being that which determines membership in that particular group of possibilities; or as being constituted by the structure of constraints on membership in such a group; or, finally (and more simply), as being made up of those of i's, and specifically i's, (nonmodal) properties possession of which by i brings the possibilities in question about and bestows, so to say, distinctness on them. (We should get a less demanding and more liberal kind of modal nature, of course, were we to let in partly distinct and nearly distinct possibilities for i.) Just as, then, there is something metaphysically quite significant about the fact that certain possibilities count as distinct possibilities for i, so, given, in particular, the third of the three ways of conceiving of the notion of a modal nature, there is something *modally* quite significant about possession, by i, of certain specific sets of nonmodal properties.

We emphasize it by saying, as I have done two paragraphs back, that each such set is both what brings a certain possibility (for i) about, and (part of) what renders that possibility a *determinate,* and eventually distinct, possibility for i. We emphasize it, further, by pointing out that we are not dealing here with just any 'casual' subset of the set of i's (nonmodal) properties: not just any subset of that set will do. Each of the subsets at play here, rather, has the 'distinction' of being involved in a well-defined (causal) process, involving i, whose endpoint is the acquisition, on i's part, of the object (viz., the property) to which the relevant (distinct) possibility is 'directed'. Each of those subsets, in other words, can be thought of as a set of properties that, as of a definite time t, possesses, thereby succeeding in singling out a unique and fully determinate possibility,[6] a (second-order) property—a modality of sorts—that none of the other subsets of the set of i's (nonmodal) properties possesses (as of t):[7] the potentiality—a property of sorts—to 'develop' in such a way as eventualy to yield, if the natural course of events obtains, what we should call, as it were *ex post facto,* the object of precisely that possibility. (The latter may, in effect, be identified with the second-order property just alluded to.)[8]

Nothing of the sort holds for impersonal/generic possibilities: there is no potentiality, in their case, to 'develop' in any *particular* direction. The properties and conditions in which each of them is grounded underlies, in fact, a whole *class* of possibilities, each of which is 'directed' to a different object. Unlike partly distinct, nearly distinct, and distinct, possibilities, they could hardly be said to be determinate: and this because (1) it is objectively indeterminate *which* possibility in the relevant class we are actually dealing with, and (2) the conditions of the realization of each possibility in the relevant class are themselves wholly indeterminate, or plainly nonexistent. ([1] and [2], of course, go hand in hand.) They are possibilities which pertain to an individual *i* simply, and entirely, by virtue of the fact that *i* inhabits a world at which such-and-such laws of nature prevail, or of the fact that *i* is a member of such-and-such a species,[9] or of the fact that *i* falls under such-and-such a (generic) sortal, or ... along the same lines ... : all of which may perhaps be said to ground infinitely many classes of possibilities for *i*; none of it, however, can intelligibly be said to be 'indexed' to any *particular* possibility in any one of those classes.

Fortuitous possibilities, on the other hand, occupy a sort of modal and metaphysical no-man's-land between the realm of distinct possibilities and that of impersonal/generic possibilities. They are possibilities you fortuitously 'acquire', chance, as it were, to stumble across, having done little or nothing to 'acquire' them or to bring about the conditions for their coming into existence—little or nothing, that is, *with a view* either to 'acquiring' them, or to bringing about the conditions ... etc. .... . They open up for you for no other reason than that you happen, as chance has it, to be in the right place at the right time.[10] (In this respect at least, quite a few impersonal/generic possibilities turn out to be purely fortuitous possibilities; so do, of course, quite a few distinct possibilities, provided "right place" and "right time" are understood in a sufficiently broad—and the broader, the emptier—way. The converse, however, need in no wise hold.)

Now, in order to determine the quality of a possibility that pertains to *i* (is it a distinct, or an impersonal/generic, or a fortuitous, possibility?),[11] the question must be raised, first, whether or not the bringing about of that possibility was (also) a matter of deliberate causation on *i*'s part (i.e., roughly, whether or not *i*'s doings which bore on the genesis of that possibility were "merely" incidental to the latter's coming into existence).[12] If it was, or if they—the doings—were not (which rules out both impersonal/generic and fortuitous possibilities), the question must be raised, second, whether or not those of *i*'s properties wherein the possibility at stake is grounded are at all distinctive, characteristic, typical, ... , of *i,* and specifically of *i* (I mean those properties woven into a causal structure of sorts, *if* they can be so woven). If they can and they are—which rules out impersonal/generic possibilities—the question must be raised, third, whether or not a causal chain exists whose last link is the object of that possibility, and whose 'initial' segment is made up of (at least) those properties (room must be made here, or course, for deliberate causation). If it is—which entitles us to speak of a determinate possibility—the question must be raised, finally, whether or not the object is within reach.[13] If it is, the possibility at stake will have to be counted as a *distinct* possibility for *i*. (Given, at any rate, an intuitively quite plausible, and possibly much too exacting, sense of "distinct possibility." Weaken ever so slightly the "within reach" clause, and what you get is a *nearly* distinct possibility for *i*. Weaken the second and the third clause, and what you get is a *partly* distinct possibility for *i*.)[14]

Get rid of the first and the third clause, weaken the second, and what you get is a whole spectrum of impersonal/generic possibilities for *i*: some, if not quite all, of the latter may come to acquire, of course, in the course of time, the status of partly distinct, or of nearly distinct, or of distinct possibilities for *i* (most of *i*'s distinct possibilities probably originated, anyway, as purely impersonal/generic possibilities). Thus, for example, an impersonal/generic possibility for *i*, although not 'originally' grounded in properties that are/were distinctive of *i* (and specifically of *i*), may come both to be so grounded (shaking off, thereby, a good deal of its 'original' indeterminacy), *and* to possess the characteristic traits either of a partly distinct, or of a nearly distinct, or of a distinct, possibility. It is essentially, if not entirely, a question of (degree of) (in)determinacy: both as regards the conditions, properties, and so on wherein a given possibility is grounded (they may not be determinate enough to ground exactly one possibility, thereby opening up, so to say, an entire galaxy of possibilities), and as regards the conditions which relate to the realization of that possibility (their degree of (in)determinacy being partly a function, obviously, of the degree of (in)determinacy of the grounding conditions).

The more determinate (in both respects) a possibility, the nearer to distinctness: the less, of course, the less—and the less *of* a possibility *überhaupt,* and the less truly a possibility *for* a specific individual. Now the same contrast—between determinacy and indeterminacy, distinctness and impersonality—is rather vividly brought out by consideration of the (simple and yet quite delicate) way in which "might" 's and "might have" 's interact: normally, the present truth of a given "might have" statement (say, "Tal might have won the tournament") presupposes the past truth of the corresponding "might" statement (in this case, "Tal might win the tournament").[15] Nothing could be simpler than that. But the change of temporal perspective (from the present to the past, and from the past back to the present) must be handled with a certain amount of delicacy: not any true "Tal might win the tournament," plainly, will do. The claim that Tal might have won carries with it, implicitly but very definitely, a suggestion to the effect that there was a time, in the course of the tournament, at which either the possibility to win was *at least* a nearly distinct possibility for Tal, or else (more weakly) the conditions wherein that possibility was grounded (and, hence, those relating to its realization as well) were sufficiently determinate for it.

Now the problem, of course, is that "Tal might win (the tournament)" was true *also* at the beginning of the tournament: purely and simply (and trivially) on account of the fact that Tal falls under the sortal *chess-player* (and that, say, tournaments are usually won by, at least, one player). As of the beginning of the tournament, that is, nothing makes it impossible (in a sufficiently strict sense of "impossible") that Tal should, in fact, win. Clearly the same holds for all the remaining players, and for the very same reason(s) for which it holds for Tal. Two points deserve comment here.

First, the conditions wherein the possibility to win is grounded (for Tal and for each of the other players) 'underlie' quite a few other possibilities as well (for Tal and for each of the other players): the possibility to *lose* the tournament (this is nothing to do with the platitude that the truth of ''*i* might φ,'' however distinct the possibility the latter expresses, is perfectly consistent with that of ''*i* might not φ'': as of the beginning of the tournament, the fact that the two possibilities—the possibility to win, the possibility to lose—are, as it were, both there, cannot certainly be accounted for in terms of the platitude just described); the possibility that each of the players should draw all of his games; the possibility that each of the players should win at least one game; ... ; and so on; and so forth.

Second, even were we to take other parameters into account (say, how good or bad a player each of the players is), we should in no way manage to reduce the original degree of indeterminacy: all we should get to say—for example as regards the possibility to win—is that the realization of the latter has a higher degree of likelihood in the case of e.g. Tal than in the case of any one of the remaining players. This, of course, leaves the possibility in question as indeterminate, with respect to the conditions of its realization, as it originally was. Now suppose the claim was made, at the beginning of the tournament, that Tal might win: such a claim is indeed true (we have just seen) but is of no relevance whatsoever to Tal's (individual: modal) nature—the grounding of the possibility expressed by ''might (win)'' was (at that point) no more specific to Tal than to any one of the other players, and no more specific to that possibility than to any one of the possibilities I have described in the previous paragraph.

Suppose, however, that—not long before the end of the tournament—the possibility to win has become a distinct possibility for Tal: the change of quality (from impersonal/generic to distinct) must be deemed to bring about quite drastic a change of perspective on Tal's (individual: modal) nature. For ''Tal might now (really) win/Victory is now at hand for Tal/Tal is now on the verge of victory'' (notice the important role played by ''now'' here) ascribes to Tal something—a possibility—that is quite distinctive of him—both in the sense that it points (as it were) to what is now a fairly definite future (at least as concerns Tal and the conditions of realization of the possibility at play), and in the sense that the grounding and history of that possibility are (virtually) unique to Tal. Were we to assert, then, once the tournament is over, that Tal might have won (such an assertion normally suggests that he has failed to win), [16] we could only be taken to have said something significant—modally and metaphysically speaking—about Tal provided the truth of our assertion is tied to the truth of the corresponding ''might'' assertion near the end of the tournament: not, obviously, if it is tied to the truth of the corresponding ''might'' assertion at the beginning of the tournament (in which case we should probably be dealing with a purely epistemic ''might,'' or something of the sort).

Now, it will be recalled, on the conception of individual natures I have put forth in the previous pages natures must be acknowledged to be contingent: the (individual:

modal) nature of a given individual *i* could have been different (in such-and-such respects)—that is, more specifically, it could have consisted of a different subset of the set of *i*'s (nonmodal) properties than the subset it actually consists of—and have, thereby, determined a different set of (distinct) possibilities for *i* than the set it actually determines. Thus suppose, for instance, there was only one point in the course of *i*'s life at which the possibility to φ was a (distinct) possibility for *i*. Suppose, further, something had interfered, earlier on, in a way that would have prevented *i* from acquiring the properties that brought that possibility about. Then, obviously, *i*'s individual nature (viz., what I have referred to above as *i*'s *modal* nature) would, had those interfering factors obtained, have been different than what it actually was (and is).

Not, of course, that the lack of interfering factors is to be counted as *part* of *i*'s (individual: modal) nature, as it actually is: but, rather, that the way *i* (actually) is and, hence, the (kind of) individual nature *i* (actually) has *depend,* sometimes crucially so, on conditions the obtaining (or nonobtaining) of which is/was (*a*) purely a contingent matter and (*b*) wholly beyond *i*'s power and/or control (cf., "*i* would not have had such-and-such a (distinct) possibility, if/if only … ," where the antecedent describes conditions that satisfy both (*a*) and (*b*)). Hence, plainly, the kind of contingency—for individual (modal) natures—I have talked about in the previous paragraph. Contingency or no, however, the fact that certain possibilities were once, and that certain other possibilities are now, distinct possibilities for *i* clearly plays a very basic role in one's grasping, and understanding, of a metaphysically very basic kind of individual nature *i* possesses: let us look more closely into the notion of a possibility, then, and attempt to bring to light the structure of possibilities in general—and thereby, indirectly, that of (individual: modal) natures as well.

2. THE STRUCTURE OF POSSIBILITIES

A possibility, we have seen, is typically 'directed' to an object—typically, a (nonexemplified) property. It also has a history: a definite past; a present; and a (more or less) clear future. (I am in no way suggesting here that there is such a thing as the 'actual' future: "(more or less) clear" just means "open"—whatever the latter exactly means.) The distinction between possibilities and their objects, then, to begin with: consider the following two examples:

(1) Tal might sacrifice the exchange two moves from now.
(2) (At this point) Stella might (really) break away: which is/would be dreadful.

(1) is clearly ambiguous: "two moves from now" can be taken either to modify "might" (so that (1) comes to be read, "As of two moves from now: Tal might sacrifice the exchange"), or to modify "sacrifice the exchange" (so that (1) comes to be read, "Tal might, as of now, sacrifice the exchange, as of two moves from now"). If it is taken to modify "might," "two moves from now" must be taken, also, to pick out the time at which the possibility to sacrifice the exchange will be acquired by Tal: our main interest here is rather in the possibility "might (sacrifice the exchange)" expresses (we assert that Tal will acquire it two moves from now, but we do not specify

when Tal will be in a position to realize it), than in the object of the possibility—viz., the property of *sacrificing the exchange*. If it is taken to modify "sacrifice the exchange," on the other hand, "two moves from now" must be taken, also, to pick out the time at which the possibility to sacrifice the exchange can be realized by Tal: our main interest here is rather in the object (or in the realization) of the possibility than in the possibility itself, which we regard as something already acquired by Tal.

So much for (1). (2) is a rather more peculiar and intriguing business. Depending on whether "is" or "would be" is employed, we get a different answer to the (obvious) question: "which" (in "which ... dreadful") *what,* exactly? Let us suppose "is" gets to be employed: then what is deemed to be dreadful is (not, of course, the possibility of Stella's breaking away, but) the fact that *that* possibility—of all possibilities—with *that* object—of all objects—should (exist and) belong to Stella—of all people. Our main interest here is in the possibility itself, in its object, in its subject, *and* (really) in the fact that it relates that particular subject to that particular object. (A similar analysis also applies, I believe, to surprising, unexpected, unusual, atypical, exceptional, ... , possibilities, whose structure is essentially relational.)

Let us suppose, on the other hand, "would be" gets to be employed: then, clearly, "dreadful" applies to Stella's breaking away (or to Stella's realizing the possibility to break away), not to the possibility of her breaking away (the existence of such a possibility we have already acknowledged in the first part of (2): hence the fact that "which," in "which would be dreadful," can only intelligibly be taken to pick out "break away"). Our main interest here, accordingly, is rather in the object of the possibility expressed by "might (break away)" than in the possibility itself. In both cases—"is," "would be"—the same possibility is ascribed to Stella; in both cases we take the possibility apart, break it down into its 'constituents': the possibility to break away (a unit of sorts), on the one hand, and the object to which it is 'directed', the property of *breaking away,* on the other. In the first case ("is") we focus partly on the present and partly on the future, hence on both constituents; in the second case ("would be") we focus specifically on the future, hence on the second constituent, and we take little or no heed of the first.

I have been speaking of a possibility's being acquired by an individual; of a possibility's belonging, as of now, to an individual; and of the object—as well as of the time of possible realization—of a possibility: I have been relying, in effect, on the view—put forth earlier—that possibilities have a past, a present, and a future. It goes roughly like this. A possibility typically comes into existence at a given time t;[17] it has, typically, a life span of its own; the latter, typically, is the interval of time throughout which the possibility can be realized; the first endpoint of the interval is, typically, the point at which the possibility begins actually to be realizable; the second endpoint, on the other hand, is, typically, the point past which the possibility vanishes (or cannot be realized any more).[18]

Now the time t at which a given possibility comes into existence and the first of the two endpoints just described need not, of course, coincide at all: for the possibility may well be there at t, but only begin actually to be realizable at a time later than t—[19]

all the more so, in fact, if what we are dealing with is an impersonal/generic possibility. Two intervals, then, are at play here: an interval, whose first endpoint is t, in which it is a question of whether or not the relevant possibility manages to become determinate (and eventually distinct); and, supposing it does, the interval itself of possible realization (notice that talk of possible realization would be quite out of place in the absence of determinacy and either partial, or near, or absolute, distinctness). A good many possibilities may, of course, never even begin to be realizable:[20] they have, in this sense, no life span of their own (think of them as still-born, as it were). They 'originate' as purely impersonal/generic possibilities, undergo no change of quality at all (remain, that is, completely indeterminate), and end up in a sort of modal never-never land. In their case reference to two intervals, let alone to the way of distinguishing between them I have just described, would, plainly, be wholly inappropriate. We need to say no more, about them, than that there is a time t at which they come to pertain to a given individual: the rest is silence.

Well, not quite: for, be it impersonal, fortuitous, partly distinct, nearly distinct, or distinct, a given possibility must be grounded in actual traits (properties, conditions) of actual individuals at a given time. Possibilities of different qualities will normally require different (nonmodal) groundings; and what we take to be one and the same possibility—relative at least to its object—will very likely have different (nonmodal) groundings at different times in its career (or, more precisely, in the career of its subject). A tie subsists, accordingly, between a given possibility (at a given time) and a certain subset of the set of (nonmodal) properties of the individual i to whom it belongs (at that time).[21] Let us say that the subset in question is that which *grounds*— or that which makes it possible for i to have—the possibility in question.

None of this, of course, gives us any way of telling whether or not the possibility at stake is, say, a distinct possibility for i: the answer to that question depends to a large extent—we have seen—on the (kind of) role played by i in the genesis of the possibility. Let us say that in the case of a distinct (or of a partly, or of a nearly, distinct) possibility a causal chain is involved whose 'initial' segment (i.e., roughly, the first of the two intervals described two paragraphs back) is essentially if not exclusively made up of (nonmodal) properties which are distinctive, characteristic, typical, ... , of i (and specifically of i), and whose last link is the object of that possibility. Those are precisely the properties which, were i in fact to acquire the object of the possibility, we should have to appeal to in an explanation and account of how (and why) i, and specifically i, has actually managed to 'acquire' that object.

No such 'initial' segment, no such causal chain, is involved in the case of a purely (and persistently) impersonal/generic, or else of a fortuitous, possibility—although the former may, I have already remarked, come to be associated, in the course of time, with a causal chain of the sort just outlined and, thereby, change in quality. The best the latter can do, on the other hand, is to get to be distinct, but only in the (quite aberrant and rather limited) sense of "distinct" in which one's assertion that such-and-such a possibility is distinct comes exclusively of the fact that the object of the possibility is "within reach."

Now talk of 'initial' segments and causal chains is talk, in effect, both of the (kind of) tie that holds between a possibility and the properties wherein it is grounded, *and,* what is especially important at this point, of the (kind of) relation that holds between those properties—more generally, the individual i who possesses them—and the *object* of that possibility (the idea of the future of a possibility comes into its own precisely at this point). In the case of distinct possibilities, it is a very tight relation we are dealing with:[22] in the sense that (1) the object of the relevant (distinct) possibility is only a step away from actuality, (2) the possibility is perfectly determinate, and (3) its realization would, on the whole, be accounted for in terms of the very properties, conditions, and so on that have rendered the possibility determinate (and then distinct).

In the case of impersonal/generic possibilities, on the other hand, we could hardly meaningfully speak of a relation between i and the object(s) of those possibilities: for one thing, the relation between them—if relation there be—fails to satisfy both (1) and (2) of the previous paragraph; for another, the conditions of realization of the possibilities in question are wholly indeterminate (and objectively so). Let us say, accordingly, that the object of an impersonal/generic possibility (for i) is *remote* from actuality, meaning thereby that indefinitely many things would have to happen—most of which we could not even begin to describe, however much we knew—in order for that object to become a member of 'the actual' (the possibility already is). Finally, in the case of fortuitous possibilities the relation between i and the object(s) of those possibilities may, in some cases, turn out to satisfy (1)–(3) of the previous paragraph: two (quite crucial and related) differences beween fortuitous and distinct possibilities would, however, still remain—first, the (kind of) role played by i in their coming into existence and in their becoming determinate (it is at most a "concurrent" role when fortuitous possibilities are at play: see section 1 above), and second, the fact that fortuitous possibilities, unlike distinct possibilities, tend to be spuriously determinate (that is, one and the same fortuitous possibility tends to have the same grounding for the different individuals to whom it pertains).

Now, I have pointed out above, the kind of grounding a given possibility requires is a function of the quality it has: and, as the grounding changes, the quality is likely to change, too. Neither change, however, need affect the identity of the possibility: since its object stays the same, we are entitled to claim that, at least in *that* respect, we are still dealing with the same possibility (or with the same modal property), for the same individual. What of the case in which *two* individuals (and one possibility for them) are involved? Analogous considerations apply, with the added consideration that the grounding of 'the' possibility is bound to vary from one individual to the other, even if the quality of 'the' possibility is the same in the two cases (unless we are dealing with a purely impersonal/generic, or with a fortuitous, possibility).

Thus suppose we say, of Kleist, that he might not have committed suicide; suppose we say, of Lucretius, that he, too (like Kleist), might not have committed suicide; suppose, finally, the quality of the possibility at play is the same in the two cases (either a partly distinct, or a nearly distinct, or a distinct, possibility: but neither a fortuitous nor an impersonal one). Have we ascribed the same possibility (or modal property) to Kleist and Lucretius? It depends. We certainly have if we take *just* the corresponding modal property into account, without bothering to look at the way in which it came to be acquired by Kleist and Lucretius, or, more simply, if we take only the (pure) object of 'the' possibility into account—for the latter is 'directed' to the same object. We (probably) have not, on the other hand, if we look *also* at the grounding of 'the' possibility (or of the corresponding modal property): for it is bound to be different in the two cases. 'The' possibility at stake here, that is, has a certain history (i.e., past)—hence grounding—in the case of Kleist, and a quite different history (i.e., past)—hence grounding—in the case of Lucretius.

"... (like Kleist)" (in "he, too (like Kleist)": see the previous paragraph), accordingly, cannot be understood univocally. In the first of the two cases just described (same object), "like Kleist" is shorthand for "like Kleist in this, that a possibility pertained to Lucretius whose *object* was the *same* as that of a possibility that pertained to Kleist." In the second of the two cases (different grounding), on the other hand, "like Kleist" is shorthand for "like Kleist in this, that the possibility not to commit suicide was *grounded* for Lucretius, as it was for Kleist, in a specific set of nonmodal properties" (one set for Lucretius, of course, and a different one for Kleist).

Hence, also, the fact that "Kleist and Lucretius might *both* not have committed suicide" and "Kleist and Lucretius might *each* not have committed suicide" cannot be used interchangeably. The former merely ascribes a 'joint' possibility to Kleist and Lucretius; it merely asserts that Kleist and Lucretius had (have?) a certain possibility in common—not being intended, obviously, to single out either of them in particular, or else to single out each of them in turn (it is concerned, primarily, with a *group* of two people).[23] The latter accomplishes quite a bit more: it singles out Kleist *and* it singles out Lucretius (and it is specifically intended to do that); it is in no way concerned with a group of people (there is little or no question of a 'joint' possibility here), and the correcting reading of it exactly parallels the second of the two readings of "like Kleist" I have described in the previous paragraph. (The same remarks apply to such pairs of statements as, e.g., "*i, j, i'*, and *j'* might *all* have φ'd" and "*i, j, i'*, and *j'* might *each* have φ'd.")

But to revert to possibilities and their qualities: as I said earlier, the three principal qualities possibilities should be taken to have, insofar, at least, as the question of individual natures is concerned, are the quality of distinctness (degrees thereof included), the quality of impersonality, and the quality of fortuitousness. But what of remoteness (cf., the fairly common—and misleading—"remote possibility," "remotely possible," and the like)?

3. REMOTENESS FROM ACTUALITY

It is not, strictly speaking, a quality of possibilities at all, or of the corresponding modal properties—not, anyway, if by a remote possibility be meant a possibility that is not a trait, or a constituent, of actuality. No possibility with an actual subject, outlandish as it (the possibility) may be, is remote from actuality[24] in *that* sense of "remote"—the object to which it is 'directed', rather, properly qualifies as such.[25] There is a different sense of "remote (from actuality)," however, in which "remote (from actuality),'' although it still primarily applies to the object of a possibility, can also meaningfully be taken to apply, via the object, to the possibility itself. Thus, for example, of an impersonal/generic possibility it can correctly be asserted (we have seen earlier) that it is remote from actuality as of the time t at which it 'first' comes to be acquired by a given individual i (it may still so count, of course, at $t + 1, t + 2, \ldots ,$ $t + n, \ldots$). As of t, that is, we have (at most) what might later turn out to be the 'initial' constituents of the 'initial' segment of what might later turn out to be a/the (causal) process whose endpoint is the object of that possibility (recall the indeterminacy of impersonal/generic possibilities here).

It might be maintained—rightly so, I believe—that ascription to an individual i of possibilities of this sort is a perfectly pointless affair, since such possibilities are too remote from actuality (in the sense just explained); since it is not at all clear that we are really dealing with possibilities in such cases; and since such an ascription depends so little on i's (and specifically i's) particularities. But, however remote the possibilities and however pointless the ascription, the realization of any one of them, had it been realized, would have been a matter of a perfectly natural development of events. There is nothing especially extravagant, nothing grossly far-fetched, nothing 'unnatural' about those possibilities (and/or their objects). Extravagance, far-fetchedness, and 'unnaturalness' set in, however, as soon as the pointlessness of ascription of a possibility to i comes not only of the fact (1) that that possibility is not (yet) tied to i's (and specifically i's) particularities and that it is hopelessly remote from actuality, but also of the fact (2) that the object of the possibility's becoming (or being) a trait of i would make/have made unreasonably exorbitant and perfectly gratuitous demands on the way i and i's environment actually—'naturally'—are (or were).[26]

Not so exorbitant or gratuitous, it might be retorted, if the (kind of) possibility I have just alluded to is taken to owe its existence to its (alleged) subject's falling under such a nondiscriminating sortal as *being,* or as *entity,* or as *thing,* and if the passage of time is left out of the picture altogether. But this goes precisely to showing how exorbitant and gratuitous those demands would indeed be, were we to take an ever so slightly less circumspect view of i's characteristics, and to put the passage of time back into the picture. We are dealing here with possibilities[27] that—or whose objects—qualify as remote (from actuality) in a sense of ''remote'' that is clearly different, and stronger (in a way), than the sense of ''remote'' I have previously discussed.

The remoteness now at play occupies one of the two extremes in a spectrum of—past and present—possibilities (for an individual i) whose other extreme is occupied by distinctness. More precisely, the spectrum is a spectrum of *objects* of—past and present—possibilities (for i), and each object has a rank in it—the rank being a function of the degree of remoteness from actuality of the object. But it need not (and in general will not) be unique, since the possibility which is 'directed' to that object may change in quality; and a change in quality carries with it, naturally enough, a change in rank of the object. The objects of distinct possibilities are the exception here: for a possibility, once distinct, cannot come back any more—either it gets to be realized, or it does not. If it does not, it simply vanishes; there is no question of a change in quality for it. (Well—vanishing, or going out of existence, may be held to entail as drastic a change in quality as could possibly be asked for: but it would not yield the kind of change in quality I have been talking about; nor would, of course, the realization of a distinct possibility.)

Remoteness, then, as the considerations just made may have suggested, is exclusively to do with the (possible) process of realization of a given possibility. It bears in no wise, although it depends,[28] on the *way* in which that possibility has come into existence or has been acquired by such-and-such an (actual) individual: and, in this respect at least, "remote" must be acknowledged to belong in a different metaphysical category than "distinct" ("partly distinct," "nearly distinct"), "impersonal," and "fortuitous." Remoteness is fundamentally a matter of how much, and of *what*, would have (or would have had) to happen in order for the object of a given possibility to become a trait of 'the actual': it is thus essentially concerned with the future of that possibility,[29] unlike distinctness, impersonality, and fortuitousness, which are a matter, rather, of the past—and the present—of that possibility. We first determine, then, having taken its object into account, the quality of a given possibility (as of a given time t): this is the metaphysically (and modally) primary way of ranking possibilities with respect to their degree of representativeness of their subjects' (individual: modal) nature (call it an *absolute* ranking). We raise the question, next, of how remote from actuality (as of t) the object of that possibility is (this yields a ranking, or an ordering, of possibilities *within* an already established ranking): the answer will be couched, typically, in purely counterfactual terms—*but for*'s, *if only*'s, *if*'s, ... , and the like.

Just like *might*'s and *might have*'s, such *but for*'s, *if only*'s, *if*'s, ... , should be taken to be (describe, express) purely objective traits of the world (or of a specific region thereof, or of a specific inhabitant thereof, at t), and to give rise to—perfectly objective—truths which are grounded in the way the world (or a specific region thereof, or a specific inhabitant thereof) actually is (at t): such as the truth, say, that, if such-and-such (and then if ... , and then if ---) were to occur/had occurred (at a time later than t, ... , ---), then a certain possibility would be/have been realized. Counterfactuals of this sort (or, as we should rather say: counterfactual *facts* of this sort), besides telling us how much, and what, would have/have had to occur in order for a given possibility to be realized, also enable us to compare possibilities (of a given quality) with respect both to how truly a possibility each of them is for its subject (within the given quality), *and* to how representative each of them is of its subject's nature (within, again, the given quality). What we thus obtain is a merely *relative* ranking of possibilities, as contrasted with the absolute ranking thereof I have alluded to in the previous paragraph.

For example: the stably high degree of remoteness from actuality of the object of an impersonal possibility (for an individual i) definitely—that is, intuitively—suggests that the possibility in question is less truly a possibility for i, and less representative of i's nature, than an impersonal possibility for i whose object has a degree of remoteness from actuality that keeps decreasing (viz., keeps decreasing as a result of i's own doings). Analogously, a past—unrealized—distinct possibility for i qualifies as a possibility that was less truly a possibility for i, and less representative of i's nature, than a past—unrealized—possibility for i whose realization would have made less demands on the way i, and i's environment, actually were. (The extreme case: a past—unrealized—possibility for i whose realization would not have been possible after a given time t, and whose object was—say, not long before t—at least as remote from actuality as it was at the time $t - n$ at which i originally 'acquired' the possibility. Clearly such a possibility could hardly have been held to be—say, as of not long before t—either truly a possibility for i, or representative of i's nature: certainly a lot less so, at any rate, than it was at $t - n$.) Absolutely speaking, of course, only distinct possibilities count as truly possibilities for their subject(s), and as representative of anything that might plausibly be called an individual nature (or a kind thereof).

Although, then, the remoter from actuality the object of a possibility is, the less representative (absolutely speaking) of the nature of its subject that possibility is, it in no way follows that, the closer to, or the less remote from, actuality the object of a possibility is, the more representative (absolutely speaking) ... etc. ... . For, clearly, the object of a fortuitous possibility (or, for that matter, of an impersonal possibility that is about to be fortuitously realized) may be as close to actuality as the object of a possibility could ever get to be, and yet, for all that, the possibility may completely fail to be representative of the nature of its subject. Closeness to actuality of the object of a possibility, then, is at most a necessary condition for that possibility's being representative of the nature of its subject: a further (and plainly more basic) condition must be satisfied—the possibility must, in some sense, have originated from,[30] and find the springs of its development in,[31] the subject to which it belongs. (This, of course, only leaves room, when it comes to the question of (individual) natures, for distinct possibilities.)

A yet different sense of "remote (from actuality)" (which I have, in fact, implicitly relied on in the last three paragraphs) can now be introduced: according to it, talk of the remoteness (from actuality) of a given possibility (for an individual i) is talk, in effect, not only of the remoteness (from actuality) of the object of that possibility, but also, and principally, of the (kind of) *relation* that holds between the possibility in question—*qua* 'directed' to a certain object—and i. Understood this way, "remote (from actuality)" comes to mean something like "remote from the way i actually is (= loosely tied to the way i actually is)" (recall the notion of an indeterminate possibility here). Thus, for instance, an impersonal possibility for i will count as more remote from actuality (in the present sense of "remote") than a partly distinct, or a nearly distinct, or a distinct, possibility for i—so will, of course, a fortuitous possibility for i.

"Remote (from actuality)" is, thereby, almost brought into line with "distinct," "impersonal," and "fortuitous": at least in the sense that it can now correctly be taken to express a (second-order?) quality of possibilities (*qua* 'directed' to such-and-such objects). It turns out, in effect, to express the very quality of possibilities in terms of which we can get—indirectly—at (individual: modal) natures themselves. The idea, which I have already mentioned a couple of paragraphs back, is roughly this: consider a sequence of less and less remote possibilities for an individual i (ranging from impersonal to distinct possibilities). On the present understanding of "remote," the sequence will be a sequence of possibilities that are more and more tightly tied to the way i actually is (and the more tightly tied, the more representative of that way). As they become less remote and approach distinctness, the possibilities in the sequence are likely to get to be representative of something more specific than just "the way i actually is"; that is, as we finally enter the realm of distinct possibilities, we come to grips, in effect, with possibilities that are likely to be representative of a very specific and distinctive way i actually is—viz., i's own (individual: modal) nature.

Otherwise, and more cautiously put: let there be such things as (individual) natures; let there be, next, traits of actual individuals that represent them (the natures)—then the traits in question are quite plausibly identified (for a certain kind of individual nature) with possibilities that qualify as distinct for those individuals. The conception of (individual) natures I have just put forth crucially relies, of course, both on the notion of a distinct possibility I have characterized in section 2 above, and—more generally—on the analysis of the notion of possibility I have outlined in that section. By way of conclusion, I shall now provide a different (and more precise) analysis with a view to showing what a possibility—if not an individual nature—*really* is.

4. AVAILABLE PROPERTIES

Let us consider, to begin with, the following fairly typical instance of a modal predication *de re*:

(3) Stella might overcome her psychosis.

(Never mind, for the moment, the quality of the possibility expressed by "might" here.) A very simple,[32] and simple-minded, parsing of (3) we easily obtain by literally taking it for what it is claimed to be—a modal *predication de re*. Let us break (3) down into its constituents (a subject and a modal predicate), then, and provide the following (obvious) representation for it:

(3a) $\hat{x}\Diamond O(x)s$,

("$\Diamond$" stands for "possibly," "O" for "overcome her psychosis," and "s" for "Stella.") In almost plain English: "Stella has (the property of) *possibly overcoming her psychosis*" (never mind the rather tricky indexical "her" here). Such a representation, however, clearly will not do: it completely misses the fact (a) that the possibility involved in (3) may have come into existence today, and not have been there at all, say, yesterday, (b) that it is has a fairly definite life-span, and finally, (c) that it is 'directed' to a very specific object. A more satisfactory representation, in which both (a) and (b) are taken into account, is as follows:

(3b) $\hat{x}\Diamond_{<t,[i,\,j]>}O(x)s$ (equivalently: $\hat{x}\Diamond_t O_{[i,\,j]}(x)s$).

Here "t" (= "now") picks out the moment of time at which (3) is 'first' true (instead of a single time t we should actually speak, we have seen in section 2 above, of an interval: but never mind), and $[i,\,j]$ is the interval of time throughout which the possibility expressed by " ... might (overcome ...)" can be realized. Now, I have remarked earlier, *t* and *i* need not (they usually do not) coincide at all: think of *i,* accordingly, as the moment of time at which the possibility involved in (3) begins actually to be realizable (or at which the corresponding modal property begins actually to be realizable),[33] and of *j* as the time past which the relevant possibility cannot be realized any more, is no more, vanishes. (3b), then, goes into something like "Stella has (= has now) *possibly overcoming her psychosis*/the possibility to overcome her psychosis, which she can realize between *i* and *j*." We do not have to—sometimes we simply cannot—be very precise about *j* (or about *i,* for that matter): the context—roughly, a set of perfectly objective background conditions relating to Stella and to the object of the possibility—will usually settle the question for us.

Context or no, at any rate, it should be clear that (3b)—by 'indexing' it, in particular, to [*i, j*]—in effect treats "might" as a weak "will" of sorts. I simply mean that, according to (3b), "might," just like "will," is future-looking; unlike "will," of course, it is a present tense (and its aspect, a kind of quasi-'futurate' progressive);[34] unlike "will ϕ," of course, "might ϕ" can be taken apart, thereby yielding something like "might, as of now, ϕ, as of then (= later than now)," which is the syntactic counterpart of the metaphysical distinction between possibilities and their objects.

The passage of time having now been looked after, let us attempt, next, to find a representation for (3) in which possibilities and their objects (= (*c*) of a couple of paragraphs back) are properly distinguished. The following two points are worthy of notice here: first, the object of a possibility (or of a modal property) is rather naturally thought of as a nonexemplified property (given a sufficiently inclusive conception of properties); and second, the claim that possibilities have objects is really a (second-order) claim about the objects themselves. Bring the subject of a given possibility into the picture, and that claim gets to be understood as follows: such-and-such a property (the object of the given possibility) is *available* to the subject of that possibility.[35] Reference to a possibility in the claim I have just made is, of course, wholly redundant: "available" expresses most (if not quite all) of what we need by way of modalities, and statements of possibility (such as (3) above) should, accordingly, be regarded as assertions to the effect that a certain modal *relation*—the relation of availability—holds between a certain (nonexemplified) property and a certain individual *i*.

We can easily make sense, in terms of that relation, of some cases of 'iterated' modalities *de re* (e.g., "might possibly"): (A) "Stella might possibly love Powell again," for instance (with "might possibly love" parsed as "possibly [might love]"), goes into something like (B) "The property of *possibly loving Powell again* is available to Stella," where "available" translates "possibly" in (A); where "possibly," in (B), translates "might" in (A); and which says, in effect, that a certain nonmodal property (*loving Powell again*) is availably available to Stella. (Cf. also the analogous—and more intriguing—"The property of *loving Powell again* might become available to Stella.") Each 'iteration' corresponds, as it were, to a different layer of availability; each layer, in turn, is associated with a different interval of time: a certain property *F* is now available to Stella (first layer and first interval, relative to *F*), whose acquisition by Stella would make a yet different property *G* available to her (second layer and second interval, relative to *G*), whose acquisition ... (third layer and third interval, relative to ...) and so on. (Thus, in the example just given, the property of *loving Powell again* involves two layers of availability, and it is acquired by Stella, if it is acquired by her at all, *past* the second of the two layers.)

We can, further, intelligibly say, of a given (nonexemplified) property, that it has now *become* available to i, and may later *cease* to be available to i; that is is *now* unavailable to i, but need not be so *later*; that it is available to i from t to $t + n$ (either throughout the interval, or at some moments in the interval, or ...); that, available to i as it may now have become, it cannot—not yet—be acquired by i; and so on; and so forth: all of which, plainly, perfectly captures the temporal understanding of modality I have been presupposing in the previous pages. It also enables us to take the first step in the direction of the representation for (3) we were after, as follows:

(3c) $[\lambda x \lambda \mathcal{P} \mathfrak{M}(\mathcal{P}(x))]s, \hat{x}O\,(x)$.

(Here "$\mathfrak{M}$" stands for "available," and "$\mathcal{P}$" ranges over properties—one of them being, precisely, $\hat{x}O(x)$.) (3) is represented this way[36] with a view, among other things, to bringing out the fact that a modal predication *de re* is not implausibly taken, in a fair number of cases at least,[37] to be *de re* with respect both to its subject *and* to its predicate. We can, accordingly, read (3c) as "Stella and the property of *overcoming her psychosis* are such that the latter is (has now become) available to the former" (more naturally: "The property of *overcoming her psychosis* is (has now become) available to Stella").

Strictly speaking, the two parenthetical remarks—"has now become," "has now become"—are really quite out of place until temporal indices have been added to (3c) (for three reasons: the presence of "now" in "has now become"; the fact that "become" signals the completion of a process whose endpoint is the availability, to Stella, of a certain property; and the fact that "available," just like "might," is future-looking). True, (3) has no (explicit or implicit) temporal modifiers either: but it could hardly be expected to, without a context (or without the appropriate background information). No context, of course, except the bare fact that Stella is psychotic, may at all be intended or presupposed—or indeed exist—in some uses of (3). In those uses, (3) comes simply to be regarded as shorthand for something like "Stella is psychotic, yes: but she might overcome her psychosis—nothing makes it impossible that she should." There is nothing wrong, of course, with this way of understanding (3) and hence, in particular, "might." It would, however, force us to give "$\mathfrak{M}$" in (3c) a sense that is modally wholly nondiscriminating: in which case, clearly, we should be dealing with purely impersonal/generic possibilities, and "has now become" would be definitely out of place, temporal indices or no.

But let us suppose that a less impersonal/generic possibility is at play in (3)—that Stella has, in fact, wittingly played the main role in a process whose terminus can now be identified as the property of *overcoming her psychosis*: which may, therefore, be said to be available to her in a tolerably nonvacuous, nontrivial, and discriminating sense of "available" (recall the notion of a distinct possibility). We need two, plainly different, temporal indices here: one for the time at which the property has 'first' become available to Stella (this we may also think of as an interval: the property has 'first' become available to Stella at t, and it will be available to her until, but not after, $t + n$); and the other for the time at which—more correctly: the interval in which— Stella can (actually) proceed to acquire that property. I propose, accordingly, the following representation for (3):

(3d) $[\lambda x \lambda \mathcal{O} \mathfrak{M}_t(\mathcal{P}(x))]s,\ \hat{x}O_{[i,\ j]}(x)$.

Here "t" picks out the time at which the property of *overcoming her psychosis* has 'first' become available to Stella (the present, normally: cf., "From now on, and until ... , such-and-such a property is available to --- ''), and $[i, j]$ is the interval in which Stella can (actually) proceed to acquire that property—the latter, of course, is available to her *throughout* (and in) that same interval. Two comments here: first, we have seen in the case of (3b) above, t and i need not coincide at all; the property in question may well be available, as of t, to Stella, and yet it may not (i.e., not yet) be possible for Stella, as of t, actually to proceed to acquire that property. Second, although the property of *overcoming her psychosis* is available to Stella throughout $[i, j]$ (in fact, more precisely: from t on, until j), it in no way follows that Stella can actually proceed to acquire that property *throughout* $[i, j]$, since she may be able so to proceed only at some moments—or somewhere, by no means everywhere—in the interval.

(Thus, consider the claim that it is true that Stella might, as of now, overcome her psychosis two years from now: then the property of *overcoming her psychosis*, even though it is now available to Stella, and will be so until [at least] two years from now, can be acquired by Stella only, if at all, two years from now. Things would have been different, of course, had we claimed, instead, that it is true, as of now, that Stella might overcome her psychosis between now and two years from now: then the interval throughout which the property of *overcoming her psychosis* is available to Stella will also be the interval throughout which Stella can actually proceed to acquire that property.) In order formally to capture these distinctions, we need something like this:

(3e) $[\lambda x \lambda \mathcal{O} \mathfrak{M}_{[i',\ j']}(\mathcal{P}(x))]s,\ \hat{x}O_{[i,\ j]}(x),$

where i' is the (moment of) time at which the property of *overcoming her psychosis* has 'first' become available to Stella; j' is the (moment of) time past which that property is not available to Stella any more, and $[i, j]$ is either any one of the proper subintervals of $[i', j']$ throughout which that property can be acquired by Stella, or else it is identical to $[i', j']$. A simpler (and perhaps more perspicuous) version of (3e), with a more explicitly relational $\mathfrak{M}$, but not meant explicitly to bring out the fact that (3) can be taken to be *de re* with respect to both its subject and its predicate, would have been the following:

(3f) $\mathfrak{M}_{[i',\ j']}(\hat{x}O_{[i,\ j]}(x),\ s)$.

We are almost home now. What remains to be done is to say something about the fact, alluded to in section 2 above, that "might" (in e.g. "Stella might ϕ") has a past—or, as we should rather put it at this point, that certain properties (e.g., the property of ϕ'ing) become available to certain individuals (e.g., Stella). Let us look more closely, then, into the relation of availability: what makes it so that it comes to hold beween e.g. the property of ϕ'ing and e.g. Stella? What makes it so that that property has now become available to Stella (or that it is now, but was not before, available to her)? Obviously—and minimally—the properties and character of the members of the range of that relation; the very same things, in fact, that we took, in the preceding sections, to underlie possibilities: the grounding of possibilities becomes now the grounding of the relation of availability itself. The claim that e.g. Stella has acquired the possibility e.g. to overcome her psychosis is just the claim, we have seen earlier, that she has (now) reached a state in which the property of *overcoming her psychosis* is (now) available to her: that is, more precisely, Stella is now in a state which is simultaneously the endpoint of a (causal) process wherein Stella and a certain subset of the set of her (nonmodal) properties have played a very basic role, and the starting point of a (causal) process, continuous with the first, whose destination is Stella's conquering her psychosis.

What makes the property of *overcoming her psychosis* available to (i.e., such that it can come to be acquired by) Stella,[38] then, is the grounding itself of the relation of availability, relative to that particular property—and to Stella—at a particular time *t* in the course of her life: possession on Stella's part, namely, of a determinate set of (nonmodal) properties which, were Stella in fact to acquire the property of *overcoming her psychosis,* would constitute a large, and possibly the most significant, part of the causal grounds for—and of the explanation of—her acquisition of that property. (This is far too strong, if we take it to apply to *all* of Stella's available properties: it certainly holds, however, for those of Stella's available properties that are, or were, the object of distinct possibilities for Stella. I shall return to this in a moment.)

It is a matter, essentially, of considering and evaluating the actual course of Stella's life from the inside, as it were:[39] a given property *F* has now become available to Stella because Stella has by now acquired properties of the 'right' kind (viz., properties such that, were Stella in fact to acquire property *F,* would constitute ... and so on—as in the previous paragraph). In other words, we determine the availability—or, as the case may be, the unavailability—to Stella of a given property *F* from the perspective of a specific segment (and of the properties possessed by Stella therein) of the actual course of Stella's life. In roughly the same way, we determine the availability—or, as the case may be, ... —to Stella of a given *modal* property ℱ—the only difference is that, when it comes to modal properties (we have seen above), *two*—at least—layers of availability must be taken into account. (Thus possession, by Stella, of such-and-such nonmodal properties renders a certain modal property, or a specific set of nonmodal properties, available to her; acquisition by her of that modal property, or of those nonmodal properties, in turn, renders—or, better, would render—the nonmodal property corresponding to ℱ available to Stella. The same treatment applies, in the opposite temporal direction, with the obvious changes, to modal properties that were once available to Stella.)[40]

Let me attempt to show, finally, how talk of partly distinct, nearly distinct, distinct, impersonal/generic, and fortuitous, possibilities can be made sense of in terms of talk of available properties. (Remoteness will be dealt with later.) The claim that such-and-such a possibility is a distinct, or a partly distinct, or a ... , or a ... , and so on, possibility for an individual *i* is now to be understood as the claim that the object of that possibility—a property, we have seen—has become available to *i* in a certain *way*: for distinct possibilities, in a way that involves both deliberate causation and a causal chain of the sort described in section 2 above (so that the property is within reach: call such properties distinctly available properties); for nearly distinct possibilities, in a way that involves both deliberate causation and a causal chain whose last link is not—yet—within reach; for partly distinct possibilities, in a way that involves both deliberate causation and a less demanding (kind of) causal chain; for impersonal/generic possibilities, in a purely impersonal/generic way, which involves neither deliberate causation nor causal chains; and for fortuitous possibilities, in a purely fortuitous way, which may involve a causal chain of sorts, but involves no deliberate causation whatsoever (cf., the example discussed in note 10). In a word: different qualities of possibilities correspond to different *ways* in which the objects of those possibilities (have) become available to the subjects of those possibilities. ("Become available" is, of course, quite out of place in the case of purely impersonal/generic possibilities.)

And now for remoteness from actuality. To say, of the object of a possibility for an individual *i,* that it is remote from actuality is to say, in the present context, that no connection, of the kind that could be described in terms of the notion of an ongoing (causal) process, holds between the properties, conditions, and so on, which make that object available to *i* and the object itself: all we have are properties, conditions, and so on, which might—in *some* sense of "might"—turn out to be the (rudimentary) initial stage of a process whose terminus is *i*'s 'acquisition' of that object. Otherwise put (switching now to the remoteness of possibilities themselves): the claim that such-and-such a possibility (for *i*) is remote from actuality is simply the claim that the *relation* of availability (between the object of that possibility and *i*) is somewhat loosely grounded in, or tied to, the way *i* actually is—the less loosely grounded the relation of availability, the more available the object of the possibility is to *i*. (A distinct possibility for *i*, for example, can be taken to 'correspond' either to a relation of availability that is as tightly grounded in the way *i* actually is as a relation of availability could ever get to be, or to a property that is as available to *i* as a property could ever get to be.)

And so it goes: the less loosely grounded the relation of availability between a given property *F* and *i* is, and (hence) the more available *F* is to *i*, the more representative the relation of availability between *F* and *i* is of the way *i*, and specifically *i*, actually is—until we reach the point of *perfect*, as it were, availability (recall the notion of a distinctly available property). This is also the point at which *i*'s (individual: modal) nature enters the picture. We might conceive of it as being represented by all, and only, the properties that are distinctly available to *i*: or better, we might take the *fact*—and no more than the fact—that such-and-such properties are distinctly available to *i* to be representative (and indirectly constitutive) of *i*'s individual nature. (The latter, in turn, following the suggestion made in section 1 above, we may think of as being constituted by the structure of constraints on membership in the set of *i*'s distinctly available properties; or as being that which determines membership in such a set; or, finally, as consisting of that proper subset of the set of *i*'s—nonmodal—properties in which the availability to *i* of all *i*'s distinctly available properties is grounded.)

Two steps remain now to be taken, neither of which I shall, however, take here: first, to show that, and how, surprising, unexpected, unusual, ... , possibilities can be understood and analyzed in terms of the relation of availability. And second, to bring to bear the notion of an available property on that of an available (or of a possible) life: each of, say, Stella's presently/past available properties is the way into a whole galaxy of lives that are now/were once available to Stella; the fact that each of the lives in the lot of those galaxies is available to Stella, in turn, opens up a new perspective both on the sense of one's attribution to Stella of an individual nature, and on the (metaphysical as well as formal) sense of ''available'' itself.[41]

Notes

1. I mean possibilities *de re*: I have nothing to say about possibilities *de dicto*. Also, no distinction will be drawn between possibilities *de re* and the modal properties 'corresponding' to them: thus, e.g., ''*i* might ϕ'' may indifferently be taken to ascribe to *i* the possibility to ϕ or the modal property of *possibly ϕ'ing*.

2. As ordinary and intuitive, at any rate, as something thought up by Henry James could possibly get to be: ''it's only a question of what fantastic, yet perfectly possible, developments of my own nature I mayn't have missed. It comes over me that I had then a strange *alter ego* deep down somewhere within me, as the full-blown flower is in the small bud, and that I just took the course, I just transferred him to the climate, that blighted him for once and forever.'' ''The Jolly Corner,'' reprinted in *Dark Company,* edited by L. Child (New York, 1984), 58. According to the notion of individual nature I have in mind, further, an individual nature counts as unique to an individual very much in the sense in which a way of doing something, a certain style of performance, is sometimes said to be unique to a certain individual, and specifically to that individual: for example, ''In a position full of attacking opportunities we expect Tal to come through, but the unique twist he gives the task each time is truly remarkable.'' R. Byrne, ''Their Man in Havana,'' *Chess Life and Review* 22 (1967):122.

3. Like hopes, desires, beliefs, ... , possibilities, too, must be acknowledged to have objects. Thus, for example, the object to which the possibility expressed by ''might ϕ'' (in ''*i* might ϕ'') is 'directed' is the (nonexemplified) property of ϕ'ing. (I return to this point in section 2 below.)

4. A character, or a personality, understood in a sufficiently strict way, just *is,* of course, an individual nature (or a kind thereof).

5. In this connection, see Kripke, *Naming and Necessity* (Cambridge, Mass., 1980), 111–13.

6. I mean that, given those properties, one—and exactly one—possibility is (so to say) possible (as of *t*): it is not only fully determinate (given those properties), but also, in a sense, *determined.* A view of this sort captures the spirit, if not quite the letter, of what David Lewis has dubbed *Stalnaker's Assumption* in *Counterfactuals* (Oxford, 1973), 78.

7. This may get around a difficulty raised by Andrew Woodfield: namely (if I remember correctly)—what do we need (the existence of) possibilities for, once we already have the properties that 'underlie' them?

8. We can then, naturally enough, putting the metaphysical and the modal side together, conceive of each of the subsets alluded to in the main text as constituting—and of each of *i*'s distinct possibilities as *representing*—a part of *i*'s modal nature.

9. It is possibilities of this sort (or even more abstract ones) Dummett appears to have in mind when he claims that ''Of Moses as a new-born baby, ... , almost anything that a man could become could have been truly said to be something that that baby might become; and hence, of any such thing, we may say that Moses might have become it.'' *Frege: Philosophy of Language* (London, 1973), 131. Thus characterized, Moses's possibilities are clearly as impersonal/generic, and as unrelated to Moses (*precisely* as a new-born baby), as a possibility could ever get to be. For one thing, they also pertain to (almost) any baby that was born around the time Moses was born (and to quite a few other babies as well); for another, they are only related to Moses via the two sortals *new-born baby* and *man,* neither of which picks out an *especially* revealing trait of Moses, or of any one of those other babies, at least insofar as each of those (hopelessly indeterminate) possibilities is concerned: and, quite apart from the two points just made, it is by no means evident

that, supposing it was true of Moses (as a new-born baby) that he might become (an) F, is is *now* true of him that he might (I mean: might in fact, really, actually) have become (an) F. (''Might,'' of course, is being employed equivocally here.)

10. Here is an example: the owner of the newly opened travel agency has just decided that the forty-seventh customer to enter the agency today will win a trip to Ulan Bator; the forty-fifth customer has just left, and i and j are only a few steps away from the agency, where they are supposed to pick up a ticket. Clearly the (fortuitous) possibility to win a trip to Ulan Bator belongs to both of them: and the ''grounding'' of the possibility is exactly the same in the two cases (be it the owner's decision, taken together with the fact that i and j are on their way to the agency and that the forty-fifth customer has just left, or i's and j's being on their way to the agency and the forty-fifth customer's having just left, taken together with the owner's decision). Equally clearly, however, neither the owner nor i and j could intelligibly be regarded as the deliberate cause of that possibility's coming to pertain to i and j: even though his decision *and* their being on their way to the agency (*and* the forty-fifth customer's having just left, and ...) do indeed bring the possibility about (for i and j).

11. The other qualities one can ascribe to possibilities (see the first paragraph in the main text) require a somewhat different treatment, which I cannot give here: notice, however, that ''distinct (nearly distinct, partly distinct),'' ''impersonal,'' and ''fortuitous'' single out the three principal qualities of possibilities, at least as regards the notion of individual nature I have been talking about in the main text.

12. Cf. here Aristotle's idea of a ''cause by virtue of concurrence.'' *Physics* 196b 22 ff., 197a 12 ff.

13. Cf. here Aristotle's idea of ''things that are in our own power'' and ''can be brought about by our own efforts.'' *Nicomachean Ethics* 1112a, 30–31; see also Ben Jonson, ''Potentiall merit stands for actuall, / Where onely oportunitie doth want, / Not will, nor power.'' *Cynthias Revels* act V, scene vi, 87–89.

14. This paragraph issued from a conversation with David Johnson.

15. In this connection, see F. Mondadori and A. Morton, ''Modal Realism: The Poisoned Pawn,'' *Philosophical Review* 85 (1976):10–13 [3–21]; and my ''Remarks on Tense and Mood: the Perfect Future,'' in *Studies in Formal Semantics*, edited by F. Guenthner and C. Rohrer (Amsterdam, 1978), 223–29 [223–51].

16. Never mind the so-called epistemic ''might (have)'' here. It expresses no (real) modality of its subject anyway; it says something, rather, about the speaker (just as the permissive ''may''—''You may release the cobra now,'' ''Yes, you may flush the toilet,'' ... —ascribes no real modality to the referent of ''you,'' but says something about the speaker).

17. I take this to be a more general claim than the claim that a possibility comes to be *acquired* (by a given individual) at t. Talk of acquisition (in a fairly strict sense of ''acquisition'') should be reserved for the cases in which the relevant individual has played an especially prominent role in bringing the possibility about—which is not so, for instance, when fortuitous and most (if not quite all) impersonal possibilities are involved.

18. I ignore here the possibility of recurring possibilities: which come into existence, vanish, recur, vanish again, recur, vanish once more, ...

19. Cf., for an analogous case, ''As of now the money is yours, but you can only touch it when you come of age.''

20. I mean really, actually realizable: talk of an unrealizable possibility (i.e., unrealizable no matter what the conditions) makes no sense.

21. The properties of i's environment should, of course, also be taken into account. On a sufficiently broad (and modally almost vacuous) notion of environment, such properties will include the entire history of the world.

22. The relation is less tight, of course, in the case of nearly distinct possibilities: even less tight, in the case of partly distinct possibilities.

23. Cf. also ''i and j might both have ϕ'd; *and i'* and j' might both have ϕ'd'': this is clearly different than ''i, j, i', and j' might *all* have ϕ'd.''

24. David Lewis's terminology. See *Counterfactuals*, 49, 52.

25. In this connexion, see my ''Kleist,'' in C. Normore and F. Pelletier, eds., *New Essays in the Philosophy of Language, Canadian Journal of Philosophy* Supp. Vol. 6 (1980):196–97.

26. Consider the claim, for example, that Kleist might have been a seraph (or an angel of a lower angelic order); or the claim that Tal might still have won, as of the penultimate round, the Leningrad Interzonal (it could be held, of course, that the claim in question is true because it was true, as of the beginning of the Interzonal, that Tal might still, as of the penultimate round, win the Interzonal: I doubt, however, that such a contention can be taken at all seriously); or ... .

27. In *some* (fairly nebulous) sense of "possibility."

28. Since, clearly, how remote from actuality (the object of) a possibility is depends, to a very large extent, on the kind of grounding the possibility has and, therefore, on its quality as well.

29. Be the possibility a past or a present one: the realization of a past possibility, had it been realized, would—obviously—have occurred at a time that was future with respect to the (past) time/interval of time at which/throughout which the possibility held.

30. This is where deliberate causation enters the picture.

31. Hence the idea, introduced in section 2 above, of a causal chain.

32. "Very simple," at any rate, for those who believe in the existence of such things as modal properties.

33. Once acquired by Stella, of course, such a modal property is *exemplified* by her: it is still realizable, however, in the sense that Stella can (from *i* on, until *j*) proceed to acquire the corresponding nonmodal property (cf., " ... and now Stella has managed to overcome her psychosis").

34. That is, Stella is now engaged in a process whose terminus is her conquering her psychosis. The aspect of "might have," in turn, is a kind of 'imperfective' progressive (from the perspective of the present, at any rate). On 'imperfective' and 'futurate' progressive, see Ellen Prince, "Futurate *Be -ing*, or Why *Yesterday morning, I was leaving tomorrow on the Midnight Special* is OK," unpublished paper, read at the 1973 Summer Meeting of the Linguistic Society of America.

35. The notion of an available property I owe to David Lewis, in conversation.

36. Which—the way—I owe, again, to David Lewis.

37. But see F. Mondadori and A. Morton, "The Extension of Might," in preparation.

38. " ... can come to the acquired by Stella" does not quite mean here "It is (now) 'open' to Stella to proceed to acquire ... "; it means, rather, something like "Most of what is required of Stella in order to proceed to acquire ... is there" (it may be there, of course, and yet Stella may be unable to proceed to acquire ... : for the appropriate conditions may still be missing, the environment may not—i.e., not yet—be favorable, ... —cf. here "Conditions were ideal for ... ").

39. This means, roughly, that claims such as the claim that Stella might have lived a thoroughly different life than the life she lived (or has lived so far) only make sense provided (1) the possibility they involve can be shown to be tied to specific properties Stella had at a specific point in the course of her life, and (2) the properties in question made available to Stella, as of that specific point, a certain property which—had she acquired it—would have resulted in Stella's living (from that point on) a thoroughly different life than the life she lived (or had lived up to that point). Claims of the sort I have just discussed may, of course, be understood in a far more general way: this is when we consider the actual course of Stella's life from the outside (so to say); we conceive of it, that is, purely *in abstracto,* as just one more life, which, just like any other life, might have been completely different—never mind when, how, and why (such is life). I do not know how to handle modalities of this sort: but I doubt that consideration of the *when*'s, the *how*'s, and the *why*'s can intelligibly be abstracted from.

40. A more complex case is provided by the assertion, for instance, that a given (nonmodal) property *F,* which was once available to (and was later acquired by) Stella, might not have been/become available to her. This means that certain properties were once available to Stella which, if acquired by her, would have rendered *F* unavailable to her. The same strategy holds, clearly, for the case in which, instead of a nonmodal property *F,* a modal property $\mathscr{F}$ is at play (no matter what the order of $\mathscr{F}$ is).

41. I wish to thank David Johnson for helpful comments on an earlier draft.

Essential Properties and *De Re* Necessity

RICHARD A. FUMERTON

The most fundamental question concerning essential properties is whether there *are* any such properties. Despite the renewed interest in essentialism sparked by the presuppositions of some prominent philosophers of language, I suspect that there are still many of us who feel extremely uneasy about the very intelligibility of the concept of an essential property. It is this fundmental question I will address in this paper. I will answer it by claiming that there is indeed a sense in which it should be relatively uncontroversial that the concept of an essential property is intelligible and that things do have essential properties, but that there are no interesting metaphysical or ontological implications of this admission. Put another way, one can accommodate essential properties within a conservative ontology that recognizes only the necessity of certain *propositions*. My strategy will be to analyze the concept of an essential property in terms of the concept of *de re* necessity and, then, to analyze the concept of *de re* necessity in terms of the concept of *de dicto* necessity.

One way to get a grasp on the concept of an essential property is to define it in terms of the technical concept of *de re* necessity. *G* is an essential property of the *F* iff the *F* is necessarily *G*. In identifying the relevant necessity as *de re,* we are stressing that it is *not* the case that the *F* is necessarily *G* iff it is necessarily the case that the *F* is *G*.

Now to explicate the concept of an essential property in terms of the concept of *de re* necessity is hardly going to ease the concern of those philosophers who find essential properties suspect. Most philosophers who are suspicious of essential properties are equally suspicious of *de re* necessity. Such suspicions, I will argue, are in one sense groundless, and, in another sense, quite correct.

In what follows, I will presuppose the intelligibility of a proposition's being a logically necessary truth, where logical necessity is broad enough to include tautological necessity, analytic necessity, and even synthetic necessity (if there are any synthetic necessary truths). Although there are still philosophers who support Quinean attacks on the analytic/synthetic distinction, and although the difficulties of presenting a noncircular analysis of *de dicto* necessity cannot be ignored, it seems to me absurd to deny that there are statements whose truth is guaranteed solely by virtue of relations between the meanings of their constituent terms. In fact, I think that there are both analytic and synthetic necessary truths, but for the purposes of this paper, I will not assume the existence of the latter. Also, although I will not present a specific analysis of logical necessity,[1] I will briefly return to the question of what makes necessary truths necessary.

Assuming that the concept of a proposition being necessarily or possibly true is intelligible, is there any reason to introduce the categories of *de re* necessity and possibility? The prima facie case for the existence of *de re* modality is the apparent intelligibility of certain statements of English containing the modal operators of ordinary discourse. If I say to you that the bachelor who lives next door could have been married by now (if he had been nicer to his girlfriend, for example), you would find my assertion quite unproblematic. We may presume, therefore, that you do not understand my claim as the assertion that the proposition "the bachelor who lives next door is married" might be true. For reasons I will discuss later, uncontroversial colloquial examples of assertions of *de re* necessity that resist straightforward[2] translation into statements of *de dicto* necessity are harder to give unless one focuses on modal statements about abstract objects like properties or numbers. It is not just a lack of imagination that brings philosophers back to Quine's old example of the number of planets, but for now, it will do as well as anything else. Quine's misgivings aside, and even giving the definite description a Russellean treatment, there seems to be *some* interpretation of 'the number of planets is necessarily greater than seven' under which the statement is true. On this interpretation, the proposition cannot be asserting that it is a necessary truth that the number of planets is greater than seven.[3]

Examples like the above convince me that statements of possibility and necessity admit of both *de re* and *de dicto* readings. The most natural reading of a modal statement is often suggested by the placement of the modal operator or by a principle of charity, although sometimes neither is decisive. In any event, as I will use modal operators, the following placement of the modal operators indicates that the statements containing them are to be interpreted as statements of *de re* modality:

(1) The *F* is not necessarily *G*.
(2) The *F* is necessarily *G*.

while:

(3) It is not necessarily the case that the *F* is *G*.

and

(4) It is necessarily the case that the *F* is *G*.

are to be interpreted as statements of *de dicto* modality.

The ambiguity between *de re* and *de dicto* readings of modal statements hardly exhausts the ambiguities inherent in modal operators. Focusing on (3) and (4), the necessity and possibility referred to could be logical, nomological, epistemic, or one of the less clear (though, in ordinary discourse, more common) variants of these. One can attempt to analyze these concepts a number of different ways. As I use the terms, however, it is epistemically possible that P for S iff P is logically consistent with the justification S has for believing P. It is nomologically possible that P iff P is logically consistent with the laws of nature. The most common use of modal operators in ordinary discourse is probably derivative of nomological possibility and necessity. When one asserts that P did not have to happen, one could be taken as asserting that not-P is compatible with the laws of nature together with certain other conditions held to be constant. Which of the conditions are presupposed by ordinary modal statements involving causal (broadly construed) necessity is an extremely difficult question, the answer to which is vague and may well vary from context to context. It is this sort of problem that the philosopher trying (correctly, I think) to "reconcile" freedom and determinism is faced with in attempting to come up with intuitively plausible interpretations of ordinary statements about what people could and could not have done. As I indicated earlier, I believe that logical possibility and necessity admit of three species—tautological, analytic, and synthetic.

The ambiguity inherent in the use of modal operators on *de dicto* interpretations of modal statements is also present on *de re* interpretations. Given the classical and contemporary concept of an essential property, however, if it is possible to analyze the concept of an essential property in terms of the concept of *de re* necessity, the modal operator would have to get the strongest interpretation, that is to say, the necessity in question would have to be stronger than either nomological or epistemic necessity. We are, however, not yet in a position to interpret the concept of logical necessity in a statement of necessity *de re*. If we allowed ourselves the metaphor of possible worlds, we could say that the F is necessarily G iff the thing that is F in this world is G in all worlds in which it exists, where the possible worlds in question are all those *logically* possible worlds—the only similarity to the actual world another world must have in order to be relevant is that it be "governed" by the same laws of logic. However, I will studiously avoid talking of possible worlds in trying to explicate essential properties and *de re* necessity. All but those philosophers with a tenuous grip on reality are willing to concede that talk of other possible worlds and the individuals in them is a convenient metaphor for something else (usually counterfactual talk about what would be true if certain other things were true), and although metaphors are, in themselves, harmless, they can seduce one into believing one has an understanding of a problem when one really does not.

Where are we, then, in our search for an analysis of essential properties? I have conceded that statements of necessity and possibility (strong necessity and possibility) admit of *de re* and *de dicto* readings. That admission, I now want to stress, involves only the admission that (1) and (2) do not translate *straightforwardly* into the parallel statements of *de dicto* possibility and necessity. Specifically (1) and (2) do not translate into (3) and (4), respectively. It is obviously premature at this point, however, to conclude that there are two sorts of necessity and possibility, two sorts of modal property, one of which attaches to propositions, one of which does not. While denying the equivalence of (1) and (3), for example, I might claim that I can analyze (1) employing only the concept of necessity and possibility construed as a property of propositions. An analogy might be helpful here (and useful later on).

Considerations analogous to those involved in arguing for a distinction between *de re* and *de dicto* interpretations of modal operators have led many philosophers to recognize a *de re/de dicto* ambiguity in the interpretation of statements describing beliefs. Thus, when I say,

(5) Henry Hudson believed that Hudson's Bay was a passage to the Orient,

the most obvious interpretation of what I say will not involve my ascribing to Hudson the rather peculiar belief in the proposition that a bay is a passage. If (5) is interpreted as ascribing to Hudson belief in the proposition named by the noun clause (the *de dicto* interpretation), (5) is false. If it is given a *de re* reading, it might well be true. Recognizing that we can interpret (5) in one of two ways, and agreeing to mark the ambiguity as one between a *de re* and a *de dicto* interpretation, does not, however, commit us to the view that one can have as the object of a belief something other than a proposition.[4] A plausible analysis of the *de re* interpretation of (5) might construe (5) as ascribing to Hudson a belief in some proposition other than the one named by the noun clause following 'believed'.

Suppose one wanted to admit an ambiguity between *de re* and *de dicto* interpretations of modal operators, but wanted to maintain that *de re* readings of modal operators could be fully analyzed employing only the concept of *de dicto* modality. How might one proceed? Perhaps the most tempting move is simply to interpret the *de re/de dicto* ambiguity as it occurs in statements whose subject terms are definite descriptions by employing Russell's distinctions of scope. Thus, the difference between (2) and (4) is that in (2), the definite description is outside the scope of the modal operator:

(2a) There exists one and only one thing that is F and necessarily (it is G).

In (4), the definite description is inside the scope of the modal operator,

(4a) Necessarily (there exists one and only one thing that is F and it is G),

where the parentheses in (2a) and (4a) surround the propositions that have the property of being necessarily true. This explication of the *de re/de dicto* distinction, however, should be anathema to the philosopher trying to understand talk of *de re* necessity in terms of talk of *de dicto* necessity. The paraphrase of (2), (2a), leaves one with the task of explaining how the ''proposition'' in parentheses could be necessarily true. I have 'proposition' in scare-quotes, for it is not clear that one can even attach sense to the claim that the words in parentheses constitute a proposition. One cannot take the 'it is G' out of its context in (2a) and even ask a sensible question about its modal status. What would it *mean* to say that 'it is G' expresses a necessary truth? The sequence of words 'it is G' can only express a proposition when there is a noun or definite description for the 'it' to refer back to, and it is tempting to suggest that in such contexts, the proposition it expresses just *is* the proposition that would be expressed were the 'it' replaced by the noun or definite description to which it refers back. But if this is correct, then (2a) as a paraphrase of (2) would not render (2) distinct from (4).

One could argue at this point against the view that 'it is G' as it occurs in (2a) has the sense of 'The F is G'. One could argue that the pronoun referring back to 'the F' has its referent determined by 'the F' but then functions as a "pure" referring term, i.e., a term whose sole meaning is its referent. We might (should) object, of course, to the existence of a referential magic wand enabling one to "convert" a pronoun whose successful use is obviously parasitic upon a definite description into a term whose meaning is quite distinct from that definite description.[5] But in the present context, I am content to focus on the modal status of a proposition that has the form 'a is G' where 'a' functions as an expression whose only sense is its referent, in this case a *thing*. What would it *mean* to say that the proposition expressed by 'a is G' is necessarily true? Providing an answer to this question would be extremely difficult on certain classical attempts to understand *de dicto* necessity. Let us look at two such views more closely.

On one view, propositions that are necessarily true are either truth functionally complex tautologies or are true by virtue of relations that hold between properties or universals. Let us focus on the latter on the assumption that the former is relatively unproblematic. On this view, what makes it necessarily true that all squares have four sides and that all red things are colored are, respectively, relations that hold between the property of being a square and the property of having four sides, and the property of being red and the property of being colored. If one thinks that the first necessary truth is analytic while the second is synthetic, one may try to mark the difference by trying to indicate some difference in the respective relations. Thus, to employ a familiar metaphor, one might say that the property of being a square "contains" the property of having four sides, while being red "determines" the presence of color even though it does not "contain" it. The relations between properties that make necessary truths necessarily true might be thought of as "internal" relations in that they hold solely by virtue of the intrinsic (nonrelational) character of the relata (propertics). As such, one can immediately see how such relations could generate necessity. Our criteria for identifying properties do not allow a property to change intrinsically. If F is intrinsically different from G, then F and G are not *precisely* the same properties. And if the intrinsic character of F and G alone grounds a relation between them, a relation that, in turn, grounds the truth of a certain proposition, one need not worry about the possibility of the relation (and the truth) holding at one time or in one situation, and not at another time or in another situation. At least, one need not worry about this as along as the relata exist. On one view of *universals*, they are not only immutable but eternal and, as such, eliminate this last concern. However, one can think of properties as immutable but not eternal, in which case one would have to worry about a sense in which a sentence that expresses a necessary truth might not have expressed that truth were the world so constituted that there were no properties to which the predicate expressions could refer. On the other hand, if properties are the meanings (and referents) of predicate expressions, such a world could also be thought of as simply one in which the relevant sentence would fail to express a proposition: hence, we still would not have found a possible world in which a proposition necessary in some other world is false.

Historically, one of the main alternatives to an account of necessary truth in terms of relations between properties or universals is the radical empiricist's attempt to ground necessary truth in relations between concepts or ideas. Hume, for example, held that all truths could be divided into truths with two sources, those that depend on relations between ideas, and those that depend on matters of fact. Hume, no doubt, had an imagist conception of idea, but one can endorse the same general approach by replacing images with the more abstract notion of a concept.[6] Again, even if ideas or concepts are not eternal entities (at one time, no doubt, there were not any minds, concepts, or ideas and, hence, if necessary truths are dependent on these, no necessary truths), there is, nevertheless, a sense in which concepts or ideas are immutable in terms of their intrinsic character. If an idea or concept X at time t differs intrinsically from an idea or concept Y at time $t + 1$, then they are not, strictly speaking, the same idea or concept. So long as two ideas or concepts stand in a certain relation by virtue of their intrinsic character, they will always stand in that relation as long as they exist. The view does leave open the possibility that the world could have been such as to contain no ideas or concepts, and in such a world, the radical empiricist would probably say there would have been no necessary truths: but, then, in such a world, there would have been no propositions to be true in the first place.

The above is only a crude sketch of a sketch of two classical accounts of what makes certain propositions necessarily true. My concern here is not to defend either view, but to point out that a philosopher who holds anything even remotely like either of these two views will have a difficult time understanding the sense in which a proposition of the form ''a is G'' could be necessarily true. If such a proposition were necessarily true, it would seem that it would have to be made necessarily true by virtue of some relation between the *particular, a,* and a *property, G*. On the classical views of necessary truth discussed above, the kind of necessity that attaches to such a proposition would have to be of such a dramatically different sort that it would simply obfuscate the issue to admit the existence of such necessity and to go on to insist that there is only one sort of necessity, necessity as a property of propositions. The relation holding between a and G generating the necessary ''proposition'' that ''a is G'' just *is* the sort of necessity that the philosopher insisting on an ontologically significant *de re/de dicto* distinction wants us to admit. (I will say something more about this sort of view in my concluding remarks.)

The interesting question, then, is whether one can reduce the concept of *de re* necessity to a traditional concept of *de dicto* necessity. Put another way, is there a way of analyzing (2) so as to avoid commitment to necessary truths more problematic than 'All bachelors are unmarried' and 'All red things are colored'? Let us see.

In granting that there is an interpretation of (2) that does not involve the claim that the proposition that the F is G is necessarily true, we need not deny that (2) is a claim about the necessity of some proposition. Perhaps we should simply construe statements of *de re* possibility and necessity as existential statements quantifying over propositions. Specifically, we could construe (2) as asserting that there exists *some* proposition bearing a certain relation to the proposition that the F is G such that that proposition is necessarily true. An analogous move can be made with respect to the *de re* interpretation of belief statements. In saying that Hudson believed of Hudson's Bay that it was a passage to the Orient, perhaps I am asserting only that there is some proposition whose predicate picks out the property of being a passage to the Orient and whose subject term[7] describes the thing that is Hudson's Bay, such that Hudson believed that proposition. Similarly, in saying that the *F* is necessarily *G*, perhaps I mean only to assert that there is *some* proposition that has a subject term, alpha, describing the *F* such that the proposition that alpha, if it exists, is *G* is necessarily true. Neither view, however, is plausible as it stands. Consider statements of *de re* belief first. Hudson may have had a premonition that he would someday die in a bay. Believing this, he would presumably also have believed that the body of water in which he would die would not be a passage to the Orient. By hypothesis, he also believed that the body of water (Hudson's Bay) in which he was sailing was a passage to the Orient. So, given the above analysis of *de re* interpretations of belief statements, we would have to conclude not only that Hudson believed of Hudson's Bay that it was a passage to the Orient, but also that Hudson believed of Hudson's Bay that it was not a passage to the Orient; and this seems wrong. I am not assuming that it is *impossible* for a person to believe of a thing that it is *F* and to also believe of that thing that it is not-*F*. One can describe a hypothetical situation in which, as a result of mirrors and trick lighting, a person simultaneously perceives one thing as being red while perceiving what he or she mistakenly believes is a different thing to be not red. Hudson's belief based on his premonition, however, would not seem to establish an ''intimate'' enough connection between Hudson and the bay to attribute to him the relevant ''inconsistent'' *de re* beliefs. The difficulty, put simply, is that there are too many definite descriptions denoting Hudson's Bay that figure in statements expressing propositions believed by Hudson.

An exactly analogous problem affects an attempt to construe statements of necessity *de re* as existential statements about the necessity of certain propositions. For any *F* and for any *G*, if it is true that the *F* is *G*, then it will also be true that the thing that is *F* and *G* is *G*, and, of course, it will be necessarily true that if there is a thing that is *F* and *G*, then it is *G*. Unless (2) is to become utterly trivial, we cannot simply say that it is true provided that there is some proposition that has a subject term ''alpha'' referring to the *F* such that it is a necessary truth that if alpha exists, then alpha is *G*.

We need not, however, abandon this general approach to understanding *de re* belief and necessity in terms of propositional belief and necessity. We may simply have to narrow down the *range* of relevant propositions that Hudson's belief in which will ensure the truth of (5), and that the necessity of which will ensure the truth of (2). Here the approach one takes to the two problems must, I think, differ. In analyzing statements of *de re* belief, the most plausible move is to restrict the relevant propositions to those whose subject terms denote Hudson's Bay by way of descriptions involving Hudson's experience. Thus, one might plausibly suggest that Hudson believed of Hudson's Bay that it was a passage to the Orient provided that there was a proposition expressed by a sentence of the form 'Alpha is a passage to the Orient' such that Hudson believed it, and such that 'alpha' is a definite description that uniquely described Hudson's Bay by virtue of some direct relation that Hudson's Bay bore to Hudson's experience. So if Hudson believed the proposition that the body of water he saw before him was a passage to the Orient, then he believed of Hudson's Bay that it was a passage to the Orient. We are obviously not going to be able to find something directly analogous to this in our search for plausible interpretations of statements of *de re* necessity, but we can search for alternative ways of narrowing down the relevant class of propositions, the modal status of which is relevant to the truth of (2).

There is one way, however, in which we must *not* try to restrict the scope of the propositions quantified over in our analysis of (2) *if* we are determined to defend the view that the property of necessity attaches only to propositions. We must not say that the *F* is necessarily *G* provided that there is some proposition expressed by a sentence of the form 'Alpha is *G*' such that it is necessarily the case that if alpha exists, then alpha is *G,* where 'alpha' is a logically proper name, or a ''pure'' referring term whose only sense is its referent.[8] All of the comments made concerning the plausibility of analyzing away *de re* modality relying on scope distinction would apply here as well. We would be left wondering what could ground the necessity of the proposition that alpha is *G,* where the only meaning 'alpha' has is its referent. But how, then, are we to use a general statement to analyze statements of necessity *de re*?

We might do well to remember that the concept of an essential property and the concept of *de re* necessity are intimately connected to the concept of identity. If a thing is necessarily *G* or has the property *G* essentially, it could not lose that property and continue to exist, nor could it have existed at any point in the past without that property. Now one who thinks that there is an ontologically significant distinction between *de re* and *de dicto* modality might argue that if *a* is necessarily *G,* there is something in the nature of *a* that precludes it from existing without *G.* But how are we to understand this talk about the ''nature'' of *a* except in terms of other properties that *a* exemplifies? Whether one adopts an ontology of bare particulars, substances, or particular properties, one must surely be tempted to acknowledge that a thing is the kind of thing it is at any time it exists solely by virtue of the kind of properties it exemplifies at that time. Now, in the ordinary way of speaking, we do allow that things endure and survive change. The car I own today is the same one I owned yesterday, despite the fact that it has many properties today that it did not have yesterday. Even the philosopher who maintains (plausibly, I think) that, in a strict philosophical sense, all particulars are momentary existents will acknowledge that there is at least a ''loose,'' no doubt vague, sense of 'same' that allows us to say that things change but endure. Throughout the history of philosophy, philosophers have tried to provide plausible analyses of our criteria for the identity of things through time, although any attempt to be precise always seems to run into the insurmountable obstacles of the vagueness and open texture of language, and of the pragmatic and conventional character of our decisions concerning identity through time. We often allow that a thing can survive rather substantial change aprovided that the changes are gradual enough, but we do regard some properties as more important than others. If a human loses the dispositional property of being conscious, for example, many of us would be inclined to regard that person's existence as terminated. Which properties a thing can lose at *t* and continue to exist seems to depend very much on which other properties the thing has at that time. Despite the fact that the vagueness of ordinary language and thought will not permit the discovery of precise necessary and sufficient conditions for the identity of things through time, we do use the expression 'same' meaningfully, and we do have rough-and-ready criteria for deciding when to say that something has ceased to exist. The question of which properties a thing has essentially or necessarily can be only, I think a question about the meaning of the "loose" sense of 'same' as applied to the identity of objects through time.[9] Which properties a thing has essentially is a function of the analyticity of certain propositions involving identity through time.

Now if the F is necessarily G, it *may* not be because it is necessary that anything that is F is G. This is precisely why so-called *de re* modal claims resist *straightforward* translation into statements about the necessity of propositions. My suggestion, however, is that if the F is necessarily G, it is because there exists some set of properties, S, exemplified by the thing that is F such that it is a necessary truth that anything that has S at t has G at all other times. Suppose, for example, that at t, the F has, in addition to G, the properties L and M. We have rules for identity through time, and one of these rules might be that anything that is F, G, L, and M at time t has existed at $t - n$, and continues to exist at $t + n$ only so long as it had at $t - n$, and will have, at $t + n$, the property G. Put more precisely, we may have the following sort of rule: If an x at t is F, G, L, and M, and if there is a y at $t + n$ that is not-G and a z at $t - n$ that is not-G, then x is not the same as either y or z. In evaluating the question of whether we actually follow such a rule governing the identity through time of things with this set of properties, we must be careful to consider the many possible ways in which things that are F, G, L, and M can have changed in the past and can change in the future. It may be, for example, that our semantic rules governing identity through time are quite complex. It may be that if a thing x has F, G, L, and M at t, and if a thing y has F, L, M, and not-G at $t + 1$, we will not call x and y the same thing. We might allow, however, that a thing x that is F, G, L, and M at t can be identical with a thing y that is F, G, L, N, and not-M at $t + 1$; and we might further allow that a thing y that is F, G, L, N, and not-M at $t + 1$ can be the same as a thing z that is F, L, N, not-M, and not-G at $t + 2$. Put less formally, the question of whether a thing that is G at t can be identical with a thing that is not-G at $t + n$ may hinge in part on what other sorts of changes have occurred in the interim. In fact, our criteria for identifying things through time often do hinge on just such considerations as reflected by the fact that the gradual character of a change is sometimes relevant to our deciding that the same thing has existed throughout the change. Note also that the relevance of such considerations precludes the possibility of simply specifying some individual in some possible world and asking intelligibly whether it is or is not the same as some individual in this world.

At this point the reader might well want some examples of properties that things have essentially. The reader, however, will be disappointed. To be sure, I can show how the philosopher's trivial examples of essential properties satisfy the analysis. Being green or not-green is an essential property of my car, for there is some set of properties exemplified by my car such that it is analytic that if a thing with those properties ceases to be green or not-green, it ceases to exist. I said earlier that I would not presuppose the existence of synthetic necessary truths, but if there are such truths, there will be essential properties derived from them. If it is a synthetic necessary truth that whatever is red is colored, then the property of being either not-red or colored will be an essential property of my car. Its being an essential property will follow from the fact that there is a set of properties my car has such that it is a (synthetic) necessary truth that anything with those properties at one time is either not red or colored at all other times that it exists. It is also relatively easy to give examples of essential properties for abstract entities like properties or numbers. The number 3 has the property of being less than 4 essentially. At any time 3 exists, there is some set of properties S that 3 has such that if a thing x has S at t and a thing y is not less than 4 at $t + n$, then y is not identical with x. The relevant member of S might simply be the property of being less than 4. Our criteria for the identification of numbers through time trivially precludes the possibility of a number's relation to other numbers changing while the number remains the same.

Suggesting plausible nontrivial examples of essential properties for ordinary physical objects exemplifying familiar properties is a much more difficult task. Earlier, I noted that it is harder to find examples of (logical) *de re* necessity than possibility. One of the reasons is simply that our criteria for the identity of things through time are so very flexible. We have *comparatively* precise criteria allowing us to say when a thing is no longer of a certain kind—allowing us to say, for example, when the thing in my driveway is no longer a car. We have far less precise criteria for determining when it is no longer a thing, i.e., when it no longer exists. This is not surprising. Given our purposes in classifying and categorizing, it is usually only under some concept that we worry about the survival of a thing. My insurance company only needs criteria for determining when the thing in my driveway ceases to be a functioning car. I am relieved of my contractual obligations to the person who cosigned an agreement with me when that individual ceases to be a person. When the priceless clay statue in my possession is accidentally smashed into a thousand little pieces, I just do not care much whether the thing that was the clay statue still exists, but in a quite different (rather scattered) form. Now I am not saying, as some might, that the question of whether a thing has endured through time is senseless unless we are identifying the thing under some sortal.[10] We have the expression 'same' that we can use meaningfully in asking the question whether the clay statue of a horse—when remodelled into a cat, when smashed into a thousand pieces, or when slowly evolved into a substance with a different chemical composition—is the very same thing. When it comes to the identification of a thing (just as a thing) through time, however, do not look for our conceptual framework to provide nice, neat answers. As long as the change is gradual enough, be it merely a change in color or shape, or a change in chemical composition, I suspect we would be hard put to identify any point at which the one thing ceased to exist and another thing, with ever so slightly different properties, began to exist. Philosophers who worry about such things all have their favorite examples of properties that are essential to a thing, and many of us know the experience of simply having to shrug our shoulders when it comes to evaluating these suggestions. The above account of essential properties has the merit of suggesting precisely why it is so difficult to come up with interesting, uncontroversial examples of essential properties. Most things can at least make out a case to have survived (in the loose sense of 'same') just about any change provided that the change has been gradual enough.

It has been suggested to me[11] that there may be far more precise criteria for the identification of the (physically) more fundamental sorts of entities out of which ordinary objects are constituted. Thus, although one might find it difficult to say what properties this table has essentially, one might be better off trying to say what properties an electron has essentially. For all I know this is true. Since most people do not even know what properties an electron has, I daresay they would not be able to say which of those properties an electron could lose and still exist. (Remember, this is a different question from the question of which properties an electron could lose and still be an electron.) When it comes to questions of identity involving things having properties with which we have no dealings, we naturally enough defer to the "experts." They are not experts because they have better insight into fundamental ontological questions, of course, but because they are the only ones who even have rules governing the identity of these sorts of things through time. The account of essential properties sketched above applies equally well, however. If an electron has a certain property F essentially, it is because a certain proposition is necessarily true: it is because the electron has some set of properties S at t such that necessarily, if an x has S at t and a y is not-G at either $t + n$ or $t - n$, then x is not the same as y.

Before I look at alternatives to the view I have sketched above, let me make one qualification of that view in the face of an obvious objection. A view of essential properties is obviously inadequate, one might argue, if it entails that the car in my driveway is necessarily red. On my account of essential properties, I take it the car would not be necessarily red. But might it not be necessarily red-at-t? After all, if x is red at t and there is a y at $t + n$ that does not have the property of being red at t, then x is not the same thing as y. I am not exactly sure how to respond to this objection. One might well challenge the claim that there is a property of being red-at-t that a thing that is red at t exemplifies at all other times during its existence. Contemporary philosophers feel free to posit properties corresponding to any well-formed predicate expression, and such ontological promiscuity can certainly be challenged. Rather than provide criteria for distinguishing genuine from spurious properties, however, I will simply stipulate that if being red-at-t is a property, a thing has it necessarily only if it has the property of being red necessarily. This may seem *ad hoc,* but my purpose is to suggest a way of understanding the use of *de re* modality as it might find coherent experession in things we actually say. And if there is no time at which a thing has the property red necessarily, i.e., if it did not have to be red at all, if follows that it does not have necessarily the property of being red at t.

Let me briefly summarize the view I have put forth. The concept of an essential property is intelligible because it can be defined in terms of statements of necessity and possibility *de re*. *De re* modality can, in turn, be defined in terms of *de dicto* modality.

The *F* is necessarily *G* iff there is some set of properties *S* that the *F* has such that necessarily, if an *x* is *S* at *t* and a *y* is not-*G* at t + n or *t* − *n*, then *x* is not the same thing as *y*. The species of necessity employed in the analysis of *de re* necessity is no more problematic than classic conceptions of *de dicto* modality. If we have rules governing the identity of things (considered only as things) through time, it is such rules that ground the truth of statements of necessity *de re* and statements describing properties of a thing as essential. Even though the concept of an essential property is thus made intelligible, we may have trouble coming up with interesting examples of essential properties for contingent objects because our tolerance of change, when it comes to identifying things through time (considered only as things), is virtually unlimited provided that the changes take place gradually enough.

Before concluding, I want to consider very briefly the question of why anyone would reject at least the general approach I have taken to analyzing the concept of an essential property and the concept of *de re* modality in terms of the concept of *de dicto* modality. The argument for the above view is simply that it eliminates all of the mystery to the discussion of essential properties and leaves us with a clean ontology. While recognizing that there are statements of necessity and possibility that can get a *de re* reading, we can insist that necessity and possibility are always properties of propositions. I am, indeed, genuinely puzzled about why one would be even tempted to move in another direction.

The answer, I suspect, may depend on the other ontological and epistemological assumptions a philosopher makes. As you may have gathered by now, I have been implicitly supposing that our only access to a thing is through its properties. Whether things are just "bundles" of properties, bare particulars, or substances, it seems to me that one can recognize the presence of a thing only in terms of the exemplification of certain properties. What is more, and what is particularly relevant to our present discussion, is that it seems that one can "trace" the careers of things only through the exemplification of various properties at different times. There is a thing before me now exemplifying certain properties. A moment later, there is a thing in the same place, exemplifying most of the same nonrelational properties, or at least most of those that catch my attention. Is it the same thing? Well, whatever the answer to this question, it seems absurd to suggest that one can find it by ignoring the properties and by paying closer attention to the "unclothed" thing that exemplifies these properties. There simply is no access in experience or in imagination to a thing stripped of its properties: consequently, any criteria we can use for answering our question of identity must be defined in terms of property exemplification. And if one defines identity through time in terms of the exemplification of certain properties at different times, and if one further acknowledges that talk of identity through possible worlds is intelligible only in terms of talk of identity through time, one must surely adopt the general approach I have taken to understanding the concept of an essential property.

Perhaps, though, my critic will not hold that one can trace the careers of things independently of their properties. Rather, the critic might suggest, we can in some sense "see," or be brought dialectically to the realization that, however properties are "tied" to individuals, some are "tied" in a way quite different than others. It seems hopeless, however, to rest this claim on phenomenological grounds. To be sure, there is a huge difference between relational and nonrelational properties, but let us focus on nonrelational properties, for our critic will hold that some of these are essential, others inessential. The color and shape of a thing (usually thought of as inessential properties) seem to me as intimately connected to the thing as it is possible for any properties to be. I cannot imagine finding a property that is "tied" more strongly to the particular that exemplifies it (if, indeed, one distinguishes the particular from its properties).

There are philosophers who purport to find in things haecceities or individual essences. An individual essence is a property that a thing has essentially and that no other thing could have. If the concept of an individual essence were intelligible, one could view all other essential properties as parasitic upon this fundamental essential property in the sense that their exemplification is determined by the property that is the thing's individual essence. Such a view, however, still leaves unexplained the concept of an essential property, for we still need an account of what makes an individual essence an essential property. Even if we could find phenomenologically such a property, we would still need an account of the "tie" between the property and the individual that exemplifies it, an account that distinguishes that property exemplification from others. I do not think one could ground such a distinction phenomenologically. (Of course, my own view is neutral about what properties things have. Although I cannot find any such properties, one could hold that among the other properties a thing has, there is this peculiar property, the individual essence. And one could adopt my theory of what makes this property essential, i.e., could claim that it is analytic that if *a* has this property, then anything before or after that does not is not the same thing as *a*.)

Not all distinctions are grounded phenomenologically. One can advance dialectical considerations in support of the view that property exemplification admits of this fundamental distinction between essential exemplification and inessential exemplification, and I am certainly open to suggestions. I must confess, however, that I simply do not know of any reasonable dialectical arguments for the distinctions needed. In fact, the only dialectical grounds that could convince me of the need to recognize two different ways in which nonrelational properties are "tied" to the individuals that possess them would be a plausible refutation of the general approach I have taken in this paper to understanding talk of essential properties, *de re* necessity, and the identity of things through time. If one could develop and defend an ontology of substances or particulars that allows that substances or particulars can have *natures* where these natures are not to be understood in terms of the exemplification of certain properties, then, perhaps, one could make intelligible the view that these natures are related to certain properties in ways in which they are not related to others. I do not understand such a view, and I seriously doubt that many *contemporary* philosophers who feel so comfortable endorsing an ontologically significant commitment to essential properties are willing to make or defend the sort of (mistaken) ontology of natured substances or particulars necessary to make their commitment intelligible.

294   RICHARD A. FUMERTON

Notes

1. I briefly present such an analysis in my *Metaphysical and Epistemological Problems of Perception* (Lincoln, 1985), 62–65.

2. More about the importance of stressing "straightforward" later.

3. Again, the proposition cannot be necessarily true *if* the definite description gets Russell's analysis. If the definite description is used referentially in Donnellan's sense of the term (see his "Reference and Definite Descriptions," *Philosophical Review* 75 [1966]: 281–304), the issue is more complicated, although even under this interpretation, I do not think the statement could be necessarily true.

4. John Searle makes this point eloquently in *Intentionality* (Cambridge, 1983), 208–17.

5. I have argued elsewhere against the intelligibility of the closely related concept of fixing reference. See *Metaphysical and Epistemological Problems of Perception*, 121–30.

6. As I use the term, concepts are properties of minds and, unlike images, do not have such properties as shape and color.

7. If propositions are nonlinguistic, talk of the subject term of a proposition is obviously problematic. I am assuming here that if there are nonlinguistic propositions, they are complex in the way sentences are complex, and we can talk about the elements of the proposition that correspond to the grammatical subject of a sentence.

8. I take this to be the *kind* of approach taken by David Kaplan in "Quantifying In," in *Reference and Modality*, edited by Leonard Linsky (Oxford, 1971), 112–44, and endorsed by Alvin Plantinga in "World and Essence," *Philosophical Review* 79, no. 4 (1970):461–92, when he argues on page 462 that *de re* modality can be reduced to *de dicto* modality. See also Plantinga's "De Re et De dicto," *Nous* 3, no. 3 (1969):235–58.

9. This general approach to understanding essential properties is not novel. In "Why Settle for Anything Less than Good Old-Fashioned Essentialism," *Nous* 7, no. 4 (1973):351–65, B. A. Brody argues that the concept of an essential property is no more problematic than the concept of identity through time. However, he does not conclude, as I will, that one can therefore reduce *de re* modality to *de dicto* modality.

10. One of the classic defenses of this position is P. T. Geach's paper "Identity" in his *Logic Matters* (Oxford, 1972). There are also excellent presentations and defenses of closely related views in Nicholas Griffin's *Relative Identity* (Oxford, 1977), and in Reinhardt Grossmann's *The Categorical Structure of the World* (Bloomington, Ind., 1983), 133–43.

11. By my colleague, Evan Fales.

Against Constitutional Sufficiency Principles

THOMAS J. McKAY

In discussions of possible worlds and essential properties, several principles of "constitutional sufficiency" have played an important role. These are principles that say that the having of certain properties is sufficient to "secure the identity" of an individual. In other words, only that particular individual could have those properties. An example would be this:

If, at possible world w_1, a certain table b_1 is made from a chunk of wood m, then if a table b_2 is made in the same way from m at w_2, then $b_2 = b_1$.

(This is a principle that Saul Kripke appeals to in "Naming and Necessity."[1]) This principle makes the very strong essentialist claim that every table x other than b_1 fulfills this condition:

x could not have been made from m in just the way that b_1 was made from m.

More general principles of constitutional sufficiency might have this form:

(CO) for any object x that had a beginning in time, if x's origin had features F_1, $\ldots, F_n$, then in any possible situation (or world), anything with an origin with features $F_1, \ldots, F_n$ would be x.

$F_1, \ldots, F_n$ might be filled out in various ways.

(a) For sexually reproducing creatures, coming from a particular pair of gametes (without twin division or with twin divisions, as the case may be) is often thought to be a constituting feature.[2]

(b) for nonliving things, being constituted from a particular bit of matter with a particular shape is often thought to be a constituting origin.[3]

And a more general schema for such principles might not require an appeal to considerations of origin.

(C) for any object x, if x has features $G_1, \ldots, G_n$, then in any possible situation (or world), anything with features $G_1, \ldots, G_n$ would b x.[4]

A more global constitutional sufficiency principle is appealed to even more often.

(CW) If w_1 and w_2 are possible worlds consisting of exactly the same matter in exactly the same patterns of configuration throughout their history, then $w_1 = w_2$.[5]

The essentialist claim associated with (CW) is in some ways more limited.

If $o_2 \neq o_1$, and if o_2 exists in w, then: for any history of o_1 or its possible worlds, there is something different in the history of o_2 or in the history of w.

For this to be nontrivial, we must keep such properties as "being identical to o_1" out of the histories. This principle formulates the idea that the facts about what objects there are should be somehow based on more primitive qualitative facts about the possible world. The idea here is that the object o_2 cannot have the same qualitative history as o_1 and yet be a distinct object: "*bare* [irreducible] distinctness across worlds does not arise."[6]

I will suggest that the general constitutional sufficiency principles are false, or at least groundless. Their appeal seems based solely on the erroneous "Jules-Verne-O-Scope" attitude to modal semantics.[7] More particular principles might have some appeal, but it is very difficult to see how to argue for them, just as it is difficult to see how to argue for almost any nontrivial essentialism. I will go on to discuss how denying these constitutional sufficiency principles allows us to resolve some modal sorites-style paradoxes. In addition, I will offer a conception of modal ontology that accords well with the denial of such constitutional sufficiency principles.

AGAINST JULES-VERNE-O-SCOPES

Philosophers have often argued as though modal judgments require a certain special feat of perceptual or pseudoperceptual identification—cross-world identification. Given a possible situation, its (in-principle) perceptible qualities, or at least its qualitative physical properties, determine whether a particular individual o_1 is there.

Such a view seems quite untenable. The most extreme forms of it run into difficulty simply from the possibility of twins. If Bobby and Billy are genetically identical twins and Bobby goes into a store, it is still possible that Billy might have gone into that store in just the same way (wearing just the same clothes, and so on). The perceptible features of the situation might not distinguish them. But there are clearly two distinct possible situations, Bobby's going in and Billy's going in, that might occur. The distinction in these situations is based on the distinctness of Bobby and Billy. Bobby and Billy's distinctness need not be determined by the purely perceptible properties of the situation. Nor can it be based solely on the purely physical properties of the situation. If Bobby and Billy had had different histories of ingestion, there might even be a particle-for-particle match between Bobby's entering in one possible situation and Billy's entering in the other situation. It might be true that "Billy might have come to be constituted by all of the same particles that in fact constitute Bobby."

Of course, there is *something* that *makes* Bobby and Billy different. (The particular products of cell division they originated from, perhaps.) Even though there is nothing in the situations of going into the store that differentiates them, there is something in the history of the world that differentiates Bobby and Billy. So even if we can conclude that a *local* Jules-Verne-O-Scope will not work for identifying individuals, perhaps a total-history Jules-Verne-O-Scope could distinguish Bobby and Billy. There might be nothing qualitative *within* certain situations that differentiates them in all possible worlds. But there is something *outside* those situations that differentiates Bobby and Billy and thereby constitutes the difference between the two distinct possible situations (Bobby's going in and Billy's going in).

Perhaps this very limiting view about cross-world identification (i.e., the view that the local Jules-Verne-O-Scope works) is a straw man. Perhaps almost everyone will agree that there can be distinct situations differing only in what objects exist within those situations. Many would say that distinguishing objects requires a look at their origins, not just their temporary qualities within some situation that involves them after their identities are established.

But even when origins are taken into account, there seem to be possibilities that are distinguished only by the objects that exist in them.

It seems that two distinct individuals could originate at different times from the same matter configured in exactly the same way. (I am not suggesting that this is likely, merely that it is possible.) Individual O_1 might cease to exist, its matter become disorganized, and then its originating matter m might, by chance, come together in exactly the same configuration at t_2. A new object O_2 would then come into existence at t_2.

Now find a time t halfway between t_1 and t_2. Object O_1 could have originated at t. Object O_2 could have originated at t. These might be facts about the potentialities of O_1 and O_2 that ought to be respected by a modal system. But the possible situations, O_1's coming into existence at t (without O_2 existing at all) and O_2's coming into existence at t (without O_1 existing at all) are qualitatively indistinguishable. No features of origin distinguish these two, even though they are clearly distinct objects.

It is easy enough to imagine "ship-of-Theseus" cases fulfilling these conditions. If the first ship s_1 is made from set of planks p at t_1, and if the planks are replaced gradually but saved and put together into a new ship s_2 at t_2, it will be true that s_1 could have been made later (at t) and also true that s_2 could have been made earlier (at t). (Although, not both can happen at the same possible world.) The situations of s_1's being made at t and s_2's being made at t might be alike in all of their physical characteristics and yet be distinct situations because they involve distinct objects.

I see no reason why such a situation could not occur with organisms (at least simple organisms) as well. Suppose that some organism o_1 originates from certain genetic material arranged in a certain way. The atoms constituting o_1's genetic material might become independent of o_1 (after o_1's death, if not sooner) and by chance be reconstituted in the same configuration, originating o_2 at t_2. (This is bizarre and unlikely, but not logically impossible.) Yet it also seems that o_1 could originate later (at t_2), making these two possible situations of origin just alike. (If o_1's parents outlive o_1, then o_1 and o_2 might even have the same parents.)

The attractiveness of denying some principles of the type (CO) can be seen in the response to some sorites-like puzzles.

It is sometimes contended that the following view is incoherent.[8]

I made table b_1 from a chunk of wood m_1. If I had cut a chunk of wood m_2 overlapping 98% with m_1, then I could still have made table b_1. But if I had cut a chunk of wood m overlapping less than 5% with m_1, then I could not have made table b_1. If I had made a table, it would have been a table distinct from b_1, because it would not have had enough of its matter of origin in common with m_1.

The argument to show incoherence is familiar: we set up a chain of possible worlds in which tables are made from chunks of wood differing only 2% from the chunk in the preceding world of the chain. By the 48th link, the chunk has less than 5% in common with the starting point. Thus, according to the view here espoused, the table in w_{48} is not b_1. But, by transitivity of identity, it is b_1. Thus the incoherence.

But this argument for the incoherence need not be correct if the principle (CO) is denied. I could have made b_1 from m_2 instead of m_1. It does not follow that I could make b_1 from m_3, where m_3 is some chunk overlapping 98% with m_2. The explicitly stated principle is this:

$$Mb_1m_1 \rightarrow \forall y(Sym_1 \rightarrow \Diamond Mb_1y).$$

'Mxy' means x is made from y; 'Sxy' means x overlaps 98% or more with y. The argument for incoherence requires a generalization of this:

$$\Box\forall z(Mb_1z \rightarrow \forall y(Syz \rightarrow \Diamond Mb_1y)).$$

But to establish this generalization, we seem to need to appeal to a principle like (CO).

Suppose that a table b_n were made from a hunk of wood z, and suppose that hunk y overlaps 98% or more with z. Then the table b_n could have been made from y (just as b_1 could have been made from m_2). But the thought-experiment shows only that we can imagine a table made from z (or m_2) that might have been made from y (or m_3). It does not show that because b_1 might have been made from a chunk m_2, then b_1 might also have been made from m_3. It shows at most that there could have been *a table* made from m_2 that might also have been made from m_3. But b_1 need not be one of the tables with this feature.

Let me make the connection with (CO) more explicit. If we deny (CO), then imagining a world in which a table is made from m_2 is not the same as imagining a world in which b_1 is made from m_2. There might be qualitatively similar worlds in which tables are made from m_2, the only difference being that in some, b_1 is made from m_2, and in others, some other table is made from m_2. Because of this, our thought-experiment yields only a weaker principle:

$$\Box\forall z(Mb_1z \rightarrow \forall y(Syz \rightarrow \Diamond\exists v(Mvz \& \Diamond Mvy))).$$

But such a principle will not suffice to show the incoherence of the commonsense view sketched earlier.

There is nothing obviously incoherent about this new position. We are required to deny the simple modal generalization

$$\Box \forall z \, (Mb_1 z \rightarrow \forall y \, (Syz \rightarrow \Diamond Mb_1 y)).$$

This in itself might seem unfortunate. After all, if we had made b_1 from m_2, couldn't we have made it (b_1) from a slightly different chunk, m_3? Thus, it appears that there is a possibility of its being made from m_3. The need to deny that we could do this (at some point in the chain) might seem like too much to swallow. But I do not believe that it is too much to swallow. Certain possibilities exist for *this table*. It could have been made from m_2, for example. The fact that it could not have been made from m_3 (or from m_{48}) shows that the general principle above is wrong. As long as we are sure that it could have been made from m_2 but not from m_3 (or m_{48}), then we can be sure that the above principle is wrong. The pull of the simple generalization is based solely on the thought-experiment together with the principle (CO). Without (CO), imagination cannot be relied upon for information about particular individuals, since the image alone cannot determine what individuals exist in situations of the imagined type.

We should not ground our modal judgments in constitutional sufficiency principles if the constitutional sufficiency principles conflict with firmly held modal judgments. Modal semantics is a systemization of modal judgments. When the semantics (including such auxiliary principles as (CO)) leads to the conclusion that the judgments are wrong, then there are two possibilities. Perhaps the judgments are wrong, but perhaps the modal semantics is an incorrect (or even incoherent) systematization. There seems to be every reason to think that the modal semantics without the constitutional sufficiency principles would give us a more adequate systematization of modal judgments, for it would allow us to preserve pretheoretical judgments about possible differences of constitution.

These problems for (CO) seem to apply equally to (CW). Distinct possible worlds might be particle-for-particle alike if these possible worlds include different individuals. Two possibilities exist: o_1's coming into existence out of m at t and o_2's coming into existence out of m at t (or b_1's being made from m_2 and some other table's being made from m_2). These two possibilities are not physically distinguished, and it seems that they can be embedded in larger contexts in which there is no physical difference. There is no evident limit to this embedding. Two possible worlds might differ only in that one has o_1 at t (and after t) and the other has o_2 at t (and after t). One is a possible way for o_1 to be, the other a possible way for o_2 to be. But certainly o_1's being that way and o_2's being that way are distinct possibilities.

Nathan Salmon has presented a nice simple version of the problem (though my solution differs from his). His "four-worlds paradox" is based on a ship-of-Theseus story. Suppose that the ship a has one hundred planks ($p_1, \ldots, p_{100}$), that a could have had up to two of its planks replaced, but that any replacement of more than two planks would have constituted a distinct ship. Consider a ship b that could have been built of $p_1, \ldots, p_{97}, p_{101}, p_{102}, p_{103}$. Ship b could also have varied by up to two planks, so it could have been constituted of $p_1, p_2, \ldots, p_{97}, p_{98}, p_{102}, p_{103}$ by use of p_{98} in place of p_{100}.

Ship a could have been constituted of $p_1, p_2, \ldots, p_{97}, p_{98}, p_{102}, p_{103}$ (by replacement of p_{99} and p_{100}). This produces the following:[9]

$$
\begin{array}{ccc}
w_1 & & w_2 \\
<<p_1, p_2, \ldots, p_{97}, p_{98}, p_{99}, p_{100}>> & & <<p_1, p_2, \ldots, p_{97}, p_{101}, p_{102}, p_{103}>> \\
a & \neq & b \\
\| & & \| \\
a & \neq & b \\
<<p_1, p_2, \ldots, p_{97}, p_{98}, p_{102}, p_{103}>> & & <<p_1, p_2, \ldots, p_{97}, p_{98}, p_{102}, p_{103}>> \\
w_3 & & w_4
\end{array}
$$

Worlds w_3 and w_4 consist of the same matter arranged in the same way, yet they are distinct worlds because w_3 includes a's being made of $p_1, p_2, \ldots, p_{97}, p_{98}, p_{102}, p_{103}$ and w_4 does not include this. (It includes b's being made of $p_1, p_2, \ldots, p_{97}, p_{98}, p_{102}$, and p_{103} instead).

Although Salmon regards this conclusion as initially paradoxical, he concludes, as I have, that distinct worlds w_3 and w_4 are acceptable. He points out that w_3 is possible relative to w_1 and that w_4 is possible relative to w_2, and he concludes that this difference in accessibility relations constitutes the distinction between these worlds. On this view, some modal system other than $S5$ or $S4$ must be the correct representation of the relative possibilities among possible worlds. (Salmon suggests that the relation is B-like).[10]

But there are two difficulties with such an approach. First, there are considerations in favor of $S5$ that should be addressed. Second, this approach does not solve the difficulty, for there is not always an appropriate difference in accessibility relations whenever two worlds are particle-for-particle alike. Thus, this does not solve the ''paradox'' of individuation.

Salmon's approach requires the existence of possible worlds that are not accessible from the actual world. Assume that the actual world is like w_1. Ship a is made from $p_1, \ldots, p_{100}$. The possibility of b's being composed of $p_1, \ldots, p_{98}, p_{102}$, and p_{103} is not accessible. If we make a ship from $p_1, \ldots, p_{98}, p_{102}$, and p_{103}, it will be a. The constitutional sufficiency principle is saved. Every possible way of making a is such that nothing else can originate in that way. World w_3 represents a way of making a, and w_4 is inaccessible.

But what should we say about the possibility of b's being made from $p_1, \ldots, p_{98}$, p_{102}, and p_{103}? Does such a possibility exist or not? If we are considering modal semantics from a superglobal perspective, it might seem that this is simply another possible world, not accessible from the world in which a is made from $p_1, \ldots, p_{100}$. But if we assume that a is some *actual* ship made from $p_1, \ldots, p_{100}$, and we recognize that we ourselves are in some possible situation, like w_1, what do we then say about the possibility of b's being made from $p_1, \ldots, p_{98}, p_{102}$, and p_{103}? It is not a possibility that exists. The notion of an inaccessible possibility (a possibility that is not possible from here) is very puzzling once we put ourselves into the picture rather than above it. Such considerations favor $S5$, because $S5$ requires no differential accessibility relations. A possibility exists or not; there are no possibilities that exist but are inaccessible. These considerations certainly do not constitute a conclusive argument against the coherence of such ideas as modal accessibility relations, but they do suggest a need for clarification before such accessibility relations can be taken as elements of a solution to a paradox.

But there is a more serious objection to Salmon's proposal. It does not seem to avoid the problem. The proposal is intended to preserve the following version of a constitutional sufficiency principle:

> Consider any ship S_n. Any way that S_n might have originated from a certain set of planks is such that no other ship could originate in that way from that set of planks.

This is intended to hold from the standpoint of any selected world. But there is no apparent reason to believe that this is true. Earlier we considered a ship-of-Theseus example that would falsify it. If S_1 is constructed at t_1 from $p_1, \ldots, p_{100}$, and S_2 is constructed on the same plan at t_2 from $p_1, \ldots, p_{100}$, it still seems that each had the following potentiality: it could have been constructed at t ($t_1 < t < t_2$) from $p_1, \ldots, p_{100}$. (We suggested that similar cases exist for organisms as well.)

The constitutional sufficiency principles in general entail an essentialist claim:

(ECO)   Consider any objects o_1, o_2, where $o_1 \neq o_2$. Any possible way that o_1 might originate (with respect to, for example, the planks that constitute it and their configuration) fulfills this condition: it is an essential property of o_2 that o_2 did not originate in that way.

That claim seems false. It is at least in need of substantial support in the case of the four-worlds paradox to which it leads. Salmon's attempt to resolve the paradox in a way that maintains (ECO) is misguided because (ECO) is itself suspect.

It should also be noted here that similar considerations apply even if origins are not taken to be the sufficiency factors. Thus, (CW) had this essentialist consquence:

(ECW)   Consider objects o_1, o_2, where $o_1 \neq o_2$. There is some set of qualitative or physical properties P such that it is an essential property of o_1 that it has some property in that set and it is an essential property of o_2 that it does not have any property in that set.

If such properties as *being identical to* o_1 are ruled out of consideration, this is nontrivial essentialism in need of defense. I see no reason to believe that it is true.

SOME ELEMENTS OF A NEW VIEW

There is a view about possibilities and possibilities for objects that accords with the denial of constitutional sufficiency principles. We will allow that two distinct possibilities can differ solely with respect to the identities of the objects existing in them. At the level of basic particles and their motions, there might be a perfect match between these possible situations (or worlds).

I want to raise questions about the relationships among possible worlds and about the relationship between possibilities for objects and physical possibilities within this framework. Such a discussion might help to make all of this more comprehensible and, thus, more acceptable.

Salmon argues against $S5$ on the basis of (ECO). Although I have questioned that argument by challenging (ECO) and have even questioned the clarity of its conclusion, I want to argue on a different basis that some such conclusion is needed. It is needed because of certain fairly clear modal and counterfactual judgments.

If ship a had been made from $p_1, \ldots, p_{98}, p_{102}$, and p_{103}, then a would have had different potentialities than it now has. In particular, if a had been made in that way, then it would have been possible for a to have been made from $p_1, \ldots, p_{97}, p_{101}, p_{102}$, and p_{103}. Of course, that is not a possibility for a, but it would have been a possibility for a if things had been different.

There are three modal claims here:

It is not possible for a to be made that way. $\sim \Diamond Ma$.

If things had been different, then it would have been
      possible (and things could have been different). $\Diamond D \ \& \ (D \ \Box\!\!\rightarrow \Diamond Ma)$.

Thus, it might have been possible for a to be made that way. $\Diamond\Diamond Ma$.

This means that $S5$ and $S4$ are inadequate, because in those systems, '$\sim\Diamond Ma$' and '$\Diamond\Diamond Ma$' are contradictories. It seems like a mistake to conclude '$\Diamond Ma$' from '$\Diamond\Diamond Ma$'; thus, the $S4$ and $S5$ accounts of modality seem wrong after all.

We are left, then, to interpret these reiterated modal operators. There seem to be two possibilities. The usual way would be to introduce a nontransitive accessibility relation, as Salmon does. There are possibilities that exist but are not accessible given this approach.

Alternatively, we might take seriously the arguments given earlier—that for something to be possible is for a certain possibility to exist. Thus, we would have to say that the possibility of a's being made from $p_1, \ldots, p_{97}, p_{101}, p_{102}$, and p_{103} does not exist, but would have existed if a had been made from $p_1, \ldots, p_{97}, p_{98}, p_{102}$, and p_{103}.

The second way has the advantage of doing away with the puzzling relationship of modal accessibility. It has the disadvantage of making it unclear how a modal semantics is to be given. So I will outline one way to consider.

We could give a semantics by directly linking the possibilities for an individual with the properties it has. For example, we could say that '$\Diamond\Diamond Fa$' is true under the following circumstances:

There is a property G such that
   (i) $\Diamond Ga$.
   (ii) If a were G, then a would have the potential to be F.
   (ii') If a were G, then the possibility of a's being F would exist.

We assume here that (ii') is a paraphrase of (ii). More generally, we would say this (where '$\Diamond_n$' stands for a sequence of n occurrences of '$\Diamond$'—e.g., $\Diamond_5 = \Diamond\Diamond\Diamond\Diamond\Diamond$):

$\ulcorner \Diamond_n A \urcorner$ is true if and only if there is some sentence B containing all of the individual constants and free variables of A such that
   (i) $\ulcorner \Diamond_{n-1} B \urcorner$ is true.
   (ii) If B were true, then $\ulcorner \Diamond A \urcorner$ would be true.
   (ii') If B were true, then the possibility of A's being true would exist.

There is an evident disadvantage here. The semantics employs subjunctive conditionals (perhaps even counterpossibles) in giving the truth-conditions. This means that our semantical metalanguage is less well understood than the standard metalanguage for modal logic. Clause (ii) is best understood as resting on a connection between situations of the type of which B is true and the possibility of A's being true. That connection should be a general fact about possibilities, not particular to the individuals referred to in A (and B).

In developing this idea, there is a metaphysical principle that we should consider. Let Fx be any sentence with no free variables other than x and with no individual constants, and let 'y' stand for some variable not occurring in Fx.

$$\exists x \Diamond_n \exists y (y = x \ \& \ Fy) \rightarrow \Diamond \exists x Fx$$

If "being F" is a "remote possibility" for some actual object, it should be "immediately possible" that something is F. Every configuration of basic particles that could be even a "remotely" possible configuration for some individual is an "immediately" possible configuration. The picture engendered here is this. There are a number of physically possible configurations of matter. Some of those constitute situations involving a, others do not. Of the situations that do not involve a, we can say the following about *some* of them: if a had been different in certain ways, a would have been involved in a situation just like that ($\Diamond Fa$). Still others are situations that a does not have the potential to be part of, but if a had been different, it would have had that potential ($\Diamond \Diamond Fa$). Perhaps there are others (situations in which hydrogen is the only matter, for example) in which a could never have had the potential to exist ($\sim \Diamond \Diamond Fa$).

If we break the link between $\Diamond$ and $\Diamond_n$ ($n \neq 1$) as applied to sentences with names or free variables, essentialist questions become even richer than they were before. Not only is there the question of which properties an individual a has essentially ($\sim \Diamond \sim Fa$), but there is also the question of which properties (if any) it has superessentially ('$\sim \Diamond_n \sim Fa$' is true for all n). (There is even the question of which properties it has 37-essentially ($\sim \Diamond_{37} \sim Fa$), plus a few others if we start to go that route.)

This might be the right set of metaphysical questions to be asking. Given the set of qualitatively possible situations, which are possible situations for Jones to be in? Which are possible for Smith? How do the essential natures of Jones and Smith produce differences in the possible situations they can appear in? If Jones had been different in a certain way, would that have changed the range of qualitative possibilities for him?

The view proposed here has an affinity with some versions of counterpart theory. There one recognizes a basic set of possibilities and imposes a set of counterpart relations producing transworld pseudoidentities. A single possibility, for example "Squrk's being F" (where Squrk is some otherworldly fellow), might represent a potentiality for both Smith and Jones, if one counterpart relation makes Squrk a counterpart of Smith and another counterpart relation makes him a counterpart of Jones. The picture we are considering would also recognize a basic set of qualitatively possible situations, in effect "multiplied" by the number of sets of individuals that have the potential to jointly fill the individual roles in those situations. But the view I suggest allows that I could have failed to finish this paper, whereas the counterpart view says only that there could have been someone a lot like me who did not finish it.[11]

Notes

1. In *Semantics of Natural Language*, edited by D. Davidson and G. Harman (Dordrecht, 1972), 350–51.

2. This version of (CO) is employed by Colin McGinn, "On The Necessity of Origin," *Journal of Philosophy* 73 (1976):127–35, for example.

3. For example, Nathan Salmon calls this "exceedingly plausible" in *Reference and Essence* (Princeton, 1981), 211. (Salmon goes on to question this, 228–29, however.)

4. Appeal to (C) but not to (CO) seems to be unusual, but such an appeal seems to be required for the argument of Robert Elliot and André Gallois, "Would It Have Been Me?," *Australasian Journal of Philosophy* 62 (1984):292–93. They assume that being made of certain elementary particles in a particular configuration is sufficient for identity.

5. For example, Harold Noonan, "The Necessity of Origin," *Mind* 92 (1983):1–20, calls the denial of (CW) "a very mysterious view indeed" (p. 3). Among the few philosophers denying (CW) are Hugh Chandler, "Rigid Designation," *The Journal of Philosophy* 72 (1975):363–69, and Nathan Salmon, *Reference and Essence*, app. I (219–52). I will argue that they do not go far enough. Arthur Prior has some interesting remarks in opposition to (CW) in "Identifiable Individuals," chapter VII of *Papers on Time and Tense* (Oxford, 1968), 66–72.

6. This is Graeme Forbes's formulation in "On the Philosophical Basis of Essentialist Theories," *Journal of Philosophical Logic* 10 (1981):73–99. He uses the term '*C*-principle' ('*C*' for 'constitutive') for the principle that modal statements are not barely [irreducibly] true or false.

7. The term 'Jules-Verne-O-Scope' is due, I believe, to David Kaplan.

8. For example, Graeme Forbes says that "if we agree that necessarily, any object made of parts could have been made of slightly different parts but not completely different parts, we contradict ourselves." From his review of Nathan Salmon's *Reference and Essence*, (*Mind* 93 [1984]:305–6). See also William Randolph Carter, "Salmon on Artifact Origins and Lost Possibilities," *Philosophical Review* 92 (1983):223–31.

9. Nathan Salmon, *Reference and Essence*, 231.

10. This approach was first suggested by Hugh Chandler, "Rigid Designation."

11. The writing of this paper has been supported by a grant from the Syracuse University Senate Research Committee. I thank Jonathan Bennett and Mark Heller for their useful comments on a draft.

Essential Properties and Philosophical Analysis

DIANA F. ACKERMAN

Why have contemporary philosophical discussions of essential properties focused on essential properties of *contingently* existing objects? Two explanations suggest themselves. First, it may seem that once a distinction is admitted between accidental and essential properties at all, the philosophically problematic cases of deciding which properties fall into each of these categories will arise mainly for properties of contingently existing objects. But this view would be mistaken. Many traditional philosophical problems can be rephrased as problems about specifying the essential properties of necessary entities. For example, the question of whether proposition *p* is logically necessary can be rephrased as the question of whether truth is an essential property of *p*.[1] The question of whether *p* is indubitable for person *J* can be phrased as the question of whether not being doubted by *J* is an essential property of *p*. And questions about philosophical analyses of the sort that concern me in this paper can be phrased as questions that are partly about the essential properties of certain concepts.[2]

Of course, as their more traditional formulations illustrate, the foregoing questions can also be phrased in terms making no explicit reference to issues about essential properties. This fact may seem to offer a second possible answer to this paper's opening question. But if Kripke[3] and others are right that proper names are rigid designators, even such questions as whether Socrates is essentially human can be phrased in such ostensibly nonessentialist terms as , "Is it logically possible that it is true that Socrates is nonhuman?"

Now consider the following proposition.

(1) To be an instance of knowledge is to be an instance of justified true belief not essentially grounded in any falsehood.

Proposition (1), if true, exemplifies an important type of philosophical analysis—the type I will consider in this paper. (For purposes of illustration, I will assume (1) is true, but nothing in my views will hinge upon this.) If (1) gives a philosophical analysis of the sort in question, (1) is a necessary truth, and thus it is an essential property of knowledge that it is exemplified by all and only cases of justified true belief not essentially grounded in any falsehood. (Of course, I am taking 'knowledge' here as a rigid designator of the property of knowledge.) But to suppose that such propositions give analyses leads to a notorious problem often called "the" paradox of analysis,[4] as follows. If the property of justified true belief not essentially grounded in any falsehood is the *analysans* of the property of knowledge, then it would seem that they would have to be the same property, in which case

(2)   To be an instance of knowledge is to be an instance of knowledge

would be the same proposition as (1). But (1) and (2) do not seem to be the same proposition; for example, (2) is trivial (i.e., understanding it entails believing it), and (1) can be informative.

Different types of solutions have been proposed to this problem. In this paper I am concerned with one type, the type holding that *analysans* and *analysandum* in an analysis giving rise to this sort of paradox are concepts or properties, rather than linguistic entities, and holding that they are different concepts. (I am using the terms 'concept' and 'property' interchangeably in this paper.) There are some important advantages to this type of solution. It resolves the paradox; it also allows us to hold that analysis is entirely about properties, not about expressions,[5] and, at least in the present case, it is intuitively satisfying, since the concepts at issue appear on the face of it to be cognitively quite different: one is relatively easy to understand, one relatively hard and complicated; one is thought about by many people, the other by relatively few, perhaps only by professional philosophers and their students; and so on. But this type of solution also raises problems. Perhaps the most obvious and immediate is as follows: if knowledge and justified true belief not essentially grounded in any falsehood are actually distinct properties, how can they be closely enough related to count as *analysans* and *analysandum*? If the relation between *analysans* and *analysandum* is not one of identity, what is it? Precisely what does this sort of analysis do? I say 'this sort of analysis' because the term 'analysis' has a long and diverse philosophical history. Not all its uses seem to be referring to the same thing. In this paper, I am concerned only with the sort exemplified by the paradox of (1) and (2), and my use of the term 'analysis' should be taken as restricted in this way.

I will start by discussing a recent solution that is suggested by the work of Kendall Walton.[6] This solution, like the proposal of my own I will present afterward, holds that the relevant relation between *analysans* and *analysandum* is importantly a cognitive one. But I will argue that Walton's solution fails to give a correct account of what this cognitive relation is. Conceptual and linguistic relativity, rather than the nature of philosophical analysis, are Walton's main concerns in his writings that I will consider. But his ideas have clear applications to the notion of analysis, and he does make some such applications.

Walton is interested in the fact that it is possible for a person J to identify entity x as having property Q based on x's features $f_1, f_2, f_3, \ldots$, and so on, even when J is not inferring (or, as some would rather put it, even when J is not explicitly and consciously inferring) that x has Q from the fact that x has $f_1, f_2, f_3, \ldots$, and so on, and even when J might not recognize this as a correct rule of inference were it presented to him. For example, suppose that J visually identifies a bird as a swallow based on its beak, wing configuration, and so on, but that there is a sense in which he does not really "take note" of these features. He identifies the bird as a swallow just by looking and cannot readily say (or recognize as true) that the features in question are what provide the basis for his identification. He cannot explain *how* to identify a bird as a swallow. In this sort of case, Walton would say J is using a *non-rule-applying test* for determining the bird is a swallow. As Walton points out, this case is similar to the common situation of recognizing one's friends just by looking rather than by "noting their facial and bodily characteristics and applying a rule of inference, even though it is these characteristics which make it possible for us to recognize them."[7] Walton also gives the example of identifying an activity as a game based on a description of its features, even though one would be hard put to come up with an account of the property of being a game based on these features that could serve as a justification for such identifications.

It is not difficult to draw upon Walton's explicit account of the notion of a difference in conceptual schemes to come up with a related account of analysis. (Although Walton says much that supports this analysis of analysis, he does not explicitly propose it, so it is probably best to think of it as suggested by his work rather than as something he is committed to or would be sure to accept.) This analysis of analysis requires one preliminary definition that Walton puts as follows: "a property of an object is *apparent* to a person if and only if either (i) the person is in a position to observe that the object has that property (as we are in a position to observe the features of a bird when we tell just by looking that it is a swallow), or (ii) he knows the object has that property."[8] Then $(P_1$ and P_2 and P_3 and $\ldots P_n)$ (or $(P_1$ or P_2 or P_3 or $\ldots P_n))$ is an *analysans* of the appropriate sort of J's concept of Q if and only if all of the following conditions are satisfied:

(a) Q is extensionally equivalent to $(P_1$ and P_2 and P_3 and $\ldots P_n)$ (or to $(P_1$ or P_2 or P_3 or $\ldots P_n))$ where each of $P_1, P_2, P_3, \ldots, P_n$ is logically independent of each other.

(b) J's ability to apply a predicate expressing Q without using rules (in the sense I have described) is dependent in each particular case on some (if the *analysans* is disjunctive) or all (if the *analysans* is conjunctive) of $P_1, P_2, P_3, \ldots, P_n$ being apparent to him.

(c) Whether or not J is willing to apply Q in a particular case when his state of mind, sense organs, and nervous system are normal is a function solely of which of $P_1, P_2, P_3, \ldots, P_n$ and non-P_1, non-P_2, non-P_3, $\ldots$, non-P_n are apparent to him.

(d) J gives priority to non-rule-applying tests of whether something has Q; i.e., even if he believes that something has Q if and only if it has $(P_1$ and P_2 and P_3 and $\ldots P_n)$ (or if and only if it has $(P_1$ or P_2 or P_3 or $\ldots P_n))$, if he were to discover an apparent exception to this biconditional, he would decide whether the exception had Q by whether it just struck him as Q rather than by whether it had $(P_1$ and P_2 and P_3 and $\ldots P_n)$ (or by whether it had $(P_1$ or P_2 or P_3 or $\ldots P_n))$.

This account has several features I consider both correct and important. It analyzes analysis in terms of a cognitive relation between diverse properties. It represents the *analysans* as, in some sense, conceptually richer and less simple than the *analysandum*. It also has the virtue of giving a role to the relation between the properties that are constituents of the *analysans* in Russell's sense of the term 'constituent' and the way *J* determines that something has *Q*.

Yet I think there are two important problems with Walton's sort of views. For one thing, Walton says.

> In attributing mental states, personality traits, motives, etc. to other people, their behavior (verbal and nonverbal) and physical circumstances serve as our data. But we virtually never consult rules in doing so, and non-rule-applying tests clearly have priority. The data may be either unnoticed cues (e.g., subtle details of gestures and facial expressions) or facts we are aware of (e.g., the fact that Jones walked out of a meeting), or both. It is evident also that any of an immense variety of different combinations of behavioral/circumstantial data may lead us to attribute a single psychological property to a person. The behavior and circumstances of angry people in different instances are diverse in the extreme. Thus, being angry is perhaps a simple property for us, which is based on the property disjunctive for us, of having one among a large (perhaps infinite) number of combinations of behavioral/circumstantial features (and/or dispositions thereto). This suggests what is wrong, and what right, about behaviorist analyses of psychological properties. Psychological predicates are not just behavioral/circumstantial predicates in disguise. People who recognize only behavior and circumstances would not see a respect in which the many and various cases of anger are alike; instances of anger would constitute an arbitrary class for them. (We might plausibly say that they do not have the concept of anger.) But on the other hand, there is nothing to look for *behind* the behavior and circumstances; seeing what angry persons have in common is just seeing their behavior and circumstances in a certain way. The anger of another person is not some mysterious transcendent property which for some peculiar metaphysical reason we cannot observe "directly," but only via the (questionable) mediation of behavior and circumstances. His behavior and circumstances (including dispositions) might reasonably be said to *constitute* his being angry, through the mediation of our conceptual scheme.[9]

But this seems wrong. It raises obvious problems about how the concept of being angry (in the sense of occurrent, conscious anger) can be the same in first-person and third-person cases. It raises similar problems about how the skeptic's concept of anger can be the same as the nonskeptic's, as it certainly seems to be, since skeptical arguments are intelligible to the unconvinced, and such arguments get whatever initial plausibility they may have precisely by drawing upon our ordinary concepts. And if someone's behavior and circumstances really "constitute" his being angry, what constitutes the anger of someone who is angry in circumstances no one else would be inclined to recognize as anger-producing, and who conceals his anger and would continue to do so no matter what because concealment is his top priority and he is an excellent actor? Moreover, consider the opposite sort of case: that of an excellent actor who is not angry but who feigns anger in circumstances everyone else is inclined to identify as anger-producing and who gives highest priority to keeping up *his* pretense no matter what. How can his behavior and circumstances constitute his anger when he is not even angry?

This objection is relatively superficial because it can be attributed to a misapplication of the account—specifically to Walton's conflation of the property of being angry and the property of appearing angry. My second objection, I think, is deeper. It is simply that on the present account, knowledge and justified true belief not essentially grounded in any falsehood do not turn out to be related as *analysandum* and *analysans*. This is shown by the fact that condition (c) does not apply, as follows. Suppose *J* has a situation described to him simply as a case of justified true belief not essentially grounded in any falsehood and is asked whether he considers this a case of knowledge. By condition (c), his answer should be affirmative, given that his mind, sense organs, and nervous system are normal; but, of course, this cannot be assumed to be the case. For example, someone who wrongly suspects that a proposed *analysans* is too broad may attrribute the *analysans* to something without attributing the *analysandum* to it. Whether this proposed *analysans* actually is too broad is not something that will be clear to everyone who understands the *analysans*. The proposition that whatever is a case of justified true belief not essentially grounded in any falsehood is a case of knowledge is not invariably recognizable as true. Instead, its truth must be *tested* by seeing if anyone can come up with any counterexamples. Thus, I think that although Walton's account is right in holding that there must be some special epistemic relation between the *analysans* and the *analysandum,* he does not seem to have succeeded in specifying it.

What direction might an improved account take? I think it is clear that an adequate account of the *analysans-analysandum* relation exemplified by the property of knowledge and the property of justified truc belief not essentially grounded in any falsehood must include the condition that *analysans* and *analysandum* are necessarily coestensive, or, to put the matter in essentialist terms, that the *analysandum* has the essential property of applying when and only when the *analysans* does. Moreover (since some philosophers deny that necessity and *a prioricity* are necessarily coextensive),[10] I should add that *analysans* and *analysandum* must be knowable *a priori* to be coextensive. But, by themselves, these conditions are not adequate. For example, they do not make analysis asymmetrical, they allow circularity (the most obvious and glaring sort of illustration here would come from taking, e.g., knowledge as both *analysans* and *analysandum*), and they apply to many pairs of concepts that do not seem closely enough related epistemically to count as *analysans* and *analysandum,* such as the concept of being 6 and the concept of being the fourth root of 1296.

What is the missing condition? I think the intuitive idea here is something along these lines: analysis is supposed to get at the properties one in some sense "goes by" or "has in the back of one's mind" in applying a concept. This is, in effect, recognized by the Walton-inspired account. But the problem, of course, is to say in just what sense one "goes by" or "has in the back of one's mind" these properties, since in applying the *analysandum,* one need not be thinking about the *analysans,* nor need one even be able to recognize as correct a statement to the effect that it applies to all and only the cases that fit the *analysandum.* Some philosophers would say one *is* thinking of the *analysans,* not consciously, but "implicitly" or "unconsciously." But the problem of specifying the appropriate sense in which implicitly or unconsciously one thinks of the *analysans,* but not of all the properties that are necessarily and *a priori* knowable to be coextensive with it, is simply a reformulation of the question at issue.

I think that a promising approach to the missing condition is to investigate what actually seems epistemically distinctive about analyses of the sort under consideration—a certain way in which they can be justified. This can be done by the philosophical example and counterexample method, which, in general terms, goes as follows. *J* investigates the analysis of *K*'s concept of *Q* (where *K* can, but need not, be identical to *J*) by setting *K* a series of armchair thought experiments, presenting *K* with a series of simple described hypothetical test cases and asking *K* questions of the form "If such and such were the case, would this count as a case of *Q*?" *J* then contrasts the descriptions of the cases where *K* answers affirmatively with the descriptions of the cases where *K* does not, and *J* generalizes upon these descriptions to arrive at the properties (not including the *analysandum*) and their mode of combination that constitute the *analysans* of *K*'s concept of *Q*. *K* answers the questions based solely on whether the described hypothetical cases just strike him as having *Q*. *J* observes certain strictures in formulating the cases and questions. He makes the cases as simple as possible, to minimize the possibility of confusion, and also to minimize the likelihood that *K* will draw upon his philosophical theories (or quasi-philosophical, rudimentary notions if he is unsophisticated philosophically) in answering the questions. For this reason, if two hypothetical test cases yield conflicting results, the conflict should *ceteris paribus* be resolved in favor of the simpler case. *J* makes the series of described cases wide-ranging and varied, with the aim of having it be a *complete* series, while I say a series is complete if and only if no case that is omitted is such that, if included, it would change the analysis arrived at. *J* does not, of course, use as a test case description anything complicated and general to be the *analysans.* There is no requirement that the described hypothetical test cases be formulated only in terms of what can be observed. Moreover, the use of described hypothetical situations as test cases enables *J* to frame the questions in such a way as to rule out extraneous background assumptions to a degree. Thus, even if *K* correctly believes that all and only *P*s are *R*s, the question of whether *P, R,* or both enter the analysis of his concept of *Q* can be investigated by asking him such questions as "Suppose (even if it seems preposterous to you) that you were to find out that there was a *P* that was not an *R,* would you still consider it a *Q*?"

Taking all this into account, I suggest the following as a promising approach to specifying the missing condition. If *P* is the *analysans* of Q, the proposition that necessarily all and only what is *P* is *Q* can be justified by generalizing from intuitions about the correct answers to questions of the sort I have described about a varied and wide-ranging series of simple described hypothetical situations. (Of course, I mean by the term 'intuition' not the result of any special mysterious faculty, but merely one's beliefs about whether certain described situations "just seem to be" or "just strike one as" cases of Q.) Actually, this would be only part of the missing condition; for example, there would be additional strictures to guarantee such things as noncircularity, the absence of superfluous additions, the greater complexity of the *analysans* than the *analysandum*, and so on. I am glossing over these and some other details because what really interests me here are some epistemic problems this whole sort of approach faces, and what these problems show about the epistemology of the sort of analysis under consideration.

The attraction of this approach comes largely from the fact that it does seem that analyses can be justified in the way indicated, as opposed to mathematical equivalences like the proposition that 6 is the fourth root of 1296, which cannot. Moreover, this account, like Walton's, gives a role to the properties actually used in determining whether a described hypothetical case fits the *analysandum*, and, unlike Walton's, it does not require that the properties that are constituents of the *analysans* also be the ones mentioned in the test descriptions. Thus, this account seems true to the intuitive idea I have mentioned that analysis, in some sense, captures what "goes by" or what is "in the back of one's mind."

But it might be objected that this account does not really tell us what this sense is either. This is because of the weight it puts on an unexplained notion of generalization. Given that the properties constitutive of the *analysans* will not be those mentioned in the test descriptions, exactly what is the process that is supposed to take us from one set of properties to the other? My intuitive idea was somewhat as follows. J contrasts the test descriptions that K identifies as cases of the *analysandum* with those he does not, and J generalizes to find the combination of properties (not including the *analysandum*) that fit the cases K identifies positively, but not the cases he does not. These are supposed to be the properties K is in some sense "going by" in applying the analysans, and the sense in which he is "going by" them is supposed to be given by the fact that they are the result of the generalization procedure. But the problem is that whatever properties *a priori* imply property Q will also *a priori* imply any property *a priori* knowable to be necessarily coextensive with Q, and the whole point of specifying the missing condition was to get beyond necessary and *a priori* coextensiveness. It might be tempting here to say that the generalization should be made to the general properties that are "epistemically closest" in some sense to those properties that figure in the positively identified test cases. But the problem of specifying in what sense these properties are epistemically closest is precisely the point of issue.

A related problem concerns people with extraordinary mathematical or philosophical abilities who can grasp in a flash relations normal people must figure out. Such people may have different results on the test I have suggested for an *analysans*, yet it is not at all obvious they would have different concepts. (One possibility here might be to make analysis a three-place relation between two properties and a person.)

Another possible approach that may seem tempting comes from considering the relation between generalizations and particular cases. The following contrast may seem to hold. In analysis, the inference is from the particular to the general; for example, the proposition that knowledge is justified true belief not essentially grounded in any falsehood is justified by the fact that it seems to fit the cases we have come up with so far. But a mathematical generalization such as the proposition that every prime number is smaller than some other prime is what justifies particular cases, rather than what is justified by them.

However, this distinction will not hold up. Some unproven mathematical propositions, such as the Goldbach conjecture, are in fact justified by cases to the extent that we currently have justification for them at all. Moreover, Carl Posy has confirmed in discussion that it is an open question in philosophy of mathematics whether every true mathematical generalization will be provable by some mathematically acceptable means.

Where do we go from here? Faced with the difficulty of giving an adequate analysis of analysis, some philosophers have argued in favor of abandoning the notion altogether. Anything that can be done with the notion of analysis, they claim, can also be done with necessary, *a priori* equivalences. Other reasons the notion of analysis has fallen into some disfavor include the fact that it is virtually impossible to produce an interesting and generally accepted example of a true one, and, of course, many philosophers nowadays also reject the whole apparatus of necessary truth and *a priori*-knowledge that underlies the notion of analysis.

I think these objections are at least questionable. I cannot undertake anything as large as a defense of necessity and *a prioricity* here, but I will say something about the other objections. First, analyses are what many philosophers traditionally have tried to produce, and it is worth trying to get as precise a view as possible of just what these philosophers have been trying to do. The Gricean account of meaning, the account of knowledge I have considered, and the causal theory of perception are all fairly recent attempts at the sort of analysis, the confirmation of which seems to hinge in a way not yet fully specified on the results of intuitions about simple described hypothetical test cases. The process of trying to establish biconditionals of this sort of analysis is one fundamental philosophical process, and although I am not claiming that all philosophy fits this model, specifying it fully would help epistemically distinguish a substantial portion of philosophical inquiry from other *a priori* disciplines, such as mathematics. This is true even if, as is generally the case, we cannot give full analyses and have to settle for less, such as one-way conditionals, partially circular accounts (e.g., knowledge is justified true belief supported by a chain of *known* reasons that do not essentially involve a falsehood), and accounts like that of being a game that are justified in the same general way as analyses but that are too open-ended even to purport to yield necessary and sufficient conditions. And there does seem to be a sense in which being justified true belief not essentially grounded in any falsehood is intimately connected epistemically with being knowledge, and being 6 is not so intimately connected epistemically with being the fourth root of 1296, although it may be that the cases are just at different points along a continuum.[11]

Notes

1. See Alvin Plantinga, *The Nature of Necessity* (Oxford, 1974), 28.

2. The original questions may seem different from these reformulations in that the latter involve ontological commitment to properties. But this does not raise a problem for my treatment of philosophical anal-

ysis, since I share Moore's view that philosophical analysis is the analysis of (and, thus, involves ontological commitment to) properties in any case. See G. E. Moore, "A Reply to My Critics: Analysis," in *Readings in Twentieth Century Philosophy,* edited by W. Alston and G. Nakhnikian (London, 1963).

3. See S. A. Kripke, *Naming and Necessity* (Cambridge, Mass., 1980).

4. Calling this problem "the" paradox of analysis is actually a misnomer, as I demonstrate elsewhere by distinguishing two independent paradoxes of analysis. See my "Two Paradoxes of Analysis" (abstract), *Journal of Philosophy* 78 (1981):733–35, and "Analysis and Its Paradoxes," in *Proceedings of the 1985 Israel Colloquium for the History, Philosophy, and Sociology of Science,* forthcoming.

5. See G. E. Moore, "A Reply to My Critics: Analysis," for some difficulties with supposing analysis is about expressions.

6. See Walton's "Linguistic Relativity," in *Conceptual Change,* edited by Glenn Pearce and Patrick Maynard (Dordrecht, 1972) 1–29, and *Conceptual Schemes: A Study in Linguistic Relativity and Related Philosophical Problems* (Ann Arbor, Mich., 1967).

7. Walton, "Linguistic Relativity," 10.

8. Ibid., 21–22.

9. Ibid., 26–27.

10. See Kripke, *Naming and Necessity.*

11. Forerunners of this paper were read at several meetings and colloquia. I am indebted to many people, especially Alvin Plantinga, Carl Posy, Philip Quinn, Ernest Sosa, and James Van Cleve, for valuable discussion of the issues, and to Kendall Walton for valuable correspondence.

Time and Thisness

ROBERT MERRIHEW ADAMS

I have argued elsewhere that there are facts, and possibilities, that are not purely qualitative.[1] In a second paper, however, I have argued that all possibilities are purely qualitative except insofar as they involve individuals that actually exist. In particular, I have argued that there are no thisnesses of nonactual individuals (where the thisness of x is the property of being x, or of being identical with x), and that there are no singular propositions about nonactual individuals (where a singular proposition about an individual x is a proposition that involves or refers to x directly, perhaps by having x or the thisness of x as a constituent, and not merely by way of x's qualitative properties or relations to other individuals).[2] I am also inclined to believe that there are not yet any thisnesses of individuals that will exist but do not yet, nor any singular propositions about future individuals—and, hence, that all possibilities are purely qualitative except insofar as they involve individuals that already do exist or have existed (counting timeless individuals, if any, as already existing). This thesis about the relation of time to thisness is the subject of the present paper, in which the conclusions of my previous papers will be presupposed.

I. SOME ARGUMENTS FOR THE THESIS

A similar view has been maintained by Arthur Prior. "Julius Caesar," he said, "a certain now-identifiable individual, did at a certain time begin to exist. But before that time, the possible outcomes of what was going on did not include the starting-to-exist of *this* individual." What they did include was "the possibility that there should be *an* individual born to these parents" who would have the qualitative properties that Caesar actually had. We may begin by considering an argument Prior offers for this view:

> Suppose there is some person living before the existence of Caesar or Antony who prophesies that there will begin to be a person who will be called "Caesar," who will be murdered, etc., and another person who will be called "Antony," who will dally with Cleopatra, etc. And then suppose this prophet to say, "No,

I'm not sure now that it *will* be like that—perhaps it is the *second* of the people I mentioned who will be called 'Caesar' and will be murdered, etc., and the first who will be born later and be called 'Antony', etc.'' This, it seems to me, really would be a spurious switch; and after Caesar and Antony had actually come into being and acted and suffered as prophesied, it would be quite senseless to ask ''Are these, I wonder, really the two people he meant?'' and if possible more senseless still to ask, ''Is it—if either of them—our man's first prophecy, or his suggested alternative, that has now come to pass?''[3]

I think that virtually everyone will feel the intuitive appeal of Prior's contention that these questions are senseless; but the force of the argument needs to be explained.

Prior's explanation of why the questions are absurd, I take it, is that the prophet cannot have made his predictions about either the right or the wrong individuals because he cannot have predicted either that Caesar would be called ''Caesar'' and be murdered or that Antony would be called ''Caesar'' and be murdered. He cannot have predicted either of these things because to predict them would have been to assert certain singular propositions about Caesar and Antony, and those propositions did not yet exist and, therefore, were not available to be asserted by him at the time of the supposed prophecy. Here we can distinguish two claims:

(1) The prophet could not yet assert any singular proposition about Caesar or Antony.

(2) No singular proposition about Caesar or Antony existed yet.

It is (1) that provides an explanation of the absurdity of the question mentioned by Prior; and that fact will count as evidence for (1), unless a better explanation can be found. I think that Prior's implicit argument is that (1) is explained in turn by (2), and, therefore, the example is evidence for (2) as well as (1).

This is not a very powerful argument for (2). If the prophet was unable to assert any singular propositions about Caesar or Antony, the nonexistence of such propositions would surely not be the only plausible explanation of the fact. There already were such propositions, it might be said, but the prophet was cut off from them because no causal chain could have run from the then future individuals to his thoughts and utterances at that earlier time; Prior's argument has no force against this hypothesis.

Other issues could be raised about the argument. Is (1) true? Or, more generally, are singular propositions about future individuals *available* to us to be asserted, believed, or known now? Does (2) provide an explanation of (1)? Or, conversely, if we can now assert or believe singular propositions about future individuals, does it follow that those propositions already exist? These questions are of interest in their own right, and we will return to them in section IV; but our first order of business is to look at another, and I think better, argument for the thesis that thisnesses of future individuals, and singular propositions about them, do not yet exist.

I was born in 1937. Among the many metaphysically possible continuations of the actual history of the world up until, say, 1935, there are surely some in which I would never have existed. It is plausible to conclude that I could have failed to exist even given everything that existed in 1935, or that had existed before then, or that exists timelessly—and, conversely, that all of those things could have existed even if I had never existed. But, as I have argued, neither my thisness nor any singular proposition about me exists in any metaphysically possible world in which I never exist; they are not among the things that could have existed even if I had never existed. It follows that they are not among the things that existed in 1935, or before, or that exist timelessly. My thisness, and singular propositions about me, cannot have preexisted me because if they had, it would have been possible for them to have existed even if I had never existed, and that is not possible.

I find this argument persuasive, but I do not want to exaggerate its force. It employs the principle,

(3) For any beings x and y and time t, if x existed before t or exists timelessly, and y exists contingently and comes into existence at t, then it would be metaphysically possible for x to have existed even if y had never existed.

This principle is plausible. It is natural to think, for example, that it is quite open and undecided what people will come into existence in the future, even given everything that has existed up to now, and everything that exists timelessly; but this principle is not uncontroversial, and there are points at which we may want to raise questions about it.

In 1935, there existed millions of people who were born before I was, but that would not have been true if I had never existed. It may, therefore, be objected against (3) that in 1935, there existed something that could not, logically, have existed if I had not later come into existence—namely, a person that was born before I was. The correct reply to this objection is that a person that was born before I was is not, in the relevant sense, something that could not have existed if I never did. Such a person (Montgomery Furth, for example) could perfectly well have existed without my coming along afterward—although in that case, of course, he could not have had the property of being born before I was. What is true in the objection is that the existential generalization "There existed in 1935 a person that was born before I was" is, in fact, true but that it could not have been true (indeed, could not even have existed) if I had never existed. But principle (3) is not concerned with such generalizations. It is concerned, rather, with possibilities *de re* about the existence of beings that instantiate such generalizations in some possible worlds and not in others.

An inventive objector will not be stopped by this reply. It may be suggested, for example, that *Furth's living before Adams was born* is something that did exist in 1935 but that could not have existed if I never had. Some may doubt, of course, whether this is something that is properly said to "exist" at all. But rather than getting into a debate about the criterion for admitting types of entities to the category of "existents," let us allow that *Furth's living in 1935* did exist in 1935. That concession does not undermine principle (3), for Furth's living in 1935 could have existed even if I had not come along later. And, perhaps, *Furth's living* (in 1935) *before I was born* is nothing more nor less than Furth's living in 1935, characterized in terms of a relation that it, in fact, has but that it could have lacked. If Furth's living (in 1935) before I was born is something more than that, a distinct existent, I am inclined to view it as constructed from Furth's living in 1935 and my birth in 1937, and to say that it did not exist before I did. An issue arises here, of the time at which transtemporal relations exist, about which I will have more to say in the next section.

I have mentioned timeless existence in (3) because thisnesses and singular propositions might be classified as abstract objects, and many philosophers think that abstract objects exist timelessly rather than at any time. It may be controversial to apply a principle such as (3) to timeless entities. But it seems to me very odd to classify as timeless a being that, though it may be immune to certain kinds of change, depends metaphysically for its existence on something that occurs at a certain time, so that it has to wait until that time, so to speak, to be assured of existence. Suppose you are considering whether to have children; in such a case, you assume that your future children may never exist, in a sense in which it is no longer true that you may never exist. If you agree with me about the metaphysical dependence of thisnesses on individuals, you will also assume that the thisnesses of your future children may never exist, in a sense in which it is no longer true that your thisness may never exist. Would it not be odd to classify as timeless something of which it is first true and later false that it may never exist?

This depends, no doubt, on the sense of 'may'. The sense in which your future children and their thisnesses may never exist is not just that there are possible worlds in which they do not. For it is still true that there are possible worlds in which you and your thisness do not exist, whereas it is not still true, in the relevant sense, that you and your thisness *may* never exist. Those who are most strongly inclined to reject (3), and to hold that thisnesses and singular propositions exist timelessly, may think that the relevant sense of 'may' here cannot be anything but epistemic. *For all you know,* your future children and their thisnesses may never exist, but you know that you and your thisness do exist. I think, however, that there is more to it—that when we say that your future children and their thisnesses may never exist, we (or at any rate I) mean that it is not merely unknown, but metaphysically open and unsettled, whether they will exist. The merely epistemic difference would hardly keep us from thinking of thisnesses as existing timelessly, but something that is first open and later settled, metaphysically, does not seem timeless.

It emerges quite clearly here that my position, like Prior's, rests on an intuition that the future, or an important part of it, is metaphysically open in a way that the present and the past are not. This is a widely shared, but controversial, intuition. Principle (3) can be seen as a partial specification of the way in which the future is to be thought of as metaphysically open. I suspect, myself, that it is too strong a specification. Maybe there are stronger bonds of metaphysical necessity between earlier and later things than it allows. Perhaps, indeed, there must be, if causal determination of later events by earlier events is to be understood. The thesis I am defending, however, is one that appeals mainly to indeterminists, who think that many events, presumably including the coming into existence of most persons, are not causally determined by earlier events. For such events, we want to exclude the sort of bonds of metaphysical necessity that (3) excludes. And to individuals coming into being in such events, the argument based on (3), that their thisnesses do not exist until they do, may be seen as applying.[4]

II. THISNESSES OF PAST INDIVIDUALS

The question naturally arises, whether the same things I am saying about future things that do not yet exist should not also be said about past things that no longer exist. I think not; there is a better case for thisnesses of past than of future individuals.

Perhaps an objector will offer me the mirror image of the argument that I find persuasive against thisnesses of future individuals. Any example we choose of an individual that exists no longer may be subject to doubts—that it is really immortal, or that it was not really an individual. I choose an example that I believe was an individual that no longer exists: the first pain that I felt on the one occasion when I was stung by a wasp. Let *i* be that pain (or anything *you* believe was an individual that no longer exists). Now the objector will say, ''Surely everything that now exists could still have existed—numerically, and not just qualitatively, the same—even if the history of the world before now had been very different—in particular, even if *i* had never existed. So if the thisness of *i* is among the things that exist now, it could have existed even if *i* had never existed. Since you deny the latter, you should also deny the former.'' This argument does not persuade me, because I do not believe that the same things could, logically and metaphysically, have existed now no matter what had existed earlier. There is a temporal asymmetry in our modal intuitions here. It is very plausible to say that the existence and identity of anything that exists now cannot depend logically or metaphysically on anything occurring later, but much less plausible to say that it cannot depend on what occurred earlier. Indeed, theses making the identity of individuals depend logically or metaphysically on various facts about their origins or antecedents have great intuitive appeal to many of us. Hence, I have no strong objection to saying that the thisness of *i* exists now without *i* existing now, but that if *i* had not existed earlier, that would have been impossible.

Whatever may be the case regarding future individuals, it seems that thisnesses of past individuals, and more particularly singular propositions about them, are still *available* to us as objects of propositional attitudes. We think that we can entertain, assert, and believe singular propositions about individuals that no longer exist. The possibility of our asserting and believing singular propositions about George Washington and Abraham Lincoln, for example, is not thought to depend in any way on the truth of immortality.

It is tempting to argue from the present availability of thisnesses of past individuals and singular propositions about them to their present *existence*. If we can entertain, assert, and believe singular propositions about individuals that no longer exist, must not these propositions exist? But I think we must be as cautious about this argument from present availability to present existence as we were about Prior's implicit inference from present *un*availability to present *non*existence. For there certainly are relations that can obtain between things that exist or occur only at different times. For example, a brush fire in September may *cause* a mud slide the following January. Perhaps entertaining, asserting, and believing are relations that can obtain between thoughts or utterances occurring at one time and propositions that exist only at earlier times.

There is a difficulty in this hypothesis of continued availability without continued existence, however. Suppose I am sitting in the dentist's chair, i' is a particular pain I felt five minutes ago, and i'' is a particular pain I am feeling now. Surely I can entertain, and indeed believe, the singular proposition about i' and i'', that i'' is more intense than i'. But when does this proposition exist? If singular propositions can exist after individuals they are about have ceased to exist, then this proposition can exist as soon as i'' begins to exist, although i' no longer exists then. But if singular propositions about an individual exist only when that individual exists, the proposition that i'' is more intense than i' cannot exist at any time, since there is no time at which both i' and i'' exist.

To be sure, this difficulty is analogous to difficulties we cannot escape in any event. If a brush fire in September causes a mud slide in January, when does the causal relation between them exist? If a relation cannot exist at a time when one of the terms it relates does not exist, then this causal relation cannot exist at any time. Perhaps it is a mistake to think of transtemporal relations as existing *at* a time at all; perhaps they do not need a time to exist at. On the other hand, they seem poor candidates for timelessness, since they depend for their existence on things that occur only at certain times, and they must therefore wait until those times to be assured of existence, as I have put it.[5] Maybe they exist—whole in the whole, but not whole in the part—in an extended period of time; on this view, the causal relation between the brush fire and the mud slide would exist in the period from September to January, but not *at* any instant or *on* any day during the period. Similarly, we could say that singular propositions about individuals that exist only at disjoint times exist in an extended period, but not at any instant within the period. It would be simpler, however, to just allow that singular propositions continue to exist after individuals they are about have ceased to exist.

The one compelling reason for denying that thisnesses of past individuals, and singular propositions about them, still exist would be the belief that the thisnesses and the singular propositions have the individuals themselves as essential constituents. One hesitates to hold it as a universal law that an entity cannot occur at a time when one of its essential constituents does not exist; a performance of a symphony is occurring while the second movement is being performed, even though other essential parts of the performance are not occurring at that time. But we would not expect thisnesses and singular propositions to be related to time in the same way as musical performances. If individuals are constituents of their thisnesses, then presumably there exist thisnesses neither of past nor of future individuals. In that case, the difference between thisnesses of past and of future individuals is not in their existence, but, at most, in their availability. If thisnesses do not have the individuals themselves as constituents, however, I see no convincing argument for denying that thisnesses of past individuals still exist, and some advantage in holding that they do.

III. EXISTING AT A TIME

This is a natural point at which to pause for an examination of one of the central concepts of the present discussion, the concept of existing *at* a particular time. My previous essays in actualism have produced no divergence from Quine's dictum ''To be is to be a value of a bound variable.'' $\ulcorner(\exists y)(y = x)\urcorner$ is equivalent to the one-place propositional function $\ulcorner x$ exists $\urcorner$. For actualism, the two-place propositional function $\ulcorner x$ exists in $w\urcorner$, where w is a possible world, is not primitive but is understood as meaning that $\ulcorner(\exists y)(y = x)\urcorner$, or $\ulcorner x$ exists $\urcorner$, is included in the world-story[6] of w, or that x would have existed if w had been actual. (Here 'would have existed' is a form of the ordinary one-place predicate 'exists'.) But $\ulcorner x$ exists at $t\urcorner$, where t is a time, is a two-place propositional function for which actualism, as I understand it, provides no such reduction.

A reduction is offered by a view that is sometimes called ''presentism'' by analogy with ''actualism.'' As the actualist holds that there are no merely possible things, but only things that actually exist, so the presentist holds that there are no merely past or future things, but only things that exist now. For presentism, 'exists' in its sole primitive sense is a one-place predicate equivalent to 'actually exists now', and the presentist's primitive quantifiers range only over things that actually exist now. And as the actualist may say that there are, in the actual world, primitive facts of the form $\ulcorner$It could have been the case that $p\urcorner$, even though there are no nonactual things that could have existed, so the presentist may say that there are, now, primitive facts of the form $\ulcorner(n$ years ago) it was the case that $p\urcorner$ and/or $\ulcorner(n$ years from now) it will be the case that $p\urcorner$, even though there are no nonpresent things that did or will exist. On this view, $\ulcorner x$ existed in 1935 $\urcorner$ can be understood as equivalent to $\ulcorner$In 1935, it was the case that $(\exists y)(y = x)\urcorner$, where 'in 1935' is subject to further reduction.

Presentism complicates the treatment of transtemporal relations. Let us say that x causes* y if and only if x and y exist at disjoint times and x causes y.

(4) $(\exists x)(\exists y)(x$ causes* $y)$

seems to be true; but the presentist cannot accept it as it stands. For by the very meaning of $\ulcorner x$ causes* $y\urcorner$, (4) cannot be true unless its quantifiers range over things that exist at disjoint times; whereas the presentist's quantifiers range only over things that exist at the present time. Presentism's nearest equivalent of (4) will be something like

(5) It was, is, or will be the case that $(\exists y)(\exists\phi)(\sim(\exists x)[y$ is occurring because it was the case that $\phi(x)]$ & y is occurring because it was the case that $(\exists z)(\phi(z)))$.

This complication of transtemporal relations might be acceptable if supported by strong enough metaphysical intuitions. Actualism requires analogous complications in the treatment of modality. But actualism rests, I believe, on strong intuitions to the effect that modal facts must have their whole ontological basis in the actual world, and that the ontological basis of the fact that there could have been, for example, a huge battle fought at Arcola, Illinois, on June 18, 1978, is not something that is or could have been a battle. The corresponding metaphysical basis for presentism would be the view that facts about the past and future must have their whole ontological basis in the present, and that the ontological basis of the fact that an important battle was fought at Waterloo on June 18, 1815, is not something that is or was a battle. This view about time, however, unlike the corresponding view about possibility, seems strongly counterintuitive. Surely the ontological basis of the fact I mentioned about Waterloo is, or includes, something that was a battle and that does not exist now and is not occurring now.

I am therefore inclined to reject presentism and to suppose that our quantifiers should be understood as ranging, at least, over past as well as present things. This leaves us, however, with $\ulcorner x$ exists at (a time) $t \urcorner$ as a primitive two-place propositional function that must be distinguished from $\ulcorner (\exists y)(y = x) \urcorner$.

IV. NAMES FOR FUTURE INDIVIDUALS

I promised to return to the question whether we can assert, believe, or know singular propositions about future individuals that do not yet exist. It has recently been suggested that we can; and the suggestion is couched in terms of the technical concept of a "rigid designator," which must first be explained. In explaining it, I will make use of a distinction I have developed elsewhere between truth *at* and truth *in* a possible world.[7] A singular proposition about an individual x cannot be true *in* a world in which x would not exist, because the proposition also would not exist there. But we can say that it is true *at* such a world if it correctly characterizes that world from our vantage point in the actual world. For instance, the singular proposition that I do not exist is true at, but not in, possible worlds in which I would not exist.

A name or other expression *n rigidly* designates an object x if and only if n designates x at (though not necessarily *in*) every possible world.[8] 'Robert Merrihew Adams', for example, rigidly designates me. I am what it designates at every possible world, including worlds in which I would not have existed. It does this designating, however, in the actual world, and, indeed, only in a certain "language" or "dialect." There could possibly, and may actually, be people who use 'Robert Merrihew Adams' as a name of some other person, or perhaps of a lake or a river. On the other hand, 'the chairperson of the UCLA philosophy department in 1978' designates me, but not rigidly. There are possible worlds in which David Kaplan bears the burden of satisfying that particular description.

There are also indexical and demonstrative expressions, such as 'I' and 'this', which rigidly designate different individuals in different contexts. On any given occasion of use, they designate the same individual at all possible worlds; but on different occasions, they designate different individuals, according to the context.

What proposition a sentence expresses depends on whether its terms designate rigidly. Thus, it is because 'Robert Merrihew Adams' rigidly designates me that 'Robert Merrihew Adams does not exist' expresses a proposition that is true at all and only those possible worlds in which I would not exist. In order to express a singular proposition about an individual, a sentence must normally contain a rigid designator for that individual.

It is widely held that once we have grasped the concept of rigid designation, we can introduce rigid designators simply by giving a description that is satisfied by exactly one thing and *stipulating* that the name we introduce is to designate rigidly the thing that in fact satisfies that description. In such a case, the description is said to "fix the reference" of the name. But, normally, it is not analytically equivalent to the name, for the name designates its object even at worlds in which the object would have failed to satisfy the description.

This brings us to the idea that particularly concerns us here, which is that in this way, we can introduce proper names that rigidly designate *future* individuals. In David Kaplan's elegant example, we introduce the name 'Newman 1' by declaring, "I hereby dub the first human being to be born in the twenty-first century 'Newman 1'."[9] Having done so, it might seem, we can already express, assert, and believe singular propositions about the first child of the twenty-first century, if there will be exactly one such person. By assertively uttering 'Newman I will be bald', for instance, we can express, and assert, a singular proposition about Newman 1, that he or she will be bald—or so it has been claimed.[10] Here we face two issues: whether we can indeed express, assert, and believe singular propositions about future individuals in this way; and whether, if we can, that shows that there do after all exist singular propositions about future individuals.

Let us begin with the second issue, the one about existence. We have already observed that there are relations that obtain between things that exist at disjoint times. It was this that kept us from regarding the present existence of singular propositions about past individuals as proved by the fact that we entertain, assert, and believe such propositions; and I think it should also keep us from inferring the present existence of singular propositions about future individuals from the fact (if it is a fact) that we can entertain, assert, or believe them. For perhaps the relations of entertaining, asserting, and believing can obtain between thoughts and utterances occurring at one time and propositions existing only at a later time. Maybe an utterance occurring in 1985 could express, and be an assertion of, a proposition that will not exist until 2001. Likewise, it has not been shown that the utterance of a rigid designator in 1985 could not express a thisness that will not come into being until the next century.

If by uttering 'Newman 1 will be bald' now, we express a proposition that will not come into being until fifteen years or so from now, it follows that what proposition, if any, we express now depends on what happens much later. But that is exactly as it should be in this example. Those who think that utterances of 'Newman 1 will be bald' in 1985 express a singular proposition about Newman 1 would certainly agree that what proposition that is depends on obstetrical events at the turn of the twenty-first century.

Those who believe that we can assert and believe singular propositions about future individuals in this way can answer Prior's argument against their opinion. For they have an alternative explanation of why it would be absurd for Prior's prophet to ask whether "perhaps it is the *second* of the people I mentioned who will be called 'Caesar' and will be murdered, etc., and the first who will be born later and be called 'Antony', etc." If we are to make sense of the question at all, or of Prior's argument, we must take it that 'the *second* of the people I mentioned' and 'the first' are meant to be rigid designators (rather like demonstratives) designating the mentioned individuals both at worlds in which they satisfy the descriptions in the order in which they were originally given, and at worlds in which their roles are reversed. Indeed, they presumably designate the same individuals at more widely variant worlds as well; for surely the prophet would be prepared to say, 'It could have been, though it won't be, that both the first and the second of the people I mentioned die of natural causes'. In the actual world, therefore, according to the prophet's intention, 'the second of the people I mentioned' designates the same individual at worlds in which he satisfies either of the two descriptions, or neither of them. It does not follow, however, that the actual world may turn out to be one in which he satisfies the first description instead of the second. For if 'the second of the people I mentioned' is a rigid designator here, its reference is fixed by the second description the prophet gave. According to the convention by which it is introduced, 'the second of the people I mentioned' designates at all possible worlds the individual (if there will be exactly one) who satisfies the prophet's second description in the actual world. That is why the suggestion that perhaps he (actually) will fail to satisfy it is senseless, though it is correct to say that he *could have* failed to satisfy it. This, at any rate, is the answer that ought to be given to Prior by anyone who thinks we can use rigid designators to assert singular propositions about future individuals.

Similar things can be said about 'Newman 1'. Because the reference of 'Newman 1' is fixed by the description 'the first human child born in the twenty-first century', it makes no sense to ask whether perhaps Newman 1 will really be born in the twentieth century. We can know on purely semantical grounds (and, hence, perhaps *a priori*) that

(6)   Newman 1 will be the first human child born in the twenty first century

expresses a true proposition, if it expresses any proposition at all, and that

(7)   Newman 1 will be born in the twentieth century

expresses a false proposition if it expresses any proposition at all. But

(8)   ◇(Newman 1 will be born in the twentieth century)

expresses a truth if it expresses any proposition at all; for if there will be exactly one first child of the twenty-first century, he or she will doubtless be born only a few second after midnight on the first morning of the century, and could surely have been born five minutes sooner.

Keith Donnellan has recently presented a better argument than Prior's against the view that we can assert, believe, or know singular propositions about future individuals. Donnellan deals explicitly with the 'Newman 1' example, focusing on the claim that (6) expresses a truth that we can know *a priori*. He agrees, in effect, that we could introduce the name 'Newman 1' by stipulating that it rigidly designates the first human being born in the twenty-first century, and that if we did, it would designate that individual, if there turns out to be exactly one such person.

Let us now imagine that just after midnight on New Century's Eve a child is born who is firmly established to be the first born of the century. He is baptised "John," but those of us who are still around, remembering our stipulation, also call this child "Newman 1." Now it seems to me that it would be outrageous to say that some twenty-five years or so before his birth, we knew that John would be the first child born in the 21st century. Suppose one of us, living to a ripe old age, were to meet John after he has grown up a bit. Would it be true to say to John, "I call you 'Newman 1' and Newman 1, I knew some twenty-five years or so before your birth that you would be the first child born in the 21st century"?[11]

Donnellan's view of this case is that by virtue of having introduced the name 'Newman 1' in the way described, we can know (perhaps even *a priori*) that if there will be exactly one first child born in the twenty-first century, the sentence 'Newman 1 will be the first child born in the twenty-first century' expresses a truth, but that we cannot know the truth of what is expressed by the sentence. He suggests that "we are in the somewhat odd position of possessing a mechanism for introducing a name that rigidly designates something, but a mechanism that is not powerful enough to allow us to use the name!"[12] We cannot *use* the name in the sense that having the name in our language does not put us "in a position to have *de re* propositional attitudes toward the entity rigidly designated" by it. It does not enable us to know or believe, nor even to assert, any proposition expressed by means of it. For it would be "just as incorrect to say to . . . the first child born in the 21st century, 'I believed about you some twenty-five years before your birth . . .', 'I asserted about you some twenty-five years before your birth . . .', etc.," as to say to him 'I knew about you some twenty-five years before your birth . . .'"[13]

I think it is clear, intuitively that Donnellan is right in holding that it would not be true to say any of these things to the first child of the twenty-first century, on the basis of our "use" of 'Newman 1'. But several explanations could be offered of *why* he is right about this. We shall consider four.

(i) Donnellan's own explanation—or partial explanation, as he himself suggests—is that in order for an entity to be an object of a *de re* propositional attitude, "the entity must enter into the 'genetic' account of how the speaker [or thinker] came to acquire the name, the beliefs he would express using the name, etc."[14] Since future entities that do not yet exist cannot enter into such genetic accounts of our present thoughts and utterances, such entities cannot be objects of present propositional attitudes *de re*. Singular propositions about them cannot now be asserted or believed. Donnellan adds,

Having indicated the direction in which I am inclined to go, I find myself wanting to ask the question, why, if indeed it is true, is one in a position to assert and know *de re* things about an entity when the entity becomes (in the right way) a part of the history of one's use of the name? What does *that* accomplish that allows for this possibility? But perhaps that is a misconceived question. Perhaps the only answer is that that is just when we do ascribe *de re* propositional attitudes.[15]

(ii) It is also possible to offer an explanation that is consistent with the claim that we can have knowledge and beliefs *de re,* and can make assertions *de re,* about future individuals. Suppose there will be exactly one first child of the twenty-first century, and about a month before her birth, her parents will begin to call her ''Jan,'' having decided to call her ''Jan'' whatever her sex turns out to be. Suppose further that at 11:30 P.M. on the last night of the twentieth century, her parents believe

(9)   Jan will be born in the twentieth century.

At that time, if these suppositions are correct, (9) will certainly express a singular proposition, and one that the parents can believe and assert. As it will turn out (if our suppositions are correct), this singular proposition will also be the proposition expressed by

(7)   Newman 1 will be born in the twentieth century.

Will Jan's parents therefore believe (7)? Certainly not. Being knowledgeable (as we may suppose) about the analytical philosophy of the 1970s and 1980s, they will know, on purely semantical grounds, that (7) expresses a falsehood, if it expresses any proposition at all.

We find ourselves in a familiar situation, which does not always involve future individuals. To take the most hackneyed example, where 'Phosphorus' is a (rigidly designating) name for the Morning Star, and 'Hesperus' for the Evening Star, it seems that many people have known

(10)   Hesperus = Hesperus

without knowing

(11)   Phosphorus = Hesperus

—even though (10) and (11) express the same singular proposition. Here it is assumed that a singular proposition is constituted by one or more individuals, or their thisnesses, together with one or more qualities or relations, and logical connectives, in such a way that there could not be two distinct singular propositions of exactly the same logical structure in which exactly the same qualities or relations are held to be satisfied by exactly the same ordered n-tuples of individuals.

In order to provide a plausible solution for problems of this sort, I believe we must say that the objects of propositional attitudes *de re* are not always singular propositions in this sense. There are several philosophical theories in the field that could provide us with alternative objects for the attitudes. They are all too complicated to be developed here; perhaps the simplest to mention is the view that the objects of assertion and belief are sentences.[16] Whatever theory is adopted, it ought, I think, to accommodate the following: In some contexts, what people are said to have believed or asserted *de re* depends only on what singular proposition (in my sense) is expressed by their thought or utterance. If I say, ''I was born in Philadelphia,'' for instance, and you say, ''Robert Merrihew Adams was born in Philadelphia,'' we will commonly be held to have asserted the same thing. But, in other contexts, what people are said to know or believe or assert depends also on other features of their state of mind or utterance or its context. If I were suffering from amnesia and had read a biography of myself without realizing it was about me, I might know that Robert Merrihew Adams was born in Philadelphia without knowing that *I* was born in Philadelphia.[17]

Whatever theory is adopted, it seems likely that it could be used to explain our intuitive data consistently with the doctrine that *de re* assertions, belief, and knowledge about future individuals are possible. If the first child of the twenty-first century will be named "Jan," why wouldn't it be correct for us to say, after her birth, "We knew twenty years ago that Newman 1 would be the first child of the twenty-first century, but we did not know twenty years ago that Jan would be the first child of the twenty-first century"—and to Jan, "We did not know twenty years ago that *you* would be the first child of the twenty-first century"? And if it would be correct for us to say these things, why wouldn't the three 'that' clauses still express the same singular proposition? After all, there have been people who did not know that Phosphorus = Hesperus, although they knew that Hesperus = Hesperus, and those two sentences express the same singular proposition (in my sense of 'singular proposition').

(iii) Both Donnellan and the position just discussed agree that 'Newman 1' can now be used to express singular propositions about the first child to be born in the twenty-first century, if there will be exactly one such child. The other two views to be considered here deny this. One of them regards 'Newman 1' as expressing not the thisness of an individual but an essence of an individual. If the first child of the twenty-first century will be Jan, then on this view, 'Newman 1' will express not the property of being identical with Jan but some other property necessarily coextensive with it—perhaps the property of being the first human child born in the twenty-first century in α, where 'α' rigidly designates the actual world. This, of course, will not keep 'Newman 1' from rigidly designating Jan.

This alternative treatment would be metaphysically interesting if we could suppose that 'Newman 1' expresses a *purely qualitative* essence, but that is doubtful. It is far from clear that 'human', 'twenty-first century', and, above all, 'α' have purely qualitative equivalents. Indeed 'α' may introduce worse problems than 'Newman 1'. At least there will be a time when it will be settled which individual, if any, 'Newman 1' designates; but if the actual world will go on forever, will there ever be a time at which it is settled which possible world 'α' designates?

(iv) It is possible to regard 'Newman 1' as a variable bound by an existential quantifier that in most contexts is not expressed. On this view, for example,

(8) $\Diamond$(Newman 1 will be born in the twentieth century)

is an informal abbreviation of

(12)   It will be the case that $(\exists x)(x$ is the first human child born in the twenty-first century & $\Diamond(x$ is born in the twentieth century)).

And, in general, $\ulcorner \phi$ (Newman 1)$\urcorner$ will be regarded as an informal abbreviation of

(13)   It will be the case that $(\exists x)(x$ is the first human child born in the twenty-first century & $\phi(x)$).

This treatment of 'Newman 1' does not disturb the point that 'Newman 1' is a rigid designator; for it is well known that variables designate rigidly within any context of use.[18] In (12), for example, it is crucial that within the scope of the existential quantifier, x designates or represents the same individual at the actual world and at all other possible worlds, including one in which that individual is born in a different century. But (12) is a general proposition and is clearly distinct from the singular proposition that the first child of the twenty-first century would express by saying, "I might have been born in the twentieth century."[19]

I am not sure which, if any, of these four accounts of the use of 'Newman 1' is correct. But that is a semantical, rather than a metaphysical, issue. For most metaphysical purposes, the situation is clear enough. If there will be exactly one first child of the twenty-first century, there will be a singular proposition about him or her, that he or she is the first child of the twenty-first century. All of that we already know; and there is nothing more informative that the use of 'Newman 1' can enable us to know or believe now. If we try to express our knowledge in a form that looks more informative (e.g., 'that *you* would be the first child of the twenty-first century'), it becomes clear that in 2015, we could not rightly claim in that form to have known it now. Nevertheless, from the perspective of the twenty-first century, our present knowing and speaking will rightly be seen as standing in some transtemporal relations to the singular proposition that will exist then. Whether some of these relations should be regarded as espression, assertion, belief, and/or knowledge is a question that can be debated in semantics without, I think, affecting the metaphysical picture very much.[20]

Notes

1. R. M. Adams, "Primitive Thisness and Primitive Identity," *The Journal of Philosophy* 76 (1979):5–26.

2. R. M. Adams, "Actualism and Thisness," *Synthese* 57 (1981):3–42.

3. A. N. Prior, "Identifiable Individuals," *Review of Metaphysics* 13 (June 1960):690.

4. Issues that arise about this argument are in several ways analogous to issues that have arisen in philosophical theology regarding the possibility or impossibility of divine foreknowledge of free human actions. Thus, the question whether *Furth's living before I was born* is something that existed in 1935 corresponds to the question whether it is a *fact* about 1935 that Furth was alive before I was born. Questions of the latter form, in the context of the foreknowledge problem, have given rise to considerable controversy about attempts to distinguish between "hard" and "soft" facts *about* a given time. [All the following articles appeared in *The Philosophical Review:* Nelson Pike, "Divine Omniscience and Voluntary Action," vol. 74 (1965):27–46, "Of God and Freedom: A Rejoinder," vol. 75 (1966):369–79, and "Fischer on Freedom and Foreknowledge," vol. 93 (1984):599–614; John Turk Saunders, "Of God and Freedom," vol. 75 (1966):219–25; Marilyn McCord Adams, "Is the Existence of God a 'Hard' Fact?" vol. 76 (1967):492–503; John Martin Fischer, "Freedom and Foreknowledge," vol. 92 (1983):67–79.] Likewise, the suggestion that thisnesses and singular propositions maybe timeless parallels the famous proposal that the foreknowledge problem could be solved by regarding God as timeless; I regard a solution in terms of timelessness as unpromising in both cases, for reasons that are somewhat similar. Perhaps the problem of the present paper *is* a form of the foreknowledge problem—if thisnesses are God's concepts of individuals. I would want to explore these connections more fully before coming to final conclusions about either problem, but this is not meant to be a paper about divine foreknowledge.

5. This is obviously an adaptation of an argument given in the previous section against the ascription of timelessness to the thisnesses of contingent individuals that come into existence. Principle (3) of the previous section also clearly requires that transtemporal relations not be allowed in general to exist timelessly.

6. The world-story of a possible world *w* is, roughly, the set of all those propositions that exist in the actual world and that would exist and would be true if *w* were actual. See my "Actualism and Thisness," 21–22.

7. R. M. Adams, "Actualism and Thisness," 20–32.

8. The term 'rigid designator' is due to Saul Kripke, but the interpretation presented here does not claim perfect conformity with any historic precedent.

9. This is a slightly modified version of an example first introduced by Kaplan in "Quantifying In," *Synthese* 19 (1968–69):201. In that paper, Kaplan rejected the possibility (or at least the propriety) of such a dubbing.

10. By David Kaplan, in a later paper, "Dthat," in *Syntax and Semantics,* vol. 9: *Pragmatics,* edited by Peter Cole (New York, 1978), 241.

11. Keith S. Donnellan, "The Contingent *A Priori* and Rigid Designators," in *Midwest Studies in Philosophy* 2 (Minneapolis, 1977), 20.

12. Ibid., 24.

13. Ibid., 23–24.

14. Ibid., 25.

15. Ibid.

16. A recent sketch of a version of this view is found in Tyler Burge, "The Content of Propositional Attitudes: Abstract," *Nous* 14 (1980):53–58. Another approach is to ascribe different "nondescriptive connotations" to some sentences that differ (for instance) only by containing different proper names for the same individual; see Diana Ackerman, "Proper Names, Propositional Attitudes, and Non-Descriptive Connotations," *Philosophical Studies* 35 (1979):55–69, and "Proper Names, Essences, and Intuitive Beliefs," *Theory and Decision* 11 (1979):5–26. Alternatively, we might say that what people assert or believe often depends on other facts about the "character" of their thought or utterance, as well as on the proposition (in my sense) that constitutes its "content"; the distinction is drawn, with respect to sentences containing indexical expressions, by David Kaplan, "On the Logic of Demonstratives," *Journal of Philosophical Logic* 8 (1978):81–98.

17. This example, and argument, are adapted from John Perry, "Frege on Demonstratives," *The Philosophical Review* 86 (1977):474–97.

18. On this Kaplanesque point and its present application, see Nathan U. Salmon, "How *Not* to Derive Essentialism from the Theory of Reference, *The Journal of Philosophy* 76 (1979):708 n.

19. This treatment of 'Newman 1' is inspired by a similar treatment of proper names in fiction developed by Alvin Plantinga, *The Nature of Necessity* (Oxford, 1974), 159–63.

20. An analogous treatment of broader issues connected with the truth of statements about "future contingents" is worthy of consideration. (I do not mean that I am prepared to endorse it.) We could think of the meaning of the future tense as consisting largely in the way in which it determines transtemporal relations in which acts of speech or thought performed by means of it will rightly be seen as standing to future events when they have occurred. Among these relations might be *correctly predicting* or *being verified by* and, conversely, *being falsified by*. Could this relational understanding of the truth of statements about the future help in resisting the pressure to think of them as timelessly true? This is a pressure we may wish to resist if the timeless truth of such statements seems to us incompatible with a metaphysically open future.

Acknowledgment: A draft of this paper was presented to a conference on the thought of David Kaplan, held at Stanford University in March 1984. Terence Parsons responded to the paper. I am indebted to him, and to other participants in the conference, particularly Paul Benacerraf, Kit Fine, and Hans Kamp, for comments that were helpful in revising the paper. I do not pretend to have done justice to all the questions that they raised.

Time and Essence

GEORGE MYRO

A need for a notion of essence seems to arise when one adopts a certain solution to a certain problem.[1]

The problem is: What is the relationship between (for example) a bit of wax and various statuettes, vases, and so on, into which it is successively shaped, or between a ship and the wood out of which it is initially made but which is, in the course of time, replaced by other wood and is used to make another ship. Confronting the fact that the original ship and the original wood have different life histories with the conditions on identity imposed by Leibniz's Law may lead one to the conclusion that the ship is not identical with, but is, rather, a distinct object from, the wood. However, further reflection may lead one to be dissatisfied with the multiplication of entities and other uncomfortable results this conclusion brings in its train.

The solution[2] that I, on the whole, favor is to subject systematically all predicates, *including identity* (or rather, *sentences* in which they may occur), to temporal qualification. The idea is that just as we accept without a blink that A might be larger than B at t but not larger than B at t', so we should accept that A may be *identical with B* at t and *not* be *identical with B* at t'. The immediate cost of this is to subject Leibniz's Law itself to temporal qualification:

If A is identical with B *at t,* then *at t, A* and B share all of their properties that, so to speak, *do not result from possession of properties at times other than t.*

The idea seems to be capable of being systematically worked out without too uncomfortable results. It makes the wax successively identical with the various objects into which it is successively shaped, and the original ship originally identical with the original wood and later identical with the new wood, while the original wood is then identical with the second ship.

A brief sketch of some features of System $G,$ a very minor modification of the standard predicate-calculus with identity, may help clarify this idea. It will also enable us to make subsequent points clearer, perhaps, by using the notation of System $G.$ (I shall be conveniently lax throughout about use and mention.)

Very roughly, the formulas of System G are the familiar ones of the predicate-calculus with identity, but subjected to temporal qualification:

$$t|Fa, \quad t|(Fa \vee \exists xGx)$$

—and also those that are built up of the former and the new ones in familiar ways (including quantification over times) and subjected, where needed, to temporal qualification, and so on:

$$t|(Fa \& t'|(Fa \vee \exists xGx)), \forall t \ t|(Fa \supset \exists t' \ t'|\exists y (Gy \& y = a))$$

—always provided that every formula of the *standard* predicate-calculus with identity occurs within the scope of some temporal qualification or other.

The inference rules are pretty much the familiar ones (though modified to allow for the new formulas), coming in two versions, "internal" and "external," illustrated, respectively, by the first trio and the last pair:

$$k|(Fa \& k'|\exists xFx) \vdash k|Fa, k|k'|\exists xFx$$
$$k|\forall x \ (Fx \& k'|Gx) \vdash k|(Fa \& k'|Ga)$$
$$k|\forall t \ t|Fa \vdash k|k|Fa$$
$$k|Fa \& k'|\exists xFx \vdash k|Fa, k'|\exists xFx$$
$$\forall t \ t|Fa \vdash k|Fa.$$

Among the additions (or a notable revision) is the analogue of temporally qualified Leibniz's Law:

$$k|a = b, k|\phi \vdash k|\phi',$$

where ϕ results from ϕ' by some replacements of 'a' by 'b' or *vice versa, provided no such replacement takes place within the scope of any temporal qualification other than by* 'k'. In view of the proviso, we may expect such formulas as

$$k|\exists x \exists y \ (x = y \& \phi x \& \sim \phi y)$$

—where 'x' and 'y' occur in ϕ within the scope of some temporal qualification other than by 'k'—to be, in general, *consistent* (as, indeed, they are). Let us say (with some imprecision) that such formulas express "*time-bound*" properties of (or conditions on) x.

I shall not say anything here about the semantics of System G.

Subjecting Leibniz's Law (like "all else") to temporal qualification allows one to think of A and B as identical at one time, though differing in their properties at another:

$$k|(a = b \& k'|Fa \& k'|\sim Fb).$$

But a closer look *seems* to show that this is not possible. If the ship in the middle of the marketplace[3] (today) is identical today with the wood in the middle of the marketplace (today), there is today only *one* object in the middle of the marketplace, and will this *one* object be tomorrow in the middle of the marketplace (as the ship will be) or in the lumberyard (as the wood will be)?

The general answer to this and similar puzzles is, I believe, a general principle to the effect that to talk of what is the case with respect to any given object at a given time, one must (be able to) identify that object by a condition which that object satisfies uniquely *at that time*.[4]

In the example being envisaged, the condition of being in the middle of the marketplace (today) is (we may allow) satisfied *uniquely today*. But this condition will *not* be satisfied *uniquely tomorrow*. *Both* the ship and the wood, which will be *distinct* tomorrow, will satisfy the condition of having been (uniquely) in the middle of the marketplace today.

Letting $1\gamma\phi\gamma$ be short for $\forall y\,(\phi y \equiv y = \gamma)$, we have:

$$d\,|(s = w\ \&\ 1sMs\ \&\ 1wMw\ \&\ 1s\ \ d\,|1sMs\ \&\ 1w\ \ d\,|1wMw)$$
$$m\,|(s \neq w\ \&\ d\,|1sMs\ \&\ d\,|1wMw\ \&\ \sim 1s\ \ d\,|1sMs\ \&\ \sim 1w\ \ d\,|1wMw).$$

Thus, to engage properly in the interrogation involved in the puzzle, we must supply *further* conditions (*in addition* to being uniquely in the middle of the marketplace today: $d\,|1xMx$) to construct conditions C and C', which will be satisfied *uniquely tomorrow* $(:m\,|(1xCx\ \&\ 1yC'y))$. For example, since the ship will still be a ship tomorrow, but the wood will not be (though both are a ship today), we may, in the one case, conjoin being a ship with our original condition and, in the other, being not a ship with that same original condition in order to obtain (1) being (tomorrow) a ship and having been (uniquely) in the middle of the marketplace today $(Cx : (Sx\ \&\ d\,|1xMx))$ and (2) being (tomorrow) not a ship and having been today (uniquely) in the middle of the marketplace $(C'x : (\sim Sx\ \&\ d\,|1xMx))$ as conditions *uniquely* satisfied *tomorrow*, respectively, by the ship and by the wood:

$$m\,|(1s(Ss\ \&\ d\,|sMs)\ \&\ 1w(\sim Sw\ \&\ d\,|1wMw)).$$

The original unanswerable question splits into two answerable ones (suggestively)—

$$m\,|\exists x(1x(Sx\ \&\ d\,|1xMx)\ \&\ ?x)$$
$$m\,|\exists x(1x(\sim 5x\ \&\ d\,|1xMx)\ \&\ ?x)$$

—and the puzzle vanishes.

It is at this point that the need for a notion of essence begins to be felt.[5] In the example envisaged, we resolved the one unanswerable question into two answerable ones in an *ad hoc* manner: relying, in particular, on the presumed knowledge that the wood will not be a ship tomorrow (and the ship will be). But what if we did not know this; or what if we *wanted to know* whether the wood was going to be a ship tomorrow? It would seem that *merely* knowing that there is a wooden ship (uniquely) in the middle of the marketplace today should *suffice* to enable us to talk about what will be the case with respect to the ship and what will be the case with respect to the wood tomorrow. It would seem that it should suffice for knowing some condition K such that its conjunction with the condition of being today uniquely in the middle of the marketplace is "*guaranteed*" to be satisfied *uniquely at all times*[6] by the ship "no matter what may happen," and, similarly, some condition K', such that its conjunction with the condition of being today uniquely in the middle of the marketplace is *guaranteed* to be satisfied *uniquely at all times* by the wood "no matter what may happen."[7]

It is not yet clear to me just how this plausible idea is to be formulated in full generality and precision. It is much easier to merely *label* it: Principle to Stick-to-itive Conditions (PSC).[8] In any case, it is extremely tempting to connect PSC with the ancient and intuitive notion of essence. In our example, the two conditions K and K' are, respectively, being *essentially* a ship and being *essentially* (a bit of) wood.

Perhaps speaking of *the* ancient and intuitive notion of essence is too sanguine: "the" notion seems by now to be a congeries of ancient (and modern) ideas and modern (and ancient) intuitions. So I shall merely wend a single exploratory path through this congeries, guided partly by PSC and partly by various intuitions and traditions in the congeries.

What I find striking is that thinking about essence in the context of PSC and of the thesis that all predicates, including *identity,* are subject to temporal qualification, which pulls PSC in its train, both generates special difficulties in getting clear about essence and facilitates the task by making the resolutions of the difficulties into stepping stones in this getting clear. Also, the thesis about temporal qualifications, by its very *being in need, via* PSC, of some notion like that of essence, seems to derive from this very need epistemic support, as if *explaining* an independently appealing notion, that of essence.

My exploratory path will have roughly two parts (and a few speculative fadings-out). The two parts will be presented, in a sense, in the reverse order. The part to be presented first will deal with that "part" of PSC that has to do with conditions K and K' being such that in conjunction with the condition of being today uniquely in the middle of the marketplace, they are *at all times** satisfied *uniquely,* respectively by the ship and by the wood. The part to be presented second will be some elaboration of that "part" of PSC that deals with its being "*guaranteed*" that K and K' have the feature dealt with in the first part. This seems to be a natural order of exposition. What suggests that it is, nevertheless, in some sense, the reverse order is that, intuitively (and, perhaps, technically), the result of the second part needs to be incorporated into the working out of the first part. To let a bit of the cat out of the bag: in the second part, an attempt will be made to specify what it is for a property (or condition) to be *an essence*—in the sense of being *capable* of being a property F such that something is *essentially F*—in terms of its *necessarily* satisfying certain conditions. (Recall that the corresponding "part" of PSC deals with its being "*guaranteed*.") In the first part, an attempt will be made to specify, roughly, how to select from among the properties of an object that property F such that the object is *essentially F*—in terms of how the object is *in fact* related to other objects. (Recall that the corresponding "part" of PSC deals with an object's having a certain property, satisfying a certain condition, *uniquely at all times.*) But, intuitively (and, perhaps, technically), only properties that are *essences* in the sense to be specified in the second part are even capable of being properties F such that an object is essentially F. So, the result of the second part is to be anticipatorily incorporated into the first part.

Let us, then, attempt to specify ("define"?) a notion: x is essentially F ($:[Fx]$).[9] We shall use, in the course of this, a notion: F is an essence ($:[F]$)—to be specified subsequently—and, indeed, we shall begin by making the latter notion into the first conjunct (of the clauses) of the specification of the former notion. Let us be guided by the example of the ship(s) and the wood(s).

We should make one point clear at once. Our aim (as can be seen by reviewing the genesis of PSC) is to have the ship, but *not* the wood, *at all times* uniquely* something that both is essentially a ship and was today uniquely in the middle of the marketplace, and to have the wood, but *not* the ship, *at all times* uniquely* something that both is essentially (a bit of) wood and was today uniquely in the middle of the marketplace, so as to provide a means of identifying each uniquely throughout its career, while allowing for the fact (or possibility) that each is distinct at some times (and identical at others). But this seems to require that it should be the case even today, when the ship and the wood are *one,* that the ship, but *not* the wood, be essentially a ship, and that the wood, but *not* the ship, be essentially (a bit of) wood.[10] But how is this possible, since today the ship and the wood are one and the same thing?

Well, this has already been taken care of in subjecting Leibniz's Law to temporal qualification: things identical at a time need agree only in properties that they have at that time and *that are not* "time-bound"[11]—i.e., *not dependent upon possession of properties at other times*. The issue has been further explored in discussing the puzzle that ushered in PSC. Just as the temporally qualified Leibniz's Law allows the ship, but *not* the wood, to have the property of going to be in the marketplace tomorrow, even though the wood and the ship are *one* today, so it will allow the ship, but *not* the wood, to be essentially a ship, and the wood, but *not* the ship, to be essentially (a bit of) wood, even today—if we contrive to make the properties of being essentially a ship and of being essentially (a bit of) wood "*time-bound*." As will be seen, we shall contrive just that.

What else should we conjoin with the first conjunct (i.e., *F* is an essence) in specifying the notion: *x* is essentially *F* - ?

We may observe that the ship is *at all times** a ship, and the wood is *at all times** (a bit of) wood. Alas, the ship is also (we may suppose) at all times* (a bit of) wood, though the wood is *not* at all times* a ship.

We may examine a somewhat more complex example. Not only is the original wood replaced by new wood in the original ship, and the original wood is used to construct a new ship,[12] but the new ship subsequently replaces the original ship as the historical monument in the middle of the marketplace. Now, not only are both ships at all times* (bits of) wood, but the monument is at all times* a ship, and at all times* (a bit of) wood.

So, being *F* at all times* does not suffice as the second conjunct of our specification. But the fact that neither (bit of) wood is at all times* a ship, or at all times* a monument, and that neither ship is at all times* a monument provides a clue. And the clue grows into the following plan.

1. The specification is to have the form of an inductive definition, as it were. The monument (in the example being considered) is to be assigned an essence—viz., being a monument (of such and such a sort)—*at the first stage.*

2. The fact that the monument is *at all times** a monument is to be employed and augmented by the fact that the monument does *not* "*properly overlap* "—i.e., is

not at some time identical with and at another time distinct from—*anything that is at all times* a monument*.

3. At subsequent stages, such as those at which the ships are assigned essences—viz., being a ship (of such and such a sort)—and later the woods are assigned essences—viz., being (a bit of) wood (of such and such a sort)—such facts are to be employed as that although each ship *does* "properly overlap" something that is at all times* a ship—viz., the monument—*neither* ship "properly overlaps" anything that both is at all times* a ship *and has not been assigned an essence at an earlier stage* (the monument having been assigned an essence at an earlier stage); similarly, the woods do *not* "properly overlap" anything that both is at all times* (a bit of) wood *and has not been assigned an essence at an earlier stage* (since the ships and the monument *have* been assigned essences at earlier stages).

4. It must be ensured that essences that have already been assigned do not come up for consideration again at later stages, and that the assignation proceeds in successive stages.

So we may propose:[13]

(1) *x* is essentially *F at the first stage* iff *F* is an essence, *x* is *F* at all times*, and *x* does not "properly overlap" anything that is *F* at all times*:

$[Fx]_1$ iff $[F]$ & $\forall t\ t|Fx$ & $\sim\exists y\,(x][y$ & $\forall t\ t|Fy)$

where

$x][y$ iff $\exists t\,\exists t'\,(t|x=y$ & $t'|x \neq y)$.

(2) *x* is essentially *F* at the $(i + 1)^{\text{th.}}$ stage $(:[Fx]_{i+1})$ iff
   (a) *F* is an essence: $[F]$;
   (b) *x* is *F* at all times*: $\forall t\ t|Fx$;
   (c) *x* does not "properly overlap" anything that both is *F* at all times* and is not, for any *G* and any $j \leq i$, essentially *G* at the $j^{\text{th.}}$ stage: $\sim\exists y\,(x][y$ & $\forall t\ t|Fy$ & $\sim\exists G\,\exists j\,(j \leq i$ & $[Gy]_j))$;
   (d) *x* does not "properly overlap" anything that, for some $k \leq i$, is essentially *F at the* $k^{\text{th.}}$ stage: $\sim\exists z\,(x][z$ & $\exists k\,(k \leq i$ & $[Fz]_k))$; and
   (e) *x* "properly overlaps" something that, for some *H*, is essentially *H* at the $i^{\text{th.}}$ stage: $\exists u\,(x][u$ & $\exists H\,[Hu]_i)$.

(3) *x* is essentially *F* iff *x* is essentially *F* at some stage:

$[Fx]$ iff $\exists i\,[Fx]_i$.

Because of the role of the phrases "at all times*" and "properly overlaps" (i.e., is *at some time* identical with and *at some time* distinct from), the notion (property, predicate) of being essentially *F* is "*time-bound*" (i.e., dependent on possession of properties at other times), and so the ship can be essentially a ship but *not* essentially (a bit of) wood, and the wood essentially (a bit of) wood but not essentially a ship even today when the ship and the wood are *one*.[14]

Let us, next, attempt to specify ("define"?)[15] a notion: *F* is an essence—in the sense of its being possible that something should be essentially *F*, the sense we employed in the specification of the latter notion. Let us begin with the (fairly) traditional notion that the essence of something is a property it needs to have in order to exist. Does the thing in the middle of the marketplace need to be a ship in order to exist? Does it need to be (a bit of) wood? We are back to the puzzle with which we began our discussion, and the resolution is that the ship in the middle of the marketplace needs to be a ship in order to exist but does not need to be (a bit of) wood in order to exist, and the wood in the middle of the marketplace needs to be (a bit of) wood and does not need to be a ship in order to exist—even though the ship and the wood are one.

The point is that necessarily, at all times*, a *ship* is identical with *something* that needs to be a *ship* in order to exist; but it is *not* the case that necessarily, at all times*, a *ship* is identical with something that needs to be (a bit of) *wood* in order to exist.[16] And, conversely, for a *bit of wood*. This suggests the following "definitions." [17]

(1) F is *adhesive* iff necessarily, at all times, if something (existing) is F, then it is identical with something that at all times* is F:

iff $\Box \forall t \; t | \forall x \, (Fx \supset \exists y \, (x=y \; \& \; \forall t' \; t' | Fy))$.

But we do not want (especially in view of our assigning essences to objects by stages—consider, especially, the "last" stage) "universally necessary" properties (such as self-identity) to count as essences (in the sense that we are attempting to specify). So:

(2) F is *minimally adhesive* iff (necessarily) if it is possible that at some time an (existing) object should be F and "properly overlap" with something, then it is possible that at some time t some (existing) object x should be F and "properly overlap" with something y *and* be such that for every object identical with x at t, if this last object is F at all times*, then it is identical with x at all times:

iff $\Diamond \; \exists t \; t | \exists x (Fx \; \& \; \exists y \, x][y) \supset$
$\Diamond \; \exists t \; t | \exists x \, (Fx \; \& \; \exists y \, x][y \; \& \; \forall z \, (z = x \supset$
$\forall t' \; t' | Fz \supset \forall t'' \; t'' | z = x))$.

Nor do we want properties that are "time-bound" (such as being a ship *on Monday,* or being a ship *at some time*) to count as essences. "Time-bound" properties, we have noted, do not obey the unrestricted form of Leibniz's Law. So:

(3) F is *absolutely Leibnizian* iff necessarily, if at any time something x is identical with something y, then x is F if and only if y is F:

iff $\Box \; \forall t \; t | \forall x \, \forall y \, (x \equiv y \supset Fx \equiv Fy)$.

And we do not want properties that are, so to speak, absolutely Leibnizian "because of a technicality"—such as being *identical* with something that is a ship *on Monday,* or being *identical* with something that is a ship *at some time* to count as essences. So:

(4) F is *not parasitically absolutely Leibnizian* iff there is no property G that is *not* absolutely Leibnizian such that F is equivalent to being identical with something that is G:

iff $\sim \exists G \, (\sim PL(G) \; \& \; \Box \forall t \; t | \forall x \, (Fx \equiv \exists y \, (Gy \; \& \; x = y)))$.

Finally, we must take into account that *genus*-properties (such as being a conveyance, or being an animal) satisfy the above conditions as well as *species*-properties (such as being a ship, or being a ship of such and such a kind, or such as being a cat, or being a cat of such and such a kind. And although we may wish to count *genus*-properties as essential properties in *one* sense, difficulties would arise in our specifying what it is for *x* to be essentially *F* in stages if we considered *genus*- and *species*-properties as on a par essences in the sense being sought.[18]

So, essences in the desired sense (used in specifying: *x* is essentially *F*) are the *logically strongest* properties that are adhesive, but minimally, and absolutely, Leibnizian, but not parasitically (AMALNP):

[*F*] iff AMALNP(*F*) & $\sim\exists G$ (AMALNP(*G*)
& $\Box\forall t$ *t* |$\forall x$ (*Gx* $\supset$ *Fx*) & $\sim\Box\forall t$ *t* |$\forall x$ (*Fx* $\supset$ *Gx*)).

Combining the two portions of our exploratory path so far, we may hope to have reached (or, at least, approximated) a notion of being essentially *F* that is tolerably plausible.[19] We may also hope that given a principle to the effect that necessarily everything (at least, within the relevant range) at all times* has an essence, i.e., is essentially *F*, for some *F*, the satisfaction of PSC will be assured.[20] That is, we may hope that PSC will *follow* from:

$\Box\forall t$ *t* |$\forall x$ $\exists F$ [*Fx*]

(subject to reconstrual in connection with ''Descartes' Principle'' about to be discussed).

There remains, however, a further problem. Although PSC, as so far considered, would suffice to underpin all *nonmodal* discourse, it might not suffice to underpin *modal* discourse. To see the difficulty, consider the following situation. A plastic toy ship is made in a mold in such a way that the toy ship and the (bit of) plastic of which it is made come to be at the same time. Furthermore, the toy ship is so destroyed that it and the (bit of) plastic cease to be at the same time. Here, since the toy ship and the (bit of) plastic do *not* ''*properly* overlap,''[21] our procedures are incapable of assigning different essences to the toy ship and to the (bit of) plastic. Yet, it seems, we might wish to say (modally) that the toy ship could have failed (at least for part of its existence) to be a (*that*) bit of plastic but could not have failed to be a toy ship; while, on the other hand, the (bit of) plastic could have failed (at least for part of its existence) to be a (*that*) toy ship but could not have failed to be a bit of plastic.

The solution I am inclined to propose is a disturbingly minor exploitation of the technical resources of System *G* that is reminiscent of a principle Descartes appears to be hinting at.[22] We have already noted that in System *G*, a formula of the sort: $\exists x \exists y$ (*x* = *y* & ϕx & $\sim\phi y$) does not yield: $\exists x$ (ϕx & $\sim\phi x$), and may be consistent when ϕx is ''*time-bound*.'' We have also noted that being essentially *F* (:[*Fx*]) is ''*time-bound*.'' This allows one to postulate what I shall call ''*Descartes' Principle*'':

If *F* and *G* are essences such that it is possible that something should be essentially *F* but not essentially *G* and possible that something should be essentially *G* but not essentially *F*, then (necessarily) if at any time, something is both essentially F and essentially G, then it is at that time identical with something that is essentially F but not essentially G, and identical with something that is essentially G but not essentially F.

Strictly speaking, this seems to amount to "introducing" a new notion: $[[Fx]]$—on the basis of the "defined" $[Fx]$—by means of:

(1) $\forall x \,([Fx] \ \& \ \exists G \,(G\,])][[F \ \& \ [Gx]).\ \supset$
$\exists y \,\exists z \,([[Fy]] \ \& \ {\sim}[[Gy]] \ \& \ [[Gz]] \ \& \ {\sim}[[Fz]] \ \& \ y = x \ \& \ z = x)).$

(2) $\forall x \,([Fx] \ \& \ {\sim}\exists G\,(G\,])][[F \ \& \ [Gx]).\ \supset [[Fx]]).$

(3) $\forall x \,([[Fx]] \supset \exists y \,(y = x \ \& \ [Fy])$
—where: $F\,]][[G \equiv \Diamond \ \exists x ([Fx] \ \& \ {\sim}[Gx])$
$\& \ \Diamond \ \exists x ([Gx] \ \& \ {\sim}[Fx]).$

Various related previous remarks are to be reconstrued in accordance with this emendation—e.g., on the connection between PSC and the postulation that, necessarily, everything has an essence (PSC itself might be rethought and strengthened in this connection e.g., by inserting "$\Box$" in front of the consequent) and note 18.

We can now speak of the thing that is in the mold and essentially a toy ship $(:[[Tx]])$—and not essentially (a bit of) plastic—and of the thing that is in the mold and essentially (a bit of) plastic $(:[[Px]])$—and not essentially a toy ship—and consistently predicate *modal* properties of the former that we do not predicate (and may consistently deny) of the latter, and *vice versa*, while maintaining that the former is, in fact, identical—indeed, at all times—with the latter and shares with it all *nonmodal* properties.

Presumably, once we go on to such modal predication, we shall want to accept *something* like

$$\Box \forall t \ t |([[Fx]] \supset \Box \forall t' \ t' |[[Fx]])$$

and, perhaps,

$$\Box Fx \equiv_\Box \exists G \,([[Gx]] \ \& \ \Box \forall t \ t |\forall y \,(Gy \supset Fy)),$$

though there may be worries about necessary properties of things that are not implied by their essence, and the relationships between temporal qualification and modality are not clear.[23]

Let me end with two sketchy, tentative, and speculative suggestions.

1. It may be that some such scheme as the one discussed in this paper will turn out to be overall more clean-shaven by Occam's razor than its alternatives (e.g., those postulating coincident but nonidentical objects or space-time worms and their slices). If so, this might justify our acceptance of a scheme of essences that might be involved in or needed by it, as suggested above, whatever scruples against essences one might have had initially. Ontological economy in one area might justify an ontological splurge in another.

2. On the other hand, if may be felt that *which* set of properties are to be regarded as the/a set of essences (as specified in the *second* part of our exploratory path) is not an objective matter—not a matter of discovery, but of choice. Under certain circumstances, one might feel, the property that is (equivalent to) the conjunction of being a

pencil and being yellow might count as an essence, and so, something, a yellow pencil, would be regarded as ceasing to exist when a yellow pencil either ceased to be a pencil *or ceased to be yellow*. And conversely, a pencil would not be regarded as an object that came to be when a (nonyellow) pencil was made and ceased to be when that pencil was destroyed. One might, of course, look around for "objective" principles, criteria, or considerations that might dictate which properties are (to be regarded as) essences. But failing to find such, one might opt for a sort of relativity of ontology, in accord with which the very *"significance"* of quantifiers and/or words expressing existence would be *determined* by the set of essences chosen, so that there could not be a genuine disagreement about whether *there are* yellow pencils, or pencils, between parties subscribing to suitably different sets of essences.

Notes

1. But, perhaps, not only then. See footnote 5.

2. See my "Identity and Time" in *Grounds of Rationality: Intentions, Categories, and Ends,* edited by R. Grandy and R. Warner, (Oxford, 1985), for an exposition of the solution (including System *G*—see below) and the dissatisfactions that prompt it. The solution was first proposed (in conversation), in my ken, in 1971 by H. Paul Grice.

3. Because it is a historical monument. Incidentally, notice the felt need for the additional temporal qualification in parentheses.

4. This obviously impinges on the disputes about the semantics (and so on) of proper names, of indexicals, and so on, but I cannot follow that tangent here.

5. The views of various theorists, such as, perhaps, David Wiggins (*Identity and Spatio-temporal Continuity* [Oxford, 1971] and *Sameness and Substance* [Cambridge, Mass., 1980]) and John Perry ("The Same F," *Philosophical Review* 79 [April 1970]:181–200), seem to be construable *within* System *G* by equating their various relations that seem to be (special cases of) "coincidence" or "cooccupancy" with identity ('=', subject to temporal qualification) of System *G,* and their identity with the relation expressed by '$\forall t \ t | x = y$' in System *G* (or, perhaps, by '$\Box \forall t \ t | x = y$' in a possible modal extension of System *G*). If so, then by equating the notions thus, we can, perhaps, raise again various problems and rerun various lines of reasoning from the present discussion. It may turn out that a notion of essence is needed independently of the presently endorsed proposals about time and identity but, otherwise, more or less as proposed here.

6. It is not clear enough to me how to deal with times at which, for example, the ship *does not exist.* One is pulled in a number of directions. One direction is to simply treat existence as expressed by a predicate that (because variables and quantifiers are now regarded as "ranging also over perhaps-nonexistents") seems (so far) not to have any distinctive logical properties. Another is that one wants to be able to talk about what is the case with respect to a thing at times at which it does not exist (if only to say that it does not exist then). A third is the venerable doctrine that nonexistents have no properties. I shall mark the lacuna in understanding here by supplying the expression 'at all times' with an asterisk to suggest that one might wish in those cases to add upon consideration such a phrase as 'at which it exists'.

7. Evidently, a weaker condition is obtained by changing the order of the existential quantifier on conditions and the universal quantifier on times, but this form of the requirement seems implausible—somehow *because* of its greater weakness.

8. A possible formulation of PSC might be to the effect that (necessarily) if a thing is at all ("in principle") uniquely identifiable at some time, then it is ("in principle") uniquely identifiable at all times:

$$\Box \forall t \ t | \forall x \ (\exists F \ 1xFx \supset \exists G \ \forall t' \ t' | 1xGx).$$

Or one might consider omitting the antecedent condition. But other formulations might appeal, especially in connection with "Descartes' Principle" discussed below.

9. A reconstrual will be subsequently proposed in connection with "Descartes' Principle."

10. For how are we, otherwise, to construe the very statement of our aim, if made today; how are we to construe the phrases 'the ship' and 'the wood'? We must not suppose that we always have proper names (as

might be suggested by our heuristic use of the individual constants '*s*' and '*w*'). And even if we did, how is it ensured that 'Sally' is the name of the ship and 'Wilbur' the name of the wood, rather than, say, the other way around? Even today we must be able to affirm

$d|\exists x\,(1x\,([Sx]\,\&\,1xMx\,\&\,\forall t\,\;t|1x([Sx]\,\&\,d|1\,xMx))$
$d|\exists x\,(1x\,([Wx]\,\&\,1xMx\,\&\,\forall t\,\;t|1x([Wx]\,\&\,d|1\,xMx)).$

without being committed to the results of interchanging the right conjuncts within the existential generalization.

11. See the paragraph on inference rules of System *G*, above.

12. I am here taking it for granted that the ship remaining (so far) in the marketplace is the original ship.

13. All such specifications (or "definitions") are always to be regarded as subjected to the temporal qualification: $\forall t\,\;t|$—and, perhaps, to an initial '□'. Note that if there is a time at which $x=y$ and a time at which x exists and y does not, then x and y "properly overlap" *eo ipso*.

14. Note, however, that at a time when the ship and the wood are identical, the former and the latter *are alike* with respect to ("*just*") being a ship and ("*just*") being (a bit of) wood. But the former and the latter *do differ* with respect to being *essentially* a ship and being *essentially* (a bit of) wood. The intuition that something that is a ship (a bit of wood) must continue to be a ship (a bit of wood), at least if it continues to exist, is more properly that something that is *essentially* a ship (a bit of wood) must continue to be (essentially) a ship (a bit of wood), at least if it continues to exist.

15. I am deeply grateful to, and hereby thank, Professor Neil Thomason, Mr. Alan Walworth, and Professor Richard Warner for numerous helpful counterexamples to an earlier attempt at this in a seminar; Professor George Bealer for effecting the writing of this whole paper and its publication; and Professor H. Paul Grice for engendering the thought that gave rise to its substance. Final thanks to Bealer for valiant last-minute attempts to improve this paper and to Noa Latham for insightful proofreading.

16. Though, perhaps, it must be identical with something that needs to be, for some sort *S*, (a bit of) "material" or "stuff" of sort *S* in order to exist. I cannot pursue this tangent here.

17. Perhaps the proposed "definition" does not quite capture the traditional idea. Perhaps we need to insert another 'necessarily' in front of the second occurrence of 'at all times*'. But there may be motives for not doing this—see footnote 22. Also, recall that the asterisk on 'at all times' records, in effect, my uncertainty whether to follow tradition and require a thing's possession of its essence *only* at times *at which it exists*. More or less, the same uncertainty prompts the parenthetical 'existing'.

18. E.g., assign being a ship as essential to the ship at stage 1, being organic matter as essential to the wood at stage 2, and being wood as essential to the ship at stage 3.

19. In line with our brief discussion of *genus*-properties, above, we may form a *derivative* notion of "being essentially$_2$F": being essentially *G*—in the sense "defined" above—for some *G* such that *F* is an AMALNP property implied by *G*. This carries over *mutatis mutandis* to the subsequent reconstrual in connection with "Descartes' Principle."

20. *G* in the formulation of PSC in footnote 8 being the conjunction of *F* with [*Hx*], for some *H*.

21. An attempt to insist that the toy ship and the (bit of) plastic are *distinct* when they *do not* exist fails for lack of specification of conditions under which *one* existing thing "becomes" (or "comes to be from") *two* nonexistent things, rather than only one, or some other number. *Cf* footnote 10.

22. E.g., in section 60 of part 1 of his *Principles of Philosophy:* -And even if we supposed that God had conjoined some corporeal substance to such a conscious substance so closely that they could not be more closely joined and had thus compounded *a unity out of the two*, yet even so they remain really distinct." (Translated by E. Anscombe and P.T. Geach in their *Descartes Philosophical Writings*, Indianapolis, 1971. Emphasis mine.) Perhaps, the *x* such that [*Fx*] and [*Gx*] in the "Descartes' Principle" I am about to state is a case of his "substantial union."

23. E.g., shall we say that: $□\forall t\,\;t|P$, is equivalent to: $\forall t\,\;t|□P$—or: $□\exists t\,\;t|P$, to: $\exists t\,\;t|□P$? And should we even allow constructions like the second in each pair? I am inclined to favor "iterating" System *G* or "applying it to itself," as it were, to produce a modal temporal logic—see end of "Identity and Time" (cited in footnote 2). Note, however, that in the preceding explication (setting aside footnote 17) of being essentially *F*, modality *de re* has appeared only with respect to *properties* (*predicates*); no modality *de re* with respect to *individuals* (*individual-symbols*) has been employed.

Actuality and Essence

WILLIAM G. LYCAN AND STEWART SHAPIRO

In this paper we shall construct a system of possible worlds out of familiar (if not unproblematic) abstract entities. Specifically, developing a proposal made in Lycan (1979), we identify ''worlds'' with certain sets of structured propositions, and ''nonexistent objects'' with certain complex properties. Thus, we take our place among those whom David Lewis (1973, 1986) has dubbed ''Ersatzers'': We treat possible worlds neither as blooming, buzzing, flesh-and-blood, albeit literally *nonactual,* universes nor in any other forthrightly Meinongian way. Instead, we furnish a stock of actual, this-worldly, though abstract, entities to take over the formal jobs that ''worlds'' have been supposed to perform.[1] These jobs include explicating the structure of modal and counterfactual discourse, clarifying puzzles about identity and individuation, and affording semantics for propositional attitudes. Let us make clear at the outset that neither of us endorses any particular semantics thus afforded;[2] our aim is only to make available an Ersatz apparatus for the use of theorists who wish to draw on the resources of possible-worlds semantics but who shrink from brazen Meinongianism considered as back-to-the-wall ontology—theorists in search of ''paradise on the cheap,'' in Lewis's phrase. Our reason for pursuing the Ersatz approach is that we take it to be the most satisfactory alternative to any theory of modality that takes Meinongian quantification as primitive and posits genuinely nonactual or nonexistent ''entities'' without construing these somehow just in terms of actual objects and their properties and relations. Our arguments against such brazen or ''relentless'' Meinongianism, and our objections to further competing deflationary accounts of ''possibilia,'' are given in Lycan (1979) and will not be repeated here; but we shall reply to some current criticisms of the Ersatz approach.

In discussing the presuppositions of our account, we intend to display some options available to investigators of the alethic modalities, and we shall clarify the often vexing tradeoffs involved in talk of necessity and possibility. We shall also begin to expose some connections between the alethic modalities, counterfactuals, and propositional attitude constructions.

343

Other theorists have proposed actualist accounts of possible worlds that resemble ours in some respects, so it is worth noting the differences. Some, like McMichael (1983b), take an axiomatic approach; certain abstract or structural properties of "possible worlds" are stipulated and defended, and then a modal language is interpreted in (arbitrary) models of the axioms.[3] Our approach is rather to *construct* worlds from stipulated sets of objects, properties, and relations; the modal language is then interpreted in the constructed structure. One advantage of our approach is that questions of consistency and overcardinality do not arise; our semantics is consistent provided only that the background set theory is.[4] Other writers who have construed possible worlds as collections of propositions (or sentences), such as Fine (1977) and Roper (1982), have taken worlds to be sets of propositions in a modal language, i.e., a language with at least one modal operator.[5] By contrast, the present approach is to construct worlds from the propositions of a nonmodal language, and only then to interpret a modal language in the resulting structure. Possibility is not (directly) taken as primitive. (Possibility is for us closely related to satisfiability, however; this is a consequence of the standard use of set theory to provide semantics for formal languages. We shall have more to say on the question of modal primitives.)

1. PROGRAM, PRESUPPOSITIONS, AND PRELIMINARIES

The following entities are assumed:

(a) A set α of actually existing concrete individuals. This could be limited to the collection of physical atoms or physically basic constituents of matter, but we prefer to include ordinary physical objects, organisms, and people. (Readers who believe in immaterial Cartesian egos or other nonspatial entities that nonetheless are contingent and/or located in time should feel free to add these on their own.) Every element of α exists in the actual world; each alternative, "nonactual" world contains the members of a (possibly empty) subset of α.

(b) A set β of abstract entities including (perhaps) sets, integers, and real numbers. To avoid cardinality problems, β is taken to be a set. This limitation is no defect even though the collection of all abstract objects does not form a set. The only abstract entities needed for present purposes are those that bear, or can bear, contingent relations to members of α. It seems reasonable that this collection of abstract objects is not a proper class. For simplicity, neither α nor β contains "mixed" entities such as sets of physical individuals or functions from numbers to physical individuals; thus, we sidestep problems raised by the contingent existence of such items (see Fine [1977], Chisholm [1981]). All members of β exist in all worlds. (Readers who think of sets, universals, propositions, and the like as theoretical posits that may or may not really exist and that therefore inhabit some worlds but not others will accordingly hold that β is empty. Let us mark the difference between this and the foregoing way of conceiving nonspatiotemporal entities by stipulatively reserving the term "*formal* entity" for members of β; thus, by definition, any "formal" entities there may be exist in all possible worlds.[6] Conversely, those who believe that some concrete items—Tractarian objects, perhaps, or God—necessarily exist and inhabit every possible world can feel free to include those items in β.)

(c) A set Γ of properties and relations, including those applying to members of α (such as personhood), those applying to members of β (such as primeness), and those applying to appropriately constituted sequences containing both kinds of entities (such as weight in grams and number of molecules). For simplicity, Γ contains neither infinitary relations nor properties of propositions.[7]

A *primitive proposition* is a member of Γ together with an appropriately constituted sequence of members of α and β. *Propositions* are constructed from primitive propositions in the usual way. We limit ourselves here to the usual finitary operations. In addition, no higher-order quantification is countenanced, until it is introduced much later as a special extension of our semantics.

We stipulate at the outset that neither α nor β contains properties, relations, propositions, or sets of propositions. Thus, for example, the present account does not countenance propositions about other propositions, or propositions about sets of propositions (such as worlds). To do so would prematurely bring on conceptual, and perhaps logical, difficulties. (We shall return to this issue in section 6.1 below.)

We accommodate the transworld identity, in the strict sense, of actually existing individuals: Since "worlds" are sets of propositions, it is easily determined which members of α inhabit a given nonactual world; individual i is in world W iff W has as an element some proposition about i. Thus, actually existing individuals are identified directly with themselves, and not with properties or with sets of properties.

We treat the transworld identity of "nonactual individuals" differently, since we do not countenance their existence in any robustly Meinongian sense (see, again, Lycan [1979]). To say that "the present king of France" could exist is to say only that it is possible for there to be at present a king of France, which on our account is, in turn, to say that some possible world has as a member the proposition $\exists x (x$ is at present king of France). Unlike actuals, merely possible individuals are identified with certain properties or *essences,* an "essence" being in part a property that necessarily applies to, at most, one individual.[8] Moreover, the essences at each possible world are stipulated. A given individual's essence serves to pick out that individual at other worlds. Suppose, for example, that F is an essence at world W and, thus, that $\exists x F x$ is a member of W. Suppose also that another world W' contains $\exists x (F x \& P x)$ for some property P; then we would say that the merely possible individual indentified by F in W has P in W'. However, it does not follow that F is an *essence* in W'. Let "the funniest person" be an essence in W, the idea being that there might have been (and is in W) a person distinct from any actual person who was also funnier than anyone in his or her own world.[9] Then the property of being the funniest person does not apply *in* W to anyone who exists at the actual world @; as we have said, actual individuals are not identified by their contingent properties at any world. But it may happen that "the funniest person" may apply to, say, John Cleese *in* @, or at another world W'. This is not contradictory, for "the funniest person" is not Cleese's essence in @, or in any other world for that matter.

Thus, we pejoratively distinguish the individuation of nonexistents from that of actuals, at least for the official purposes of this paper. We want to be traditional essentialists concerning the former, though haecceitists concerning the latter (but we shall consider alternatives to this policy later on). Against rabid realists of Lewis's stripe, we are inclined to hold that the two sorts of individuals differ sharply: (i) Actual individuals are given; by definition, they are part of the world we live in. They can be perceived and ostended. (And we assume that the proper names of actual individuals neither abbreviate flaccid descriptions nor are equivalent to them in any other semantical way.[10]) Mere possibilia are not given or (*pace* Routley [1980]) encountered, but specified, stipulated, or constructed. Moreover, (ii) the only way to specify a nonexistent is to proffer a description—"the golden mountain," "the present king of France," "the winged horse ridden by Bellerophon," "Jimmy Carter's older brother."[11] (It is these specifying descriptions that are taken for now as the essences.) And consequently, (iii) it is arguable that nonexistents figure in no "singular propositions," and that they are the objects of neither *de re* modalities nor *de re* propositional attitudes.[12] We see no clear sense in which one can have a particular nonactual object in mind as opposed to one that is qualitatively just like it (though we shall take a tentative step toward providing such a sense for those who want one in the appendix).

Our dichotomy between haecceitism for actuals and qualitative essentialism for "nonexistents" can be formally bridged despite the differences just mentioned, so long as the haecceities of actuals are taken to be *their* essences. That is, for each actual individual c, there is a property that applies to c alone in those worlds in which c exists and to nothing at any other world; in effect, it is the property of *being (identical with)* c, expressible by the predicate $x = c$.[13]

2. THE CONSTRUCTION

We find it convenient to introduce a *language* of sorts, with each "sentence" taken as denoting or specifying, rather than expressing, a proposition. Members of α and β are taken as constants denoting themselves, and members of Γ as predicate and relation "letters." The language is two-sorted, with lowercase roman letters acting as constants and variables ranging over α, and uppercase roman letters as constants and variables ranging over β. For each subset $\alpha_0 \subseteq \alpha$, let $L\alpha_0$ be the language constructed from α_0, β, and Γ. Notice that $L\alpha_0$ is not a modal language. Modal operators will be added below and interpreted by the present structure.

We need to stipulate a set E of formulas of L, each with one lowercase variable. Various members of E serve as essences of nonactual objects in the various worlds. A formula ϕx of E will be thought of as specifying (or naming) the one object satisfying ϕ at a given world. For each $c \in \alpha$, E contains the formula $x = c$. As above, this formula is c's haecceity and only essence. Some restrictions on E will be needed in light of other facets of the structure. In what follows, the term "individual" will be used to refer to entities named by members of E; "actual individual" will refer only to members of α (i.e., to entities named by the haecceities).

We also require the stipulation of a set N of sentences of $L\alpha$. These are the necessary or essential truths. A sentence ψ is a *necessary* truth iff ψ holds in (is a member of) every possible world; ψ is an *essential* truth iff ψ holds in every possible world containing those members of α occurring in ψ. The set N should include all true statements concerning only members of β (such as the truths of mathematics) and all sentences regarded as analytic truths. For each possible essence ϕx, N should also contain the sentence $\forall x \forall y (\phi x \,\&\, \phi y \rightarrow x = y)$; that is, it is necessary that each essence apply to, at most, one individual at each world. The set N may contain sentences about actual objects that express properties and relations taken to be essential to those objects, such as "Socrates is human"—our haecceitism does not preclude actual objects' having essential properties, but only the identification of actual individuals with those properties. N may also contain statements expressing purported metaphysical laws (e.g., "Everything is either material or ideal," "Time travel does not occur"), ordinary physical laws, or the like. Different stipulations of the set N will reflect different notions of necessity. For example, a minimal N reflects logical necessity, while a rather full N might reflect, say, physical, chemical, and biological necessity all in one. It should be noted, finally, that N need not be closed under deduction. Even if "Socrates is human" is an essential truth, it does not follow that "There are humans" is either an essential or a necessary truth, since "There are no humans" may be true at worlds that lack Socrates entirely. However, the details of the possible-worlds structure guarantee deductive closure within worlds.

One might object that by requiring the set of essential truths to be stipulated, we throw away the explanatory advantage of standard accounts. But we are only bringing out what is already implicit in the standard treatments. On any possible-worlds semantics, a sentence expresses a necessary (or essential) truth just in case it is true in all the relevant worlds. But how is it to be determined whether such truths as "2 + 2 = 4," "All physical objects attract," "Socrates is human," or "This table is made of wood" hold throughout all worlds? Imagine two people disputing whether there is a world at which $2 + 2 \neq 4$, or at which Socrates is crustacean rather than human. There is no obvious way to adjudicate such a question.

At such a juncture, one of the disputants might frustratedly and frustratingly fall back and assert that even if "2 + 2 = 4" fails at some worlds, it still holds at every *mathematically* possible world; that "All physical objects attract" holds in every *physically* possible world; and, perhaps, that "Socrates is human" is true in every world in which Socrates is as he (essentially) is in @ (i.e., in all "Socratic" worlds). But what makes a world "mathematically possible," other than its containing or validating all the truths of mathematics; what makes a world "physically possible" save its supporting all the laws of physics; and wherein is a world "Socratic" but for its containing Socrates's purported essential properties? So far as we can determine, the only way to specify a certain relative modality by reference to a special type of world is to stipulate the set of propositions distinctively contained by every world of that type. If so, then stipulation of this sort is essential to *any* account of possible worlds.

We arrive, finally, at our key definition. A *possible world* is a structure $<\alpha_W, E_W, S_W>$ in which:

  (1) $\alpha_W \subseteq \alpha$.
  (2) (a) $E_W \subseteq E$,
      (b) the members of E_W are all in $L\alpha_W$, and
      (c) for each $c \,\epsilon\, \alpha_W$, the haecceity $x = c$ is in E_W.

(3) S_W is a set of sentences of $L\alpha_W$ such that

    (a) S_W is maximally consistent (that is, S_W is satisfiable and if $S_W \subseteq S$ is in $L\alpha_W$, then either $S_W = S$ or S is not satisfiable),

    (b) every element of N in the language $L\alpha_W$ is in S_W,

    (c) if ϕx and ψx are in E_W, then $\exists x \phi x$ and $\forall x\,(\phi x \rightarrow \sim \psi x)$ are in S_W,

    (d) if $\exists x \chi x \in S_W$, then there is an essence $\phi x \in E_W$ such that $\exists x (\phi x\ \&\ \chi x) \in S_w$, and

    (e) if $\exists X\ \pi(X) \in S_W$ then there is an $A \in \beta$ such that $\pi(A) \in S_W$.

We allow the possibility that α_W is null, or in other words, the possibility that W contains no actual individuals. We also allow (or at least do not disallow) the possibility that E_W is null, in which case W contains *no* individuals (but in light of (3b) and (3d), this is ruled out if N contains an existentially quantified sentence, such as $\exists x (x = x)$, that does not contain any actual individuals). If E_W is empty, we call W *the empty world*. (Assuming that there are neither structureless propositions—propositions having no predicates as parts—nor 0-adic predicates, there is at most one empty world. In such a world, any sentence of the form $\forall x\ \chi$ is true, and any sentence of the form $\exists x \chi$ is false.) Note that if there is an empty world, then the definition of satisfaction must be modified to allow satisfaction in an empty domain. The definition of modal satisfaction that we shall offer includes special clauses for this purpose.

One world $W(@)$ is designated the *actual world* (we shall use the latter phrase indifferently as between the abstract structure $<\alpha_W, E_W, S_W>$ and the one flesh-and-blood universe we have already called $@$, except where confusion would result). We have $\alpha_{@} = \alpha$ and $E_{@} = \{x = a \mid a \in \alpha\}$.

The set α_W is the collection of actual individuals ($\in @$) that exist in W. The set E_w is the collection of essences of the individuals (actual and nonactual) that exist in W. Clause (2b) prevents a sentence like "x is the older brother of Jimmy Carter" from being an essence in a world lacking Jimmy Carter. Of course, this does *not* prevent "the older brother of the first President from Plains" from being an essence in such a world. Clause (2c) guarantees that the essence of each actual individual is its haecceity.

The set S_W is the class of propositions true in W. Clause (3a) ensures that W is completely determined. For each sentence ψ of $L\alpha_w$, either $\psi \in S_w$ or $\sim\psi \in S_w$. (3b) entails that each necessary or essential truth about actual individuals that are contained in W is true in W. (3c), together with the foregoing properties of N, guarantees that each essence of W names exactly one individual that "exists" in W and that no two essences name the same individual. Thus, there is a one-one correspondence between the essences of W and the individuls existing in W. Clause (3c) also entails that if b and c are distinct members of α_w, then $b \neq c$ is a member of S_w. For example, we do not consider it possible for Jimmy Carter and Billy Carter to be identical. Obviously, it is possible for Lillian Carter to have had just one son who became an alcoholic, peanut farmer, gas station owner, human rights champion, beer promoter, Libyan sympathizer, and President; it is possible for this son to have been Jimmy Carter and possible for him to have been Billy Carter (and it is possible for him to have been someone who does not exist), but it is not possible for this son to have been both Jimmy and Billy. On our view, to *be* Jimmy is (*inter alia*) to be distinct from Billy. (3c) also entails that if ϕx is an essence of W that is not a haecceity and $b \in \alpha_W$, then $\sim\phi b$ is in S_w. Notice that this does not prevent ϕb from holding in a different world (in which ϕ is not an essence). Finally, (3d) guarantees that each "individual" predicate satisfied in W is satisfied by an essence of W and that each "abstract" predicate satisfied in W is satisfied in W by a member of β.

Despite our quick remarks in its defense, our tendentious differential individuation policy (as between existents and nonexistents) is questionable, to say the least. One may be particularly dissatisfied with our essentialistic assumptions that there are no singular propositions involving nonactuals and that (accordingly, or *vice versa*) there are no attitudes or modalities *de* nonactuals. Among others, David Lewis and Alan McMichael have maintained that an adequate modal semantics must accommodate all these features, contrary to our assumptions;[14] we shall consider their arguments in section 5 below and also in the appendix.

3. MODAL LANGUAGE AND SEMANTICS

The language $M\alpha$ is obtained from $L\alpha$ by adding two sentential operators:

(1) For each formula ψ, $\Box\psi$ is a formula, read "ψ is essential." If ψ is a sentence without lowercase constants, then $\Box\psi$ may be read "ψ is necessary." Informally, if ψ is any sentence, then $\Box\psi$ is true if ψ is true in every world that contains all of the actual individuals named in ψ.

(2) For each formula ψ, $\Diamond\psi$ is a formula, read "ψ is possible." Informally, if ψ is a sentence, then $\Diamond\psi$ is true if ψ is true in some possible world.

There is little need for an additional operator for necessity, or truth in all possible worlds. Concerning sentences that lack lowercase constants, such an operator would be equivalent to our "$\Box$," and concerning sentences with lowercase constants, such an operator would be empty. The above structure entails that there is no member of α that is contained in every possible world.

Before proceeding with the strengths and weaknesses of our structure and modal language, we shall develop the semantics. This involves assigning a truth value to each sentence at each world *containing the actual individuals named in the sentence*. The semantics is bivalent in that there are only two truth values. The only "gap" is that no truth value is assigned to a sentence in a world that does not contain all of the relevant actual individuals. Notice, incidentally, that it follows that every sentence of $M\alpha$ is assigned a truth value in the actual world.

We employ the usual technique of assigning truth values to formulas in terms of valuations of the free variables. For a given possible world W, let a W-*valuation* v be a function that assigns an essence $[v/x](y)$ in E_W to each lowercase variable x, and assigns a member $\{v/X\}$ of β to each uppercase variable X. In the case in which W is the empty world, E_W is null, so, of course, no assignment can be made to the lowercase free variables. Thus, an empty world valuation is limited to an assignment of members of β to uppercase variables. (If also β is null, then there are no empty world assignments.)

For each world W, each W-valuation v, and each appropriate formula ψ, we define $W, v \models \psi$, read "v satisfies ψ at W: We proceed by induction on the "complexity" of formulas. Formula ψ is said to be *more complex* than χ iff either ψ contains more modal operators than χ or the two formulas have the same number of modal operators and ψ has more connectives and quantifiers. Thus, for example, if R is a predicate, then $\Box Ra$ is more complex than $\forall x \forall y (Rx \rightarrow Ry)$.

A. If $\psi (x_1 \ldots x_n X_1 \ldots X_m)$ is an atomic formula, all of whose free variables are indicated, then $W, v \models \psi$ iff the sentence

$$\forall y_1 \ldots \forall y_n (([v/x_1] (y_1) \& \ldots \& [v/x_n] (y_n)) \rightarrow$$
$$\psi(y_1 \ldots y_n \{v/Y_1\} \ldots \{v/Y_m\}))$$

is in S_W. Notice that if W is the empty world and $n > 0$, then this case does not arise—there are no appropriate W-valuations. In such cases, an ad hoc decision is in order; we prefer to say that in such situations, "$W, v \models \psi$" is not a legitimate metalinguistic formula.

B. $W, v \models \sim\psi$ iff $W, v \not\models \psi$; and similarly for the other connectives.

C. $W, v \models \forall x \psi$ iff $W, u \models \psi$ for each W-valuation u that agrees with v on every variable except possibly x (relettering if necessary); and similarly for the other quantifiers over uppercase and lowercase variables.[15]

D. If $\psi(x_1 \ldots x_n)$ is a formula, all of whose lowercase free variables are indicated, then $W, v \models \Box\psi$ iff $W', u \models$

$$\forall y_1 \ldots \forall y_n (([v/x_1] (y_1) \& \ldots \& [v/x_n] (y_n)) \rightarrow \psi(y_1 \ldots y_n)),$$

for all possible worlds W' containing the actual individuals named in $[v/x_1]$ $\ldots [v/x_n]$, and ψ, and all W' evaluations u that agree with v on uppercase variables (relettering if necessary).[16]

E. If $\psi(x_1 \ldots x_n)$ is a formula, all of whose lowercase free variables are indicated, then $W, v \models \Diamond\psi$ iff $W', u \models$

$$\exists y_1 \ldots \exists y_n ([v/x_1] (y_1) \& \ldots \& [v/x_n] (y_n) \& \psi(y_1 \ldots y_n)),$$

for some possible world W' containing the actual individuals named in $[v/x_1] \ldots [v/x_n]$, and ψ, and some W' evaluation u that agrees with v on uppercase variables (relettering if necessary).

If ψ is a sentence and W a world containing the actual individuals named in ψ, then ψ is *true at W*, written $W \models \psi$, iff $W, v \models \psi$ for every W-valuation v; ψ is *essential*, written $\models\psi$, iff $W \models \psi$ for every world W containing all of the actual individuals named in ψ. Finally, if ψ is a sentence containing no lowercase constants, then ψ is *necessary* iff $\models\psi$.

Recall that each essence of a world W names exactly one individual in W. Thus, informally, if R is a predicate, then

$$W, v \models R(a_1 \ldots a_m x_1 \ldots x_n A_1 \ldots A_p X_1 \ldots X_q)$$

iff S_W contains the sentence asserting that R is satisfied by $a_1 \ldots a_m$, the essences named by $[v/x_1] \ldots [v/x_n]$ and the abstract objects $A_1, \ldots, A_p, \{v/X_1\}, \ldots, \{v/X_q\}$.

4. PROPERTIES OF THE STRUCTURE AND SEMANTICS

To shed light on which sentences of $M\alpha$ are essential and which inferences are valid, we present the following theorems. The omitted proofs are straightforward, but some are tedious.

4.1 Logic

The first group of results concern the logic of the structure.

T1. If $\psi(x_1 \ldots x_n X_1 \ldots X_m)$ is a formula all of whose free variables are indicated, and v, u are two W-valuations such that $[v/x_i] = [u/y_i]$ and $\{v/X_J\} = \{u/Y_J\}$ for $1 < i < n$, $1 < J < m$, then $W, v \vDash \psi(x_1 \ldots x_n X_1 \ldots X_m)$ iff $W, u \vDash \psi(y_1 \ldots y_n Y_1 \ldots Y_m)$.

C1a. If ψ is a formula and v, u two W-valuations that agree on the free variables of ψ, then $W, v \vDash \psi$ iff $W, u \vDash \psi$.

C1b. If χ is a sentence, then $W \vDash \chi$ iff $W, v \vDash \chi$ for *some* W-valuation v.

T2. If $\psi(X_1 \ldots X_m)$ is a formula some (or all) of whose free uppercase variables are indicated, then $W, v \vDash \psi(X_1 \ldots X_m)$ iff $W, v \vDash \psi(\{v/X_1\} \ldots \{v/X_m\})$.

T3. If $\psi(x_1 \ldots x_n X_1 \ldots X_m)$ is a formula of $L\alpha_W$ (i.e., a formula with no modal operators), all of whose free variables are indicated, then $W, v \vDash \psi$ iff the sentence

$$\forall y_1 \ldots \forall y_n (([v/x_1](y_1) \& \ldots \& [v/x_n](y_n)) \rightarrow$$
$$\psi(y_1 \ldots y_n \{v/X_1\} \ldots \{v/X_m\}))$$

is in S_W (relettering if necessary).[17]

Proof: We proceed by induction on the complexity of ψ. If ψ is atomic, then the theorem is the relevant clause in the definition of satisfaction. The cases of the induction step concerning the connectives are straightforward applications of first-order logic to the induction hypothesis and the conditions on S_W. The only cases of interest concern the quantifiers. We present here the case of the universal quantifier over lowercase variables. Suppose, then, that the theorem holds for $\psi(x, x_1 \ldots x_n X_1 \ldots X_m)$. We show that it also holds for $\forall x \psi$. Fix a W-valuation v and let $v*$ and $\psi*(x)$ abbreviate

$$[v/x_1](y_1) \& \ldots \& [v/x_n](y_n) \text{ and } \psi(x, y_1 \ldots y_n \{v/X_1\} \ldots \{v/X_m\})$$

respectively. (1) Suppose, first, that $\forall y_1 \ldots \forall y_n (v* \rightarrow \forall x \psi*(x))$ is in S_W. Let $\phi(y)$ be any essence of W. By deductive closure, S_W contains the sentence $\forall y \forall y_1 \ldots \forall y_n (\phi \& v* \rightarrow \psi*(y))$. Thus, by the induction hypothesis and C1a, we have that $W, u \vDash \psi$ for any W-valuation that assigns ϕ to x and agrees with v on the other free variables of ψ. Since ϕ is arbitrary, we have $W, v \vDash \forall x \psi$. (2) Suppose, now, that $W, v \vDash \forall x \psi$. Then $W, u \vDash \psi$ for every W-valuation u that agrees with v except possibly at x. Thus, by the induction hypothesis, $\forall y \forall y_1 \ldots \forall y_n (\phi \& v* \rightarrow \psi*(y))$ is in S_W for each essence ϕ of W. To obtain a contradiction, suppose that $\forall y_1 \ldots \forall y_n (v* \rightarrow \forall x \psi*(x))$ is *not* in S_W. Since S_W is maximally consistent, we have that $\exists y \exists y_1 \ldots \exists y_n (v* \& \sim \psi*(y))$ *is* in S_W.

By one of the conditions on S_W, there is an essence ϕ such that $\exists y \exists y_1 \ldots \exists y_n (\phi(y) \,\&\, v* \,\&\, {\sim}\psi*(y))$ is in S_W. This contradicts the consistency of S_W.

C3a.   If ψ is a sentence of $L\alpha$, then $W \vDash \psi$ iff $\psi \in S_W$.

C3b.   If ϕ is an essence of W, then $W,v \vDash \phi(x)$ iff $[v/x]$ is ϕ.

Proof: By T3, we have $W,v \vDash \phi$ iff $\forall y([v/x](y) \to \phi(y)) \in S_W$. If $[v/x]$ is ϕ, then the latter formula is a logical truth and is thus contained in S_W, whence $W,v \vDash \phi(x)$. If, however, $[v/x]$ is not ϕ, then, by the conditions on S_W, we have that $\forall y([v/x](y) \to {\sim}\phi(y))$ and $\exists y[v/x](y)$ are both in S_W. Thus, $\forall y([v/x](y) \to \phi(y))$ is not in S_W and, hence, $W,v \nvDash \phi$.

T4.   If $\psi(x)$ is a formula (of $M\alpha$) with x (and possibly other variables) free, and v is a W-valuation in which $[v/x]$ is a haecceity $y = a$, then $W,v \vDash \psi(x)$ iff $W,v \vDash \psi(a)$.

The following is a straightforward corollary of T1 and C3b (but see note 17):

T5.   If $\psi(x_1 \ldots x_n X_1 \ldots X_m)$ is a formula, some (or all) of whose free variables are indicated, then $W,v \vDash \psi$ iff $W,u \vDash$

$$\forall y_1 \ldots \forall y_n (([v/x_1](y_1) \,\&\, \ldots \,\&\, [v/x_n](y_n)) \to$$
$$\psi(y_1 \ldots y_n \{v/X_1\} \ldots \{v/X_m\}))$$

for some (or, by C1a, every) W-valuation u that agrees with v on the remaining free variables of ψ (relettering if necessary).

T6.   Let W be a nonempty possible world and $\psi, \chi_1, \ldots, \chi_n$ be formulas of $M\alpha$. If ψ is a logical consequence of $\chi_1 \ldots \chi_n$ and if $W, v \vDash \chi_i$ for all W-valuations v and all $1 < i < n$, then $W,v \vDash \psi$ for all W-valuations v.[18]

Proof: We proceed by induction on the length of a derivation of ψ (from the χ_i) in a standard axiomatization of first-order logic. The only interesting cases are the axioms and rules involving the quantifiers. As examples, we present instances of the rule of existential instantiation, $\psi(x) \to \chi \vdash \exists x\psi \to \chi$, and universal instantiation, $\vdash \forall x\psi(x) \to \psi(a)$, both for lowercase variables: (1) Suppose, then, that $W,v \vDash \psi(x) \to \chi$ for all W-valuations v. Suppose also that $W,u \vDash \exists x\psi(x)$ for some W-valuation u. Then we have $W,u' \vDash \psi(x)$ for some W-valuation u' that agrees with u except possibly at x. By assumption, $W,u' \vDash \psi(x) \to \chi$ and, hence, $W,u' \vDash \chi$. Since, by the restrictions on existential generalization, χ does not contain x free, we have (by C1a) $W,u \vDash \chi$. (2) Suppose $W,v \vDash \forall x\psi(x)$ for some W-valuation v. Then $W,v' \vDash \psi(x)$ for every W-valuation v' that agrees with v except possibly at x. Let u be such a valuation in which $[u/x]$ is the haecceity $y=a$. By T4, we have $W,u \vDash \psi(a)$. Since v and u agree on every variable except x, and x does not occur free in $\psi(a)$, we have $W,v \vDash \psi(a)$.

C6a.   If ψ is a logical truth that is true in the empty world, then $\vDash \square\psi$.

C6b.   If ψ is a logical truth, then $\vDash \exists x(x=x) \to \square\psi$ and $\vDash \square(\exists x(x=x) \to \psi)$.[19]

So much for the purely logical aspects of our structure and semantics. To sum up, corollary C3a indicates that the only nonmodal sentences satisfied at a given possible world are those it ''contains''; theorem T5 reduces the satisfaction of a formula by a W-valuation to the truth at W of a corresponding sentence; and theorem T6 entails that every nonempty possible world satisfies every logical truth and that satisfaction at a given possible world is closed under logical consequence.

4.2. Propositional modal logic

We turn now to modal formulas. Our structure and semantics validate some common laws:

T7a. $W,v \models \Box\psi \leftrightarrow \sim\Diamond\sim\psi$ and $W,v \models \Diamond\psi \leftrightarrow \sim\Box\sim\psi$, for all worlds W and W-valuations v.

T7b. $W,v \models \Box\psi \rightarrow \psi$ and $W,v \models \psi \rightarrow \Diamond\psi$ for all worlds W and W-valuations v.

These, of course, are rather minimal properties of essentiality and possibility. Other common modal formulas apply only in restricted forms:

T8. If ψ has no lowercase free variables, then (a) $W,v \models \Box\psi \rightarrow \Box\Box\psi$ and (b) $W,v \models \Diamond\psi \rightarrow \Box\Diamond\psi$, both for all appropriate worlds W and W-valuations v.

The formula indicated in (a), of course, is the main axiom of S4; (b) concerns the main axiom of S5.

It is worth noting that neither of these hold generally if the main formula ψ contains free variables. Informally, the problem is that the possible essences are not "rigid." If ϕ is an essence (of a nonactual) in W, it may happen that ϕ is not an essence in W' and, moreover, may refer in W' to an (actual or nonactual) individual with different essential properties. For example, suppose that (1) a formula $\phi(x)$ (say, equivalent to "x is the funniest person") is an essence in world W; (2) there is a formula $\chi(x)$ (perhaps, equivalent to "x is funny") such that $\forall x(\phi \rightarrow \chi)$ is a necessary truth; (3) $\phi(c)$ $\epsilon S_@$ (if c is John Cleese, then this amounts to Cleese being the funniest person in the actual world); and (4) $\sim\chi(c) \epsilon S_V$ (i.e., Cleese is not funny in V). For world W, let $[v/x]$ be ϕ. Under these conditions, $W,v \models \Box\chi(x)$. (In W, it is essential that the funniest person is funny.) However, since $V \models \sim\chi(c)$, we have $@ \models \sim\Box\chi(c)$ (Cleese is not essentially funny) and, thus, $@ \models \phi(c)\& \sim\Box\chi(c)$ and so $@ \models \exists x(\phi(x)\&\sim\Box\chi(x))$. Thus, $W,v \nvDash \Box\Box\chi(x)$. (That is to say, even though "the funniest person is funny" is necessary, it does not follow that in every world, the individual who satisfies "x is the funniest person" is *essentially* funny.) A somewhat similar construction refutes the unrestricted version of T8b.

The situation concerning the haecceities, however, is different:

T8'. $W,v \models \Box\psi \rightarrow \Box\Box\psi$ and $W,v \models \Diamond\psi \rightarrow \Box\Diamond\psi$ for all worlds W and W-valuations v that assign haecceities to all lowercase free variables of ψ.

In particular, both formulas are always satisfied at the actual world $@$ (or any world that contains only actuals). Theorem T8' holds because each haecceity refers to the same individual (with the same essential properties) in each possible world that it refers at all.

There are some common modal formulas that are not generally satisfied here. The most notable of these, perhaps, are $\Box(\psi \rightarrow \chi) \rightarrow (\Box\psi \rightarrow \Box\chi)$ and $\Box(\psi \& \chi) \rightarrow \Box\chi$. Let $\eta(x)$ be a formula (say, equivalent to "x is male") such that $\eta(c)$ is essential (i.e.,

Cleese is essentially male). Let Z be a world in which $\sim\exists x\,\eta(x)\in S_Z$ (there are no males in Z). Notice that $\eta(c)\rightarrow\exists x\,\eta(x)$ is a logical truth and, thus, $@\vDash\Box(\eta(c)\rightarrow\exists x\,\eta(x))$. Also, $@\vDash\Box\eta(c)$. However, since $Z\nvDash\exists x\,\eta(x)$, we have $@\nvDash\Box\exists x\,\eta(x)$. Notice that we even have $@\nvDash\Box(\eta(c)\,\&\,\exists x\,\eta(x))\rightarrow\Box\exists x\,\eta(x)$.

The problem with these formulas is that the satisfiability of the compounds $\Box(\psi\rightarrow\chi)$ and $\Box(\psi\,\&\,\chi)$ involves those worlds containing the actual individuals named in *both* ψ and χ, while the satisfiability of $\Box\chi$ involves the (wider) class of worlds containing only the actual individuals named in χ. A similar problem results if ψ has free variables not free in χ. We do, however, have

T9. $W,v\vDash\Box(\psi\rightarrow\chi)\rightarrow(\Box\psi\rightarrow\Box\chi)$, provided that χ contains all of the lower-case constants and free variables that occur in ψ.

Notice that T9 holds in case the formulas in question have no lowercase free variables or constants. Thus,

T10.   If ψ is a sentence containing no lowercase constants that is a theorem of S5 (and, if appropriate, true in the empty world), then $\vDash\psi$.

Theorem T10, however, cannot be extended to the appropriate S5 consequences of N. As above, it does not follow from $\eta(c)\in N$ that $\vDash\exists x\,\eta(x)$. Let N' be the set of formulas of N that have no lowercase constants.

T10a. If ψ is a sentence containing no lowercase constants that is an S5 consequence of N' (and, if appropriate, true in the empty world), then $\vDash\psi$.

4.3 The quantifiers

We turn now to the various formulas that express relationships between the quantifiers and the modal operators. If δ is a variable, these formulas include (a) the Barcan formula $\forall\delta\Box\psi\rightarrow\Box\forall\delta\psi$, equivalent to $\Diamond\exists\delta\psi\rightarrow\exists\delta\Diamond\psi$; (b) its converse $\Box\forall\delta\psi\rightarrow\forall\delta\Box\psi$, equivalent to $\exists\delta\Diamond\psi\rightarrow\Diamond\exists\delta\psi$; (c) $\exists\delta\Box\psi\rightarrow\Box\exists\delta\psi$, equivalent to $\Diamond\forall\delta\psi\rightarrow\forall\delta\Diamond\psi$; and, finally, (d) $\Box\exists\delta\psi\rightarrow\exists\delta\Box\psi$, equivalent to $\forall\delta\Diamond\psi\rightarrow\Diamond\forall\delta\psi$.

We begin with lowercase variables. The only formula generally valid is the converse of the Barcan formula.

T11. $W,v\vDash\Box\forall x\,\psi(x)\rightarrow\forall x\,\Box\psi(x)$ for every (appropriate) possible world W and W-valuation v.

That is, if $\forall x\,\psi$ holds in every (appropriate) possible world, then ψ holds of every possible individual in every (appropriate) possible world.

The Barcan formula itself, for lowercase variables, does not generally hold. Let χ be a property (perhaps, "having causal relationships with physical objects") that holds essentially of all individuals in the actual world. Thus, $@\vDash\Box\chi(a)$ for all $a\in\alpha$ and, thus, $@\vDash\forall x\,\Box\chi(x)$. This does not preclude a world V in which $\exists x\sim\chi(x)\in S_V$ (a world that contains a purely nonphysical individual). If so, then $@\nvDash\Box\forall x\,\chi(x)$. In short, if the Barcan formula did hold in a world W, then any property essential to every individual of W would hold of every possible individual in every (appropriate) possible world.

A similar example illustrates that the lowercase version of formula (c) is not generally satisfied. In the above example, since $@ \models \Box\chi\,(g)$, we have $@ \models \exists x \Box\chi(x)$. If Z is a world in which $\forall x \sim\chi(x) \in S_Z$ (i.e., in which every individual is nonphysical), then $@ \not\models \Box\exists x\chi(x)$. (Notice that this example also refutes $\forall x \Box\chi \to \Box\exists x\chi$, even if there are no empty worlds.)

Concerning formula (d), let $\chi\,(x)$ be a formula equivalent to "either x is the oldest child of Lillian Carter, or Lillian Carter has no children and x is Lillian Carter." It is reasonable to assume that $@ \models \Box\exists x\chi(x)$ and that $\models \forall x \forall y (\chi(x)\ \&\ \chi(y) \to x = y)$. In the actual world, Jimmy Carter j satisfies χ, or, in other words, $@ \models \chi(j)$. Let V be a world in which j exists but does not satisfy χ (such would be the case if Ms. Carter had had a child before Jimmy). Thus, $V \models \sim\chi(j)$. It follows that $@ \not\models \exists x \Box\chi(x)$. There is no actual individual that is essentially either-childless-Lillian-Carter-or-the-oldest-child-of-Lillian-Carter.

The main aspect of lowercase variables involved in these considerations is that they range over different sets in different worlds. Uppercase variables do not share this aspect—by definition, every world has the same set of abstract objects. That is, each world has the same set of natural numbers, real numbers, and so on. Moreover, each uppercase constant denotes the same individual (itself) in each world. A consequence is that three of the four formula forms presently under consideration are generally valid for uppercase variables:

T12. $W,v \models \forall X \Box\psi \to \Box\forall X\psi.$
    $W,v \models \Box\forall X\psi \to \forall X \Box\psi.$
    $W,v \models \exists X \Box\psi \to \Box\exists X\psi.$

Suppose, for example, that $W,v \models \forall X \Box\psi$. Then ψ holds essentially of each element of β and, thus, $W,v \models \Box\forall X\psi$.

Concerning uppercase variables, the only formula not generally valid is (d) $\Box\exists X\psi \to \exists X \Box\psi$. This is because abstract objects can have contingent relationships with concrete individuals. To mimic our previous example, suppose that $\psi(X)$ is equivalent to "X is a natural number and Lillian Carter has exactly X children." It seems reasonable to assume that $@ \models \Box\exists X\psi$ and that $\models \forall X \forall Y (\psi(X)\ \&\ \psi(Y) \to X = Y)$. Unless Ms. Carter has the same number of children in every world in which she exists, we have $@ \not\models \exists X \Box\chi$.

4.4. Cardinality

Since possible worlds here are sets of "linguistic" entities, it is not difficult to compute an upper bound on the number of possible worlds. Presuming a robust, but tempered, attitude on abstract objects, the limiting factor on world cardinality is the set β of abstract objects. Let κ be the cardinality of β and, for cardinality γ, let $P\gamma$ be the cardinality of the powerset of γ.

Recall that the only types of abstract objects required here are those that have, or can have, contingent relationships with concrete individuals. First, to account for number relationships, such as "number of offspring" or "number of molecules," β must contain natural numbers. It seems reasonable to include the entire set of natural numbers because, otherwise, there would be a fixed upper bound on the possible number of individuals. Thus, $\kappa > \aleph_0$. Second, to account for such relationships as "weight in grams" or "distance," β may have to include real numbers. If β contains "continuum many" real numbers, then $\kappa \geq P_{\aleph_0}$. It may be possible, however, to restrict β to rational numbers (or algebraic numbers) and to rely on approximation. For example, instead of "the weight of x, measured in grams, is (real number) X," we may be able to use "the weight of x, measured in grams, is within (rational number) Y of (rational number) Z." If this is possible, then $\kappa = \aleph_0$. On the other hand, if β does not contain all of the real numbers, it may not be possible (or convenient) to formulate enough of the laws of physics for the set N of essential truths. Third, β *may* contain functions from real numbers to real numbers in order to formulate such items as possible trajectories or weight as a function of time. If so, then it seems that $\kappa > PP_{\aleph_0}$. We hold, at least tentatively, that $PP_{\aleph_0}$ is an upper bound on the cardinality of β. At least for now, we cannot conceive of a larger collection of abstract objects all of which can have contingent relationships with concrete individuals. Thus, $\aleph_0 \leq \kappa \leq PP_{\aleph_0}$.

The set α of actual individuals is probably finite and certainly, at most, countable.[20] We assume, further, that the set Γ of properties and relations is, at most, countable. Thus, the cardinality of the set of expressions of $L\alpha$ is κ, and since a possible world is a set of sentences of $L\alpha$, there are at most $P\kappa$ possible worlds.

Thus, the complete upper bound on the number of possible worlds is $PPP_{\aleph_0}$. This, of course, is a rather large cardinal number, but we may at least assert that it is neither a proper class nor inaccessible.

Assume, for the moment, that β contains all of the real numbers and nothing else. It seems, then, that there must be *at least* "continuum-many" (i.e., $P_{\aleph_0}$) possible worlds. For example, let $\chi(X)$ be equivalent to "X is a real number between 60 and 100" and let $\psi(X)$ be equivalent to "the weight of Jimmy Carter, at the time of his nomination, measured in kilograms, is X." It seems reasonable to say that for each real number X between 60 and 100, Jimmy Carter could have weighed X kilograms at the time of his nomination. This amounts to @ $\models \forall X(\chi(X) \rightarrow \Diamond\psi(X))$. Now, if $\forall X \forall Y(\psi(X) \& \psi(Y) \rightarrow X = Y)$ is in N, then, for each real number X between 60 and 100, there must be a different possible world in which Jimmy Carter weighs X at the indicated moment. Thus, there must be at least $P_{\aleph_0}$ possible worlds.

Even though (under present assumptions) an uncountable set of abstract objects is needed to express every possibility, perhaps it can be assumed that in *any given world W*, all relationships between individuals of W and abstract objects are consequences of essential truths and a countable set of "simple" relationships (such as weight, height, and so on) between individuals and abstract objects. More formally, the proposal is that for each world W, there is a countable set of sentences C_W such that both $C_W \subseteq S_W$ and every member of S_W is a consequence of C_W and the sentences of N that are in $L\alpha_W$. If this proposal is correct, then (under the prevailing assumptions) the set of possible worlds has cardinality $P_{\aleph_0}$.

Against this conclusion, consider the relationship "the weight of Jimmy Carter X seconds after his birth, in kilograms, is Y" (both X and Y being real number variables). It seems clear that in each world, Jimmy Carter's weight is a function of his age. Mathematically, at least, there are more than $P_{\aleph_0}$ such functions.

5. FURTHER OBJECTIONS

We shall now mention some problems for our account.

5.1. Contingent existence

It is a feature of our semantics that a sentence ψ can be evaluated at a world W only if W contains all of the actual individuals named in ψ. But consider "Either Socrates was a professional boxer or there are people." If personhood is essential to Socrates, then the disjunction is satisfied in every world at which Socrates exists. It comes to count as an essential truth despite its disjuncts' being respectively false and contingent.

A cognate shortcoming is that our language $M\alpha$ cannot express contingent existence. For example, there is no sentence equivalent to "It is not necessary that Jimmy Carter exist." A straightforward attempt at such an expression would be $\sim\Box\exists x\,(x=j)$. But the latter is an essential falsehood, for $\exists x\,(x=j)$ holds at every world containing Jimmy Carter. Nor would it help at this stage to introduce a predicate $\eta(x)$ expressing "x exists." The predicate would be trivial, since we would have $\vDash \Box\forall x\,\eta(x)$, $\vDash \forall x\Box\eta(x)$, and $\vDash \eta(b)$ for each actual individual b. The third formula amounts to "b exists in every world that contains b."

These difficulties can be overcome by introducing a free logic (in which evaluated formulas can fail of truth-value) and extending the definition of $W,v \vDash \psi$ to all formulas ψ of $M\alpha$. A meaningful existence predicate could then be introduced. We would have $W,v \vDash \eta(b)$ if $b \in \alpha_W$ and $W,v \vDash \sim\eta(b)$ otherwise. Many formulas would then be seen as ambiguous regarding existential import of its constants; no new conceptual difficulties would arise.

5.2. Object language and metalanguage

Recall our stipulation at the outset that neither α nor β contains properties, relations, propositions, or sets of propositions. Its purpose was to provide the language L with a well-founded recursive definition and, incidentally, to allow a straightforward calculation of the number of possible worlds. A resulting feature of $L\alpha$ is that $L\alpha$ cannot express propositions about other propositions or about sets of propositions; thus, our modal language, $M\alpha$, is unable to make directly modal statements concerning either possible worlds or possibility itself.

$M\alpha$ does allow some indirect statements about possible worlds and possibility through iterated modal operators. For example, the interpretation of a formula in the form $\Box\Diamond\psi$ amounts to "For every possible world W, there is a world V that satisfies ψ." What cannot be expressed, even indirectly, are the straightforward senses of such statements as "There is a type of necessity relative to which '2 + 2 = 4' is contingent," "Every logical truth is essential," and Plantinga's "It is necessarily true that Socrates is snub-nosed in the actual world."

This difficulty could be overcome by a metalinguistic move: we might formalize the language used to discuss the present structure and develop a system of "metapossible worlds'' to interpret this metalanguage. If this were done, then many of our stipulations concerning L and the sets E, N, and S_W could be formulated as ''metanecessary'' truths to be included in the counterpart to N. The foregoing sample statements could be made in the metalinguistic modal language that serves as the counterpart to $M\alpha$.

We suggest that the present shortcoming and its somewhat cumbersome resolution are only a special case of the usual need for stratification of languages; no language is able to express its own semantics entirely.

5.3. Primitive modality

It might be complained (as by Lewis [1973, 85]) that our account is circular. We claim to explicate the notion of possibility, but we do so in terms of logical *consistency,* and what is ''consistency'' but the possibility of joint truth, or the impossibility of deducing a contradiction?

To this we reply (see Lycan [1979, 314]) by declining to understand consistency in any such way. As we have already made clear, we understand it rather in terms of satisfiability, which understanding affords us either of two quite tolerable options. First, we may define satisfiability as it is normally defined, in set-theoretical terms; satisfaction is simply a relation between models, the only primitive notion involved being that of membership. This stance has a steep ontology—the set-theoretical hierarchy, or at least enough of it to include all of the formal entities and the propositions, individuals, and so on. And it has the effect of reducing possibility to a *prima facie* nonmodal notion. But set theory is usually taken as grounding formal validity, consequence, and the like; we are only following standard practice on this construal. (Should another semantics come along, our framework could presumably be rewritten in its terms.)

But it may be fairly suspected that some modal primitive is still lurking in the neighborhood—perhaps, the admissibility of the models. Alternatively, then, we might exercise our second option: countermorphologically, we could take ''satisfiability'' as primitive. Admittedly, it would then be a *modal* primitive, which means we would have succeeded, at best, in explicating a few modal notions in terms of another. Would it not be better to disdain modal primitives and hold out for defining all modal notions in entirely nonmodal terms?

Indeed it would, and a wonderful trick it would be if anyone could do it. But unless our own model-theoretic option resists objection, no one ever has done it, and we gloomily doubt that anyone ever will, though we have no non-question-begging argument to show it impossible.[21] Every other system of modal metaphysics we know rests on at least one modal primitive, however bland. One might think that, in particular, Lewis uses no modal primitives, since his treatment of worlds as flesh-and-blood avoids the sorts of abstraction that actualists resort to, but not so: Lewis's primitive is the notion of a 'world'' itself. ''World'' for him means ''*possible* world,'' since he admits no impossibilia, and he no more provides an account of how it is that some sets of sentences correspond to ''worlds'' and some do not than we do of how it is that some are satisfiable and some are not.[22] Thus, we are no worse off, even if our earlier option is seen to fail.

5.4. Essences of nonactuals

Let us take up Lewis's and McMichael's question regarding modal properties of nonactuals. It arises in several different forms, but we think the most trenchant version of the objection is a simple modal one: Given such and such a nonexistent object introduced and universally accepted as being "the F," *could that object have failed to be F*?

Intuitions differ from case to case, and from person to person even within cases. We find three main types of case: (a) "nonexistents" generated solely by definite description made up on the spot, such as "the golden mountain" or "the town just north of Mayberry in which Marie Curie discovered the secret of eternal life"; (b) fictional objects already well entrenched in literature and/or in culture; (c) nonactual items endowed with their own modal properties by initial stipulation. Let us consider these *seriatim*.

Could *the golden mountain* have been made of aluminum, or of marshmallow? Could *the town just north of Mayberry* . . . never have been remarkable in any way at all? We do not know what to make of these questions. They seem senseless, or at least to have no answers, since the descriptions they involve have been introduced brutely, without context, and there is no background story or other information against which to measure modal stretch. For nonexistents of type (a), descriptive or qualitative essences of the sort we have posited seem entirely appropriate. However, types (b) and (c) are less straightforward.

Consider Perry White, fictional editor of the *Daily Planet*. Might he have gone into bricklaying, philosophy, or nursing instead of journalism?[23] We are pulled two ways here. On the one hand, "Perry White" is only a fictional *character,* a creation of a human author; all there is to him, so to speak, is his two-dimensional role in the story as Clark Kent's unsympathetic, cigar-chomping boss. Had the author left out this "boss" character entirely and, at the same time, introduced a janitor, or an itinerant drunk who wanders in off the street, and happened to name the character "Perry White," this new character would not *be* Perry White in the sense in which we now use that name, but would simply be a different character despite the accidental sameness of moniker.

On the other hand, as is well known, fictional characters do not have only the properties explicitly ascribed to them in their native works, but also those that may be extrapolated or assumed on the basis of the text and its setting. Now, the original character Perry White is (in the story) a man. Presumably, he has toes, even though we never see them, and even though there is no specific toe length that he has. Similarly, like any man, he presumably has a genetic code, even though there is no specific genetic code that he has. And why not suppose that he has the everyday sorts of modal properties that ordinary men have as well? Every actual man is such that he might have pursued a different occupation, so why not Perry White? In one episode or another, White might even be moved to remind Clark Kent of this possibility, saying something like, "I should have listened to my mother when she told me to stay out of journalism because of idiot milquetoast jerk reporters like you!"

But if we grant (for this or any other reason) that White might have joined a different trade, it seems we are saying that at a world other than that described in the Superman stories, White does go into bricklaying, or whatever, instead of editing the *Planet*. And this conflicts with our assumption about his qualitative essence. If his editorship is not a reliable transworld identifying mark, the same can be said of any other feature attributed to him by his creator; and so it seems we must award him a haecceity, just as if he were actual. Yet this would be extremely problematic, as our original argument for qualitative essences implies, and as we shall further consider below. (Can we imagine a story just like the Superman corpus except that in it, Perry White's and Clark Kent's haecceities are switched?)

It will help to distinguish two sorts of truth, in a thoroughly familiar way: truth *simpliciter* from truth-in-fiction. We want to say it is not *true* (period), even though it is indisputably true-in-fiction, that there is a person (Clark Kent) who can leap tall buildings at a single bound.[24] If this distinction is sound, it facilitates the accommodation of our occasional haecceitist feelings about fictional characters. It is indisputably true-in-the-comics that Perry White has toes, genes, and modal properties. It is not true in reality—or, less tendentiously, true *simpliciter*—that "he" does. Whatever account we might be moved to give of truth-in-fiction, what concerns us in fashioning semantics for natural language is truth, period, and it is not true in this sense that there is someone called "Perry White" who is a newspaper editor but who might have been a bricklayer. What is true, at the outside, is that there is a character, Perry White, who is (designated as) Clark Kent's editor, and that is all there is to it; he has modal properties only in-the-story.

Unfortunately, the matter cannot be settled so easily. For we have granted at least that White has his modal properties *in-fiction,* and the semantics of this "in-fiction" operator remains to be determined. When provided, it may be found to cause trouble for our brand of actualism. Indeed, we may expect it will, for the only natural possible-worlds interpretation of "It is true-in-fiction that *P*" is something like "It is true that *P* at every world compatible with the implications and presumptions of the (relevant) story,"[25] and *this* seems to establish one or more worlds at which White becomes a bricklayer.

The objection is reinforced by an argument of McMichael's that is not tied to the vexing vagaries of fiction but is based on plain iterated modalities of type (c). Again, (almost) indisputably, there might have been someone having such and such a property *F* that also had, but might have lacked, a further property *G*; for example, Rose Kennedy might have had a son, distinct from Jack, Robert, and Ted, who went into philosophy but who might, instead, have gone into bricklaying. Thus, on anyone's possible-worlds semantics, fiction and its awfulness completely aside, it seems there is a world *W* containing the supernumerary philosopher Kennedy, and a further world *W'* also containing that very Kennedy but at which he went into bricklaying instead of philosophy—not because of any work of fiction but simply because the envisioned possibilities seem genuine. Thus, we are forced to consider transworld identity-conditions for McMichael-individuals.

We might, naturally, try to assimilate such individuals to cases of type (a). That is, we might insist that the imagined philosopher-son of Rose Kennedy must remain a philosopher throughout all the worlds he inhabits, just as the golden mountain must remain golden, since he has, in effect, been stipulated on the spot in the same way. But this would be to deny the truth of our original iterated modal sentence, and that sentence still seems true (in reality, not in fiction of any sort). We must grant that "Rose Kennedy's fourth son" is a philosopher at some worlds, and not at others. We can get away with granting that, so long as we are allowed to split the original description "Rose Kennedy's fourth son who is a philosopher" into essence and accident: let that individual's essence be simply "x is Rose Kennedy's fourth son," abbreviated "$R(x)$." One world ($\neq$ @) contains $R(x)$ as an essence and "$\exists x(R(x)$ & x is a philosopher)" as an element; another world containing $R(x)$ has "$\exists x(R(x)$ & x is a comedian)" as an element instead.

But if the philosopher-son is only contingently a philosopher, might he not also be only contingently a *son*? It would seem that just as there might have been an F (distinct from every actual individual) who is but need not have been G, there might have been an F (ditto) who need not have been F. Consider "There might have been someone in the doorway who need not have been in the doorway." If context provides an extrinsic essence for the supposed person (say, "The person we are about to say hello to"), there is no difficulty, but if no such extrinsic essence is ready at hand, the person is stuck in the doorway at least *pro tem*. If we are to respect these iterated singular modalities in the absence of "extrinsic" essences, it seems we must move to nonactual haecceities of some sort after all; we must grant that there is a property of *being N*, where N is a proper name of our imaginary philosopher, that persists from world to world despite variation of all his ordinary features.[26] If there is a nonqualitative property of *being Perry White*, for example, and a nonqualitative property of being Clark Kent, then there *is* after all a world just like that of the Superman stories in which everything is the same except that White has all of Kent's qualitative features, and *vice versa*.

Numerous objections may be brought, and have been brought, against this idea of nonqualitative haecceities for nonexistents. We think that the objections can technically be circumvented, albeit with some considerable effort, and that there is more to be said in defense of such haecceities than might at first appear; we take this up at some length in the appendix. But we are not very well satisfied by the token defenses of unexemplified haecceities that we shall muster there, and so we officially stick by our essentialism regarding nonactuals. This means that we do not take the alleged modal properties of fictional characters and of McMichael-individuals seriously, despite the argument we have tentatively advanced on their behalf. We shall make available a harmless variation on our original formalism, to those theorists who do insist on taking the iterated modal properties seriously (since we maintain that the idea is coherent even if unattractive). But if we are to disdain them ourselves, we must explain why the relevant iterated modalities are specious despite the argument we gave, or rather, why someone might be tempted to accept the argument despite the speciousness of the iterated modalities; we shall attempt this in the appendix.

Incidentally, McMichael presents his troublesome argument as a problem for *actualism* specifically, as if the Meinongian/Lewisian "possibilist" were not to be troubled by it. Initially, we can see why: it is the Ersatzers or other actualists like ourselves who deny that nonactual individuals are *in propria persona* constituents of other worlds, and so have trouble accounting for the transworld identity of nonactuals. But we do not see why McMichael's problem does not, upon examination, infect "possibilist" semantics as well. Consider Lewis's hyperrealist view. Superficially, it offers a straightforward account of singular iterated modalities: Perry White might have gone into nursing iff he has a counterpart at some other world (still distinct from @) who does go into nursing; the counterpart is a flesh-and-blood individual similar to White, just as robust a constituent of his or her own world as White is of his, and so there is no embarrassing ontological asymmetry of the sort we are peddling in this paper. But, we contend, McMichael's dilemma rears its head when we ask what counterpart or similarity relation is operative. Not an effable, qualitative relation, since to set up the dilemma at all, we need the assumption that White could have lacked any of the features conventionally associated with him by the stories. But, presumably, not a nonqualitative, *sui generis* property either, for this would be (as Lewis himself agrees[27]) to leave a mystery as the sole ground of modalities *de* nonactuals. Thus, we do not see that, as regards McMichael's problem, Lewis is any better off than we are.

5.5. Intentional identity

It may be, and should be, wondered what our account has to say about Geach's (1967) problem of "intentional identity." Crudely, the problem is that a nonexistent individual may be the topic of each of two different propositional or other psychological attitudes—attitudes of the sort we would usually think of as *de re,* even though there is no actual *res* toward which the attitudes are directed. Geach's example is

(1)   Hob thinks a witch has blighted Bob's mare, and Nob thinks that she (the same witch) has lamed Cob's sow.

Another example might be

(2)   Gonzo fears there is a burglar at the door and hopes that that very burglar has not stepped on his turtle.

Each of these sentences is open to any number of interpretations,[28] some of which are obviously unproblematic from anyone's point of view. But according to Geach, there is a further sort of reading that resists being displayed by any standard logical means: that on which both of the attitudes in question are directed toward *nonspecific* individuals, yet, in some sense, their foci are *the same*. For example, Gonzo fears that there is a burglar at the door (that is all he fears—there is neither any actual individual nor any particular predesignated nonactual such as Raffles that he suspects of burgling); yet he hopes that *that* burglar has not stepped on his turtle, not just that there is no burglar who is at the door and has stepped on it, or that there is no burglar who he fears is at the door and has stepped on it, or the like.

Geach's problem seems to us cognate with Lewis's and McMichael's, addressed in the previous section, in that it turns on the transworld identity of nonactuals who are not presumed to share their most salient properties. It is another case of a non-actual individual introduced by one modality, which is said to have further modal properties (here, nonalethic *de re* attitudinal properties) in its own right: (1) says that Hob thinks there to be a witch who did so-and-so, which witch is also thought by Nob to have yet another attribute; (2) says that Gonzo fears there to be a burglar, which burglar is also hoped by him to be a nonchelonicide. The natural possible-worlds semantics for each sentence takes us to one or more worlds in which there is an individual of such and such a description (≠ any existing individual), and then to another world in which *that same* individual has some further property, yet (perhaps) may not satisfy the previous description, thus forcing our earlier question of transworld identity for nonactuals.

If Geach's problem is cognate with Lewis's and McMichael's problem in this way, that would predict a corresponding intuitive reaction on our part. In response to Lewis and McMichael, we were inclined to doubt that the putative iterated modalities really had sense, on the grounds that (roughly) the initial hypotheses determine only generic individuals that are not nonqualitatively distinguishable; the individuals do not, except possibly by virtue of further imaginative and stipulative activity on our part, have any qualitative or modal reach beyond what is provided by the initial hypotheses. The same is true of Geach-individuals, and so we should expect to find ourselves with the same suspicion of senselessness.

Prediction confirmed: we do find ourselves with that suspicion. Once the various unproblematic readings have been set aside, we do not hear any natural or intuitive and coherent interpretation of (1) or (2). (The same is argued by Dennett [1968].) Indeed, we have more trouble hearing such an interpretation for examples of Geach's sort than we do for McMichael individuals. And when we consider the matter in terms of possible worlds, an explanation of this difference in tractability readily presents itself: McMichael's examples begin with statements of *possibility,* which semantically are associated with existential quantifiers—at *some* world, there is some individual that has such and such a further modal property. But Geach's examples begin with propositional-attitude verbs, which call for *universal* quantification over worlds (cf. Hintikka [1962])—at *every* world compatible with what Hob thinks, there is some individual that has the further attitudinal property. In Geach's case, we are explicitly forced to envision a multiplicity of worlds, each inhabited by a witch, the various witches being quite different and presumably distinct from each other across the various worlds. This makes it even harder intuitively to attach sense to the suggestion that Nob's thought picks out any one of these different witches to the exclusion of the others, and so harder to understand how Nob could, in any sense, have in mind "the same" witch as Hob has.

We concede that, with some ingenuity, sense might still be *given* to (1) and (2) on some more subtle understanding than the unproblematic ones. We shall say a few words more about this in the appendix.

6. EXTENSIONS

The present structure can be adapted to yield accounts of several constructions other than the alethic modalities. In this concluding section, we provide brief sketches of possible directions for some of these extensions.

6.1. Higher-order possibility

As presently formulated, our language does not countenance the contingent existence of properties and relations. That is, each world is constructed from just the same set (Γ) of properties and relations. However, it is straightforward to extend our account to handle "possible but nonactual properties" and the like.[29]

The idea is to use a second-order "language," with uppercase Greek variables ranging over properties and relations (involving concrete individuals).

We take the second-order language with a standard semantics in which, for a given domain d, predicate variables range over the entire powerset of d. Since the completeness theorem does not hold for such languages, we must distinguish between semantic notions of satisfiability and syntactic notions of consistency. (Cf. our earlier response to Lewis regarding modal primitives.) In section 2 above, the definitions were formulated in terms of the semantic notions because we believe these to be the fundamental ones. Here it makes a difference.[30]

To follow the lead of section 1, we are haecceitists concerning this-worldly properties and relations (i.e., members of Γ). For example, if $P \in \Gamma$, then P is in world W just in case W includes a proposition containing P. For much the same reasons as above, "nonactual" properties and relations are stipulated through formulas $\phi(\Sigma)$ with one free higher-order variable.

Modification of the semantics is straightforward. A set E' of possible property and relation essences is added to the construction. (To accommodate the haecceities, for each $P \in \Gamma$, $\forall x (\Sigma x \leftrightarrow Px) \in E'$.) Also, the set N of essential truths is expanded to include such sentences as $\forall \Sigma \forall \Pi (\phi(\Sigma) \ \& \ \phi(\Pi) \rightarrow \forall x (\Sigma x \leftrightarrow \Pi x))$ for each possible essence ϕ (corresponding to the requirement that each possible essence name at most one individual at each world).[31] Each world is specified by a *subset* $\Gamma_W \subseteq \Gamma$ and a subset $E_W' \subseteq E'$, together with the items of section 2 above. The only other addition is the counterpart to the (extensional) uniqueness of the essences: If $\phi(\Sigma)$ and $\psi(\Sigma)$ are in E_W', then $\exists \Sigma \phi(\Sigma)$ and $\sim \exists \Sigma (\phi(\Sigma) \ \& \ \psi(\Sigma))$ are in S_W.

Note that the only sort of nonexistence we envision for actual properties and relations in a world W is their absence from propositions in W. Concerning properties and relations generally, it is a consequence of the set-theoretical semantics that we distinguish between a property's being unexemplified (having the empty extension) at a world and its being absent from that world. For example, if $\phi(\Sigma)$ is a possible property essence, then the absence of ϕ from a world W amounts to $\sim \exists \Sigma \phi(\Sigma)$. This means that ϕ is false no matter what property is substituted for Σ (including the empty property). The emptiness of ϕ amounts to $\exists \Sigma \phi(\Sigma) \ \& \ \forall \Sigma \forall x (\phi(\Sigma) \rightarrow \sim \Sigma x)$.

One bonus of this extension is that it may be possible to dispense with the set β of abstract objects. Recall (note 6) that we regard abstract objects as places within a structure. Moreover, most common mathematical structures admit categorical descriptions in second-order languages (with standard semantics). Thus, for example, reference to the natural numbers can be eliminated in favor of reference to the objects that have a certain property. The drawback of this approach is that one cannot apply a branch of mathematics in a world W unless W contains enough concrete objects to model that branch. It seems that similar considerations led to Hartry Field's (1980) decision to include an uncountable continuum of space-time points as concrete objects (see Shapiro [1983a]).

6.2. Conditionals

On many "possibilist" accounts, a conditional "If ψ then χ" is satisfied at a world W just in case χ holds in the world V that is most like W except that ψ holds in V. Of course, if ψ is false in W, there may not be such a world V (or there may be more than one relevant world V). An alternate account would have χ holding in every world most like W except that ψ holds.

In the present framework, there is a rather natural way to formulate this notion of "most like—except." If W, V, and V' are possible worlds, we say that V' is *closer to W than V*, written $V <_W V'$ iff $S_W \cap S_V \subset S_W \cap S_{V'}$ (here we take $A \subset B$ to entail $A \neq B$). If ψ is a sentence of $L\alpha_W$, then V is *most like W with* ψ iff $\psi \epsilon S_V$ and there is no world V' such that $\psi \epsilon S_{V'}$ and $V <_W V'$.[32]

As things stand, it is not necessarily the case that for every ψ consistent with the set N of essential truths, there is a world that is most like W with ψ. Suppose, for example, that α consists of the set $\{a_1, a_2, \dots\}$ and that Γ has only the predicate Px and the binary relations Rxy and identity. (To make the example definite, let Px be "x has a normal nose" and Rxy be "x is older than y.") Let the set N contain only the sentences Ra_ia_j for all $i < j$ and the sentence $\forall x(\phi(x) \rightarrow Px)$ for every possible essence ϕ that is not a haecceity. (This makes it essential that all nonactuals have normal noses. Alternately, it may be assumed that there are no nonactuals.) Now, let α_W be α and let S_W contain $\forall xPx$ (everyone has a normal nose) and, thus, $Pa_1, Pa_2, \dots$ Finally, let ψ be $\forall x \exists y(Rxy \, \& \sim Py)$ (for each person, someone younger lacks a normal nose). Notice that for every world V, $\psi \epsilon S_V$ if and only if there are infinitely many i such that $\sim Pa_i \epsilon S_V$. For any such V, there is a V' that is closer to V and also satisfies ψ.

The "problem" here is that the possible worlds structure does not preclude the existence of a set S such that S is consistent with the essential truths, but S is not contained in any possible world. In the present example, such a set is $T = \{\psi, Pa_1, \dots\}$. This facet of our framework may be appropriate. The properties of "possibility" and "consistent with all appropriate essential truths" may not be equivalent.

On the other hand, the reason the set T is not contained in any possible world is that it implies the existence of an individual with a particular property ($\sim Px$) for which there is no essence. That is, the structure described above does not contain "enough" essences. Since the possible essences are stipulated at the outset, it can certainly be stipulated that there be enough of them. Consider, then, the following thesis:

(*) For each $\alpha' \subseteq \alpha$ and each set S of sentences in $L\alpha'$, if S is consistent with the sentences of N that are in $L\alpha'$, then there is a possible world W such that $\alpha_W = \alpha'$ and $S \subseteq S_W$.

The thesis (*) implies that every maximally consistent set containing the appropriate essential truths is the set S_W of a possible world.

If (*) holds, then for every world W and every sentence ψ in $L\alpha_W$ consistent with N, there is a world V most like W with ψ. This is established by the following construction:

Choose an arithmetization of the sentences of $L\alpha_W$. Let ψn be the sentence with Gödel number n. Define a sequence $<Sn>$ of sets of sentences as follows:

$S0 = \{\psi\} \cup \{\chi \mid \chi\epsilon N \text{ and } \chi \text{ is in } L\alpha_W\}$.
If $\psi n \epsilon S_W$ and ψn is consistent with Sn, then $Sn + 1 =$
$Sn \cup \{\psi n\}$. Otherwise, $Sn + 1 = Sn$.

Let $S = \cup Si$. Since S is consistent with the appropriate members of N, (*) implies that there is a world V with $\alpha_V = \alpha_W$ and $S \subseteq S_V$. This world V is most like W with ψ.

It does not follow, however, that for each world W and appropriate sentence $\psi \notin S_W$ that there is a *unique* world most like W with ψ. Notice that in the above construction, the arithmetization determines the order in which the sentences of S_W are considered. Different arithmetizations may produce different worlds V.

For any sentence χ, if $\chi \notin S_W$, then χ is *missing* from *some* world most like W with ψ iff $\sim\chi$ is consistent with ψ and the appropriate essential truths. Inversely, χ is *in every* world most like W with ψ just in case ψ, together with the essential truths of W, implies χ. On the other hand, χ is *in some* world most like W with ψ iff there is a set $S \subseteq S_W$ such that $\{\psi\} \cup S$ is consistent with the essential truths of W and, together with those essential truths, implies χ.

To take an example, consider the conditional ''if this match is struck, it will light,'' vis-à-vis the actual world. The consequent, ''the match will light,'' is true in *some* world most like the actual world with the match being struck, just in case there is a set S of sentences true in the actual world (such as ''the match is dry,'' ''the chemical composition is correct,'' and so on) that is consistent with ''the match is struck'' and the essential truths (such as the laws of chemistry) such that S, together with ''the match is struck'' and the essential truths, implies that the match will light.

One who is impressed with the analysis of this example might be led to conclude that a conditional ''if ψ then χ'' is true in world W just in case χ holds in *some* world most like W with ψ. The trouble with this is that we could then have ''if ψ then χ'' and ''if ψ then not χ'' both holding in the same world, even if ψ is consistent with the essential truths of that world.

The foregoing account, then, needs to be improved. This might be accomplished if it can be specified that the order in which the sentences of S_W are considered in constructing the ''most like'' possible world is to be determined by some sort of ''closeness,'' ''similarity,'' or ''relevance'' to ψ (vis-a-vis χ).

6.3. Propositional attitudes

For simplicity and brevity, we restrict ourselves to belief and knowledge and provide only an outline of an account. Assume that the original language $L\alpha$ does not contain any knowledge or belief sentences. Consider a new series of languages $P\alpha_W$ that contains for each person $a \in \alpha_W$, two operators aK and aB. A sentence $aK\psi$ is read "a knows that ψ"; $aB\psi$ is read "a believes that ψ."

Recall that, above, a possible world is a structure $<\alpha_W, E_W, S_W>$. We add to this a pair of functions k_w and b_w from the set of people in α_W to the powerset of the set of sentences of $P\alpha_W$. For each person a, $k_W(a)$ is the set of sentences known by a in W; $b_W(a)$ is the set of sentences believed by a in W. It is *not* stipulated that either $k_W(a)$ or $b_W(a)$ be deductively closed.

It is a straightforward matter to define satisfaction $W, v \vDash \psi$ for sentences ψ of $P\alpha_W$ similar to the above treatment of modality. One of the new clauses is:

$$W, v \vDash aK\psi(x_1 \ldots x_n X_1 \ldots X_m) \text{ iff the sentence}$$
$$\forall y_1 \ldots \forall y_n ([v/x_1] (y_1) \& \ldots \& [v/x_n] (y_n) \to$$
$$\psi(y_1 \ldots y_n \{v/X_1\} \ldots \{v/X_m\}))$$

is in $k_W(a)$.

The clause for b_W is similar.

At this point, a stipulation should be added: The framework is *knowledge-sound* iff for each world W, each sentence ψ of $P\alpha_W$, and each person a in α_W, $\psi \in k_W(a)$ only if $W \vDash \psi$. This, of course, is the common dictate that only true sentences can be known. It is hereby stipulated that all structures under consideration are knowledge-sound.

Some common facets of possible worlds and knowledge can now be defined. World V is *accessible to* W concerning the knowledge of a iff $V \vDash \psi$ for each $\psi \in k_W(a)$. In short, V is accessible to W concerning the knowledge of a iff, as far as a knows, V may be the case.

Notice that if V is accessible to W concerning the knowledge of a and $W \vDash aK\psi$ then $V \vDash \psi$. However, it does not follow that $V \vDash aK\psi$. That is, if a knows ψ in W, then ψ is true in all worlds accessible to W concerning the knowledge of a, but it may be that ψ is not known by a in some of those worlds. We may define V to be *superaccessible to* W concerning the knowledge of a just in case $k_W(a) \subseteq k_V(a)$. Of course, if V is superaccessible to W, then V is accessible to W.

Suppose that an operator were added to the present language to represent the *consequences* of the knowledge of an individual a (as in Hintikka [1962]). The relevant set of "knowable" propositions would be deductively closed. If a semantics for this operator were formulated in terms of superaccessibility, the logic would resemble S4 much as the above modal logic resembles S5.

6.4. Impossibilia

It seems to us a notable virtue of our Ersatz apparatus that it accommodates impossible "objects" and worlds nearly as readily as it does possibilia (see Lycan [1979], 313–14). Meinong accepted impossibilia for just the reasons for which he embraced ordinary nonexistents—that they are referred to in everyday speech and in literature, that they are common objects of thought, and so on—and so do we (so long as we are allowed to be actualists about them). Moreover, impossibilia are needed for technical purposes as well; although epistemic and alethic modal logic can do without them for obvious reasons, doxastic logic and the theory of conditionals have need of them for equally and coordinately obvious reasons: inconsistent beliefs and counter-logical conditionals are otherwise a closed book to the possible-worlds semanticist.[33] In fact, any argument for the positing of ordinary nonexistents, plausible or implausible, extrapolates automatically to impossibilia unless it is qualified *ad hoc* against such extrapolation;[34] so a theory of nonactuality ought to allow for them. The Lewisian possibilist cannot do so as comfortably as we, for if "worlds" are flesh-and-blood universes operating according to (immanent) laws of nature, it is hard to imagine how they could contain contradictions. (Lewis himself, of course, does not countenance impossible worlds, presumably for this reason, and hence offers no theory of counter-logicals.)

Naturally, we want more than one impossible world, for otherwise the resulting treatments of counterlogicals and belief sentences would be both trivial and incorrect. Therefore, the inconsistent sets of sentences or propositions that constitute our impossible worlds cannot be closed under deduction but must be less prodigally fleshed out from their antecedent suppositions in some conservative and discerning way. An inconsistent believer must believe only the relatively immediate consequences of his or her inconsistencies; a counterlogical antecedent must take us to a neighborhood of impossible worlds containing the same inconsistency but not many others. There are a number of formally different ways of limiting closure for inconsistent systems: dialectical logic, paraconsistent logic, relevance logic, the contrasting method of Rescher and Brandom (1980), and so on;[35] we do not choose between them here.

Unlike Meinong, our leading contemporary Meinongians tend to shun impossibilia and show surprising respect for Russell's argument that contradictoriness is the best proof of untruth.[36] Meinong himself patiently reminded his critics that contradictoriness is a vice only in putative existents, and we agree. We cannot see how the positing of impossibilia leads to logical trouble *unless one thinks of Meinongian predication as true* simpliciter: that is, unless one assumes that contradictory objects *really* have their contradictory properties. But they should not really have them, on anyone's view, and they certainly do not really have them on our view. It is not true (*simpliciter*) that the golden mountain is gold, that Sherlock Holmes lives in Baker Street, or that the round square is round. It is perhaps true-in-fiction that Holmes lives in Baker Street, but it is equally true-in-fiction that Watson has a jezzail-bullet wound that is in his shoulder and also in his leg rather than in his shoulder.[37] There is no reason to suppose that "truth-in-fiction," for those who insist on it, is logically well-behaved—on the contrary. Thus, we see no reason to exclude impossibilia from our constructed modal paradise.

APPENDIX: MODAL PROPERTIES OF NONEXISTENTS

Let us go more deeply into our objection (5.4) based on modal properties of nonexistents. So far as we can see, there are just four possible ways of handling the (alleged) transworld identity of nonactuals. Of these, one is our official essentialist view; another is haecceitism, already briefly discussed, which can be fit into our formal framework rather easily. The third will fit only by the loftiest fiat, and the fourth can be made to fit by suitable modification.

Let us begin by stating the main objections to haecceitism for nonactuals. One is that with which we began in section 1: that nonexistents can be introduced only by description.[38] A second (closely related) objection is that even if we can coherently think of a world just like this one save for the switching of Adam and Noah, we simply *cannot* distinguish two worlds that differ only in the switching of the alleged haeccei-ties of Rose Kennedy's philosopher son who might have gone into bricklaying and her fifth, bricklayer son who might, instead, have gone into philosophy, or, as in Adams (1981), two worlds that differ only in the switching of two nonactual electrons. Third, if nonactuals have haecceities and can differ numerically without differing qualita-tively, then it ought to be possible for us to have a particular object in mind, or to have a propositional attitude toward that object, without having in mind a qualitative twin; yet this does not seem possible.[39]

Fourth, as Adams observes ([1981], 11–12), an ordinary haecceity (assuming real people have them) bears a special relation to its owner: it could not exist without its owner's (that very person's) existing also. But if actualism is correct, no nonactual "individual" can enter primitively into any relation, and in particular, there can be no state of affairs that consists simply in Perry White's exemplifying Perry-Whiteity. To put the point slightly differently: Predicates that express the haecceities of actual indi-viduals are syntactically and semantically complex, consisting of the identity sign concatenated with a rigid designator whose reference has been fixed by a process in-volving causal contact with the referent itself; but a "nonactual individual" is not gen-uinely an individual on our view, and cannot stand as a term in a genuine identity predication. Fifth, it is not easy to see the difference between an "unexemplified haec-ceity"[40] and a good old Meinongian *nonexistent possible,* once there is no visible residue of familiar qualitative properties to go proxy for the noxious Meinongian ob-ject; McMichael (1983a, 61) asserts that the introduction of haecceities for nonactuals "seems tantamount to acceptance of possibilism."

All five of these objections have force,[41] and accordingly, we have fashioned our semantics without recourse to unexemplified haecceities.[42] But for those who find themselves driven to take the putative modal properties of nonexistents more seri-ously, we offer an approach that will take at least some of the sting out of our objec-tions to haecceities for nonactuals. Most of the objections stem from the fact that nonactual individuals stand in no causal relation to us and are known only by descrip-tion. But it is possible to frame a causal-historical theory of reference, even for empty singular terms, that affords a finer-grained individuation scheme. Consider fictional characters again. One thing that makes Perry White the character he is is the circum-stances of his creation. We might say that a fictional character qualifies as being (iden-tical with) Perry White if and only if the relevant use of his name is connected in the right historical way with Jerry Siegel's original act of writing (in the real world). Sev-eral sorts of cases fall nicely into line with this suggestion. (i) If some writer or car-toonist in Mayberry, North Carolina, who has miraculously never heard of the Superman comics just as miraculously happens to invent a character also named "Perry White," that character is not the same character as Mr. Siegel's Perry White, even if he or she is similar in remarkable respects to Clark Kent's editor. However, (ii) if someone undertakes to write a spinoff strip about the original Perry White's journalistic triumphs and tribulations or about his private life (as George Macdonald Fraser has brilliantly written about Thomas Hughes's Flashman), with the original firmly in mind and with the intention of grafting the new stories smoothly onto the old, we are willing to count the new White as being the same character as the old.[43] (iii) Mr. Siegel could have written a new Superman story in which Superman (or another character) discovered that the *Planet* editor was an imposter, and that the real Perry White had years ago decided against journalism and gone into philosophy instead (but changed his name for reasons of euphony to "Hilary Putnam"). This would stick, it seems to us; after the new story had been published, it would be true-in-fiction that Perry White was really a philosopher and had only erroneously been thought to be Clark Kent's editor.[44]

If some such causal-historical criterion could be made to work, it would provide a means of distinguishing qualitatively identical characters and so lessen the pressure of our objections to unexemplified haecceities. The initial problem was that nonactuals are identified only by description because they are causally unconnected to us; but as we have seen, their names, their dubbings, and subsequent acts of referring or "referring" to them are not so unconnected. Potentially, they can be used to distinguish descriptively identical characters. If this conjecture is sound, our first objection fails.[45] So does our second; for transworld identities in the "nonactual" analogue of Chisholm's "Adam"/"Noah" example can be established similarly, when pegged to real-world fictive acts and authors' intentions. In particular, we can extrapolate Kripke's emphasis on *stipulation* to the case of nonactuals. What distinguishes the White-and-Kent-switched world from its progenitor is simply stipulation backed by the right historical connection and the right intentions, just as for existents.[46] The same can be said even for McMichael-individuals: Rose Kennedy's philosopher-son is himself at another world, even if he has shed his philosophizing for bricklaying and so on, if the utterer of his original supposition so stipulates under the right conditions. Our third objection goes wide as well. Odd as it may seem, I can want Pegasus rather than a descriptively identical winged horse, if I know that the latter nonexistent's name (homonymously "Pegasus") has a different ancestry from that which figures in the classical myth, e.g., if it was made up last week by my highly and coincidentally imaginative plumber.

(The causal-historical idea promises to help give sense to Geach's "intentional identity" sentences also. For if, say, Hob's witch can be pegged to his original mental act, then Nob's witch may be pegged in turn to Hob's witch by virtue of the (presumed) historical connection between his (Nob's) mental act and Hob's. There is still the problem of Hob's semantically mandated multiplicity of witches, but a sufficiently clever and detailed causal-historical criterion might be able to surmount it.)

Our fourth and fifth objections are harder to turn aside, even with the aid of our causal-historical idea, but we can say at least a bit in response to each of them. Regarding the fourth, Adams is bothered by the fact that an ordinary (exemplified) haecceity is identified by reference to its owner and could not exist in the absence of singular states of affairs involving that owner, while no actualist ontology can provide a genuinely singular state of affairs involving a nonexistent. But the causal-historical account can help at least with the identification problem; the haecceity of a nonexistent could now be identified by reference to a fictive act or other quasi-dubbing. Moreover, we do not have to suppose that a haecceity exists in the absence of its owner, for we can say that at the relevant nonactual world, its owner does exist—the presence of the haecceity and the existence of its "owner" are one and the same state of affairs there. (Neither the robust haecceitist nor the Lewisian possibilist will be satisfied by this account, of course; the unexemplified haecceities and "nonexistent individuals" it provides are pale shadows or feeble imitations of real haecceities and individuals. That is as it should be, for an actualist. All we claim is that the account is itself formally coherent[47] and affords a tenable identifying criterion for unexemplified haecceities.)

Regarding the fifth and final objection, the question of what advantage unexemplified haecceities have over bare Meinongian possibilia, we would point to one key difference (for a fuller discussion, see section XII of Lycan [1979]). The real trouble with possibilia is that (a) they force us to disambiguate the existential quantifier as between actual existents and nonexistents, but that (b) at the same time, we are allowed no expressible means of doing so; their defenders merely assert that the quantifier *is* ambiguous and arrogantly decline to discuss the matter further.[48] By contrast, an unexemplified haecceity is an actual item, a property, that does not differ in ontological status from any other property despite being "blank"—it is part of the transmundane framework. (What marks it as exemplified at a world where the "corresponding individual" exists is just the relevant existential proposition's being an element of that world; thus we sidestep Adams' objection. Of course, these "haecceities" for nonactuals are not like those of real individuals, since they are not composed of the identity relation concatenated with the individuals themselves; they are watered down. That is to be expected from Ersatzers.)

We mentioned two further options. Both involve denying that nonactuals can be literally identical across worlds. One is to make all nonactuals worldbound, and import a counterpart relation to replace transworld "identification." This is, of course, Lewis's (1983) choice, and in effect Morton's (1973) and McMichael's (1983b);[49] each suggests some sparse structural axioms governing the posited relation. This goes against our constructivist grain; we could not in good conscience take something so crucial as primitive. (And we have no idea how the relation might be defined without thereby giving rise to a qualitative essence; remember again our contention that iterated modalities pose just as nasty a problem for Lewis as they do for actualists.)

The final option is to bite a very obdurate bullet and deny flatly that there is any way *at all* to identify nonactuals across worlds[50]—our essences would serve to identify individuals within worlds but never across worlds. This would make our iterated modal predications *essentially false:* necessarily, Perry White could not have been a philosopher, nor Rose Kennedy's fourth son a bricklayer, nor the person in the doorway somewhere else, period. Formally, the only changes required would be in the definition of satisfaction.[51] But we see no advantage of this option over our official essentialist view.

As we said above, if we are to eschew unexemplified haecceities and unexplicated counterpart relations alike, we need to explain away the contrary haecceitist intuition. What we are inclined to say is that (some) people's imaginative faculties are prone to supply definiteness and determinacy where there is none. If the name "Smedley" is introduced as being that of a possible fat man in the doorway, one's imaginative faculty may ignore the fact that no determinate genetic code nor any other true individuator has been supplied along with the bare description, and suppose that an individuator *has* been fixed even though we do not know it. *On this false supposition,* we may then accordingly (seem to) attribute modal properties to the "individual." But since there is in fact no individuator, the modal properties are unreal.

Notes

1. G. H. Merrill (1978) speaks of "proxies," and offers a methodological account and defense of their use.

2. For Lycan's own views on the semantics of propositional attitudes in particular, see 1981, 1984a, 1985; on conditionals, see 1984b.

3. Similarly, but less formally, Adams (1981) defends basic principles regarding possibilia and urges that these principles be incorporated in any account of possible worlds.

4. The latter is an informal and relatively weak theory—Zermelo set theory will do. And as we shall show in section 4.4, it is straightforward to calculate the number of worlds. In any case, a relatively modest set is obained. (Thus, we avoid the criticism of Lewis posed by Forrest and Armstrong [1984].)

5. Fine takes the notion of possibility as primitive and defines a "world-proposition" to be a maximally possible proposition: a proposition that is possible and either implies P or implies $\sim P$ for any proposition P (the envisioned "language" being infinitary). Roper's interest seems limited to providing structures to play the roles of the worlds in the standard Kripke structures for various languages.

6. The current use of the term "abstract" is neologistic in any case. As D. M. Armstrong has observed, an "abstract entity" is, for most contemporary philosophers, no longer something abstract*ed*, essentially a one-over-many, but rather something not in space-time. Here, we recognize a further distinction between either of the latter conceptions and the modal conception of something not even in *logical* space, something that is formally part of the framework in which all worlds are set rather than inhabiting this world or that one. (See David Kaplan [1969], sec. VIII.) Readers inclined to accept different nonspatiotemporal objects at different worlds are free, of course, to include such items in α.

Some of the Quinean temptation to think of "abstract" objects as contingent comes from the assimilation of arithmetic, set theory, and the like to geometry construed as a very general theory about the physical world. But this is, in one way, a confusion. Suppose we construe numbers, sets, and so on as *places within structures* (Resnik [1981, 1982], Shapiro [1983b]). The question of whether a structure *exists* at a given world is separate from that of whether the structure is *exemplified* by any system of concrete objects at that world. For example, both Euclidean geometry and the various nonEuclidean geometric structures exist, *qua* structures, here at @ if any sets and/or numbers do; but this is not to say anything about the actual nature of space, which is a question of physics.

7. But see our remarks in sections 5.2 and 6.1 on higher-order abstract entities.

8. We, at least tentatively, mean to include fictional characters as nonexistents and as inhabitants of possible worlds. This is neither unproblematic nor uncontroversial. Some writers, such as Peter van Inwagen (1977), decline to treat "fictional characters" as nonexistent; others, including Kripke (1972), Kaplan (1973), and Fine (1984), deny them possibility. We shall not join the labyrinthine issues involved here (see also Parsons [1980]; Routley [1980]; Castañeda [1979]; Howell [1979]; Fine [1982]; Bertolet [1984a, 1984b]; and all the multifarious works further cited in these). But we shall recall the status of fictional characters in our response to objection 5.4 (section 5 below), and pursue it at some length in the appendix.

9. This is not to say that that nonactual person is essentially funnier-than-anyone; see below.

10. See Lycan (1984a).

11. For similar and more extended defenses of an inegalitarian attitude towards the individuation of nonexistents, see Kaplan (1973, 505–6) and Rescher (1975, chs. III and IV) (also Kripke [1972, 763–65] and Plantinga [1974, 154–55]). Robert Howell questions this argument, albeit programmatically and somewhat obscurely, in section 7 of 1979. Somewhat different defenses may be found in Skyrms (1981) and in Adams (1981, sec. 2).

12. *Pace* Howell (1979), Routley (1980), Lewis (1983), and others; see our reply to objection 5.5 in section 5.

13. N.B., we here abide by our earlier intention to duck questions of contingent abstract entities by making our haecceities formal or framework entities. One might think of complaining that a haecceity cannot now be composed of its individual constituent concatenated with the identity relation, since the individual exists only at some worlds while the haecceity is transmundane. But such is the way of framework entities: the haecceities (like everything else) are actual items, and are transmundane only in that they are part of the framework used to *describe* "possible worlds." One can also form the more restrictive notion of "inhabiting" a world, and think of haecceities as *inhabiting* only those worlds containing propositions that include the relevant individual as a constituent. (Adams [1981] proposes a related distinction between "truth *in*" and "truth *at*" a world.)

14. Lewis (1983); McMichael (1983a, 1983b). Their concern is glancingly anticipated by Morton (1973).

15. Notice that if W is the empty world, then $W, v \models \forall x \psi$ and $W, v \not\models \exists x \psi$ (provided that these are "well-formed").

16. The $[v/x_i]$'s do not have to be essences in the worlds W'. Notice, incidentally, that the relevant formula does not have any lowercase free variables, and, thus, the possibility that W' is empty is unproblematic. The next clause is similar.

17. One "exception": Notice that if $n > 0$ and W is the empty world, then the left-hand side of this biconditional is ill informed. Theorem T5 is similar.

18. Concerning the restriction on W, recall that in the standard semantics for first-order languages, each domain is nonempty. Hailperin (1953) and Quine (1954) have presented deductive systems for a first-order logic without the assumption that each domain is nonempty. The restriction on W in T6 may be dropped if "logical consequence" is interpreted as in those papers.

19. Note that $W \models \exists x (x = x)$ if and only if W is not the empty world.

20. The countability of α can be proved from the premises that (actual) space is Euclidian (or "Einsteinian"), that each member of α occupies a space of nonzero measure, and that the members at α do not overlap. If it is *necessary* that there is a one-to-one function from the points of space-time to R^4 such that the image of the space occupied by each object has nonzero measure, then each set of essences E_w is also, at most, countable.

21. If our pessimism is justified, the prospects for naturalism are dimmed considerably. For precisely this reason, D. M. Armstrong is expressly trying to work out a theory of possibility without employing any modal primitives whatever (the only germ of the theory published to date appears in 1984). It is a version of combinatorialism in the sense of Lycan (1979).

22. Lewis might respond that we grasp the concept of a "world" independently, by knowing that an alternative world is the *same kind of thing as* the world we live in (see [1973, 85, 87]). But this would be simply to assume that a possible world is of the same kind as @ while a putative impossible world is not— and what warrants that?

23. This is not intended as a question about what Jerry Siegel (the author of Superman) might have chosen to *do* with the character, as when we ask whether he might have made White a health nut.

24. This observation strikes us as intuitively and strictly correct, but we admit we have encountered some hardy bibliophiles who maintain that Kent truly and literally works at the *Daily Planet* and doubles as Superman and so on.

25. For key refinements, see Lewis (1978).

26. McMichael offers two more subtle arguments against pinning nonexistents of his sort to "qualitative essences": that given a suitably bifurcated and symmetric world, any alleged qualitative essence might fail to discriminate an inhabitant from its doppelganger, and that two nonactual worlds might be connected by a chain of individually small changes that gradually switch two characters' properties (as in Chisholm's

original "Adam"/"Noah" case [1967], though McMichael's own argument relies on less aggressive assumptions). We think both arguments can be resisted by enforcement of the alternative view of nonactual-individuation that we shall sketch in the appendix, but we shall not pursue them here.

N.B., it is also open to a granite-jawed actualist to deny after all the truth of McMichael's iterated modal sentences on the grounds that they would make good sense only on a strong version of realism about possibilia. One might imaginatively stipulate that Rose Kennedy had a philosopher son in addition to the three we know, and count it true-in-the-stipulated-scenario that the son might have gone into bricklaying, but refuse to give a standard possible-worlds semantics in turn for truth-in-a-scenario, and refuse to grant it true *simpliciter* that the imaginary son might (literally) have gone into bricklaying. Actually, this stipulation would be illicit in our system as presented here, since we have specified that the language contains no modal operators; we prize the system's well-foundedness. In order to carry out the strategy just mentioned, the granite-jawed actualist would have to create a new hierarchy of languages.

27. Lewis (1983, sec. V). To accommodate iterated singular modalities for the case of intentional objects of sensation, Lewis is forced to increase the -adicity of his already strained and bulging counterpart relation (secs. VI and VII), in a dauntingly baroque way: Object X *for* subject U is a transworld counterpart of object Y *for* subject Z (31). We find this extra relativization objectionable on several grounds, but cannot pursue them here.

28. See Geach's own paper, Dennett (1968), and Saarinen (1978).

29. *Contra*, perhaps, Lewis; in conversation he has hinted that the Ersatzer will have trouble making room for alien properties, i.e., properties that might have existed but do not exist at our world. We suspect that by "properties" here, he may mean something like physical magnitudes or Scotist scientific universals of Armstrong's sort (1978), rather than the far more ubiquitous predicate-meaning-like Platonic entities that we have in mind; we doubt that he would object to our present strategy.

30. It is straightforward to reformulate the current construction in terms of a nonstandard Henkin semantics. Here, of course, a completeness theorem holds, but we still insist on the semantic notions.

31. If something more than extensional equivalence is desired here, it may be modified accordingly.

32. Notice that if $\psi \epsilon S_W$ then the only worlds V most like W with ψ are those in which $S_V = S_W$, and if ψ is not contained in any possible world, then there is no world most like W with ψ. To handle the latter situation, one would have to develop a structure of impossible worlds (see section 6.4 for some preliminary remarks in this direction). It might be pointed out, incidentally, that it is straightforward to extend the present account to deal with conditionals that contain modal operators.

33. Though Robert Stalnaker (1984) at least tries to do without.

34. Lewis's main argument (1973, 84–85) that we should take apparent existential quantification over nonexistents at face value "unless . . . taking them at face value is known to lead to trouble" is no exception, "unless [to quote Lewis out of context] you beg the question by saying that it already *is* trouble [to posit impossibilia]."

35. See, respectively (and only representatively), Da Costa (1974); Arruda (1979); Anderson and Belnap (1975); and Rescher and Brandom (1980), which also contains a convincing philosophical defense of impossibilia. Urn models have also been urged in aid of impossible worlds, by Hintikka (1979) relying on Rantala (1975).

36. E.g., Parsons (1980). Routley (1980) and Lambert (1983) are more sanguine.

37. Formally, N.B., we have made no explicit provision for truth-in-fiction or any other sort of truth "at" a nonactual world; officially, we confine our semantical attention regarding nonactual worlds to satisfaction alone, though it would be easy to define "truth at" a world either in terms of satisfaction or simply as set membership.

38. Robert Howell (1979, sec. 7) protests that specification by description is not the only alternative to introduction by ostension; but his positive hint of a *tertium quid* is so far very obscure. (It seems structurally similar to Lewis's method of perceiver-relative counterparts in 1983.)

39. Robert Kraut (1979, 213) notes the peculiarity of someone's (truly) claiming to want *Pegasus* but denying that he or she would be satisfied by just any winged horse that was ridden by Bellerophon, and so on.

40. Note the ambiguity of "unexemplified" here as between "not instantiated at @," "not instantiated at such and such a world in which it exists," and "not instantiated at any world." In the absence of qualification, we shall always mean the first of these.

41. Lewis (1983, 22–23) poses a sixth: that he can make no sense of the idea of an object's existing *in its own person* at each of two different worlds and nonetheless having properties at one that it does not have at the other. (He rejects the analogy of a thing's having a property at one *time* but not at another.) This intuition of bad craziness is, of course, the same as that which has always driven Lewis to counterpart theory as opposed to literal transworld identity; and it enables him to return at least some of the "incredulous stares" he is accustomed to receiving from complacent actualists.

For our part, we have no difficulty at all with the notion of having properties relative to worlds; we find the time analogy entirely supportive here even if, in other respects, it is imperfect. And for Ersatzers who believe in singular propositions, actual individuals are literally and unproblematically constituents of "other worlds" anyway; the only problems are those created by the assigning of haecceities to nonactuals, and we have already listed those special problems.

42. For McMichael's own semantics, see again 1983b.

43. Obviously, there are vexing borderline cases here. We are inclined *not* to treat pastiches in the way described; the character called "B*nd" in Christopher Cerf and Michael Frith's Ian Fleming parody, *Alligator* (*Harvard Lampoon*, 1962) is not James Bond, even though he is directly inspired by Fleming's creation. For that matter, we do not countenance the protagonist of John Gardner's recent, comparatively respectful "Bond" books, for the reason that Gardner's hero is very distinctly Hollywood Bond—just good fun—as opposed to Fleming's own very serious character. (Fleming presciently made this distinction himself, in *The Man with the Golden Gun*, when Bond, amnesic, is being vetted for authenticity by members of his own Service: his suspiciously new clothing and his choice of the Ritz hotel, both in fact dictated by his KGB brainwashers, are described by the Chief of Staff as "sort of stage Bond.") We are more amenable to the Bond of Kingsley Amis (in *Colonel Sun*, written under the pseudonym "Robert Markham"), who seems totally genuine save for the interjection of one or two unmistakable and presumably irrepressible Amisisms. The difference in identity between Gardner's and Amis/Fleming's characters is due, we surmise, to differences in the authors' respective metalinguistic intentions, but the latter would be very hard to spell out.

44. It may seem that our own case (presented earlier) of the absence of the editor figure and the presence of an entirely different character who happens to be named "Perry White" is a counterexample, since the distinctness of the two seems to consist in the difference between their descriptive roles in the story. This again depends on Siegel's intentions. If he had never created the editor figure in the first place, his alternative invention of the janitor or itinerant bum would have been simply a different fictive act, and so would have had a different character as its issue in any case. If, on the other hand, Siegel had written in the editor figure to begin with but (for some peculiar reason) then decided that White would not have been like that but would have pursued a very different sort of life plan, eventuating in a janitor's job or in vagrancy, the new White *would* count as the same character as the old despite his drastic transformation.

45. As McMichael has pointed out in conversation, this requires that we conceive of fictional characters and worlds as being created by authors rather than as having existed from time immemorial. That is all right with us (especially since we have no stake in the haecceitist view we are now adumbrating); the view takes fictional characters to be something like fictive acts with qualitative stereotypes appended.

46. Fine (1982) relies heavily on the author's "sayso" in the individuation of fictional characters.

47. Here are the modifications needed to add unexemplified haecceities to our system: (a) Stipulate a set $\triangle$ of "blank" properties or predicate letters, to be included in Γ, the original set of properties and relations. (b) The set E of possible essences should consist of $\triangle$, the actual haecceities (formulas of the form "$x = c$"), and nothing else. That is, all essences are (actual and merely possible) haecceities. (c) The set N of essential truths should include $\forall x(Px \rightarrow \sim Qx)$ for each pair P,Q of distinct members of $\triangle$, and $\sim Pc$ for each member P of $\triangle$ and each $c \in \alpha$. N may also contain essential truths about some of the essences; for example, some of the unexemplified haecceities may be stipulated to apply only to humans, or to ping-pong balls. Our framework works exactly as before.

48. A possibilist of Lewis's sort would deny that his quantifier *per se* is ambiguous, since on the surface his quantifier is univocally Meinongian, while real existence and this-worldly ontological commitment are marked by what are superficially grammatical predicates, such as "actual" or "exists." But this terminological scheme differs only orthographically from an ambiguous quantifier.

49. McMichael takes as primitive an accessibility relation among maximally consistent "roles."

50. This is Adams's (1981) view. We agree, incidentally, with almost everything Adams says that is applicable to our framework, excepting his denial of essences.

51. The clause for the diamond would have to be modified as follows:

(a) if v assigns a nonactual to any free variable in ϕ, then $W, v \vDash \Diamond\phi$ iff $W, v \vDash \phi$.

(b) if v assigns actual individuals to all the free variables in ϕ, then $W, v \vDash \Diamond\phi$ iff $W', v' \vDash \phi$ for world W' and valuation v' that agrees with v on the variables free in ϕ.

The clause for $\Box\phi$ is obtained analogously.

References

Adams, R. M. 1981. "Actualism and Thisness." *Synthese* 49:3–41.

Anderson, A. R., and N. Belnap. 1975. *Entailment*. Vol. I. Princeton.

Armstrong, D. M. 1978. *Universals and Scientific Realism*. Cambridge.

—————. 1984. "Metaphysics and Supervenience." *Critica* 16.

Arruda, A. 1979. "A Survey of Paraconsistent Logic." In *Proceedings of the Fourth Latin-American Logic Conference*. Amsterdam.

Bertolet, R. 1984a. "Inferences, Names, and Fictions." *Synthese* 58:203–18.

—————. 1984b. "Reference, Fiction, and Fictions." *Synthese* 60:413–37.

Castañeda, H.-N. 1979. "Fiction and Reality: Their Basic Connections." *Poetica* 8:31–62.

Chisholm, R. 1967. "Identity through Possible Worlds: Some Questions." *Nous* 1:1–8.

—————. 1981. *The First Person*. Minneapolis.

Da Costa, N. 1974. "On the Theory of Inconsistent Formal Systems." *Notre Dame Journal of Formal Logic* 15:497–510.

Dennett, D. C. 1968. "Geach on Intentional Identity." *Journal of Philosophy* 65:335–41.

Fine, K. 1977. "Postscript." In A. N. Prior and K. Fine, *Worlds, Times and Selves*. London.

—————. 1982. "The Problem of Nonexistents, I." *Topoi* 1:97–140.

—————. 1984. "Critical Review of Parsons' *Nonexistent Objects*." *Philosophical Studies* 45:95–142.

Forrest, P., and D. M. Armstrong. 1984. "An Argument against David Lewis' Theory of Possible Worlds." *Australasian Journal of Philosophy* 62:164–68.

Geach, P. 1967. "Intentional Identity." *Journal of Philosophy* 64:627–32.

Hailperin, T. 1953. "Quantification and Empty-Individual Domains." *Journal of Symbolic Logic* 18:197–200.

Hintikka, J. 1962. *Knowledge and Belief*. Ithaca.

—————. 1979. "Impossible Possible Worlds Vindicated." In *Game-Theoretic Semantics*, edited by E. Saarinen. Dordrecht.

Howell, R. 1979. "Fictional Objects: How They Are and How They Aren't." *Poetica* 8:129–77.

Kaplan, D. 1969. "Quantifying In." In *Words and Objections: Essays on the Work of W. V. Quine*, edited by D. Davidson and J. Hintikka. Dordrecht.

—————. 1973. "Bob and Carol and Ted and Alice." In *Approaches to Natural Language*, edited by J. Hintikka, J. Moravcsik, and P. Suppes. Dordrecht.

—————. 1975. "How to Russell a Frege-Church." *Journal of Philosophy* 72:716–29.

Kraut, R. 1979. "Attitudes and Their Objects." *Journal of Philosophical Logic* 8:197–217.

Kripke, S. 1972. "Naming and Necessity." In *Semantics of Natural Language*, edited by D. Davidson and G. Harman. Dordrecht.

Lambert, L. 1983. *Meinong and the Principle of Independence*. Cambridge.

Lewis, D. 1968. "Counterpart Theory and Quantified Modal Logic." *Journal of Philosophy* 65:113–26.

—————. 1973. *Counterfactuals*. Cambridge.

—————. 1978. "Truth in Fiction." *American Philosophical Quarterly* 15:37–46.

—————. 1983. "Individuation by Acquaintance and by Stipulation." *Philosophical Review* 92:3–32.

—————. 1986. *On the Plurality of Worlds*. Oxford.

Lycan, W. G. 1979. ''The Trouble with Possible Worlds.'' In *The Possible and the Actual*, edited by M. Loux. Ithaca.

_____. 1981. ''Toward a Homuncular Theory of Believing.'' *Cognition and Brain Theory* 4:139–59.

_____. 1984a. ''The Paradox of Naming.'' In *Analytical Philosophy in Comparative Perspective*, edited by J. L. Shaw. Dordrecht.

_____. 1984b. ''A Syntactically Motivated Theory of Conditionals.'' *Midwest Studies in Philosophy* 9:437–55.

_____. 1985. ''Thoughts About Things.'' In *The Representation of Knowledge and Belief*, Arizona Studies in Cognition, No. 1, edited by M. Brand and R. M. Harnish. Tucson.

McMichael, A. 1983a. ''A Problem for Actualism About Possible Worlds.'' *Philosophical Review* 92:49–66.

_____. 1983b. ''A New Actualist Modal Semantics.'' *Journal of Philosophical Logic* 12:73–99.

Merrill, G. H. 1978. ''Formalization, Possible Worlds and the Foundations of Modal Logic.'' *Erkenntnis* 12:305–27.

Morton, A. 1973. ''The Possible in the Actual.'' *Nous* 7:394–406.

Parsons, T. 1980. *Nonexistent Objects*. New Haven.

Plantinga, A. 1974. *The Nature of Necessity*. Oxford.

Quine, W. V. 1954. ''Quantification and the Empty Domain.'' *Journal of Symbolic Logic* 19:177–79.

Rantala, V. 1975. ''Urn Models: A New Kind of Non-Standard Model for First-Order Logic.'' *Journal of Philosophical Logic* 4:455–74.

Rescher, N. 1975. *A Theory of Possibility*. Pittsburgh.

Rescher, N., and R. Brandom. 1980. *The Logic of Inconsistency*. Oxford.

Resnik, M. 1981. ''Mathematics as a Science of Patterns: Ontology and Reference.'' *Nous* 15:529–50.

_____. 1982. ''Mathematics as a Science of Patterns: Epistemology.'' *Nous* 16:95–105.

Roper, A. 1982. ''Toward an Eliminative Reduction of Possible Worlds.'' *Philosophical Quarterly* 32:45–59.

Routley, R. 1980. *Exploring Meinong's Jungle and Beyond*. Canberra.

Saarinen, E. 1978. ''Intentional Identity Interpreted: A Case Study of the Relations Among Quantifiers, Pronouns, and Propositional Attitudes.'' *Linguistics and Philosophy* 2:151–223.

Shapiro, S. 1983a. ''Conservativeness and Incompleteness.'' *Journal of Philosophy* 80:521–31.

_____. 1983b. ''Mathematics and Reality.'' *Philosophy of Science* 50:523–48.

Skyrms, B. 1981. ''Tractarian Nominalism.'' *Philosophical Studies* 40:199–206.

Stalnaker, R. 1984. *Inquiry*. Cambridge.

van Inwagen, P. 1977. ''Creatures of Fiction.'' *American Philosophical Quarterly* 14:299–308.

Sources of Essence

HUGH S. CHANDLER

Almost everyone believes in modality *de dicto*. Necessarily, puppies are young dogs. The necessity here derives from the meaning of "puppy." The term *means* young dog. *Essentialism* is belief in a more exotic sort of modality, one that does not derive from meaning in this direct and simple way. In the next two sections, I will consider indexical and nonindexical kind terms and the sort of modality applicable to each. In the last section, I will consider individuals and proper names.

I

It is widely believed that terms for 'natural kinds' are indexical. The relevant sense of 'indexical' is explored a bit in section II. Our present concern is the meaning of 'natural kinds'. Here is Peter Strawson explaining David Wiggins's view. (Wiggins takes himself to be defending the theories of Hilary Putnam and Saul Kripke.)

> To be an instance of a natural kind is to possess whatever inner make-up science reveals, or will reveal, as constitutive of that kind and causally responsible for the manifest properties, the characteristic development and mode of activity of its instances.[1]

Recasting this suggestion: N is a 'natural kind' in the 'inner makeup' sense if and only if (1) there is a particular inner makeup that is causally responsible for the characteristic manifest properties of *N*s, and (2) any given entity, actual or possible, is an *N* if and only if it has this inner makeup. The sort of inner makeup Strawson probably has in mind is anatomical or molecular structure. Notice that he says "or *will* reveal." The suggestion is that sometimes we have a concept of the kind, and perhaps a name for it, without having any idea what the relevant 'inner makeup' might be.

In its deepest sense, a 'natural kind' is "any kind comprehended by a basic law of nature."[2] But basic laws of nature are not easy to come by. Hence, on this interpretation, it is far from clear that we now recognize any natural kinds.

In its loosest sense, a 'natural kind' is just a kind, specimens of which can be found in nature—toadstools, pebbles, and bird's nests, not beer cans. Clearly there can be 'natural kinds' in this sense that are not natural kinds in the inner makeup sense. Consider worms. My dictionary says that a worm is "any small, slender, creeping or crawling, limbless animal." If by 'inner makeup' is meant something like characteristic anatomical structure, or characteristic DNA, worms as such do not have *an* inner makeup. They have various inner natures, depending upon what kind of worm they are.[3]

Hilary Putnam has an interesting way of dealing with putative natural kinds whose member have more than one sort of inner structure.

> If there is a hidden structure, then generally it determines what it is to be a member of the natural kind; . . . but the local water, or whatever, may have two or more hidden structures—or so many that 'hidden structure' becomes irrelevant, and superficial characteristics become the decisive ones.[4]

Putnam's suggestion might be something like this: worms do not form a natural kind in the inner makeup sense. Nevertheless, the term 'worm' is a natural-kind term in that it *would* designate a natural kind in the inner makeup sense if there were some one characteristic hidden structure shared by local worms. Since there is not, the meaning of "worm" relates to the superficial characteristics of worms.

The idea is that at least some natural-kind terms have a sort of built in 'default' device. If local members of the designated kind have a characteristic inner nature, then the extension of the term is determined by that nature. If, on the other hand, those members lack a characteristic inner nature, the extension is determined by superficial characteristics.

Surely there are many terms for natural kinds (in the loosest sense) that do not comply with Putnam's suggestion. Consider sand, for example. Most grains of sand are composed of silicon oxide (silica). But this does not reveal something about the essence of sand. On the contrary, sand mostly composed of stuff other than silicon oxide (say small diamonds) is physically possible. The extension of the term is governed by superficial characteristics, and we know the rough definition. Sand is made up of loose grains of rock between .05 and 2.0 millimeters in diameter, varying in color from white to brown or dark grey, and is found, characteristically, along the shores of large bodies of water or in deserts. I do not see how there can be a 'default' device in such a case. The extension of the term "sand" is governed by known superficial characteristics even though local sand *has* a typical inner structure.

No doubt there are noteworthy necessary truths about worms and sand. Necessarily, worms do not look like rabbits. Or, at least, they do not do so when they are in their normal form. (Perhaps there could be worms that go through rabbit-like phases.) Certainly sand cannot be composed of boulders. It seems clear that these necessities are consequences of the known meanings of "worm" and "sand," and that they are necessarily true *de dicto*.

The most radical way in which a putative natural kind can fail to have a characteristic inner nature is by the kind turning out to have no members. Consider unicorns.

Kripke, as is well known, argues that "no counterfactual situation is properly describable as one in which there would have been unicorns."[5] As I understand it, the argument goes like this:

(1) "Unicorn" is meant to be a natural-kind term.

(2) Hence, any possible unicorn would have the characteristic inner makeup of unicorns.

(3) The alleged superficial characteristics of unicorns could spring from various radically different inner makeups, and which of these, if any, is *the* inner makeup of unicorns would be determined by the nature of actual unicorns.

(4) But there are no unicorns.

(5) Therefore, there is no characteristic inner makeup of unicorns.

(6) Therefore, unicorns are impossible.

Putnam has given us grounds for rejecting this argument. Why shouldn't we say that the term "unicorn" has defaulted? Unicorns are possible. If they existed, they would just be creatures having the *superficial* characteristics we imagine unicorns to have. Possible unicorns have various inner structures and belong to various possible species (as do possible worms). It might be said that a putative natural-kind term cannot default unless local members of the kind force it to do so. But why should we accept this doctrine? Why shouldn't the discovery that there are no unicorns do the job?

Unicorns would look something like horses—except that they would always be white and have one horn. Necessarily, in their normal form, they would not resemble worms. This necessity springs from the meaning of "unicorn."

Putnam holds that the picture he advocates applies to a wide variety of cases.

So far we have only used natural-kind words as examples; but the points we have made apply to many other kinds of words as well. They apply to the great majority of all nouns, and to other parts of speech as well.[6]

Thus, we come to pencils. According to a bit of science fiction invented by Rogers Albritton, pencils are really organisms. When one cuts them open and examines them under an electron microscope, one sees delicate little nerves and tiny organs. The idea that people manufacture pencils is an illusion. In fact, they spawn and grow.

Putnam's theory of pencils goes like this: It is epistemically possible that the Albritton hypothesis is correct. If it is, then pencils have an inner makeup that makes them necessarily (i.e., essentially) organisms. On the other hand, if local pencils are artifacts as we devoutly believe, then pencils are necessarily artifacts.

It follows that 'pencil' is not *synonymous* with any description—not even loosely synonymous with a *loose* description. When we use the word 'pencil', we intend to refer to whatever has the same *nature* as the normal examples of the local pencils in the actual world. 'Pencil' is just as *indexical* as 'water' or 'gold'.[7]

I think Putnam is plainly wrong here. The extension of the term "pencil" is determined by a cluster of relatively superficial characteristics. (Putnam believes that holders of the cluster theory are necessarily committed to the idea that *being an artifact* is an essential property of pencils. I cannot see any reason to think this is true.)

Putnam does not hold that there could be pencils that are organisms. On Putnam's view, we can be almost certain this is *not* possible. And we can be almost certain that it is possible for a pencil to be an artifact. I think, on the contrary, that we *know* it is possible for a pencil to be an artifact simply by knowing what we mean by ''pencil.''

Think of inventing, and naming, a new device, say a kind of mousetrap. How do we know that at least some such mousetraps could be artifacts? Well, we know we can build them. We know we could make them out of various materials, in various ways. If we know anything at all, we know that the devices we have in mind need not be organisms.

On the Putnam theory, before there were any pencils (or any mousetraps), there was nothing to index—hence, no determinate nature. I hold that when we see how to construct such things, we see that the things *are possible*. Their nature is given (and probably exhausted) by what we have in mind.

If in fact, local pencils are organisms, then, certainly, pencils that are not artifacts are possible. But this is not too surprising. Perhaps somewhere things we should call ''pencils'' grow on trees. In any case, pencils that *are* artifacts are certainly possible. This bit of knowledge does not depend in any way upon the inner nature of local pencils. I take this to show that Putnam's indexical interpretation of ''pencil'' is incorrect.[8]

A similar point can be made about invented plants and animals. Suppose, for example, we invent animals that run on bony wheels (let's call them ''rotarians''). We design the appropriate sort of anatomy and DNA. And we make it a necessary truth that rotarians have this inner nature. There is no reason why we should not be able to provide the term ''rotarian'' with a complete, descriptive, nonindexical definition, either before or after the creation of rotarians. (Once rotarians exist, the members of some tribe could have an indexical term for them.)

It looks as though terms for many natural kinds (in the loosest sense), terms for mythological species, and ordinary terms for artifacts (living and nonliving) are *not* indexical. Necessary truths about such kinds are presumably true *de dicto*.

II

A kind term is *non* indexical if and only if either (1) there is no final characterization of the designated kind, or (2) expert speakers can explain the meaning of the term by providing such a characterization.[9] Thus, for example, the meaning of the term ''Bostonian'' can be finally explained by saying it means someone who lives in, or comes from, Boston. Notice that a final characterization can contain an indexical element. In this case, the definition of the nonindexical term ''Bostonian'' includes the proper name ''Boston.'' It seems likely that some nonindexical kind terms are so messy they lack a final definition. The term ''game'' may be an example. In such a case, one can at least describe typical members of the family.

A kind term is *indexical* if and only if (1) there is a final characterization of the kind, but (2) expert speakers explain the meaning of the term by 'pointing to' the kind rather than by providing a final characterization of it. For example, suppose the members of a certain family use the term ''Billsvillian'' to designate anyone who lives in, or comes from, Bill's hometown, but they do not know what town that is. The family intends the term to be necessarily coreferential with the correct characterization. If Bill comes from Chicago, then necessarily Billsvillians are Chicagoans. So far as the family is concerned, it is epistemically possible that Bill comes from Boston, or Peoria, or ..., and so on. Thus, there are alternative epistemically possible final characterizations of Billsvillians. Perhaps the notion of 'indexical' just sketched is a bit eccentric. It is meant to capture the peculiar feature of kind terms that enables them to pay their part in the generation of exotic necessary truths. [10]

When we name a kind blindly, we may be indulging in a 'definition lottery'. It is not easy to distinguish between this procedure and the introduction of an indexical kind term.

Suppose a coin has been flipped. It lies unexamined in a corner of the room. We decide that if it landed heads up, a 'wem' is a toy run by a windup motor. If the coin landed tails up, a 'wem' is toy run by an electric motor. Thus, it is possible that wems necessarily contain windup motors. Whether or not this is necessary depends upon how the coin fell, i.e., depends upon a fact that remains to be discovered.

This is not an example of an indexical kind term. Nor is it a demonstration of essentialism. It is a definition lottery. If it is necessarily true that wems run on windup motors, that necessity derives from our *conditional definition* of ''wem.'' When we examine the coin, we may discover that it landed heads up, and, thus, we may learn that a wem necessarily runs on a windup motor. But it would be misleading to say we had found, or discovered, a necessary truth. It would be better to say we had discovered what we meant by ''wem.''

Suppose that ''wems necessarily run on windup motors'' is true. Is it true *de dicto*? Of course, we have to look at the coin in order to find out whether it is true. We do not know *a priori* that wems necessarily run on windup motors. But why shouldn't we say the position of the coin shows that the statement is true *de dicto*? If we knew what we meant by ''wem,'' then we would know that wems necessarily run on windup motors.

There are probably some philosophers who will say that the term ''wem'' does not denote a particular kind of toy *before* we look at the coin. The term hangs fire. Certainly, one must admit a hint of bad magic in the idea that the term denoted toys that run on windup motors before we checked the coin. If we had then been asked what we meant by ''wem,'' we might well have said we did not know.

After we look at the coin, we can provide a final definition of ''wem.'' Notice that the definition will not include mention of the coin. That is to say, the coin plays no part in the meaning.

Now let us consider an indexical term. Suppose we have noticed some toys running about the house, but have not examined them. We decide to call these toys, and all others that operate on the same sort of motor, ''wems.'' (If the toys have different sorts of motors, then ''wem'' does not designate anything—it is a misfire.)

One difficulty in regard to this case is the vagueness of "same sort of motor." What taxonomy do we have in mind? Are we counting electric motors with different sorts of armatures as different sorts of motors? I assume we can make the background taxonomy sufficiently clear. *Some* vagueness is certainly permissible.

Before we discover what is inside local wems, we can explain what a wem is only by saying something like "wems are toys like *these*—ones that run on *this* sort of motor (whatever sort that is)." The fact that we can thus explain our meaning shows that we are not in a definition lottery. But such talk does not provide a final characterization of wems. The description, together with facts about the toys, may determine such a characterization, and we intend that characterization to be necessarily coreferential with the term.

When it becomes known, for example, that wems are toys that run on electric motors, the term may come to have just this meaning and, thus, cease to be indexical. Apparently, there could be an indexical kind term such that being indexical is not an essential property of that term. Perhaps this is true of all indexical kind terms.

Suppose it is necessarily true that wems run on electric motors. Where does the necessity come from? That is to say, how does it come about that this is a necessary truth? Its sources are (1) our stipulation that wems must have the sort of motor found in the local specimens, and (2) the fact that these specimens contain electric motors— convention plus fact.

Here is a clearer case. Imagine a team of contemporary scientists studying planet x. They are reasonably sure there is some sort of liquid on its surface, but they have no idea what the liquid is. In their discussions of the planet, they have taken to calling that liquid (to be identified chemically) "glop." The background taxonomy is fairly precise. If the liquid on the planet's surface is pure water, then glop is H_2O. The scientists can explain what they mean by "glop." They say, for example, "By 'glop' we mean the liquid on the surface of planet x (identified chemically)." But there is a modal ambiguity here. Suppose that during some geological periods, the liquid on the surface of planet x is water, and that during others, it is ammonia. Do the scientists intend that, in such a case, the term "glop" sometimes designates water and sometimes ammonia? No doubt that could be their intention. But I assume the case is different. Or, suppose that the liquid is water; in that case, *could* glop be ammonia? Again, I assume not. "Glop" is meant to be necessarily coreferential with the chemical characterization of the liquid now on the surface of planet x.

Suppose that glop is H_2O. In that case, glop has the property of being H_2O necessarily—glop and H_2O are necessarily coextensive. If we like, we can even say that "glop" *means* H_2O. But the necessity is not *de dicto*; it is exotic.

Now suppose the scientists *discover* that glop is H_2O. Will "glop" change its meaning? It need not do so. The scientists may explain the meaning of the term just as they did before, and then add that glop is H_2O. In this case, "glop" is indexical, but the final characterization is known.

III

A 'natural individual' might be one that came into existence through natural processes; one that was not assembled, carved, or molded, for some purpose—a nonartifact. A bird, or an atom of gold, is likely to be a natural individual in this sense. It is easy to assume that the members of a 'natural kind', in some sense or other, must be 'natural' in this way. But the assumption is plainly false. Worms can be assembled from various clone parts. An individual worm thus assembled is 'nonnatural' in that it came into existence through nonnatural processes. Nevertheless, it may be a worm of some ordinary sort (say a roundworm) and, thus, a member of a natural kind (in some sense).

Some philosophers suggest that individuals can be 'natural' in a more profound sense. Perhaps the idea is that the individual members of a natural kind (in some deep sense) are delineated by nature itself rather than by us. Their essences are discovered—not the product of convention. Leibniz apparently believed in individuals of this sort. He calls them ''perfect substances.''[11] In any case, let us think about individuals that are *not* natural in a deep sense.

Imagine a computer screen upon which little spots of light appear and 'move about'. We want to set up a system for delineating individual 'dots'. They are going to be *continuents*. And let us have them be individuals of a kind such that it is logically possible that they should do things other than the things they actually do. Thus, we will be able to say things like ''If this dot had been traveling at a slightly faster speed, it would have collided with that one.''

We need an appropriate set of rules for tracking particular dots from one place to another, and for determining when a dot has come into existence or ceased to exist. For example, we have to decide whether or not the same dot can disappear on one side of the screen and appear on the other. And if a spot of light disappears from the screen at a particular place and, after a moment, a spot appears at that same place, are we to say that the same dot is back again or that the original dot has been destroyed and a new one created? The system can be developed in many different ways.

Of course, the rules will not be 'complete'. They may not tell us whether a is the same dot as b under all possible circumstances. Or, there may be cases in which the rules do not tell us whether a given dot has ceased to exist. We need rules only for circumstances that tend to arise.

Suppose a particular dot is at the center of the screen, and we wish to know whether that dot could now have been in the lower right-hand corner. The procedure would be to trace the dot back, perhaps all the way to its origin, and then see whether there is a way the dot could have gotten from there to the lower right-hand corner by now.

Let us make it a rule that a dot originating at a given time and place could not have originated at a very different time and place. If a given dot originated at the middle of the left-hand side of the screen at 10:32 Tuesday morning, then *that* dot could not have originated in the upper right-hand corner at noon on Monday. Unless we have some such rule, any dot could be anywhere at anytime.

We have the beginnings of a system for delineating individual dots. Some such system, however crude, must underlie any naming of dots. Different systems make 'dots' different sorts of things. Unless some system is presupposed, nothing definite will get named. With a system in place, the procedure might go as follows. Someone points to a particular spot of light on the screen and says, "I name this dot 'Jill'." Saying that the *dot* will be named 'Jill' lets the world know which system of individuation is at work.

Suppose that Jill came into existence at the center of display screen S 1 at 10:03 A.M. on June 5, 1985. Our system is such that if this is true, it is necessarily true. Jill could not have had a different origin. The necessity is exotic. It is not simply a consequence of what we mean by "Jill." It springs from the system in the background plus the facts about Jill's time and place of origin.

If someone points to Jill and says, "This dot necessarily came into existence at the center of S 1 at 10:03 A.M. on June 5, 1985," the statement is true; but it is not true *de dicto*.

The background system for dots permits exotic necessary truths. I believe that other possible systems would not do so. For example, we might decide that a 'blot' is much like a dot, except that it need not have had the origin it did have—it could have had any origin we can imagine it having. Blots can be named by pointing at a spot of light and saying, for example, "let's call this blot 'Fran'." Necessary truths about Fran are generated by the background system. Thus, it may be a necessary truth that Fran has not recently expanded so as to include the whole screen and then contracted back to normal size. Our rules may say that this sort of expansion destroys a blot (and, for that matter, a dot). A necessary truth of this sort is not exotic. The necessity is a consequence of what we mean by "blot" (and "dot") and is no surprise to expert speakers. The point is that *all* interesting necessary truths about blots may be of this sort.

The name "Fran" may be indexical in an ordinary sense—it was introduced by pointing—but it is not meant to be necessarily coextensive with a final characterization. In fact, the background system for blots may be such that there is no final characterization for Fran, or for any other blot.

We hold that Jill is the only dot that could have originated at the center of S 1 at 10:03 A.M., June 5, 1985, and headed off (say) due east. Pretend that some dot had come into existence there and then and headed east, but had then gone on to lead a life quite unlike the one Jill actually led. Might that have been some other dot—not Jill? Some systems would permit this. But we will say that what has been pretended is that Jill led a life very different from her actual one. The description "the dot that originated at the center of S 1 at 10:03 A.M. on June 5, 1985, and headed due east" is necessarily coreferential with the name "Jill" as we are now using it.

I suppose the background system for blots will not permit us to name possible, but nonactual, blots. The system for dots permits this. Perhaps, for example, we do not know whether a dot came into existence at the center of display screen S 1 at 6:42 P.M., on June 4, 1985, and headed due west. Since this description is rigid—it designates the same *dot* under all possible circumstances—nothing prevents us from referring to such a dot as "Jack." The name permits us to say things like "If Jack ever existed, and always has moved west, then Jack still exists." In a case like this, a proper name is understood nonindexically. How could it be otherwise? The name is taken as an abbreviation for a final characterization of a possible dot.[12]

If Jack is real, then, necessarily, Jack came into existence on June 4. What sort of necessity is this? It is certainly not exotic. The fact is that by ''Jack,'' we just mean the dot that came into existence on June 4, ... and so forth. It is not surprising that if there is such a dot, it originated on June 4. But is the necessity *de dicto*? I do not know how to answer this question. On the one hand, if there is such a dot, we are saying *of it* that it necessarily came into existence on June 4. We are not saying something about Jack *under some description*. On the other hand, the necessity is an uninteresting consequence of what we now mean by ''Jack.''

The enterprise just described is rather artificial. The point of the artifice is to magnify our role in delineating individuals. In regard to dots and blots, it is clear that the delineation is largely a matter of convention.

The delineation of individual plants and animals is also, at least partially, conventional. Suppose a worm— Charlie—is assembled by grafting together three clone parts: *a, b,* and *c.* Could Charlie have come into existence by the fusion of two of those parts and one substitution? Well, perhaps; we have not definitely decided this yet. Our rules are 'incomplete'.

Where there is such indeterminacy, the final characterization of the individual (if there is such a characterization) must be equally indeterminate. I take it that the name ''Charlie'' (as we are using it) and ''the worm that comes into existence through the grafting together of pretty much all three parts *a, b,* and *c* '' are necessarily coreferential. Where the applicability of one is indeterminate, so is the other.

Suppose we have three worm parts—*d, e,* and *f*—that could be grafted together to form a worm. The background system tells us that there is only one worm that can be so formed. Let us call that possible worm ''Ralph.'' By ''Ralph,'' we just mean the worm we might create out of those parts. (''Has Ralph been put together yet?'' ''No. We're hoping to do it tomorrow.'') At the moment, the name is operating nonindexically. We know that if Ralph exists next week, then, necessarily, Ralph originated through the grafting together of at least two of the worm parts *d, e,* and *f*; but this necessity is unsurprising.

A similar case could arise in generating worms from carefully identified spermatozoa and ova. By ''Walter,'' we might mean the worm to be generated by the union of spermatozoon $S1$ with ovum $O1$.[13] (The possibility of twins adds an extra twist. If two worms are generated by the process, perhaps we should say that neither one is Walter.)[14]

After Walter has been created, we can explain who or what Walter is in part by 'pointing'. We can say things like ''Walter is the large worm in jar number six.'' Perhaps everyone forgets which spermatozoon and ovum produced him. In that case, the name becomes indexical in something like the sense used in section II.

Nonindexical proper names, if there are any, might well contain an indexical element. For example, when ''Walter'' is nonindexical, it is taken as an abbreviation for some such description as ''the worm generated by the union of $S1$ with $O1$.'' But ''$S1$ and ''$O1$'' are proper names. I assume that *they* are understood indexically (at least, in the ordinary sense of 'indexical').

Can a proper name begin its career indexically (in my peculiar sense) and become nonindexical? Normally, we are not particularly interested in final definitions for proper names. But, for example, in biological research, final characterizations of individual worms might be crucial. In such a lab, names for particular worms might often be used as abbreviations for final characterizations. Perhaps, then, it is a great misfortune that "Alfred" is an indexical name of a worm. Records are anxiously studied in hopes of uncovering the names of the worm parts from which Alfred was created. The names are discovered, and "Alfred" comes to mean "the worm made from $P6$, $P18$, and $P20$." (Eventually, the researchers may forget whether Alfred was actually created.)

So far as I can see, it is even possible that a nonactual worm, like Ralph, should have an indexical name. Suppose that the biology lab explodes. The crucial worm parts die, and all of the members of the team that was to create Ralph have total amnesia. No one now knows which parts were to have formed Ralph. But Ralph is still a subject of conversation. By "Ralph," we mean the worm that the unfortunate team was about to create.

Thus, there may be proper names that are not indexical, and indexical proper names that are not essentially indexical. Furthermore, there may be nonindexical names that are not essentially nonindexical, and there might even be indexical proper names for individuals who never actually exist.

Most ordinary proper names are indexical (in my sense). Expert speakers are aware (perhaps vaguely) of the appropriate background system, and there is a final characterization of the named individual; but expert speakers cannot provide such a characterization. The meaning of the name is explained indexically—that is, *via* some gesture or description that points to the individual ("that dot there," "the worm in jar number three," and so forth). The name and these gestures or descriptions are contingently coreferential.

Some necessary truths about individuals are simply consequences of the background system for the individual in question. But some systems of this sort interact with certain contingent facts to yield hybrid necessary truths. When our devices for referring to such individuals do not depend upon knowledge of the relevant contingent facts, those hybrid truths become exotic.[15]

Notes

1. Strawson, "Critical Notice of *Sameness and Substance* by David Wiggins," *Mind* CX (Oct. 1981):605.

2. See Paul M. Churchland's "Conceptual Progress and Word/World Relations: In Search of the Essence of Natural Kinds," *Canadian Journal of Philosophy* (Mar. 1985) 15:1–17, n.1.

3. Worms are found in three different phyla, namely platyhelminthes, nematoda, and annelida. Annelids (e.g., earthworms) are no more closely linked to platyhelminths (e.g., flatworms) than are mollusks (e.g., oysters).

4. Hilary Putnam, "The Meaning of 'Meaning'," in *Mind, Language, and Reality, Philosophical Papers,* Vol. 2 (Cambridge, 1975), 240–41.

5. Saul Kripke, *Naming and Necessity* (Cambridge, Mass., 1972), 156.

6. Putnam, "The Meaning of 'Meaning'," 242.

7. Ibid., 243.

8. Much of what I say about pencils is taken from Stephen P. Schwartz, "Putnam on Artifacts," *The Philosophical Review* 87, No. 4 (Oct. 1978):566–74.

9. The idea of a 'final characterization' is a garbled version of a suggestion made to me by my colleague Tim McCarthy.

10. My use of the phrase "exotic necessary truth" is derived from the work of Keith Donnellan. See his "Kripke and Putnam on Natural Kind Terms," in *Knowledge and Mind,* edited by Carl Ginet and Sydney Shoemaker (Oxford, 1983), 84–104.

11. G. W. Leibniz, *New Essays on Human Understanding,* abridged edition, translated and edited by Peter Remnant and Jonathan Bennett (Cambridge, 1982), 328–29.

12. See David Kaplan's "Bob and Carol and Ted and Alice," in *Approaches to Natural Language,* edited by K. J. J. Hintikka, J. M.E. Moravcsik, and P. Suppes (Dordrecht, 1973), 516–17, n. 19.

13. Nathan Salmon reports that both David Kaplan and Saul Kripke hold that we can have names for such possible but nonactual animals. See his *Reference and Essence* (Princeton, N.J., 1981), 39, n. 41. Salmon doubts that there can be such names.

14. A worm that is one of a pair of identical twins is necessarily a product of a particular spermatozoon and ovum. But a final definition of such a worm will have to distinguish it from its twin. How can this be done? The trick might be managed by naming the first cells that are fated to belong to one of the twins rather than the other.

15. Charles Caton, Tim McCarthy, and Patrick Maher read an earlier draft of this paper and provided valuable comments and corrections. I also received helpful advice from Leslie Chandler.

Essentialism and the Elementary Constituents of Matter

EVAN FALES

Essentialism begins with reflection upon intuitions that all of us share: that the world is organized into different kinds of things; and that the life of a thing is bounded by changes that, unlike those it survives, usher it into and out of existence. Essentialism ends with a puzzle: to account for the connection between particulars and their properties in such a way as to explain how some properties, but not others, attach to a thing by necessity. Part of the challenge is to provide philosophical credentials for this kind of necessity. The other is to determine when it applies, or to show how this can be determined.

I shall propose a solution to the puzzle, one that supports the philosophical *bona fides* of essentialism but that, ironically, gives little encouragement to the intuitions that initially motivate the doctrine. Those intuitions (as I have called them) derive from attention to examples of a sort that do not sustain any solution to the puzzle. The intuitions can be accounted for, but not in a way that really touches the deep ontological question of necessity.

The solution I propose to the deep question is that the essential properties of a genuine substance are its monadic properties; the accidents, its relations. This is bound to seem preposterous:[1] it ill accords with the intuition that some monadic properties are accidents, and it does not correspond in general to taxonomic practice. Yet the proposed solution was initially suggested to me by actual taxonomic practice—or, rather, by the classifying strategies of a special group of practitioners, namely physicists. I shall comment presently upon the relationship between these actual policies and the philosophical status of the essentialist thesis I shall defend.

It will be apparent that the form of essentialism I am defending here is a version of the claim that there are natural kinds. That claim will need to be refined, and I shall need to elucidate what I mean by 'genuine substance'. Once I have explained the doctrine to be discussed, I shall consider its modal and epistemological status, and then show how the distinction between monadic properties and relations might explain the essence/accident distinction.

Someone who holds that there are natural kinds need not, of course, deny that human purposes, interests, and linguistic habits are relevant, even properly relevant, to the construction of systems of classification. But the essentialist should take one human enterprise to be central to the question whether there are natural kinds. That enterprise is science, the purpose of which is, or includes, the discovery of objective principles of classification. I have argued elsewhere that the business of devising taxonomies lies at the very heart of scientific theorizing.[2] There is little novelty in the reflection that scientists produce taxonomies, or that the generation of classifying schemes is somehow a theory-laden process. But the implications of this fact, from the standpoint of scientific realism, are sometimes overlooked.

Suppose there is an intimate connection, a connection of a conceptual sort, between the nomological structure of a physical theory and the associated taxonomy that provides a set of sortals in terms of which the domain of the theory may be exhaustively specified. Suppose there is, in other words, a reciprocal relation between laws and the entities governed by them, such that the laws narrowly constrain acceptable principles of classification for the entities they govern. If one takes a realist view of a theory, one must then equally be a realist respecting the taxonomy. The problem is to show in some detail how, in general, a theory can serve to dictate a natural ontology of kinds. That is a matter of discovering what the constraints are and why they obtain.

The first major step in the argument is to concede that not every sort of scientific theory can dictate a taxonomy that meets the requirements of a philosophically adequate conception of natural kinds. Thus, not all scientifically useful taxonomies will be of interest to the essentialist. If the concept of a natural kind tells us that things of that kind cease to exist when they lose certain properties, then the application of the concept is clear only to the extent that we have clear criteria for whether something has or lacks the properties in question. If we do not have clear criteria for this, or for when an individual begins and ceases to exist, then we have no clear conception of a natural kind under which it falls.[3]

But most, if not all, of the familiar individuals of our world are not such that we can nonarbitrarily specify conditions that sharply demarcate when they cease to exist, or when they begin to exist. Nor can improvements in scientific understanding be expected to remedy this circumstance. For the familiar entities of our world are fuzzy: they do, or can, gradually come into being and gradually fade away. There is no point in the progressive dying and decay of a maple tree at which it ceases to be a maple, and no set of properties, the loss of which is both necessary and sufficient to turn the tree into something else. And how are we to handle borderline cases? Are they of no natural kind whatever?

But there is an underlying, and quite general, explanation for this fuzziness. It is that familiar objects are composed of very many smaller parts, bound into complete structures whose features can be gradually changed by removing or adding parts or by rearranging them. Although laws constrain the ways in which parts may be added, subtracted, or rearranged, they do not do so in a way that confines permissible variation in structure to varieties sufficiently distinct and few in number to generate a genuine taxonomy. This fact invites the sorites paradoxes that, since Locke, have constituted one of the chief objections to natural kinds.[4]

If sorites paradoxes wreak havoc with the genidentity of familiar objects, they simultaneously suggest a strategy for outflanking the obstacle they create. If most theories do not generate suitable taxonomies because their domains are complex entities, perhaps we can hope for better if we consider only theories that describe, or purport to describe, the simplest bits of matter, those bits from which everything else is composed. And, if modern physics may be consulted to provide evidence in this regard, we shall indeed get something better. For elementary particle physics holds the promise of a sharp and nonarbitrary classification of the basic constituents of matter— fundamental entities, or *FE*s, as I shall call them. It is, indeed, these *FE*s that I had in mind when I spoke earlier of genuine substances. We may now say that 'genuine' in the required sense just means 'noncomposite'. Moreover, any complete theory of elementary particles holds a special position among theories generally. Since everything (everything material, at least) is composed of such entities, a theory that describes them is fundamental to our understanding of the physical universe as a whole. A theory that describes them describes everything (material) that there is. If, then, *FE*s can be classified into natural kinds, it follows that essential properties have a deep role to play in the structure of the world, and *a fortiori* in a proper understanding of it.

To be sure, if *FE*s were themselves capable of gradual change, we would not by the strategy just outlined be able to save essentialism from the Lockean objection. It is not an *a priori* matter whether the differences between *FE*s are discontinuous or not. And so essentialism, in the form I propose, is in one sense not an *a priori* thesis. What *is a priori* is the conceptual connection between essentialism and theories that have a certain form. What is *a posteriori* is whether any theory of the requisite form correctly describes the world.

What, then, must the form of a theory be, and how does it generate an associated taxonomy? It is not sufficient that the domain of the theory be *FE*s, and that these *FE*s have sharply distinguishable properties. For that is not enough to determine which properties of an *FE* are essential and which are accidental. At best, it tells us that any property of an *FE* that can change continuously must be reckoned contingent. We are not entitled to the converse proposition.

A fundamental theory of matter must accomplish at least two things. It must specify (or contain an algorithm for determining) the physically possible states of any collection of matter, and it must determine the permissible transitions between states of any system, together with their associated probabilities. Thus, such a theory must specify which sets of properties can be coinstantiated by *FE*s. As such, it prohibits certain sortals; but this leaves untouched the problem of how it distinguishes accidental from sortal-determining properties.

One can think of a fundamental theory as being expressed by an (infinite) two-dimensional array. The vertical and horizontal positions of the matrix stand for physically possible states of affairs, and the matrix entry at a given position represents the transition probability that the "horizontal" state will be succeeded by the "vertical" one. Alternatively, the same information could be supplied by an infinite set of conditional laws specifying the probabilities associated with transitions between states. Either formalization would be equally impossible to carry out in practice, but it appears that each would, in principle, express all the factual content of the theory. But in fact it would be wrong, or at least misleading, to draw this conclusion. Such a formalization would obscure crucial features of theories of the sort we actually employ. These features are brought out when those theories are expressed (as they are) in terms of finite sets of more general laws. But the gain achieved by the style of formalization actually employed is by no means simply, or even at all, that of finite expressability.[5] What is brought into the open is, rather, the fact that the uniformities of nature are independent of, or generalizable over, certain physical variables, and not others. And this bears on the distinction between essential and inessential properties. Let us see how.

In the present context, the essentialist's problem boils down to this. He must show which of the theoretically possible state transitions that any physical system can undergo are ones that involve substantial change, and which do not. Initially, it might seem impossible to do this without invoking some arbitrary or conventional rule. For, to take the simplest sort of case, suppose the essentialist regards a change in a single FE to constitute a substantial change—the destruction of a particle of type A, and the creation in its place of a particle of type B. A conventionalist might reply that this description of the situation is neither more nor less acceptable than an alternative description, according to which the change in question marks successive phases of one and the same particle. Thus the property that disappears in the change is an essence of A-type particles only in the sense of being a nominal essence, an essence relative to the convenient or conventional decision to classify particles into types A and B.

To this argument an essentialist must respond by showing that certain taxonomic strategies are not merely arbitrary or pragmatic but are determined by features of the world, or, to put it more cautiously, by what fundamental theory tells us the world is like. And in order to avoid begging the question, we must be able to extract from fundamental theory a description of the world that does not already incorporate or presuppose a classification scheme for FEs. But this is just what the transition matrix achieves. The matrix can be formulated so as to describe the transition probabilities between states specified simply as bundles of properties or structures of related property bundles. There need be in this no commitment as to what the conditions of identity through time are for particles, nor need there be any introduction of kind names for particles. So the transition matrix provides one way of formulating the information content of a theory in classification-free form.

Because it merely enumerates in plodding detail the infinitely many possible states, a transition matrix leaves implicit any generalizations over relevant variables that a theory embodies. Such generalizations are of crucial significance to our inquiry. Take, for example, a physical system that transforms to a different later state. The transition probability associated with this transformation may be insensitive to certain alterations in the specification of the involved states. If, for example, the entire system is translated in space, while all the other variables remain fixed, we may find (indeed, do find) that this does not affect the transition probabilities. That this is so is an *a posteriori* discovery, built into contemporary theories. It could have turned out differently. But if it is so, then the spatial coordinates assigned to a system, or, alternatively, mere translation within a set of coordinates, do not affect its behavior. And this means that the laws of nature can be generalized with respect to spatial location.

But there is a corollary. Any *part* of a system, insofar as it is "isolated," can be translated with respect to other parts of the system, without the mere fact of new relative location affecting physical behavior. The generalizability of laws with respect to spatial location is tied, therefore, to a claim about what "does not matter" to the intrinsic nature of a piece of the world. This provides a basis for the conclusion that (relative) spatial location is a contingent property of matter and, *a fortiori,* of *FE*s.

Other generalizations are in the offing. What they are is a matter for the physicist to discover. Present physical theory counts among the contingent properties of *FE*s, orientation in space, velocity, and position in time. The arguments are similar in each instance. Essential properties are, by default, those with respect to changes in which the behavior of *FE*s is not invariant. At present, these are taken to include rest mass, charge, spin, and a variety of other quantized properties. Thus, those properties whose values serve to restrict the possible states of a system, or which affect transition probabilities, are ones that nature distinguishes from ones that do not do so. This is no function of our conventions.

Physicists classify *FE*s. The principle that underlies their classifying strategy is, I believe, the one just explained. But what has all this to do with essentialism? To be sure, the principle in question is a general one, and it is one that makes use of what physicists have a right to regard as objective features of the world. These features, moreover, are used to determine a sorting of particles into kinds and hence to provide criteria for judging the creation and decay of individual particles. But conventionalists need not deny that classification makes use of objective properties or general principles. What they deny is that we have any intelligible notion of substance, or any reasons transcending pragmatic ones, for picking one principle rather than another as the generating rule for constructing taxonomies that distinguish what we call substances. A satisfactory answer to the conventionalist must therefore show that the proposed principle latches onto the things themselves; and it must show that the creation and extinction of individuals are processes that, determined by this principle, are objectively distinguished from mere change. Put another way, such a principle must be able to give substance to the notion that properties attach to an individual in two fundamentally different ways: some necessarily, and others not. Conventionalists are at a loss to explain such claims about necessity (and contingency) except as an artifact of the rules of language. Essentialists must find a different explanation than this one.

Seeking such an explanation, an essentialist might notice the fact that the "contingent" properties of the physicist are all relations, whereas the taxonomy-determining properties are all monadic. This is the interesting empirical fact with which we began. (Of the properties that current theory ascribes to *FE*s, I have mentioned only a few. There would be little point in attempting to complete the list, since our understanding of elementary matter is still so incomplete.) The main task is to show what, on the one hand, this fact has to do with the "underlying principle" of classification used in physics, and what, on the other, it has to do with supplying a distinction between essential and accidental properties.

First, let us examine the underlying principle. Given a system of *FE*s, clearly the relations that obtain between them can play a causal role in the evolution of the system. What the taxonomist makes use of is the fact that they need not do so. Relations can be changed in ways that do not alter the behavior of individual *FE*s. This fact underlies the possibility of approximating, at least ideally, the situation of a closed or isolated physical system. It also underlies the possibility of explaining the enormous variety of things and changes in the physical world in terms of a much smaller number of stable constituent bits of matter and their shifting relations. In its purest form, this explanatory strategy postulates *FE*s that can be neither destroyed nor created, which indeed can undergo no internal change. But this extreme, Democritean form of atomism is not required. Even a theory that allows *FE*s to undergo law-governed changes in monadic properties and/or creation and destruction can avail itself of the explanatory power of atomism.

Now why should the underlying principle, and the fact that it leads physicists to classify in terms of monadic properties, be relevant to the issue of essentialism? At this point, arguments that are more properly philosophical can be brought to bear. First, it is perhaps an unsurprising result that relations are not essential properties of an *FE*, even if other properties are. It is unsurprising because relations cannot be thought of as intrinsic to a thing, constitutive of what it is. For a relation can change, not by virtue of any change in the thing itself, but by virtue of changes in the other relatum or relata. This is part, if not all, of what is implied by the idea that a substance has its existence independently of anything else. Hence, there is a strong reason for not regarding relations as contributing to the nature of a thing.

Most essentialists would find this first aspect of the taxonomic policy of physicists congenial. On the other hand, it is far less initially plausible to hold that every monadic property of a thing is essential to it, i.e., that there are no monadic accidents. To hold this might indeed seem to trivialize essentialism; moreover, it seeems clearly implausible when the paradigmatic examples of natural kinds are chosen, as they commonly have been, from among biological species. For if the essence/accident distinction can be applied to animals and plants at all, it is clear that some monadic properties must be counted as accidents. But I have rejected the notion that the distinction can be so applied;[6] and it would hardly be justifiable to draw lessons from the biological sphere when the nature of fundamental entities is at stake.

There is ample reason for holding each of the monadic properties of an *FE* to be contitutive of its nature. Every property (*a fortiori,* every monadic property) that is discoverable by us—indeed every property that can have any physical bearing upon the interactions of an *FE* with the rest of the world—must be one that influences some of the causal connections between that *FE* and its environment: thus, one that influences some transition probabilities. And if the causal role of a fundamental bit of matter does not constitute its nature, what could do so? It is causal roles that make a particle what it is, so far as physics is concerned; and if two particles are interchangeable *salva* causal roles, then they are of the same kind. Moreover, there are no grounds here for discriminating between monadic properties, elevating some but not others as essences; or anyway no grounds so long as the properties in question are not continuously variable. There may be practical reasons for regarding certain causal roles of an *FE* as more important (more useful for human purposes, for instance); but under the impartial eye of physical theory such distinctions vanish. The underlying principle of elementary particle taxonomy, then, accords equal status to each monadic property of an *FE*.[7]

If the distinction between essences and accidents is what I have claimed it to be, then it is a clear distinction. Yet the business of determining essences is not thereby freed of subtleties, for the question whether a given property is monadic or a relation is sometimes obscure and quarrelsome. Indeed, physics provides such cases. One example of this involves the distinction between determinable properties and their determinations. If a determinate property is a relation, it is natural to assume that every determinable of which it is a species is also a relation. But that assumption is overhasty. That a particle is at a specified location in space-time is a relational fact and is accidental, but that it is somewhere or other in space-time is, we suppose, of its essence. Is *being in space-time* a relational property? To so construe it would amount to taking space-time to be a particular; and it is doubtful that this is correct. It is more plausible to regard *being spatiotemporal* as a monadic property. So I doubt that we have here a counterexample to my claim.

A further example of this kind concerns the spin of elementary particles. An electron has a spin whose magnitude is $1/2\hbar$, and whose direction can be either ''up'' or ''down'' relative to an axis of measurement. The direction of the spin vector is a relation between it and a coordinate system, and by present lights ought to be regarded an accidental property of electrons. The magnitude of the spin is intrinsic and hence ought to count as an essence. (Physicists agree.) Now one can regard the two types of spin—''up'' and ''down''—as determinate values of the determinable property of having a spin of $1/2\hbar$. But if this is so, then the determinate properties are relations; the determinable one, monadic.

The fact that two particles that differ only with regard to spin direction (and spatiotemporal location) should be treated as belonging to the same species nicely illustrates the main argument. One can transform a spin-down particle into a spin-up particle by active means: by rotating it. But one can achieve the same substitution by means of a passive transformation, one that rotates not the particle but the coordinate system. Clearly this choice reflects the fact that a relation can be changed by changing either relatum. Therefore, we expect that in general transformations that *can* be achieved by passive means correspond to accidental properties; those that require an active transformation indicate that the change in question involves an essential property. (There is, however, one exception to the rule concerning active transformations, which will be noted below.)

It follows form all this that two particles are not of the same type unless a passive transformation exists that transforms particles of the first kind into ones of the second, and vice versa. Moreover, such transformation must be characterizable as passive in terms of operations performed in real physical space, not in some abstract space whose coordinates are other physical parameters; and the operations must be physically possible ones. Were the operations not physically possible, we would be determining essences relative to a physics that does not characterize our world and its constitutents. The result is that essences would be torn loose from the actual causal roles of their owners.[8]

Now the current theory of elementary particles introduces several symmetries and near-symmetries that prompt classification of *FE*s by physicists into species and into closely allied groups of species, or genera. In some cases there has been debate over whether the transformations that determine a symmetry group are active or passive. It is not my purpose here to enter the lists on such particular technical questions. But the general nature of these difficulties may be illustrated by a purely geometric example. Consider two scalene triangles that are congruent mirror images of one another. They are different, in a way they would not have been had they not been mirror images. Its their difference a difference in some monadic property, or in a relational one? Intuitively, one is inclined to say that the difference is intrinsic or monadic. But whether or not a transformation exists that takes the one triangle into the other depends upon the type of space in which they are embedded. In an orientable space, no passive transformation will transform one triangle into the other. But in a nonorientable space, both active and passive transformations exist that achieve this. Moving to a case that is both physical and three-dimensional, should we say that whether the difference between a right-handed glove and a left-handed glove is monadic or relational depends upon whether physical space is in fact orientable?[9]

Finally, mention must be made of the one type of active transformation such that symmetry under it is a criterion for comembership in a natural kind. Take a closed system. If an *FE* in that system can be replaced, other things being equal, by another— and if the resulting system is physically indistinguishable from the original one—then the replaced and replacing *FE*s are of identical type. I noted above some complexities in the application of the distinction between monadic properties and relations; let me now remark that these do not seem to undermine in any way the clarity of the distinction itself, or the metaphysical lucidity that it confers upon the distinction between essences and accidents.

Nevertheless, the conclusion I have reached can be regarded in two ways. One might conclude that it disembowels essentialism: if every monadic property (of an *FE*) is equally an essence, then the thesis that some entities—*FE*s—have essences becomes the unexciting claim that they have monadic properties. That they have monadic properties, and that there is a distinction between monadic properties and relations, are hardly front-page philosophical news. Have I then formulated an ''essentialism'' so eviscerated that empiricists can swallow it? Or is even this sort of essentialism too bitter a pill to go down empiricist throats? Well, if the doctrine is to have substance, it requires realism with regard to universals; and most empiricists are nominalists. Moreover, the doctrine has no bite unless one can accept (on the evidence) realism with regard to the elementary particles of present or future microphysics. Those empiricists who are realists in both senses, however, can accept my proposal with a clear conscience. What will they gain? Let us see.

A different attitude toward this outcome—my own, in fact—is that the view I am proposing is philosophically interesting and formualtes a nontrivial sort of essentialism. It is interesting, first, because the world might have been such that there were, in this sense, no natural kinds—either because there were no elementary bits of matter not further decomposable, or because the monadic properties of those bits did not assume discrete values. It is interesting, second, because it is a kind of essentialism that applies only to *FE*s, and not to composite entities, so that it is not a trivial or purely conceptual matter that the essence/accident distinction should be linked to that between monadic properties and relations. Third, it is interesting because it is a form of essentialism that permits a solution to the deepest problem essentialism faces. It permits an explanation of just what the special relation is that essential properties bear to the substances that have them. I shall conclude by elaborating upon these three points in the order given.

Point one raises the question of the philosophical status of the essentialist hypothesis defended here. Is the claim a properly philosophical one, or is it really a scientific hypothesis, decked out in philosophical robes? This question is most likely to disturb those philosophers who, whether sympathetic to the hypothesis or not, conceive philosophy to be a strictly *a priori* discipline. Whatever the status of the other arguments I have given, the suspicion of empirical content is surely fostered by my having cited factual evidence concerning features of quantum mechanics as confirming the claim that all and only monadic properties of *FE*s constitute their essences.

But in certain parts of ontology, at least—the philosophy of space and time, for example—philosophical analysis and empirical findings are sufficiently intermeshed that it is not particularly useful, even if it were possible, to distinguish purely philosophical issues from purely scientific ones. It should not be surprising if a similar blurring of disciplinary boundaries attends concern with the fundamental character of matter. But no matter. The hypothesis at hand is partly philosophical, in a sense that would be accepted by those who insist upon the distinction, and partly empirical.

For it is not an *a priori* truth that the decomposition of matter comes to a halt with a set of material particles (or material what-have-you) that are not further divisible. In fact, we do not know this to be true, though present evidence seems to favor it; and there have been speculations that matter is infinitely divisible.[10] Also, as already mentioned, it is not an *a priori* truth that *FE*s, if they exist, exhibit discrete differences, rather than grading continuously into one another. What if some monadic properties should vary continuously, but not others? I think it is not clear what sort of taxonomic policy such a hybrid case ought to dictate. On any of these alternative possibilities, some form of essentialism might yet be true—but the present essentialist hypothesis would not apply.[11] To that extent it is not *a priori*.

On the other hand, the relation between a fundamental theory and the taxonomy, if any, of *FE*s that it generates is not an empirical matter but one that depends upon formal and conceptual considerations. And the ontological question of the nature of the "tie" between essential properties and the *FE*s that instantiate them is not an empirical question.

How, then, can it be appropriate to make an appeal to current physical theory to decide this last question? Two points need to be made. First, it is one thing for empirical findings to suggest a philosophical hypothesis; it is another for such findings to constitute the sole warrant for the hypothesis. The primary basis for identifying the essence/accident distinction with the monadic/relation distinction is not the empirical evidence, but the conceptual relation between fundamental theories of the taxonomy-generating sort, and the sort of taxonomies that they can generate.

Second, it is false that *a priori* truths can in no sense be given to us through empirical means. Most philosophers agree that '7 + 5 = 12' is an *a priori* truth. But it is a fact that can be discovered empirically that when one counts together seven oranges and then five more, one counts twelve oranges; for the *a priori* truth has empirical embodiments. In some cases it is empirical findings of this sort that first suggest an *a priori* truth. If the geometry of the universe is Riemannian, then the empirical theories that embody a correct description of the world must incorporate a Riemannian geometry, and they must be consistent with empirical facts that correspond to the abstract theorems of that geometry. Similarly, if the essentialism proposed here is true, then the essential properties of *FE*s are the monadic ones. A correct physical theory of *FE*s must reflect that fact, and may suggest it to us in the first place.

The second point of interest regarding the sort of essentialism proposed here is that it does not apply to composite entities. This enables the essentialist to circumvent the difficulty that composite structures can grade into one another in minute steps or continuously through rearrangement or substitution of parts. Only where theory dictates discontinuous and sizable differences between allowable composite structures (as is approximately the case with atomic species) is there any hope of motivating a natural taxonomy for them.

However, the matter cannot quite be left there. If the distinction between essences and accidents is explained in terms of the distinction between monadic properties and relations, it remains a puzzle why the latter distinction applies to composite entities, whereas the former does not. The solution to this puzzle lies, I believe, in denying that composite structures have, strictly speaking, monadic properties. Properties that apply monadically to composite structures have as "constituents" relations that are instantiated by their component parts; this disqualifies them from playing the role of essences. Take for example the monadic macroscopic property of temperature. To be at a certain temperature is to consist of molecules that have a certain distribution of relative velocities. Temperature, therefore, is a composite property among whose constituents are relations. Similar remarks apply to color, and so on. If we wish to regard these properties as monadic nevertheless, we must at least say that they are not atomic monadic properties. So the essentialism I have been proposing should be more precisely formulated thus: the class of essential properties is identical to the class of atomic monadic properties.

Consider finally the third point of interest. In his famous diatribe against modal logic,[12] Quine raised the specter of Aristotelian essentialism, which, he declared, it was no part of his plan to defend. It is not part of my plan either; but this is not because

I think *no* ontologically grounded distinction can be made between the way in which whiteness inheres in Socrates and the way in which humanity does. Such a distinction could be motivated by biological theory, since according to that theory certain traits play a deeper role in the functioning of organisms—and organisms function in such a way that these traits tend to cluster, more or less, in discontinuous fashion. This is an objective matter. But I share Quine's skepticism insofar as I doubt whether this distinction can bear the weight of the modal distinction between *de re* and *de dicto* necessity, for the reasons already given. Possibly there are other sorts of essences that composite individuals have: for example, essences of origin. But these, too, seem plagued by paradoxes of the ship-of-Theseus type.

The distinction to which I have been drawing attention, the one that applies only to *FE*s, is a deeper one. Yet it is not one that requires an appeal to some new and mysterious "tie" between particulars and their properties, a tie somehow stronger, more necessary, than the ordinary one. That tie, admittedly, is itself freighted with philosophical puzzles; but these do not obscure the distinction between monadic properties and relations on which the present argument depends. Though I have not attempted here any deep analysis of the distinction, there can be no doubt that there is such a distinction, and that monadic properties are "in" the things they characterize in a more intimate and complete way than their relations are. When we add the fact that any monadic property that can correctly be attributed to an *FE* constitutes part and parcel of what determines the way that particle enters into the system of the world, we have clear grounds for saying that a monadic change is a change in nature. And thus, provided the monadic changes are discrete, we can underpin the *de re*/*de dicto* distinction after all. So on the essential point, I believe that Quine was wrong.

Notes

1. Unless, perhaps, one is a Bundle Theorist. But what follows is no Bundle Theory, nor any kin to it.

2. In Evan Fales, "Relative Essentialism," *British Journal for the Philosophy of Science* 30 (1979):349–70. I am no longer happy with the way in which that paper connects theory to taxonomy.

3. I am assuming that *existence* is not itself a fuzzy concept.

4. At the same time, theory may justify a *rough* demarcation into species, e.g., for animals and rocks—one that is not arbitrary but that is, nevertheless, subject to slippery-slope objections. Because of the objections, such taxonomies cannot give much substance to the notion of an essential property.

5. Expressibility by means of a finite set of laws is, after all, bought at the price of generalization over variables that can take an infinity of values. The possibility of generalization, however, betokens more than notational compactness.

6. This is, once again, not to say that there could be no theoretical grounds for grouping animals and plants into species. But the ontologist who seeks to justify essentialism would do best not to look here, where, at most, we might speak of a kind of quasi-essentialism obtaining.

7. To talk of causal roles may prompt a question, for if causation is a relation and causal roles are essential to *FE*s, have we not here a relational essence? The question is the more acute for those who, like myself, take causation to be a relation that is real, external, and necessary. My view of the matter is that causation is grounded in a second-order relation that obtains between first-order physical properties (universals). This—except for the necessity—is the Tooley/Armstrong/Dretske theory of causation. I hold that every physical universal has a set of associated causal connections to other physical universals that is essential to it. The connections are relations, but they are essences of universals, not of particulars. Whether a particular causally interacts with other particulars is, of course, a contingent matter, depending not only

upon the causal connections of the monadic properties that it instantiates, but also upon the contingent spatiotemporal relations in which it stands to those other particulars.

8. For debate about this point, see Michael Redhead, "Quantum Field Theory for Philosophers," in *PSA 1982: Proceedings of the Biennial Meeting of the Philosophy of Science Association,* Vol. 2, edited by P. Asquith and T. Nickles (East Lansing, Mich., 1983); Robert Weingard, "Grand Unified Gauge Theories and the Number of Elementary Particles," *Philosophy of Science* 51 (1984):150–55; and Redhead's reply, forthcoming in *Philosophy of Science.* I am indebted to Professor Redhead who, in conversation, alerted me to the difficulty I mention in the following paragraph. See also Michael Redhead, "Symmetry in Intertheory Relations," *Synthese* 32 (1975):77–112, on the role of physical symmetries and the distinction between active and passive transformations.

9. The suggestion is admittedly strange; I am not sure it can be made coherent. In any case, this example needs further discussion. However, the analogy to *FE* symmetries is attenuated by the fact that the property *being scalene* is a complex property that contains relations (instantiated by the parts of the triangle) as constituents: see below on this. For further discussion of the example, see Graeme Nerlich, *The Shape of Space* (Cambridge, 1976).

10. A prominent contemporary advocate of this view is David Bohm.

11. On the other side, if the Democritean hypothesis were true—if *FE* s were indestructible and uncreatable—then a different, more direct ground for essentialism would be at hand. To put it in a way that does not beg the question: if some properties are such that if an *FE* has them ever, it has them always, whereas other properties are such as to come and go, then there will be a causal explanation of how the ephemeral properties change; but the persistent properties will have no explanation, or at least none of that sort. A world of this kind would be one in which persistent properties are kind-defining and ephemeral ones are accidental.

12. W. V.O. Quine, "Reference and Modality," in Quine, *From a Logical Point of View* (Cambridge, 1953):139–59.

Essentialism without Individual Essences: Causation, Kinds, Supervenience, and Restricted Identities

BERENT ENÇ

Suppose a scientist alters slightly the DNA molecule of a unicellular organism by genetic splicing. Is the resulting organism *one and the same individual* as the original? Suppose a piece of lead is bombarded by a sufficient number of alpha particles to turn into a piece of gold. Is the piece of gold *the same thing* as the piece of lead? Suppose I raise my arm and salute. If I had moved my arm slightly higher, instead of just so, would I have done *one and the same thing*? When Segovia plays the Bach chaconne on the guitar, is he playing *one and the same piece* as the chaconne that is played on the violin? If my parents' only child had been conceived a month earlier, would it have been me?

These are questions about individual identity. And I suspect that answers to them rest ultimately on answers to questions about individual essences.

I must confess that I do not know the answers to questions about identity or about individual essences. Not only do I not know the answers, I also do not know how one goes about looking for the answers, or how one goes about evaluating the answers that have been proposed by philosophers from Aristotle to Kripke. Part of my puzzlement arises from the fact that I cannot connect the intellectual endeavor in which one seeks these answers to others areas of metaphysics, to questions like, what sorts of things exist? what is the structure of the universe? what is causation? It seems to me that the discipline in which these latter questions are asked is intimately tied to science, and that one can hope to learn how to approach them by trying to understand the nature of the scientific enterprise and of the structure of scientific theories. And, in turn, if answers are found to these latter questions, these answers will teach us significant facts about science. It is just because questions about individual essences seem so protected from what happens in science that I despair of discovering an acceptable philosophical method of approaching them.

In what follows, I propose to develop an essentialist view and to argue that such a view enables us to understand better that aspect of our universe that makes scientific explanation possible, to grasp one facet of causation, and to develop one way of distinguishing between the identity and supervenience relations among properties. The essentialist view I develop will be isolated from individual identity and individual essences, but it certainly will belong to that part of metaphysics that will be open to influences from the sciences.

The view I will develop below may be roughly described by contrasting the questions of the opening paragraph with the following questions: Suppose a scientist alters slightly the DNA molecule of a unicellular organism by genetic splicing. Is the resulting organism one and the same *kind* of organism? Suppose a piece of lead is bombarded by alpha particles and turns into a piece of gold. Is the piece of gold the same *kind* of substance as the original piece? Suppose I raise my arm and salute. If I had moved my arm slightly higher, would I have done one and the same *kind* of thing? And so on. Although we may, again, not know the answers to these new questions, we can, I think, say what we need to know, where we need to look, and how to proceed in order to discover the answers.

These questions may, perhaps, be answered in the framework of roughly the following type of essentialism: Our universe is made up of a multitude of kinds of things, and the kinds cut across each other so that an object may be of (indefinitely) many different kinds at the same time, or an object may be one kind of thing at one time and change into a different kind of thing at a later time. These kinds are defined by some of the properties shared by the objects.[1] These properties are essential to the kind of thing an object is at a given time. And the essential properties determine, in turn, the causal powers of these objects and some of the other properties they may share. Insofar as they determine such things, the kinds whose essences they are are *real*. Since our best scientific theories inform us which properties determine what, these scientific theories may enable us to locate the essential properties of kinds. Hence, the best answer to questions like "is it the same kind of thing?" can be found in the true scientific theory that deals with the relevant subject matter. For example, it is argued by some biologists and philosophers of biology that species do not have essences, that population genetics teaches us that essentialism is untenable in biology.[2] On the view I am characterizing here, this would have the consequence that species are not kinds of organisms, even, perhaps (by the nature of the arguments offered), that there are no biological *kinds of organisms*. If so, then the question "is the unicellular organism after splicing the same kind of organism?" will have been shown to have no answer; it will have been shown to be the wrong question to ask. It is quite possible that a similar fate will befall all the questions on my second list, except the one about lead and gold. In the case of atomic elements, our best chemical theory tells us that when a piece of lead turns into a piece of gold, its atomic structure is altered; and according to the view I will develop below, certain features of the atomic structure will turn out to be essential to chemical kinds, hence the piece of lead, when bombarded, will become a different kind of thing.

I. DEVELOPMENT OF THE VIEW THROUGH EXPLANATION

Consider the following two pairs of putative explanations:

1a. The barometer reading dropped three hours ago. Whenever the barometer reading drops, a storm follows within three hours.
     Hence, there is a storm now.
1b. The atmospheric pressure dropped three hours ago. Whenever the atmospheric pressure drops, a storm follows within three hours.
     Hence, there is a storm now.
2a. The coefficient of electrical conductivity is proportional to the coefficient of thermal conductivity. Object c has a greater coefficient of thermal conductivity than object d.
     Hence, object c has a greater coefficient of electrical conductivity than object d.
2b. The electrons in the molecules that make up object c are bound with weaker forces than those of object d. The weaker these forces, the higher the electrical conductivity.
     Hence, object c has a greater coefficient of electrical conductivity than object d.

Intuitively, it is clear that the valid deductive inferences represented by 1a and 2a are not good explanations.[3] (I think they are not explanations at all.) But 1b and 2b, with the proper filling in of details, are perfectly adequate explanations.

The traditional diagnosis of what goes wrong in 1a is familiar: The premises fail to identify the proper *cause* of the storm. They refer to a side effect that happens to be a sufficient condition for the storm. In other words, the barometer's dropping is not what causes the storm; rather a drop in atmospheric pressure causes it. Hence, it is the latter, not the former, that *explains why* there is a storm.

What is wrong with 2a is perhaps harder to explain.[4] Traditional understanding of causation makes it wrong to speak of the molecular structure of these objects as *causing* their disposition to conduct electricity. However, intuitively, the pattern of explanation in 2a seems to suffer in some deep and basic way from the same defect as that of 1a. If the diagnosis of the fault of 2a does not lie in its using the wrong causal ties, and if 2a does share the same type of defect with 1a, then perhaps the fact that no causal connection exists between barometer droppings and storms is not the correct diagnosis of why 1a fails as an explanation.[5]

What exactly is the defect shared by 1a and 2a? It seems that in both, we can point out that what is referred to in the explanans is not *what makes it the case that* the explanadum is true. Thus, it is not the barometer's dropping that makes it the case that there is a storm; what makes it the case that there is a storm is a drop in atmospheric pressure. It is also not the thermal-conductivity coefficient's being high that makes it the case that the electrical-conductivity coefficient is high; rather, the weak forces in the molecular structure make this the case.

What is the nature of the relation designated by the expression "makes it the case that"? We have already observed that it includes both a causal connection and the relation wherein an object's having a certain (structural) property constitutes its having some other (manifest) property. The causal relation and the constitutive relation seem to be quite distinct from each other. Apart from the intuition that made us think there was something common to the defects in the explanations 1a and 2a above, is there any reason for thinking that there is some underlying structure to these two relations?[6]

First, we must note that the relation "makes it the case that" (henceforth, M) needs to have as its left-hand relatum an event's instantiating some property (as I will later suggest, a constituent of a *kind-designating property*) of the event, or the state of affairs, in question. So the proper form of the relation is "*a*'s being F is what makes it the case that *b* is G."

When the M relation has causal force, it does not merely express the fact that one event-token is the cause of a second event-token. For, as Donald Davidson[7] and Michael Levin[8] have emphasized, sentences that express event causation are purely extensional. For example, if the tornado caused the destruction, and if "the event that occurred two hours after I left Wisconsin" is coextensional with "the tornado," then it will be true that the event that occurred two hours after I left Wisconsin caused the destruction. However, I think it is clear that "the event's being a tornado is what made it the case that the town was destroyed" may be true, while "the event's occurring two hours after I left Wisconsin is what made it the case that the town was destroyed" is false. I take this to show that the M relation in its causal capacity has in its content something stronger than mere event causation. In fact, substitution of *nomically* coextensional properties into the left-hand side of the M relation does not always retain truth value. For example, suppose that a piece of metal is placed across the wires of a circuit. Although all and only metals with high thermal conductivity have high electrical conductivity, it is clear that the metal's having *high electrical conductivity,* and not its having *high thermal conductivity,* is what made it the case that a short circuit occurred.[9] On the other hand, the relation is preserved if expressions that refer to the *same property* are substituted into the left-hand side. For example, if the metal's having high electrical conductivity is what caused the short circuit, and if having high electrical conductivity is the property that interests electrical engineers most, then the metal's having the property that interests electrical engineers most is what caused the short circuit. A second aspect of the M relation, used with causal force, is that the right-hand side of the relation is purely extensional; it admits of substitution of nomically coextensional properties. If my altering the chemical composition of the alloy is what made it the case that it has high electrical conductivity, then given the coextensionality between high electrical conductivity and high thermal conductivity, it also made it the case that it has high thermal conductivity.

Now the first piece of evidence that the relation M has an identity of its own, not fully captured by conceiving of it as a mere disjunction of two distinct relations (causal and constitutive), is the fact that $M,$ used in its constitutive capacity, has the same degree of nonextensionality as M used in its causal capacity. For example, if a substance's having the crystalline structure it has is what makes it the case that it has a refractive index $i,$ and if all and only substances mined in Timbuktu have that crystalline structure, it does not follow that a substance's having been mined in Timbuktu makes it the case that it has the refractive index i.[10] Furthermore, if a substance's having that crystalline structure is what makes it the case that it has a refractive index i, and if all and only things that have a refractive index i are the most precious stones, then the substance's having that crystalline structure is what makes it the case that it is a most precious stone.

A second piece of evidence lies in the fact that in order for the relation M to hold, the event, or state of affairs, described by the right-hand relatum needs to be "tuned" to or "sensitive" to the property designated in the left-hand relatum. And this requirement covers both the constitutive and the causal instances of M. Some examples may give a feel for what I mean by the metaphors "tuned to" or "sensitive to."[11]

Consider, first, a red berry and an electronic detector that rings a bell when a bright red object is presented to its photosensitive "eye." Let us assume that what makes it the case that the bell rings when the berry is presented to the detector is the berry's being red. Suppose now that the total chemical composition of the berry is sufficient to give it a bright red color. Now, I think, there is a reading on which the following is *false:* "The berry's having that chemical composition is what makes it the case that the bell rings." The detector is not "sensitive" to the chemical composition of the berry. What makes the detector respond in this way (or the thing that has the capacity to elicit this response) is the *color* of the berry, and as far as the ringing of the bell is concerned, any chemical composition that would give the berry that shade of red would do. So, on the reading I have in mind, it is *not* the berry's having the chemical composition that it actually has, as opposed to one of those "functionally equivalent" compositions, that makes the bell ring.[12]

Consider, second, Emperor Tom who dies because he has taken arsenic. Suppose that his dying is what makes it the case that twenty-one cannon shots are fired. Again, there is a reading, parallel to that of the previous example, on which it is *false* that Tom's having taken arsenic is what makes it the case that twenty-one cannon shots are fired. This is false because the firing of the cannon shots is not "tied to" Tom's taking arsenic, in the sense that the same shots would have been fired (i.e., one and the same event as that referred to by the right-hand relatum would have occurred) if Tom had died a natural death instead.

The pattern according to which these examples of "sensitivity" are generated may be formulated as follows:

That a is F is causally (or constitutively) sufficient for b's being G.

b's being G is what makes it the case that c is H.

But a's being F is not what makes it the case that c is H.

where,

(i) b or c (or both) may be identical with a,

(ii) a's being F is only *one* of the ways in which b can be G.

Notice that it is (ii) above that is doing all the work in the generation of these examples. If a's being F is the *only* way in which b can be G (or is the unique cause of b's being G), then a's being F will always make it the case that b is G. If this is right, then the notion of sensitivity may be captured by requiring that the left-hand relatum designate a property that is not only sufficient but also *necessary* for the occurrence of the right-hand event (or, for the right-hand state of affairs to obtain). The basic intuition here is this: for a's being F to make it the case that b is G, the following subjunctive has to be true: "If a were not F, the event (or the state of affairs) in which b is G would not have occurred (obtained)."

It might appear that what I have called "the basic intuition" just flies in the face of common sense. It mght, for example, be pointed out that Tom might still have died even if he had not taken arsenic (i.e., even if the subjunctive, the truth of which was offered as a necessary condition for the M relation to hold, is false); yet, it seems quite clear that Tom's taking arsenic is what made it the case that he died (or, caused him to die). However, the objection relies on the ambiguity involved in our event talk. The truth conditions of the sentence "Tom might have died" would be satisfied if some event or other might have occurred in which Tom dies (not at any *particular time* nor under any *particular circumstances*). But the subjunctive requires that if Tom had not taken arsenic, *this particular event* in which he died would not have occurred—and that, of course, is quite true.[13]

It might also seem that what I have called "sensitivity" makes the relation M nontransitive, but that appearance is misleading for reasons similar to those involved in the previous objection. Although it is true that Tom's taking arsenic is what made him die this particular death, and that his dying is what made it the case that twenty-one cannon shots were fired, his taking arsenic is not what made it the case that those shots were fired. But that is so only because the event in which Tom died this particular death is *not* what is being referred to by the left-hand relatum in the true sentence "Tom's dying is what made it the case that twenty-one cannon shots were fired." That relatum refers to that particular event's instantiating some property; and the property in question is not dying this particular death, it is, rather, dying. Clearly, the sentence "Tom's dying this particular death is what made it the case that the cannon shots were fired" is false: what made the cannon shots to be fired was this particular event's instantiating one specific property, i.e., that of being an event wherein Tom died, and not its instantiating the indefinitely many properties that Tom's dying *at this moment, under these circumstances, in this very way in fact instantiated.*[14]

The same point about transitivity can be made by the red berry example: It is false that for any berry of this kind of plant, its having the *total* chemical composition is what makes it red. Furthermore, if there are several different chemical compounds, any of which is sufficient for a berry to be red, then having one of these compounds, as opposed to having some other one in its chemical composition, is also not what makes the berries red. So when it is said that any berry's having the chemical composition that this berry has is not what makes the bell ring, again the transitivity of the M relation is not violated.[15]

These two features of the relation M (i.e., its nonextensionality and its sensitivity) amount to a mere suggestion that there is some uniform underlying structure to the relation; and unless a plausible account of such an underlying structure can be given, this suggestion will remain inconclusive.

II. POSSIBLE WORLDS

Both the nonextensionality and what I have called the "sensitivity" of the relation M indicate that the sentences that assert this relation to hold have some modal force.

Consider, first, a case that, for reasons that will become apparent below, I take to be paradigmatic of the M relation. Liquid hydrochloric acid has a large number of properties that are "typical" of it: it is clear; it has a distinctive odor at room temperatures; it solidifies at t degrees Celsius; and so on. It also has a number of causal consequences: if ingested, it kills; if lead is placed in it, the lead dissolves; and so on. Let us designate these properties $P_1, P_2, ..., P_n$. In addition, it has a distinctive molecular structure. This molecular structure is essential to it, that is, in any possible world in which a pool of liquid is hydrochloric acid, that pool has that particular molecular structure; if the molecular structure is altered, it will *cease to be* hydrochloric acid. Now, intuitively, it seems plausible to expect that for any P_i of the set of Ps, there is some component of the molecular structure that is essential to hydrochloric acid, which makes it the case that a given pool of hydrochloric acid has that P_i. For some other P (e.g., P_j), there may be some *other* component of that molecular structure such that a pool of hydrochloric acid's having *that* component property is what makes it the case that it is P_j. What is important to notice here is that the liquid does not have that P in *all* the possible worlds in which it has the molecular structure essential to hydrochloric acid. The liquid has that P only in that set of possible worlds in which the relevant natural kinds of the actual world also exist. For example, in a possible world in which the liquid is hydrochloric acid, but in which there is *schmight* instead of light, and where *schmight* is the medium that makes vision possible, except that it is *reflected* by objects that transmit light, that body of hydrochloric acid will *not* be clear.[16] Or in the possible world in which atmospheric pressure is much higher than that of the actual world, the acid will not vaporize at room temperature and, hence, will have no odor, and so on.

The same pattern may be read into the causal instances of the M relation. For example, if anyone ingests hydrochloric acid, that thing's having the molecular structure it has is what makes it the case that that person dies.[17] Here, when we take the set of possible worlds in which the thing ingested is hydrochloric acid (i.e., in which the thing ingested has that molecular structure) and consider the subset of that set in which the thing that has done the ingesting is an organism with the kind of digestive system and metabolism that people have in the actual world, *and also* in which the relevant conditions that have obtained in the period between the ingestion and the death in the actual world are kept constant (e.g., in which the stomach is not emptied or an antidote is not administered), then we find that the person dies in *each* of the possible worlds in that subset.

In other words, I am proposing the following as the underlying pattern for all instances of the M relation:

a's being F is what makes it the case that b (or a) is G if and only if:
   (i) a is of kind K; and
   (ii) F is a component of the property that essentially defines K; and

(iii) each possible world in which a is (has) F, and in which the relevant kinds of the actual world exist and the relevant conditions of the actual world obtain, contains the event (or the state of affairs) in which it is true that b (or a) is G; and

(iv) each possible world in which a is not (fails to have) F, and in which the relevant kinds of the actual world exist and the relavant conditions of the actual world obtain, does not contain the event (or the state of affairs) in which it is true that b (or a) is G; and

(v) in any possible world in which any object of whatever kind is F, and in which the relevant conditions hold, there exists some object that is G; but it is not the case that in every possible world in which any object of whatever kind is G, there exists some object that is F.

A few words of explication and qualification are in order here.

1. *Laws*: It is assumed that the fundamental laws of the actual world governing things of kind K hold in *all* the possible worlds that are being considered here. But since not all the kinds of the actual world are assumed to exist in each possible world containing Ks, some of the so-called derived laws of the actual world may not hold in all of them.

2. *Relevance*: Conditions (iii) and (iv) make liberal use of the notions of relevant kinds and relevant conditions. Appeal to relevance is notorious in philosophy as a move typically made when the analysis being offered is incomplete in some respects. And I admit that the present context is no exception. I do not know how to characterize these notions precisely and noncircularly. If my aim had been that of giving a complete possible-world semantics for the relation M, I would have to admit to failure. However, my aim here is a more modest one: I want to argue that *if* a complete account for the relation M can be given along the lines suggested here, *then* we will be able to see that M is quite central to several seemingly unrelated issues in metaphysics. On the other hand, some tentative remarks about the factors that determine what is relevant are certainly in order:

(a) Consider the barometer-storm case that was discussed above.[18] If in describing the possible worlds for condition (iii), we assumed all the conditions and the kinds of the actual world to be relevant, then there will not be a possible world in which barometer readings drop and no storms follow, simply because the conditions in the actual world *include* a drop in atmospheric pressure. As a result, the analysis offered for the M relation will turn out not to be sufficient. On the other hand, if we do not specify any conditions whatsoever as being relevant, then there will be possible worlds in which the atmospheric pressure drops but, because of other meteorological interferences, a storm does not follow. As a result, the analysis will turn out not to be necessary. What should be clear from this example is that the relevant kinds and conditions should *exclude* all those factors that are among the determinants of the property referred to by the left-hand relatum. In other words, the relevance clause of condition (iii) will require examining possible worlds in which the physical and logical determinants of a's being F (as well as their physical and logical consequences) are allowed to vary, and in which all the other conditions of the actual world are kept constant. The basic idea is that we want to examine whether, under the conditions that hold in the actual world, it is (physically) possible for b not to be G when a is F *regardless of how a gets to be F*. It is easy to see that this gloss on relevance gives us the correct answers with regard to the barometer case. In some of the possible worlds in which the barometer reading drops, there will not have been a previous drop in atmospheric pressure (because the drop in atmospheric pressure of the actual world is one of the determinants of the drop in the barometer reading), and none of the meteorological events that are consequences of the drop in atmospheric pressure will take place; hence, a storm will not occur in those possible worlds. (Presumably, the drop in the barometer reading would be due to a faulty spring, or a drop in room pressure, and so on.) On the other hand, in every possible world in which the atmospheric pressure drops (regardless of what causes such drops) and in which all the conditions of the actual world hold, a storm will occur.

It is important to notice here that which conditions are kept constant in the possible worlds will depend on whether the event (or state of affairs) in which b is G is an individual (token) event or an event type solely characterized by the kind of thing b is and by the property G. Suppose John, a healthy sixty-five-year-old man, goes out to shovel snow on a cold night after having consumed a fifth of scotch and dies of a heart attack. By condition (iii), it will not be incorrect to say that what made him die (what caused that particular event to occur) was his shoveling snow,[19] because the conditions that are to be kept constant in the possible worlds will include the outdoor temperature, as well as his having consumed a large quantity of alcohol. However, condition (iii) blocks our having to say that what causes people like John (i.e., sixty-five-year-old healthy males) to die is shoveling snow. The right-hand relatum here is no longer a particular event; it is, rather, an event type characterized by a kind of thing instantiating a property (i.e., death of sixty-five-year-old healthy males). And condition (iii) blocks this judgment because, consistent with the laws of the actual world, such people will shovel snow when it is not that cold, or when their cardiovascular system is not impaired, and so on. Hence, in the possible worlds we examine, not all the conditions that surrounded John's death are to be kept constant. In other words, when b's being G is a *type* of event, the relevant conditions will be specifiable by an examination of that type (i.e., the kind of thing b is presumed to be and by the property G[20]) and by a determination of those conditions that are nomically inconsistent with a's being F. In simpler terms, we look for laws that connect a's being F with b's being G, and in the possible worlds we examine, we keep constant only the conditions that are covered by the *ceteris paribus* clauses of such laws. If there had been a law that stated that, other things being equal, healthy sixty-five-year-old males die if they shovel snow, and if drinking large quantities of alcohol and the cold air were part of what was implied by "other things being equal," then conditions (iii) would not block the judgment that shoveling snow is what makes such men die.

(b) Consider, once again, John who dies shoveling snow. This time, suppose that the alcohol in his bloodstream was sufficient to bring about a heart attack but that the shoveling accelerated it—he died two hours earlier than he would have had he not shoveled snow. Did his shoveling snow make him die? The answer has to come from condition (iv). And the correct answer depends on what we take to be the right-hand relatum.

First, let us suppose that what we are interested in is the particular death that occurred. In accordance with condition (iv), we examine the possible worlds in which John does not shovel snow. What conditions do we keep constant in these worlds? Again, we obviously cannot be allowed to keep all the conditions of the actual world, for his shoveling snow is one of them, and carrying that to the possible worlds would make these worlds internally inconsistent. Furthermore, his shoveling snow in the actual world has led to a number of physiological events in John, like his heart beat going up to 150, the occlusion of the left ventricle at 1:05 A.M., and so on. If we carried *these* conditions over to the possible worlds, we would find that John suffers the very same death that he suffered in the actual world, in spite of the fact that he does not shovel snow in these possible worlds. So it seems that in the possible worlds in which John does not shovel snow, all the conditions that are (physically or logically) determined by his shoveling snow in the actual world have to be changed so as to make the possible world nomically consistent with the actual world. In other words, the relevance clause of (iv) requires our keeping all the conditions and kinds that hold in the actual world constant, *except* those that are determined by a's being F. If we do that, then, in the case we are considering, John does not die that particular death in any of the possible worlds in which he does not shovel snow; his death in those worlds is a different event, one that occurs two hours later, one in which a different kind of heart failure is implicated, and so on. Consequently, conditions (iii) and (iv) jointly yield the verdict that his shoveling snow is what made John die.

However, when we are asked the question "Did shoveling snow make John die?" the interest usually does not lie in finding out what made it the case that this individual event, with its indefinitely many properties, occurred. The interest lies, rather, in discovering what made some event or other occur that instantiates the property of John's dying.[21] If this is so, then the possible worlds in which John does not shovel snow, and in which all the relevant conditions as specified in the previous paragraph are kept constant, will contain events that do not instantiate that property. As a result, condition (iv) will not be satisfied, and it will turn out to be *false* that John's shoveling snow is what made him die.[22]

(c) A final remark about the relevance clause of condition (iii) may be of interest here. Consider a roulette table. The croupier starts the wheel turning and propels the ball; a minute or so later, the ball lands in slot number twenty-one. What made it the case that the ball landed in twenty-one? Let us suppose that the question involves, as it would normally be understood to involve, our explaining the occurrence of some event or other that instantiates the property of landing in slot twenty-one.[23] The correct answer surely is not the croupier's propelling the ball in the way he or she did. This is not what made it the case that the ball landed in slot twenty-one. And the way the relevance clause was explicated above in (a) should bear out this result. According to that clause, the relevant conditions that are to be kept constant across the possible worlds will include all the conditions of the actual world except (i) those that are the determinants of the croupier's propelling the ball *and* (ii) those that are nomically consistent with the ball's being propelled just that way. What (ii) means in this context is just this: we look for laws that govern the ball's being propelled that way and its landing at some (particular) slot. If there are any such laws, these laws may include a *ceteris paribus* clause. The relevant conditions will consist of all the conditions covered by such a *ceteris paribus* clause, and any condition that holds in the actual world that is not covered by the *ceteris paribus* clause will be said to be nomically consistent with the ball's being propelled just that way. These latter conditions will be allowed to vary in the possible worlds in which the ball on a roulette table is propelled just that way. Since, in the case we are examining, there is no law of the required kind, conditions like the rotational speed of the wheel, the position of the ball relative to the wheel at the time the ball is released, coefficients of friction involved, and so on will all be allowed to vary in the possible worlds; and it will be false that the ball lands in slot twenty-one in each of these worlds.

Consider, in contrast with the roulette example, a case in which a light switch is flipped and the light goes on. Does my flipping the switch make it the case that the light goes on (some event happens that instantiates the property in question)? In this case, there is a (derived) law that connects the flipping of the switch with the light's going on under certain conditions, i.e., the power being on, there being no break in the circuit, the bulb's being good. These (*ceteris paribus*) conditions will now constitute the relevant conditions that are to be kept constant in the possible worlds; hence, condition (iii) will be satisfied.

The boundary between these two types of cases is far from being sharp. And both of the examples I have used above may fall in the large gray area. The difficulty in deciding whether a condition falls under the *ceteris paribus* clause of a derived law arises from the fact that the *ceteris paribus* clauses of laws are rarely explicitly stated. And, in many cases, what counts as a *ceteris paribus* clause may have to be decided by pragmatic considerations.[24] However, there are two sets of extreme cases that are of interest here. The first involves the contribution of random occurrences to the causal chain between two events (or to the relation that holds between a structural property and a manifest property of an object). If we changed the roulette example to one in which the wheel was replaced by an electronic computer that determined the outcomes in a genuinely random way, then not only would no law connect the pressing of the button that starts a roll and the particular outcome, but also no set of conditions that obtain in the actual world would determine the outcome. Here, it will be clearly false that pressing the button is what makes it the case that twenty-one comes up.[25] The second type of case involves events (or states of affairs) governed by what we might call *ideal laws*. These laws state what happens under certain ideal conditions. Consider the Aristotelian view of sexual reproduction. According to this view, the phenotypic characteristics of the offspring are ideally derived from the characteristics of the male parent. Only if interfering factors are present, does the result deviate from the ideal. The Aristotelian law involved here has, as part of its content, a specification of a set of ideal conditions. And when we consider the set of possible worlds in which the sperm contains the information it does in the actual world, the conditions we have to keep constant will include the ideal conditions specified by the law. In such a case, it will be true that the sperm's being the way it is is what makes the (ideal) offspring have the phenotypic characteristics it has.[26]

As I stated earlier, the purpose of the foregoing was to provide a rough guideline for the relevance clauses of conditions (iii) and (iv). It was not intended to function as a full-fledged possible-world semantics for the M relation. The explication of relevance I have given relies heavily on the notions of the determinants of a property and of the nature of the laws that govern that property. Both of these notions are directly tied to the M relation. At best, the account I have provided will generate an infinite regress if it is used to determine the truth value of a sentence of the form "a's being F makes it the case that b is G." For in order to specify the relevant conditions involved, we would have to know what determines a's being F, what a's being F determines, and what type of laws connect a's being F with b's being G. Each of these three considerations will most likely require our figuring out the truth value of several other sentences that involve the M relations that a's being F enters into, and so on *ad infinitum*.[27]

3. *Asymmetry*: The relation M is obviously asymmetric. And condition (v), in connection with the notion of relevance discussed above, is designed to capture this asymmetry. Consider the hydrochloric acid example once again. If having the component F of the molecular structure is what makes hydrochloric acid clear, then in any possible world in which something has F and in which the relevant kinds exist, that thing will be clear. But it will not be the case that in any possible world in which something is clear (and the relevant kinds exist), the property F will be instantiated in the microstructure of that thing. Similarly, if hydrochloric acid's having the structure F' is what makes people who ingest it die, then in every possible world in which something has that structure (and the relevant kinds exist), people who ingest it die. But it will not be the case that in every posible world in which a person who ingests something dies, the thing ingested has F'.

Condition (v) generates the desired result when used in conformity with the aspect of relevance discussed above under 2(a), i.e., the requirement that the relevant conditions must *exclude* all those conditions that figure among the determinants of the left-hand relatum. In other words, if a's being F is what makes it the case that b is G, then b's being G will not make it the case that a is F. This is because, by condition (v), b's being G will, in general, have determinants other than a's being F, and in the possible worlds where b is G, these determinants will be allowed to be different from the determinant of b's being G in the actual world. Hence, it will not be true that a is F in all of these possible worlds.

It may be worth remarking that in cases of genuine property identity, condition (v) is violated.[28] Suppose "being water" and "being made up of H_2O molecules" refer to the same property. Then whenever something is water, that thing will be made up of H_2O molecules; and as a result, it will be false that this thing's being made up of H_2O molecules is what makes it the case that it is water.[29]

One final example may illustrate how condition (v) operates in less obvious cases. Consider Euclidean figures. An object's being a closed and four-sided figure is what makes it the case that it has four angles,[30] but an object's having four angles is not what makes it the case that it is closed and four-sided, because although anything that is a four-sided closed figure has four angles, it is not true that anything that has four angles is closed and four-sided. (It could be an open figure with five sides.[31])

III. KINDS

As I have been suggesting above, appealing to a discovered M relation is one of the most powerful ways we have to explain why a particular event instantiates some specified property, or why a type of event occurs under specified conditions.[32] Such explanations take the form of asserting that a's being F is what makes it the case that such events occur. The truth of these assertions is dependent on the existence of appropriate laws,[33] because it is these laws that guide the possible world evaluation of the assertions. (However, the laws need not be cited in the explanations.[34])

One essential component of such explanations is the asymmetry of the relation between the explanans and the explanandum. In other words, if a's being F stands in some symmetric relation to b's being G, then the relation cannot help us explain in this way why b is G by citing a's being F. Clearly, the asymmetry of the M relation makes it a suitable candidate for such explanations. A further discussion of the factors that contribute to the asymmetry of the M relation (i.e., of the way condition (v) operates) will help develop the main point of this paper.

Condition (v) requires the existence of possible objects that are G, but not F. For example, if hydrochloric acid's having the molecular structure it has is what makes it transparent, then there are possible worlds in which some objects are transparent, but do not have the molecular structure of hydrochloric acid. If the relation between two properties were such that an object's (*any* object's) having the first lawfully guaranteed the object's having the second, *and also* any object's having the second lawfully guaranteed the object's having the first, clearly this relation would violate condition (v) and would therefore not be the M relation. For it to be possible to satisfy condition (v), there have to be certain (possible) kinds of objects that have one of the two properties and lack the other. So conditions (iii), (iv), and (v) can be jointly satisfied only if their application is restricted to certain *kinds* of things. (And this restriction explains the need for conditions (i) and (ii).) To return to the hydrochloric acid example, the nature of the relation that holds between molecular structure and transparency is just this: The pool of liquid is of some kind; that kind of thing's having the component of the molecular structure it has is necessary and sufficient for the pool's being transparent; but although other kinds of things may not have that structure without being transparent, other kinds of things may be transparent without having that structure. In other words, the M relation holds between the instantiation of two properties only *modulo* certain *kinds* of things.

Thus, kinds play a crucial role in the type of explanations that involve the M relation. But what is it for an object to be of a certain kind? It would seem that the object's having a certain property that is associated with that kind is required. And the property has to be such that if any object had that property, it would be of that kind; *and* if the object ceased to have that property, it would cease to be of that kind. Although this seems necessary for an object's being of a kind, it certainly cannot be sufficient. Not any property we choose to concoct will constitute a real kind. For example, being gold is being a kind of substance, but being within the fifty-mile radius of the Eiffel Tower is not really being a kind of object. One obvious difference between things that are gold and things that are within the fifty-mile radius of the Eiffel Tower is that the former have some property in common that is both necessary and sufficient for being gold (e.g., some atomic structure) *and* that explains, by means of the *M* relation, both other properties they have in common and their causal powers. On the other hand, the latter share only the property of being within the fifty-mile radius of the Eiffel Tower, which explains little; if an object's having this property is used as a left-hand relatum in the *M* relation, few event types, or states of affairs, can fill in as the right-hand relatum.[35]

So a second necessary factor that is involved in an object's being of a certain kind is that the property that constitutes the kind be "rich" enough to stand as the left-hand relatum in the *M* relation to a large variety of event types and states of affairs. Leaving aside, for the moment, the obscurity of the notion of *richness,* and the vagueness involved in the expression 'a large variety', this second factor, too, seems insufficient to yield the intuitively graspable concept of a kind. Consider the property of being at 110 degrees Celsius. On at least some standards of richness, this seems to be a rich property: water's being at 110 degrees (at certain pressure levels) is what makes it boil; sugar's being at 110 degrees is what makes it turn into soft ball; plastic's being at 110 degrees is what makes it melt; a metal's being at 110 degrees is what makes it burn flesh on contact; and so on. But given our intuitions about kinds, being at 110 degrees Celsius is hardly the right property to define a real kind. What then is the difference between the property that defines gold and the property that determines the class of objects that are at 110 degrees Celsius?

When we examine the property that defines gold, we discover that it is a complex property, and that it is *not* this complex property as a whole that enters into *M* relations; it is, rather, distinct components of that complex property that are brought in as the left-hand relatum for various right-hand relata in the *M* relation. For example, what makes a piece of gold wire a good conductor of electricity is not its having the (total) atomic structure it has but, rather, its having some particular part of that structure, e.g., that part that it shares with silver and copper and that is necessary, as well as sufficient, for being a good conductor. A different part of its structure might be what makes it yellow, a third part might be what makes it dissolve in a mixture of hydrochloric and nitric acids and so on.[36]

If this is right, then what I have been calling "kind-designating properties" rarely enter as a whole into the *M* relation; only *components* of such properties do.[37] Thus, one way of characterizing real *kinds* is to say that they are defined by a cluster of properties and that each part of the cluster is such that an object's having that part is what makes it the case that that object (or some other kind of object with which it interacts) has some other property. It is this cluster that I have been referring to as "the complex property," and its "richness" consists in the fact that an object's having a component of this complex property is what makes it the case that some (kind of) thing has, or comes to have, some property. Such a complex property is made up of component properties that function as the left-hand relatum of the M relation, each component entering into an M relation with a different property. And when a sufficient number of these component properties are, under the conditions of the actual world, *compossible,* the complex property they make up defines a kind.[38] The complex property, thus, becomes the essence—the identity of the kind—any object that has that complex property is an object of the kind defined by that property.

A more formal characterization of kinds may be formulated as follows.

A cluster made up of a sufficient number of properties defines a kind if and only if:

> (i) it is nomologically possible for the cluster to be instantiated;
> (ii) each component property of the cluster is such that for every object that instantiates the cluster, that object's having that component property is what makes it the case that the object (or an object of some other kind) has (or comes to have) some property.[39]

What is important here is that objects of a kind do not need to have the property that defines the kind as part of their essence. Objects can migrate through kinds without ceasing to be. A chunk of gold can become a chunk of lead; wood can become ash; food can, because of the growth of bacteria, turn into something harmful to the body; and so on. Furthermore, since kinds are not mutually exclusive, an object can be of several kinds at once. A piece of gold wire is a metal, a conductor of electricity, and the kind of thing that dissolves in a mixture of hydrochloric and nitric acids. Kinds need not be any more mysterious entities than the properties that define them. For our purposes, they may be thought of as classes of possible objects that possess the defining property. If a kind is construed as a class of *possible* objects, they do not cease to exist when all (or any of) the actual objects cease to exist (or, cease to be of that kind).[40] The only way a kind can go out of existence is for the circumstances of the actual world to change in such a way as to make it impossible for the component properties of the complex that defines the kind to coexist in an object. For example, destroying all the gold in the world does not get rid of the kind of thing gold is; for that kind to go extinct, it is necessary that something in the world makes the formation of gold atoms impossible.[41] Finally, kinds do not change. But that does not mean that there must always be some unchanging property among the actual and possible members of a kind. There is no theoretical difficulty in acknowledging a kind whose defining property has a built-in "program" for a prescribed path of change in that property. If the world were such that gold atoms were transformed into heavier and heavier isotopes every millenium or so, with a concomitant change in the manifest properties of chunks of gold, that would not be a reason to deny that gold as a kind existed.[42]

The pronouncements I have made in the last two paragraphs have not been backed by any arguments. What reason do we have, therefore, for thinking that kinds are as I have declared them to be? The only type of reason I can offer here is a systematic one. I have argued that the M relation is one of the most important keys to understanding the structure of our universe. Our attempts at explaining regularities presuppose a universe where M relations hold among appropriate relata. And the logical structure of this relation requires the existence of kinds that are more or less as I have characterized them. If one accepts the M relation in the way it has been developed here, as a significant building block of our universe, one can hardly deny most of what I have claimed about kinds.[43]

Finally, it may appear that a vicious circularity threatens my account of the M relation. The relation depends on the existence of kinds, and kinds are defined in terms of the M relation. It is quite true that there is such an interdependence between the M relation and kinds. However, the existence of this interdependence does not vitiate the views I have defended here; it just underlines what I have been suggesting in these pages—that kinds, on the one hand, and properties that stand in the M relation, on the other, are two logically related aspects of what is essential to the structure of the uniformity of nature.

IV. SUPERVENIENCE, REDUCTION, AND IDENTITY

A property is said to supervene on a second just in case the presence of the second necessitates the presence of the first, but not conversely.[44] The M relation may be used to explicate this notion and to draw some of the distinctions that have become familiar in the literature.[45] Consider the following three examples:

(i) The aesthetic quality of *this* painting supervenes on the composition of figures and colors.
(ii) The goodness of kitchen knives supervenes on the quality of the blade, the construction of the handle, and the balance between the blade and the handle.
(iii) The coding of a musical passage on an audio tape supervenes on the arrangement of the magnetic particles that make up the surface of the tape.

In each of these examples, if we let the supervenient property be G, and the property on which it supervenes be F, it should be clear that something's being F is what makes it the case that it is G.

However, there are important differences among these examples. In (i), only in *this painting* does the composition of figures and colors stands in the M relation to a particular aesthetic quality. Since in a different painting, something quite different (e.g., use of chiaroscuro) might make it have the same aesthetic quality, it would be false to assert that any painting's having the composition of colors and figures this painting has is what makes it the case that it has that aesthetic quality. The M relation that holds in this example is of no use in the type of explanation that has been spotlighted in this essay, i.e., it does not explain whay kinds of things *regularly* have the properties they have.

In example (ii), it is also false that having the type of blade, the particular handle construction, and the balance *this* knife has is what makes *any* kitchen knife good. A different type of blade with a different handle construction might produce *equally* good results. However, there is an important difference between this case and example (i). I am assuming that here nothing other than these three determinables (quality of blade, balance, and handle construction) will contribute to the goodness of a kitchen knife, although in each good knife a different set of determinates of these determinables may jointly be the contributing factor.[46] It is this difference that imparts some explanatory force to the *M* relation. Thanks to the *M* relation, when we have a good knife, we know where to look for the factors that make up its goodness; but since the relation has as its left-hand relatum determinable properties, we do not know what specific (determinate) type of blade or handle to expect in that particular knife. When we are given the blade and handle specifications of a totally new style of knife, knowing that the type of blade and handle construction of kitchen knives is what makes them good does not help us in predicting whether this style of knife will be good. This point is perhaps better expressed in the more familiar terminology of functionalism: The goodness of a kitchen knife consists in an *open-ended disjunction* of properties.[47]

The type of relation exemplified by kitchen knives embodies an important feature: When we discover that the blade, handle, and so on, are what make a kitchen knife good, we discover that the goodness of a kitchen knife *consists in,* is *nothing but,* the type of blade, the handle construction, and so on, that it has. So, in some way, an ontological reduction is achieved. This is a minor achievement, though, because the reduction does not thereby render 'the goodness of kitchen knives' dispensable. The open-endedness of the disjunction makes it impossible to refer to any one of the disjuncts in order to explain the *regularities* a kitchen knife's being good gives rise to. For example, what makes a kitchen knife ideally suited for chopping vegetables is its being a good knife, *not* its having the particular type of blade it has, and so on.[48] It being *good,* not its having this type of blade, stands in the *M* relation to a host of regularities.[49] And this fact requires our retaining the property of goodness of kitchen knives in our ontology.[50]

The third example, that of audio tapes, introduces a new factor. There, what makes *any* tape contain the coding for this sequence of sounds (say, the opening bars of Beethoven's Fifth Symphony) is its having the magnetic particles on its surface arranged in this way. Whenever this sequence of sounds is coded on an audio tape, the magnetic particles must be arranged just that way. Here, *modulo* the kind of thing in question, namely, magnetic audio tapes, the five conditions I offered in explicating the *M* relation are all satisfied. As a result, because of the transitivity of the *M* relation, every regularity that can be explained via the *M* relation by the tape's having a coding for such and such musical passage can also be explained by the tape's having its magnetic particles arranged that way. The ontological reduction achieved here is of greater significance than that achieved in the second type of case. Not only do we know that the coding of numerical passages on a magnetic tape consists in (is nothing but) the arrangement of the magnetic particles, but we also recognize that the relation between these two properties of the kind of thing magnetic tapes are renders the former property, in principle, dispensable in the explanatory scheme of things. Such in-principle dispensability is all that is required for the success of intertheoretic reductions in science.

The history of science provides us with vivid examples of the type of discovery that makes intertheoretic reduction possible. For instance, when it was conjectured that gases were collections of molecules, it became reasonable to suppose that the thermodynamic properties of gases consisted in (were nothing but) the mechanical properties of the molecules. This supposition is tantamount to the thesis that the thermodynamic properties of gases supervene on the mechanical properties of the gas molecules in the way the goodness of kitchen knives supervenes on the properties of the blade and the handle. But this supposition, by itself, is never sufficient for theoretical reduction. What is also needed is that of supplementing the vocabulary of the reducing science (i.e., mechanics) with formalisms that will transform the supervenience into the type exemplified by the magnetic tape case. The formalisms in question consist of equating temperature with the mean kinetic energy of the molecules, and the pressure with the mean rate of change in their translational momentum. These concepts are added to the theory of mechanics in response to pressures generated by reductionist concerns, and in conformity with the constraints imposed by the laws of the reduced theory and of the reducing theory.[51] In other words, successful reduction of thermodynamics to mechanics requires discovering what specific mechanical property of the molecules makes it the case that gases have each of the thermodynamic properties they have (e.g., discovering that the molecules' having a mean kinetic energy e is what makes it the case that the gas has temperature t). And this discovery, in turn, requires discovering the appropriate formalisms to be added to the reducing theory.[52]

When such a reduction is achieved, and the in-principle eliminability of the properties of the reduced theory is demonstrated, the M relation between the formalisms added to the reducing theory and the properties of the reduced theory acquires a new dimension. First, we realize that *in gases,* it is necessary that they have temperature t when and only when their molecules have mean kinetic energy e, and second, we see that every regularity that can be explained by the gases' having that temperature can be explained by the molecules' having that mean kinetic energy.[53] These two insights are all that are needed to declare that an *identity relation* holds between the temperature of gases and the mean kinetic energy of their molecules.[54] But the identity is a *restricted* identity; it is an identity that is derived from the relation that holds between the properties of the *kind of thing* gases are, and hence, it is restricted to only the kind of thing gases are.[55] Furthermore, since the restricted identities are derived from an M relation, and from the type of supervenience the relation generates, the asymmetry of the M relation (and of supervenience) carries over to our discourse about these properties. For example, it is true that the temperature of gases is nothing but the mean kinetic energy of the molecules, but it is false that the mean kinetic energy of the molecules is nothing but the temperature of the gases that are constituted by those molecules.[56]

What, then, is the difference between genuine property identity and restricted property identity? If what has been said above about restricted identity is basically right, it would seem that two expressions F and G that refer to properties will refer to one and the same property *simpliciter,* not a property of a kind of thing, only if it is necessary that whenever one of F or G is instantiated by *any* kind of object, then the other one is also instantiated by an associated kind of object. Satisfaction of this requirement clearly entails the violation of condition (v) for the M relation (and it renders conditions (i) and (ii) irrelevant). Hence, the existence of an M relation between two properties is inconsistent with there being a genuine identity between them. What is, perhaps, less obvious is that the machinery by means of which intertheoretic reductions are achieved in science seems particularly ill suited to discovering genuine identities. Scientific theories embody laws, and these laws are generally confined to kinds of things and to the properties of *those kinds.* Reduction of a theory is almost always carried out with reference to the kinds that form the domain of that theory. Hence, it is difficult to see how such a reduction can establish the *necessity* of the following conditional: if the reduced property is to be instantiated by some kind of thing *outside* the domain of the theory, then that kind of thing will also instantiate the reducing property.[57] Scientific reduction is not equipped to demonstrate this necessity simply because the reducing theory does not have jurisdiction over *all possible kinds.*

V. CONCLUSION

I have attempted to argue that one important element in the structure of regularities in nature is the M relation that holds between properties. If these arguements are sound, then the existence of this relation has certain natural consequences: (i) it commits us to kinds and to clusters of properties that form the essence of those kinds; (ii) it helps us to understand the structure of supervenience; and (iii) it gives us an insight into scientific reduction and into the nature of restricted identities.

If our grasp of the universe requires our discovering appropriate M relations, and if M relations are logically tied to kinds that have essences, then it seems that we must admit these kinds into our ontology. Until a similar sort of argument is provided for individuals, I, for one, will be happy to live without individual essences.[58]

Notes

1. I shall be using 'define' throughout this paper in the nonlinguistic sense.
2. See Elliott Sober (1980) and David Hull (1976, 1978).
3. These two pairs are closely parallel to the nonexplanations discussed by Baruch Brody (1971, 1980). His example in which one tries to explain why stars are far by the fact that they twinkle has a structure similar to 1a. He also has a second example that has a structure similar to 2a. This second example is: anything that combines with bromine in a one-to-one ratio combines with chlorine in a one-to-one ratio, and sodium combines with bromine in a one-to-one ratio; but these two facts do not explain why sodium combines with chlorine in a one-to-one ratio.
4. Brody (1980) explains the failure of his sodium example by pointing out that combining with bromine in a one-to-one ratio is not an essential property of sodium. I have sympathy with his diagnosis.
5. My purpose here is not to deny that the causal order of things sometimes plays an important role in explanation. It is, rather, to suggest that there may be a deeper account of the failure of 1a.
6. As will become apparent below, what I am suggesting is that Aristotelian efficient causes and formal causes have a common underlying structure.
7. Davidson (1963, 1967)

8. Levin (1976).

9. See Dretske and Enç (1984) for a discussion of the nonextensionality generated by such contexts.

10. I borrow this example from Dretske (1977). He uses the example to show that the context generated by "It is a law that . . ." is nonextensional in exactly the way I am suggesting the left-hand relatum of the *M* relation is nonextensional.

11. Later I will try to replace these metaphors with a more illuminating account.

12. I am not relying on a hidden intentionality that may exist in "detectors." If all of those "functionally equivalent" compositions had the *same* ingredient (e.g., some specific compound), then I would admit that the berry's having that ingredient is what makes the bell ring.

13. I am relying on a Davidsonian view about the idividuation of events. See Davidson (1969).

14. I am concerned with motivating the formal characterization of the *M* relation by appealing to the ordinary usage of the expression "makes it the case that." However, there will be contexts in which the expression is used with a different force, in which our linguistic intuitions about the expression do not conform exactly to the formal characterization. I do not take the existence of such contexts to constitute a refutation of what I will offer as the formal characterization.

15. An ambiguity similar to the one in the arsenic case exists in this example. If the question is "what makes *this particular* berry red?" (or, "what makes *this particular* berry capable of causing the bell of the detector to ring?"), a correct answer might be "its having the chemical composition it has." But if the question is "what makes the berries of this kind of plant red (or, capable of causing the bell to ring)?" then I suggest that "their having this chemical compound," where this chemical compound is one of several functionally equivalent compounds, is not the correct answer.

16. I am assuming that 'clear' means 'can be seen through', and not 'transmits light'.

17. As in my discussion of the typical properties. I am here assuming that the left-hand relatum of the *M* relation refers to a property of the molecular structure that is *necessary* for death, and not to the totality of the molecular structure that is essential to hydrochloric acid. If this assumption is violated, then the person's death would not be "sensitive" to the property in question, and the relation *M* will fail to hold between the acid's having the property and all those events in which the people who ingest the acid die. What makes this point important in this context is that we are interested in the causal powers of hydrochloric acid, not in the explanation of a particular death. In other words, we want to locate a property of the molecular structure of the acid, the having of which makes it the case that people (in general) who ingest the acid die.

18. I am assuming, for the purposes of this example, that a fully deterministic tie exists between pressure drops and storms.

19. Here, I am assuming that neither drinking alcohol nor shoveling snow was, by itself, sufficient, but that each was a contributing factor to the death. Under this assumption, it would also not be incorrect to say that what made him die was his drinking a fifth of scotch.

20. In many cases, whether *a*'s being *F* is what makes it the case that *b* is *G* seems to be dependent on pragmatic considerations related to the context in which the question is asked. These considerations usually determine whether *b*'s being *G* is a particular event or an event type, and also, if it is an event type, what kind and what property are being presumed to determine the type.

21. I think that when a request for an explanation of an event is made, what is to be explained is the occurrence of some event (which particular event, we do not care) that instantiates a property. (Or, perhaps I should say, it is generally the case that what is to be explained is the event's instantiating a property.) For example, when we ask "What makes this berry red?" we usually want to know what makes it the case that this berry is in some or other state in which it is red. Rarely do we want to know what makes it the case that this berry is in the particular (total) state it is in, in which it is red. Naturally, there are notable exceptions. Requests for a historical explanation of an event (e.g., what caused the Civil War?) and requests for the explanation of an aesthetic quality of a work of art (e.g., what makes this painting beautiful?) are among the most obvious cases of such exceptions.

22. Conditions (iii) and (iv) will yield a similar negative answer in all cases of overdetermination, and I find this result not at all inconsistent with my intuitions about the proper use of the expression, "makes it the case that."

23. Again, it may be less confusing to describe what is to be explained as "the instantiation of the property of landing in slot twenty-one by the particular event in which the ball lands in slot twenty-one." This is

a different explanandum from "the event in which the ball lands in slot twenty-one." The latter can be adequately explained by citing a salient factor in the causal chain that actually resulted in that event (salience to be determined by the pragmatics of the case). But, as I have been arguing, the former requires more.

24. The importance of pragmatics in explanation is a well-recognized fact. But I do not think that acknowledging this fact commits me to placing an essential role on pragmatics in the account of the M relation. Whether the relation itself holds is free from pragmatic considerations. Pragmatic considerations play a role (a) in deciding what precisely the relata are and (b) in figuring out what laws are presumed to hold.

25. Dretske and Snyder (1972; 1973) have argued for an account of causation according to which causes need not be sufficient for their effects. They would say that since pressing the button is "all that is necessary" (their phrase) for the outcome, pressing the button is what causes the outcome. What I am suggesting is that regardless of what the correct account of event causation (or agency) may be, the M relation fails to hold in those cases where the right-hand rlelatum is an event's instantiating a property, and where the left-hand relatum is merely "all that is necessary" for the right-hand relatum.

26. According to Sober (1980), the availability of such ideal laws about the propagation of phenotypic characters is one of the factors that supports theses about the essences of species. He then argues that in modern population genetics, no such ideal laws exist, and consequently, species essentialism is a less plausible position in modern biology than it was in Aristotelian biology.

27. David Lewis's analysis of causes (1973) has been criticized for suffering from a similar problem in that it appeals to the notion of possible worlds that are *closest (most similar)* to the actual world. For a criticism of Lewis's theory of counterparts, see Feldman (1971) or Brody (1980, 106).

28. Let us assume here that what I am calling "genuine property identity" holds between F and G *only if* in every possible world where anything is F, that thing is G, and in every possible world where anything is G, that thing is also F. I will have more to say about genuine property identity later.

29. Condition (v) is also violated when we consider "a's being F is what makes it the case that a is F."

30. Suppose "angle" means "angle less than 180 degrees."

31. It might be pointed out, quite correctly, that by my conditions, an object's being *closed* and four-angled is what makes it the case that it is four-sided. This result does not violate the asymmetry of the M relation. All it could possibly violate are our intuitions about reading the M relation as "makes it the case that." I suggest that the intuition that may incline some to think that an object's being closed and having four angles is *not* what makes it the case that it has four sides may be due to envisaging the act of drawing quadrangles. In drawing them, we *give* them four sides, and they end up having four angles, and not the other way around. This raises interesting questions about how the M relation operates in geometry and about the role of constructive (explanatory) proof in mathematics. I do not propose to address these questions in this context.

32. See note 21 for an (incomplete) list of contexts in which explanations require a different pattern.

33. I tend to think that the notion of laws has been unduly inflated by philosophers and has been pressed to serve too many needs. It might be less inflationary (at least in the context of evaluating these assertions) to conceive of laws as connections among properties, along the lines suggested by Dretske (1977), Tooley (1977), and Armstrong (1978, 149–57).

34. Of course, when we give such an explanation, we may be asked why a's being F makes this the case. And the appropriate response may be to cite the relevant laws. But this further task involves that of trying to show that our original assertion was true.

35. Suppose that a strong field of atomic radiation is centered right under the Eiffel Tower. Then it might seem that an object's being within the fifty-mile radius of the Eiffel Tower *would* function as the left-hand relatum in the M relation for a large variety of right-hand relata. But condition (iv) shows this to be false. For example, what will make it the case that an object produces a certain number of clicks on a geiger counter is not its being within the fifty-mile radius of the Eiffel Tower; what makes this the case is, rather, the object's having been in a field of radiation.

36. Apart from the fact that the total structure is not necessary for these results and, hence, violates condition (iv), the point can be supported further by the following type of consideration. Suppose "having such and such atomic structure" and "being gold" refer to the same property. Anyone who thinks that having that structure is what makes a piece of wire be a good conductor of electricity will, by substitution of identicals, be committed to thinking that being gold is what makes this piece of wire be a good conductor of electricity. And this latter thought seems to be arguably false.

37. Perhaps entities that are the simplest building blocks of the universe, if any such entities exist, are an exception here.

38. There is clearly no magic number of such component properties below which they fail to constitute a kind. At one extreme, we have properties, such as being bigger than a bread box or being at 110 degrees Celsius, that fail to constitute a kind. (The former fails because it does not enter into M relations in which the right-hand relatum is a type of event or state of affairs, the latter because it enters into M relations with different right-hand relata depending on what kind of thing instantiates it.) At the other extreme, we have clear cases, like gold, metal, and so on, the components of which enter into a rich variety of M relations. And between these two extremes is a vast area where the cluster is small and where we do not know what to say. (Do brittle objects make up a kind? Is sugar that is at the soft-ball stage a kind of sugar?) The existence of this vast area reflects, I think, the difficulty of saying precisely what kinds are.

39. Kinds characterized this way may not conform to our intuitive notion of kinds. For example, the characterization given above does not exclude sugar that is at 110 degrees Celsius from being a kind of sugar. To secure a closer match with our intuitive notion of kinds, a third condition may need to be added to the above two:

(iii) For each component of the cluster, and for any object that instantiates the cluster, what makes it the case that the object comes to have that component is *not* some *other* object's having some property.

This condition will allow sugar to be a kind but will exclude sugar at the soft-ball stage from being a kind. It will also allow vegetable matter with high carbon content to be a kind but will exclude coal, or diamonds, from being a kind. However, I propose to be quite liberal about kinds, and for the purposes of this essay, I will confine myself to the first two conditions.

40. For an interesting discussion of whether biological kinds (i.e., species) are sets, see Kitcher (1984a; 1984b) and Sober (1984a).

41. If species are kinds, then to speak of extinct species is to acknowledge the (practical) impossibility of evolution's ever again giving rise to members of such species.

42. Evolutionary change has often been offered as one of the reasons for denying that species are kinds. (See Hull [1976; 1978] and Ghiselin [1974].) I want to avoid the controversy over the question whether species are kinds or individuals. However, given my characterization of kinds, the fact that there is change would not by itself be a decisive factor in this controversy.

43. However, my suggestion that kinds be equated with classes of possible objects is not forced on us by the structure of the M relation. Indeed, many different conceptions of kinds are compatible with what I have argued for here.

44. See Kim (1984) and Sosa (1984).

45. Prompted by issues in the philosophy of psychology, the literature of the last ten years is full of interesting studies of supervenience. See, e.g., Horgan (1978), or the essays in Horgan (1984).

46. Speaking of determinables and determinates may be misleading. What is at issue is more the level of the specificity of the properties.

47. When philosophers of psychology suggest that each token mental state (of higher organisms) is identical with a state of the central nervous system, but that there is no type-type identity, they envisage the kind of relation I have imagined to exist between the goodness of kitchen knives and their constituent properties.

48. This point is just a reiteration of my earlier discussion of ''sensitivity.''

49. I do not think that I am saying anything novel here. The point has been developed and defended more fully by many philosophers. For a classic treatment of it, see Jerry Fodor (1975). Introduction.

50. If mental states (e.g., believing that this is water and wanting to have water) supervene on the states of the central nervous system in exactly this way, then it will be true that my being in this particular neurological state is what makes it the case that I have this particular belief-desire pair. However, what makes it the case that I produce a piece of behavior of this type (e.g., drinking water) is not my having this particular belief and desire; it is, rather, my having a belief of this *kind* (a belief with this content) and a desire of this kind. Hence, it will be false that my being in the neurological state I am in is what makes me act the way I do. This demonstrates the explanatory indispensability of mental-state types—indeed, the indispensability,

or irreducibility, of the contents of mental states in the explanation of behavior. Furthermore, explanatory indispensability is not a purely epistemological phenomenon. Its orgins lie in the way the relevant properties are structured in our universe.

51. By speaking of *adding,* I do not mean to suggest an element of arbitrariness or of conventionalism here. What makes the discovery of these formalisms possible is the nature of the properties as they are understood in the reduced theory, and the approximate correctness of the laws of the reduced theory.

52. If we were to pursue my fantasy about kitchen knives, we could imagine a resourceful engineer coming up with a formula that, for example, defined the gamma factor of a kitchen knife as a function of the three variables that took as values the specific type of blade, the handle, and the balance. Such a discovery would make the goodness of kitchen knives supervene on a range of values of the gamma factor in exactly the way the temperature of gases supervenes on the mean kinetic energy of the molecules.

53. It may also be of some interest to note that the in-principle eliminability of a property in explanatory contexts seems to be generally associated with discovering that the laws of the theory that refer to such properties are true only under specifiable *ideal* conditions—indeed, with discovering what (in the vocabulary of the reducing theory) those ideal conditions are.

54. These identities used to be called "contingent identities" (see, e.g., J. J. C. Smart [1962] and Causey [1972]). Thanks to Kripke, contingency of an identity relation has come to be recognized as a contradiction. The way I have described the relation, there is nothing contingent about it. The essentialism of kinds that I have been developing here, and the modality of the *M* relation, makes it clear that these restricted identities have all the modal force of "genuine identities."

55. It is a known fact, for example, that the temperature of solids is not the mean kinetic energy of their molecules.

56. I argued for a similar point (1976). There I suggested that property identities established in intertheoretic reduction were based on what I called a "generative relation" (necessary and sufficient causation). I was later criticized for confusing epistemic asymmetry of explanatory contexts with the ontological symmetry of identity relations. What I did not realize then was that I was dealing with restricted property identities and that such identities inherit the asymmetry of the generative relation (or of the *M* relation, as I have been calling it here).

57. The only way the necessity of such a conditional can be established is by *fiat*: When a property *G* is reduced to *F,* one can, perhaps for good theoretical reasons, declare by *fiat* that if any object were to lack *F,* it could not have *G.* This issue overlaps with the question of how expressions refer to properties—a question to which I do not have even the beginnings of an answer.

58. I am indebted to Geoffrey Joseph, Palle Yourgrau, and Elliott Sober for being willing to discuss with me the issues involved in this paper, and to Fred Dretske and Dennis Stampe for their comments on an earlier version. The research for this paper was made possible by a grant from the graduate school of the University of Wisconsin-Madison during the summer of 1984.

References

Armstrong, David. 1978. *A Theory of Universals.* Cambridge.

Brody, Baruch A. 1971. "Towards an Aristotelian Theory of Scientific Explanation." *Philosophy of Science* 39:20–31.

_____. 1980. *Identity and Essence.* Princeton, N.J.

Causey, Robert. 1972 "Attribute Identities and Microreductions." *The Journal of Philosophy* 69:407–22.

Davidson, Donald. 1963. "Actions, Reasons, and Causes." *The Journal of Philosophy* 60:685–700. (Also in Davidson [1980].)

_____. 1967. "Causal Relations." *The Journal of Philosophy* 64:691–703. (Also in Davidson [1980].)

_____. 1969. "The Individuation of Events." In *Essays in Honor of Carl G. Hempel,* edited by Nicholas Rescher. Dordrecht. (Also in Davidson [1980].)

_____. 1980. *Essays on Actions and Events.* Oxford.

Dretske, Fred. 1977. "Laws of Nature." *Philosophy of Science* 44:248–68.

Dretske, Fred, and Aaron Snyder. 1972. "Causal Irregularity." *Philosophy of Science* 39:69–71.
_____. 1973. "Causality and Sufficiency: Reply to Beauchamp." *Philosophy of Science* 40:288–91
Dretske, Fred and Berent Enç. 1984. "Causal Theories of Knowledge." In *Midwest Studies in Philosophy,* Vol. IX, edited by Peter A. French, Theodore H. Uehling, Jr., and Howard K. Wettstein, 517–28. Minneapolis.
Enç, Berent. 1976. "Identity Statements and Microreductions." *The Journal of Philosophy* 73:285–305.
Feldman, Fred. 1971. "Counterparts." *The Journal of Philosophy* 68:406–9.
Fodor, Jerry. 1975. *The Language of Thought.* Cambridge, Mass.
Ghiselin, Michael. 1974. "A Radical Solution to the Species Problem." *Systematic Zoology* 23:536–44.
Horgan, Terence. 1978. "Supervenient Bridge Laws." *Philosophy of Science* 45:227–49.
Horgan, Terence, ed. 1984. *Spindel Conference, 1983: Supervenience. The Southern Journal of Philosophy,* Vol. 22 Supplement.
Hull, David. 1976. "Are Species Really Individuals?" *Systematic Zoology* 25:174–91.
_____. 1978. "A Matter of Individuality." *Philosophy of Science* 45:335–60.
Kim, Jaegwon. 1984. "Epiphenomenal and Supervenient Causation." In *Midwest Studies in Philosophy,* Vol. IX, edited by Peter A. French, Theodore H. Uehling, Jr., and Howard K. Wettstein, 257–70. Minneapolis.
Kitcher, Philip. 1984a. "Species." *Philosophy of Science* 51:308–33.
_____. 1984b. "Against the Monism of the Moment: A Reply to Elliott Sober." *Philosophy of Science* 51:616–30.
Levin, Michael. 1976. "The Extensionality of Causation and Causal Explanatory Contexts." *Philosophy of Science* 43:266–77.
Lewis, David. 1973. "Causation." *The Journal of Philosophy* 70:556–67.
Smart, J. J. C. 1962. "Sensations and Brain Processes." In *The philosophy of Mind,* edited by V. C. Chappell. Englewood Cliffs, N.J.
Sober, Elliott. 1980. "Evolution, Population Thinking, and Essentialism." *Philosophy of Science* 47:350–83.
_____. 1984a. "Sets, Species, and Evolution: Comments on Philip Kitcher's 'Species'." *Philosophy of Science* 51:334–41.
_____. 1984b. *The Nature of Selection.* Cambridge, Mass.
Sosa, Ernest. 1984. "Mind-Body Interaction and Supervenient Causation." In *Midwest Studies in Philosophy,* Vol. IX, edited by Peter A. French, Theodore H. Uehling, Jr., and Howard K. Wettstein, 271–82. Minneapolis.
Tooley, Michael. 1977. "The Nature of Laws." *Canadian Journal of Philosophy* 7:667–98.

MIDWEST STUDIES IN PHILOSOPHY, XI (1986)

I'm Going to Make You a Star

ROBERT SCHWARTZ

The belief that the world is a product of our conceptualizations, that facts are as much made as found, has an air of otherworldliness. And a forceful "But people don't make stars" is often thought to be the simplest way to bring proponents of such metaphysical foolishness back to their senses. For isn't it obvious that the stars in the firmament are not of our doing? There were stars long before sentient beings crawled about and longer still before the concept "star" was thought of or explicitly formulated. Indeed, there would have been stars, with all their properties, had there never been organisms with minds. The claim that we make our world is thus untenable. We do create concepts and theories, but not the facts they purport to describe. These are mind-independent, a matter of the world just being as it is.

Now the thesis that we participate in making our world would not be worth serious consideration if, for example, the claim were that we physically fashioned stars from earth, air, fire, and water, and, having given them their shape, placed them in the heavens above. Rather, the claim is that in fashioning and shaping theories, we make stars. This latter version of the thesis has the advantage of not being patently false, and the disadvantage of being more puzzling. For if we do not actually take raw material and work on it until it has starlike properties, surely we cannot be said to literally make stars. So at best the thesis of world-making would seem to come to no more than a play on the word 'make.' Perhaps so, but plays on words can be revealing. In this case, it may help us appreciate that the alternative picture of a world readymade, of facts waiting out there to be discovered, of objects that are at one and the same time mind-independent and Self-Identifying, is no less a play on words and no easier to spell out.[1] Still, for those who bridle at using the phrase 'making stars' in anything but a robust physical crafting sense, we can grant the point and, thus cautioned, go on to explore whether there is some additional construal of 'making' that may serve to elucidate the integral role conceptualization plays in constructing our world.[2]

THE LIMITS OF POWER?

Even the staunchest Realist allows that parts of the world are of our making. Tables, chairs, the Eiffel Tower, Pepsi Cola, and telephones are things we produce, states of affairs that come about only through human intervention. Bringing such objects into existence, however, would seem to require the kind of physical manipulation all would agree is not possible in the case of stars. If we make stars, it must be by doing something cognitive or mental, not by shifting matter around. But no argument is needed to show that we do have some power to create by conceptualization and symbolic activity. Poems, promises, and predictions are a few obvious examples, their very embodiment being achieved through symbolization. Moreover, our cognitive powers to shape the world do not stop here. We can make people healthy, wealthy, and wise by doing no more than offering sound advice, inside information, and intellectual insight. And notice, too, that it is only fitting that the designer of the Eiffel Tower and the inventor of the telephone be considered among their prime makers, although neither may have ever bolted a single girder or headset into place. So just as no on can reasonably assert that we physically hoisted the stars up high and set them aglow, no one can deny we can bring facts about by words and thought as well as by deeds of pushing and pulling.

TRUTH IN MAKING

What, then, is the point of the challenge to make a star? Several different issues, ideas, and intuitions tend, I think, to be run together here. And we shall explore various of these matters as we go along. For many, though, a major reason for issuing this challenge is to help reiterate some important, albeit obvious, facts about the objectivity of truth—facts that are thought to conflict with the notion that we play a role in making our world. Truth and falsity, we are reminded, are properties of sentences, properties that are "independent of us," independent of what we believe or are willing to assert. We do not make sentences true or descriptions apply just by uttering them sincerely. If wishing will not make it so, neither will wholehearted assent. 'P' is true if what 'P' says is how things *really* are, and not because 'P' happens to be included in some theory we propose or hold. Persons so benighted as to think otherwise, who harbor subjectivist or idealist fantasies that truth somehow depends on our states of mind or is a matter of communal agreement, can be made to see the error of their ways by reflecting on their powerlessness when it comes to making or altering the facts about stars. Let them repeat as often and sincerely as they can "There's a bright star glowing straight above" and notice that such affirmations can do nothing to make the sentence true, since there is no star so placed.

But a proponent of the view that we partake in making our world by our activities of symbolization and cognition need have no qualms with any of this. Acknowledgment of our role in constructing the world does not entail a subjective account of truth and certainly does not require denying that 'P' is true if and only if P. Indeed, when it

comes to accounts of truth, the whole question of making really does not make a difference. We do, after all, readily take credit for making chairs. Yet the truth of such sentences as "Some chairs float on water" and "There are more chairs than tables"
depends on whether what the senetences say is so. These sentences are true or false
"independent of us," independent of what we are willing to assert or accept. The situation is the same with lengthy poems or wealthy persons. We may make them, and the
making may be primarily a verbal doing, but whether the predicates 'contains 150
lines' and 'is a millionaire' actually apply is not up to us. It is not a matter of our merely
saying they do. Willingness to assign humans credit for things being as they are does
not entail adopting a solipsistic attitude toward truth.

To claim that in fashioning concepts and categories, we partake in making our
world is compatible with the idea that sentences purporting to describe the products of
our work are true or false independent of us. Although we may have a hand in making
stars through our conceptual activities, sentences about stars, just like sentences about
chairs and poems, are true if and only if they tell it like it is. Truth is no less objective
because we may have a role to play in making it so that things are as they are.

What's more, our undoubted failure to place a star above at the drop of a hat is
itself of no pressing significance. That we play a role in making our world, and, in
particular, in making stars, does not mean that we are able to create objects or states of
affairs by wish or whim. We may fail at cognitive construction as often and as badly as
we do at physical making. The ether and phlogiston are two prominent examples of
vigorous intellectual attempts that did not pan out. Devising useful categories and insightful theories is an arduous business and not a matter of unconstrained talk. We
have no guarantees that things will turn out as planned. Nevertheless, I wish to maintain that in shaping the concepts and classification schemes we employ in describing
our world, we do take part in constituting what that reality is. For whether there are
stars, and what they are like, are not facts that the world can either wear on its surface
or keep hidden from us until we become smart enough to discern them. They are facts
that are carved out in the very process of devising perspicuous theories to aid in understanding our world. Or to put the thesis in an alternative form: until we fashion star
concepts and related categories, and integrate them into ongoing theories and speculations, there is no interesting sense in which the facts about stars are *really* one way
rather than another. Or so I would claim.

But can this be right? The idea that *we* in any way determine whether there are
stars and what they are like seems so preposterous, if not incomprehensible, that any
thesis that leads to this conclusion must be suspect. Perhaps, however, clarity can be
gained here, and some of the mystery removed, if we come down to earth for a while
and first examine some more homey cases of conceptual making.[3]

THE GAMES PEOPLE PLAY

One warm, starry August night, Allison's luck turned. She had the good fortune to
draw all the blank Scrabble tiles and win her final game by a wide margin. Thus concluded a glorious week at the New Jersey shore. Now the point of telling this brief

vacation tale is not to promote the splendors of New Jersey as a tourist haven. Instead, I wish to explore how much, if any, of this idyllic portion of reality it makes sense to see as existing readymade, independent of our activities of cognition and categorization.

Let's begin simply with the blank Scrabble tiles Allison drew. These are standardly pieces of wood, approximately $3/4'' \times 3/4'' \times 1/8''$, with no markings; they serve as wild cards or jokers in the game. A Scrabble joker can stand for any letter of the alphabet. And the facts are that Allison came up with all of these little pieces of wood and that she used them wisely to win. But are there facts about Allison's fortunate draw, or about Scrabble jokers in general, that just are what they are and would have been so had the game not been invented and the rules and roles of the blank tiles never specified? It would seem implausible, for example, to claim that the facts that Scrabble jokers are worth zero points and that there are two jokers to the game are eternal aspects of Reality, independent of human doings. Nor is it clear that there could even be Scrabble jokers had the concept never been devised and given its shape and content. Of course, merely formulating the concept "Scrabble joker" will not bring it about that the world contains blank pieces of wood of the specified kind. Fashioning a concept is one thing, and carving lumber is another. On the other hand, merely making pieces of wood of a given size and shape would not be enough to create Scrabble jokers either. For had the game never been devised, what could possibly make it so that these pieces of wood rather than those pieces of coal, rather than nothing at all, were of the right sort? Under such circumstances, there would be no basis for its being the case that certain features are the ones that really are constitutive of being a Scrabble joker or that certain items have what it takes to be really of that kind. Similarly, had the game not been invented, what could possibly make it the case that the property also extended to take in some smaller bits of magnetized metal, like those found currently in Scrabble travel sets? Surely, it is not a pure and simple matter of the way the world is that all and only these items, and not those, are of a kind, the kind made up of the true or real Scrabble jokers.

I do not mean to belabor the obvious, that the English phrase 'Scrabble joker' could have no use until given one by speakers of the language. Rather, the property itself, or better perhaps, which objects actually have the property of being a Scrabble joker, is not a fact that it makes good sense to conceive of as existing out there all along, independent of how we might fashion what that property is or to what it applies. In devising the game of Scrabble, we create the very possibility of their being such things as Scrabble jokers.[4]

Paradox might seem to loom, however, if looked at from another perspective. Suppose prior to anyone's coming up with the idea of Scrabble, there happened to be scattered about blank wood chips $3/4'' \times 3/4'' \times 1/8''$. These tiles would have had the appropriate features to be Scrabble jokers all along. At a later date, they may even have been collected and packaged as pieces in official Scrabble sets. So unless some mysterious form of backward causation is countenanced, the existence of these Scrabble jokers cannot be dependent on our cognitive activities, activities that, by hypothesis, took place after the fact.

But resolution of this seeming paradox lies ready at hand and requires no violation of our standard notion of causation. Had the game of Scrabble not been devised, one of the properties these chips could not have possessed is the property that concerns us, the property of being a Scrabble joker. These bits of wooden reality could no more be Scrabble jokers without the cognitive carving out of the features and dimensions of the concept, than they could be Scrabble jokers had they never been carved from the tree. Admittedly, in the latter instance, the dependence is more obvious. We would be reluctant to claim that an undetached piece of tree trunk is a Scrabble joker unless it is physically separated from its surround, although there is a sense in which *it*, the particular expanse of material stuff, existed, was square, was $3/4'' \times 3/4'' \times 1/8''$, and was blank before it was milled. One might say that all the carpenter did was make *it* portable and, in so doing, make its other Scrabble features stand out. Putting matters this way, however, seems quite perverse. Yet it may not be much more perverse than the idea that this section of tree trunk, milled or not, could have or would have been a Scrabble joker without our cognitively shaping the concept and giving it its form. For in drawing the boundaries of the property and setting them one way rather than another, we make it that the features of this object, and not that, are the right ones, the ones that go to make it a fact that it is a Scrabble joker. By conceptually highlighting some of the literally countless features any two items possess, and the countless others they share, while downplaying the rest, we help determine that it is appropriate or correct to group this object, rather than that, with certain other items as members of the Scrabble joker kind.[5]

Those who devised the game, then, may not have physically made this particular Scrabble joker; it would have been out there, in the world, without them. They did not make *it*. They did have a hand, nonetheless, in bringing it about that *it* is a Scrabble joker. They contributed toward making ''its being a Scrabble joker'' a fact, or true. Moreover, in the absence of such work of mind, the facts about Scrabble jokers—how many there are, how many points they are worth, how many are contained in a regulation game, and so on—are facts that could have no substance or factuality. The idea that the Scrabble facts are *independently* this way, and not that, fades away not for lack of accuracy, but for lack of intelligibility.

So it may seem that at least some of the facts about Allison's vacation could not have been what they are had there not been human cognitive intervention. This will not come as much of a surprise, since the part of the story on which we have been focusing, the Scrabble game, involved an obvious artifact. And who would have thought to deny the importance of a human contribution in making the facts about artifacts what they are? Perhaps, then, it would be best to move on to some other aspects of our vacation tale and see how things fare there.

IS NEW JERSEY AN ARTIFACT?

Allison, it should be recalled, was to be found in New Jersey. And various facts about her final vacation day involve her being there. So some of the facts about Allison's summer idyll are what they are because New Jersey is what it is. It could not be the case that Allison was vacationing at the New Jersey shore were New Jersey a landlocked state. But we may ask once more, how many of the facts about New Jersey are what they are independent of any conceptual work—in this case, independent of our conceptually marking off boundaries betweeen land masses and reaching agreement to divide the country into political or social units of a particular sort?[6]

New Jersey, for example, is small when compared with Texas and Montana. New Jersey has a specific, distinctive shape, it lies on the Atlantic Ocean, and it contains more than 120 lakes but no major coal deposits. These are the facts. These, though, are not facts about they way the world is, features the world possesses in and of itself, that we merely seek to uncover. For had our forefathers not decided that New Jersey began here and ended there, there would be nothing to determine or make it so that New Jersey is pointy at its southern extreme or that New Jersey abuts the Atlantic, has so many bodies of inland water, and has only so much coal within its confines. If the boundaries of New Jersey had been drawn differently, or if they were to change, the New Jersey facts, perforce, would not be the same. The properties New Jersey has depends, in part, on what, if anything, we make of New Jersey.

There is, though, a sense in which it may be said that this is not so—that New Jersey may have had some of its features eternally, or at least without regard to any of our doings. The particular clump of matter that the label 'New Jersey' picks out, *it*, tautologically—or, perhaps, necessarily—always had its specific size and shape and contained within itself all it contained. One might even be tempted to say that it had its very same form and place before ocean erosion and glacial activity made its boundary features manifest. *That* mass of stuff has whatever shape and location *that* mass of stuff has. Or, in general, whatever is, is as it is. Still, it does not follow that the sundry New Jersey facts initially cited were out there all along, independent of our bringing it about that there is such a geographic unit as New Jersey and setting its dimensions. By drawing the boundaries differently, we might have made it so that New Jersey was more rectangular, had two more lakes, and had no immediate access to the Atlantic.

Thus, we play a role in fashioning what the New Jersey facts are. To maintain that, in this way, we help make New Jersey what it is, or is like, goes beyond the claim that all words, 'New Jersey' included, are meaningless marks without human practice or convention. For not only do we partake in determining how the phrase 'New Jersey' is to be used, at the same time, we help determine the way the world is—that New Jersey's features are as they are. Admittedly, we no more physically make *it*, the stuff out of which New Jersey is carved, than the sculptor makes the marble from which the statue emerges. But as the sculptor shapes what the figure is like, we shape what New Jersey is like. And, in so doing, we contribute toward its being the case that *it* is New Jersey and, hence, toward what the New Jersey facts really are.

Our fashioning of New Jersey, however, is not entirely arbitrary or simply a matter of wish or fiat. There are physical as well as political constraints on what we can do. Attempt to draw all the boundaries 150 miles east, and there no longer is a land mass suitable to be an inhabitable territory or state. Instead, we have a piece of the Atlantic not within United States borders. Likewise, we could not merely decide and, by so doing, make it the case that New Jersey has all the features we would want it to have. We did all right in making New Jersey a seaside state and, accidentally perhaps, in including a lot of lakes, but we could not set the boundaries where they are and make it so that New Jersey has plentiful coal. What's more, coastal erosion may affect the facts about New Jersey's size and shape in ways that go beyond our conceptual resources to resist.

But is New Jersey an artifact? Notice that our contribution toward the facts about New Jersey required no physical fabrication. We did not physically carve New Jersey from its background matter to make its shape and other features stand out. Nor is New Jersey like a poem or a promise, an artifact whose very embodiment is in words. If New Jersey is an artifact, it is of a different sort. But is it an artifact? Fortunately, there is no need here to resolve the question of New Jersey's metaphysical status. Artifact or not, the facts about New Jersey are dependent on our activities of categorization and classification. If we are to look for states of affairs untinged by cognitive intervention, we must, again, look elsewhere.

THIRTY DAYS HATH SEPTEMBER

Our brief story located Allison in time as well as space. To be more specific, we may now record that Allison's triumph occurred at 9:00 P.M. on August 31, 1985. These are the temporal facts. But what is it that makes these facts so? What is it that makes the day the event took place really part of August rather than part of September, or determines that 9:00 P.M. is not already into the next day? More generally, where are we to assign responsibility for such temporal facts as: August precedes September, September has thirty days, the number of days in a month varies but the number of minutes in an hour is constant, and sixty seconds make a minute?

As opposed to Scrabble jokers and New Jersey, the lack of material bulk and substance tends to make us less ready here to think of months, days, hours, and so on, as eternally in the world, just waiting to be accurately described. The mind boggles at the idea of Agusut with its thirty-one days, being following by September, and each constituting one month of a twelve-month year, as entities and properties inherent in the very way the world is. In turn, there is little attraction to view true statements about these temporal matters as simply reflecting Reality correctly—a testimony to our ability to cut up the universe at its pregiven or natural joints. Indeed, there is a strong temptation to think of these facts as matters of mere convention. In seeking to give order to our experiences, we impose a temporal framework on the world and locate events in this human-made network. The length, size, and order of temporal units are themselves, then, facts about our imposed framework.

To the extent that temporal facts are thus seen as conventional, our original claim that in fashioning concepts and categories, we help determine how things are, could not possibly be controversial. For on this account, cognition is given *full* credit for these facts. There is, however, a price to pay in making this move. The price is that these temporal facts are no longer understood as being "about the world"; rather, they are just descriptions of our cognitive constructs. But surely we cannot assume that all states of affairs with a temporal component are simply matters of convention. The fact, for example, that Allison's lucky draw was on August 31, and not September 1, is as much a function of how she spent her time as of how we drew up the calendar. Analogously, that it is the case that I missed my dental appointment by one-half hour depends, in part, on how we shape and delimit the boundaries of the hour and related temporal units. Nevertheless, adopting a different set of time conventions will not, by itself, make me on time and the dentist now free to see me. So how much, if any, of these facts is conventional?

This question is an old one, and the moral to be drawn from the difficulties resolving it is of some vintage too. The appropriate place to draw the line between truths of convention and truths of fact is anyone's guess and might itself best be seen as a matter of convention. Moreover, wherever the line is drawn, it will remain, at most, a fragile border. And this fragility is only heightened when we reflect on facts with a temporal dimension. The hope of finding a fixed solid demarcation between the conventional and the nonconventional would seem no more likely to be fulfilled than the hope of finding a significant boundary between the analytic and synthetic, artificial and natural kinds, and kindred notions.

But this is not the place to argue that no serviceable conventional/nonconventional distinction can be drawn. Nor is it necessary to deny that, for certain purposes at least, truths can be placed at different points along a spectrum between the two extremes. For our concerns, it is enough to note that the world no more comes ready-built with months, days, minutes, and seconds than it does with Scrabble jokers and New Jersey. Which expanses of time are Augusts and which are minutes is as much a function of our cognitive activities as which pieces of wood are Scrabble jokers and which expanses of land constitute New Jersey. Accordingly, the pure and simple temporal facts about Allison's vacation are not to be found out there, all complete, independent of our doing. Rather, in fashioning our categories of temporal order, we help carve out what the temporal realities of the world really are. Admittedly, to maintain that the events of Allison's vacation could have no temporal place independent of our activities of cognitive organization may seem paradoxical. It's just that the alternative of seeing them as having definite temporal dimensions independent of any scheme of ordering is not such an appealing idea either.

Our construction and choice of temporal frameworks is not, however, arbitrary, the result of free flights of fancy. Nor is successful adoption of a scheme constrained solely by the demands of felicitous conversation. We could not set up twelve-month years with thirty-five days to each month and keep the seasons in their place. Likewise, we could not allow the number of months in a year to vary annually, without giving some yearly elected officials more power than others.[7] The existence of such constraints, though, does not mean that the time schemes we have adopted are unique or sacrosanct. Alternates have been proposed, and incompatible systems are even today found in use. Furthermore, there may not be one best way to meet all the demands and constraints we would like to meet. The Gregorian calendar will make it so that the shortest and longest days of the year are regularly six months apart, but then the phases of the moon will occur at varying times. With other systems, the moon will be found to be on a more regular schedule, while the solstices may lose their "natural" periodicity. Intercalating with occasional "leap seconds" (i.e., seconds with more milliseconds in them) might make calendars simpler and the seasons more constant, yet it would complicate our efforts to describe the speed of light, or to determine and compare the radiation frequencies of distant stars. Compromises may have to be made, but what else can we do? To attempt to determine the temporal patterns and regularities of these astronomical phenomena, as they really are in and of themselves, independent of any time scheme, is to attempt to resolve questions that can no more be sensibly asked than answered.

STARS AND THEIR HEAVENLY BODIES

Talk of astronomical phenomena points us skyward, raising once again thoughts about our power to make and create heavenly bodies. Moreover, this issue could not have been avoided. For Allison's vacation ended on a starry night, and there could not have been a starry night without stars, and glowing ones at that.

But people don't make stars! Any claim that they literally do, would require stretching our understanding of the word 'make' beyond reasonable bounds. Now, I am not convinced that this is so, nor am I clear how one might resolve this linguistic point. Still, I see nothing to be gained in arguing over the correct English usage of this term. I do wish to maintain, nonetheless, that the facts about stars are inextricably enmeshed in our cognitive and theoretical enterprises. Such facts can no more be divested entirely of their conceptual shaping and molding than can the various other facts discussed hitherto. Whether there are stars, and what they are like, are facts that can *emerge* only in our attempts to describe and organize our world. The world is not given to us readymade with stars, any more than it is given to us readymade with Augusts and Septembers. As we play a role in delineating what part or parts of the earthly universe are New Jersey, so we help determine what bits of heavenly stuff are stars. And as the very property of being a Scrabble joker (or what it is to be an object having this or related properties) would lack form and content out of its setting in the sphere of human activity, so the property of being a star would lack definitive character and boundaries until fashioned in the course of describing the heavens and accounting for its doings.

Each of the objects that falls under the label 'star' exhibits an unlimited number of features, but what makes them each a star has to do with the commonalities among the set. Yet, commonalities are all too easy to find. Any set of items can be understood to be a grouping based on some commonality or other. What is important for being a star is sharing the right features. But which features are the appropriate ones, and what makes this grouping or kind the star-kind, is not to be found written in the stars. Rather, the significant likeness we find among stars *derives* from our efforts to come to terms with our heavenly environment. What counts for real likeness and makes an object really of the star-kind depends on which features are taken as salient or worth paying attention to.

Unless our theories made prominent the features they do, there would be no basis for seeing the sun and the North Star as being more alike than the Evening Star

(Venus) and the North Star. By assigning importance to some features and downplaying others, our descriptive schemes shape what constitutes astronomical sameness—that which members of the star-kind must share. The property of being a star is not preformed, merely awaiting a verbal label. The property itself—or, better perhaps, which items have the property—requires cognitive construction and molding. In seeking interesting ways to classify heavenly bodies and to make alliances between these kinds, we thus provide a basis for its being the case that this and not that, the sun and not the Evening Star, are stars.[8]

The sun is a member of the class of stars, in part because we have brought it about that the features the sun has count. We help make it that it is reasonable or right or appropriate to group the sun, but not Venus, with the North Star as members of the same astronomical class or kind. In so doing, we also help select or carve out just which class is the class of stars, the class to which the label 'star' truly applies. In this sense, then, we may be said to play a role in making this class the class of stars.

There is, of course, another sense in which the class of stars existed and always contained the members it does, independent of any human intervention. Classes, after all, are tenseless abstract objects, individuated on the basis of the members they contain. So conceived, class identity and class membership do not depend on the foibles of our activities of categorization and classification. Still, whether the members of this class, rather than that class, are stars is not so independent. The question as to which class constitutes or is the star class, the class whose members really are stars, requires a human touch. Prior to our efforts to group, describe, and interrelate our groupings, no one particular class could possibly lay claim to being the class of stars. For in what would such a fact lie?

But stars existed long before anyone thought up the idea of a star and elaborated theories as to their nature. So unless we are willing to countenance some mysterious type of backward causation, how can their existence depend on our doings? Well, in much the same way as, and in the same sense that, Scrabble jokers, New Jersey, and Augusts depend on our conception for their being, or rather for their being what they are. There would seem to be nothing particularly puzzling, for example, in the fact that our temporal constructions establish the basis for precalendar Augusts as well as more recent ones. In the process of fashioning classificatory schemes and theoretical frameworks, we organize our world with a past, as well as a future, and provide for there being objects or states of affairs that predate us. Although these facts may be about distant earlier times, they are themselves retrospective facts, not readymade or built into the eternal order. They are facts that "fall out" of our attempts to give structure to our world. In the absence of such cognitive work, the facts about stars—how many there are, whether the sun is a star, whether stars are sources of light—lack the wherewithal to be facts, to be the way the world really is.

But surely we are not free to conceive of stars any way we like or, as a matter of whim, to decide that some arbitrary class is the class of stars, or that some randomly chosen item belongs to that class? Certainly not! There are constraints on our scientific schemes of classification and organization, as there are on any conceptual system that is to serve a useful purpose. And in earlier sections of this paper, several of the different sorts of constraints that impinge on our constructive activities have been noted. Yet, must it not be admitted that the constraints on devising adequate astronomical concepts are quite different from those involved in setting up a system of rules for Scrabble or in mapping our territories or in ordering time? Right again! The constraints on creating intellectually interesting games differ from those we attempt to satisfy in devising insightful explanatory and predictive theories about the heavens. But, then again, the constraints on game-making also differ from those involved in organizing land masses into socially coherent subdivisions or in ordering time into usable units. In turn, these latter differ from each other, as well as from the pushes and tugs that constrain our shaping of stars. What's more, there is little reason to assume that the practices, needs, assumptions, interests, and types of data that impinge on astronomical theorizing can in any rich, illuminating sense be seen as all the same as those that influence our cognitive efforts in mathematics, taxonomy, geology, psychology, economics, computer science, and history, let alone those that influence and shape our attempts at making serviceable maps, revealing portraits, or frutiful moral codes.[9]

Doesn't the important or real difference lie in the fact that our efforts to organize the heavens are constrained by the way the world is, by an unyielding Reality? Well, aren't our other acts of conceptual fabrication also so constrained? Establishing workable boundaries for New Jersey and practical orderings of time can not be accomplished without taking into account how things are. Even in the case of Scrabble, an unyielding Reality obtrudes. We would not have a viable game were the rules to tax the limits of our memory or require levels of visual acuity not humanly possible. And physical law precludes stipulating that Scrabble jokers have a specified size and shape but no mass. In fashioning our categories and concepts, whether in science or in games, we must keep one eye on our world, to see how we are doing. As the sculptor is ever heedful of the limits imposed by the materials he or she wishes to shape, so the theorist must be responsive to such forces when attempting to carve order into our world.

All useful making, physical or conceptual, is the result of construction and constraint, of give and take. This is abundantly clear. Trouble arises only when it is assumed that there is some unique way to split the process of making into two distinct parts, assigning so much credit to us and the rest to an entirely independent realm— to the world complete with all its properties. For this would require a problematic shift in the nature of the give and take just mentioned. It would require that cognitive construction be simply a matter of *taking* into account what is *given,* and conversely, that what is given is fixed and finished, the way Reality is independent of any of its takings. The difficulty, though, is that this latter notion of the given—the eternal readymade version of the world, untinged by our cognitive efforts—is not a notion we can have much confidence in making sense of. It comes off little better in the case of stars than it does with Scrabble jokers, New Jersey, and August.

But people don't make stars! Of course they don't! We never compressed huge quantities of gas and set them aglow in the heavens above. We did not in this sense make the sun. Similarly, we did not make New Jersey. We never hauled earth masses to a spot between New York and Pennsylvania and there gave it shape. Nor did we ever string together thirty-one days, insert them before September, and, thus, make an August. All of these things existed in the world before we or, perhaps, any fellow conscious creatures stalked about. Our conceptual work was work on what-was-already-there. The stuff or matter or substance was not of our doing, and it had whatever features it had. After all, whatever is, is, in all its full glory. In formulating our concepts and categories, we merely seek to bring some order to what-is-already-there. In the course of this process, though, we help shape the properties by which this organization is to be effected. We lend a hand in carving out the star-kind, along with the Scrabble joker–kind. With the aid of such schemes, it then becomes feasible to see and justifiably claim that these, and not those, are Scrabble jokers; that this, and not that, is New Jersey; that so much, and no more, is one of the Augusts; and that the ones over here, but none of them over there, are the stars. In turn, we give significance and content to the facts these properties are used to describe. *It,* the sun, was in the readymade world all along. Yet, independent of our fashioning the relevant properties and kinds, questions about what *it* is really like have neither any force nor any answers. We did not make *it,* we only helped determine what the facts about it are, which properties it can reasonably be said to possess, and, in particular, whether one of the classes it belongs to is the class of stars.

Put this way, the Realist regains the world—a world untouched either by human hand or mind. It is, however, a stark world, stripped of its facts and properties, bereft of any definite character or nature. If this, then, is all the Realist has to show for denying us the boast of making our world, it is really worth the effort?[10]

Notes

1. The expression "mind-independent and Self-Identifying" is taken from Hilary Putnam, *Reason, Truth and History* (Cambridge, 1981), 54. Various of my views fit in with some of the themes Putnam develops, especially in chapter 3. They also have strong affinities with ideas Nelson Goodman has promoted and defended over the years. And, to an extent I had not realized until recently, they do little more than echo William James. See, for example, *Pragmatism* (New York, 1907), lectures 6 and 7.

2. I wish to stress that my goal is not to convince the reader to be happy with the locution 'making stars'. Instead, like James, it is primarily to contrast "the belief that the world is still in the process of making with the belief that there is an 'eternal' edition of it ready-made and complete." ("The Absolute and the Strenuous Life," *Journal of Philosophy* 4 [1907]:547). Those who cannot bring themselves to countenance my use of 'making' should feel free to substitute such phrases as: 'without such doing there could be no fixed fact of the matter', or 'without such doing our world would no more be *really* this way than that'. These phrases are harder to swallow stylistically but, conceptually, may go down more easily.

3. I believe that the constructive role we play in these next examples interestingly parallels our contribution in the astronomical domain. My hope is that if it begins to seem implausible that the facts in these nonstar cases are entirely independent of us, our confidence that the facts about stars are readymade and complete may also become less firm. Needless to say, I do not wish to deny that there are significant differences among these various cases. But, I think, the differences themselves should be conceived of differently, and when this is done, a better picture emerges of the ways our cognitive efforts help fashion our world.

4. This may seem trivially true to anyone who maintains, as I do not, that in order to be a Scrabble joker, an object must have been used or intended for use in the actual play of a game. I believe, however, that my remarks could be recast citing properties that clearly lack this requirement, properties such as "has all it takes to be a Scrabble joker, save for intended game use" or "physically resembles Scrabble jokers in shape and markings." For without our cognitive contribution, there would be no basis for its being a fact which items had these latter properties too.

It is also important to note that I use the notion of a ''property'' throughout in an everyday sense, with no rich metaphysical or ontological implications. Those committed to the idea that properties are complete, eternal, abstract objects will find my talk of shaping properties out of place. For such persons, my argument would have to be put a bit differently, although its thrust would remain the same. Suppose all the properties $P_1, \ldots, P_n$ are readymade, fixed, and out there prior to our intellectual work. The issue then becomes which of these properties is the property of being a Scrabble joker. My contention is that there would be no basis for singling out one particular property as the property had the game of Scrabble not been devised. That P_{10}, rather than P_{24}, is the property of being a Scrabble joker is not independent of how we fashion and take to applying the concept.

5. To so describe the situation may be misleading if it is thought to suggest that the features themselves just are what they are independent of cognitive construction. But, as I hope becomes clearer in the later sections of this paper, my argument is that what holds for the property ''Scrabble joker'' applies all the way down, to the constitutive features as well.

6. I do not mean to claim that our constructive role with respect to New Jersey is the very same as it is with Scrabble jokers or the other cases to be discussed. I have included a variety of examples because they highlight different points and exhibit interesting differences in the constraints on making. In addition, I use the term 'New Jersey' as short for 'the territory that comprises the state of New Jersey'. As such, it would seem to function more like a definite description than a proper name. I think, however, claims like those presented in this section could be made while construing 'New Jersey' as a proper name, but then there would be some differences in point and argumentation.

7. For an interesting discussion of how these sorts of factors affected the construction of calendars, see *The Encyclopedia Britannica*, 11th ed. (New York, 1910), ''Calendar.''

8. Anyone uncomfortable with talk here of making properties is reminded of footnote 4. And let me briefly repeat the point made in footnote 5. The distinction between a property and the features that go into it is a transient one, used only for purposes of discussion. The character of the features, too, is the result of cognitive crafting.

9. I have examined the role pictures may play in making our world in ''The Power of Pictures,'' *Journal of Philosophy* 82 (1985):711–20. Nothing in that paper, any more than in this, demands that we ignore the significant disparities and contrasts among the examples discussed. Indeed, I think a study of the varying kinds of constraints that guide and delimit our cognitive construction in different domains would be most revealing. It is in this context, for example, that I believe interesting questions could be raised as to where, if anywhere, the constraints might be rich enough to rule out all but one organizational scheme, where, as is the case with temporal and geographical mappings, they are likely to allow for a variety of acceptable solutions, and where they may not even preclude alternative systems that irresolvably conflict.

10. This paper was written while I was a Fellow at the Center for Twentieth Century Studies, University of Wisconsin-Milwaukee. I wish to thank Margaret Atherton, Paul Coppock, Mark Kaplan, and John Koethe for their comments and criticism.

Sex, Gender, and Essence

JOHN DUPRÉ

INTRODUCTION

The primary aim of this paper is to show why the assumption that real essences under-lie the kinds we distinguish in scientific investigation is mistaken. I want to claim that this assumption is not merely empirically unwarranted, but necessarily at odds with a genuinely empirical approach to science. Briefly, unless one supposes the discovery of a kind to imply the discovery of an essence, there is nothing more to the discovery of a kind than the discovery of the correlations of properties characteristic of the members of the kind. Since I do not believe that essences are to be found so easily, I shall argue that the importance of the discovery of kinds to the progress of science is much less than is generally supposed.

Although I shall illustrate this argument with a fairly detailed discussion of some specific classificatory concepts, I would like to emphasize at the outset that the role of this discussion is just that—illustration. It would be possible to understand the basic thrust of this argument by reading only the introduction and the conclusion of the paper. However, the cases that I shall discuss should certainly assist in the understanding of the argument (as well, I hope, as having some intrinsic interest of their own). The significant point about the concept of sex is that although it is undoubtedly a concept that has major significance for biology, and although it is also a concept that divides the natural world into well-defined classes, the scope of the generalizations to which it gives rise is at every stage an empirical matter. In its briefest outline, the force of my argument will be that if a real essence is to serve any purpose, it must at least determine the scope of generalizations covering the entities that realize it. But, for a serious em-piricist, there is never any reason to suppose that this can be done.

The case of sex is particularly revealing because despite the extreme sharpness, by biological standards, anyway, of the cleavages it makes in the organic world, it turns out that there is neither evidence nor reason to expect that it gives rise to any general-izations across the broad categories that it defines. The concept of gender, a concept that has received a good deal of elaboration and clarity from the last fifteen to twenty years of feminist scholarship, has been developed in ways that demonstrate that one cannot assume that the intersection of biological sexual categories with some smaller biological category will give one the appropriate scope for generalization. Even as applied to one species, *Homo sapiens,* the scope of generalizations restricted to male or female is a purely empirical matter and, in most interesting cases, far narrower than that of the entire species.

I shall begin the paper with a brief explanation of what I understand by essentialism, or, at any rate, of the sense in which I shall claim that it is objectionable. I shall also mention some immediate difficulties that it presents in the context of biology. I shall, then, discuss first sexual categories, and then gender categories, as illustration of the impossibility of extrapolating from the existence of a kind to the scope of any generalizations about its members. In the discussion of the latter categories, I shall mention some of the reasons for confidence that the sex/gender distinction cannot be dissolved. In conclusion, I shall argue that the cases considered point to fundamental defects in the essentialist point of view, and that this point of view should be abandoned rather than modified.

ESSENCES

In thinking about essences, it is first necessary to distinguish two very different functions that they may be supposed to serve. First, essences are often conceived as properties that determine the answer to the question to what kind the object that instantiates them belongs. But, second, essences are also thought of as determining the properties and behavior of objects that instantiate them.

Within the first type of function, we can introduce the familiar Lockean distinction between real and nominal essences. The view that nominal essences determine the kinds to which objects belong amounts to little more than the introduction of a bit of technical terminology. A nominal essence is connected to a kind by some sort of linguistic convention. Since it is obvious that we could not refer generically to members of any kind without the existence of some linguistic convention determining the (at least approximate) limits of that kind, the existence of nominal essences as characterized above is not controversial. More detailed description of nominal essences may certainly commit one to more or less powerful semantic theses—for example, to the view that there must be necessary and sufficient conditions for the application of every classificatory term—but will carry no metaphysical commitments.[1] My concern in this paper will be solely with real essences.

To assert that there are real essences is, in part, to claim that there are fundamental properties that determine the existence of kinds that instantiate them. The existence of such properties will have profound metaphysical consequences: in particular, it will imply that the existence of kinds of things is as much a matter of fact about the world as is the existence of particular things. Such kinds are quite independent of our attempts to distinguish them, and their discovery is part of the agenda of science. It is consistent with at least the majority of modern usage to take the previous sentence as providing a necessary and sufficient condition for the existence of a *natural* kind, and I shall hereafter use that expression in that way. It is important to note, however, that although the existence of a real essence is, then, sufficient to determine the existence of a natural kind (ignoring possible problems about noninstantiation), it does not follow that a real essence is necessary. As a matter of fact, I believe that there are natural kinds without real essences, unless perhaps in an almost vacuously attenuated sense.[2]

I would also like now to emphasize a point that will be central to the argument I have in mind against essentialism. This is the observation that even if a kind *is* determined by a real essence, it is hard to see what route there could be to the *discovery* of essences other than the prior discovery of kinds. This should immediately lead one to entertain serious doubts about the empirical credentials of such essences. In particular, if this epistemological point is correct, we should be very suspicious of any practical consequences that appear to follow from the existence of a real essence. In the remainder of this section I shall develop the concept of a real essence so as to try to show that if the existence of a real essence amounts to anything, it does, indeed, have practical consequences—specifically, in entitling us to anticipate the existence of laws governing the behavior of objects that partake of it. In the following two sections, I shall illustrate the fact that the differentiation of kinds entitles us to no such anticipation. The conclusion that will be developed in the final section of the paper is that discovering kinds does not involve discovering essences; and so, given that there is no other way of discovering them, nothing does.

However, to return to the main thread of the argument, it does seem that, barring the most radical and implausible nominalism, there must be *something* to the doctrine of real essences as so far described. Some kinds are, at the very least, more natural than others. The class of creatures with wings and feathers, for example, is more natural than that of creatures that are gray and over one foot long. This is so because when we know that a creature belongs to the first class, we can make numerous further reliable predictions about it—that it, or its female relatives, lays eggs, is warm-blooded, and so on. Membership of the second class carries no such benefits. Depending on how deeply we can explain such clustering of features, we can adduce more or less powerful characterizations of real essences. If, to take one extreme case, God had simply chosen to assemble creatures in the light of some preconceived ideas of which features went well together, the real essences might amount to no more than conjunctive, or perhaps partially disjunctive, descriptions of God's aesthetic preferences. Since these descriptions would still reflect genuine clusterings of properties, they would at least be natural kinds and would exhibit, in a sufficiently weak sense, real essences. However, we naturally believe that the discontinuities in nature admit of somewhat deeper explanations, and this leads us finally to the second, and much more problematic, function of real essences, that of explaining the nature of the members of the kinds that such essences determine.

The strongest possible notion of a real essence would be that of a property, or group of properties, that determined—and, hence, in principle could be used to explain—all the other properties and behaviors of the objects possessing them. Although such a notion *might* be defensible for individual essences (Locke seems sometimes to have envisaged the microstructural description of an object potentially playing such a role), it cannot work for the type essences that are my present concern. This is for the simple reason that there is no kind (with the possible exception of the ultimate microphysical kinds), the members of which are identical with respect to all of their properties, even their intrinsic ones. I say "intrinsic" properties because it is obvious that the *behavior* of an object will typically depend on both its intrinsic properties and its external environment. Clearly, the strong view I am considering should claim only that essence determines behavior as a function of some set of external variables, or, in other words, determines precisely specifiable dispositions to behavior. However, variation in intrinsic properties requires a more fundamental retreat from the strong position. Specifically, some distinction between essential and accidental properties, that is, between properties that can and those that cannot vary between members of a kind, is unavoidable.

A promising and natural modification of the strongest conception of real essence, which provides a way of drawing just the distinction mentioned above, is the following: the essence of a kind determines just those properties and dispositions of its instances for which it is a matter of natural law that members of the kind will exhibit those properties or dispositions. The essential properties of members of a kind will then be, first, the real essence itself, and, second, those properties and dispositions nomically determined by the real essence. The rest will be accidental. Thus, for example, it is clearly no law of nature that squirrels are gray, since many are black. On the other hand, perhaps it is a law that squirrels have tails,and, hence, tailedness is an essential property of squirrels. An essentialist holding the position I am now suggesting would explain this by saying that the essence of squirreldom, perhaps a particular genetic structure, determined the growth of tails, but not a particular color of coat. The suggestion that the essence might be the genetic structure illustrates another important aspect of such a position, the way that the essence itself is to be distinguished from other essential properties. Presumably, the genetic structure causally determines the growth of a tail, and not vice versa. Thus, the essence itself is that property that is explanatorily primary among the set of essential properties.

Making such an essentialism applicable to any part of biology—and, probably, to most other parts of science—requires some important qualifications. To begin with, it is very difficult to find really sharp distinctions anywhere in biology; generally, there is a range of intermediate cases. Certainly, as far as taxonomic distinctions are concerned, sharp boundaries are the exception rather than the rule. Thus, a theory of essences would have to be considered as applying to typical members of kinds rather than to all members. Assuming that it remains desirable to attribute individuals to kinds despite their abnormality, the laws applying to such kinds could be only probabilistic. The probability that something has a tail, given that it is a squirrel, would then reflect the frequency of the abnormality of tail-lessness. The modified essentialist position could be maintained by insisting that there is, nevertheless, some standard genetic structure that constitutes the essence of squirreldom, and that anything that perfectly realizes this structure would, as a matter of nomic necessity, have a tail. Less-than-ideal squirrels would then be judged to be squirrels, or not, on the degree of similarity of their genetic structure to this standard form. It will be apparent, however, that this unavoidable modification leaves the essential/accidental distinction rather more arbitrary than might have been wished. It is, at least, unclear whence the fundamental difference between blackness and tail-lessness of squirrels derives—apart from a patently question-begging appeal to the essential nature. If it comes to no more than a quantitative difference in frequency, then a fairly arbitrary decision is required to include one (or its genetic basis), but not the other.

Many philosophers of biology would wish to mitigate this difficulty by denying that taxonomic distinctions define kinds at all, and a fortiori, that they are natural kinds that could admit of real essences.[3] I myself believe that species (higher taxa I assume to be purely nominal kinds) are kinds rather than individuals. However, I doubt that the present problem will be much mitigated by denying that species are kinds. Whatever kinds one happens to favor in biology (e.g., ecological or evolutionary), one is unlikely to find the sharp boundaries that would evade the present difficulty. A striking illustration, which will be discussed in detail in the next section, is that of sex. It would be hard to imagine a more obviously natural division within biology than that between male and female. Yet in sexually dimorphic species there are typically variations with respect to sexually specific characteristics, and even genuinely intermediate individuals. At any rate, the distinction btween fairly sharp boundaries between kinds and absolutely sharp ones is itself an absolutely sharp one, so that the advocate of biological kinds that completely evade the present problem will have a difficult task.

Part of my reason for emphasizing this difficulty is to stress the detachability of a belief in natural kinds from a belief in essences. The belief that there are discontinuities in nature to be discovered rather than invented is quite independent of the question whether these discontinuities are sharp or gradual. Moreover, the relation of natural kinds to questions of explanation does not depend on a doctrine of essences. One might suppose, for example, that there was some optimal set of laws (perhaps maximally deterministic and/or explanatory) governing a domain, and that the classes of entities recognized by those laws should be considered as natural kinds. Such a view does not require that any fundamental distinction be drawn between the essential and accidental properties of the members of such kinds. Since it will typically be the case that the frequencies of such properties in a kind will vary continuously from almost one hundred percent to almost zero percent, such a distinction appears inevitably arbitrary. But, as I have tried to show, without this distinction, the point of essentialism becomes obscure.

I shall return to the idea that natural kinds should be treated strictly as derivative from the discovery of laws in the final section of this paper. But, for now, I shall move on to discuss more specific cases in detail. This will demonstrate some further and compounding difficulties with the essentialist perspective.

SEX

As promising an essential distinction as one is likely to find in biology is that between male and female. The distinction can be drawn successfully for a very large number of organisms, and although, as I have suggested is true of almost any biological distinction, there are borderline cases, the vast majority of organisms of types to which the distinction applies can be assigned unambiguously to one category or the other.

Another relevant feature of the distinction, although now only for as long as we look at a particular type of organism, is that there are systematic differences between males and females at various levels of structural organization, and that these are causally and explanatorily related. More specifically, for most species, males and females differ genetically, physiologically, and behaviorally; and we are fairly confident that the genetic differences cause the physiological ones, and that the physiological differences cause the behavioral ones.

However, further consideration shows that the situation diverges greatly in certain respects from the essentialist scenario I sketched in the previous section. The properties that are causally fundamental in explaining sexual dimorphism between the members of a species are unquestionably not the properties that realize the real essences (if any) of maleness and femaleness. A microstructurally oriented essentialist might be inclined rashly to assume that the essence of maleness and femaleness for humans was/is the possession, respectively, of an XY or an XX chromosome. But many animals that can be divided into males and females as clearly as humans can have no XX or XY chromosomes. Indeed, this view would seem to imply that to say that there are both female humans and female geese would be a gross equivocation on the word ''female,'' since in each case the word refers to a quite different microstructural property; and this would patently be absurd.

Surely the correct way of describing the situation is to say that *for humans,* having XY or XX chromosomes *causes* individuals to be male or female. What it is to be male or female, on the other hand, is a property at a higher level of structural organization, that of producing relatively large, or small, gametes. It is *this* distinction, based on the fact that most types of organisms have individuals of two kinds distinguishable by a major dimorphism in the size of the gametes they produce, that is referred to by the general categories of male and female, and that in particular species is caused by a particular genetic dimorphism.[4] Thus surprising, and even paradoxical, though it may seem, it is correct to say that physiological differences between the sexes, and any genetically determined behavioral differences that there may be, are not, in fact, caused by the sex of the organism; rather, these differences and the sex of the organism are joint effects of a common cause.

In this light, it is *not* surprising that the sexual categories have little explanatory power. It is very doubtful, that is, whether there are any very significant laws relating to males and females in general. It seems plausible that every generalization about a sexually specific characteristic is limited to some narrower group than that of all sexually dimorphic species. In some cases, there is a recognized taxon over which the generalization applies, either because the character concerned is an evolutionary novelty in a phylogenetically demarcated taxon, typically a species, or because that very character is used to define the higher level grouping, as with mammals, or placental mammals.

Although the possibility cannot be ruled out a priori that there might be some properties universally, or almost universally, correlated with large or small gamete production, there seems to be no reason to expect that this will be the case. This observation invites reconsideration of my claim that sexual categories are exceptionally promising candidates for biological natural kinds. The intuitive basis for that claim certainly has nothing to do with a knowledge of laws pertaining to males and females in general. It is based, rather, on two kinds of observation. First, that within any species, and often within much larger taxa, there are very pervasive sex-specific generalizations to be made. Men grow or shave beards, and women have breasts; males and females of large numbers of (related) species have relatively similar genitalia. And, second, for enormous numbers of species, it is possible to distinguish males from females. However, what these observations properly suggest is that sex is a very significant property that may be appealed to in the analysis of innumerable different taxonomic groupings but that, nevertheless, it is not a property that is sufficient to define any significant kind. Alternatively, if one wishes to insist that males and females *do* form natural kinds, then there are natural kinds with little or no explanatory power.

The fact that nature can be "carved at the joints" without yielding explanatorily significant categories is worth a moment's reflection. The explanation in this case is not hard to find, deriving from a very fundamental fact about biology: biological kinds reflect historical similarities as much as they indicate similarities of causal power. The divide between males and females, as general categories, derives not from characteristic properties or dispositions of the two classes but, presumably, from the existence of a very pervasive evolutionary tendency toward sexual dimorphism.[5] But it seems likely that the common evolutionary pressure may do no more than favor a simple dimorphism of gamete size, and that subsequent elaborations of the dimorphism may well be much more specific to particular evolutionary lineages, and not susceptible to large-scale generalization.

Two responses to the preceding argument need to be considered. First, I have so far ignored a trend in contemporary biology that *does* want to maintain the general explanatory power of sexual categories. By this, I mean a major area of sociobiology. And, second, one may accept the general conclusion that I have argued for above and yet explore the possibility of defining narrower, but still explanatorily powerful, sexually delimited kinds. I shall now briefly discuss these positions. The second will lead conveniently into the topic of gender.

I cannot hope to give an adequate treatment here of the highly problematic and controversial discipline of sociobiology.[6] However, one major area of sociobiological theorizing does assert precisely what I have said there is no reason to believe: that the simple fact of gamete size dimorphism strongly disposes species to certain subsequent evolutionary developments, specifically, to quite well-defined behavioral dimorphism. At its most general, the theory asserts that those organisms with smaller gametes (i.e., males) will tend to develop behavioral strategies that maximize the dispersion of their gametes, while the females will develop strategies that tend to increase the chances of successful development for those offspring that they are able to assist. At this very general level, the theory is based simply on the idea that a large gamete is a more significant investment of resources than a small one, and this will give dispro-portionate encouragement to strategies that tend to further its development. If there is any force to this argument, there is obviously a lot more to it when the reproductive physiology of the organism requires that much larger investments of resources are de-manded for the female to have any chance of reproduction, as is the case of viviparous animals or animals that lay large eggs. Additionally, in such cases it is argued that when the offspring, or egg, is produced a substantial time after fertilization and re-quires further care to have any chance of survival, the female will find herself playing an evolutionary game with no cards. The male, it is argued, will by then have taken off to attempt to impregnate more females, and the only way that a female can expect to have any reproductive success at all will be to provide at least the essential minimum of parental care.

The most obvious defect with this argument is that the predictions to which it gives rise do not turn out to be true. Many species, even of birds and mammals, are quite monogamous in both sexes, and there are many species in which the male pro-vides as much parental care as the female, or even more. But I shall not attempt any evaluation of the general force of this sociobiological argument, since the preceding simple observation is sufficient to demonstrate the conclusion I wish to draw for my present purpose. This is simply that however significant a *force* in evolution these ar-guments may indicate, that is all they indicate. Clearly, if there is such a force, it is one capable of being overridden by other forces that operate in an opposing direction; oth-erwise, there could not exist the many exceptions just mentioned. (The same point can, and will, be made in connection with alleged systematic differences beetween men and women.) It might be thought that since I have allowed that dispositions com-mon to members of a kind suffice to give that kind explanatory power, the above con-cession would be sufficient to constitute sexual categories as natural kinds. But this would be a confusion based on the failure to distinguish historical from causally ex-planatory categories. It may be that in every species there has been an evolutionary tendency for males to acquire dispositions to promiscuity and females to acquire dis-positions to parental care. But in many cases those dispositions have not been actual-ized; and, hence, the members of many species do not have those dispositions. A drake, say, may have no disposition whatever to desert his mate. And it would be ab-surd to say that he must have such a disposition merely on the grounds that his ances-tors had some, in fact unrealized, tendency to evolve such a disposition. So, in short, whatever the force of these sociobiological arguments, though they may help to ex-plain the particular behavioral dimorphisms in particular species, they do nothing to make males or females into genuinely explanatory kinds.[7]

The second response I described above was to accept that sexual categories are not themselves explanatory kinds but to argue that more narrowly defined sexually specific categories might, nevertheless, be so. Thus, male and female mammal, goose and gander, and man and woman may constitute sex specific natural kinds with ex-planatory force regardless of whether male and female are themselves such kinds. Two general points should be made about this proposal. First, assuming, which I would be very reluctant to do for any taxonomic level above the species, that the taxon that is being sexually restricted is a genuine kind, this is not a case of the intersection of two kinds, but one of the subdivision of one kind. This is simply the application of the main conclusion of the present section about general sexual categories. But second, there is certainly no a priori objection to the internesting of natural kinds. There is nothing incoherent, for instance—though there is, almost certainly, something false—in conceiving biological taxonomy in this way. Metal and iron provide one plausible example. Human and woman might be another.

It is worth mentioning that the viability of this proposal will depend on accepting that some taxonomic groupings are, indeed, natural kinds. For one who believes that species are individuals (see note 3), it would be quite extraordinary to suppose that these individuals might be formed from the union of two kinds. However, this is not the place to pursue that issue.

It seems that there is nothing deeply wrong with this idea provided one registers some important qualifications. In particular, it would be absurd to suppose that man and woman, say, were "better" kinds than human. To admit that species are kinds is to admit that kinds may encompass very considerable variation and, hence, license only probablistic nomic generalization. Moreover, as I have argued earlier, it is to admit that kinds can be considered as defined by essences only in the most attenuated sense of "essence." It would, again, be absurd to suppose that the essence of woman was any more clearly definable than the essence of human. But, in fact, one would predict the opposite. Since the similarities between men and women are vastly more numerous than the differences, one would expect the latter kinds to be "worse." And the problems with defining an essence of woman must surely, then, be more severe than those of defining an essence of human.

My final point follows, once again, from the fact that male and female are not themselves explanatory kinds. The explanatory significance of sexually specific kinds must be wholly empirically determined. No systematic differences between the males and females of a particular species can be assumed beyond those that are used to distinguish the sexes. This does need slight qualification. Sometimes one can appeal to higher-level generalizations. If one discovers a new species of mammal, one will reasonably anticipate that dissection will reveal an approximately familiar and sexually dimorphic type of reproductive physiology characteristic of mammals. However, I know of no other type of property for which, in the case of higher animals at least, such broader generalizations would be of any use. Certainly, there are none in overt morphology beyond similarities of external genitalia in related taxa; and more importantly, there are none in the area of behavior, or again, none that extend beyond very narrowly defined phylogenetic groups. And, as I have insisted, none can be deduced from the mere fact of subsumption under the broad sexual categories. Accepting, then, the possibility, if highly qualified, that species as kinds may be subdivided into sexually specific subkinds, it is now time to look in more detail at the human case and to turn to the topic of gender.

GENDER

The term "gender," as it has been developed in contemporary feminist theory, refers to the sexually specific roles that are occupied by men and women in various societies.

The most obvious reason for insisting on a sharp distinction between sex and gender[8] is that whereas whatever properties may follow from the sex of their bearers, such as reproductive physiology and secondary sexual characteristics,[9] must be equally prevalent in all societies, it is quite clear that gender roles, on the contrary, are highly variable and culture specific in many respects. So even if man and woman as biological categories are modestly explanatory natural kinds, it is clear that much of the behavior encompassed under gender roles is no part of what they explain.

It is not altogether easy to assess the *extent* of variability in gender roles. One reason for this is that a great deal of the relevant research is particularly susceptible to the kinds of problems to which feminist critics of science have drawn attention; if there is any part of science for which the accusation of distortion by male-biased preconceptions seems particularly plausible, this is surely it.[10] But both anthropological and historical evidence leaves little doubt that such variability is extremely widespread.[11] Some particularly noteworthy areas are those that have been of special prominence in attempts to reduce gender specific behavior to a causal consequence of sex. Promiscuity, and the extent to which it is a male prerogative, provides one important example. Also of interest is the variability in the extent to which the generally socially approved form of gender specific behavior is adhered to or insisted upon. The prevalence of, and attitudes toward, homosexuality and incest, both subjects that have received a great deal of attention from sociobiologists, appear to be highly variable. The prima facie evidence seems to be that in most of the aspects of behavior that suggest sexual dimorphism in the context of a particular culture, there is a great deal of cross-cultural variation.

Before continuing this discussion, it will be useful here to recapitulate a little, and explicitly to reintroduce the topic of essentialism. One traditional view might be the following. Both humans and males constitute natural kinds with a certain essential property. To be a male human is to partake of both the relevant essential properties, and much of the behavior of a male human can be explained by reference to the causal powers of one or both of these essential properties. Against this I have argued that the most that can be sustained is the claim that male humans form a subkind of humankind. If this kind has an essential property, it is presumably a combination of the essential genetic structure of humans with the specifically sex-determining genetic features of male humans. The reason that the essentialist is forced into this specific, and, I suspect, rather unpromising, form of genetic determinism is precisely that maleness in general is not an explanatory category, and the only available candidate for an explanatory essence for the kind of human males must be their distinctive genetic features. Unpromising or not, there are certainly those, certain sociobiologists providing their theoretical wing, who want to maintain a position of this kind and trace the behavioral differences between men and women to the genetic.

A major thrust of the feminist research that has emphasized the historical and anthropological variability of sexual differences in behavior has been explicitly directed against positions of this kind. Its aim has been to establish that these differences are to be understood in terms of social forces, which are fairly specific to particular

cultures. It has also offered alternative schemes of explanation, perhaps the most influential and interesting of which are those that trace these differences primarily to the
action of economic forces and conditions.

It would be an oversimplification to suppose that feminist scholarship fits uni-
formly into this agenda. To begin with, there are some feminists who would pretty
much accept the essentialist structure that I have just outlined, while objecting only
that the details have been filled out in a way revealing profound male bias. Most noteworthy in this category are a small number of feminist sociobiologists.[12] But more significantly, a markedly essentialist flavor has often been detected in a good deal of
more mainstream feminist thought.[13] Indeed, it may even be suggested that the very
intelligibility of feminism depends on construing women as a natural kind and, hence,
on accepting essentialism. Although there may be some feminist projects that do, indeed, depend on this assumption, in most cases such suspicions are ill grounded. It
will be worth a short digression to indicate why this is so.

It is easy to overestimate the prevalence of essentialist assumptions in feminist
writing by failing to identify its primary goals. A great deal of emphasis in feminist
work has been accorded to one observation that strongly appears to be a cross-cultural
universal, namely, that men seem invariably to have achieved a position of domination over women. I do not think it would be unfair to say that this is often seen as the
central theoretical problem of feminism. And if the central theoretical problem is one
of explaining a universal fact about the relation of men and women, it is not surprising
that much of the writing has a rather essentialist flavor.

But it is crucial not to overlook the fact that feminism, perhaps more than any
other area of academic interest, is at least as much a political movement as a theoretical
inquiry. From a political point of view, the universality of male domination is clearly
of paramount importance. The political achievement of feminism may be described
without exaggeration as the discovery and definition of an entire political class ignored by traditional theories. Nevertheless, the political significance of patriarchy
should not blind us to the fact that from the point of view of the purely theoretical task
of understanding sex and gender categories, this fact is anomalous rather than central.
A brief consideration of the reasons for this will also help to forestall any tendency for
the universality of male domination to serve as a motivation for a crudely biological
theory of gender differences.[14]

Although I would readily concede that if male domination is a universal or near
universal phenomenon throughout human societies, it is a phenomenon well worth
theoretical study, there is no reason whatsoever for taking this as contradicting the basic variability in human sexually differentiated behavior. In the first place, it is only
one case to set against many. But even this way of putting the case is misleading; male
domination is a phenomenon on a higher level of abstraction than is the characterization of particular forms of behavior in particular societies. There is no reason to suppose that the exercise of male domination is itself something that has always been
implemented by the very same kinds of behavior. On the contrary, the kind of labor
that women perform for men is quite different in, say, feudal societies, hunter-gath-
erer societies, and modern industrial societies; and the social institutions and personal

interactions that enforce such performance are equally variable. Hence, the *implementation* of male domination—which is what we should consider, rather that its mere existence, if we are evaluating the plasticity of behavior—far from contradicting the variability of gender roles, graphically illustrates it. Analogously to my conclusion for the case of sex, there may be good reason to suppose that human sex differences give rise to forces that have some tendency to bring about male supremacy. But, as in the previous case, although the existence of such a force may be of use in explaining the genesis of a particular gender-differentiated society, it does not pick out any property that characterizes the present state of that society. In this case, even if male supremacy is genuinely universal, the enormous variability in the form that it takes indicates extensive interactions with more specific forces that, in turn, show that there are no grounds for assuming that even the abstractly characterized consequence is in any way inevitable.

Returning now to the main theme of my argument, as in the broader case of sex in general, the question we should consider is whether even man and woman (in their biological sense) are genuinely useful explanatory categories. I have conceded that as purely biological kinds, they are largely unobjectionable; it may be allowed as a modest nomic generalization, for example, that humans born with penises will tend to grow facial hair later in their lives. But there is a very powerful tendency to extend the relevance of explanatory categories beyond their empirically determined limits—a tendency, I am suggesting, that derives philosophical nourishment from the idea that when one has distinguished a kind, one has discovered an essence. If, in fact, the empirical significance of the kinds man and woman does not go beyond some systematic, if quite variable, physiological differences and the observation that men appear to have achieved a dominant position in all or most societies, the kinds distinguished seem of very modest significance. Certainly, nothing in those empirical facts provides the slightest motivation for thinking that these categories should be accorded fundamental importance in explaining the particular forms of behavior found in very different social systems, whether such explanation is motivated by sexist apologetics or (misplaced) feminist ardor.

The conclusion I want to defend might be stated as follows. Just as the concept of sex in general will do very little to explain why peacocks, but not turkeys, have long tails, or why the prairie chicken, but not the goose, is polygynous, so the notion of woman will do nothing to explain why Oriental women once had their feet mutilated, or why twentieth century Western women are more likely to become nurses than doctors. In principle, the same move is open to one as was suggested at the conclusion of th discussion of sex in the previous section. It would be possible to suggest that the appropriate explanatory categories were again to be narrowed, so that for behavioral explanations, the relevant classes would be as specific as female 'Kung or male Spaniard. At this point, however, the claim to have identified even the most attenuated natural kinds would be impossible to sustain. The claim to have identified a natural kind must involve the idea that the behavior of its instances depends, in some cases, on intrinsic properties of the individual characteristic of members of that kind. But it would be hard to find even the most bigoted racist nowadays prepared to assert that the social interactions characteristic of a man raised in, say, rural Spain would have been just the same if that individual had been brought up in a wealthy California suburb. To concede that explanations must appeal to kinds with that degree of specificity is to concede beyond serious argument that it is local, presumably cultural, factors that determine the relevant forms of behavior.

MORALS FOR ESSENTIALISM

I would like to take the discussion of the preceding two cases to illustrate a general argument against essentialism. The main thrust of this argument is to plea for complete empiricism with regard to the explanatory potential of particular kinds. My suggestion is that a belief in real essences either is vacuous or violates this demand. In partial reaction to this point, I shall also suggest that attention be drawn away from the attachment of fundamental importance to the delineation of kinds, and directed toward the identification of properties, dispositions, and forces. To connect these points, what makes a kind explanatorily useful is that its instances share the same properties or dispositions and are susceptible to the same forces. But since we have no way of deciding how much of such concomitance to expect in any particular kind, the discovery of a kind adds nothing to the discovery of any correlations that may turn out to characterize it. An essence, as I characterized it in the first section of this paper, can be seen as a promissory note on the existence of such correlations. It is a promissory note that empiricists should reject. I take the preceding discussion to illustrate this point in the following way: it is easy enough to distinguish classes at many different levels of generality—males, male vertebrates, men, Irishmen, and so on—but there is nothing in this process of differentiating classes that provides any basis for predicting the extent to which its members will be amenable to lawlike generalizations. Finally, this in no way impugns the theoretical significance of the *properties* on the basis of which such classes are differentiated (I shall elaborate on this remark with regard to sex below).

The most powerful example I have offered in support of this plea is the case of sex in general. As I said in the course of discussing sex, what we see is that there are major seams in nature that not only fail to distinguish robust natural kinds, but also fail to distinguish classes that realize any general lawlike regularities. The explanation in this case is simple enough: the seam reflects a presumably uniform type of historical process rather than the discrimination of any causally uniform type of entity. But it is hard to see what could be the basis for postulating the existence of a natural kind, in the strong sense of a set of common possessors of a real essence, except either the perception of a natural seam among phenomena, or the discovery of one or more laws satisfied by a class of phenomena. In the first case, as the example of sex shows, the inference to a natural kind would be illegitimate; and in the second case, unless it constituted a quite ungrounded assumption that further hitherto undiscovered laws were in the offing, it would be wholly redundant.

Having rejected the idea that general sexual categories could provide a basis for lawlike generalization, I then considered the possibility that far more restricted sexually specific categories might still constitute natural kinds in the strong, essentialist sense. I do not mean to claim that this possibility has been—or, for that matter, could have been—rigorously explored in the space I have allowed. However, the issue of gender shows, at least, that it cannot generally be assumed that such kinds are discoverable. Here again, it is not difficult to see what is going on. Many factors affect human behavior, including behavior that is gender differentiated. Looked at in this obvious way, it would be foolish to assume that there were forms of behavior that were determined simply by the agent being, say, a human male—still less by the agent being merely a male. Nevertheless, unless we are careful to restrict the import of our categories to the empirical, we are in danger of being led into just such an assumption.

I should emphasize that I do not take myself to have shown any particular limits on the nomic significance of sexually defined categories in general. In the case of humans, there are good reasons for doubting whether this significance extends beyond the purely physiological. In many other species, there are undoubtedly good generalizations to be made about sexually dimorphic behavior. My point is not that sex is a scientifically useless concept, but rather that from a conceptual standpoint that seeks kinds and their underlying essences, one is very likely to misrepresent that significance. I should now, therefore, say something very briefly about how I do understand its significance.

To begin with, nothing I have said contradicts the idea that sex is a highly significant *property*. By that, I mean that sex is a property that, in a sufficiently specific context, is frequently susceptible of lawlike generalization. At a certain time of year, for instance, the males of a particular species of bird produce very characteristic and predictable noises. If you know the time of year and the species of bird, what you additionally need to know, if you want to predict whether it will make that noise, is what sex it is.

No doubt of more theoretical interest are the ways that sex connects with evolution. At the most theoretical level, there is the question of the origin and maintenance of sexual reproduction. Since sex seems, prima facie, such an extraordinary waste of reproductive energy from the point of view of most females, this is a very baffling question. On the other hand, this very problematic nature of the phenomenon makes it likely that there is some powerful evolutionary process at work. At a less general level, as Darwin emphasized at great length, the existence of sex can have profound effects on the particular course of the evolution of a species. Thus, I am far from denying the biological interest of sex. What I want to claim is that the way in which the basic sexual categories—male, female, neuter, hermaphrodite—divide the natural world tells us nothing about either the extent to which such categories will give rise to general laws or, more importantly, what will be the scope of whatever interesting laws do involve those categories. It is the denial of this latter point that, I believe, is required to provide any motivation for an essentialist position and that, I have argued, is very difficult to reconcile with the range of phenomena I have been discussing.

Let me conclude with a word about natural kinds. There is certainly no harm in calling a set of objects that are found to have a substantial number of shared properties a natural kind. I want to insist that the discovery of such a kind provides no basis for the supposition that some particular property or properties can nonarbitrarily be singled out as essential. But, as I remarked earlier, there is no reason why the term "natural kind" should be wedded to essentialism—or, anyway, no more reason than an accident of linguistic history that can readily be rectified. With this proviso, I am quite happy to refer to species as natural kinds. This case is unusual, in that we do have reason to expect that members of species will share a large number of properties, this reason being that we suppose the members of the species to have come about through an extremely homogeneous historical process. However, this in no way contradicts my insistence that the extent of homogeneity within a kind should be treated wholly empirically. Members of a species, as I have remarked, also vary greatly. And we cannot know a priori how variable any particular feature will turn out to be.

The only thing that could provide grounds for dispensing with this empirical stance would be if we were somehow to know that the members of certain kinds were completely homogeneous in all respects. Many people seem to believe that this is true of the kinds distinguished by physics and chemistry, though I find this doubtful.[15] If it is, physics and chemistry are in a very important respect different from biology. But even if this is the case, it is surely an empirical fact, not anything that could be known a priori. It is surely possible to conceive of a world composed of indivisible atoms, each as different from one another as one organism is from the next. Such would not appear to be the case; but *how* homogeneous physical or chemical particles may be remains an empirical matter. If this is correct, even microphysics cannot provide a hiding place from the categorial empiricism that I am advocating.[16]

Notes

1. This claim is, of course, controversial in the light of the well-known views to the contrary of Kripke (1972) and Putnam (1975). I have argued against these views elsewhere (1981). The possibility of deriving essentialism from semantic considerations has also been attacked at length by Salmon (1981).

2. This is a reasonable way of interpreting the conclusion I formerly defended about species (1981).

3. Classic statements of the view that species should be treated as individuals have been made by Hull (1976) and Ghiselin (1974). An excellent sense of the present state of the debate can be gleaned from Kitcher's (1984) attack on the view and Sober's (1984) reply.

4. An interesting paper by Michael Lavin (unpublished), primarily addressed to some philosophical problems that arise from gender reassignment surgery, includes a persuasive argument for the view that what we mean in ordinary language by "male" and "female" has nothing to do with either genetic or general biological considerations, but is derived wholly from considerations of gender, that is, of socially constructed conceptions of what it is to be male or female in our society. Although I am entirely sympathetic to this view, I hope it is clear that it is these more technical considerations that are relevant to my present discussion.

5. The nature of this pressure, however, remains surprisingly obscure. Excellent sources on the problem are Williams (1975) and Maynard-Smith (1978).

6. The classic text on sociobiology is Wilson (1975); a highly readable popular introduction is Dawkins (1976). The enterprise has come under devastating attack from Lewontin, Kamin, and Rose (1984) and, perhaps a little more sympathetically, from Kitcher (1985).

7. Kitcher (1985, especially 166–76) shows clearly the internal weakness of this sociobiological argument.

8. Some feminists, notable among them Alison Jagger (1983, 112) now want to resist drawing such a distinction between sex and gender, on the grounds that it erroneously suggests that the sexual side of the dichotomy is rigid and unchanging; and that, in fact, there is a continuous dialectical interaction between

cultural and biological aspects of gender differentiation. Nancy Holmstrom (1982) develops a similar position and defends the conception of a distinctively female nature, on the basis that ''nature'' should be understood in a way that encompasses both biological and culturally determined aspects, since she also denies that these can be intelligibly disentangled. Although I do not want to take issue with this view and willingly disavow any implication that there is some readily distinguishable set of immutable biological differences between men and women, I believe that my appeal to this distinction in the present context is both useful and harmless.

9. Secondary sexual characteristics—for example, the distribution of body hair—in fact show considerable geographic variability. If Darwin was right in attributing the majority of geographical variations among humans to a process of sexual selection (see Darwin [1981], especially chs. 7, 19, 20), this is hardly surprising.

10. See, e.g., Longino and Doell (1983); Reed (1978).

11. A good illustrative source is the collection of essays in Ortner and Whitehead (1981). It should, perhaps, be mentioned that these authors have more interesting and ambitious goals than merely establishing gender role variation. Ortner and Whitehead's introduction *begins* with the sentence: ''It has long been recognized that 'sex roles'—the differential participation of men and women in social, economic, political, and religious institutions—vary from culture to culture.'' Nevertheless, for anyone who doubts this claim, these essays include ample evidence.

12. See, e.g., Hrdy (1981). At a more popular level, an entertaining feminist answer to Desmond Morris is Morgan (1972).

13. Jagger (1983) suggests that a commitment to biological determinism is a characteristic defect of the school of feminist thought she describes as ''Radical Feminism.''

14. As that, e.g., of Steven Goldberg (1973). Unfortunately, it is also my impression that some feminists have been led by the same observation in the same direction though certainly those who, like Goldbertg, see male aggressiveness as the crucial, and even biologically grounded, factor are likely to point out that aggressiveness is not necessarily an unqualified virtue.

15. I have briefly defended this claim elsewhere (1983, 326–27).

16. I would like to thank the Pew Memorial Trust for a grant that supported the initial stages of this research, and the Stanford Humanities Center where it was completed.

References

Darwin, Charles. 1981. *The Descent of Man, and Selection in Relation to Sex*. Princeton.

Dupré, John. 1981. ''Natural Kinds and Biological Taxa.'' *Philosophical Review* 90:66–90.

——————. 1983. ''The Disunity of Science.'' *Mind* 92:321–46.

Ghiselin, Michael. 1974. ''A Radical Solution to the Species Problem.'' *Systematic Zoology* 23:536–44.

Goldberg, Steven. 1973. *The Inevitability of Patriarchy*. New York.

Holmstrom, Nancy. 1982. ''Do Women Have a Distinct Nature?'' *Philosophical Forum* 14:25–42.

Hrdy, Sarah. 1981. *The Woman Who Never Evolved*. Cambridge, Mass.

Hull, David. 1976. ''Are Species Really Individuals?'' *Systematic Zoology* 25:174–91.

Jagger, Alison. 1983. *Feminist Politics and Human Nature*. Totowa, N.J.

Kitcher, Philip. 1984. ''Species.'' *Philosophy of Science* 51:308–33.

——————. 1985. *Vaulting Ambition: Sociobiology and the Quest for Human Nature*. Cambridge, Mass.

Kripke, Saul. 1972. ''Naming and Necessity.'' In *Semantics of Natural Language*, edited by D. Davidson and G. Harman, 253–355. Dordrecht.

Lavin, Michael. Unpublished. ''On the Moral Permissibility of Sexual Reassignment Surgery.''

Lewontin, Richard, Steven Rose, and Leon Kamin. 1984. *Not in Our Genes: Biology, Ideology, and Human Nature*. New York City.

Longino, Helen, and Ruth Doell. 1983. ''Body, Bias, and Behavior: A Comparative Analysis of Reasoning in Two Areas of Biological Science,'' *Signs* 9:206–27.

Maynard Smith, John. 1978. *The Evolution of Sex*. Cambridge and New York.

Morgan, Elaine. 1972. *The Descent of Woman*. London.

Ortner, Sherry, and Harriet Whitehead. 1981. *Sexual Meanings*. Cambridge and New York.

Putnam, Hilary. 1975. "The Meaning of 'Meaning'," "Is Semantics Possible?" and "Explanation and Reference," In *Mind, Language, and Reality, Collected Papers, Vol. II*. London and New York.

Reed, Evelyn. 1978. *Sexism and Science*. New York and Toronto.

Salmon, Nathan. 1981. *Reference and Essence*. Princeton.

Sober, Elliott. 1984. "Discussion: Sets, Species, and Evolution: Comments on Philip Kitcher's 'Species'." *Philosophy of Science* 51:334–41.

Williams, George C. 1975. *Sex and Evolution*. Princeton.

Wilson, Edward O. 1975. *Sociobiology*. Cambridge, Mass.

Part-Time Objects

PAOLO DAU

The claim that enduring objects have temporal parts, that is, that they are made up of temporal slices, segments, stages, or phases, has had distinguished exponents and critics alike. The exponents—McTaggart and Quine come readily to mind[1]—appeal to temporal parts in order to explain a number of otherwise puzzling phenomena, notably the problem of persistence through change. Critics—good examples being Chisholm, Geach, and Thomson[2]—have responded by charging that the view that enduring objects have or are made up of temporal parts is a "crazy metaphysic," in Thomson's phrase.

Temporal parts have also been connected with mereological essentialism in interesting ways. Some have suggested that mereological essentialism—the thesis, in Chisholm's words, that for all objects x and y, "if x is ever part of y, then y is necessarily such that x is part of y at any time that y exists" (1976, 149)—follows from the claim that objects are made up of parts *at all*;[3] others have claimed that mereological essentialism can be avoided only by espousing the thesis that enduring objects have temporal parts;[4] and still others may think that understanding enduring objects to be made up of temporal parts (or in any case of temporal slices) is, in effect, to *concede* mereological essentialism in the strict sense.

In this paper, I shall explore the connections between mereological essentialism and the thesis that objects have temporal parts. I shall first set out several formulations of the view that enduring objects have temporal parts, and consider some of the objections typically raised against that view. I shall then go on to examine the implications of that view for mereological essentialism.

I. TEMPORAL PARTS

It is important to be clear from the start about what it is that we are entitled to expect from a doctrine of temporal parts. We are entitled to be told what a temporal part of a continuant *is,* and to be given examples of temporal parts. And we are owed an account of the connection between temporal parts and the continuants of which they are parts, an explanation of what is meant by calling such things *parts* of their continuants.

Each component of the doctrine depends directly on the conception of an enduring object—specifically, of a physical object—with which we begin. Here is Quine's (1982) view:

> A physical thing—whether a river or a human body or a stone—is at any one moment a sum of simultaneous momentary stages of partially scattered atoms or other small physical constituents. Now just as the thing at a moment is a sum of these spatially small parts, so we may think of the thing over a period of time as a sum of temporally small parts which are its successive momentary stages. Combining these conceptions, we see the thing as extended in time and in space alike; the thing becomes a sum of momentary stages of particles, or briefly particle-moments, scattered over a stretch of time as well as space. (269)

Quine's position combines two quite independent ingredients. The first is the conception of a physical object as "the material content of a portion of space-time" (1981, 92); indeed, on a strong version of this Quinian view, any portion of space-time with some material content determines a unique physical object. The second is the view that physical objects are sums of "successive momentary stages." (The notion of 'sum' employed here is that developed in the calculus of individuals (*CI*). It is discussed in some detail below.) Although the two views are independent, there is, of course, a connection between them: thinking of physical objects spatiotemporally is apt to lead us to regard time as spacelike and, therefore, to predispose us to be more receptive to temporal parts, construed now on a close analogy to spatial parts. In fact, the conviction that space and time are similar in important respects, so that lasting through time is understood as analogous to extending through space, is often the principal support for the metaphysics of temporal parts.[5]

This view of physical objects is, however, not the only one possible. It is not even the ordinary view. David Wiggins (1980), no friend of temporal parts, recommends instead the conception of enduring objects as "three-dimensional continuants—things with spatial parts and no temporal parts, which are conceptualized in our experience as occupying space but not time, and as persisting whole *through* time" (25). Thus, according to the picture Wiggins defends, there is a fundmental asymmetry between space and time. Whereas at each (spatial) point occupied by an object, what we find is a part, and not the whole, of the object, at each instant at which a continuant exists, we find the whole continuant, and not a part or phase or stage of it.[6]

Now it is certainly more difficult to make sense of the notion of a temporal part on the three-dimensional view of physical objects than on the four-dimensional, spatiotemporal view. If for no other reason, this is because we ordinarily understand the notion of a part materially, or more precisely spatially, so that parallels with and analogies to the spatial properties that underlie the applicability of this notion of a part become very important. Thus, to the extent that extension and duration are held to be disanalogous, we will find it proportionately more difficult to make sense of the notion of a temporal part. This is not to say, however, that a different notion of part (for example, that appropriate to the claim that Canada is part of the United Nations, or that respect for one's elders is part of good manners) could not be invoked in explicating the concept of a temporal part.

Moreover, even within the confines of Wiggins's rigid conception of continuants, it is still possible to make sense of the concept of a temporal part. To begin with, the notion can be introduced by stipulating that each continuant counts as a temporal part, albeit an improper one, of itself. The notion of a temporal part becomes particularly apposite when we expand our ontology of individuals to include agglomerative physical objects of various kinds. Some of these will intuitively have proper temporal parts. For example (niceties aside), Congress has a natural decomposition into two-year temporal segments: here, the notion makes good sense, and is not unmotivated. Of course, it is possible to maintain that collective entities such as Congress are best understood as abstract objects (for example, sets, either of persons or of sets of persons). But this will require the introduction of special senses for the predicates we customarily and unproblematically use in talking about such entities. Congress began some two hundred years ago and will eventually no longer exist; it deliberates, sometimes procrastinates, listens to the President, and is presently located in Washington. Introducing special senses for such predicates (set-deliberates, set-listens) is both counterintuitive and ad hoc. Whether amoebas, dogs, and automobiles also have proper temporal parts—perhaps by being themselves regarded as aggregative entities of the right kind—is something that should be left to the appropriate experts to determine. (I also leave open for the moment whether agglomerative physical objects are always best understood as fusions, that is, sum individuals in the *CI* sense, of their parts.) In any case, there is room in Wiggins's three-dimensional account of physical objects for the notion of temporal parts.

II. PART-OBJECTS

The attempt to introduce the notion of a temporal part into the three-dimensional account of physical objects also serves to isolate a secondary thesis that is evidently a source of considerable discomfort for many critics of the metaphysics of temporal part. We can best set out this thesis by taking up the three-dimensional view once more.

On *any* viable conception of physical objects, it must be true that ordinary physical objects have physical parts. But this truism does not decide the ontological status of the parts into which ordinary physical objects can be fragmented, sundered, or decomposed. Granted that a table, to take a simple and straightforward example, could be broken down into adjacent vertical strips one inch in width, or, indeed, into any one of a large number of different classes of arbitrarily selected, jointly exhaustive, regional subparts, it is not at all clear that it would be correct to claim that the table is presently made up or composed of those parts. By contrast, it seems right to say that the table is made up of a top and (let us suppose) four legs, and that *these* parts are genuine objects in their own right. To be sure, the marks of 'genuineness' in the sense in question here are both varied and vague. For an undetached part to be a genuine object, it must in some sense be a unitary thing, independent and self-subsistent.[7] Not all the parts into which a physical object can be broken down will have these traits. The intuition with which we are working, then, is that ordinary physical objects have *some* decompositions yielding proper parts that are genuine objects, substances in their own right, even if other possible decompositions do not. Let us call such undetached constituent parts of a physical object its *part-objects*. The thesis that all viable accounts of physical objects must validate is, then, that (ordinary) physical objects are made up of part-objects. The temporal analogue of this thesis is that continuants are made up of temporal part-objects—part-time objects, so to speak.

Now, in each case, for the notion of physical parts and for the notion of temporal parts, it is possible to make a much stronger claim. The *plausibility* of this claim will depend both on the general conception of physical object with which we are operating, and on the particular kind of physical object we have in mind. To take the most favorable case, consider a quantity of some substance, say a glassful of water. Supposing that we take the matter making up this portion of water to be a genuine object in the first place, it seems intuitively correct to say that it is arbitrarily decomposable into part-objects. *Any* subregion of the region occupied by that matter determines a part-object of the original chunk of matter.[8]

I see no reason why the advocate of physical (or temporal) parts must make comparable claims about trees, automobiles, or people. They need not deny that any subregion of the region occupied by the stuff making up such an object corresponds to a legitimate part—a genuine part-object—of the stuff making up the object. This does not mean that it corresponds to a legitimate part of the object. In espousing the thesis that ordinary physical objects are made up of parts, they need not accept the claim that such objects are made up of arbitrary undetached parts. To force on them the stronger claim is *ab initio* to privilege the view that such an object is to be identified with its stuff: an identification certain to make much more difficult any subsequent distinction between constitution and identity, for example, or, for that matter, a rejection of mereological essentialism, at least for those who think of the matter making up an object in spatial, and not spatiotemporal, terms.

Of course, opponents of the notion of a temporal part have typically directed their criticisms at a theory that they construe as claiming that continuants are made up of arbitrary temporal parts. The theory to which they object, in other words, is (roughly) one according to which *any* subinterval of the interval of time during which a continuant exists corresponds to a temporal part-object of that continuant. Such critics are, therefore, likely to be unimpressed by the modest role for temporal parts that I have suggested could quite naturally be introduced even within the three-dimensional conception of physical objects. Perhaps a sufficiently modest ontology of temporal parts would prevent some of the characteristic applications of the notion. Certainly a theory of temporal parts according to which each continuant is made up of infinitely many, arbitrarily demarcated temporal part-objects is much more powerful, and is a much more attractive target for criticism. But we are entitled to be told in clear terms just what the objections to such a theory amount to. There seems to be two quite different kinds of objection one could direct against such an account. The first is the objection that the very notion that a continuant is made up of temporal parts is incoherent; incoherent, for example, in the way in which it has historically been claimed that the very notion that a substance—hence, monadism—has parts is incoherent. The second kind of objection is directed at the claim that each of the infinitely many different possible temporal subdivisions of a continuant corresponds to a part-object of that continuant; compare, the claim that each of the infinitely many different possible spatial subdivisions of a physical object corresponds to a part-object of the physical object in question. As a matter of fact, critics of the theory of temporal parts have claimed that their objections are to the very *notion* of a temporal part. Hence, if the difficulties they produce are actually due to an arbitrary ontology of temporal parts, their criticisms are, at the least, misleading, if not outright misplaced. Conversely, a theory that proposes an arbitrary ontology of temporal parts is not licensed in its profligacy by the very notion of a temporal part. It must look for a defense of its ontological excesses in the service of temporal parts elsewhere, in other features of the theory.

III. THE SPATIOTEMPORAL VIEW

A combination of the spatiotemporal conception of physical objects and an identification between such objects and the matter making them up provides us with the framework needed in order to make some sense of arbitrary temporal parts.

On the ordinary, three-dimensional conception of physical objects, an object occupies a certain spatial region at each instant it exists. For our purposes, spatial regions can be thought of as point sets, specified by means of tuples of reals. Of course, a considerable amount of idealizing is necessary in order to suppose that the region occupied by a typical physical object is at all precisely defined, but we may let that pass. Now, on this conception, it would clearly be a mistake to think that the entire object is to be found in any proper spatial subregion of the region it occupies at any time. The entire object occupies the entire region and is bounded by its outer surfaces: it is what fills the whole region at that time. A similar point will form part of the four-dimensional version of the account of physical objects.

It is also worth noting from the start that in speaking of objects as occupying regions of space, we are committed neither to the claim that matter is indefinitely divisible, nor to the claim that all the subregions of an occupied region are themselves occupied. A great deal depends on how the region associated with a physical object at a time is conceived. Perhaps the most natural picture here is that proposed by van Inwagen (1981, 135): start with the material object (at a time), and define the region it occupies as the set of points 'within' it. If we do this, then we shall certainly have to hold that many of the subregions in question are neither occupied nor occupiable.[9] This means that if we intend to define our arbitrary spatial or temporal parts by reference to associated subregions, we shall need to be more careful. The machinery developed by Cartwright (1975), following suggestions of Tarski (1983, 24–29), can be employed to this end. Very roughly, we should think of the region occupied by an ordinary physical object at a time as obtained by taking the union of a large class of disconnected small open balls (in the topological sense). The idea is that we take only the regions occupied by the small particles making up the object, and leave out the spaces in between. If current scientific accounts of material objects are even approximately correct, then ordinary objects turn out to be what Cartwright calls 'scattered' objects. Since this result does not at all presuppose the notion of a temporal part, it will be useful to keep it in mind throughout later discussion.

On the four-dimensional account, too, we can regard a physical object as the material content of a region, but now a region of space-time. Thus, the region in question bounds the object not only spatially, but temporally. On the three-dimensional conception, the entire object is to be found at each instant that it exists. On the four-dimensional conception, this is a mistake. The object fills the region of space-time; the entire object no more exists at one instant and lasts whole to another than, on the three-dimensional picture, the object begins at one place and lasts whole to another. Just as we would reject the claim that the entire pencil exists at the tip and at the eraser—rather, the pencil is the object extending from the tip to the eraser—so, too, we should reject the claim that a physical object exists at this instant and at that—rather, it is the object existing from the first instant to the second.

In terms of this conception of physical objects, the notion of temporal part is easily enough introduced. A temporal part of a physical object is, intuitively, a temporal slice or cross section of that object. Thinking of physical objects as the material content of regions of space-time, we may define temporal parts of such objects as the material contents of the temporal cross sections of the region filled by the object.[10] The thesis that physical objects have arbitrary temporal parts comes from holding that each temporal subregion determines a temporal part of the object: keeping in mind that we are talking about the material content of a region that can be so defined as to be completely filled will help this thesis sound less implausible. It may, perhaps, be worth noting that the three-dimensional notion of a spatial part can also be introduced within this framework.

The parallels between extension and duration exploited by the temporal parts theorist should not be taken as suggesting that there are no differences between spatial and temporal parts. The spatial parts of an ordinary object are usually objects of a different kind, while the temporal parts of an ordinary object are objects of the same kind with most of the properties of the whole object. Thus, although the spatial parts of my automobile are not themselves automobiles, its temporal parts are merely shorter-lived automobiles:

> The temporal parts of an enduring thing would have been perfectly good things of that kind if they had existed on their own, without the other phases which in fact preceded and followed them, while this is very seldom true in the analogous spatial case: the spatial parts of a thing, conceived as existing in spatial disconnection from each other, are not things of the same kind.[11]

By combining the notions of temporal and spatial parts, we get the notion of a spatiotemporal part, which, applied to filled regions of space-time, then yields the notion of a concrete space-time portion of matter. This is Quine's particle-moment. In the manner suggested by Quine, it can serve as the building block by means of which we can work our way back to ordinary objects, construed now as temporally and spatially segmented sums.

IV. "A CRAZY METAPHYSIC"

A theory along these lines makes a convenient focus for the objections to the notion of temporal part recently developed by Thomson (1983). Thomson has a quite different conception of physical objects, but it is not entirely clear what her views come to. She seems to hold that a (possibly quite large) number of different physical objects can coincide spatially, and even that two physical objects can agree completely in respect to their positions and their physical properties. Whatever the details of her account may be, two things are reasonably clear. The first is that some of the more peculiar features of her account result from trying to avoid mereological essentialism; the second is that she rejects the metaphysics of temporal parts.

Thomson's objections to the "crazy metaphysic" of temporal parts deserve careful examination. As we shall see, they also call for considerable care in disentangling their various sources. One such source is Thomson's conviction that if temporal parts of physical objects are to be taken seriously, they must really be *parts* of physical objects, concrete objects in their own right. In particular, for Thomson, any account that treats a temporal part as a set-theoretical entity (for example, as an ordered pair made up of an object and a stretch of time),[12] or as merely a *façon de parler*,[13] is of no interest. Thomson's requirement that temporal parts turn out to be concrete objects seems to me reasonable. Its imposition is the business of her first metaphysical thesis, issued on behalf of the 'friends of temporal parts' (1983, 206):

(M1) If x is a temporal part of y, then x is part of y.

This thesis also points the way to the solution to a problem exacerbated by Thomson's generous ontology of temporal parts: what is the relation between a continuant and its infinitely many different temporal parts? The answer is to be found in the calculus of individuals,[14] in which Thomson embeds her version of the theory of temporal parts. The calculus of individuals is supposed to characterize the part-whole relation, and thanks to the mediation of the thesis (M1), it can be applied to temporal parts. This application proceeds by means of one of the characteristic notions of the calculus, that of the *fusion* of individuals. One individual fuses others just in case anything discrete from—having no common content with—the first is also discrete from all the others, and conversely. That is, where '$x \, D \, y$' symbolizes 'x is discrete from y', and '$x \, \mathrm{Fu} \, S$' symbolizes 'x fuses [the set of individuals] S',

$$x \, \mathrm{Fu} \, S =_{\mathrm{df}} (y) \, [y \, Dx \equiv (z)(z \in S \supset y Dz)].$$

Now one of the axioms of the calculus of individuals is what we may call the *fusion principle*,[15] which states that

(FP) $(\exists x) \, (x \in S) \supset (\exists y) \, (y \, \mathrm{Fu} \, S)$.

(Uniqueness can be proven within the calculus.) It is by means of this machinery that a continuant is related to its temporal parts, namely, as their fusion.

Of course, all this still leaves the exact nature of a temporal part unspecified and imprecise. Thomson proposes the following reconstruction. Letting 'P' range over places, 't' over instants, and 'T' over stretches of time (including instants), Thomson defines a *cross-sectional temporal part* (1983, 207):

D1.: x is a cross-sectional temporal part of $y =_{\text{df}}$
$(\exists T)$ [y and x exist throughout T & no part of x exists outside T & (t) (t is in $T \supset (P)$ (y exactly occupies P at $t \supset x$ exactly occupies P at t))].

(Here 'x' and 'y' are variables ranging over physical objects and their parts.) Then Thomson's version of the thesis that continuants have temporal parts is given by what we may call her *fission principle,* the metaphysical thesis that

(M2) (T) [y exists throughout $T \supset (\exists x)$ (x exists throughout T & no part of x exists outside T & (t) (t is in $T \supset (P)$ (y exactly occupies P at $t \supset x$ exactly occupies P at t)))].

So it would seem that, according to Thomson, a cross-sectional temporal part of a continuant y is an object that comes into existence no earlier than y, ceases to exist no later than y, and coincides with y perfectly at each instant that it exists. Her fission principle, then, asserts that a cross-sectional temporal part of y corresponds to each stretch of time throughout which y exists.

Plausible though this reading is, it is not entirely correct. A sure sign of this is the fact that Thomson goes on to give a second definition of what she calls a *temporal part*:

x is a temporal part of $y =_{\text{df}}$
$(\exists T)$ [y and x exist throughout T & no part of x exists outside T & (t) (t is in $T \supset (P)$ (y exactly occupies P at $t \supset x$ exactly occupies P, or a place in P, at t))].

This cannot be right. From the lump of clay in my basement, I make a crude statue of Winston Churchill. His right hand is the bit I do last. One could argue that the statue exists even before the right hand is finished; no matter, under the circumstances, the right hand begins to exist no earlier than the statue. Dissatisfied with the results, the next day I destroy the statue. I am careful to begin by destroying the right hand first. One could argue that the right hand ceases to exist before the statue does; no matter, under the circumstances, the right hand ceases to exist no later than the statue. Of course, at all times that it exists, the right hand of the statue is a (spatial) part of the statue. According to Thomson's definition, the right hand is, therefore, a temporal part of the statue. Something has gone wrong.

Now it is not enough just to discard Thomson's definition D2 of a temporal part. Friends of temporal parts may wish to maintain that St. Paul's Cathedral in 1801 is a cross-sectional temporal part of St. Paul's Cathedral—in any case, McTaggart does (1921, 176). It seems that Thomson's definition D1 won't let him. Surely St. Paul's Cathedral in 1801 was made up of stones that existed long before 1801. Given Thomson's definition, this means that St. Paul's Cathedral in 1801 is not a cross-sectional temporal part of St. Paul's Cathedral for 1801. Something else is, by the fission principle. Moreover, if we give Thomson the additional assumption that for each enduring object, there is a stretch of time T having the property that the object and all its parts exist at all and only the instants in T, we get the conclusion that each object is a cross-sectional temporal part of itself. But, if this is so, then no part of any object can have existed before—or can exist after—the object. In particular, given that the stones that originally made up St. Paul's Cathedral existed before the cathedral, we must conclude that they are not parts of the cathedral. Thomson forces the exponent of temporal parts to precisely such an "absurd result" (1983, 210).

She does so, however, by using a questionable definition and an implausible assumption. It is quite natural, particularly for someone thinking of a physical object as the material content of a region of space-time, to construe the conjunct in Thomson's definition of a cross-sectional temporal part that reads, "no part of x exists outside T," as meaning simply that x does not exist at any instant t not in T. This is not what Thomson has in mind. She means, quite literally, that no physical part of x can exist before or after x. It is because this is built into the definition that, in order to get the apparently plausible conclusion that each continuant is a cross-sectional temporal part of itself, we need to make the additional assumption that each such object exists at all and only the instants at which any of its parts exist. Clearly, this assumption is terribly implausible; it is tempting to suppose that it can be avoided simply by changing the definition to read as follows:

D1*. x is a cross-sectional temporal part of $y =_{\text{df}}$
$(\exists T)$ [y and x exist throughout T & x does not exist outside T & (t) (t is in $T \supset (P)$ (y exactly occupies P at $t \supset x$ exactly occupies P at t))].

Notice that we still need an extra assumption in order to get the desired conclusion that every object is a cross-sectional temporal part (henceforth, temporal part) of itself. But this is now just the assumption that for each physical object x, there is a stretch of time during which x exists and outside of which x does not exist. This amounts to the claim that physical objects exist temporally. With this change, the counterintuitive result that no part of an object can precede or survive the object *seems* to be avoided.

Unfortunately things are not so simple. There is still a problem ahead, but it is because of the calculus of individuals and the fission principle, and *not* because of the notion of a temporal part. The difficulty is this: in the calculus of individuals, every individual is a fusion of all its parts, and the identity of individuals can be shown to amount to their having exactly the same parts. Now, the notion of part is introduced by means of the definition[16]

$x < y =_{\text{df}} (z) (z \text{D}y \supset z \text{D}x)$.

That is, x is part of y just in case everything discrete from y is also discrete from x. So, in the calculus of individuals, objects are individuated by means of their parts, and what counts as a part depends on what sort of overlap there is among other objects. Consequently, the addition of the fission principle to the calculus of individuals, which (intuitively) adds new objects overlapping continuants, forces a finer individuation of those continuants.

Consider my new automobile, which contains an old fuse I got from my neighbor. Surely we want to say that the fuse is part of the automobile. But the automobile is new, and the fuse is several years old. There is, therefore, a stretch of time, say T, during which the fuse exists and the automobile does not. The fission principle tells us that there is an individual x that is the temporal part of the fuse precisely corresponding to that interval T. Notice that this temporal part is an individual in the range of the variables of the system, and that—at least it is plausible to suppose this—it is discrete from my automobile, even if the fuse as a whole is not, since the temporal part in question does not exist at any instant at which my automobile exists. But then, by the definition of 'part' developed within CI, it follows that if the fuse is part of the automobile, that temporal part of the fuse must be discrete from the fuse. This is inconsistent with the assumption that the temporal parts of an object are parts of that object, that is, with thesis (M1) above.

Clearly, there are a number of ways of avoiding this problem. For example, one could reject (M1) and look for another way to ensure that temporal parts are concrete objects. More interesting is to deny that the temporal part of the fuse for the interval T is discrete from the automobile. One way to do this is to construe the automobile as a *scattered object,* made up of continuants that are 'gathered' in different combinations at different periods, then partly scattered again. Thus, the whole fuse is part of the automobile, but it only becomes juxtaposed to the bulk of the automobile's parts after the period T. On this picture, what we call an automobile in our ordinary use of the term is a special stage in the automobile, that temporal part that coincides with the relative cohesiveness of the automobile's parts.

Although not ruled out by CI, this response nonetheless misses the point. The point is that *given* the assumption that the automobile comes into existence after (some of) the continuants that eventually make it up, CI forces us to take *temporal stages* of those continuants as the parts of the automobile. More precisely, given the fission principle and the thesis that individuals that do not overlap temporally are discrete, we are forced to conclude that the automobile has as one of its parts not the fuse but a temporal stage of my neighbor's fuse, namely, the stage that corresponds to the period during which the fuse is located within the automobile. And, in general, we are forced to the conclusion that *all* the parts of a continuant are temporal parts of its continuant part-objects. Thus, returning to the example of St. Paul's Cathedral in 1801, we can see that the parts of this individual are not the stones in the cathedral, but the 1801 stages of those stones. So, too, for the cathedral itself: its parts are not the stones of which it is made, but (roughly) the temporal parts of those stones coinciding with the cathedral's existence. In short, no part of any object either precedes or outlives that object, and Thomson's definition D1. of a cross-sectional temporal part turns out to be correct after all.

The major culprits in all this are CI and the fission principle. Certainly CI has its own independent difficulties: to mention only one, not all agglomerative physical objects can be handled by means of the resources of the calculus of individuals. A central thesis of CI is that although both classes of F's and fusions or sums of F's divide up the universe into the F's and the non-F's, classes have a preferred and unique decomposition into parts, while sums do not. Indeed many complex physical objects have no preferred decomposition; yet it seems equally clear that the notion of part appropriate for other aggregative physical objects is ill served by CI. Canada is part of the UN, and Saskatchewan is part of Canada, but not of the UN. Some might doubt that such collectives are really physical objects, in spite of their having many straightforwardly physical properties; but other examples of aggregative physical entities with a preferred decomposition are easy enough to come by: star clusters, molecules, flocks of geese, and the like.[17] (Compare the answer to the question "How many parts (members, components, constituents) does it have?" asked in such cases as with the answer to the same question asked about a glassful of water.) Perhaps some of the difficulties Thomson finds with her version of the theory of temporal parts are due to the inadequacy of the CI account of the part-whole relation for such cases.

In any case, it should be clear that given a sufficiently rich stock of parts, use of CI will inevitably lead to departures from our ordinary views. Ordinarily, we would say that the United States is part of North America; since Hawaii is not part of North America, we must revise this claim. A correction of this sort is not apt to seem implausible: we commonly decompose geopolitical entities into constituent states, provinces, and counties. But given an ontology of arbitrary undetached geographical parts, we will need to make less intuitive revisions as well. Ordinarily we would say that Lake Champlain is part of New York state; but the northern tip of Lake Champlain is discrete from New York, since it is discrete from the United States. So if we admit such individuals as the northern tip of Lake Champlain and accept the characterization provided by CI, we shall have to conclude that our ordinary way of speaking is inaccurate: Lake Champlain is not part of New York. Strictly speaking, only part of Lake Champlain—the New York part—is part of New York. The similarities between this case and the case of temporal parts of continuants are obvious. Of course, it is possible to avoid having our discourse about geographical parts regimented in this way by reinterpreting the part-whole relation as a three-place relation holding among two individuals and a place. This lets us admit that not all of Lake Champlain is in New York without having to countenance such individuals as the northern tip of Lake Champlain. The entire Lake Champlain, we could then say, is part of New York *here*, but not *there*. Compare: the whole fuse is part of my automobile *now*, but not *then*. Whether this option is attractive depends precisely on the strength of our aversion to the part-objects in question.

Now friends of temporal parts will most likely be entirely dissatisfied by such concessive responses to the intuitive difficulties produced by combining CI and the fission principle. They will insist that a great deal more can and should be said on behalf of the theory Thomson criticizes, and that, indeed, her objections stem precisely from having failed to apply the very conception of physical objects that makes the notion of a temporal part most plausible. It seems to me that a strong case can be made for their claim.

To begin, notice that the very point of the notion of temporal parts is to introduce temporal subdivisions for continuants. Having done so within the scope of CI, we should expect the parts of continuants to be treated in like fashion. Nor is this objectionable: after all, we were to think of physical objects as the material contents of regions of space-time. Surely there is nothing strange about a notion of part that holds that the parts of a physical object are contained *within* the object. But, then, if the whole object is bounded temporally as well as spatially, its parts must be bounded likewise. Now that we can measure along the temporal dimension, we can tell where the parts begin and end temporally. Far from being unreasonable or counterintuitive, Thomson's D1. quite correctly expresses the facts of the matter. Finally, inasmuch as physical objects are thought of as being made up of concrete space-time portions of matter, we should keep firmly in mind a conception of physical objects that treats them as complexes of spatiotemporal particles. Therefore, the parts of physical objects will themselves be such spatiotemporarlly extended complexes. Thomson's (1983) objections derive much of their force from refusing to apply this conception:

> I said this seems to me a crazy metaphysic. It seems to me that its full craziness comes out only when we take the spatial analogy seriously. The metaphysic yields that if I have had exactly one bit of chalk in my hand for the last hour, then there is something in my hand which is white, roughly cylindrical in shape, and dusty, something which also has a weight, something which is chalk, which was not in my hand three minutes ago, and indeed, such that no part of it was in my hand three minutes ago. As I hold the bit of chalk in my hand, new stuff, new chalk keeps constantly coming into existence *ex nihilo*. That strikes me as obviously false. (213)

To be sure, exponents of temporal parts have themselves made similar claims. Salmon writes[18]

> A time-slice of an enduring object, such as a statue, is a temporal "part" of the statue, in much the same way that a cross-sectional slice of the statue is a spatial part of the statue. The enduring statue is "constructed" through time, as it were, from its time-slices. A time-slice of an enduring object may have a very fleeting existence. The statue-during-interval-t exists throughout t, but the statue-at-moment-t' comes into existence in a flash and just as quickly disappears never to be seen again.

The fact remains, however, that any residual puzzlement about Thomson's example is directly due to thinking of physical objects as existing at instants, and not through regions. What Thomson describes as "new chalk constantly coming into existence *ex nihilo*" is actually just different complexes of matter in different places. It is no more surprising, on reflection, that there should be different chalk part-objects at different times than that there should be different bits of chalk at different places (at a time). Misled by her three-dimensional conception of continuants, the friend of temporal parts would say, Thomson is doing the equivalent of looking in different places and finding different objects there. Once again, the four-dimensional conception prevents this kind of confusion.

Although Thomson's objections lose much of their force when applied to a consistently worked out spatiotemporal account of material objects, a great deal of conceptual and linguistic revision awaits us if we try to work extensively within the spatiotemporal view. Perhaps a positive inducement is needed in order to move us to contemplate such wholesale revision.

V. OVERCROWDING

Such inducement may be found in an argument developed by Cartwright, which we shall consider briefly.[19] Suppose that A is any complex physical object, that is to say, one having proper physical parts. For convenience, we may suppose that A has proper part-objects, one of which is B. (Perhaps A is a human body, and B is one of its cells.) Suppose that at time t_1, A loses B—it is simplest if we imagine that B is destroyed at t_1, though nothing vital hinges on this detail. Suppose we let C be the part of A exclusive of B at an earlier time, say at t_0. Our puzzle is as follows.

First, consider the situation at t_0. By assumption, both A and C exist, and it seems entirely clear that A and C are different objects, since they have different physical properties—at the very least, they differ in size and mass, for example. Thus, we have

(1) $A \neq C$.

Next, consider the situation at t_2. It seems clear enough that C survives A's loss of B at t_1: after all, nothing has happened to C itself. Rather, something that was adjacent to C has been removed, and C itself was left untouched. So C exists at t_2. The question of A's existence at t_2 is less clear. Of course, if mereological essentialism is correct, then A does not exist past t_1; but we should be reluctant to accept this thesis in general. We have a strong intuition that ordinary physical objects survive the loss of parts, not in all cases, but in many. A human body, for example, surely would survive the loss of a single epidermal cell. Imagine that we have a case of this sort: then we may suppose that A, too, exists at t_2.

This raises the question of the connection between A and C at t_2. To suppose that A is C, that is,

(2) $A = C$,

will obviously not do. But to deny that A is identical with C seems equally difficult. After all, A and C coincide perfectly at t_2; indeed, we may even suppose that they continue to do so for as long as each exists.

Now, none of these difficulties arise on the four-dimensional conception of physical objects. Thinking of A and C in terms of the spatiotemporal regions they fill, we can readily see that (1) above holds. Moreover, the description of A and C as 'coinciding perfectly' at t_2 will no longer do. The strongest claim that can be made is, instead, that A and C share a temporal part, which we may suppose begins at t_1 and extends for as long as each exists. This is no more problematic than the claim, on the three-dimensional conception, that two objects can have a common spatial part (during a given interval of time). Moreover, use of the notion of temporal parts allows this response when physical objects are understood to be the material content of given regions (where material content is, in turn, to be construed in terms of the fusion or sum of spatiotemporal particles). Of course, it is not essential to the notion of a temporal part that it be developed in this way. The thesis that continuants are made up of proper temporal part-objects is quite independent of the thesis that they are composed of arbitrary temporal parts. Embedded in an appropriate account of physical objects, the latter thesis is attractive on account of the solutions it suggests to difficult puzzles; and if it is unattractive because of the revisions in our conceptual framework that the global theory would bring, this is to a considerable extent mitigated by the realization that at bottom, we are faced with a choice of *which* commonsense views to reject.

Notes

1. See, for example, McTaggart (1921, 175–78). See Quine's version of the thesis, which is cast in terms of spatiotemporal parts (1982, 269; 1963, 65–66; 1960, 114–18, 171–73).

2. Geach first set out his objections (1965), and then summarized them (1979, 69–71). (The first work is reprinted in Geach [1972, 302–18].) Thomson's criticisms are worked out in 1983; her arguments are examined in detail in part IV of the present paper. Chisholm's objections may be found concisely and conveniently summarized (1976, 138–45).

3. Carter defends a version of this claim (1983). His arguments are similar to those examined in part V of the present paper.

4. This is an overstatement. There are, of course, a number of other ways of avoiding mereological essentialism, including denying the transitivity of identity, distinguishing identity and identity across time, insisting on a distinction between the 'is' of identity and the 'is' of constitution, and conceding that distinct objects can occupy the same space at the same time. The appeal to temporal parts as a way of avoiding mereological essentialism was first suggested by Cartwright, who opts for this move in preference to the other alternatives (1975, 169–70). Heller couples his version of Cartwright's move with a spatiotemporal conception of physical objects (1984, 264–65).

5. Russell was already arguing as early as 1897 for a completely symmetrical analysis of time and space: see his unpublished article. Through the later influence of G. E. Moore, Russell's early views resulted in the position articulated in *The Principles of Mathematics,* according to which each object is eternally and immutably associated with the times and places it occupies (1903, 470–73). In its rough outlines, both this position and the account of change to which it leads would be quite congenial to the modern-day exponent of the four-dimensional conception of physical objects.

6. Wiggins makes much of the contrast between continuants and events or processes. Events and processes have temporal parts, continuants do not. Unlike enduring objects, events may be said to occupy stretches of time: to get "the whole event you must trace it through its historical beginning to its historical end" (1980, 25, n. 12). (It is by contrast with this position that we are to understand Wiggins's claim that continuants persist *whole* through time.) It is certainly true that events and processes are quite naturally thought of as having temporal parts. It is also true that the *career* or *history* of a continuant can naturally be held to have temporal parts in that same sense. This makes it tempting to assimilate continuants to their histories, and, in general, objects to (special kinds of) events or processes. Hence, Quine (1960):

> Physical objects . . . are not to be distinguished from events or, in the concrete sense of the term, processes. Each comprises simply the content, however heterogenous, of some portion of space-time, however disconnected and gerrymandered." (171)

It seems to me that Geach and Wiggins are right to protest this assimilation. But this is not to say that we can make no sense of a continuant's being made up of temporal parts. And one of the ways that we can make sense of this notion is by relying on *analogies* between the ordinary concepts of objects having spatial parts and processes having temporal parts, on the one hand, and of continuants having temporal parts on the other. (See Hirsch's position [1982, 139–41, 187–88].)

7. Or, perhaps, as van Inwagen suggests, possessing their own entelechy (1981, 133). The measures of independence and self-subsistence may well pull apart. One measure reflects the extent to which we think that the part-objects can survive their association with the original whole. A table leg, for example, can clearly continue to exist even if the table does not, and can become part of another table. It is less clear whether the surface of a solid wooden table top, or a knife's edge, can properly be said to pass this test. To the extent that we feel they do not, we will be disinclined to treat them as genuine parts of the objects concerned. A second measure of independence is provided by the extent to which we think that the parts in question could not be individuated save as parts of the whole they help constitute. The internal organs of an animal, for example, are clearly (most of them) detachable, can survive the dissolution of the whole, and can even become parts of other physical objects. But, unlike the table leg, they do not exist before the whole they originally help constitute. We may put the difference here counterfactually by saying that whereas, unproblematically, the very same table leg might have been used to make up another table instead of this one, there is no clear sense at all in which Jones's heart might, from the start, have been someone else's heart. To the extent that we measure the legitimacy of a part in this way, we will be disinclined to treat as genuine objects those parts whose individuation can proceed only by means of the whole they originally help constitute. So, too, in the case of temporal parts: we should leave open the possibility that the 'genuineness' of the part is a matter of degree.

8. Depending on how the associated region is defined, this claim may need to be weakened: see part III below for discussion.

9. Van Inwagen gives the example of the subregion of a spherical region S whose elements are the points in S with rational distance from the center (1981, 135, n. 2).

10. A more detailed presentation of this standard approach may be found in Heller (1984, 325–28).

11. Quinton (1973, 77).

12. For an illustration of this approach, see Pollock (1974, 139).

13. Even though he recommends an extreme version of the multidimensional analysis of physical objects, this is the approach taken by Schlesinger (1903, 256).

14. The calculus of individuals was originally developed by Leonard in 1930, and then elaborated on by him and Goodman (1940). (See also Goodman [1966, 42–51].) Their work was anticipated by Lesniewski and, in a somewhat different formulation, by Whitehead. To be precise, Thomson's account of temporal parts is embedded in *mereological predicate logic,* that is, the conjunction of the calculus of individuals and ordinary predicate logic.

15. The name comes from Cartwright (1975, 161) and is also used by Thomson. In Cartwright's approach, the fusion principle is a special case of a thesis he calls the *covering principle* (ibid., 160), which also generates objects by division (or *fission,* as it is termed by Cartwright and in the text above).

16. Of course, formalizations of the calculus of individuals can take different primitive predicates, including one whose intended interpretation is 'is part of'. (See, for example, Tarski [1983, 24–29].) This does not alter the intuitive point being made in the text, which is that given *CI,* the more finely one individuates parts, the more finely one will have to individuate continuants. (Technically, what matters is not the introduction of parts, but the introduction of common parts.)

17. See Burge (1977) for criticisms of *CI* and an alternative account of aggregates and a (corresponding) nontransitive part-whole relation.

18. Salmon (1981, 108).

19. Cartwright (1975, 164–69). The same kind of example is widely discussed in the literature. Van Inwagen sets out a version (1981) and uses it to argue against the thesis that arbitrary parts of a physical object are part-objects. Carter uses his version to develop a plausibility argument for mereological essentialism (1983). Thomson's version is resolved by her proposal that different physical objects can coincide spatially (1983). Wiggins proposes to respond to the puzzle by distinguishing between constitution and identity (1980). Cartwright sees the example as supporting the metaphysic of temporal parts: this is the position defended in this section.

References

Brody, B. 1980. *Identity and Essence*. Princeton.

Burge, T. 1977. "A Theory of Aggregates." *Nous* II:97–119.

Carter, W. R. 1983. "In Defense of Undetached Parts." *Pacific Philosophical Quarterly* 64:126–43.

Cartwright, R. 1975. "Scattered Objects." In *Analysis and Metaphysics,* edited by K. Lehrer, 153–73. Dordrecht.

Chisholm, R. 1973. "Parts as Essential to Their Wholes." *The Review of Metaphysics* 26:581–604.

——————. 1976. *Person and Object.* La Salle.

Geach, P. T. 1965. "Some Problems about Time." *Proceedings of the British Academy.* London.

——————. 1972. *Logic Matters.* Berkeley.

——————. 1979. *Truth, Love and Immortality: An Introduction to McTaggart's Philosophy.* Berkeley.

Goodman, N. 1966. *The Structure of Appearance.* 2d ed. Cambridge, Mass.

Heller, M. 1984. "Temporal Parts of Four Dimensional Objects." *Philosophical Studies* 46:323–34.

Hirsch, E. 1982. *The Concept of Identity.* Oxford.

Leonard, H. S., and N. Goodman. 1940. "The Calculus of Individuals and Its Uses." *Journal of Symbolic Logic* 5:45–55.

Massey, G. J. 1976. "Tom, Dick, and Harry, and All the King's Men." *American Philosophical Quarterly* 13:89–107.

McTaggart, J. M. 1921. *The Nature of Existence.* Vol. 1. Cambridge.

Pollock, J. 1974. *Knowledge and Justification.* Princeton

Quine, W. V. O. 1960. *Word and Object.* Cambridge, Mass.

——————. 1963. *From a Logical Point of View.* New York.

——————. 1981. "What Price Bivalence." *The Journal of Philosophy* 77:90–95

——————. 1982. *Methods of Logic.* 4th ed. Cambridge, Mass.

Quinton, A. 1973. *The Nature of Things.* London.

Russell, B. A. W. Unpublished. "Why Do We Regard Time, but Not Space, As Necessarily a Plenum?" Manuscript in the Bertrand Russell Archives.

——————. 1903. *The Principles of Mathamatics.* Cambridge.

Salmon, N. U. 1981. *Reference and Essence.* Princeton.

Schlesinger, G. N. 1985. "Spatial, Temporal and Cosmic Parts." *The Southern Journal of Philosophy* 23: 255–72.

Tarski, A. 1983. *Logic, Semantics, Meta-Mathematics.* 2nd ed. Indianapolis.

Thomson, J. J. 1983. "Parthood and Identity Across Time." *The Journal of Philosophy* 80:581–604.

van Inwagen, P. 1981. "The Doctrine of Arbitrary Undetached Parts." *Pacific Philosophical Quarterly* 62:123–37.

Wiggins, D. 1980. *Sameness and Substance.* Cambridge, Mass.

MIDWEST STUDIES IN PHILOSOPHY, XI (1986)

Identity, Modal Individuation, and Matter in Aristotle

NICHOLAS WHITE

This paper is concerned with an aspect of Aristotle's views on identity and individuation. Under individuation, I do not here include problems about identifying an object from one time to another, which will not directly concern me at all, but questions about what difference of features, if any, is thought by Aristotle to distinguish objects that he takes to be distinct. To a degree, this paper deals with Aristotle's views on the principles of the Indiscernibility of Identicals and of the Identity of Indiscernibles, though my main aim is not to determine to what extent he accepted either of these principles. Rather, the focus is on cases in which he took certain objects to be distinct and thought that they could be discriminated, and questions are raised about what he thought made for the discriminability.

Some of Aristotle's views on these cases will appear, at least at first sight, odd or even perverse. That is not a disadvantage of examining them. On the contrary. When they are considered in the right way, they can help reveal much more about what presuppositions underlie the views we ourselves take as obvious than would a banal attempt to assimilate his views to our own. Furthermore, we often end up discovering, as in this case, that some of our ideas are far more similar to his exotic ones than we otherwise would have realized.

I shall begin by expounding some features of what Aristotle calls "accidental sameness," a relation between objects that sometimes seems to be identity but that in his view is not. I shall then explain how this relation differs from identity, and what distinguishes its relata from each other. By then, we shall have seen most of what is strange about his view. Next, I shall compare some of Aristotle's views about accidental sameness with some of Saul Kripke's views, particularly his thesis that all identities are necessary. There will be some points of agreement and some of disagreement. For a more direct contrast with Aristotle, I shall then take up some views of Allan Gibbard, who argues against Kripke that there are contingent identities. It turns out that where Gibbard sees contingent identity, Aristotle does not see identity but distinctness with accidental sameness. By asking why this disagreement arises, we shall see some interesting divergences between Aristotle and many of us nowadays in some fairly basic assumptions about how particular physical objects may be specified. That divergence will lead us to some questions about Aristotle's concept of matter. There, as usual, things will become very difficult, and I shall not have space for a full treatment of the problems. But there will emerge in what Aristotle says about matter an important resemblance between our own views and the features of Aristotle's notion of accidental sameness that initially seem the oddest, and this resemblance will throw light on the role of the notion of matter in our own scheme of ideas.

I

It is not difficult to see in Aristotle some ideas about identity very close to our own. At one point in the *Topics,* he says that if A and B are the same, then whatever is predicated of the one is predicated of the other (152b25-28),[1] and this looks very much like the kind of principle, sometimes labeled ''Leibniz's Law'' or ''The Indiscernibility of Identicals,'' that is often taken to govern the notion of identity as we use it. That is, we tend to take it as clear that whatever else identity might involve (such as the converse principle, the Identity of Indiscernibles), it must obey the rough principle,

(I)   If $A = B$, then whatever holds of A holds of B too.

Refining the principle, of course, involves clarifying what the range is of things that ''hold of'' A and B in the intended sense. But even without any such refinement, we might well be happy to take Aristotle to have in mind a version of (I) such as we might accept.

The problem of refining (I) arises in another passage, *Sophistical Refutations* 179b1–4. It might be the case, Aristotle says, that I know Coriscus, but do not know the man approaching over there, even though it seems right to say that the man approaching—or ''the approacher,'' as Aristotle actually puts it, for reasons we shall see—is Coriscus. (Note in passing that Aristotle uses the verb ''know'' here with a direct object, not a propositional construction.) What to do? We are familiar with various options. Say that in the relevant sense I do know the approacher? Or say that in the relevant sense I do not kow Coriscus? Or say that more than one sense can be given to 'know'? Or say that Coriscus is not, after all, identical with the approacher, in spite of the fact that when he comes closer, lo and behold, there is Coriscus? Or say that in the relevant sense for (I), being known by me or not being known by me are not things that ''hold of'' or fail to ''hold of'' other things?

Aristotle's response to the problem is to give what looks like a restriction of his principle to certain cases of sameness. He says, ''Only to things that are undifferentiated and one in substance (*ousia*) do the same things seem to belong'' (179a37–39), and much the same apparent restriction emerges in *Sophistical Refutations* 166b31–32 and 169b3–6, and in *Physics* 212b14–16, where he says, ''It is not the case that all the same things belong to things that are the same in just any way, but only to those things whose being (*einai*) is the same.''

But if we agree that Aristotle is here enunciating some kind of restriction on his version of (I), just what restriction is it, and what is its result? Two alternatives come to mind immediately. According to one, he is saying that things that are not the same in substance or being are not identical. That is, we should construe his 'same in substance' and 'same in being' as fairly equivalent to ' = ' in (I), and take his other uses of 'same' to express something other than identity. This would have the consequence that in his view, Coriscus and the approacher are not identical, notwithstanding the fact that, again, when he comes closer, there is Coriscus, right there. Such an idea seems a bit disturbing, as if Frege had told us that whatever astronomers may say, the morning star and the evening star are not identical. The obvious alternative construal of Aristotle's point avoids this consequence. It is easy to say that although Coriscus and the approacher *are* identical, really and flatly identical, nevertheless, of that thing—i.e., Coriscus, i.e., the approacher—being known by me does and does not hold. For, the alternative continues, only of things that are the same in substance do all the same things hold, and Coriscus and the approacher, although they are *identical,* are not *the same in being,* and it is only sameness in being, not identity, that is governed by (I). But this alternative also has a very disturbing consequence. If (I) governs sameness in being, then what is identity, and what principle governs it? If having the same things hold of an object is not necessary for identity, we need to find some other explanation of it. This seems like a difficult project, to say the least.

There is one way of regarding identity that may make it possible for us to accept this latter construal of Aristotle's restriction. For example, Jonathan Barnes makes the sensible suggestion that in Aristotle's view, Coriscus and the approacher are identical after all, but only *contingently* so, whereas things that are the same in being or substance are necessarily identical, or something like it.[2] Aristotle would be pointing out, in a somewhat oblique way, that if you allow modal and intensional predicates to express things that "hold of" a thing in the sense of (I), then, of course, (I) will fail, except for objects that are not merely identical but that are, in some way, noncontingently so. The point would then be roughly like the point that even if $A = B$, you cannot infer 'Necessarily $A = B$' or 'Everybody knows that $A = B$' from, respectively, 'Necessarily $A = A$' or 'Everybody knows that $A = A$'. Rather, something stronger than '$A = B$', something more like sameness "in substance or being" between A and B, would seem to be required to license the inferences. But Aristotle might still accept (I) as governing identity, provided that only nonmodal and nonintensional predicates be included among the things that "hold of" objects in the sense that (I) expresses.[3]

But it does not seem that Aristotle's restriction can be successfully construed in this way. As Gareth Matthews notes, Aristotle never suggests that we could explicate the relation holding between Coriscus and the approacher, which relation he calls "accidental sameness," as a nonnecessary or contingent sameness.[4] More important, as Matthews also points out, Aristotle consistently conveys the idea that if A and B are accidentally the same, they are, in a way, *not* the same, whereas, on any customary account of contingent identity, if A and B are contingently identical, then they *are* identical, though it is contingent that they are so, just as someone who contingently eats beans *does* eat beans, though it is contingent that he does, and it is not thereby true, in a way, that he does not eat beans. In addition, Aristotle's talk of accidents frequently conveys a picture under which objects that we might think of as identical are, at least in one sense, compounds of entities joined by a kind of connection of accidence. Instead of the object—i.e., Coriscus, i.e., the approacher—being regarded merely as a single object that can be described by a variety of different words or phrases, or that possesses different attributes, we have a kind of compound of objects, Coriscus and the approacher (and others as well).[5] This picture is encouraged partly by a feature of the Greek language, which allows an adjective or participle, often with the definite article, to stand by itself as a substantive expression without the addition of any noun, so that my phrase 'the approacher' is a word-for-word rendering of the phrase *ho prosiōn,* which could also be translated as "the approaching" (with the participle in this case carrying masculine gender, though, in some similar cases, it is in the neuter). When the noun is added, the resulting phrase, like 'the approaching man', can easily have the look of a designation of a compound entity, consisting of the man and the approacher. The structure of the phrase then seems to mirror the structure of the object designated, though Aristotle says that the structure of phrases is not always an accurate index of the structure of objects (e.g., *Metaphysics* VII.4). (Unfortunately, Aristotle uses proper names in examples so infrequently that it is impossible, I think, to be sure how he thinks, e.g., 'Coriscus' and 'the man' or 'the approacher' are associated.) And, sure enough, in the *Physics* and the *Metaphysics,* Aristotle frequently suggests that when we have a case of a man who is (accidentally, of course) musical and pale, we can speak of a kind of compound object, made up of "the man" and "the musical (one)" and "the pale (one)," which—the things, not the phrases—are joined by the relation of "accidental sameness" into something that is "accidentally one."[6] For example, at *Physics* 190a18–21, he speaks of "the man" and "the unmusical" and "the compound of them, . . . the unmusical man," and at 190b20–22, he says, "In a way the musical man is a compound of man and musical, for you will analyze it into the definitions of them." None of this has the look of a modern notion of a single object designated by contingently codesignative phrases that can be linked in straightforward identity statements. One might, of course, hold to sanitize Aristotle's texts by insisting on construals that meet certain modern standards of logical or ontological tidiness. For some pedagogical purposes, it might be nice to encourage students to understand Aristotle in such a way, sometimes.[7] But I think the texts themselves finally resist such sanitizing, and that it actually succeeds in obliterating not only something historically important but also some ideas of real philosophical interest and suggestiveness.

So far, then, it looks as though Aristotle holds onto the Indiscernibility of Identicals by taking things that are "accidentally the same" to be, in an important way, nonidentical.[8] As Matthews notes, this interpretation is reinforced in the *Topics* itself by the fact that Aristotle contrasts accidental sameness with sameness of the "leading and primary" sort (103a25–39),[9] exemplified by the sameness of a cloak and a mantle, or of a man and a two-footed animal, which are no doubt intended as cases of sameness in substance. It is most striking that he evidently feels a need to actually *argue* for the claim that the musical (one) is, in any sense, the same as Socrates in one of these sorts of cases (103a32–39). Although not all of his examples are as clearly formulated as one could wish,[10] it is clear that reservations are being expressed about the way in which Coriscus and the approacher are the same, by contrast to cases of sameness in being or substance.

II

If we accept that in Aristotle's view, accidental sames are not identical in a straightforward modern sense, we urgently need to understand better what sorts of things they are, and what he takes their relationship to be. At one time, I supposed that we might think of them as things much like space-time worms, even though Aristotle does not use such a notion.[11] If our example of an accidentally unitary compound is "the musical man," then the man would be a worm of which the musical (one) is a temporal part, corresponding to the period of the man's life during which he is musical. This interpretation reverses the part-whole relation indicated by Aristotle, but that might not seem too great a price to pay for an otherwise straightforward reading. Alan Code developed such an interpretation, along with a way of seeing in Aristotle some of the parallels between modal logic and tense logic.[12] But Matthews pointed out that the interpretation will not work. For there is no reason why things that Aristotle would count as accidentally the same might not have just the same temporal extent, and, thus, count (for all that has been explained) as flatly identical (see sec. IV of this paper).[13] So construing accidental sames as space-time worms will not help us understand the sense in which they are nonidentical, since Aristotle never warns us that, for example, the man and the pale (one) are merely accidentally the same only if the man is not pale from precisely the beginning of his life to precisely the end of it. Thus, if we are to take the man and the pale (one) as always discernible, as Aristotle evidently does, the discernibility must be of a different sort from what is given merely by difference of spatiotemporal boundaries. So, in order to develop an interpretation of Aristotle's treatment of (I), we need a way of understanding accidental sameness as a relation between nonidenticals, but this temporal way of understanding that matter does not seem to work.

I think we may go further and draw a stronger conclusion. The idea of space-time worms provides the only likely way in which we might have hoped to interpret accidental sameness within a straightforwardly nonmodal and nonintensional framework. Since it seems inadequate, I doubt whether there is any explanation of Aristotle's way of distinguishing accidental sames that is not, somehow, modal or (if one differentiates) intensional. This is the view of Russell Dancy, and in spite of some considerations raised against it by Frank Lewis, it seems to me correct.[14] When Aristotle explains how accidental sames differ from each other, he says that they differ in *logos*, in account or (in this case) *definition* (see *Met.* 1024b29–31, 1015b24–26; *Phys.* 190b22–24). This comes to the same as saying that they differ in being or (in one sense) in substance, since a definition is what conveys the being of a thing (see, e.g., *Soph. Ref.* 179a37–b2). Now, although there is much obscurity surrounding his notion of a definition, I think it would be agreed universally to be clearly some kind of modal notion. To give the definition of what it is to be an *X*, it is evidently not sufficient to give a term or phrase that is merely coextensional with the term represented by 'X' (see, e.g., *Topics* 101b38 ff. with 102a18 ff.). Since Aristotle plainly intends that accidental sames not merely may but must differ in definition,[15] but that no further difference between them is required, it is clear that accidental sameness is a modal notion of some sort. Although he does not explain the idea in terms of our alethic modalities,[16] he clearly believes, as we have seen, that if the man and the pale (one) are accidentally the same, this may be in virtue of, not the fact that they have different spatiotemporal extent or anything of that sort, but merely the fact that their definitions are different, and thus that they *could,* in some sense, have been spatiotemporally distinguishable, since, for example, the man in question *could* have ceased to be pale. It is difficult to see what sense we could make of his notion of difference of definition in general if we deny that it approximates some sort of modal thought as this. So, in our terms, the distinction between accidental sames is somehow to be explained modally. To put the point so as to make it appear paradoxical, and thus, perhaps, to explain why some interpreters like Barnes have preferred to try to interpret accidental sameness differently, accidental sames are distinct not necessarily because they are distinct in the actual state of affairs, but because they are distinct in some possible state of affairs.[17]

Notice that we do not automatically quail at the idea of an object whose identity conditions depend in part on what is the case in possible, but not actual, states of affairs. For we allow such modal individuation, as I shall call it, for some types of abstract objects, notably attributes (or properties, in our sense as opposed to Aristotle's). The attribute of being a featherless biped can be distinct, we take it, from the attribute of being human even if in the actual world the things possessing the one are just the things possessing the other. Perhaps the relevant notion of possibility contains problems, but we do not seem to mind, in and of itself, the fact that these can be distinct objects actually, even if what makes them distinct, so to speak, is facts about which things possess them in other possible worlds.[18]

The idea of physical or material objects that are modally individuated in this way seems far more problematical than that of modally individuated abstract objects, so we need some way to understand how Aristotle could have accepted the former idea. We had better see why it might fit more easily into his scheme of things than it seems, at first sight, to fit into ours.

III

Why does it seem strange to suggest that the man is not identical with the pale (one), on the ground that the man might not be or have been pale, or that the pale (one) might not be or have been a man? (Perhaps Aristotle does not believe in the latter possibility, but the former one makes for just as much oddity.) Or why would it seem so strange to suggest that in spite of all that astronomers produce as evidence, the morning star is not identical with the evening star, simply on the ground that the morning star might not have risen in the evening, or might cease to do so, or vice versa?

Before attacking this question, we ought to notice that in certain respects, Aristotle's position shows affinities with a view that has been advocated by Saul Kripke. Unlike Frege, for one, Kripke believes, first, that all identities are necessary and, second, that identity statements linking rigid designators (i.e., terms designating the same object in all possible worlds) are necessarily true if true at all.[19] In order to deal with such statements as

(1)   The morning star = the evening star

Kripke holds that either they do not involve rigid designators, or they are necessary after all. And, in fact, he argues that in the case of (1) in some of its uses, it is, indeed, necessary (when the descriptions are used to "fix the reference"[20]), while in the others, its singular terms are not rigid. Aristotle's treatment of his own examples can escape the consequence of admitting any contingent true identity statements at all, by so construing the word 'same' that

(1′)   The morning star is the same as the evening star,

when taken as true, never turns out to be a genuine identity statement, but only a statement of accidental sameness between distinct objects modally individuated. This strategy ends up admitting objects and styles of individuation that Kripke does not. Kripke, after all, has strategies that were not available in Aristotle's day, notably ways of arguing that a phrase like 'the morning star' or 'the pale (one)' might not in all contexts designate the same object in every possible world.

To what extent is Aristotle's treatment of these issues motivated by a belief like Kripke's that all identities are necessary? It would be nice to have more evidence to go on, especially since Aristotle's use of both proper names and alethic modalities when dealing with these topics is so sparse that we have to use other clues. Unfortunately, he almost never discusses certain cases that might be revealing, trivial identity statements of the form '$A = A$', or, for that matter, statements of the form 'the F = the F'. Still, he does say something that seems to bear on them in one of his treatments of sameness, *Metaphysics* x.3, at 1054a33–b3. Here, he distinguishes (1) sameness in number, (2) sameness in both definition and number, and (3) sameness in definition ("of first substance"). We need not settle all of the questions that can be raised about this classification, which does not well fit the other account of sameness in the *Metaphysics,* the one in V.9.[21] It seems plain that the condition laid down in (2) is the conjunction of the conditions in (1) and (3), and that, at least in the case of material substances, (1) amounts to sameness of matter, a notion we shall come to shortly.[22] What is interesting, though, is Aristotle's example under (2): "You are the same as yourself in form and in matter." Perhaps we may take this to suggest that for Aristotle, a statement of trivial selfsameness like 'You are the same as you' or 'Socrates is the same as Socrates' will typically express sameness in being, and, thus, perhaps we can infer that he thinks there is a kind of necessity in your being identical with yourself or in Socrates's being identical with himself, as Kripke does.

In passing, we should notice that Aristotle faces a difficulty of saying how his treatment really will help him deal with problems arising out of epistemic and other intensional notions, like our original problem about knowing Coriscus and the approacher. Even if we say that as accidental sames, they differ in *logos,* and so in being, we may not be able to thus explain why a person seems both to know and not to know the same thing. We might not be able to deal, for example, with the notorious case in which *A* and *B* are the same in being, but I do not know that they are and, thus, seem to know *A* but not *B*. At any rate, Aristotle needs to show how his solution can be applied to these problems, if it can be. On his side, Kripke observes that his views about rigid designators and proper names do not by themselves solve problems about epistemic attitudes and the like.[23]

Even if there is some similarity between Aristotle's views and Kripke's on these issues, nevertheless, Aristotle's way of individuating actual objects by modal considerations involves a peculiarity to which nothing in Kripke's position corresponds.[24] What is possible affects Kripke's account of what is actual to this extent, that if a state of affairs cannot be taken to be necessary, then it cannot be taken to consist in an identity holding in the actual world. But Kripke never allows his thesis that identities are necessary to dictate an individuation of actual objects that seems to run as directly against what we take to be commonsense individuation as some of Aristotle's ways of individuating do. So we cannot use Kripke's position alone to give us an understanding of how Aristotle could have taken up his position.

IV

Let us turn, then, to an argument against Kripke's thesis advanced by Allan Gibbard, who wishes to show that some identities are contingent:[25]

> I make a clay statue of the infant Goliath in two pieces, one the part above the waist and the other the part below the waist. Once I finish the two halves, I stick them together, thereby bringing into existence simultaneously a new piece of clay and a new statue. A day later I smash the statue, thereby bringing to an end both statue and piece of clay. The statue and the piece of clay persisted during exactly the same period of time.

Arguably, Gibbard could also have used an example more like some of Aristotle's cases of accidental sameness. Suppose that the two halves of the statue differ chemically in such a way that putting them together instantly causes the whole statue to change from brown, the original color of the two halves, to yellow. So, on one way of talking (see *Phys.* I.7 and *De Gen. et Corr.* I.3–4), we might say that a yellow (one) is created at the same moment as the statue. Suppose, then, that whatever puts the statue out of existence simultaneously ensures that no yellow (one) remains. In Gibbard's own example, he says that the statue, which he calls 'Goliath', and the lump of clay, which he calls 'Lumpl', are identical, though contingently so, because he *could* have squeezed the lump before it dried, thus causing the statue, but not the lump, to go out of existence. In the other case, Aristotle counts the statue and the yellow (one) as nonidentical, in effect, though accidentally the same. Why do Aristotle and Gibbard disagree?

Gibbard explains his reasons for thinking that Goliath and Lumpl are identical.[26] For one thing, if the statue is formed by shaping the whole lump, rather than by putting two smaller lumps together, it seems reasonable to say that the statue is a temporal segment of the lump, so in the present case, when the statue endures for the entire career of the lump, it seems reasonable to say that the two are identical. More fundamentally, he argues, the likeliest model of a systematic account of the physical world suggests that they ought to be thought of as identical. We would like to think of such physical objects, he maintains, as constituted in a simple way from fundamental physical entities, such as point instants, or else a fixed or changing set of particles. In either case, Goliath and Lumpl seem to be identical—either the same set of point instants, or the same set (or function from times to sets) of particles. If these are the sorts of resources that we are allowed to use in describing and individuating such objects, then there seems to be no way of ascribing an attribute to Goliath that is not at the same time ascribed to Lumpl, and vice versa.

Since my main aim is to show in broad terms how Gibbard' view differs from Aristotle's, I shall have to leave aside many issues raised by the disagreement between Kripke and Gibbard. (In particular, Gibbard has to give an account of proper names different from Kripke's, to show that 'Goliath = Lumpl' can be an identity statement joining names even if it is contingent.) For Aristotle, the kind of thing that Gibbard takes to be paradigmatic of a description of the physical world and that allows his identification of Goliath with Lumpl is not an open option. For one thing, Aristotle is strongly opposed to atomism (see, e.g., *De Gen. et Corr.* I.2, 8), and so would oppose an identification of objects with any description of atomic constituents. More generally, he can be called an opponent not only of atomism in the strict sense, but of microreductionism in a more general sense, since he does not believe that an adequate description of items in the physical world, notably living organisms, can be given by describing their physical parts alone. But more basically for present purposes, perhaps, he does not think of the spatiotemporal manifold in a way that would easily suggest identifying objects by specifying their spatiotemporal boundaries or by such things as point instants. As a look at his accounts of place and time in *Physics* IV.1–5, 10–14 shows, he does not suppose that there is any integrated way of giving such spatiotemporal specifications that could even begin to individuate objects. This is part of the reason why, as we have seen, he does not make use of the notion of a space-time worm. As a result, he is not subject to the kind of pull from physical theory, or a general picture of what a physical theory ought to be like, that induces Gibbard to find it plausible to identify a statue under certain conditions with a lump.

To see why Aristotle's view can seem so odd to us, and what underlies the disagreement between it and Gibbard's, start by recalling what we noted erarlier, that to the extent that we accept modal notions, we have no qualms about using them to individuate objects that are abstract rather than concrete. The idea of using modal differences to distinguish the morning star and the evening star seems very peculiar, but it does not seem peculiar to use them to distinguish, say, the attribute of being the star rising in the morning and the attribute of being the star rising in the evening. The same difference appears, I think, when we consider Descartes's argument in *Meditation* VI for the non-identity of body and soul. I take it as obvious that Descartes, in effect, relies there on a kind of modal individuation, for distinguishing objects on the basis merely of what can or could be the case about them, not by establishing antecedently anything that actually is the case about them. There is nothing odd about this procedure for modern versions of the Cartesian argument, which aim merely to show that, for example, mental *states* and physical *states* are not identical. But Descartes's own argument raises more worries, precisely because he argues for the nonidentity of soul and body as distinct *substances,* and then even goes so far as to try to find a distinct location for the soul. Similarly, when Aristotle speaks of accidental sames, he is not talking of attributes or purely abstract objects, and he clearly distinguishes things like "the musical (one)" from both universal attributes like pallor and (if he believes in them[27]) individual attributes like the individual pallor of Socrates. So, it seems to me, what makes Aristotle's view look so strange is primarily that we find in it a modal individuation of objects that are concrete.

What seems so strange about such entities, Gibbard's account might now suggest to us, is that unlike abstract objects, concrete objects are anchored straightforwardly in the physical, spatiotemporal world by their location in it. And our now-traditional and thoroughly familiar theory of the physical world accords to spatiotemporal specifications such pervasiveness, integration, and importance that it becomes easy to think that *the* leading way to specify a material object is to describe it in terms of that system (though perhaps if physics gets much stranger, all that could change). Aristotle's idea of modal individuation flouts that way of thinking, and so makes the objects thus individuated seem, in a way, not fully anchored in the physical world. I do not see any contradiction or strict paradox here (though, of course, some styles of modal individuation can lead to problems). Rather, one's rough sense of what the physical world is causes one to feel pulled in two directions, toward saying that such objects are in the physical world, and against saying it. Such objects seem to be in the physical world because they are in some sense given a spatiotemporal location in it, but they are not fully so, because their identity conditions are not given fully by that location but by modal considerations in addition (see note 18).

Arguably, there is an additional difference between Aristotle's view and the one that Gibbard expresses, which would keep the former even further from the latter's style of identifying material objects. The general statement of Gibbard's view presupposes that (something like) the respective spatiotemporal boundaries of Goliath and Lumpl are both determinate, so that if we are taking them to be objects existing at the present moment, we can take it as a determinate matter of fact whether their respective features are such that their temporal end-points coincide.[28] (Again, a certain amount of physics can make this problematical.) Although there is exegetical controversy over this matter, it can be argued that Aristotle believes otherwise, and I think that he does. On what I think is the correct reading of the famous passage about future contingents in *De Interpretatione* 9, he holds that the truth value of statements about future contingents is now objectively indeterminate. If the subject matter of our discourse now is a man and an accidentally same musical (one) existing now, then, since being musical is an accident of a man, the man's future musicality must be contingent, and not fixed by anything about the present state of affairs (see *Met*. V. 30 and IV. 2, also under what I believe to be the correct interpretation[29]). It would follow from *De Interpretatione* 9 that it is now indeterminate whether the musical (one) will last as long as the man. If so, then the truth value of many statements about the spatiotemporal coincidence—and, thus, on Gibbard's view the identity—of present cases of accidental sames would turn out to be indeterminate at any given time.

If the foregoing reflects Aristotle's view accurately, then we can see more fully why he is not drawn to the manner of individuation that Gibbard adopts for objects like Goliath and Lumpl. None of this would fully explain why, failing such a manner of individuation, Aristotle opts for the particular modal one that he does, but it certainly would help toward an explanation. At any rate, although I would be prepared to argue that this interpretation is, in fact, correct, I offer it here merely as an optional way of pushing the explanation of Aristotle's view of accidental sameness further. Those who read *De Interpretatione* 9 differently may rest content with the explanation I gave before I took up that passage.

There will be more to say about Aristotle's attitude toward future contingents when we consider his views about the individuation of particular material substances in the next section of this paper.

V

As the reader has no doubt been thinking impatiently for some time now, Gibbard's example of Goliath and Lumpl is strikingly reminiscent of Aristotle's discussions of the relation between form and matter. Let us follow that lead now. I shall try to show both the role of modal individuation in Aristotle's doctrine, and its place in our own ways of thinking.

For lack of space, I shall have to fudge one important issue in the comparison between Aristotle and Gibbard. It is not entirely clear what Aristotle would say about Lumpl. He has a contrast between a statue and "the clay" of the statue, and he might take Lumpl, i.e., "the lump of clay," to be what he means by "the clay" of the statue. But not all philosophers take matter terms like 'the clay' to designate things like lumps, especially in Gibbard's sense, which requires a certain degree of cohesiveness (Gibbard stipulates that smashing the statue to bits puts not only Goliath but also Lumpl out of existence). So perhaps Aristotle would have denied that Lumpl is what he thinks of as "the clay" of the statue, and would have, instead, regarded it as a kind of low-level, not fully formed or unitary substance. (Clearly, though, the fact that the lump is not what Aristotle or others mean by the phrase 'the clay' by no means shows that there is no such thing as the lump, and it seems clear that there is such a thing.) In either case, though, Aristotle evidently does not regard the matter of a statue and the statue as the same in being or substance (*Met*. VII, passim).

What is important for our purposes is that the distinction between the statue and either the clay or the lump of clay would, for Aristotle, have to be some sort of modal distinction, as in the case of accidental sames. For, as before, when Aristotle says that the matter "underlies" the formed substance and is not the same in being, there is no sign that if only we suppose that the matter is brought into existence and put out of existence simultaneously with the substance, then we will be able to say that they are the same in being. (Note that bringing the matter into existence would not be the same as bringing the lump into existence, but it can be accomplished, in Aristotle's view, by cooking the matter up out of some other sort of matter.[30]) That they are different in being is independent of their status in the actual spatiotemporal scheme of things.[31]

So far we have seen that Aristotle relies on modal attributes to distinguish accidental sames from each other, and to distinguish the matter of a material substance from the material substance itself. But there are other kinds of individuation, involving both these and other kinds of entities, that Aristotle also needs to explain. I am not assuming here that he must be adopting some form of the principle of the Discernibility of Nonidenticals, i.e., of the Identity of Indiscernibles. Whether he does will be touched on below, though only briefly. Rather, I am simply assuming that when he holds that two entities are distinct, there will be something of some sort to say about what their distinctness consists in. For example, we shall want to ask what distinguishes from each other like things that are, respectively, accidentally the same as distinct substances. What distinguishes, say, the pale (one) that is accidentally the same as Glaucon from the pale (one) that is accidentally the same as Adeimantus (let us assume that both are pale)? For another thing, we need to know what distinguishes the matters (so to speak) of distinct material substances, for example, the matter of Glaucon from that of Adeimantus. Third, what distinguishes one material substance from another, especially when they are cospecific and, thus, have the same form (*eidos*) and the same definition corresponding to their form? Thus, what distinguishes Glaucon from Adeimantus? For Aristotle, finding the answers to these questions is tied up with a metaphysical project of giving "principles and causes" (see, e.g., *Met.* IV.1, VI.1., *init.*; VIII.1, *init.*), so he sometimes insists that the answer to questions about "what distinguishes" (as I have put it) one thing from another have certain sorts of explanatory force. Insofar as I can, however, I shall try to bypass such issues here, and simply ask what kinds of things, in Aristotle's view, might possibly hold of one thing that do not hold of the other.

In the case of accidental sames, orthodox interpretation generally has it that what Aristotle thinks of as "nonsubstances," like the musical (one) and the pale (one), are individuated only by their relations to particular substances. Thus, the one pale (one) differs from the other simply because the former is accidentally the same as Glaucon, while the latter is accidentally the same as Adeimantus. Possibly Aristotle believes that the one might also, simply by virtue of its relation to Glaucon, accidentally have features that the latter lacks, such as being (accidentally) in motion if Glaucon is walking but Adeimantus is not (see, perhaps, e.g., *Phys.* 211a21–23). The general idea, in any case, is that the distinctness of the nonsubstances of this sort depends on a prior distinction of the material substances from each other. This interpretation probably requires some elaboration, but seems to be essentially correct. (I shall here sidestep the philosophical problems arising from the idea of individuation that requires relational attributes in this way.)[32]

The distinctness of particular material substances, however, raises more overt problems. Aristotle argues explicitly in *Metaphysics* VII. 15 that there is no definition of any material (or any other) particular. That is, he holds that no appropriate group of general terms together serve to distinguish any material particular from every other thing in the way that he demands of a definition. His reasoning is notable in relying solely on the fact that material particulars contain matter and are, therefore, subject to change (1039b27–31, 1040a2–5, 27–b4; cf. 1036a5–9), and in imposing certain modal conditions on an adequate definition. He insists that a definition be as a whole necessarily true of the object to be defined, in the special sense that it *cannot cease* to be true of that object, and *cannot come to be* true of any other object (1042a27–b2). In the case of the sun, for example, Aristotle holds that it cannot be defined, because whatever features of it you care to mention that together distinguish it at the present moment from all other existing objects, (a) the sun *could lose* enough of them so that the remainder would not distinguish it from everything else (1040a30–33), and (b) some other object *could come to have* all of them (1040a33–b2). Interestingly, the argument does not rely on the idea that something else could *have had* all of the features in the definition, or that the sun could *have lacked* some of them. It depends only on possibilities from the present time onward. It is also clear that, as in general in his writings, Aristotle considers no features incorporating dates or demonstrative references to times (e.g., "the source of the most light for the earth in 1984" or "the closest star to Buffalo now").[33] A definition is, thus, defeated if no set of dateless general terms *must* forever hold of the object, and it alone.

As a way of specifying one of a number of cospecific material particulars, the only alternative to a definition that Aristotle gives explicitly is a very problematical claim about matter. What distinguishes Glaucon and Adeimantus, according to orthodox readings of his doctrine, is that Glaucon has one (lump of?) matter and Adeimantus another (e.g., *Met.* 1034a5–8, 1054a34–35, 1071a27–29, 1074a33–34). (It is often held, with justification, that Aristotle sometimes writes as though he thinks that each particular, or at least each "natural" particular, has its own form, rather than there being only one form for all members of a given species; but he does not always follow this view, and even when he does, he does not maintain that each particular form has its own definition, which is what is important for present purposes.)

Put this view together with the view that material particulars have no definitions, and it follows pretty directly that the matter that distinguishes Glaucon from other human beings has no definition. Otherwise, Glaucon evidently could be defined by reference to the definition of his matter. Aristotle plainly endorses this conclusion, both by tracing the indefinability of material particulars to their matter (*Met.* 1039b20–31 and, more directly, 1036a2–9).

Some interpreters ascribe to Aristotle the view that the matter of a particular material substance can be distinguished from other matter only by reference to the substance itself, so that, for example, the matter of Adeimantus could only be specified by something like the phrase, 'the matter of Adeimantus'. There is room to doubt that this is Aristotle's view, but it certainly would lead to difficulty conjoined with the thesis that what distinguishes Glaucon from Adeimantus is only the distinction between their respective matters. The unhelpful result would be: what makes Glaucon distinct from Adeimantus is that the former has a certain matter, while the latter has another, and what distinguishes the two matters is that the one is of Glaucon and the other is of Adeimantus. Some trouble might be avoided by carefully explaining which claim has explanatory or ontological priority over which, but it is not plain how Aristotle resolves the problem, if, indeed, he falls into it.

The thesis that Glaucon has certain particular matter does not seem to be offered as a substitute for the definition of him that Aristotle says is unobtainable. Or, at least, that thesis would not seem to meet Aristotle's requirements for a definition. For one thing, it certainly seems that Glaucon does in due course cease to have the matter that he has today and comes to have different matter, and it is possible that by chance Adeimantus might later come to comprise the matter that Glaucon does today. So it looks as though the thesis is offered as part of a different project from that of finding a definition. That project probably has to do with saying what *right now* distinguishes one member of the species from another. Aristotle does not seem to suggest that the answer is, for example, ''Glaucon has the matter of Glaucon, and Adeimantus has the matter of Adeimantus.'' Rather, his somewhat compressed language suggests that he has in mind a situation in which both men are in front of us and present to our senses, so that we can say, ''Glaucon has [pointing] *that* matter, and Adeimantus has [pointing again, but—as is supposed to be obvious to sight alone—elsewhere] *that* matter'' (1036a5–9, 1037a1–2, 1040a2–5, 1070a9–10). Aristotle holds that the demonstrative reference to matter serves only as long as the objects are kept within view (especially 1040a2–5). Therefore, the whole project of actually explaining in any particular case what distinguishes two cospecfic particulars from each other can be carried out only when demonstrative references to matter are possible.[34] In denying such explanations the status of definitions (and, likewise, in refusing to regard statements about particulars as part of genuine ''science'' or *epistēmē*, as at *An. Post.* I.4, 8), Aristotle is casting his lot with those philosophers, such as Frege and Plato, who think of genuine science as containing no statements whose content essentially involves indexical elements.

If matter is one way, in such circumstances, of saying how one member of a species is distinct from another, are there any other ways? In particular, can one give a general specification, short of something meeting the standards for a definition, that uniquely specifies one material particular? Remember that Aristotle seems not to use dated descriptions (which, *Physics* IV.10–14 indicates, he might well think would presuppose references to particular substances existing at present), nor for that matter superlatives, which might help only in some cases. Here we have come down to a question that seems fairly basic to his views about individuation. Does he think that it is possible, in all or some cases, to give a specification, in general terms and without demonstrative references to present matter or substances, that singles out a material particular?

In some cases, he almost certainly thinks that it is possible, but I do not see any reason to say that he thinks it is possible in all cases. The cases in which it is possible are cases like that of the sun and other actual eternal things that are one of a species (1040a27–29). The difficulty in giving a definition arises in *Metaphysics* VII.15 from a possibility, in a very bare sense, of something's happening very much contrary to nature, but Aristotle firmly believes that this determinately *will not* happen (see *De Caelo* I.8, 9). However, most cases are very different. Using the kinds of terms that he seems to allow himself, it is not fully clear that he could find general terms to distinguish Bucephalus from even merely the other horses living in his day, let alone all other past and present horses, or all horses past, present, and future. (Even Quine needs to be able to fall back on 'Bucephalizes' if necessary!) Arguably, we are not generally guaranteed any such thing, unless we are granted, as something given and not requiring explanation in terms of references to particular objects, full use of locations in a spatiotemporal manifold or the like (and even that may not suffice). I see no grounds for supposing that Aristotle thought that there was such a guarantee, and we have seen that he did not use a full spatiotemporal frame of reference. Such specifications of materials particulars are not given in his texts, and *Metaphysics* VII.15 does not seem to presuppose their availability (except for special cases like that of the sun) when it denies that material particulars can be defined.

Of course, Aristotle might well have omitted mention of such specifications simply because *knowing* that a description was uniquely satisfied by a given object, from among all those in the future as well as the past and present, would never be possible for a human being with limited information. In that case, there might *be* such a specification, but it would be of no interest because of its unknowability to us. As before, it is not at all obvious why he should think that such a specification is guaranteed. In addition, if I was correct in what I said earlier about his views on future contingents (sec. IV of this paper), then, since at any given time the future accidental characteristics of all particulars are indeterminate, the future adequacy of any putative individuating specification will be not merely unknown or unknowable, but itself objectively indeterminate. I suspect that this is, in fact, what Aristotle thought, but even if I am incorrect and his views about future contingency did not positively prevent him from believing that there could be adequate individuating specifications, we have seen—to repeat—no ground for thinking that there always are such specifications for all, or even most, material particulars.

The upshot appears to be that except for references to the matter of particular substances, Aristotle believes that there is no way of uniquely specifying each such object in contradistinction to all others of its species, and no way of giving any such specification purely in general terms, or, at the least, no way in which we could know such specifications to be such. We should not conclude in either case that such objects are therefore identical with each other, since although we saw him in the *Topics* holding onto (I), the principle of the Indiscernibility of Identicals, there is no evidence that he generally accepts a principle of the Identity of Indiscernibles; and besides, he does think that his references to matter provide a way of discerning cospecific material particulars, even if it is neither a definition nor in general terms. The Indiscernibility of Identicals, though, still stands in the *Metaphysics,* as far as we can tell, in the sense that it is nowhere rejected or contravened. But interestingly, it is nowhere made explicit there, even in full-dress explanations of the word 'same' (especially V.9 and X.3), nor elsewhere outside of the *Topics*. One reason, relevant here, is that since Aristotle now holds that sometimes only a difference in matter distinguishes distinct particulars (the *Topics* does not employ the notion of matter), what seems important about identicals is no longer, in all cases, their indiscernibility by virtue of possessing the same general attributes.[35]

VI

From the point of view articulated by Gibbard, Aristotle's way of individuating accidental sames appears peculiar. Is there also something peculiar, from that same point of view, about his way of individuating particular material substances? Yes, in the way in which they are distinguished from things that are accidentally the same as they. Yes, too, in the way in which a substance is distinguished from its matter. For modal individuation is involved in both cases. What about the distinctness of cospecific material particulars, or of their respective matters? Are these distinctions drawn by what actually holds of the things to be distinguished, or does it also contain a modal element? The answer cannot be entirely clear, because Aristotle's view about what distinguishes these things is not entirely clear in relevant ways, and he may not have reached a final formulation with which he was satisfied. Evidently, though, the distinctions are not drawn by what general attributes attach to the objects to be distinguished. That means only that he rejects a certain version of the Identity of Indiscernibles, namely, a principle of the identity of things indiscernible by general attributes. If difference in matter is thought of as expressible only by demonstratives, as we have seen it might be thought of by Aristotle, then he subscribes to a type of "haecceitism," as he is often traditionally held to do. And the distinguishability of such objects may be quite limited, if he, indeed, thinks that it can be successful only for objects that exist now and are now in one's sensory field (see sec. V of this paper). But it is difficult to say whether the distinctions should be said to be drawn on the basis of what holds in the actual state of affairs. Certainly they are not drawn on just the kind of basis that Gibbard envisages, that is, constitution from fundamental physical entities in space-time, like particles or point instants. But that by itself does not settle whether the basis is nonmodal.

A good deal about both this question and other questions raised here hinges on how we should explain Aristotle's notion of matter, especially as concerns notions like that of "the matter of" this or that thing. The distinction between the thing and its matter, we saw, is, in a certain sense, modal. That does not automatically make the distinction between Glaucon and Adeimantus also require a modal explanation. Whether it does depends on how one goes on to describe the role of their respective matter in distinguishing them. And all of that is material for a different essay from this one.

It is worth noting, as food for further philosophical thought, that Aristotle comes closest to some modern philosophers, and also to certain ordinary and unscientific ways of looking at things, when he distinguishes modally between a substance and its matter. There are distinct echoes in ordinary thought, as opposed (I take it) to the way of thinking that Gibbard expresses, of the idea that what distinguishes the statue from the clay is not necessarily what *is* true of each of them but what *could* be so. And there are also echoes in philosophers who are liable to write such things as that the clay is not "as such" a statue, even though it is a statue (or, lest we think that talking of "constitution" instead of "being" takes care of the whole issue, that the clay does not "as such" constitute a statue, even though it does constitute a statue). For the phrase 'as such' suggests a thought about what follows or does not follow from something's being clay, which seems to be a modal sort of thought, about what can or cannot be the case with clay.[36] This is not to say, though, that this and other ordinary matter talk could not be given a nonmodal explication, granted enough divergence from ordinary ways of thinking or talking. But it would be the kind of explication that is done for the sake of scientific departures from ordinary styles of thought. It would be comparable, say, to W. V. Quine's recommendation that ordinary disposition terms be supplanted by nondispositional terms describing such things as microscopic structure. I am not here saying that either such explication would be advisable or even feasible, but only that they resemble each other in being attempts to revise ordinary thinking, and also in aiming at the elimination of modal notions in favor of nonmodal ones. But the elimination of a modal distinction between an object and its matter has a stronger motivation within ordinary thinking itself. For as we saw, modal individuation in other cases involving material objects seems peculiar even to ordinary thinking, at least nowadays.[37]

One interesting question to ask is why we should feel at all inclined, immersed as we are in a picture of the world in which spatiotemporal location does much of our individuating work and modality does little, to retain a notion of the matter of a thing that goes somewhat against our normal tendency. The beginning of the answer, I suppose, is along the following lines. Talk of "the matter" comes in when, for various reasons, we have difficulty drawing spatiotemporal boundaries or thinking of ways to try to draw them. It is often hard to keep track of some water or some syrup. Sometimes they are there in things that we can easily keep track of, like ice cubes or (differently) jugs, but sometimes their salient features remain when these bounds are broken. It is useful to have terms that refer to such things but leave unsettled just what sort of boundaries they must have. We tend to think of these terms as referring to objects, but objects whose spatiotemporal boundaries, especially their future ones, are not determinate, or, at least, are far from our abilities to determine. And because we do not know what may happen to the water at or after the destruction of the ice cube, then, because the former *could* remain after the latter is gone, we unhesitatingly think of them as distinct. Talking of "lumps" of clay and the like is a way of replacing talk of "the clay" by talk of entities whose boundaries are somewhat more definitely drawn, but the replacement seems clearly like a changing of the subject within ordinary thinking itself. The idea that *whatever* "the clay" might be, it is composed of—and arguably, for scientific purposes, identifiable with—sets of fundamental physical entities that have (it was earlier hoped) fully determinate spatiotemporal locations is a more definite departure from both ordinary thought and the kind of thought that Aristotle tried to develop philosophically. In that kind of thought, what is important about "the clay" or "the matter" is what *can* and *cannot* happen to it, *however* it may turn out to be shaped spatiotemporally. This thought is what is expressed in Aristotle's dictum that matter is "potentiality." It is along lines like this that I think his notion of matter is best understood, and ours too. And in this way of thinking, I have tried to show, there is a connection between his way of thinking about identity and ours.

Notes

1. Aristotle also says that the one will be predicated of whatever the other is. For our purposes, that condition does not need separate treatment.

2. Barnes, review, *Philosophical Books* 20 (1979):57–61, especially 59.

3. Here and hereafter I shall think of modal predicates (and intensional ones—I shall not usually distinguish) as being of a "*de re*" sort, expressed by open sentences within the scope of modal operators. In many contexts, it is hard to be sure that Aristotle is using such predicates—see my "Origins of Aristotle's Esseentialism," *Review of Metaphysics* 26, no. 1 (Sept. 1972):57–85—but I think that the following will amply bear out my using them to discuss the particular points at issue here, and I shall defer justification.

4. Gareth B. Matthews, "Accidental Unities," in *Language and Logos,* edited by M. Schofield and M. Craven Nussbaum (Cambridge, Eng., 1982), 223–40, especially 229.

5. See my "Aristotle on Sameness and Oneness," *Philosophical Review* 80 (1971):177–97, especially 185–87.

6. See ibid., 186, and references there, along with Matthews, "Accidental Unities." A similar interpretation of Aristotle was arrived at independently by Kit Fine, and I have benefited greatly from discussions with him on these matters. A development of a similar account of the notion of accidental sameness is offered by Frank A. Lewis, "Accidental Sameness in Aristotle," *Philosophical Studies* 42 (1982):1–36. But Lewis seems to me to go wrong in equating "the generous (one)" with, e.g., "generous Socrates," while taking the latter to be the same object as "the compound of the substance Socrates and the accident generos*ity*" (p. 5, with my emphasis). It seems to me that the message of *Met.* V. 6 and 9, along with *Phys.* 190a18–21 and 190b20–22, is pretty clearly that "generous Socrates" (perhaps equivalent to "the generous man") is a compound of Socrates and "the generous (one)," and that "the generous (one)" is not the same as either generosity or Socrates's particular generosity (see *infra,* with *Cat.* 8 and 10). Aristotle seems to me nowhere to suggest either that "the generous (one)" is a compound (he clearly says that "the generous man" *is* a compound), or that it is an attribute or to be equated with what is designated by the abstract noun, and the texts mentioned seem to me to refute this equation. (Note that here and in similar contexts, I am using double-quotation for scare-quotation. Aristotle is talking here about extralinguistic entities, not expressions.)

7. Thus, I would read, for example, C. J. F. Williams, "Aristotle's Theory of Descriptions," *Philosophical Review* 94 (1985):63–80.

8. In "Aristotle on Sameness and Oneness," I claimed that Aristotle did not retain a firm grip on this principle, and so showed confusion about the notion of identity. I thought so because I was startled that he should take such objects as the man and the approacher not to be flatly identical. But I was mistaken, as was argued by a number of poeple, including Matthews, "Accidental Unities," and Fred D. Miller, "Did Aristotle Have the Concept of Identity?" *Philosophical Review* 82 (1973):483–90. Still, I think that there is room to argue that in certain respects, Aristotle's notion of sameness is less close to the standard modern notion of identity than it is to a version of what Peter Geach calls "relative identity" (not relative to certain general terms, such as "sortals" or "count nouns," but, instead, to various different standards of indiscernibility). See especially his "Ontological Relativity and Relative Identity," in *Logic and Ontology,* edited by M. Munitz (New York, 1973), 287–302. This type of relative identity can be interestingly compared to the "relativistic" position on transworld identification expounded by David Kaplan in "Transworld Heir Lines," *The Possible and the Actual,* edited by M. Loux (Ithaca, N.Y., 1979), 88–109, especially 99–104, and also to some ideas of Jaakko Hintikka on the distinction between different kinds of individuation, in,

e.g., "On the Logic of Perception," *Models for Modalities* (Dordrecht, 1969), 151–83, and developed by Richmond H. Thomason, "Perception and Individuation," in *Logic and Ontology,* edited by M. Munitz, 261–85. But even if sameness is, in some sense, relative, in Aristotle's view, one sort of sameness is still taken to be primary (see next note).

9. I use 'leading' to translate '*kuriōtata*' at 103a25. Although it is almost universally translated as 'most strictly' (and *kuriōs* as 'strictly'), I do not see any evidence that that is its meaning. When one sense of a word is said to be the "strict(est)" sense, I take it to be suggested that the other senses are casual or loose, or the like, and that if one adhered to strict standards, one would use the word only in the "strict" sense. To call a sense of a word the "leading" or "primary" sense, on the other hand, is more vague and is also ambiguous, since different standards of priority can come into play, but it is not to say that the other senses of the word ought in any way to be dropped or not taken seriously. I think it is clear that when Aristotle takes one sense of 'same' to be primary, he does not mean that it is the only sense that "strict" standards of usge would sanction, but that it has a kind of priority that philosophical investigation must explain (see, e.g., *Met.* V. 11). My reason for taking sameness in being to be tantamount to identity is not that Aristotle calls it "primary," but rather that it is the relation that he continues to hold to be governed by (I).

10. In some cases, it is difficult to tell whether he is talking here about particulars or universals, though I think that he means to be talking consistently about particulars here.

11. White, "Aristotle on Sameness and Oneness," 195–96.

12. "Aristotle's Response to Quine's Objections to Modal Logic," *Journal of Philosophical Logic* 5 (1976):159–86.

13. Matthews, "Accidental Unities," 237.

14. R. M. Dancy, "On Some of Aristotle's First Thoughts about Substance," *Philosophical Review* 84 (1975):338–73, especially 368, and Lewis, "Accidental Sameness in Aristotle," 22–23 (I am assuming that Lewis is correct in taking Dancy's word 'formal' as equivalent to 'intensional'). Lewis's argument against Dancy appears to be simply that accidental sames "may" (p. 23, 1. 2) differ in nonmodal properties (he does not show that they *must* so differ). But the point is that even when they do not, Aristotle's standard of distinctness in *logos* still makes them distinct.

15. See *Met.* V. 6, 1015b16–34 versus 1016a32–b11, and V. 9, 1017b35–1018a2; X. 3, 1054a33–b3. The point is, of course, not that there is only a modal distinction between the general terms used to designate accidental sames, such as 'man' and 'pale', that are obviously nonequivalent in extension. But when we consider a single case of accidental sameness, the rest of the extensions of the terms is irrelevant; Aristotle insists that the terms be different in definition (*Top.* 103a29 ff. versus 25–27), and they are different in definition even if they are extensionally equivalent (102a18–30, 103a27–29). (Remember that, as is generally recognized, sameness in definition is not, in Aristotle's view, a relation between linguistic expressions, nor does it *arise from,* though it is related to, facts about linguistic usage or about what human beings actually know.)

16. See my "Origins of Aristotle's Essentialism."

17. Barnes, review. Matthews, "Accidental Unities," also makes evident his feeling that Aristotle's view is strange by calling such things as the pale (one) "kooky" objects.

18. Someone might object that it is a basic fact about the actual world that the attribute of being a featherless biped and the attribute of being a man are distinct, not something that is "made" to be so by facts about which things possess them in other possible worlds. Indeed, someone might claim that it is the distinctness of the attributes in the actual world that "makes" it the case that they are not shared in common in all possible worlds. But although I shall not argue the point here, I take it to be important and right to think of matters in the way that I have put them.

19. Saul A. Kripke, *Naming and Necessity* (Cambridge, Mass., 1972), 3–4, 5.

20. Ibid., 14–15, 53–60.

21. At *Met.* V. 6, which I think V. 9 has to be read in conjunction with, Aristotle says that "whatever is one in number is one in form" (1016b36). If oneness in number subsumes accidental oneness, then this statement almost certainly conflicts with 1054a33–b3, which plainly assumes that what is the same in number need not be the same in form. But there is no reason to think that there is a conflict, because there is no reason to think that accidental oneness here falls under oneness in number, or that at 1054a33–b3, accidental

sameness falls under sameness in number. Ross says that it must do so in the latter passage (W. D. Ross, *Aristotle's Metaphysics.* Vol. II [Oxford, 1924], 287), where he follows Alexander, but his argument seems to me plainly invalid.

22. Notice that sameness in number, whatever exactly it comes to, is not confined by Aristotle to material particulars: see *Top.* 151b28–33, 152a11–19.

23. For material in Aristotle pertinent to this difficult issue, see especially *Met.* IX.10 and VI. 4, and *De An.* III. 6.

24. Perhaps not quite nothing: it all depends on how one takes the Cartesian view that Kripke advances in *Naming and Necessity,* 144–55. I take it, though, that he is discussing states rather than substances (see sec. IV of this paper).

25. Alan Gibbard, "Contingent Identity," *Journal of Philosophical Logic* 4 (1975):187–221, especially 191.

26. Ibid., 192–93.

27. The controversy about whether he does was begun by G. E. L. Owen, "Inherence," *Phronesis* 10 (1965):97–110. I do not know how, or when, it will end.

28. Perhaps Gibbard's view presupposes something less than full determinacy, e.g., some determinate range within which there may be indeterminacy. So far as I can see, it does not matter for present purposes.

29. For a different view of *De Interpretatione* 9, see, e.g., G. E. M. Anscombe, "Aristotle and the Sea Battle," *Mind* 65 (1956):1–15. For a defense of the traditional interpretation, which I adopt, see, e.g., J. L. Ackrill, *Aristotle's Categories and De Interpretatione* (Oxford, 1963), 132–42. Ross, *Aristotle's Mteaphysics,* vol. II, 361, takes *Met.* IV.2 to deny what I take it to assert, that there are objective cases of accidental, undetermined events.

30. See *Met.* 1016a17–24, 1015a7–11, 1023a28–29.

31. As I remark below in section VI, *fin.*, this point is probably related to Aristotle's claim that matter is "potentiality" *dunamis* (*Met.* 1042a27–28, 1043a27–28, 1042b9–11, 1049a23–24) and similar doctrines. I should also add that I believe that in some contexts, the contrast between *dunamis* and *energeia* should be thought of as a contrast between, not "potentiality" and "actuality" as is customary, but "indeterminacy" and "determinacy."

32. See notes 6 and 27 for related issues. Such conditions of individuation for things like "the musical (one)" are obviously like those generally associated with individual attributes, which are traditionally seen in *Cat.* 2, though their presence there is denied by Owen, "Inherence." I am inclined to think that whether or not Aristotle really believed in individual attributes when he wrote the *Categories,* he did not believe in them in later works (if the *Cat.* is early), but he believed in things like the musical (one) instead. This issue, and the question of the exact difference between the two kinds of entity, require a long story. For present purposes, what is important is that whatever may be the case for individual attributes, the other sorts of entities are thought of as, in a sense, concrete and located, and as accidentally the same as material substances, rather than as "in" them (*Cat.* 2). Into the same discussion, one must also bring Aristotle's views on mathematical objects, on which see especially Ian Mueller, "Aristotle on Geometrical Objects," *Archiv für Geschichte der Philosophie* 52 (1970):156–71, and Julia Annas, *Aristotle's Metaphysics M and N* (Oxford, 1976), for issues that must be dealt with in this connection, which are, unfortunately, too numerous for me even to summarize here.

33. For some speculation on Aristotle's reasons for avoiding specifications with dates, see Hintikka, *Time and Necessity* (Oxford, 1973), ch. 4.

34. This seems to be the best way to take 1070a9–10. The alternatives offered by Ross, in his comment on these lines, both seem to me weak, though the one he adopts is grammatically the same as mine.

35. I have suggested, in "Aristotle on Sameness and Oneness," that part of the exlanation is also that his preoccupations have shifted to problems about identity over time (see especially pp. 191–92), though I would now withdraw the suggestion made there that it was also because Aristotle was confused about the notion of identity (see note 8).

36. See note 31. My suggestion bears important connections to, and was partly suggested to me by, some ideas of George Bealer, "Predication and Matter," *Synthese* 31 (1975):493–508, especially 499.

37. For Quine's view about dispositions and the like, see in particular his "Natural Kinds," *Ontological Relativity and Other Essays* (New York, 1969).

MIDWEST STUDIES IN PHILOSOPHY, XI (1986)

Toward an Aristotelian Theory of Abstract Objects

MICHAEL J. LOUX

Throughout his philosophical career, Aristotle insisted on the ontological priority of familiar concrete objects, and in his most mature writings, he encapsulated this category preference for the things he called substances in the thesis that 'being' has *pros hen* equivocity or focal meaning.[1] This thesis has frequently been understood as a claim about existential statements, the claim (1) that 'exists' has a different meaning or sense when predicated of logical subjects from different Aristotelian categories and (2) that, among these distinct senses, that appropriate to substances is primary or basic. The proponent of this interpretation would spell out the doctrine by telling us that 'exists' has a different meaning in each of the following:

(1) Wisdom exists
(2) Paternity exists
(3) The number two exists
(4) Socrates exists

and would supplement the story with some suitable account of the distinction between independent or subsistent and dependent or merely inherent entities, attempting thereby to justify the claim that the sense of 'exists' at work in sentences like (4) is more basic than that attaching to sentences like (1) through (3).

Although a long-standing reading of the *pros hen* nature of 'being', such an interpretation has serious shortcomings. First, it fails to recognize that Aristotle's intentions are to use the *pros hen* equivocity of 'being' as the vehicle for explaining the ontological priority of substances. On this intrpretation, we must understand the priority in advance and, then, interpret the *pros hen* nature of 'exists' in the light of that priority. Second, the interpretation takes the *pros hen* to be just another kind of equivocity; it overlooks the fact that when Aristotle insists on focal meaning for a given term, his aim is to point to semantical properties that distinguish *pros hen* expressions from our standard examples of equivocal terms.

Consider Aristotle's favorite example of a *pros hen* term, the predicate 'healthy'.[2] 'Healthy' is used in different senses when we speak of a healthy complexion, a healthy food, and a healthy man. But among the different senses attaching to the term, that in which it is predicated of a metabolically sound organism is primary or basic; and the remaining senses of the term are to be explained in terms of this core meaning. A ruddy complexion is healthy in the sense that it is symptomatic of something healthy in the basic sense, and a plateful of fresh spinach is healthy in the sense that its ingestion is productive of a thing healthy in the core sense. The central thrust of this account is that really only one sort of thing is healthy—metabolically sound organisms. Other things are called healthy because they bear some relation to the things that are properly said to be healthy. But, then, the force of applying the *pros hen* analysis to 'healthy' is reductionistic; for the analysis provides us with a recipe whereby, invoking the supplementary vocabulary specifying the various relations marked by the secondary uses of the term, we can analyze away all but the primary use of the term.

Now, we are to apply this sort of account to 'exists'. A problem, however, arises. In the case of 'healthy', we analyzed away all but the primary use of the term; but the things that serve as logical subjects of 'healthy' in its secondary uses survived the analysis. We still had our ruddy complexion and our spinach chock full of vitamins; we just withheld the predicate 'healthy' in their cases, reserving it for the things that have the complexion and partake of the spinach. But when we try out this form of analysis on 'exists', we find that the procedure of analyzing away all but the core sense of 'exists' has the effect of eliminating from our inventory of logical subjects all the things of which we predicated the term in its secondary uses. If we insist on focal meaning for 'exists' and claim that it is only in sentences like (4) that the term exhibits its core sense, then we are committed to the idea that 'exists' as applied to things like virtues, relations, and numbers can be analyzed away in favor of 'exists' as a predicate of the things Aristotle calls substances. But, then, what becomes of virtues, relations, and numbers? Strip 'healthy' away from complexions, foods, and forms of exercise, and those things survive; we just stop calling them healthy. But the logic of 'exists' is such that if we deny existence of qualities, quantities, relations, and the like, we find ourselves with nothing left but substances; and it is difficult to see just how the presumed analysis of sentences like (1) through (3) is supposed to go.

Aristotle is sensitive to this subtlety in the logic of 'exists'. His response is to agree that extending the *pros hen* analysis to 'exists' forces us to deny that what appear to be expressions referring to logical subjects in sentences like (1) through (3) are genuinely functioning as such. If only the things he calls substances really exist, then there are no such things as qualities, quantities, and relations; and a radical strategy is required for sentences like (1) through (3). The strategy, as outlined in *Metaphysics* Z.1 and hinted at elsewhere, consists in recasting such sentences, so that they turn out to be claims about substances.[3] Thus, (1) becomes

   (5) Some substance exists and it is wise;

and (2) becomes

   (6) At least two substances exist, and one is the father of the other.

What appear to be existential claims about nonsubstantial items turn out to be claims about the existence of substances and how they are qualified, quantified, and related to each other. The only use of 'exists' that survives the analysis is that appropriate to substances. Likewise, the only genuinely referring expressions are those from the category of substance; for on the analysis Aristotle provides, apparently referring expressions from other categories give way to predicate-terms enabling us to characterize substances.

Of course, Aristotle need not deny that what is expressed by sentences like (1) through (3) is true. The very point of endorsing the *pros hen* analysis in this context is to provide an account of how, when only substances exist, such sentences might manage to serve as the vehicles for making true claims. Nor should we suppose that the kind of analysis required for a sentence apparently about something other than a substance will be as straightforward as our analyses of (1) and (2) might suggest. It may be (and doubtless would be in the case of "things" like irrational numbers, socioeconomic classes, and supernovas) that the analysis would be a very complicated matter indeed. We need only suppose that the philosopher's laconic style conceals a garrulous philosophical persona.

So Aristotle's claim (and that of anyone defending a genuinely Aristotelian perspective in ontology) is that although it is surely legitimate to engage in discourse apparently about properties, relations, kinds, and the like, in the final analysis, there are no such things, and such discourse is really discourse about substances. What is called for, then, is a reductive analysis, one that preserves the features of our discourse about nonsubstantial "things," but that shows that discourse to have its foundation in a body of discourse presupposing the existence of substances and nothing else.

The project of identifying the proper form of such an analysis is both venerable and familiar. It has, however, given rise to a dialectic, the upshot of which has not proved satisfactory to the Aristotelian; for without laboring the point with technical details, the fact is that the Aristotelian has not had an easy time of providing an analysis of the required sort for even the most elementary claims about abstract entities. The difficulty is that we regard many of the claims about abstract entities as not merely true, but necessarily true. We think, for example, that it is a necessary truth that wisdom is a virtue; and, as the Platonist correctly points out, any attempt to construe such a claim as ultimately about subtances is going to founder on the fact that there is no claim about wise persons that is both a plausible substitute for the original claim and a necessary truth.[4]

But were Aristotelians to succeed in identifying such a claim, their troubles would not be over; for whereas they may have succeeded in showing the derivative character of talk about wisdom, their success here would hinge on their willingness to invoke the notion of necessary truth. On the surface, this appears innocent enough, but when probed, the strategy becomes suspect; for talk about what is necessarily true, necessarily false, possible, contingent, and so on must ultimately be construed as talk about a new species of abstract entities, propositions.

So Aristotelians are forced to confront a new species of nonsubstantial entity, the proposition; and, presumably, they must show how talk apparently about propositions, with all of its unique features, is really just talk about substances. Interpreting propositional discourse as discourse about sentences or utterances will not do; for discourse about individuals inscribing and uttering is just not rich enough to capture the full range of features we want to ascribe to propositions. The Aristotelian has realized this and has traditionally attempted to deal with propositions in conceptualist terms, insisting that talk about propositions is talk about the conceptual activities of rational beings, and that such talk, in turn, is really just talk about the conceiving rational beings.[5]

But however well motivated the move, it has its problems. The central thrust of the view is that talk about propositions is to be understood as talk about persons and their believings, conceivings, and so on. It is notorious, however, that verbs like 'conceives' and 'believes' (the so-called verbs of propositional attitude) characteristically take that-clauses as their grammatical objects. Thus,

(7) Socrates conceives that the Acropolis is on a hill

and

(8) Plato believes that Fido is a dog;

and the standard interpretation of such that-clauses construes them as names of propositions.

So how can the conceptualist strategy claim to serve the purposes of the Aristotelian whose aim is to show that there are no such things as propositions? Well, here the Aristotelian has characteristically argued that the surface grammar of intentional discourse is misleading. It suggests a relational interpretation of conceptual activity, where we have a mental state or act a person undergoes and an object that the state or act takes, that object being a proposition. The Aristotelian insists on rejecting this act-object interpretation in favor of what is often called the act theory of intentionality, according to which expressions like 'believes that Fido is a dog' and 'thinks that 2 + 2 = 4' are construed not in relational terms but as one-place predicates enabling us to say how it is with persons.

There are several different ways of filling in this very general suggestion. One obvious form the act theory can take involves an adverbial account of intentional discourse where the recalcitrant that-clauses are construed as adverbs expressing *how* a person thinks, conceives, believes, and so on. Alternatively, the act theorist can deny that verbs like 'believes' and 'conceives' are complete predicates, construing them, say, as predicate-forming functors that take declarative sentences as their arguments and yield as their values one-place predicates true or false of persons. Whichever strategy they take, Aristotelians will argue that the predicates characterizing the mental states of persons bear interesting logical relations to each other that are the result of their semantic structure rather than of any implicit reference to mutually involving mental states or logically related abstract entities of the propositional sort.

Suppose, then, we endorse this general conceptualist strategy. Just where will it take us? Not far, I would suggest, at least not if we argue, as conceptualists typically have, that all talk about propositions can be construed as talk about the intellective or conceputal lives of rational beings like ourselves. On this view, the existence of a conceputal lives of rational beings like ourselves. On this view, the existence of a proposition is to turn on the fact that some rational being or other has had the relevant thought; but the fact is that if we restrict ourselves to rational beings like ourselves, there just will not be enough thoughts to do the job. Platonists never tire of pointing out, for example, that there is a nondenumerable infinity of propositions specifying, in turn, that each irrational less than the number one is less than the number two; but for obvious reasons, we have to concede that it is just not the case that for each such proposition there has been, is, or will be, among rational beings like ourselves, one who has had, is having, or will have the relevant thought. And, of course, if for any one of these propositions, there is such a rational being with the relevant thought, this fact is merely contingent. Platonists, however, rightly point out that the existence of propositions is itself necessary and so deny (rightly again, I think) that attempts to derive discourse about propositions from a base involving the contingent goings-on in the mental lives of rational beings is bound to fail.

So things do not look too promising for the Aristotelian's attempt to get by with an ontology consisting exclusively of Aristotelian substances. Platonists with their rich ontology of properties, relations, kinds, actions, events, and propositions appear to win the day; and, of course, this is a conclusion that each successive generation of philosophers has learned to live with. But is the conclusion inevitable? Is there no way that the Aristotelian can get by with an ontology restricted to substances? My own view is that something like the Aristotelian strategy can be executed successfully; but only if Aristotelians are willing to apply their conceptualist insights to the mental life of a rational being whose range of conceptual activity, unlike ours, is in no way limited and who, unlike us, eternally and necessarily thinks. In short, what is required is a conceptualism that makes reference to God. Let me show how this is to go.

We are to suppose that there is such a being as God and that God thinks. There is, of course, no *thing* such that God thinks that thing. Just as Aristotelian conceptualists eschew an act-object analysis of human thinking, I shall insist that, as applied in the divine case, expressions like 'thinks that $2 + 2 = 4$' are nonrelational predicates enabling us to characterize God, to say how it is with God; and although I do not want to rule out an adverbial treatment of the relevant that-clauses, I shall take 'thinks that' to be a functor operating on declarative sentences to generate one-place predicates. As I shall interpret it, 'thinks that' is a generic functor in the sense that there are several more specific functors that identify the various forms thinking can take. I want to focus on three of these functors: 'conceives that', 'entertains that', and 'believes that'. Each picks out a different kind of thinking; and each serves, when applied to declarative sentences, to generate one-place predicates that characterize God, or any person for that matter, in terms of what the Platonist would call distinct attitudes toward one and the same or different propositional contents.

I would not seek to define these different functors. After all, they provide the primitive or basic ways in which we characterize the mental life of God; but I can give an idea of the sense I attach to the terms if I say that the 'conceives that' functor generates predicates that are assent- or acceptance-neutral. To ascribe such a predicate to a person has the force of saying that the person grasps, apprehends, or understands what the Platonist calls the propositional content of the relevant predicate. 'Believes that', on the other hand, generates predicates that are true only of persons who endorse, assent to, or accept what the Platonist calls the propositional content of those predicates; and 'entertains that' stands midway between these two functors. Although it does not generate predicates whose application hinges on assent or acceptance, one entertains only where, on the Platonist's account, one might have accepted a given propositional content.

I assume that, despite their Platonistic overtones, my characterizations of conceiving and believing are clear enough. It is the 'entertains that' functor that stands in need of further clarification. Entertaining, I have said, stands midway between believing and conceiving; it is weaker than the former, yet stronger than the latter. When we entertain, we focus on alternatives to what we believe, where what we believe is included among those alternatives; but there are limits to what a person is prepared to entertain. Perhaps, the closest analogy we can draw on is the epistemic attitude we take toward stories and the elements of stories. Stories, or at least the elements of stories, are often factual. Nonetheless, in assuming the epistemic attitude appropriate to stories, one prescinds from judgments of truth or falsity. But although one is willing to consider as legitimate elements in a story many things one refuses to endorse as fact, storytelling is subject to principles of plausibility; and should some element in a story violate those principles, a person refuses to take the story seriously, refuses, that is, to accord the story the appropriate epistemic attitude. In the same way, when we entertain, we focus on things we do not believe as well as on things we do believe; but we do not entertain just anything. Among the things a person conceives, grasps, or apprehends, but does not believe, some are construed as too preposterous, too absurd to merit the epistemic stance I have called entertaining.

I hope these informal remarks give some sense of the force I attach to the three functors. Toward sharpening the notions, I would point to some technical features of the relevant functors. First, when applied to one and the same declarative sentence, the functors generate predicates with interesting logical relations, relations implicit in my informal remarks on the three functors. The Platonist would characterize the relations by saying that the set of propositions a person believes is a proper subset of the propositions that person entertains, and the set of propositions a person entertains is a proper subset of the propositions he or she conceives. An Aristotelian, on the other hand, would put the point as follows: if a person, P, believes that q, then P entertains that q, but not necessarily vice versa; and if a person, P, entertains that q, then P conceives that q, but not necessarily vice versa.

Second, when predicates formed from the three functors are ascribed to God, their ascription conforms to the followign axioms:

(A) God conceives that p if and only if
    God conceives that not-p;
(B) God believes that p if and only if
    God does not believe that not-p.

The following principle, itself a consequence of (B) and the logical relations between the 'entertains that' and 'believes that' functors, governs the ascription to God of predicates formed from the 'entertains that' functor:

(C) If God entertains that p, then either God entertains that not-p or God believes that p and does not entertain that not-p.

The second disjunct of the consequent of (C) invokes a kind of belief that will play an important role in our account. For convenience, I shall label it strong belief and shall say that a person, P, strongly believes that q just in case P believes that q and does not entertain that not-q.

So there is God, and God thinks by believing, entertaining, and conceiving. Predicates formed from the relevant functors enable us to characterize God in God's mental life. Of course, the range of such predicates at our disposal does not exhaust the unlimited richness of divine thought. There are ways God is in God's conceiving, entertaining, and believing that we lack the conceptual and linguistic resources to capture. Nonetheless, the predicate-resources available to us enable us to say enough about God to get on with our Aristotelian project, that of showing how an ontology restricted to substances might provide an objective base for Platonistic discourse with its talk of propositions, properties, relations, kinds, and so on.

Let us begin with the case of propositions. I have denied that God's thought is relational. God does not think by undergoing a mental act directed toward an intentional object. God thinks by being such and such, where we capture just how it is with God by employing predicates constructed out of the various intentionality functors and declarative sentences. How could such thinking on God's part provide a base that legitimates *our* Platonistic talk of propositions? I would suggest that we look to God's conceiving for an answer.

The Platonist insists that God conceives, grasps, or apprehends all propositional contents. Being Aristotelians, we do not want to put things this way; but we have already agreed with the Platonist that the predicate-resources at our disposal fail to exhaust the richness of God's conceiving. Were God to use a language for purposes of self-characterization, God alone would have a stock of predicates of the form 'conceives that such and such is the case' sufficient to characterize exhaustively this aspect of the divine mental life.

We can further agree with the Platonist that talk of divine conceiving and talk of propositional contents are intimately related; but whereas the Platonist wants to characterize divine conception in terms of the antecedently given notion of propositional contents, as thorough-going Aristotelians we must insist that it is the activity of divine conceiving that provides a base legitimating or justifying our appeal to the notion of a proposition. Hence, we shall adopt some principle of the following sort:

(α) If God conceives that p, then that p is a proposition (where 'p' is a placeholder for declarative sentences);

and we shall insist that the 'that p' which appears in the consequent of (1) has a depth grammar quite different from that associated with the 'that p' of the antecedent. In their surface grammar, both are substantival expressions. However, the 'that p' in the antecedent is only superficially substantival; for as we have seen, a predicate like 'conceives that $2 + 2 = 4$' does not break up into 'conceives' and 'that $2 + 2 = 4$'. It is a predicate constructed out of a predicate-forming functor ('conceives that') and a declarative sentence ('$2 + 2 = 4$'). The that-clause in the consequent of (α), on other hand, is properly substantival; and what we, as Aristotelians, want to claim is that although we are justified in invoking discourse involving properly substantival that-clauses, the justification does not rest on the existence of a special category of abstract entities, propositions. In the final analysis, there are no propositions. There is simply God who is properly characterized as conceiving that this or that is the case; and the fact that God is properly so characterized is what legitimates discourse apparently (but not really) about propositions.

Now, propositions, we want to say, have a variety of characteristics: they are true or false, necessary or contingent, true or false in a possible world, and so on. How are our ascriptions of these characteristics justified within the Aristotelian framework we are delineating? Let us begin with the case of truth and falsity. According to the Platonist, there is a one-to-one correspondence between propositions and another sort of abstract entity, what the Platonist calls states of affairs. States of affairs are said to obtain or fail to obtain; and a proposition is said to be true just in case the state of affairs corresponding to it obtains.[6] This is a complicated story indeed, one that enables us to give an account of truth only by multiplying the categories of nonsubstantial objects in our primitive ontology. Aristotelians will want none of this. Theirs will be a shorter story. They will tell us that although God's conceiving provides the justification for talk about propositions, not all of those propositions are correlated with God's beliefs. God is properly characterized both as conceiving that $2 + 2 = 4$ and as conceiving that $2 + 2 = 5$; and that is as it should be. However, when we turn to the stock of predicates for characterizing God's beliefs, we must assume that although 'believes that $2 + 2 = 4$' is satisfied by the Godhead, 'believes that $2 + 2 = 5$' is not. But, then, Aristotelians have an easy time of identifying the objective basis for our ascription of truth to propositions. They will suggest that we adopt a principle of the following sort:

(β) If God believes that p, then that p is a true proposition,

insisting once again that, despite appearances to the contrary, the that-clauses in the antecedent and consequent of (β) have radically different depth grammars. To complete their account of the notions of truth and falsity, Aristotelians will appeal to axiom (B), which governs the use of 'believes that' predicates in God's case, telling us that the conjunction of that axiom and (β) provide a justification for our practice of parceling out the concepts of truth and falsity over the totality of propositions.

Likewise, the modal properties of propositions (their being possible, necessary, contingent, and so on) fall into place on this account. Consider God's entertaining. Entertaining, we said, stands midway between conceiving and believing. Although it does not involve assent or endorsement, the fact is that we entertain only with a view toward accepting. Entertaining, we might say, is a kind of option-oriented thinking, in the sense that we entertain only what we might believe. But, then, if we look to the pool of predicates characterizing God's entertainings, we find a firm basis for ascribing possibility to propositions. Indeed, some principle of the following sort seems inescapable:

(γ) If God entertains that p, then that p is a possible proposition;

and when we reflect on that fact that entertaining has a view toward believing, we see that to ascribe possibility to a proposition has the effect of ascribing possible truth to a proposition, so that the full force of this *de dicto* modality is preserved on this account.

Justifying the ascription of necessity to a proposition is only slightly more complicated. Here we must appeal to the notion of strong belief. Recall that a person strongly believes that p just in case he or she believes that p and does not entertain that not-p. Suppose, then, that God strongly believes that p. (α), (β), (γ), and the standard ties between truth and falsity (justified by axiom (B)) together justify us in saying that the proposition that p is true and the proposition that not-p is not possible. But in the light of our ordinary notion of propositional necessity, that is just to say that the proposition that p is necessary, i.e., necessarily true; and given the notions of possibility, necessity, truth, and falsity, the notions of a proposition's being contingently true or false and a proposition's being necessarily false or impossible fall out in familiar and natural ways.

So we have a justification of the standard notions of propositional modality, and that justification is strictly Aristotelian. Notice, however, an interesting fact. If we assume that God is not fickle in God's entertainings, then we can assume that if God entertains that such and such is the case, God strongly believes that God entertains that such and such is the case; but, then, it follows that if a proposition is necessarily true, it is necessarily true that it is necessarily true and, likewise, that if a proposition is possible, it is necessarily the case that it is possible. There is a parallel assumption about God's conceiving that we have no option but to endorse, namely, that if God conceives that such and such is the case, then God strongly believes that God conceives that it is the case. I would recommend that we endorse as well the relevant assumption about the stability of God's entertaining; hence, I would recommend that we accept these S-5 ish assumptions about propositional modality.

On the contemporary philosophical scene, there is a familiar connection drawn between talk of propositional modality and possible worlds. It is claimed that propositions are possible that are true in some possible world, that propositions are true that are true in the actual world, that propositions are necessary that are true in all possible worlds; and with the help of these insights, much interesting and useful work on the semantics of modal systems is rendered possible. Can these connections be justified on the Aristotelian framework I am developing? To some extent, they can. Let us begin by noting that the predicates we invoke in characterizing God's mental life can be complex. We have focused on predicates like 'conceives that $2 + 2 = 4$' and 'believes that water is H_2O'; but predicates like

'conceives that both $2 + 2 = 4$ and the earth is round'

and

'believes that both Reagan is president and if water is H_2O, then all bachelors are unmarried' also hold true of God. Indeed, there is no upper limit on the complexity of predicates characterizing the divine mental life. But however complex the predicates we invoke here, we cannot succeed in exhausting the richness of God's thinking. This comes out most poignantly when we reflect on one kind of divine entertaining, what we might call maximal entertaining. Were we to have at our disposal predicates complex enough to characterize all of God's thinking, then we could characterize maximal entertaining by saying that God maximally entertains that p just in case (1) God entertains that p and (2) God strongly believes that for any q such that God conceives that q either if God believes that p then God believes that q or if God believes that p then God believes that not-q. But given the limits of human thought and language, we are unable to identify sentences for which the 'p' in the attempted characterization is an appropriate placeholder; and since there are more ways God is in God's conceiving than we can express, our use of the expression 'for any q' in the abortive characterization looks suspiciously like the appeal to a quantifier over propositions. But although we cannot give instances of predicates that express the relevant entertainments, we are justified in supposing that God entertains in ways that satisfy a maximality condition; that is, that God entertains in ways such that the belief corresponding to that entertainment determines, for every divine conception, either that God has the associated belief or does not have the associated belief. Furthermore, we are justified in supposing that God could provide an exhaustive characterization of what the Platonist calls the contents of God's maximal entertainings and that God could run through all of the predicates of the form 'conceives that p' that hold true of God; but, then, we are justified in supposing that God can do what we cannot do, provide a characterization of the concept of a maximal entertainment that is not in the least contaminated by Platonistic notions.[7] Now, what I want to suggest is that God's maximally entertaining this or that provides us with the objective foundation of our talk of possible worlds. If we are willing to violate the canons of austerity guiding (α)–(γ) by invoking the symbol 'p' (presumably a placeholder for sentences, but one such that we cannot, but God can, identify the sentences for which it is a placeholder), then we can say that

(δ)   If God maximally entertains that p, then that p is a possible world.

So God's maximal entertainings provide the basis for discourse about possible worlds. But we have already pointed to the intimate connection between the 'entertains that' and 'believes that' functors, according to which one entertains only where one might believe. Suppose, then, that God entertains that p. Given the relevant connection, it should be clear that God strongly believes that for some q such that God maximally entertains that q, if God believes that q, then God believes that p;[8] but then we can say, in the languate of propositions, that every possible proposition is true in some possible world. Likewise, if God strongly believes that p, then God does not so much as entertain that not-p; then, God believes that p (as we might put it) no matter what; hence, the result, in the language of propositions, that a necessary proposition is true in every possible world.

Now, among God's maximal entertainments, there will be one, but only one, such that God believes that it is the case. This fact makes it legitimate to speak of one and only one actual world; and obviously, since all the propositions that are true are grounded in God's beliefs, it follows that what we call true propositions are true in the actual world.

So what we want to say about propositions can be justified on the strictly Aristotelian base of a divine substance who thinks. To see how one might find in this base the resources for legitimating our talk of properties, kinds, and relations, I would suggest that we consider the internal structure of the predicates we use to characterize God's inner mental life. Some of those predicates have the following form:

conceives that something is F-ish.

Thus,

'conceives that Socrates is snub-nosed'
'conceives that Plato is bald'
'conceives that Fido is brown',

all of which enable us to describe God as thinking that some object or other is characterized in some way. But if we take predicates of this sort as our base, then the following principle seems plausible as a rough-and-ready attempt to show how talk about properties might be justified:

(ϵ) If God conceives that something or other is F-ish then *being F* is a property.

In the same way, there are predicates of the following form true of God:

conceives that something is a K.

Thus,

'conceives that Socrates is a man'
'conceives that Secretariat is a horse'
'conceives that Fido is a dog',

all of which enable us to describe God as thinking that some object or other is to be classified in some way. But, then, it seems reasonable to suppose that

(ζ) If God conceives that something or other is a K, then K-kind is a kind.

Finally, there are predicates of the following form true of God:

conceives that one thing, a, is R with respect to another thing, b.

Thus,

'conceives that Socrates is the husband of Xantippe'
'conceives that Ronald Reagan is taller than Jimmy Carter'
'conceives that the Capitol is a mile from the White House',

all of which enable us to describe God as thinking that one thing is related in some way to another thing. Such predicates as applied to God provide an obvious foundation for our talk of relations:

(η) If God conceives that one thing is R with respect to another thing, then *being R* is a relation.[9]

Hence, the Aristotelian framework provides us with the resources for justifying talk about properties, kinds, and relations. Such things have often been lumped together and called attributes. Intimately connected with talk about attributes is the concept of exemplification. Thus, objects *possess* properties, *belong to* kinds, and *enter into* relations. In our Aristotelian framework, this talk of exemplification has a ready justification. Consider predicates of the form

> entertains that something is F-ish
> entertains that something is a K

and

> entertains that one thing is R with respect to another thing.

Many predicates of this form apply to God; it is their applicability that provides a justification for thinking that certain attributes are exemplifiable. Likewise, God's mental life is appropriately characterized by predicates of the form

> believes that something is F-ish
> believes that something is a K

and

> believes that one thing is R with respect to another thing.

Their applicability to the Godhead, I would suggest, underwrites our belief that certain attributes are exemplified.

In a similar way, if we look to the predicates characterizing God's strong beliefs, we find the resources for legitimating essentialist talk about a given object's necessarily or essentially exemplifying this or that attribute. Thus, predicates of the form

> strongly believes that if a particular substance, a, exists, then a is F-ish (a K, or R with respect to some other substance) (where 'a' is a placeholder for proper names of substances)

hold true of God. For example, it is reasonable to think that predicates like the following apply to God:

> 'strongly believes that if Socrates exists, then Socrates is rational'
> 'strongly believes that if Secretariat exists, then Secretariat is a horse'

and

> 'strongly believes that if the planet Mars exists, then Mars was created by God',

They all characterize God as strongly believing that if a given substance exists, it is a properly characterized or classified in a particular way; and their applicability to God, I would suggest, provides the objective basis for our saying that the relevant objects exemplify the relevant attributes necessarily or essentially. Of course, since God's strong beliefs are invariant across God's maximal entertainments, it follows that the applicability of such predicates provides us with the basis for thinking that an object exemplifies an attribute essentially or necessarily if and only if that object exemplifies that attribute in every possible world in which it exists.

So Aristotelians, invoking the framework of divine thought I have sketched, can provide an account of the legitimacy of Platonistic discourse about attributes as well as propositions. Assuming the existence of a rational substance, God, they can, without any appeal to Platonistic entities like propositions or properties, show how it might be that there is an objective foundation for the rich Platonistic framework that is part and parcel of our working picture of the world. What we manage to say using that framework, they can agree, is often true; but the grounds of that truth do not consist in the existence of objects of the sort suggested by a naive consideration of the framework. There are only substances, they will insist; but one substance has a mental life rich enough to support beliefs that are apparently, but not really, about entities of the sort so exotically characterized by Platonists.

Anyone who finds this strategy attractive might be tempted to count its possibility a resounding victory for traditional nominalism. But although it is true that the nominalist and I agree in denying the existence of abstract entities, the view I have sketched parts company with traditional versions of nominalism on one important issue. What I would like to call responsible nominalists (as opposed to those revisionists who would uphold nominalism even at the expense of rejecting beliefs and intuitions that lie at the core of our conceptual framework) have held that although our appeal to Platonistic language is legitimate, its legitimacy rests on the possibility of translating that language into one that is rigorously nominalistic. So, in the end, traditional nominalists have wanted to hold that our language is only apparently Platonistic. As they see it, expressions (substantival that-clauses, abstract singular terms, and so on) whose use appears to commit us to the existence of propositions, properties, and the like are replaceable, without loss of content, by expressions whose use presupposes the existence of individuals and nothing else; and those who have sought to develop an account of Platonistic discourse consistent with Aristotle's contention that only substances exist have typically endorsed this central tenet of traditional nominalism. It is, however, a tenet I reject. Although I hold that the truth of our everyday beliefs presupposes none of the abstract entities eschewed by the hard-core Aristotelian, I want to deny that our language can be recast in any of the ways that might be favored by traditional nominalists.[10]

On this score, it is easy to misunderstand the various principles, (α) through (η), that I put forward in support of my version of Aristotelian conceptualism. Those principles are meant to show how there could be an objective foundation for our various Platonistic beliefs, something other than the abstract entities championed by the Platonist by virtue of which those beliefs are true. The relevant principles are not meant as translation rubrics enabling us to replace our Platonistic language by one a traditional nominalist would recommend. Were they intended as such, they would fail, and for an obvious reason. An atheist can, without semantic incongruity or inconsistency, speak of the various abstract entities. By itself, one might object, this consideration is not decisive; and here one might point to recent debates in the philosophy of language, insisting that the upshot of those debates is that speakers of a language can employ the referring expressions of that language without a full-blooded understanding of their semantic underpinnings. But even if we assume a semantically well-informed community of language users (all of them theistic conceptualists), the fact remains that the relevant language users could not use my principles (α) through (η) as translation rubics for demonstrating the inherent nominalistic base of our conceptual scheme.

Those principles could successfully serve the reductionist enterprise only if we had at our disposal predicates of the appropriate form characterizing the divine thought in ways that will correspond with the totality of propositions, relations, kinds, and properties posited by the Platonist. But, of course, we do not have the requisite predicates. We are not omniscient. Accordingly, our language has limitations of an obvious and familiar sort. As the Platonist wants to put it, there are more propositions than declarative sentences and more attributes than predicates for characterizing, classifying and relating objects. As an Aristotelian, I would make the point by saying that our predicate-resources for characterizing God's mental life are outstripped by that mental life; and it is precisely this fact, I want to claim, that makes it necessary for us to speak of propositions, properties, and the like. Were we to have at our disposal the descriptive resources sufficient to express all the ways God is in God's conceiving, entertaining, and believing, talk of the various abstract entities would be dispensable. But we do not, and it is not, so we are stuck with an inherently Platonistic way of looking at the world.

Perhaps I can make this aspect of my view clearer by pointing to its implications for a controversy that has proved central in recent discussions between nominalists and Platonists, the controversy over the semantics of the quantifiers, in particular the semantics of the ∃-quantifier. Some philosophers (typically Platonists) have insisted that the truth conditions for sentences incorporating the ∃-quantifier are to be given in objectual or referential terms (i.e., in terms that make reference to objects satisfying open sentences); whereas, others (typically nominalists) have argued for a substitutional account of the ∃-quantifier, according to which an ∃-quantification is true just in case it has a true substitution-instance. The significance of the controversy for the nominalism-Platonism issue is familiar enough; if the substitutionalist is right, then it is possible to endorse the quantification of sentential-variables and predicate-variables free of any commitment to propositions or attributes.

The fact is that the substitutional account fails precisely because it is possible for us to make true claims involving the quantifier even in cases where we do not (in fact, could not) have the linguistic resources for constructing the relevant true substitution-instances.[11] So we have no option but to accept the objectualist's account of the truth-conditions for quantified sentences; and if we want to endorse higher-order quantification, we are forced to concede once again that our conceptual framework is inherently Platonistic.

Suppose, however, that God were to use a language. Call it Godspeak. Since it would have sufficient descriptive resources to permit an exhaustive characterization of the divine mental life, Godspeak would include, for each quantified sentence endorsed by God, a sentence that represented a substitution-instance of that quantified sentence; and that substitution-instance would itself be endorsed by God. So, for that language, a substitutional account of quantification would be appropriate. Godspeak would, of course, be a language meeting the standards of the most austere nominalism. Its substantival that-clauses, its abstract singular terms, its terms expressing the concept of exemplification, and the *de dicto* modalities would all be eliminable, without loss of content, in favor of nominalistic predicates that God would use for the purposes of characterizing God's own mental life. Using Godspeak, God could provide a complete characterization of human language, identify its deficiencies, and, thereby, give an account of its inescapably Platonistic contours. But we who lack the perspective afforded by Godspeak must make do with our own Platonistic language; and although we can agree with the traditional nominalist that our use of that language does not presuppose the existence of the abstract entities championed by the Platonist, we must deny the possibility, for us at least, of translating that language into one that does not even give the appearance of commitment to the existence of those abstract entities.

In a similar fashion, the view I have outlined provides the resources for adjudicating another important philosophical controversy, that between realists and antirealists. I shall conclude by showing how. In different forms, the debate between realists and antirealists has played an important role throughout the history of modern philosophy and has come to occupy center stage in recent philosophical discussions. A number of different (and not always clearly articulated) issues have been operative in recent discussions of realism and antirealism; but a central concern in all these discussions is the notion of truth. [12] We can express this concern by asking whether, for each proposition, there is something by virtue of which that proposition is rendered determinately true or determinately false. On the view I have been delineating, the answer to this question is straightforwardly affirmative. Within our Platonistic conceptual scheme where talk of propositions, truth, and falsity has its natural home, each proposition is such that there is something outside the web of propositions that renders the proposition determinately true or determinately false. Consider any arbitrary proposition, p. Correlated with that proposition is some belief state of the sort expressed by the various intentionality predicates I have invoked, and either God is in the state or God is not in that state. If God is in the relevant state, then p is determinately true; if God is not in that state, then p is determinately false.

It would be wrong, of course, to suppose that the relevant belief state or lack thereof serves as a criterion by means of which we are justified in concluding that the relevant proposition is true or is false. For obvious reasons, it does not. The criteria (or, as it is put nowadays, the verification and falsification procedures) we invoke in this connection are quite different. They involve tests we can perform, tests whose results are accessible to us. Of course, for some propositions, it may turn out that there are no such tests or procedures that we can appeal to; and in those cases, we cannot determinately say whether the proposition is true or false. But my axiom (B) ensures that the belief-state correlated with that proposition is such that either God is in the state or God is not in the state. So our concept of truth (and it is the only one there is) turns out to be, as contemporary realists want to claim, verification-transcendent.

Still, the view I have outlined does not represent a complete vindication of realism; for although my view construes our Platonistic conceptual framework as realist to the core, the account I have sketched characterizes the divine thought in terms that are amenable to the antirealist. If I am right, then there are no propositions for God to think; hence, talk of truth and falsity is out of place here. Consequently, divine thought does not provide a context where the central question raised by the realist/antirealist controversy can be so much as raised. But although one cannot ask whether the propositions believed by God are one and all rendered determinately true or false by some reality distinct from those propositions, one can ask a related question, namely, whether for each belief-state, such that God is in that belief-state, there is something outside the web of divine beliefs that justifies God's being in that state; and the answer, which I assume will give no small comfort to the antirealists, is negative.

Those (and I could myself among them) who hold that rational beings other than God perform free actions will insist that some of God's belief-states are grounded in some reality distinct from God's beliefs. If God believes that some rational being, P, freely performs some action, A, then presumably God is in that belief-state because P does, in fact, perform A freely. To hold otherwise, I think, is to deny that finite rational agents can engage in free action.

But if we set aside the case of God's beliefs about the free actions of rational agents, we find that the account I have outlined most naturally unfolds into a very different story. Take the case of God's strong beliefs. If one were to ask the realist why God has the strong beliefs God does, the realist would answer by referring to the necessity of the corresponding facts. Thus, the realist would tell us that God strongly believes that $2 + 2 = 4$ because it is necessarily the case that $2 + 2 = 4$. But if my account is correct, then the realist has things backward here. God is not in the relevant strong belief states because the facts are necessarily as they are. On the contrary, the facts are necessarily as they are because God has the relevant strong beliefs. So it is the case that $2 + 2 = 4$ because God believes that $2 + 2 = 4$; and it is necessarily the case that $2 + 2 = 4$ because God strongly believes that $2 + 2 = 4$.

In the same way, if we turn to the realm of contingent facts (other than those consisting in rational agents freely performing actions), then, on the account I have given, it is most natural to suppose that the facts stand as they do because God has the beliefs God does. The realist will probably tell us that God believes that the earth rotates on its axis because the earth does, in fact, so rotate, or that God believes that it rains in Buffalo, New York, on June 21, 1985, because it does, in fact, rain there on that date. However plausible it may appear, the realist's account of divine thought fails to capture the dependence of the contingent and God's role as creator and conserver. These features are, however, highlighted on the account I have provided; for I want to say that the earth rotates on its axis because God believes that it does, and that the rain falls in Buffalo because God has the corresponding belief.

The realist will insist, of course, that the antirealism coloring my account leaves God's beliefs arbitrary: "Surely, we want to say that God is a rational being; but on your account, there is no rationality to God's beliefs. God just believes any old thing." The response is, I take it, twofold. First, that God's rationality does not consist in God's beliefs satisfying some antecedently given conception of rationality but, rather, in those beliefs being the ideal and the ultimate measure of any canons of the true, the consistent, or the reasonable. Second, that God's beliefs are not arbitrary. God believes that $2 + 2 = 4$; and we say that the proposition that $2 + 2 = 4$ is true. God strongly believes that $2 + 2 = 4$; and we say that the proposition is necessarily true.

The realist will no doubt object, "But, then, you are saying that had God believed otherwise, then it would not have been the case that $2 + 2 = 4$, so the proposition that $2 + 2 = 4$ is not really a necessary truth after all." The correct response, I take it, is to grant the subjunctive conditional at work in the objection, but to challenge its relevance. We can concede the truth of that conditional without embarrassment, since its antecedent is necessarily false. God does not simply believe that $2 + 2 = 4$. God strongly believes this, and, furthermore, God strongly believes that God strongly believes this; but, then, it is difficult to see how, in spite of the truth of the relevant conditional, it follows that $2 + 2 = 4$ is not a necessary truth. Of course, many of God's beliefs are not to be counted among God's strong beliefs; but this is not to say that those beliefs are arbitrary. It is merely to make the point that we in our Platonistic framework would express by saying that God might have believed otherwise; and anyone who holds that God freely creates and conserves must grant this. God believes that it rains in Buffalo on June 21, 1985. He does not strongly believe this, however. Indeed, God strongly believes that on some (doubtless, many) of God's maximal entertainments, God believes otherwise; but given the fact that we express by speaking of the contingency of the weather in Buffalo, it would be surprising were things not to be so.[13]

Notes

A slightly abridged version of this paper formed the basis of my inaugural address as Ignatius A. O'Shaugnessy, Dean of the College of Arts & Letters, at the University of Notre Dame on October 18, 1985.

1. See, e.g., *Metaphysics* Γ.2 and Z.1.

2. See *Metaphysics* Γ.2.

3. See especially 1028a20–28.

4. For a detailed discussion of the difficulties faced by nominalistic reduction strategies, see chapter IV of my *Substance and Attribute* (Dordrecht, 1978). Although I still endorse many of the individual conclusions of that book, the reader familiar with *Substance and Attribute* will recognize that my views on the ontological status of abstract entities have changed fairly radically and that my views about methodology in metaphysics have undergone revision as well.

5. Although Aristotle is none too clear about the ontological status of propositions, this conceptualist strategy has its roots in the opening remarks of *De Interpretatione* (16a3–8).

6. The account I attribute to the Platonist is developed in Alvin Plantinga's *The Nature of Necessity* (Oxford, 1974). See especially pages 45–46. Not all Platonists would provide precisely the same story. See, e.g., chapter IV of Roderick Chisholm's *Person and Object* (La Salle, Ill. 1976).

7. It may be that the difficulties I point to here are not as serious as I suggest. If we are justified in supposing (as I think we are) that God engages in entertaining that satisfies a maximality condition, then, perhaps it is sufficient to construct (in some artificial way) a family of dummy predicates of the form 'entertains that φ' which could serve as stand-ins for predicates that only God could determinately specify. But even if this is not sufficient, the fact remains that our inability to individuate the ways God is when God maximally entertains corresponds to the Platonists' difficulty in individuating possible worlds; for they are unable to provide a purely qualitative characterization that singles out just one possible world. Of course, since the Platonists are allowed (as I am not) the luxury of quantifying over propositions, states of affairs, and so on, they can succeed in providing a general characterization of the maximality condition that they claim possible worlds satisfy. Here, though, I am not at a serious disadvantage, since (as will become clear later) my theory provides an account that, although insisting that the objective truth-maker for Platonistic discourse generally is divine thought and not a special realm of abstract entities, provides a perfectly straightforward explanation of why the Platonist succeeds on this score and I do not. But more to the point, although it would be nice to be able to account for the insights of possible worlds theorists, I would not be

terribly concerned were my theory to fail in its attempt to do so; for as I see it, possible worlds discourse is dispensable in the sense that nothing central to the Platonistic framework (other than possible worlds themselves) is lost if we cease invoking that discourse. I am, of course, suspicious of revisionistic versions of nominalism, but I think it fair to say that Kripke-style discourse does not lie at the core of our conceptual framework. At one time, I may have thought otherwise. See pages 30–31 of "Modality and Metaphysics" in my *The Possible and the Actual* (Ithaca, N.Y., 1979).

8. Once again, my use of the expression 'for some q' suggests quantification over propositions, states of affairs, or the like. I am perfectly willing to admit that there may be serious problems with my use of this locution. It is worth pointing out, however, that (like the locution 'for any q' in the abortive attempt at characterizing maximal entertaining) the expression 'for some q' here falls within the scope of the 'strongly believes that' operator as applied to God; and although we do not have at our disposal all of the sentences that generate substitution-instances of the relevant quantified sentences, God does (or would, were he to use a language). Indeed, I shall argue later that the mythical language God might use (Godspeak, I call it) is one such that all of its quantified sentences would have their truth-conditions given in substitutional terms.

An unrelated issue about the notion of truth-in-a-world. It should be obvious that if God maximally entertains that p and strongly believes that if God believes that p, then God believes that q, then the proposition that q is true in the possible world that p.

9. Strictly speaking, what I characterize in (ζ) is the notion of a dyadic relation. It should be obvious that the principle could be recast to accommodate three-term relations, four-term relations, and so on.

10. It was for this reason that I characterized my account as "something like the Aristotelian strategy." If one takes the Aristotelian approach to require strict translations of all Platonistic sentences into strictly nominalistic sentences, then my version of conceptualism should not be counted Aristotelian. I prefer to construe the Aristotelian view as one that insists on the propriety of Platonistic discourse, but denies the existence of Platonic entities, and to see the view as having several variants (strict translation versions being one kind of variant, and my own antieliminationist approach another).

11. I am thinking of the legitimacy of a formula of the following sort: $(\exists x)$ (x has no label). I take it that given the limitations of human language, the formula (as normally understood) will always express a truth; yet, on pain of paradox, it cannot have a true substitution-instance.

12. I think Michael Dummett's writings represent the central work on the issue. Although I do not pretend to understand how all of the issues he construes as relevant to the debate over realism are related, I think it is clear that the central issue in the realism/antirealism controversy, as delineated by Dummett, is the issue of truth and its grounds.

13. The approach I outline here is obviously subject to applications in ethics, the philosophy of mathematics, the theory of action, the philosophy of religion, and so on. Working out the precise details of the applications is, however, beyond the scope of the present paper.

I want to thank Thomas Flint, Michael DePaul, Alvin Plantinga, Philip Quinn, David Burrell, Aron Edidin, Richard Foley, Stephen Horst, and Howard Wettstein, all of whom read earlier drafts of this paper and provided helpful comments.

Contributors

Diana F. Ackerman, Department of Philosophy, Brown University and Hebrew University of Jerusalem

Robert Merrihew Adams, Department of Philosophy, University of California, Los Angeles

William R. Carter, Department of Philosophy and Religion, North Carolina State University

Hugh S. Chandler, Department of Philosophy, University of Illinois

Roderick M. Chisholm, Department of Philosophy, Brown University

Robert C. Coburn, Department of Philosophy, University of Washington

Paolo Dau, Department of Philosophy, University of California, San Diego

John Dupré, Department of Philosophy, Stanford University

Berent Enç, Department of Philosophy, University of Wisconsin, Madison

Evan Fales, Department of Philosophy, University of Iowa

Graeme Forbes, Department of Philosophy, Tulane University

Alfred J. Freddoso, Department of Philosophy, University of Notre Dame

Richard A. Fumerton, Department of Philosophy, University of Iowa

Eli Hirsch, Department of Philosophy and the History of Ideas, Brandeis University

Michael J. Loux, College of Arts and Sciences, University of Notre Dame

William G. Lycan, Department of Philosophy, University of North Carolina

Thomas J. McKay, Department of Philosophy, Syracuse University

Alan McMichael, Department of Philosophy, Virginia Polytechnic Institute

Fabrizio Mondadori, Department of Philosophy, University of Wisconsin, Milwaukee

George Myro, Department of Philosophy, University of California, Berkeley

Nathan Salmon, Department of Philosophy, University of California, Santa Barbara

Robert Schwartz, Department of Philosophy, University of Wisconsin, Milwaukee

Stewart Shapiro, Department of Philosophy, The Ohio State University, Newark

Robert Stalnaker, Sage School of Philosophy, Cornell University

James Van Cleve, Department of Philosophy, Brown University

Peter van Inwagen, Department of Philosophy, Syracuse University

Nicholas White, Department of Philosophy, University of Michigan

Peter A. French is Lennox Distinguished Professor of Philosophy and chairman of the philosophy department at Trinity University in San Antonio, Texas. He has taught at the University of Minnesota, Morris, and has served as research professor in the Center for the Study of Values at the University of Delaware. His books include *The Scope of Morality* (Minnesota, 1980). **Theodore E. Uehling, Jr.,** is professor of philosophy at the University of Minnesota, Morris. He is the author of *The Notion of Form in Kant's Critique of Aesthetic Judgment* and articles on the philosophy of Kant. He serves as vice president of the North American Kant Society. **Howard K. Wettstein** is associate professor of philosophy at the University of Notre Dame. He has taught at the University of Minnesota, Morris, and has served as a visiting associate professor of philosophy at the University of Iowa and Stanford University. Wettstein has published papers in the philosophy of language.